Make the Grade.
Your Atomic Dog Online Ed

W9-BBY-494

The Atomic Dog Online Edition includes proven study tools that expand and enhance key concepts in your text. Reinforce and review the information you absolutely 'need to know' with features like:

- **Review Quizzes**
- Key term Assessments
- Interactive Animations and Simulations
- Notes and Information from Your Instructor
- Pop-up Glossary Terms
- A Full Text Search Engine

Ensure that you 'make the grade'. Follow your lectures, complete assignments, and take advantage of all your available study resources like the Atomic Dog Online Edition.

How to Access Your Online Edition

- **If you purchased this text directly from Atomic Dog ....**
  Visit atomicdog.com and enter your email address and password in the login box at the top-right corner of the page.

- **If you purchased this text NEW from another source....**
  Visit our Students' Page on atomicdog.com and enter the **activation key located below** to register and access your Online Edition.

- **If you purchased this text USED from another source....**
  Using the Book Activation key below you can access the Online Edition at a discounted rate. Visit our Students' Page on atomicdog.com and enter the **Book Activation Key in** the field provided to register and gain access to the Online Edition.

Be sure to download our *How to Use Your Online Edition* guide located on atomicdog.com to learn about additional features!

This key activates your online edition. Visit atomicdog.com to enter your Book Activation Key and start accessing your online resources. For more information, give us a call at (800) 310-5661 or send us an email at support@atomicdog.com

2198279RF

PKG

International Logistics

THE MANAGEMENT OF INTERNATIONAL TRADE OPERATIONS

Third Edition

International Logistics

THE MANAGEMENT OF INTERNATIONAL TRADE OPERATIONS

Pierre A. David, Ph.D.
Baldwin-Wallace College

Richard D. Stewart, Ph.D.
University of Wisconsin-Superior

CENGAGE
Learning™

Australia • Brazil • Japan • Korea • Mexico • Singapore • Spain • United Kingdom • United States

CENGAGE
Learning™

International Logistics:
The Management of International
Trade Operations, 3e
Pierre A. David, Ph.D.,
Richard D. Stewart, Ph.D.

Developmental Editor: Sarah Blasco

Custom Production Editor: Jennifer Flinchpaugh

Technology Project Manager: David Sterkin

Permissions Specialist: Todd Osborne

Marketing Specialist: Courtney Sheldon

Manufacturing Manager: Donna M. Brown

Senior Project Coordinator: Robin Richie

Cover Image: Photo © Suresh Atapattu.
Used with permission.

For product information and technology assistance, contact us at
Cengage Learning Academic Resource Center, 1-800-423-0563
For permission to use material from this text or product,
submit all requests online at **www.cengage.com/permissions**
Further permissions questions can be emailed to
permissionrequest@cengage.com

Library of Congress Control Number: 2006909685

BOOK ISBN-13: 978-1-111-21955-0
BOOK ISBN-10: 1-111-21955-9

PACKAGE ISBN-13: 978-1-111-46498-1
PACKAGE ISBN-10: 1-111-46498-7

Cengage Learning
5191 Natorp Blvd.
Mason, OH 45040
USA

Cengage Learning products are represented in Canada by Nelson Education, Ltd.

For your course and learning solutions, visit **www.cengage.com**

Purchase any of our products at your local college store or at our preferred online store **www.CengageBrain.com**

Printed in the United States of America
2 3 4 5 6 7 14 13 12 11

to Beth

to Kathleen

Brief Contents

Contents

Preface

A User's Perspective

We wrote this book with the idea that its content should be primarily directed at the users of international logistics services. It covers all of the concepts that are important to managers who are actively exporting or importing goods or are otherwise involved in international trade operations. All of the relevant issues are thoroughly explained, including documentation, terms of payment, terms of trade (Incoterms), exchange rate exposure, international insurance, Customs clearance, agency and distributorship sales contracts, packaging, transportation, and security issues.

We strived to make this book accessible to the reader. We took great care to make certain that all of the concepts are clearly and accurately portrayed, and we spent a considerable amount of time to ensure that the vocabulary is precise and accurate, a perspective that we both gained from years of experience teaching hundreds of students, including a fair proportion of non-native speakers of English.

We have paid attention to the order in which the material is introduced, so that the approach is logical and the reader can understand a concept without having to refer to material that is presented later in the book. Given the interdependence of international logistics topics, this was a challenging undertaking, but we think we managed to achieve that goal. Nevertheless, we would strongly advise the interested reader to read the book once "quickly," before delving into some of its finer details.

Since the book introduces a number of topics that tend to be technical or unfamiliar to many readers, we included more than a hundred illustrations, tables, and figures in the text to support the core content. All were chosen carefully to accurately depict the concepts presented in the text. We used our own photographs, but we also have to thank more than 50 professional and amateur photographers who let us borrow their work.

Feedback

It quickly became apparent that this book clearly met a need. It received strong academic support and was adopted by most of the logistics programs in the United States and many abroad. It also became the official reference textbook for the international portion of the Certification in Transportation and Logistics offered by the American Society of Transportation and Logistics, and is recommended for the Certified Global Business Professional examination of the North American Small Business International Trade Educators.

We are very thankful that our textbook, which presents the information from the perspective of the users of international logistics services, is a beneficial match for courses taught in so many programs. Many faculty members and readers found that perspective useful and refreshing, and told us so. Several recommended changes and improvements and the material in the third edition has benefited from the feedback of many colleagues, who took a substantial amount of time to let us know how to improve it, and from hundreds of our students, most of whom are professionals engaged in international business, who helped us determine which aspects of the book needed to be revised.

What's New in This Edition

The third edition of this textbook includes many changes, all of which improve the text substantially. As should be expected, the text has been entirely updated to reflect the changes in the practice of international logistics that have taken place in the last few years, especially in terms of cargo security and Customs rules. All examples, statistics, and illustrations have also been updated. The chapters also incorporate a large number of suggestions made by reviewers and adopters, who helped us make the content more student friendly. We are very thankful for their contributions.

The first significant change in the third edition is the revision of the chapter on air transportation, which was completely rewritten with the help of Professor Robert Materna, Ph.D., Embry-Riddle Aeronautical University Worldwide, a certified professional logistician and airline transport pilot. We are very grateful for Robert's willingness to share his knowledge of international air transportation. He added an important practitioner's perspective in that chapter, and this book is much stronger because of his valuable expertise.

Another substantial change to this text is the inclusion of an additional chapter on security issues in the supply chain. While security requirements that are specific to each mode of transportation are still covered in their respective chapters, we thought that it was important to cover the different conceptual approaches to security in international logistics and present some coverage of the different perspectives in this important domain, as well as the theoretical support for the different approaches taken.

Chapter 1 was also expanded from the second edition, in response to those adopters who wanted to see greater coverage of international trade concepts and international trade theory. It is written for those students who need a review of the historical development of international trade and of the creation of the institutions that facilitate international trade, as well as an overview of the drivers of international commerce and of the principal economic theories of international trade. Finally, Chapter 2 was expanded to introduce the topic of reverse logistics and provide examples of its growing importance in international logistics.

Online and in Print

International Logistics: The Management of International Trade Operations, third edition, is available online as well as in print. The online version demonstrates how the interactive media components of the text enhance presentation and understanding. For example,

- Chapter quizzes test students' knowledge of various topics and provide immediate feedback.

- Clickable glossary terms provide immediate definitions of key concepts.

- References and footnotes "pop up" with a click.

- Highlighting capabilities allow students to emphasize main ideas. They can also add personal notes in the margin.

- The search function allows students to quickly locate discussions of specific topics throughout the text.

- An interactive study guide at the end of each chapter provides tools for learning, such as interactive key-term matching and the ability to review customized content in one place.

Students may choose to use just the online version of the text or both the online and print versions together. This gives them the flexibility to choose which combination or resources works best for them. To assist those who use the online and print version together, the primary heads and subheads in each chapter are numbered the same. For example, the first primary head in Chapter 1 is labeled 1-1, the second primary head is labeled 1-2, and so on. The subheads build from the designation of their corresponding primary head: 1-1a, 1-1b, etc. This numbering system is identical in the online version to make moving between the online and print versions as seamless as possible.

Supplements

Atomic Dog is pleased to offer a competitive suite of supplemental materials for instructors using its textbooks. These ancillaries include a set of PowerPoint® slides, an Instructor's Manual, and a Test Bank—all via an Instructor Resource CD available from the publisher or by contacting Pierre David at pdavid@bw.edu.

A full set of PowerPoint Slides is available for this text. This is designed to provide instructors with comprehensive visual aids for each chapter in the book. These slides include outlines of each chapter, highlighting important terms, concepts, and discussion points. The slides can be edited to reflect a particular pedagogical style.

The Instructor's Manual for this book offers lecture outlines and notes; in-class and take-home assignments; recommendations for multimedia resources such as films and Web sites; and long and short essay questions and their answers, appropriate for use on tests.

The Test Bank for this book includes over 800 carefully constructed questions in true/false, multiple-choice, and completion format in a wide range of difficulty levels. The Test Bank offers not only the correct answer for each question, but also a rationale or explanation for the correct answer and a reference—the location in the chapter where materials addressing the question content can be found.

There are also two compact discs of photographs that duplicate and supplement the photographs in this book, as well as two DVDs of material for classroom use. These photo CDs and DVDs are available to faculty members upon request, by contacting Pierre David at pdavid@bw.edu. Requests should be made from an official faculty e-mail address.

About Atomic Dog

Atomic Dog is faithfully dedicated to meeting the needs of today's faculty and students, offering a unique and clear alternative to the traditional textbook. Breaking down textbooks and study tools into their basic "atomic parts," we then recombine them and utilize rich digital media to create a "new breed" of textbook.

This blend of online content, interactive multimedia, and print creates unprecedented adaptability to meet different educational settings and individual learning styles. As part of *Cengage Learning*, we offer even greater flexibility and resources in creating a learning solution tailor-fit to your course.

Atomic Dog is loyally dedicated to our customers and our environment, adhering to three key tenets:

Focus on essential and quality content. We are proud to work with our authors to deliver a high-quality textbook at a lower cost. We focus on the essential information and resources students need and present them in an efficient but student-friendly format.

Value and choice for students. Our products are a great value and provide students with more choices in "what and how" they buy—often at savings of 30 to 40 percent less than traditional textbooks. Students who choose the Online Edition may see even greater savings compared to a print textbook. Faculty play an important and willing role—working with us to keep costs low for their students by evaluating texts and supplementary materials online.

Reducing our environmental "paw-print." Atomic Dog is working to reduce its impact on our environment in several ways. Our textbooks and marketing materials are all printed on recycled paper. We encourage faculty to review text materials online instead of requesting a print review copy. Students who buy the Online Edition do their part by going "paperless" and eliminating the need for additional packaging or shipping. Atomic Dog will continue to explore new ways that we can reduce our "paw-print" in the environment and hope you will join us in these efforts.

Atomic Dog is dedicated to faithfully serving the needs of faculty and students—providing a learning tool that helps make the connection. We hope that after you try our texts, Atomic Dog—like other great dogs—will become your faithful companion.

Acknowledgments

We are thankful for all of the help that we obtained in writing this third edition. First are the suggestions made by our colleagues William Borden (John Carroll University), Bud Cohan (Columbus State Community College), Jim Chester (Baylor Law School), Frank W. Davis (University of Tennessee – Knoxville), Charles Kerr (Long Beach City College), Jeanne Lawrence (East Carolina University), Edison Moura (Sul Ross State University–Rio Grande College Del Rio), MyongSop Pak (Sungkyunkwan University), Stephen Hays Russell (Weber State University), as well as the help provided by students Steven Baer (Weber State University), Mark Forquer, Jeffrey Halaparda, Marrisa Newsom, and Jamie Serenko (Baldwin-Wallace College).

The second edition and first editions had been enhanced by the comments made by Yavuz Agan (Western Illinois University), Syed Tariq Anwar (West Texas A and M University), Bud Cohan (Columbus State Community College), Angelica Cortes (University of Texas–Pan American), Frank Davis (University of Tennessee), Stanley Flax (St. Thomas University), Mary Jo Geyer (Robert Morris University), Tom Grooms (Northwood University), Jon Helmick (United States Merchant Marine Academy), Thuong T. Le (University of Toledo), Larry LeBlanc (Vanderbilt University), Michael Munro (Florida International University), Steve Swartz (University of North Texas), Evelyn Thomchick (The Pennsylvania State University), and Peter Weaver (Ferris State University).

Thank you all. We could not have done it without your help.

We are also indebted to Steve Scoble, Kendra Leonard, Matt Walker, and Sarah Blasco at Cengage Learning, for their enthusiasm and support for this third edition. They encouraged us along, and this book would not have been possible without their considerable help.

Finally, Pierre would like to thank his wife Beth, and children, Natalie, Caroline, and Timothy, for their patience and encouragement during the summer and fall of 2009. Richard would like to thank his wife Kathleen Collins for her continuous strong support in this project.

Berea, November 15, 2009

About the Authors

Pierre A. David, Ph.D., Baldwin-Wallace College

Pierre David is a Professor of Business Administration at Baldwin-Wallace College, a liberal arts university located in Berea, Ohio. His teaching interests include marketing and operations management, particularly as these disciplines are applied to an international environment. His primary teaching focus are the courses in international logistics and international market research offered as part of the Baldwin-Wallace College International MBA program. His regular teaching schedule also includes courses in international marketing, marketing management, market research, and operations management at the graduate and undergraduate levels. In 1998, based upon student recommendations, he received the Bechberger Award for Excellence in Teaching.

Dr. David has also had the opportunity to conduct international logistics training sessions in the United States, France, Turkey, China, and Brazil. His research interests are in international logistics and international market research, but also include statistics: he and other faculty members at Kent State University are doing very large scale computer simulations to determine sampling distributions of specific statistics.

He earned a Ph.D from Kent State University, an MBA from the University of Pittsburgh, and an MBA from l'École de Hautes Études Commerciales du Nord in Lille, France, all of which were in marketing and operations management. He has lived in four different countries (Tunisia, Switzerland, France, and the United States) and visited a dozen more.

Dr. David is active in several youth programs, the United Way, and his church. He is married to Beth, and they have three children.

Richard D. Steward, Ph.D., University of Wisconsin-Superior

Richard Stewart is a Professor at the University of Wisconsin-Superior, the Director of the Transportation and Logistics Research Center, and the Co-Director of the Great Lakes Maritime Research Institute.

He earned his Ph.D at Rensselaer Polytechnic Institute's Lalley School of Management, his master's degree at the University of Wisconsin–Green Bay and his bachelor's degree at the U.S. Merchant Marine Academy. Dr. Stewart has commanded ocean going ships and was manager of a $300 million fleet of tankers and bulk vessels trading worldwide. He was a captain in the U.S. Naval Reserve and holds a current Unlimited Ocean Master's License and STCW-95 certification.

Dr. Stewart has extensive teaching experience in undergraduate and graduate courses in the United States and overseas. He is an examiner for the American Society of Transportation and Logistics and is certified in transportation and logistics. His publications include research reports, books, and articles on transportation management, port operations, transportation education, and marine environmental management. He is a consultant for law firms and transportation companies.

Dr. Stewart is active in Boy and Girl Scouts and several professional societies, and serves on public advisory committees and nonprofit boards. Richard is married to Kathleen Collins, and they have four children.

Introduction

Chapter Outline

Key Terms

absolute advantage   (p. 11)

cluster   (p. 16)

comparative advantage   (p. 12)

euro   (p. 7)

factor endowment   (p. 13)

International Monetary Fund   (p. 5)

International Product Life Cycle   (p. 15)

outsourcing   (p. 8)

World Trade Organization   (p. 4)

The years since World War II have seen an unprecedented increase in international trade and a parallel improvement in the economic development of most nations. Countries that were barely able to feed their populations sixty years ago are now economic powerhouses where inhabitants enjoy a modern standard of living and where many companies trade internationally. In most developing countries, political concerns have shifted from famine and abject poverty to pollution and urban gridlock, once the concerns of developed countries only.

This increase in international trade was triggered by the realization that countries' economies benefit by trading with each other and that trade increases the overall well-being of the world's population. Figure 1-1[1] illustrates how much international trade has grown, and the respective shares of the twenty-five European countries, the United States, Japan, China, and the remainder of the world in international trade from 1953 to 2007. Although the economic crisis of 2008–2009 has had an impact on the overall volume of international trade, this decrease is likely to be temporary. As people's standards of living increase worldwide, so do their abilities to purchase a greater number of goods, and therefore so does international trade.

Professionals in international logistics have been the main facilitators of that trade growth. They have been the managers responsible for the safe and timely deliveries of these millions of dollars worth of goods. They are responsible for:

- arranging transportation of these goods over thousands of miles
- understanding the trade-offs between the different modes of transportation available and making the correct decision
- making sure that the goods are packaged properly for their journey
- insuring the goods appropriately while in transit, and understanding the risks they face
- minimizing the risks associated with international payments by selecting the right payment currency or the right hedging strategy
- making sure that the goods are accompanied by the proper documents so that they can clear Customs in the country of destination
- defining properly who, between them and their foreign counterparts, is responsible for which aspects of the voyage and the documents
- determining which method is most suitable for payment between the exporter and the importer

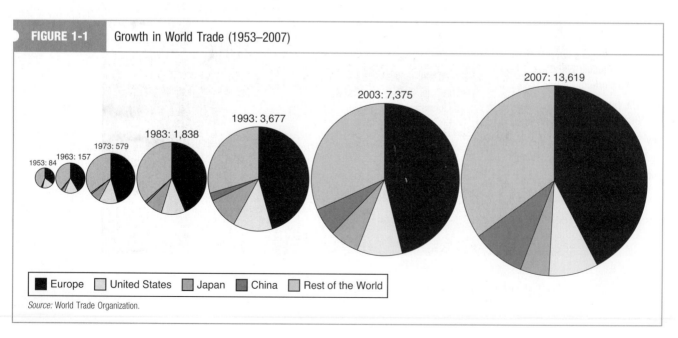

FIGURE 1-1   Growth in World Trade (1953–2007)

Europe | United States | Japan | China | Rest of the World

Source: World Trade Organization.

- following security measures designed to prevent damage to the goods while they are in transit, and following regulations imposed by the governments of importing countries and international organizations
- storing the goods in appropriate warehouses and distribution centers when they are not in transit.

While all of these responsibilities of an international logistics manager will be covered in the remainder of this textbook, this chapter gives an overview of the extent of international trade, of the economic theories of international trade, and of some of the difficulties associated with conducting business in an international environment.

The Alice Tully Theater Project

In 2008 the Lincoln Center's Alice Tully Theater in New York City underwent a complete renovation of its decorative and acoustical elements. The architectural firm in charge of the renovation collaborated with an acoustical research firm to include walls which were shaped to give the theater better acoustical characteristics. The walls were covered by panels made with a very thin wood veneer, so thin that small lights placed behind the wood could shine through it and give the theater a warm, pleasant glow when the main lights were turned off. The theater can add a light show to some of its acoustical performances.

The wood veneer used in those panels came from a single moabi tree harvested in the forests of Gabon, a country in West Africa. The tree species is endangered, so a minimal amount was used; the hundreds of plywood sheets needed for the project were created from a single log that was about 40 inches in diameter (about 1 meter). In order to achieve this enormous yield, the log was first shipped from Gabon to Ryūgasaki City, Japan, where it was cut into slices that were eight hundredths of an inch thick (two tenths of a millimeter). The wood veneer was then shipped to Miami, Florida, where it was inspected before being shipped to Salt Lake City, Utah, where it was glued to a substrate and then formed to the shapes that the acoustical engineers had designed for the theater. The resulting plywood sheets were then eventually shipped to New York City for final installation.

Patrons of the Alice Tully Theater are undoubtedly enjoying these magnificent wood-veneered walls, but few of them can fathom that the wood that was used to build them had traveled more than 25,000 miles (40,000 kilometers). The wood had traveled by road, rail, and ocean before its final destination; all along the way, international logisticians made sure that it was transported economically, packaged properly, and that it cleared Customs without difficulties.[2,3]

Figure 1-2
The Maobi Wood Panels of the Alice Tully Theater in New York City
Source: Photo © Iwan Baan. Used with permission.

1-1 International Trade Growth

In current U.S. dollars (that is, not corrected for inflation), international trade in merchandise has grown 27,000 percent between 1948 and 2008,[4] an average annual growth rate of 9.79 percent. In constant U.S. dollars (2008 dollars), the growth was 2,900 percent for the same period, an average annual growth rate of 5.8 percent.

In constant U.S. dollars, international trade in merchandise and services has more than doubled since 1998, an average annual growth rate of 8.2 percent. Tables 1-1,[5] 1-2,[6] and 1-3[7] show the **World Trade Organization's (WTO)** data for international trade for merchandise and services for the period for which it has kept that information. The differences between exports and imports reflect the different ways in which the values of exports and imports are calculated. The economic contraction of 2008–2009 is expected by the WTO to have a substantial impact on world trade; as of March 2009, the WTO was expecting to see a 9 percent decline in the total value of world trade.[8]

World Trade Organization (WTO) The international organization responsible for enforcing international trade agreements and for ensuring that countries deal fairly with one another.

TABLE 1-1	World's Total International Trade in Merchandise

International Merchandise Trade Volume in U.S.$ billions

Year	Current U.S. Dollars		2008 Constant U.S. Dollars	
	Exports	**Imports**	**Exports**	**Imports**
1948	58	62	518	554
1953	84	85	677	685
1958	110	115	819	857
1963	157	164	1,105	1,155
1968	242	252	1,498	1,560
1973	580	595	2,813	2,886
1978	1,307	1,358	4,313	4,481
1983	1,846	1,890	3,987	4,082
1988	2,869	2,964	5,222	5,394
1993	3,782	3,876	5,635	5,775
1998	5,501	5,683	7,262	7,502
2003	7,586	7,865	8,876	9,202
2008	16,127	16,415	16,127	16,415

Source: World Trade Organization.

TABLE 1-2	World's Total International Trade in Services

International Service Trade Volume in U.S.$ billions

Year	Current U.S. Dollars		2008 Constant U.S. Dollars	
	Exports	**Imports**	**Exports**	**Imports**
1983	354	383	765	827
1988	600	625	1,092	1,138
1993	942	958	1,404	1,427
1998	1,341	1,313	1,770	1,733
2003	1,832	1,781	2,143	2,084
2008	3,731	3,469	3,731	3,469

Source: World Trade Organization.

TABLE 1-3	World's Total International Trade in Merchandise and Services

International Trade Volume (Merchandise and Services) in U.S.$ billions

Year	Current U.S. Dollars		2008 Constant U.S. Dollars	
	Exports	Imports	Exports	Imports
1983	2,200	2,273	4,752	4,909
1988	3,469	3,589	6,314	6,532
1993	4,724	4,834	7,039	7,203
1998	6,842	6,996	9,031	9,235
2003	9,418	9,646	11,019	11,286
2008	19,858	19,884	19,858	19,884

Source: World Trade Organization.

This increase in international trade was triggered by a massive liberalization of international commerce following World War II and the creation of a number of international organizations designed to facilitate international commerce, as well as a significant decrease in transportation costs and transit times. During that period, a much greater consumer acceptance of things "foreign," from food to automobiles, allowed an increasing number of companies to expand their sales beyond their domestic borders.

1-2 International Trade Milestones

The development of international trade has been fostered over the years by several critical milestones, the ratification of several key international treaties, and the establishment of international organizations designed to facilitate and support international trade activities.

1-2a The Bretton Woods Conference

In July 1944, the last year of World War II, the leaders of the Allied nations met in the resort town of Bretton Woods, New Hampshire, for a conference that led to the creation of several international institutions, two of which were specifically designed to facilitate world trade:

- the *International Monetary Fund (IMF)* on December 27, 1945,[9] which established an international system of payment and introduced stable currency exchange rates
- the *General Agreement on Tariffs and Trade (GATT)*, which through multiple negotiation periods (Geneva, 1948; Annecy, France, 1949; Torquay, U.K., 1951; Geneva 1956; the Dillon Round, 1960–61; the Kennedy Round, 1964–67; the Tokyo Round, 1973–79; and the Uruguay Round, 1986–94) led to a decrease of duty rates from an average of over 40 percent in 1947 to an average slightly above 4 percent in 2008.

International Monetary Fund (IMF) The international organization created in 1945 to oversee exchange rates and to develop an international system of payments.

1-2b The World Trade Organization

The WTO was officially created on January 1, 1995.[10] It "replaced" the GATT and is the organization that is essentially in charge of "enforcing" free trade. Since 2001, the WTO has been working on the Doha Round of multilateral negotiations, whose goal is to improve trade in agricultural commodities, which is impeded by a large number of nontariff barriers, and replete with agricultural subsidies in developed countries.

The round has stalled and no progress has been made in the discussions since July 2008.

The main point of dissension concerns the agricultural subsidies that the developed countries continue to grant to their farmers. The United States and the European Union want the elimination of each other's subsidies, which the developing countries regard as trade barriers, preventing their lower-priced commodities to compete in the developed markets. Negotiations were scheduled to resume in 2009. However, because of the economic crisis that began in 2008, as well as additional conditions presented by the U.S. administration regarding sustainability practices in farming, the Doha Round was not scheduled to start again as of April 2009.[11]

1-2c The Treaty of Rome

The Treaty of Rome, signed in 1957 by Belgium, France, Germany, Italy, Luxembourg, and the Netherlands, led to the eventual creation of the European Union and was emulated by countless other groups of countries that were more or less successful in designing their own common markets. The European Union expanded in 1973 (adding Denmark, Ireland, and the United Kingdom), in 1981 (Greece), in 1986 (Spain and Portugal), in 1995 (Austria, Finland, and Sweden), in 2004 (Cyprus, the Czech Republic, Estonia, Hungary, Latvia, Lithuania, Malta, Poland, Slovakia, and Slovenia), and finally in 2007 (Bulgaria and Romania). It totals twenty-seven countries as of April 2009.

The creation of the European Union triggered many other regional economic groups and other bilateral or multilateral agreements: most notably the Association of South East Asian Nations (ASEAN), Mercosur, the Andean Community, and the North American Free Trade Agreement (NAFTA). A number of examples are given in Table 1-4.

TABLE 1-4	Economic Trade Blocs	
Economic Group	**Date of Creation**	**Current (2006) Membership**
European Union	1958	Austria, Belgium, Bulgaria, Cyprus, Czech Republic, Denmark, Estonia, Finland, France, Germany, Greece, Hungary, Ireland, Italy, Latvia, Lithuania, Luxembourg, Malta, Netherlands, Poland, Portugal, Romania, Slovakia, Slovenia, Spain, Sweden, United Kingdom
Central American Common Market	1960	Costa Rica, El Salvador, Guatemala, Honduras, Nicaragua
ASEAN (Association of South East Asian Nations)	1967	Brunei, Cambodia, Indonesia, Laos, Malaysia, Myanmar, Philippines, Singapore, Thailand, Vietnam
Andean Community	1969	Bolivia, Colombia, Ecuador, Peru
Caricom (Caribbean Community)	1973	Antigua and Barbuda, Bahamas, Barbados, Belize, Dominica, Grenada, Guyana, Haiti, Jamaica, Montserrat, Saint Kitts and Nevis, Saint Lucia, Saint Vincent and the Grenadines, Suriname, Trinidad and Tobago
ECOWAS (Economic Community of Western African States)	1975	Benin, Burkina Faso, Cape Verde, Côte d'Ivoire, Gambia, Ghana, Guinea-Bissau, Liberia, Mali, Niger, Nigeria, Senegal, Sierra Leone, Togo. Guinea is no longer a member, since the coup d'état of December 2008.
Gulf Cooperation Council	1981	Bahrain, Kuwait, Oman, Qatar, Saudi Arabia, United Arab Emirates
Mercosur (Southern Common Market)	1991	Argentina, Brazil, Paraguay, Uruguay
NAFTA (North American Free Trade Area)	1994	Canada, Mexico, United States
Economic Community of Central African States	1994	Angola, Burundi, Cameroon, Central African Republic, Chad, Democratic Republic of the Congo, Republic of the Congo, Equatorial Guinea, Gabon, Rwanda, São Tomé and Príncipe
Eurasian Economic Community	1996	Belarus, Kazakhstan, Kyrgyzstan, Russia, Tajikistan, Uzbekistan
East African Community	2001	Burundi, Kenya, Rwanda, Tanzania, Uganda
South African Customs Union	2004	Botswana, Lesotho, Swaziland, South Africa

1-2d The Creation of the Euro

The **euro** was introduced in 1999 and put in circulation on January 1, 2002 in twelve of the fifteen countries of the European Union (Austria, Belgium, Finland, France, Germany, Greece, Italy, Ireland, Luxembourg, the Netherlands, Portugal, and Spain). The adoption of the euro was extended to Slovenia in 2007, to Cyprus and Malta in 2008, and to Slovakia in 2009. It has also become the currency of a number of smaller countries not part of the European Union (Andorra, Kosovo, Monaco, Montenegro, and San Marino), as well as the currency on which a number of other countries have pegged their currencies (Bosnia and Herzegovina and the Communité Française Africaine, for example). The introduction of the euro was the first multinational effort at replacing eleven strong legacy currencies, and it has become one of the most widely traded currencies of the world.

euro The common currency of 16 of the 27 countries of the European Union.

1-3 Largest Exporting and Importing Countries

Figures 1-3[12] and 1-4[13] show the largest exporting and importing countries for 2007 according to WTO data. Most of these countries have liberal trading policies or free-trade agreements with many of their partners; more specific information about these countries' general trade policies can be found in the World Bank's "Doing Business" database.[14]

1-4 International Trade Drivers

There are many explanations for the enormous surge in international trade in the second half of the twentieth century. Some companies found reasons to expand their sales in foreign countries, and others found reasons to purchase some of their raw materials and supplies from abroad. The reasons behind this international expansion are generally divided into four main categories: cost drivers, competitive drivers, market drivers, and technology drivers.

1-4a Cost Drivers

For companies that require large capital investments in plants and machinery, there is a strong incentive to spread the costs of these fixed costs over a large number of units. For that reason, companies in the automobile industry have been among the first to seek customers outside of their domestic markets, and the companies that dominate that industry are present in just about every country: Ford Motor Company, Toyota Motors, and Volkswagen produce and sell automobiles in the most remote corners of the world. Those that do not have as strong an international presence tend to be purchased by their competitors or enter partnerships with them: Chrysler was purchased by Daimler-Benz in 1998 before Daimler sold 80 percent of the company to a private-equity firm. Nissan entered a partnership with Renault in 1999; and in late spring 2009, Chrysler was being rumored to be purchased by Fiat.

The consolidation of the automobile industry into thirteen large manufacturing groups started in the 1970s: Toyota, General Motors-Saab-Daewoo-Opel-Vauxhall-Holden, Volkswagen-Audi-Porsche-Škoda-Scania-SEAT, Ford Motor Company-Volvo-Troller, Hyundai-Kia, Honda, Peugeot-Citroën, Renault-Nissan, Fiat-Chrysler, Suzuki, Daimler, Mitsubishi, and BMW. The concentration of manufacturing capacity is even more evident: The top ten car-manufacturing countries represent more than 75 percent of all of the world's car production.[15]

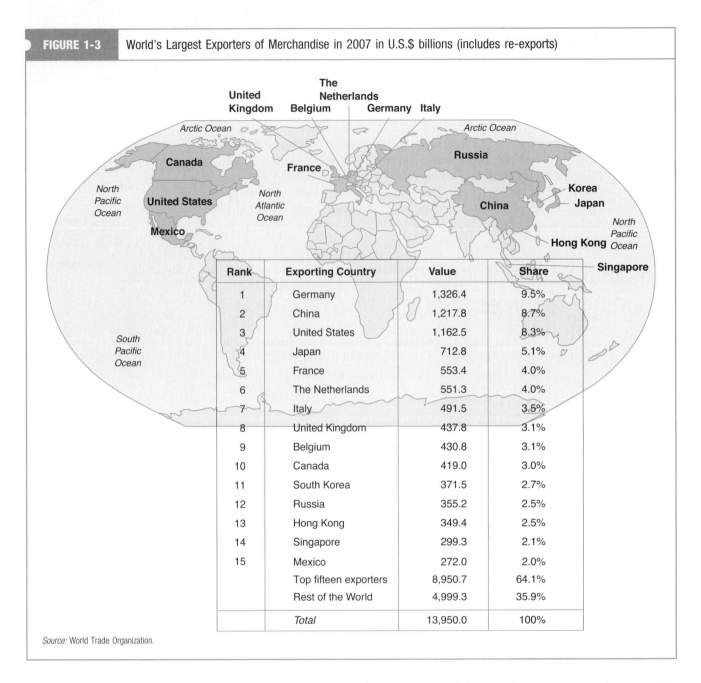

FIGURE 1-3   World's Largest Exporters of Merchandise in 2007 in U.S.$ billions (includes re-exports)

Rank	Exporting Country	Value	Share
1	Germany	1,326.4	9.5%
2	China	1,217.8	8.7%
3	United States	1,162.5	8.3%
4	Japan	712.8	5.1%
5	France	553.4	4.0%
6	The Netherlands	551.3	4.0%
7	Italy	491.5	3.5%
8	United Kingdom	437.8	3.1%
9	Belgium	430.8	3.1%
10	Canada	419.0	3.0%
11	South Korea	371.5	2.7%
12	Russia	355.2	2.5%
13	Hong Kong	349.4	2.5%
14	Singapore	299.3	2.1%
15	Mexico	272.0	2.0%
	Top fifteen exporters	8,950.7	64.1%
	Rest of the World	4,999.3	35.9%
	Total	13,950.0	100%

Source: World Trade Organization.

Such cost drivers are not limited to plants and machinery. In industries where the developmental costs are very large and the costs of manufacturing are low, such as in the software industry, companies are keen to develop their international sales to dilute their developmental costs; such is the case for Microsoft, for example.

The other cost incentives to trade are found on the sourcing side; companies that assemble products from parts and subassemblies (called *Original Equipment Manufacturers*) seek suppliers that have the lowest possible prices. They will purchase their parts from companies located in countries that enjoy low labor costs or low energy costs. Such a purchasing pattern is called **outsourcing**. For example, Royal Appliance Manufacturing, a producer of vacuum cleaners under the brand "Dirt Devil," used to manufacture all of its products in the United States. As of 2009, it produces none in the United States, having outsourced all of its production.

This outsourcing phenomenon is also called the "Wal-Mart effect" in the United States. Manufacturers are asked to provide products at certain prices, called "price points," and there is an unrelenting pressure to make these price points lower every

outsourcing A practice that consists of a business contracting with other businesses to have them perform some of the operations that it used to handle in-house.

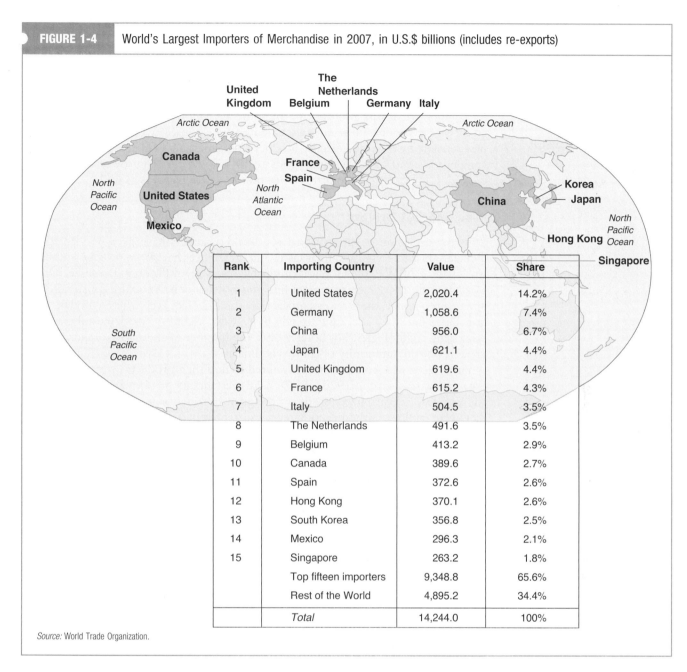

FIGURE 1-4   World's Largest Importers of Merchandise in 2007, in U.S.$ billions (includes re-exports)

Rank	Importing Country	Value	Share
1	United States	2,020.4	14.2%
2	Germany	1,058.6	7.4%
3	China	956.0	6.7%
4	Japan	621.1	4.4%
5	United Kingdom	619.6	4.4%
6	France	615.2	4.3%
7	Italy	504.5	3.5%
8	The Netherlands	491.6	3.5%
9	Belgium	413.2	2.9%
10	Canada	389.6	2.7%
11	Spain	372.6	2.6%
12	Hong Kong	370.1	2.6%
13	South Korea	356.8	2.5%
14	Mexico	296.3	2.1%
15	Singapore	263.2	1.8%
	Top fifteen importers	9,348.8	65.6%
	Rest of the World	4,895.2	34.4%
	Total	14,244.0	100%

Source: World Trade Organization.

year, in response to consumer preferences. Companies then seek the lowest-cost suppliers, invariably abroad.

The pursuit of lowest manufacturing costs has also caused a substantial shift in other industries as well, notably those that manufacture products that are sold to consumers at retail: textiles, toys, housewares, and so on.

1-4b Competitive Drivers

In some cases, it is a competitive incentive that drives companies to expand overseas. For example, a company may feel compelled to follow one of its domestic or foreign competitors into a new foreign market so as not to lose overall market share. Examples of such competitive behavior are more common in industrial goods than in consumer goods; however, this is the drive for the intense competition between the two largest retailers in the world: Carrefour of France and Wal-Mart of the United States. They compete in many different countries; however, as soon as one enters a new foreign market, the other feels compelled to follow suit.

In other cases, companies expand their sales abroad in response to moves made by non-domestic competitors. When a new overseas competitor enters a company's home market, the company may "retaliate" by going overseas and in turn competing in that newcomer's home market. An example of such behavior would be The Gap entering the Italian market after Benetton started competing in the United States.

Competitive drivers also exist on the sourcing side. If a competitor starts offering an entry-level product targeted at a segment of price-conscious consumers, a company may retaliate by offering a similar product to maintain its market share. Because the competitor's entry-level product tends to be manufactured in low-cost producing countries, the company has little choice but to source overseas as well.

1-4c Market Drivers

With the explosion of international tourism, consumers have become increasingly global in their interests, and their tastes and preferences have become almost uniform worldwide. This phenomenon was originally observed for products that reflected this consumer mobility, such as camera film and hotel rooms. Should a consumer want film in any country, there are essentially only three choices everywhere—Kodak, Agfa, and Fuji—but they are easy to purchase, with identical sizes, sensitivities, and processing technologies. For hotel rooms, the number of alternative brands is much greater, but the uniformity of choices is similar.

Firms faced with consumers who wanted to find their products everywhere had to expand overseas. In the 1970s, McDonald's restaurants in Germany, Great Britain, and France were patronized mostly by foreigners looking for an experience with which they were familiar. Although foreigners still represent a good portion of their sales today, McDonald's restaurants cater mostly to domestic consumers who have come to appreciate the convenience of fast food. This phenomenon of standardization of tastes is everywhere: in television shows, clothing, books, music, food, sports, and so on.

Finally, as consumers become increasingly knowledgeable about the products they consume, they are more likely to purchase products with which they are unfamiliar. The wine industry is typical in that respect. French and Italian wines at one time dominated the higher segments of the market, but the way they were marketed demanded that the consumer learn a complex system of classification. When U.S. vintners "simplified" the industry by labeling the bottles with the name of the grape variety they used, it expanded the market by making it less intimidating to buy wine. Consumers were less likely to make mistakes and more likely to enjoy their wines. An unintended consequence of this simplification was a substantial increase in the sales of wines from countries that traditionally had sold exclusively domestically: Chile, South Africa, and New Zealand, for example.

1-4d Technology Drivers

Another reason people are so familiar with products is that the diffusion of information has become universal. Anyone with an Internet connection can quickly access Wikipedia or any other Web site that provides information. Consumers can conveniently purchase products everywhere, and it is just as convenient to purchase from overseas as it is to purchase next door. Companies that have a presence on the Internet are enticing consumers everywhere to purchase their products. Expanding on this concept of worldwide competition between companies, Thomas Friedman writes about how the world has become flat, and that individuals are now competing with each other on a worldwide scale for jobs: Easy communications and transfer of information have made one's location irrelevant.[16]

An easy example of the worldwide availability and sharing of information is the textbook that you are reading; in order to find good illustrations of certain concepts, the authors looked for photographs on the Internet. A total of 52 different photographers, from 23 different countries, provided the illustrations for this book.

In a similar fashion, companies can easily find suppliers for just about any product on the Internet as well.

1-5 International Trade Theories

On a formal level, economists have developed several theories to explain why countries trade, and all have empirical support. The following four theories are the ones most commonly used to explain bilateral trade between two countries.

1-5a Smith's Theory of Absolute Advantage

Adam Smith's Theory of Absolute Advantage was first defined in *The Wealth of Nations* in 1776: "If a foreign country can supply us with a commodity cheaper than we ourselves can make it, better buy it of them with some part of the produce of our own industry, employed in a way in which we have some advantage."[17]

The principle of **absolute advantage** is very easy to understand. Suppose companies, located in France, can produce 20,000 liters of wine for each year of labor they employ and, also using a year of labor, can produce two units of machinery. Suppose companies in Germany produce, with the same amount of labor, 15,000 liters of wine and three units of machinery. It is clear that the French enjoy an absolute advantage in making wine and that the Germans have an absolute advantage in making machinery, and therefore it is in the best interest of both parties to have the French companies produce wine and the German companies make machinery. Table 1-5 illustrates that point.

absolute advantage An economic theory that holds that when a nation can produce a certain type of good more efficiently than other countries, it will trade with countries that produce other goods more efficiently.

Before trading, both countries use their respective resources to make wine and machinery. France produces 20,000 liters of wine and two units of machinery, while Germany produces 15,000 liters of wine and three units of machinery. If the two countries decide to trade and use their respective absolute advantages, France will take all of the resources it had been using to make machinery and divert them to make more wine, shifting production from two units of machinery to 20,000 additional liters of wine. Germany also shifts its emphasis; instead of making 15,000 liters of wine, it makes three additional units of machinery.

TABLE 1-5	Absolute Advantage		

Production Before Trading

	France	Germany	Combined Output
Wine	20,000 liters	15,000 liters	35,000 liters
Machinery	2 units	3 units	5 units

Production After Trading

	France	Germany	Combined Output
Wine	40,000 liters	0 liters	40,000 liters
Machinery	0 units	6 units	6 units

Consumption After Trading

	France	Germany	Combined Consumption
Wine	20,000 liters	20,000 liters	40,000 liters
Machinery	3 units	3 units	6 units

France then proceeds to buy three units of machinery from Germany. France would be willing to pay as much as 30,000 liters of wine (what it would have to give up in order to manufacture those three units) to purchase these units. Germany, reciprocally, proceeds to buy 20,000 liters of wine. Germany would be willing to pay four units of machinery (what Germany would have to give up to make those 20,000 liters) to purchase this wine. Overall production, consumption, and satisfaction are higher in both countries.

The theory does not concentrate on labor alone, but on the sum of all of the resources that are needed to make the product. A country (company) has an absolute advantage if it produces more goods than another, using the same amount of input; in other words, a company enjoys an absolute advantage if it is more efficient.

There are many examples of absolute advantage in international trade; countries "specialize" in specific crops or manufactures because they enjoy a worldwide absolute advantage over all other countries. For example, Kuwait produces crude oil more cheaply than any other country and imports most everything else its economy needs. Taiwan produces most of the world's supply of random access memory (RAM) chips, and uses these proceeds to import products and goods it cannot produce as efficiently, such as soybeans from Brazil.

1-5b Ricardo's Theory of Comparative Advantage

Although most frequently attributed to David Ricardo, the Theory of Comparative Advantage was first outlined by Robert Torrens in his *Essay on the External Corn Trade* in 1815.[18] It was Ricardo, though, who illustrated it with a numerical example in *On the Principles of Political Economy and Taxation* in 1817[19] and who is responsible for its great acceptance. The principle of **comparative advantage** is not as simple as that of absolute advantage.

comparative advantage An economic theory that holds that nations will trade with one another as long as they can produce certain goods relatively more efficiently than one another.

To illustrate the comparative advantage theory, suppose that companies in Great Britain can manufacture, using one year of labor, five units of machinery and 100 tons of wheat. Companies in Brazil, using the same input of labor, can manufacture three units of machinery and 90 tons of wheat. In this case, Britain enjoys an absolute advantage in both machinery and wheat, and therefore the two countries would not trade, according to the Theory of Absolute Advantage.

However, Britain enjoys a comparative advantage in the production of machinery and Brazil enjoys a comparative advantage in the production of wheat. For Britain to manufacture 100 additional tons of wheat, it has to "give up" five units of machinery; in other words, the cost of a piece of machinery is 20 tons of wheat. For Brazil, in order to produce 90 additional tons of wheat, it has to give up three units of machinery. The cost to Brazil of producing one unit of machinery is 30 tons of wheat. Therefore, it makes sense for both countries to trade with one another; Britain can sell units of machinery in exchange for wheat from Brazil. Should the agreed-upon price be between the British "value" of 20 tons of wheat for each unit of machinery and the Brazilian "value" of 30 tons of wheat for each unit of machinery, both countries will find it beneficial to trade with each other. Assuming a market price of 25 tons of wheat for each piece of machinery, Britain is better off making machinery rather than growing wheat, and Brazil is better off growing wheat than making pieces of machinery. Table 1-6 illustrates that example.

Before trading, both countries use their respective resources to make wheat and machinery. Great Britain produces 100 tons of wheat and five units of machinery, while Brazil produces 90 tons of wheat and three units of machinery. If the two countries decide to trade and use their respective comparative advantages, Great Britain may decide to take the resources it had been using to make wheat and divert them to make more units of machinery.

Britain decides to decrease its production of wheat by 20 tons and increase its production of machinery by one unit. Brazil also shifts its emphasis; it decreases its production of machinery by one unit and increases its production of wheat by 30 tons.

| TABLE 1-6 | Comparative Advantage |

Production Before Trading

	Great Britain	Brazil	Combined Output
Wheat	100 tons	90 tons	190 tons
Machinery	5 units	3 units	8 units

Production After Trading

	Great Britain	Brazil	Combined Output
Wheat	80 tons	120 tons	200 tons
Machinery	6 units	2 units	8 units

Consumption After Trading

	Great Britain	Brazil	Combined Consumption
Wheat	105 tons	95 tons	200 tons
Machinery	5 units	3 units	8 units

Using a market price of 25 tons of wheat for each unit of machinery, Britain then proceeds to buy 25 tons of wheat from Brazil in exchange for one unit of machinery. Brazil, reciprocally, proceeds to buy this unit of machinery by selling 25 tons of wheat. British companies now have 105 tons of wheat available for consumption and Brazil has 95 tons. Overall, production, consumption, and satisfaction are higher in both countries.

The Theory of Comparative Advantage is present in most of the exchanges that companies make internationally. Most firms specialize in making certain products efficiently, and these specializations give them a comparative advantage. At one point in its history, the Ford Motor Company built the River Rouge plant, where, at one end, iron ore and coal were delivered, and at the other, finished automobiles rolled off the assembly line; the company thought that it was to its advantage to make all of the parts that were needed to make an automobile. Today, Ford realized that it has gained a comparative advantage in the design and assembly of automobiles, and countless suppliers have made a business out of their own comparative advantage: Mittal Steel (India) in sheet metal, Alcan in aluminum products, TRW in airbags, and so on. Even though the Ford Motor Company is capable of producing these products, it chooses not to, and rather buys them from companies that can produce them relatively more efficiently.

1-5c Heckscher-Ohlin Factor Endowment Theory

The Factor Endowment Theory was developed by Eli Heckscher and Bertil Ohlin in 1933[20] and builds on Ricardo's comparative advantage concept. Ricardo's explanation of **factor endowment** was based on comparing the effectiveness of a country at using its labor to produce goods, and it assumed different levels of technology to account for the differences in the countries' ability to manufacture goods.

The Heckscher-Ohlin theory extends that idea by assuming that even when technology is identical, some countries enjoy a comparative advantage over others because they are endowed with a greater abundance of a particular factor of production. Since economists consider that there are four factors of production—land, labor, capital, and entrepreneurship—, countries with a greater abundance of one of these factors enjoy an advantage over others.

factor endowment An economic theory that holds that a country will enjoy a comparative advantage over other countries if it is naturally endowed with a greater abundance of one of the factors of economic production.

A country may have a relative abundance of capital but scarce labor resources. In that country, because capital is plentiful, it is inexpensive, and therefore the products made by industries that require a lot of capital tend to have a relatively low production cost. Comparatively, labor is relatively scarce and therefore expensive, and products made by industries that require a lot of labor tend to be relatively more expensive.[21]

For example, Japan has a relative abundance of capital, and therefore Japanese companies can manufacture products, such as precision machinery, that are capital intensive at a relatively low cost. However, although Japan has a heavily subsidized agriculture, it still produces rice at a very high unit cost. There are two reasons for that high production cost: Japan has a relative scarcity of land and of labor. Indonesia, on the other hand, has an abundance of labor and agricultural land, and Indonesian farmers can produce rice at a very low cost. However, capital is relatively scarce in that country, and therefore manufacturing production costs are high and there are few companies manufacturing precision machinery. Because they enjoy an abundance of capital, the output of Japanese precision-machinery companies is much greater than the output of their Indonesian counterparts. Similarly, because the Indonesian farmers have access to more labor and land, their production of rice is much greater than the output of Japanese farmers. Table 1-7 illustrates that example more precisely, with figures based on actual data.[22,23,24]

In 1978, Japan produced 6 million cars and 16 million tons of rice a year. Its automobile industry used abundant capital, and therefore it enjoyed relatively low production costs. On the other hand, rice was produced using very high priced labor and scarce land, and therefore it was a high-cost commodity. In Indonesia, the situation was reversed; the country produced fewer than 20,000 automobiles, because such production demanded a large amount of capital, which was scarce in Indonesia. However, the country also produced 26 million tons of rice because of its abundant labor and agricultural land. There was relatively little trade between the two countries.

In 2007, Japan produced only 11 million tons of rice, a decrease of more than 30 percent, but Indonesia's production reached a record 57 million tons, more than twice what it had been in 1978. Japanese companies used their capital to expand their production to satisfy the needs of the Indonesian population in terms of automobiles, producing a total of 10 million vehicles at home. However, they also made capital investments in Indonesia; automobile production in Indonesia soared to about 420,000 vehicles in 2007, many of them made in Japanese-owned plants.

The Factor Endowment Theory explains why certain countries specialize in the production of certain products. Argentina has abundant grazing land, and therefore enjoys a comparative advantage over other countries in beef production. India has abundant educated labor and therefore enjoys a comparative advantage in the staffing of call centers. The United States has an economic system in which entrepreneurship

| TABLE 1-7 | Heckscher-Ohlin (based on actual data) |

Total Country Output (1978) Before Trading		
	Japan	**Indonesia**
Automobiles	6 million cars/year	20,000 cars/year
Rice	16 million tons/year	26 million tons/year

Total Country Output (2007) After Trading		
	Japan	**Indonesia**
Automobiles	10 million cars/year	420,000 cars/year
Rice	11 million tons/year	57 million tons/year

is handsomely rewarded, and it enjoys a comparative advantage in innovation and the development of intellectual property.

1-5d Vernon's International Product Life Cycle Theory

The **International Product Life Cycle** Theory was developed by Raymond Vernon in 1966.[25] This theory explains the development of international trade in three stages, as shown in Figure 1-5.

In the first stage, a company creates a new product to satisfy a market need. This generally takes place in a developed country, as the critical number of customers

International Product Life Cycle An economic theory that holds that, over its life cycle, a product will be manufactured in different countries.

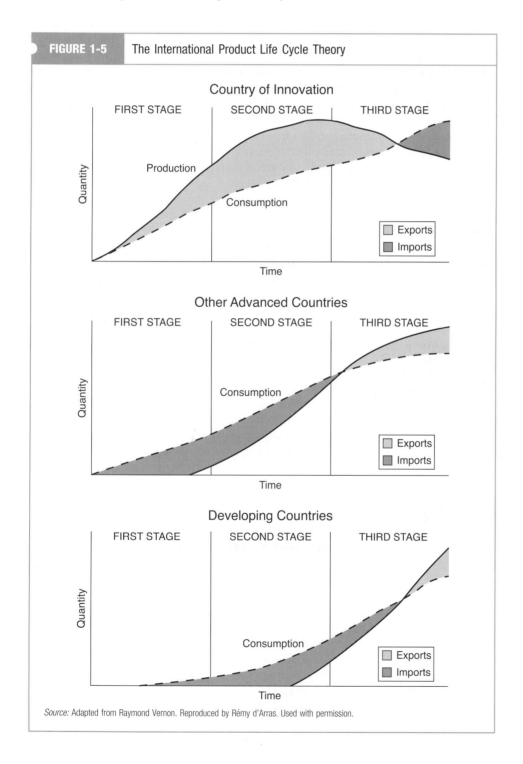

FIGURE 1-5   The International Product Life Cycle Theory

Source: Adapted from Raymond Vernon. Reproduced by Rémy d'Arras. Used with permission.

necessary for a new product launch is often found only in those countries. The product may also use proprietary technology that is available only in that country as well. The firm manufactures the product in the country of innovation because it needs to be able to monitor the manufacturing process carefully, since there are always unexpected problems in manufacturing a new product. As the product gains acceptance, the firm starts to export the product to other developed countries, where similar markets start to emerge.

In the second stage, sales in other developed countries start to grow and local competitors see that there are enough customers to justify production of products that imitate the original product or improve upon it. Alternative processes or patents are developed. Sales continue to grow, and the product manufacturing process becomes much better controlled and somewhat standardized, and many companies master the intricacies of making that product. At the same time, the higher-income segments of developing countries' markets import the product from developed countries, and a market in those countries starts to emerge.

In the third stage, the manufacturing process has become much better known and almost routine. There are pressures to lower production costs. At the same time, the markets in developing countries start to reach such sizes that entrepreneurs there start to produce, frequently under contract from firms in the developed countries. Because the manufacturing costs of a mature product tend to be mostly labor related, these firms start to export massively to developed countries, slowly replacing all of the manufacturing capacity in those markets.

There is much empirical evidence that supports the International Product Life Cycle Theory. The first televisions were manufactured and sold in Great Britain. They eventually were manufactured in other developed countries in Europe, North America, Japan, Australia, and New Zealand. As their popularity increased, all of the manufacturing facilities in those developed countries were eventually replaced by manufacturing facilities in developing countries in Southeast Asia. At the turn of the twenty-first century, there were no longer any manufacturing facilities in the United States for televisions at all.

1-5e Porter's Cluster Theory

Michael Porter's Cluster Theory, developed in 1990,[26] is not a theory of international trade, but an explanation of the success of certain regions at developing a worldwide absolute (or comparative) advantage in a particular technology or product, despite having no particular advantage in any specific factor of production.

cluster An observation that a firm can develop a substantial competitive advantage in manufacturing certain goods when a large number of its competitors and suppliers are located in close proximity.

The **cluster** theory argues that it is critical to have a cluster of companies in the same industry, as well as their suppliers, concentrated in one geographic area. The companies feed on each other's know-how, and their competitiveness pushes them to innovate faster. In addition, when such a cluster exists, the best and brightest employees are eager to move to that location, as they know that they will easily find employment. As these employees move from firm to firm, they also take with them the know-how they acquired with their previous employers, and therefore innovation "travels" from firm to firm. In some cases, these employees develop technologies and ideas that their employers may not want to pursue further and they themselves then start a company to exploit these ideas. Innovation flourishes within the area.

There are several areas of the world where such clusters can be found. The most commonly mentioned location is the so-called Silicon Valley in California, where most of the innovation in computer technology took place in the latter part of the twentieth century. However, Porter studied the cluster of Sassuolo in Italy, which specializes in ceramic tiles and produces more than 30 percent of the world's output, more than 70 percent of which is exported.[27] Another well-known cluster is the area around the Jura mountains in France and Switzerland, where, from the late eighteenth century until the mid-twentieth century, most of the mechanical watches in the world were produced.[28]

1-6 The International Business Environment

On a more practical level, the international logistics professional should have some understanding of the particularities of the international business environment. While it is impossible to replace experience in dealing with people from different countries, it is often useful to know the relevant issues. These few paragraphs are no substitute for classes in international marketing, intercultural communication, international finance, and international economics, but neither are these classes substitutes for experience in world travel and frequent contact with people from different countries and the extensive study of a foreign language.

The international environment is often first described by differences in culture, which is a term that encompasses the entire heritage of the people living in a particular country or geographical area; their language, their customs, their traditions, their morals, their beliefs, and their relationships with one another. If there is one aspect of international business about which it is difficult to generalize, it is culture. Not only are there differences between countries, but there are often differences between regions of a country (in the United States, consider New York and Hawaii), between industries within a country (consider the biotech industry and the auto industry), and often between companies within an industry (consider IBM and Apple Computers). Therefore, stating that normal business attire in the United States is a pin-striped suit, a white shirt, and a conservative tie is correct, but only in a certain industry, in a certain geographic location, and in a particular company. Normal business attire can also be a pair of khaki slacks, a polo shirt, and loafers in a different company, location, and industry. Making similar generalizations about what is standard in certain countries is just as incorrect.

The best strategy for a person interested in a career in international business would be to become familiar with the different techniques for intercultural communications. A number of excellent textbooks have been written in this field.[29] For a person interested in conducting business with a firm in the United States, there are books dealing with the American business culture.[30] For managers interested in a specific country, Brigham Young University publishes the *CultureGrams*, which are excellent synopses (a few pages) of a given country's culture.[31] Despite all of these tools, culture and cultural misunderstandings are probably the greatest sources of frustration for managers involved in international business. Several tools are presented in Chapter 17 to prevent some of these problems, but the best strategy is to be flexible and sensitive to other people's reactions.

The remainder of the international environment is simpler to understand; countries have different approaches to their legal systems, to the ways they run their governments, and to the ways their economies function. Most information about a country can easily be found in the *World FactBook* published by the Central Intelligence Agency,[32] in the *Country Commercial Guides* published by the U.S. Department of Commerce,[33] in the *Country Profiles* and *Country Reports* published by *The Economist*'s Intelligence Unit,[34] and in the Business Planet database of the World Bank.[35]

Further information on countries, of a different nature, can be found in other sources: As previously mentioned, the *CultureGrams*[36] published by Brigham Young University give excellent insights on the cultures of 190 countries in the world, in addition to the 50 U.S. states and 13 Canadian provinces. The United Nations' *Human Development Report*[37] gives a composite perspective on the quality of life in most countries.

Finally, and this is a "must see," data on multiple countries are vividly illustrated by Gapminder,[38] a Web site dedicated to illustrating data in graphic and dynamic form. This Web site is a phenomenal effort undertaken by Hans Rosling of Sweden, his son Ola Rosling, and his daughter-in-law Anna Rosling Rönnlund, who have created software that makes data come alive. The software was purchased by Google in 2007.

Review and Discussion Questions

1. Given the total volume and importance of international trade and international exchanges, describe the implications to someone's career in business, and to your education in particular.

2. Consider two countries' situations: Country A can produce either six automobiles or twelve movies with the same amount of resources. Country B, using the same resources, can produce either five automobiles or eight movies. Using Ricardo's Theory of Comparative Advantage, determine which country would produce automobiles and which would produce movies, and the range of relative prices within which these products would trade.

3. Wal-Mart is famous for requesting ever lower "price points" from its suppliers: If a supplier offers a product for $45, Wal-Mart will ask the supplier to consider introducing a similar product for $39. According to the Heckscher-Ohlin Factor Theory, which consequences do such requests have?

4. In addition to the clusters of Silicon Valley and Sassuolo, Michael Porter identified a cluster for printing presses in Heidelberg, Germany, and others have written about clusters in Limoges, France, for porcelain and in Valenza Po, Italy, for gold jewelry. What characteristics do industrial clusters have that other cities do not have? Can you think of another industrial cluster in the United States or abroad?

Endnotes

1. *World Trade in 2008—Overview*, World Trade Organization, 154 rue de Lausanne, CH-1211 Genève, Switzerland, http://www.wto.org/english/res_e/statis_e/its2008_e/its2008_e.pdf, accessed April 13, 2009.

2. Scherer, Barrymore Laurence, "Alice Tully's Pleasing Makeover," *Wall Street Journal*, April 14, 2009, p. D7.

3. Crissey, Jeff, "On Center Stage," *Modern Woodworking*, March 2009, pp. 24–29.

4. *World Trade in 2008—Overview*, World Trade Organization, 154 rue de Lausanne, CH-1211 Genève, Switzerland, http://www.wto.org/english/res_e/statis_e/its2008_e/its2008_e.pdf, accessed April 13, 2009.

5. *Statistics Database—Time Series*, World Trade Organization, 154 rue de Lausanne, CH-1211 Genève, Switzerland, http://www.wto.org/english/res_e/statis_e/its2008_e/its2008_e.pdf, accessed April 13, 2009.

6. *Ibid.*

7. *Ibid.*

8. "WTO sees 9% global trade decline in 2009 as recession strikes," World Trade Organization Press Release, March 23, 2009, http://www.wto.org/english/news_e/pres09_e/pr554_e.htm.

9. "The IMF at a Glance: A Factsheet, September 2008" http://www.imf.org/external/np/exr/facts/glance.htm, accessed April 13, 2009.

10. "The WTO in Brief: History," http://www.wto.org/english/thewto_e/whatis_e/inbrief_e/inbr00_e.htm, accessed April 13, 2009.

11. Karmarkar, Suparna, "Why Doha Round conclusion is even more crucial now," *The Hindu Business Line*, http://www.thehindubusinessline.com/2009/03/13/stories/2009031350280900.htm, accessed April 13, 2009.

12. *World Trade in 2008—Overview*, World Trade Organization, 154 rue de Lausanne, CH-1211 Genève, Switzerland, http://www.wto.org/english/res_e/statis_e/its2008_e/its2008_e.pdf, accessed April 13, 2009.

13. *Ibid.*

14. *Business Planet: Mapping the Business Environment*, The World Bank Group, 1818 H Street NW, Washington, DC 20433, http://rru.worldbank.org/businessplanet, April 13, 2009.

15. *World Motor Vehicle Production by Country and Type*, International Organization of Motor Vehicles Manufacturers—Organization Internationale des Constructeurs Automobiles, 4 rue de Berri, 75008 Paris, France, http://oica.net/wp-content/uploads/all-vehicles.pdf, accessed April 13, 2009.

16. Friedman, Thomas, *The World Is Flat: A Brief History of the Twenty-first Century*. New York: Farrar, Strauss and Giroux, 2005.

17. Smith, Adam, *An Inquiry into the Nature and Causes of the Wealth of Nations*. New York: Bantam Classics, 2003.

18. Torrens, Robert, *The Budget: On Commercial and Colonial Policy*. London: Smith, Elder, 1840.

19. Ricardo, David, *On the Principles of Political Economy and Taxation*. Mineola, NY: Dover Publications, 2004.

20. Ohlin, Bertil, *Interregional and International Trade*, 1933, reproduced in Samuelson, Paul A., *Heckscher-Ohlin International Trade Theory*. Cambridge, MA: MIT Press, 1991.

21. Suranovic, Steven M., "The Heckscher-Ohlin (Factor Proportions) Model Overview, *International Trade Theory and Policy*, http://www.internationalecon.com/Trade/Tch60/T60-0.php, accessed April 14, 2009.

22. *Paddy Rice Production, by Country and Geographical Region, 1961–2007*, Food and Agriculture Organization, http://beta.irri.org/solutions/index.php?option=com_content&task=view&id=250, accessed April 19, 2009.

23. Fuss, Melvyn A. and Leonard Waverman, "Passenger Car Production 1961–1984," *Cost and Productivity in Japanese Production: The Challenge of Japanese Efficiency*, Cambridge, UK: Cambridge University Press, 1992.

24. *World Motor Vehicle Production by Country and Type*, International Organization of Motor Vehicles Manufacturers—Organization Internationale des Constructeurs Automobiles, 4 rue de Berri, 75008 Paris, France, http://oica.net/wp-content/uploads/all-vehicles.pdf, accessed April 13, 2009.

25. Vernon, Raymond, "International Investment and International Trade in the Product Life Cycle," *Quarterly Journal of Economics*, May 1966, 80(2), pp. 190–207.

26. Porter, Michael E., *The Competitive Advantage of Nations*. New York: Free Press, 1990.

27. "Sassuolo cluster profile," *United Nations Industrial Development Organization*, http://www.unido.org/index.php?id=o4309, accessed August 10, 2006.

28. Glasmeier, Amy, "Why Switzerland?" In *Manufacturing Time; Global Competition in the Watch Industry: 1790–2000*. New York: Guilford Press, 2000.

29. Lustig, Myron W., and Jolene Koester, *Intercultural Competence: Interpersonal Communication across Cultures*. Boston: Allyn and Bacon, Pearson Education, Beamer, Linda, and Iris Varner, *Intercultural Communication in the Global Workplace*. Boston: McGraw-Hill-Irwin, Klopf, Donald W., *International Encounters: The Fundamentals of Intercultural Communication*. n.p.: Morton Publishing Company, 2006.

30. Robinson, David, *Business Protocol*. Cincinnati: Cengage Learning, 2010.

31. *CultureGrams*, Brigham Young University, http://culturegram.stores.yahoo.net/incul.html.

32. *The World Factbook*, Central Intelligence Agency, https://www.cia.gov/library/publications/the-world-factbook.

33. *Country Commercial Guides*, United States Department of Commerce, http://www.export.gov/mrktresearch.

34. *The Economist's* Intelligence Unit, http://www.eiu.com.

35. *Business Planet: Mapping the Business Environment*, The World Bank Group, 1818 H Street NW, Washington, DC 20433, http://rru.worldbank.org/businessplanet, April 13, 2009.

36. *CultureGrams*, Pro-Quest and Brigham Young University, http://www.culturegrams.com.

37. United Nations Development Programme, *Human Development Reports*, http://hdr.undp.org/en/statistics.

38. Rosling, Ola, Anna Rosling Rönnlund, and Hans Rosling, *Gapminder: Unveiling the Beauty of Statistics for a Fact-Based Worldview*, http://www.gapminder.org.

International Supply Chain Management

Chapter Two

Key Terms

Distribution Resources Planning (DRP)   (p. 27)
just-in-time   (p. 26)
Manufacturing Resources Planning
(MRP II)   (p. 26)

Materials Requirement Planning
(MRP)   (p. 26)
reverse logistics   (p. 34)

Chapter Outline

Before presenting the different aspects of international logistics, it is useful to understand how this function is currently included in the management of a firm engaged in international business. It is essential for the international logistician to understand the responsibilities of that profession and the interactions that this function has with the other operational functions of a firm, such as marketing, finance, and production.

Over the years, the responsibilities of an international logistics manager have evolved substantially. This chapter introduces a brief history of the development of the profession of international logistician, the evolution of the activities that have become his or her responsibility, and the current status of this managerial position. It should be made clear that the responsibilities of an international logistician are still changing; it is not known whether the profession will eventually include a greater number of activities or whether its responsibilities will be curtailed, especially in light of the creation of the field of Supply Chain Management.

2-1 Historical Development of International Logistics

2-1a The Early, "Slow" Days

The globalization of markets is generally understood to be a recent phenomenon, triggered by the economic development explosion after World War II; however, while international trade has certainly increased dramatically in the second half of the last century, nations have engaged in international trade for eons. However, before the twentieth century and the advent of modern transportation, trade between nations had always relied on courageous traders who ventured to faraway places in the hope of earning a living. The spice trade was well established in Roman times and flourished during the Middle Ages, bringing a vast array of different products to European consumers; a Florentine merchant listed 288 different spices that he could procure for his customers in 1400. These goods moved either by sea or by caravans of pack animals, "with many transshipments, many tolls, and much danger of loss."[1]

The adventurer-logisticians of that period were responsible for determining what goods they should take along as payment for the goods they hoped to bring back, negotiating with foreigners with whom they did not share a language, and arranging for the transportation and safekeeping of the goods while in transit. They were exposed to the risks of international travel, of market preferences, and of political instability. They were willing to be pioneers.

Can these early traders be considered to have been the first involved in international logistics? Undoubtedly. The word "logistics" comes from the Greek *logistike*, which translates as "the art of calculating"[2] using concrete items, in contrast to *arithmetike*, which was the art of calculating using abstract concepts. The latter eventually evolved into the modern concepts of arithmetic and algebra. The former gave birth to the modern term "logistics," which has evolved into the art and science of determining eminently concrete aspects of business management, from transportation and packaging to warehousing and inventory management.

The first international traders were involved in logistics; they calculated how much their ships—or beasts—could carry, how much food to bring along, and how best to package the goods while in transit, decisions that parallel exactly what a modern logistics manager does when considering how many units to place in a modern container, how to balance the load evenly, and how to protect the goods for their international voyage. Early traders had to decide which payment method was most appropriate, just as a modern exporter must select the best method of payment to ensure being paid. While many aspects of international logistics have changed, the main concerns of people involved in this field remain similar: They have to ensure that goods manufactured in one part of the world arrive safely to their destination.

Nevertheless, the modern interpretation of the term "logistics" has its origins in the military, where it was used to describe the activities related to the procurement of ammunition and essential supplies to troops at the front. It gave birth to the title of *Maréchal des Logis* in the French military, which is given to a sergeant in charge of a unit's supplies and housing. Interestingly enough, when the term applies to the branch of the military in charge of logistics on a large scale, the French use a different term altogether, *le train*.

Initially, therefore, what was understood as "business logistics" was based on the military concept and encompassed mostly the physical movement of goods (1970s). Today, the term is much broader and includes not only all the activities related to the physical movement of goods, both upstream (procurement) activities and down-stream (sales) activities, but also the management of the relationships with suppliers and customers.

Over the last thirty years, the focus of logistics has evolved substantially: Early on, and probably until the mid-1980s, the main concern of logistics managers, and specifically of international logistics managers, was to make sure that the goods arrived at their destination in good condition and at the lowest possible cost. Shorter transit times were considered, but generally only when the goods were perishable or were so urgently needed that the additional costs were justified; for most goods, however, long transit times were essentially considered normal. As time moved on, a transition was made to shorter transit times.

2-1b The Move Toward Speed

Containers—"boxes" in the logisticians' vernacular—changed the focus of international logistics. Even though they were introduced in 1956, containers had a limited impact on international trade until the early 1970s.

Before containers, the process of shipping internationally by ocean was cumbersome and very time-consuming. The traditional method was to first pack goods at the point of origin into a truck or a railroad car for their trip to the port. The goods were then unloaded at the port and loaded onto a ship using cranes and slings, as well as a large number of longshoremen who stowed them appropriately for their ocean voyage. The goods were then unloaded at the port of arrival, loaded again onto a truck or railroad car for their inland trip, and finally unloaded at their destination. Packages had to be small and light enough to be handled by humans in the ships' holds, and very sturdy to withstand their being handled numerous times. A transatlantic shipment took in excess of one month, the majority of that time spent at the ports.

With the advent of containers, shipments began to speed up. Instead of loading and unloading the goods several times, containers were loaded only once, in the shipper's plant, and unloaded only once, at the customer's facilities. Packaging did

Ocean Shipping before Containers

Before the advent of containers, stevedoring was back-breaking work. The goods to be shipped abroad would arrive to port in trucks or railroad cars in small packages or on pallets. They would then be unloaded in a warehouse located alongside the pier and counted. When the ship arrived, it would first have to be completely emptied of its current goods, and that merchandise had to be removed from the pier before any loading could start. The merchandise to be loaded was then moved from the warehouse to the quay and counted once more. A loading plan was devised to determine what should be loaded first (the heavier, tougher items), and what should be loaded last.

continued

Ocean Shipping before Containers (Continued)

Longshoremen would then assemble the goods into "drafts," which were larger parcels that could be loaded onto the ship by cranes. They did this by hand, carrying, dragging, and rolling the merchandise to a point where the crane could pick them up; they eventually placed slings under each draft before it was loaded (see Figure 2-1). The merchandise was then lifted onto the ship, where another gang of longshoremen would unpack the drafts, count the goods once again, and position them into the holds of the ship (still using muscle power), making sure that every piece of cargo was tightly braced against the others so that it would not shift during the voyage.

Many of these goods were not packaged to be handled easily; some bags of grain weighed as much as 220 pounds (100 kilograms), and bags of sugar weighed 132 pounds (60 kilograms). A single longshoreman generally carried the bags of sugar, but two shared the work of moving a bag of grain. Bananas were regularly unloaded by walking down a gangplank on the side of the ship rather than by crane. Each bundle weighed about 176 pounds (80 kilograms). With such working conditions, it is understandable that longshoreman accidents were common; every year, one in

six was injured. Between 1947 and 1957, 47 longshoremen were killed at the port of Marseille.[3]

Unloading was not much different. The results of such labor-intensive work was that there were millions of longshoremen employed worldwide, as many as 50,000 in each of the ports of New York, London, and Marseille. Most of these men were employed only part-time, working whenever there was a ship, idle when there were none, competing for work when a ship was scheduled to arrive in port. They toiled in all sorts of weather and had to learn to move anything; one day they would load and unload delicate goods, and the next, heavy, dirty, smelly bags.[4]

All this changed with the advent of containers, which allowed the mechanization of loading and unloading ships. The work of a stevedore became much less physical; although some dockworkers still have to be aboard the ship to position the twist locks that tie the containers to one another and lash down the two lower containers in a stack, many of them drive trucks to position containers alongside the ship or pick them up, or operate a gantry crane.[5]

Figure 2-1
Cargo Handling in a Port before Containers
Source: Photo © Saxon Fogarty Collection, courtesy Fremantle Ports of Western Australia. Used with permission.

not have to be as sturdy. Ship loading and unloading operations were much faster. Ships no longer had to be completely empty to load new cargo; as soon as a stack of containers was empty, the crane that was unloading containers from the ship did not have to return to the ship "empty;" it could immediately pick up another container to be loaded onto the vessel. This single difference doubled the productivity of crane operators. Because of all of these improvements, the costs of ocean shipping came down: port labor costs were lower, ships were more productive because they spent less time idling in ports, and significant investments were made in container ships that became ever more efficient.

Only a few years later, in the late 1970s and early 1980s, international logistics saw an explosion in the number of air shipments. Even though DHL had been founded in

Malcom McLean

Anyone observing one of the world's ports today would see a constellation of containers. Containers being hoisted off ships and onto trucks or trains, others being loaded onto ships, and still hundreds of others stacked and waiting their turn to be moved. Other than these boxes, there are no actual goods to be seen, and the observer would have no way of knowing what was coming and going. Inside the boxes could be televisions or shampoo, computers or potato chips. But the scene at these same ports just a few decades ago was very different.

Before the adoption of these boxes, or containers, shipping was a much different business. A business that was slow, inefficient, and rife with corruption. But the idea of one man, Malcom McLean, changed all that.

Before containerization, goods were delivered to the waterfront as separate pieces by truck or train. From there, they were taken by hand to a storage shed to wait for longshoremen to load them onto a ship. The longshoremen would take each piece and place it by hand in the cargo hold. Loading thousands of goods onto a ship could take days, and the process had to be reversed when the ship reached its destination.[6] Those wishing to export their merchandise would typically have to arrive days or even weeks before the ship was set to sail in order to ensure that their goods would be loaded. "Ships remained in port for days while longshoremen wrestled individual boxes, barrels and bales into and out of tight spaces below deck. Damage was frequent and expensive, as were losses from pilferage."[7] This process was terribly inefficient and slow, and was a major deterrent for many manufacturers who might consider transporting their goods overseas or even to other parts of the country.

This was the scene in 1937 when Malcom McLean, the owner of a small trucking company in North Carolina, had to drive a truck loaded with cotton intended for export to a port in New Jersey. Once he arrived, he had to wait for days for longshoremen to load his cotton. He knew there

had to be a better way. After this experience, he put his mind to building a better system of shipping, which would eventually grow his company into a huge force in the shipping industry.

McLean went about hiring as many experts in containerization as he could find and learning everything he could about the field. He had the idea of driving truck trailers onto ships but found that it was impractical. Eventually McLean and one of his engineers came up with a plan to use the deck space of the widely-available T-2 tanker ships, and "containers thirty-three feet [ten meters] long, a length chosen because the available deck space aboard the T-2 tankers was divisible by thirty-three."[8] The boxes were much larger than anything seen before and had to be loaded onto tankers by cranes. The tankers were equipped with specially-designed frames that would hold the containers in place.

McLean put his idea to the test on April 26, 1956, when the converted tanker ship *Idea X* set sail from Newark, New Jersey. McLean and his team watched a crane load 58 containers onto the ship, one every seven minutes. A loading process that previously had taken days now took only hours. The ship left the Port of Newark destined for Houston, trailed the entire way by the Coast Guard to ensure its safety. Six days later, the team watched the *Idea X* come into port in Houston with all 58 containers still safely aboard. This first test had been a complete success.

When the transit costs of the journey were calculated, McLean knew he had a real winner. Traditional shipping of loose cargo at the time cost about "$5.83 per ton," while *Idea X* container shipping cost only "15.8 cents per ton."[9] These dramatically reduced costs drove the development of container shipping, and an infrastructure was built to handle containers at ports around the world. McLean's company grew, as did competitors, and new technologies were developed to make containerization even more cost

Malcom McLean (Continued)

effective. Larger ships were built that could handle more containers, and the trend continues today, as bigger ships are constantly in the works. Despite the protests of longshoremen, the old way of loading ships was quickly abandoned as containerization was embraced. This encouraged more businesses to ship their products farther, thereby creating new markets. It also allowed new foods and other goods to be sent around the world to places they had never been before. The idea of containerization is what has fueled the spread of globalization (see Figure 2-2).

Figure 2-2
Thousands of Containers at Port Elizabeth, New Jersey
Source: Photo © Albert Theberge, National Oceanic and Atmospheric Administration. Used with permission.

1969 and Federal Express in 1973, neither of these services provided much coverage: DHL was strictly a San Francisco–Honolulu service until 1974, and Federal Express had only twenty-five domestic destinations until 1979. However, Federal Express sales rose quickly, and by 1983, it had become a billion-dollar corporation based strictly on domestic shipments. It started international operations in 1984 and by 2005 had changed its name to FedEx and become a $30 billion corporation. In the United States, the term "fedex" has become a verb.

The costs of air shipments also dropped considerably during this period. In the beginning, Federal Express operated with Dassault Falcon jets, which had limited cargo capacity. By the end of the 1970s, after a partial deregulation of the industry, it had acquired Boeing 727s and McDonnell-Douglas DC10s, which had much greater capacity. Further deregulation in the 1980s and open-sky agreements in the 1990s increased the number of aircrafts dedicated to freight, and air shipments became increasingly cost competitive with surface alternatives.

As customers' expectations of speedy delivery increased, it became clear that delivery speed had become one of the salient criteria in the selection of a supplier. David Hummels estimated that "each additional day spent in transport reduces the probability that [a company] will source from that country by 1 to 1.5 percent."[10]

Materials Requirement Planning (MRP) A computer-based management tool that allows a manufacturing firm to determine what to produce, and in which quantity, in function of what it sells to its customers.

Manufacturing Resources Planning (MRP II) A computer-based management tool that uses MRP at its core, but also includes other functions in the firm, such as finance, procurement, and purchasing.

just-in-time A management philosophy that consists of planning the manufacturing of goods in such a way that they are produced just before they are needed in the next step of the assembly process.

2-1c The Emphasis on Customer Satisfaction

By the early 1990s, the increased speed of ocean shipments and the availability of affordable airfreight services had effectively changed the focus of logistics managers: They began to consider the shortest reasonable transit time in response to customers' requests for speedy deliveries. Although it was still very important to make sure that the goods arrived in good condition and at the lowest possible cost, the managers' focus had shifted from these process-oriented concerns to the satisfaction of customers' requirements.

The major reason behind this change of objectives in the management of logistics was the increased focus by large manufacturers on the reduction of inventories during the 1980s. Starting in the mid-1970s and culminating in the early 1980s, interest rates climbed to unprecedented heights, triggering a concern about all the money immobilized in inventories. In the 1980s, companies emphasized reductions in their "static" inventories, or the goods they kept in their warehouses or plants. By the early 1990s, they had shifted their attentions to their "mobile" inventories, or the goods that were in transit between two of their plants or between their suppliers and their plants. The tools they used were **Materials Requirement Planning (MRP)** and **Manufacturing Resources Planning (MRP II)**, which allowed them to create **just-in-time** manufacturing processes. In turn, these processes triggered a need for "time-defined" deliveries of assembly parts; plants demanded to have parts delivered just before they were used on the assembly line, and not later. The number of goods that were "in transit" had to be curtailed as well.

 *Materials Requirement Planning*

In the late 1970s and early 1980s, Japanese manufacturers adopted a new manufacturing management philosophy that was based on reducing work-in-process inventory and delivering the goods to the assembly line just before they were needed. Such philosophy was called "just-in-time" (JIT). Toyota's system for JIT management was a technique using cards that it still uses today, called *kanban*. Other manufacturers also adopted the JIT philosophy, starting in the early 1980s, but implemented it using a technique called Materials Requirements Planning (MRP), especially in the United States.

MRP is a computer-based system that determines what needs to be manufactured on a given day, and in which quantity, and whether that order should be expedited. It creates a Master Production Schedule based upon what is currently in inventory (on-hand), what is required to be produced (orders and forecasts of sales for the final product), and bill-of-materials files that spell out precisely what each product's components are. It is a "pull" system: Nothing is manufactured unless there is an order for the final product (or a forecast of an order), and all parts and subassemblies are manufactured only to fulfill a particular order.

Although it was originally strictly a manufacturing program, MRP eventually expanded to include other functions related to production—purchasing, finance, and

so on—and computer programs that included those functions came to be known as Manufacturing Resources Planning software, or MRP II. As of 2009, MRP II programs are present in almost all North American plants.

Another derivative of the MRP programs was Distribution Requirements Planning (DRP) software. The idea behind DRP is similar: Whenever a consumer purchases a product in a retail store, that purchase is captured by point-of-sale scanners, and the DRP program orders another one to be shipped from the distribution center and one to be manufactured by the supplier. This also operates as a "pull" system: No product is manufactured or shipped by the supplier unless that product was sold by the retailer, and it minimizes the probability of unsold inventory in the supply chain.

Both MRP and DRP have strongly influenced the management of logistics; the traditional warehouse, which was once used to keep products in inventory until they were needed, has become a distribution center (DC), whose function is to take large shipments from manufacturers and separate them into smaller parcels to be delivered to retail stores. Such "cross-docking" operations, where trucks are being unloaded on one side and loaded on the other, are illustrative of the increased emphasis on JIT deliveries.

By the mid-1990s, all manufacturers had adopted such techniques and were requiring their suppliers to ship just-in-time. At the same time, large retailers and other distributors jumped on the same idea. They started to use techniques derived from MRP and MRP II to develop **Distribution Resources Planning (DRP)**, which used final consumer sales data to "pull" products through the distribution channel. Consumer sales data were collected through the point-of-sale (POS) scanners. If the products were selling briskly, then the DRP program reordered the goods from the manufacturer and had them delivered just-in-time to the appropriate warehouse or retail store. If a product did not sell well, none were ordered again. This strategy forced logistics managers to shift their attention to transit times and to become adaptable to frequent changes in their work. This came to be known as "agile logistics."

Today, the requirements of most manufacturers and large retail chains are such that they penalize financially the suppliers that do not deliver on time (too early or too late) by withholding a portion of the invoice at the time of payment.

It is fair to say that customer satisfaction is now the primary concern of logisticians: Not only does the shipment have to be accurate (the right parts, in the right quantity), complete (no back-ordered parts), and the packaging appropriate so that the goods arrive undamaged and ready to be sold, but it must also be delivered within a very specific time frame.

While international logisticians must make sure that the shipment is accurate and complete and arrives on time, they also have many other responsibilities. They must make certain that their shipment's paperwork is in perfect order so that it can clear Customs without delay. They must make sure that the packaging is sufficient to protect the goods during their long (and often eventful) international voyage. They must ensure that they meet a myriad of security requirements and must manage the intricacies of a transaction involving different currencies and different laws. They must choose the right mode of transportation and must make sure that the goods are properly insured. In short, they have many challenges with which to contend for each shipment.

Distribution Resources Planning (DRP) A computer-based management tool that allows a retail firm to determine what to order from its suppliers in function of what it sells to retail customers.

2-1d The Transformation into a Strategic Advantage

The 1990s saw the integration of logistics into supply chain management, and the early 2000s saw the emergence of the management of the supply chain as a strategic tool. By the end of the 2000s, it had clearly become a means by which corporations sought a competitive advantage, and it now commanded the attention of top managers, often with the creation of the position of Chief Supply Chain Management Officer.

The emphasis of logistics managers shifted to securing a differential advantage over competitors by providing better service to customers, offering better delivery terms, working with suppliers and customers to offer greater flexibility, and making the processes as seamless as possible. These tasks were made particularly challenging as the complexity of the global supply chain increased drastically during the same period: From 1995 to 2007, the number of companies involved in international trade (which the United Nations calls "transnational companies") increased from 38,000 to 79,000, and the number of foreign subsidiaries increased from 265,000 to 790,000.[11] This complexity increased further with the introduction of numerous new products: In 2006, the number of products in the Consumer Packaged Goods industry increased 17 percent, accompanied by a corresponding change in the number of products eliminated.[12]

A study of Chief Supply Chain Officers conducted by IBM in 2008[13] identified the six greatest challenges faced by companies involved in international trade:

- Cost containment, in view of increased fuel costs, increased need for flexibility, and increased expectations of internal and external customers

- "Visibility" to the supply chain, which refers to the management of all of the information that is generated in the supply chain and making sure it is collected, analyzed, and distributed to the appropriate manager

- Risk management, in view of renewed problems in currency fluctuations, transportation risks, product recalls, tight shipping schedules, and reduced inventory levels

- Increasing customer demands, in terms of delivery performance, cost containment, information availability, and levels of service

- The globalization of the economy, which has transformed itself into a source of additional revenues in addition to being just about cost savings

- Sustainability efforts that affect product and packaging designs, transportation choices, and supplier selections. These efforts at reducing energy and water usage, as well as waste, reflect the changing preferences of consumers and the legislative efforts of many countries.

Figure 2-3[14] shows the relative importance of sustainability practices in North America, western Europe, and the Asia-Pacific regions.

2-2 Definitions of Logistics and Supply Chain Management

As the fields of logistics and international logistics evolved, the managers working in those fields changed the definitions that they used to describe their profession. Whereas "logistics" was the most commonly accepted term for all of the activities in which they engaged, the term was broadened, starting in the mid-1980s, to include additional activities; eventually, the profession was renamed "supply chain management" in the 1990s. Today, the term "logistics" is understood to encompass a number of activities that are a subset of the activities that constitute supply chain management.

| FIGURE 2-3 | Relative Implementation of "Green" Practices in Different Regions of the World |

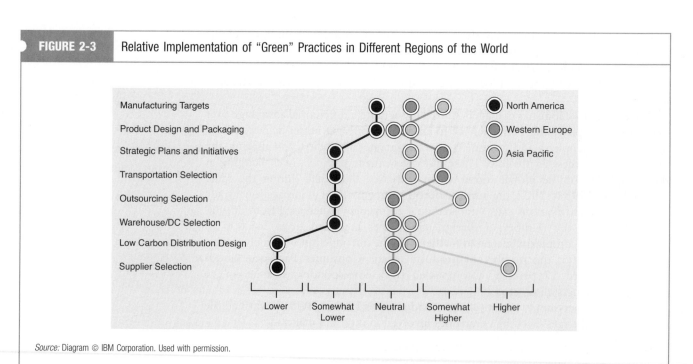

Source: Diagram © IBM Corporation. Used with permission.

2-2a Logistics

As it stands today, the term "logistics" is defined by the professionals in the field as:

> [T]hat part of the supply chain process that plans, implements, and controls the efficient, effective forward and reverse flow and storage of goods, services, and related information between the point of origin and the point of consumption in order to meet customers' requirements.[15]

From this definition, it is clear that logistics managers see that the focus of their profession lies in those activities that are related to the *physical aspects* of the movement of goods from supplier to customer. Logisticians are concerned mostly about the transportation, packaging, warehousing, security, and handling of goods that their firms purchase or sell, and they interact daily with managers who hold other responsibilities closely related to the movement of these goods: manufacturing and production, purchasing and procurement, marketing, inventory management, finance, customer service, and so on.

Figure 2-4 summarizes a slightly different opinion of the evolution of logistics, as seen by Alfred Battaglia.[16] In his view, the logistical function of a company came to include the management of materials and manufacturing somewhat earlier than the 1990s. What is clear is that most logistics professionals referred to their profession as *supply chain management* by the early 2000s.

2-2b Supply Chain Management

In an international survey of logistics educators conducted in 2001, Larson and Halldorsson[17] found that there were four different viewpoints regarding the relationship between logistics and supply chain management, three of which are shown in Figure 2-5.

Nevertheless, it seemed that by 2004, the "inclusionist" viewpoint had prevailed, as the Council of Logistics Management changed its name to the Council of Supply

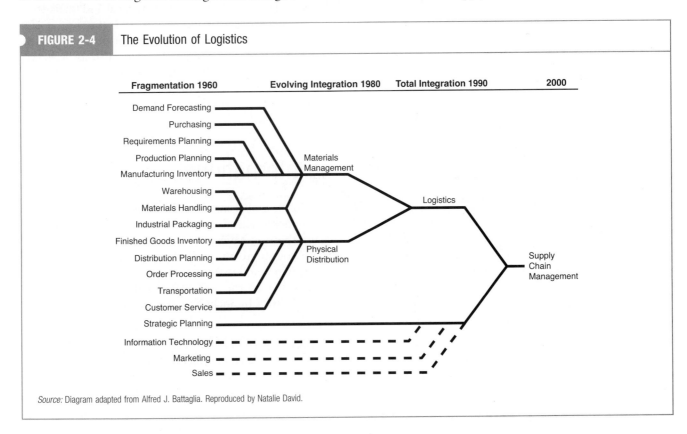

> **FIGURE 2-4**   The Evolution of Logistics

Source: Diagram adapted from Alfred J. Battaglia. Reproduced by Natalie David.

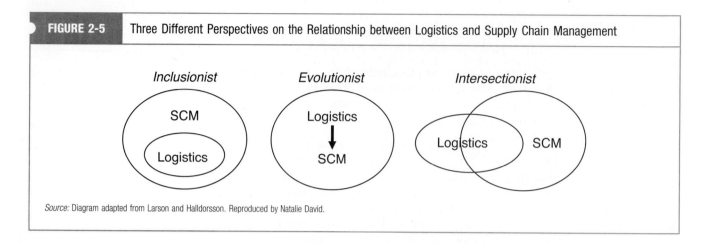

FIGURE 2-5   Three Different Perspectives on the Relationship between Logistics and Supply Chain Management

Source: Diagram adapted from Larson and Halldorsson. Reproduced by Natalie David.

Chain Management Professionals (CSCMP), to reflect what was perceived as the broader nature of the field, and produced a definition of the term "supply chain":

> Supply Chain Management encompasses the planning and management of all activities involved in sourcing and procurement, conversion, and all Logistics Management activities. Importantly, it also includes coordination and collaboration with channel partners, which can be suppliers, intermediaries, third-party service providers, and customers. In essence, Supply Chain Management integrates supply and demand management within and across companies.[18]

The most significant characteristic of this definition is that it reflects an extension of the concept of logistics to that of supply chain management. In the view of the CSCMP, the shift from logistics to supply chain management was a shift from an internal focus on the company's own processes to an external focus that includes all the firm's partners. The scope of supply chain management is therefore much broader than the scope of logistics: Not only does it include all of the tactical and managerial decisions on which logistics and operations managers tend to focus, but it also includes strategic issues that are more traditionally the domain of the managers in those top management positions that are now colloquially referred to as "C-level" positions (CEO, chief executive officer; CFO, chief financial officer; COO, chief operations officer; and so on). Several companies have created the position of chief global supply chain officer; IBM reported having interviewed 400 of them for its *Supply Chain of the Future* study in 2008.[19]

2-3 Definition of International Logistics

The role of international logistics in the global supply chain mirrors that of logistics in the domestic environment: International logistics professionals focus on the tactical aspects of the global supply chain, those activities that are inherent to the movement of goods and paperwork from one country to another, those activities that constitute the basis for export and import activities and operations.

The definition of logistics provided by the CSCMP can therefore be logically modified to define international logistics by including the elements of the international environment:

> International logistics is the process of planning, implementing, and controlling the flow and storage of goods, services, and related information from a point of origin to a point of consumption located in a different country.

The emphasis of international logistics is therefore on the creation of internal processes and strategies. These processes and activities are the focus of this textbook.

2-4 Definition of International Supply Chain Management

A characteristic of supply chain management is that it is inherently global in nature; just about every company outsources some percentage of its production abroad or sells to customers who are located abroad. If it does not, its suppliers or customers do. In 2006, *Forbes* magazine reported that the percentage of the content of the quintessential American car (the Ford Mustang) that was made outside of the United States stood at 35 percent. In contrast, the Toyota Sienna, a Japanese minivan sold in the United States, was made of 90 percent American parts.[20]

It is not clear why the CSCMP did not include this global aspect of supply chain management in its definition. The Council's definition should more accurately read:

> Supply chain management encompasses the planning and management of all activities involved in sourcing and procurement, conversion, and all logistics management activities. Importantly, it also includes coordination and collaboration with channel partners, which can be suppliers, intermediaries, third-party service providers, and customers, whether they are located in the United States or abroad. In essence, supply chain management integrates supply and demand management within and across companies.

Figure 2-6 outlines the current state of the relationships between logistics, international logistics, and supply chain management as of 2006. The activities included in the logistical function are those that include physical transportation of the goods from the supplier(s) to the company and from the company to its customer(s). Logistics also includes the warehousing and other inventory functions within the company that involve the products it purchases, manufactures, and sells.

International logistics works in a parallel form for foreign suppliers and customers. It includes additional activities, such as Customs clearance, documents handling, and international packaging, but the main function of international logistics is concentrated on the physical movement of goods from suppliers to the company and from the company to its customers. The fact that they are in an international arena makes fulfilling these activities much more complex.

Supply chain management is a much broader term; it not only includes both the domestic logistics and the international logistics functions, but it also includes the management of the relationships with suppliers and customers (domestic or foreign) and, to some degree, of their relationships with their suppliers and customers. It deals with the entire supply chain, attempting to manage a smooth flow of goods from the first supplier to the ultimate customer. A possible example of a supply chain management activity is the management of quality by the large U. S. Original Equipment Manufacturers (General Motors, Ford Motor Company, Daimler-Chrysler, and General Electric) that implemented QS-9000, which includes a process by which they certify the quality function of their direct suppliers (called Tier 1 suppliers), of these suppliers' suppliers (Tier 2), and of these firms' suppliers in turn (Tier 3).

2-5 Elements of International Logistics

There are only a few activities that are exclusively specific to international logistics; however, the traditional logistical activities are managed differently in an international environment than they are in a domestic environment.

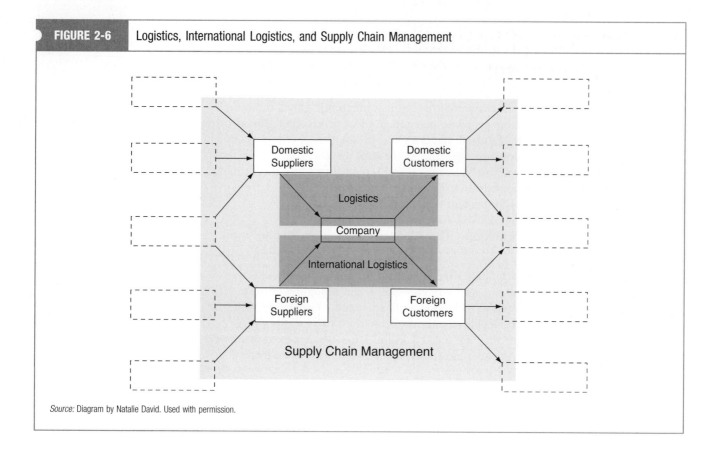

FIGURE 2-6   Logistics, International Logistics, and Supply Chain Management

Source: Diagram by Natalie David. Used with permission.

- The environment involved in international logistics is quite important. While there is obviously the issue of language and culture—neither of which should be underestimated, but which are more appropriately covered in an intercultural management textbook—the physical environment of international logistics is quite distinct. The differences in the infrastructure of international logistics and the challenges they represent are covered in Chapter 3.

- The decisions regarding international transportation are eminently more complicated. Because of the distances involved, there are different modes of transportation, different carriers, different transportation documents, and much greater transit times. Chapters 11, 12, and 13 cover these transportation alternatives.

- The number of intermediaries involved is greater. Banks, insurance companies, freight forwarders, to say nothing of the governments of the exporting and importing countries, all have different paperwork requirements. Chapter 9 covers the multitude of documents that are utilized in international trade.

- The inherent risks and hazards of international transportation are much more significant. In order to protect the goods while they are in transit, the logistics manager must have a good understanding of the packaging/packing options that are available. Chapter 14 covers the choices and decisions surrounding packing for international transport. Chapter 15 covers the management of security issues in international trade.

- International insurance is much more complex. The contracts are sometimes written using archaic language and terminology that varies in meaning depending on the country in which the insurance company is located. Chapter 10 presents the different types of insurance coverage available in an international environment.

- International means of payment are more involved. The risks of nonpayment and currency fluctuations call for specific strategies that are never used in domestic transactions. Chapter 7 explains the different alternative means of payment, and Chapter 8 presents the methods used by international traders to protect themselves against the risks presented by currency fluctuations.

- Terms of trade are much more complicated, as the greater number of nodes and links increases the number of possible alternatives for transfer of responsibility and ownership. The terms of trade used in international sales—the Incoterms of the International Chamber of Commerce—are presented thoroughly in Chapter 6.

- The crossing of borders represents specific challenges. Products sold abroad or purchased from abroad have to go through Customs, a complicated and paper-intensive process in most countries. The procedures involved in such a process are described in Chapter 16. In addition, in the conduct of business with foreign firms, issues arise in the contracts of sale, distribution agreements, and other legal documents. Chapters 4 and 5 present the options available to a firm engaged in international trade.

- Supply chain managers are becoming more conscious about sustainability issues and are therefore making decisions that reduce the energy and resources used in manufacturing, packaging, and shipping goods across borders. Each chapter of this textbook, when appropriate, deals with the sustainability issues that are relevant to the chapter's topic.

2-6 The Economic Importance of Logistics

In a yearly study of domestic logistics, Rosalyn Wilson calculates the percentage of the U.S. gross domestic product (GDP) that is spent on logistical activities (transportation, inventory, and administrative costs linked to logistical activities). In 2004, those activities stood at 8.5 percent of GDP but increased to 10.1 percent in 2007, due to rising energy costs.[21] Collectively, American businesses spend upward of $1.4 trillion on domestic logistical activities.

Until 2005, logistical costs had been steadily decreasing as a percentage of GDP: While their share of GDP was traditionally in the mid-teens in the 1960s and 1970s—with a high of 16.2 percent in 1982—they have steadily declined since the 1990s, as shown in Figure 2-7.[22] This decrease is due mostly to corporations becoming more efficient in their use of inventory; the advent of just-in-time, MRP, and their subsequent derivatives have decreased inventory levels from 24 percent of the U.S. GDP in 1981 to a low of 14 percent in 2004;[23] they increased to 14.6 percent in 2007,[24] due mostly to reduced sales rather than inefficiencies.

Some of this decrease can also be attributed to more efficient means of transportation—for example, the increased use of containers—and to the deregulation of the U.S. transportation industry, especially during the 1980s and early 1990s.

However, since the late 1990s, the costs of transportation have been slowly rising; increased fuel costs, a shortage of truck drivers, additional security costs, and a transportation infrastructure stretched to its limits have considerably increased what businesses spend collectively on transportation. Transportation costs rose almost 20 percent from 2004 to 2007, and represent 6.2 percent of the GDP of the United States.

Overall, the logistics functions of U.S. companies are much more efficient than those of its trade partners' companies. In 2000, the China Federation of Logistics and Purchasing estimated that logistics costs amounted to 20 percent of the Chinese GDP and that they had decreased only to 18.3 percent in 2006.[25] This progress is due to improvements in infrastructure and the adoption of better inventory management techniques; nevertheless, it is still about twice the relative weight of the same function in the United States.

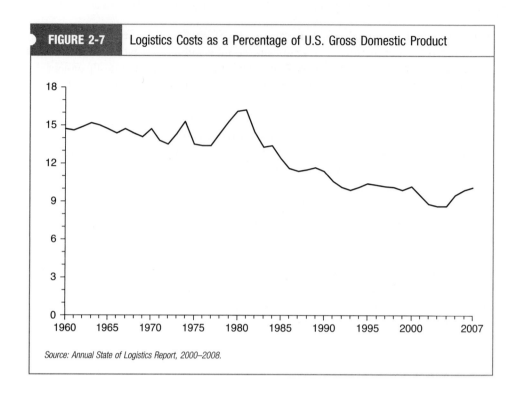

FIGURE 2-7 Logistics Costs as a Percentage of U.S. Gross Domestic Product

Source: Annual State of Logistics Report, 2000–2008.

2-7 The Economic Importance of International Logistics

While there are no comprehensive data illustrating the total value of international logistics activities, it can be conservatively estimated that the percentage spent on international logistics activities would be around 15 percent of the total volume of international trade. Because the total value of the world's merchandise trade is U.S. $13.6 trillion, the total expenditures on international logistics is approximately U.S. $2 trillion. This estimate takes into account the fact that the domestic logistical infrastructure of the North American continent is particularly efficient and that international logistics activities are typically more cumbersome and costly due to less efficient infrastructures and procedures, as well as longer distances.

There is one aspect of international logistics, though, that distinguishes it from domestic logistics regarding its impact on the world's economy: Not only are the profits of corporations involved in logistics taxed by their respective governments, but international trade also generates a considerable amount of additional government revenues, as most imports are subject to tariffs. A very conservative estimate of the "value" of duty collection and other taxes directly linked to international trade would be about 5 percent of the world's merchandise trade. International logistics activities therefore generate approximately U.S. $500 billion in additional government revenues.

reverse logistics The management of the logistical activities involved in the return of a product (or parts of it, including the packaging) to a manufacturer.

2-8 The Emergence of International Reverse Logistics

The management of **reverse logistics** involves the handling of goods after they have been sold to the final consumer or customer. Reverse logistics is the "process of planning, implementing, and controlling the efficient, cost effective flow of raw materials, in-process inventory, finished goods and related information from the point of consumption to the point of origin for the purpose of recapturing value or proper disposal."[26] Essentially, the activities of reverse logistics are the same as those of traditional logistics, except in "reverse."

Goods are returned to the manufacturer for a number of reasons:

- The goods have completed their useful life for the consumer or customer and are returned because they can be remanufactured or refurbished by the manufacturer. There are multiple incentives for both the customer and the manufacturer to do so; either there are sustainability incentives to the consumer (laws to encourage the return of obsolete or depleted goods), or the costs of returning the goods are lower than the disposal costs for the customer, or the return and reuse costs for the manufacturer are lower than the costs of manufacturing new parts.

- The goods are returned because the consumer needs them to be repaired under warranty, or the goods do not meet the expectations of the customer.

- The goods are defective and the manufacturer issues a recall of the goods so that they can be repaired or made to conform to the requirements of the market.

- The packaging that was used to ship the goods from the manufacturer's plant to the customer's facilities can be reused for another shipment.

Many companies are now realizing that a reverse logistics system combined with source-reduction processes can be used to gain competitive advantage through value creation.[27] Specific examples come from Kodak, Estée Lauder, and Caterpillar.

Kodak started a campaign in 1990 to take back, reuse, and recycle its single-use cameras, originally designed as disposables. In 1990, it collected 0.9 million cameras and by 1998, that figure had jumped to 61 million units. As of 2008, Kodak had multiple recycling facilities where up to 86 percent of camera parts are reused in manufacturing new cameras.

Estée Lauder used to dump $60 million of its products into landfills annually. In the first year of its reverse logistics program, after an initial investment of $1.3 million, Estée Lauder was able to increase the number of returned products by 24 percent, reduce the number of destroyed products from 37 percent to 27 percent of returned products, and save $0.5 million in labor costs. Estée Lauder has since created a $250 million product line from its return flows, the third most profitable product line in the company.

As for Caterpillar, it operates 14 remanufacturing plants around the world. The plants are capable of disassembling and rebuilding diesel engines—cleaning, inspecting, and repairing as many as 20,000 parts along the way. The remanufacturing division of Caterpillar is its fastest growing division, at a rate of 20 percent per year, and annual revenues exceed $1 billion.[28]

In all cases, especially in an international environment, the process of getting the goods from the customer or consumer to the manufacturer involves the intermediaries that were present at the time of the original sale. Many companies are starting to implement a "cradle to cradle" manufacturing system, in which the product is manufactured, used by consumers, recovered after use, and then reused, refurbished, resold, or some combination of these activities, to put the product back into circulation. Figure 2-8 shows the flows in a typical reverse logistics system from "cradle to cradle."[29]

Manufacturers, especially in the United States, have not typically designed products for repair, reuse, or recovery. There is a strong sentiment worldwide to change that business model with the introduction of extended producer responsibility laws. European environmental laws have been introduced with the concept of extended producer responsibility for everything from the products themselves to their packaging materials. Many firms are now realizing that designing products for not

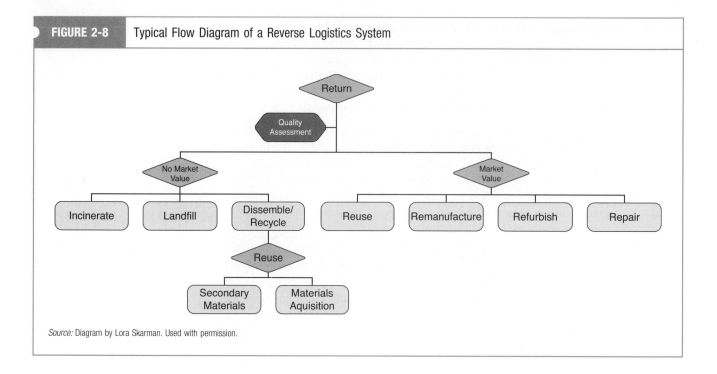

FIGURE 2-8   Typical Flow Diagram of a Reverse Logistics System

Source: Diagram by Lora Skarman. Used with permission.

only the first use, but also subsequent use provides a cost advantage because these products can be sold in secondary markets with minimal work after recovery. The cost of raw materials, transportation, storage, and other supply chain components as well as regulations will drive international logistics professionals to get the most out of their products' life cycles.

Two Different Reverse Logistics Programs

In 1991, the German government passed a law that required all manufacturers of consumer packaged goods to take back all of the packaging that they used to ship their goods, including the final consumer containers. This law triggered the creation of a dual refuse collection system, ubiquitous in the country, called *Der Grüne Punkt*, The Green Dot, designed to collect and return all consumer packaging materials to the manufacturers.

Set up by the industry, this secondary garbage collection system is made up of yellow collection bins located near retail centers and of yellow plastic bags used by households on garbage collection days that are designed to collect used consumer packages (see Figure 2-9). The materials collected are then sorted, recycled, or reused. The entire system is funded by the industry. As of 2001, German consumers recycled more than 80 percent of their packaging materials.[30]

The city of Curitiba, Brazil, has implemented its recycling program in a completely different way. It has placed recycling containers throughout the city and has encouraged families to sort their household waste (see Figure 2-10). It is an entirely voluntary program, but the city has managed to recycle more than two-thirds of its household refuse.[31]

The city hires homeless and very low income residents to collect recyclable items and exchanges what they collect for food and money. The city even has a "green exchange" program through which residents of the *favelas* (slums) that surround the city can exchange their household trash for food. This has the effect of keeping these neighborhoods cleaner and improves the nutrition and income of the city's poorest residents.

continued

Two Different Reverse Logistics Programs (Continued)

Figure 2-9
A *Grüne Punkt* Recycling Bin in Germany, Specifically
Marked "For Packaging Materials Only"
Source: Photo © Vovchychko. Used with permission.

Figure 2-10
The Color-coded Recycling Bins of Curitiba, Brazil
Source: Photo © Gilberto de Oliveira Souza. Used with permission.

Review and Discussion Questions

1. What are the elements that differentiate international logistics from domestic logistics?

2. What are the principal distinct components of international logistics?

3. What are the major costs of international logistics? Given what you read in Chapter 1 about the World Trade Organization, what trend do you expect these costs to follow?

4. MRP and DRP have allowed manufacturers and retailers to carry less and less inventory. What consequences would a major snowstorm or disruption of transportation have on such just-in-time management systems?

5. Describe the impact of international trade on your own life, using the products that you own or have purchased in the recent past.

Endnotes

1. Gies, Frances, and Joseph Gies, *Cathedral, Forge and Waterwheel; Technology and Invention in the Middle Ages*. New York: HarperCollins Publishers, 1995.

2. Klein, Jacob, *Greek Mathematical Thought and the Origin of Algebra*, translated by Eva Brann. Mineola, NY: Dover Publications, 1992. Original published by MIT Press, 1968.

3. Pacini, Alfred, and Dominique Pons, *Docker à Marseille, Récits de vie Payot*, T. S. Simey, ed. Paris, 1996.

4. Levinson, Marc, *The Box: How the Shipping Container Made the World Smaller and the World Economy Bigger*. Princeton, NJ: Princeton University Press, 2006.

5. Levinson, Marc, *The Box: How the Shipping Container Made the World Smaller and the World Economy Bigger*. Princeton, NJ: Princeton University Press, 2006. Cudahy, Brian J., *Box Boats: How Containerships Changed the World*. New York: Fordham University Press, 2006. Donovan, Arthur, and Joseph Bonney, "The box that changed the world," published by *The Journal of Commerce*. New York: Commonwealth Business Media, 2006.

6. Levinson, Marc, *The Box: How the Shipping Container Made the World Smaller and the World Economy Bigger*. Princeton, NJ: Princeton University Press, 2006.

7. Donovan, Arthur, and Joseph Bonney, "The box that changed the world," published by *The Journal of Commerce*. New York: Commonwealth Business Media, 2006.

8. Levinson, Marc, *The Box: How the Shipping Container Made the World Smaller and the World Economy Bigger*. Princeton, NJ: Princeton University Press, 2006.

9. *Ibid.*

10. Hummels, David, "Time as a Trade Barrier," Purdue University working paper, July 2001, http://www.unc.edu/depts/econ/seminars/hummels.pdf.

11. *World Investment Report 1996: Investment, Trade, and International Policy Agreements*, United Nations, August 1996, and *World Investment Report 2008: Transnational Corporations and the Infrastructure Challenge*, United Nations, July 2008.

12. "Record 182,000 new products flood CPG shelves," *Metrics 2.0*, February 19, 2007, http://www.metrics2.com/blog/2007/02/19/record_182000_new_products_flood_global_cpg_shelve.html.

13. *The smarter Supply Chain of the Future; Global Chief Supply Chain Officer Study*, January 2009, IBM Global Services,

Route 100, Somers, NY 10589, http://www-935.ibm.com/services/us/gbs/bus/html/gbs-csco-study.html, accessed May 13, 2009.

14. *Ibid.*

15. Council of Supply Chain Management Professionals, "Supply Chain Management/Logistics Management Definitions," http://cscmp.org/aboutcscmp/definitions.asp, accessed April 26, 2009.

16. Delaney, Robert V., and Rosalyn Wilson, *13th Annual State of Logistics Report: Understanding Inventory—Stay Curious*, ProLogis and Cass Information Systems, Inc., June 10, 2002, http://www.uwa.com/supply_a_004.pdf.

17. Larson, Paul D., and Arni Halldorsson, "Logistics vs. supply chain management: An international survey," *Journal of Supply Chain Management*, March 2004, pp. 17–31.

18. Council of Supply Chain Management Professionals, "Supply Chain Management/Logistics Management Definitions," http://cscmp.org/aboutcscmp/definitions.asp, accessed April 26, 2009.

19. *The smarter Supply Chain of the Future; Global Chief Supply Chain Officer Study*, January 2009, IBM Global Services, Route 100, Somers, NY 10589, http://www-935.ibm.com/services/us/gbs/bus/html/gbs-csco-study.html, accessed May 13, 2009.

20. Fahey, Jonathan, "The parts paradox," *Forbes*, May 8, 2006.

21. Wilson, Rosalyn, *19th Annual State of Logistics Report: Surviving the Slump*, Council of Logistics Management, June 18, 2008, http://cscmp.org/securedownloads/filedownload.aspx?fn=memberonly/19SoLReport.pdf.

22. Wilson, Rosalyn, *17th Annual State of Logistics Report: Embracing security as a core business function*, Council of Logistics Management, June 19, 2006, https://cscmp.org/Downloads/Memberonly/17StateLogisticsReport.pdf.

23. Wilson, Rosalyn, *19th Annual State of Logistics Report: Surviving the Slump*, Council of Logistics Management, June 18, 2008, http://cscmp.org/securedownloads/filedownload.aspx?fn=memberonly/19SoLReport.pdf.

24. *Ibid.*

25. "Several Issues in China's Logistics Industry," *Market Avenue*, January 28, 2008, http://www.marketavenue.cn/upload/articles/ARTICLES_1340.htm.

26. Hawks, Karen, "What Is Reverse Logistics?" *Reverse Logistics Magazine*, Winter-Spring 2006, pp. 12–13.

27. Jayaraman, Vaidyanathan, and Yadong Luo, "Creating Competitive Advantages Through New Value Creation: A Reverse Logistics Perspective," *Academy of Management Perspectives*, May 2007, pp. 56–73.

28. *Ibid.*

29. Stock, James R., *Development and Implementation of Reverse Logistics Processes*, Council of Logistics Management, 1998.

30. Rekacewicz, Philippe, "Packaging Production and Recycling: Selected European Countries," http://maps.grida.no/go/graphic/packaging_production_and_recycling_selected_european_countries, accessed August, 4, 2009.

31. Alvarado, Paula, "Jaime Lerner and Sustainability in Curitiba and 'Urban Acupuncture'," November 12, 2007, http://www.treehugger.com/files/2007/11/jaime_lerner_interview_planeta_sustentavel.php.

International Logistics Infrastructure

Chapter Three

Key Terms

air draft (p. 43)

berth (p. 45)

draft (p. 42)

infrastructure (p. 41)

land bridge (p. 57)

leap frogging (p. 57)

For the manager of international logistics, it is important to have a good under-standing of the challenges presented by the different levels of **infrastructure** found abroad. It is always one of the first problems encountered by an international manager; things don't work abroad like they do at "home." There are different standards and expectations of performance, things that work much better, and things that do not work as well—in some cases, not at all. Adapting to those differences and anticipating problems before they arise are among the skills of an experienced international logistics manager.

The issue with learning how to manage these differences in infrastructure is that they are difficult to generalize in one particular comment or statement. Most challenges tend to be concentrated in some small geographic areas, and in most cases are limited to a single location: A specific port is not equipped with sufficient cold-storage warehousing space, does not have an appropriately sized crane, or is experiencing delays in getting the goods from the port to the remainder of the country; a road is particularly congested, a specific tunnel has recently been closed, or a railroad is experiencing shortages of appropriate cars. These challenges force the manager involved in international logistics to recognize the possibility of serious problems. The purpose of this chapter is to present enough information and examples to encourage him or her to ask questions at the onset of a transaction, so that there are no discrepancies between the expectations of the company and what can be achieved.

infrastructure A collective term that refers to all of the elements in place (publicly or privately owned goods) to facilitate transportation, communication, and business exchanges.

3-1 Definitions

Before going much further, it would be useful to determine what is meant by "infrastructure" in the context of international logistics. A few dictionary definitions would be a good start:

> The basic facilities, services, and installations needed for the functioning of a community or society, such as transportation and communication.[1]

> A collective term for the subordinate parts of an undertaking; substructure, foundation.

> The permanent installations forming a basis for military operations, as airfields, naval bases, training establishments, … etc.[2]

In the field of logistics, the definition can be very broad: *Infrastructure* is a collective term that refers to all of the elements in place (publicly or privately owned goods) to facilitate transportation, communication, and business exchanges. It would therefore include not only transportation and communication elements, but also the existence and quality of public utilities, banking services, and retail distribution channels. To this list, it makes sense to add the existence and quality of the court system, the defense of intellectual property rights, and the existence of standards. As these concepts are introduced in this chapter, their inclusion into the concept of infrastructure will become more understandable.

The study of infrastructure is important because the movement of goods and of documents, as well as the movement of money and information, is dependent on these infrastructure components.

3-2 Transportation Infrastructure

The infrastructure that most obviously affects the movement of goods internationally is that of transport. Without a good understanding of the transportation infras-tructure that a shipment will face, a manager may package a product inappropriately, may face delays, or may even be faced with unexpectedly damaged merchandise.

3-2a Port Infrastructure

Port infrastructure is made up of several items, most of which are interconnected and obviously affect the type of ships that can call on a given port, as well as the type of merchandise that can transit through it.

With the advent of the much larger post-Panamax containerships—i.e., those too large to get through the Panama Canal—ports have been faced with many challenges. Specifically, the size of those ships is stretching the capabilities of the ports: They are wider, longer and higher above the water, and have much deeper drafts. There were 29 containerships of a capacity greater than 10,000 TEUs—twenty-foot equivalent units, or twenty-foot containers—scheduled to be delivered in 2008–2009, and as many as 200 to be built and delivered before 2012 (see Table 3-1), which represents only 14 percent of all the ships ordered for that period, but 35.8 percent of the capacity being built.[3] Most of these ships operate on the trans-Pacific routes between the United States, Japan, China, Singapore, and Hong Kong. Such large ships mean that as many as 6,000 forty-foot containers need to be unloaded and 6,000 loaded in a single port.

Depth of Water

The first issue is undoubtedly the depth of the water of a port, which has to be sufficient to accommodate the **draft** of the ships that call at that port. In many ports, the depth of the channels and of the berths, which had been sufficient to accommodate Panamax ships, is not sufficient to accommodate the newer, larger ships. Therefore, in a great number of ports, the port authorities have had to engage in dredging activities in order to allow ships with drafts exceeding 40 feet (13.5 meters) to access the port. Only a few ports with naturally deep channels have been exempt from this activity.[5]

draft The minimum depth of water that a ship needs in order to float.

TABLE 3-1	Containerships on Order as of August 2008			
TEU Size Range	**Number of Ships**	**Percentage of Ships on Order**	**Total Capacity of Ships (in TEUs)**	**Percentage of Ship Capacity**
Ships Smaller than Panamax				
0-999	131	9.4%	108,858	1.6%
1,000-1,999	283	20.4%	408,580	6.0%
2,000-2,999	142	10.2%	365,182	5.4%
3,000-3,999	84	6.0%	286,250	4.2%
Panamax				
4,000-4,999	256	18.4%	1,110,523	16.3%
Total Panamax and smaller	896	64.5%	2,279,393	33.5%
Post-Panamax				
5,000-5,999	54	3.9%	285,938	4.2%
6,000-6,999	107	7.7%	696,534	10.2%
7,000-7,999	24	1.7%	178,000	2.6%
8,000-8,999	94	6.8%	792,954	11.7%
9,000-9,999	14	1.0%	133,200	2.0%
10,000-10,999	39	2.8%	390,840	5.7%
11,000-11,999	20	1.4%	226,000	3.3%
12,000-12,999	56	4.0%	701,640	10.3%
13,000-13,999	85	6.1%	1,120,138	16.5%
Total post-Panamax	493	35.5%	4,525,244	66.5%
Total	1,389		6,804,637	

Source: Clarkson Ship Register and CompairData, as reported in *American Shipper.*[4]

Despite the fact that the dredging of channels and ports can be exceedingly expensive, ports have little alternative but to undertake this improvement of their capabilities. One of the ports that has benefited from its natural assets is the Port of Prince Rupert in British Columbia, Canada, which started handling container freight in the fall of 2007. The port enjoys terminals with a natural draft of 67 feet (20 meters), as well as a Canadian National Railroad terminal in the port giving it a direct link to the North American continent. Since it also is the North American port closest to the Asian rim ports, Prince Rupert is attempting to divert some of the traffic that traditionally called on West Coast ports in the United States; it can shorten transit times from China to Chicago by as many as 60 hours.[6]

In a parallel fashion, longer ships require longer turning circles, and therefore a redesign—and dredging—of different access channels. As ships become yet longer, wider, and heavier, the challenge for the ports will be to keep up with these ships' requirements and adapt.

Bridge Clearance

Another factor of great importance in ports is the clearance under its bridges; the ships that call on that port have an **air draft** that dictates the minimum space they need under the port's bridges. In many older ports, the bridges are too close to the water, leaving very little clearance for tall ships or ships carrying outsized cargo. In some cases, the ships have to be modified or designed so that they can clear the bridges: Several of the ships that call on the Port of New York–New Jersey were specifically designed to accommodate the Bayonne Bridge's low clearance of 151 feet (45 meters) above the water at high tide.[7]

air draft The minimum amount of space between the water and the lowest part of bridges that a ship needs in order to enter a port.

These factors—depth of channels and berths, and bridge clearance—are likely to affect how ports are used in the future. There is a strong likelihood that some ports will not be able to make the necessary infrastructure adjustments to accommodate the largest ships and that there will be a need to create large port hubs, to and from which mega-containerships will travel. Smaller ports would then be served by smaller "feeder" ships that would not tax the ports' infrastructures beyond their capacity. Such large port hubs were created in the 1990s in the Mediterranean Sea: Marsaxlokk in Malta and Cagliari in Sardinia (Italy) serve as trans-shipment ports, loading and unloading large containerships in deepwater and using feeder services to serve the local markets and shallower ports of France, Italy, and Spain. There have been discussions of a large port fulfilling the same function on the Atlantic Coast of the United States, to alleviate the constraints presented by the current older ports of New York and Philadelphia.[8]

An example of such an effort is the deepwater Port of Yangshan, part of the Port of Shanghai, in China (see Figure 3-1). It was built on several small islands near Shanghai

Figure 3-1
The Deepwater Port of Yangshan, Shanghai, China
Source: Photo © Bert Van Dijk. Used with permission.

and is linked to the mainland by the Donghai Bridge, a 20-mile-long (32 kilometers) bridge, most of which is above water.[9] As the Port of Shanghai became congested, and since it is relatively shallow and would require a lot of dredging, the government of China decided to build a deepwater port in the Hangzhou Bay, just south of Shanghai. The port was built on a large landfill between two of the uninhabited islands. A good way of seeing the work that has been accomplished is to look at Google Maps (http:// maps.google.com) and enter the following geographic coordinates: 30°37′30″ North and 122°04′00″ East. Since the program generally starts on the "map" setting of the program, the islands are shown as they were before the construction of the port, and the coordinates will yield a result which is "just water." By switching to the "satellite" view, the port becomes visible, with the landfill connecting the two islands. There are a number of Panoramio photographs linked to that page as well.

The new port is expected to rival the Ports of Hong Kong and Singapore for the title of largest port in the world, measured by the number of containers handled. As of 2009, it had 16 berths, with the capacity to handle 9.3 million TEUs per year. When it will be completed in 2020, it will have 30 berths and will be able to handle 15 million TEUs.[10]

Cranes

Port terminals have found out that the width of those post-Panamax ships can also be a challenge for their cranes. The width of a traditional Panamax ship can be loaded with up to thirteen containers (see Figure 3-2). Some of the post-Panamax ships can be loaded with as many as eighteen containers side-by-side. This presents a problem for ports in which the cranes cannot reach the far side of the ship. Early on, ports managed their lack of crane capacity by loading ships from one side, turning the ships around, and then loading the remainder of the containers. The problem was one of balance, as the ships list if they are heavier on one side. Today's ports have made considerable investments in new large-capacity cranes that can load these large ships.

Figure 3-2
A Traditional Container Berth and Gantry Cranes in the Port of Hong Kong
Source: Photo © Wong Kai Yan. Used with permission.

Figure 3-3
The Indented Container Berth of the Paragon Terminal in Amsterdam
Source: Photo © Port of Amsterdam. Used with permission.

Another obvious alternative is for ports to increase the reach of the cranes, which would be accompanied by a need to increase the height of the cranes, as the vessels are higher. These modifications can be quite costly for a port, and new cranes capable of serving these ships can cost $50 million.[11]

Another alternative, chosen by the Amsterdam Container Terminals at the Paragon Terminal, is to create an indented **berth** to allow ships to be loaded from both sides (see Figure 3-3). An advantage of this configuration is that it allows the ship to be loaded with up to twelve cranes rather than the maximum of six in a traditional port. This alternative speeds up the loading of the ship considerably, from a maximum of 160 containers per hour (the world record held by the Port of Singapore for a traditional berth) to up to 300 containers per hour, decreasing the time that a ship spends in port and therefore increasing its profitability.[12]

For shippers handling noncontainerized cargo, the cranes' capacity is a major factor in deciding through which port to send a specific cargo. Cigna Insurance published a directory called *Ports of the World* that lists the equipment of any port in the world, specifically the capacity of its cranes (see Table 3-2).[13] Unfortunately, ACE Limited, the company that purchased Cigna's international property-and-casualty insurance business, has not updated the booklet since the late 1990s, and the information has become obsolete. The best alternative to find out what the capabilities of a port are is to find its Web site; however, sometimes, especially if the port is small, the information will be incomplete or nonexistent.

From a shipper's standpoint, it should be obvious that the crane at the port of destination should have at least the same capacity as the one that was used to load the cargo. Failure to pay attention to that fact is likely to lead to a dismantling of the cargo or to the use of an overloaded crane, both of which could place the cargo in jeopardy.

berth The location, in a port, where a ship is loaded and unloaded.

Port Operations

Another issue in ports is the way the port is managed, particularly its work rules, which are often dictated by strong unions. Some ports, such as the Port of Long Beach on the Pacific coast of the United States, used to operate only eight hours a day[14] instead

TABLE 3-2   Typical Entries in *Ports of the World* Booklet

Piraeus, Greece

Facilities

Transportation Services	Truck, Rail, and Barge
Cargo Storage	Covered: 245,000 m^2
	Open: 1.6 million m^2
	Refrigerated: adequate
Special Cranes	Heavy lift: 130 tons
	Container: 2 with 40-ton capacity
Air Cargo	Hellinikon Airport: 14 kilometers

Cargo Handling

Containerized, bulk, and general cargo can be handled by existing port equipment.
2 RO/RO and 7 tanker terminal berths are available.
Specialized handling is also provided for ore and bulk commodities.

General

Winters are mild (3°C to 4°C average) with summers hot (42°C) and relatively dry (40 centimeters annual rainfall).
Container facilities are being expanded.
Plans include the development of an open area of 320,000 m^2 for the Ikonion Container facility.

Takoradi, Ghana

Facilities

Transportation Services	Truck and Rail
Cargo Storage	Covered: storage adequate; transit shed accommodate 12,500 tons of general cargo
	Open: 5,000 tons capacity
Special Cranes	Heavy lift capacity is 17.5 tons
Air Cargo	Accra Airport: 260 kilometers

Cargo Handling

Normal cargo can be handled through Takoradi. This port also has bulk, tanker, and RO/RO berths for specialized cargo handling.

General

Average rainfall is approximately 70 centimeters, with heaviest accumulations from April through August.
Temperatures range from 16° C to 30° C.
Fixed shore facilities are to be upgraded and new equipment provided.

Source: Cigna Insurance.

of the much more efficient twenty-four hours a day, seven days a week of most Asian Pacific Rim ports. Today, the port stevedores will load and unload a ship at any time, but the terminals' truck gates are open from only 7:00 A.M. to 5:00 P.M., and only on weekdays, ostensibly to accommodate the work hours of the businesses shipping goods to and from the port.[15] Nevertheless, since the immense majority of the goods transiting through the Ports of Long Beach and Los Angeles are destined for areas far beyond Southern California, the rule is very constraining.

Work rules can also be mind-bogglingly complex and hamper the efficiency of ports to the point where they are less and less competitive: In the 1950s, unions dominating the ports of South America were refusing to unload containers,[16] for example. When there are attempts at modifying these rules, strikes are common: Some Japanese and European ports are plagued with recurring work stoppages. Finally, the issue of productivity is often linked to labor practices. For example, while Japanese ports can handle routinely 45 container movements per hour per crane, most United

States ports stagnate at 25 movements per hour.[17] As productivity in the ports increases, the need for additional capital expenditures decreases. For many ports that are physically constrained by the sea on one side and by a large city on the other, increases in productivity are the only possible avenues for handling the growth in cargo volume that they are experiencing.

Warehousing Space

It is critical to understand the amount of warehouse storage space that exists in the port. In most instances, it is necessary for merchandise to be placed in some storage areas that are protected from the elements (specifically rain and sun). If these storage areas are not available or are overcrowded, then it's likely that cargo will be left exposed, leading to possible damages. Cigna's *Ports of the World* lists the amount of covered storage space available in every port (see Table 3-2).

Similarly, the shipper should pay attention to the amount of space available in the port to store containers before and after their ocean voyage; the smaller the space, the greater the probability that a container will be moved multiple times, or that it will be stored in an inappropriate location. Even if the cargo can tolerate being left exposed to the elements, another concern is the possibility of flooding in the container—or cargo—staging area. It is not unusual, when bad weather strikes, to see a port's container yard flood and the containers at the bottom of a stack partially immersed, even in a modern port. During the floods that devastated southern Brazil in 2008, hundreds of containers were affected by the water surge in the ports of Paranaguá, Itajaí, and São Francisco do Sul (see Figure 3-4).

For refrigerated cargo containers, these issues are compounded by their need for a reliable power supply and proper reefer storage areas, equipped with power outlets and personnel competent enough to monitor the temperature charts of the refrigerated containers.

Figure 3-4
The Port of Itajaí Flooded in December 2008
Source: Photo © Eduardo Marquetti. Used with permission.

Connections with Land-Based Transportation Services

Yet another issue at ports are their connections to the remainder of the country's transport infrastructure, such as rail and road access. In some cases, there is so much congestion on the access roads to port terminals that cargo can be delayed substantially. This is a major issue in just about every port in the world, but particularly in North and South America and in China. Most ports are obviously located near the ocean, and the cities that developed around these ports are located between the port and the hinterlands, which the cargo must eventually traverse. Therefore, every piece of cargo that is shipped through the port has to travel through the city, which creates a serious strain on road and railroad infrastructures to and from the port and engenders serious traffic jams and the resentment of the local population. Ports are actively looking at overcoming these bottlenecks.[18]

The Ports of Los Angeles and Long Beach inaugurated in 2002 the Alameda Corridor, a north-south, 20-mile (32 kilometers) rail link between the ports and the transcontinental rail yards on the eastern edge of the city of Los Angeles (see Figure 3-5). The Corridor is a 33-feet (10 meter)-deep trench that cuts through the city's neighborhoods and is uninterrupted by road traffic.[19]

Port Capacity

Another issue in ocean transportation is the strained capacity of ports, as many ports are operating at capacity or very near their capacity. Because ports tend to be physically located between an ocean and a city, there are limits to the ways that they can expand as their traffic increases. Many ports add capacity by gaining on the sea with landfills or by purchasing real estate that is then transformed into port terminals, both of which tend to be quite costly. For example, the port of Santos in Brazil is located on a "river" that stretches between an island and the mainland. The older port is located on the island, and it cannot expand because it is constrained by the city of Santos on one side and the river on the other side, on which it cannot gain because the river cannot be

Figure 3-5

The Alameda Corridor between the Port of Long Beach and East Los Angeles

Source: Photo © Alameda Corridor Transportation Authority. Used with permission.

made narrower. All of the port expansion has been on the other side of the river, but, there again, it is limited by the river and suburbs that are now growing along with the city.

In the United States, there is, for example, an increasing need for additional capacity in container terminals on the Pacific Coast. This extra capacity cannot come from the expansion of the ports themselves; it has to come from increases in productivity, which is difficult to achieve, or from the addition of new ports. The creation of the Port of Prince Rupert, in a city of 14,000 inhabitants unconstrained by urban sprawl, with a strong rail connection to the hinterland and a deep natural harbor, is a harbinger of what is to come.

3-2b Canal and Waterway Infrastructure

Maritime transportation is also quite dependent on the existence and proper maintenance of canals and other maritime channels. Their size, as well as the size of their locks, has a great influence on international trade. For example, ships sized to get through the Suez Canal are called Suez-Max ships, just as those sized to get through the Panama Canal locks are called Panamax ships. The current trend in shipbuilding is to create ships that are much too large to fit through the Panama Canal: These vessels are called post-Panamax ships.

The Panama Canal

On August 15, 1914, the *Ancon* became the first ship to officially pass through the Panama Canal. This unprecedented voyage ushered in a new era of shipping and international trade. The new route allowed ships to make the trans-Pacific voyage from Asia to the Americas quickly and safely. At a cost of $375 million (and 25,000 lives), the Canal immediately put Panama at the center of global trade.[20]

Today, nearly one hundred years later, the canal is as important as ever, accounting for 5 percent of world trade. However, with the launching of new mega-ships, the canal is quickly reaching its capacity. The new giant container-ships are too large to fit through it. The small number of these giant ships in use today means it is not yet a major issue, but as more and larger ships are put into service, this situation will quickly change. The increased trade between Asia and the rest of the world in recent years has also meant more ships passing through the canal, and it faces so much traffic that there is often a backup, with some ships having to wait days for their turn.[21] The Panama Canal Authority was faced with the dilemma to either improve the canal or watch it become outdated.

After years of planning, the Panama Canal Authority has decided to spend $5.25 billion to improve the canal and make it more viable for modern shipping needs, a project that will double the current canal's capacity and allow it to accept larger ships by 2015. This is a massive

engineering project that will take advantage of the techniques learned in building the original canal while implementing new methods to build the new canal faster, making it much more efficient. The new canal will replace its current locks (see Figure 3-6) with new ones that are 1,400 feet long (420 meters), 180 feet wide (54 meters), and 60 feet deep (18 meters), allowing the canal to accommodate 12,600 TEU vessels, mega-ships previously labeled as post-Panamax.

The new canal will include two new sets of locks, one set on the Pacific side and one on the Atlantic. Two new navigational channels will also be built to connect to the existing canal. One major obstacle the engineers struggled with was getting access to enough water to supply the canal, which will require two billion gallons per day. They solved this by implementing a system that will reuse 60 percent of the water flushed out during each ship's passing. This means that although the new canal holds 65 percent more water than the old one, it will actually use 7 percent less water.

The final obstacle the Canal Authority faced was how to pay for the project. The Panamanian government and citizens support the project, but the small country cannot afford to pay the multi-billion dollar price tag. Executives eventually came up with a plan that will pay for the project through increased canal tolls, cash reserves, and international loans.[22] Construction has started and authorities are

continued

The Panama Canal (Continued)

hoping that on the 100th anniversary of the original canal in 2014, the eyes of the world will once again turn to their country as the first mega-ship passes through the new Panama Canal.

Figure 3-6
The Panama Canal: The Gatun Locks on the Atlantic Side
Source: Photo © Roger Wollstadt. Used with permission.

From an international logistics standpoint, several waterways are fundamentally and strategically important. However, these waterways have lost their monopoly, as alternatives were developed to circumvent their shortcomings.

- **The Bosporus Strait in Turkey**. Joining the Black Sea to the Mediterranean Sea, it is the only water link between the Black Sea and the oceans. A large percentage of the merchandise trade between Russia and the rest of the world transits through it, creating severe congestion and raising safety concerns for the city of Istanbul, which is built on both sides of the Strait. Several efforts have been made to convert some of that traffic to a network of pipelines.[23]

- **The Suez Canal**. Located in the sandy desert of eastern Egypt (see Figure 3-7), the Suez Canal links the Red Sea to the Mediterranean Sea and allows ships to avoid traveling around the entire continent of Africa when they are going from the Persian Gulf to Europe. When it was closed after the Six-Day War in 1967, oil companies started to build much larger oil tankers, to make the voyage around the Cape (South Africa) more cost-effective. Since its reopening in 1975, the canal has recaptured some of the traffic it had lost, through a widening and deepening effort. However, it is still too shallow for many ships, and its tolls are prohibitive. The cost of a single trip through the Canal can exceed U.S. $500,000 (see Table 3-3).

- **The Panama Canal**. Designed to allow ships to avoid traveling around Cape Horn in South America, the Panama Canal allows ships to cut as many as three weeks off their journey between the Atlantic and the Pacific Oceans. However, the canal is remarkably "slow," because it is essentially running at its maximum

Figure 3-7
A Container Ship, the 8400-TEU *Maersk Taikung*, in the Suez Canal
Source: Photo © Timothy Meyer. Used with permission.

TABLE 3-3	Toll Calculation for a Large-Size Laden Containership Using the Suez Canal Northbound

Tariff for a Laden Container Ship, Northbound
Suez Canal Net Tonnage : 80,000
Gross Registered Tons : 171,000
Draft: 15.5m
Canal Tolls breakdown:

First 5000 : 5000 × 7.65	38,250.00 SDR
Next 5000 : 5000 × 5.00	25,000.00 SDR
Next 10000 : 10000 × 4.00	40,000.00 SDR
Next 20000 : 20000 × 2.80	56,000.00 SDR
Next 30000 : 30000 × 2.60	78,000.00 SDR
Next 50000 : 10000 × 2.05	20,500.00 SRD
	257,750.00 SDR
USD/SDR Exchange rate : 1.5555 USD	
Canal Tolls	400,919.72 USD
Tugs (1 tug)	12,443.68 USD
Mooring / Projector	2,352.50 USD
Pilotage	634.63 USD
Disbursements	14,389.20 USD
TOTAL	430,739.73 USD

SDR = Special Drawing Rights currency.
Source: Leth Agencies.[24]

capacity. Wait times to enter it average twenty-two hours.[25] Yet, despite the emergence of land bridges (see Section 3-2d) in the United States, and the emergence of post-Panamax ships, the canal still retains its commercial importance, and its tolls are competitive, averaging U.S. $67,000.

- **The Saint Lawrence Seaway**. Linking the Great Lakes to the St. Lawrence River and the Atlantic Ocean, the Seaway is a narrow canal, and few ships can pass through its locks. It is also plagued by ice, and the Welland Canal—which links Lake Erie to Lake Ontario and bypasses the Niagara Falls—closes from January to March. This has forced companies to find alternative means of transportation, and the traffic through the Seaway is down 45 percent from what it was twenty years ago.[26]

- **The Corinth Canal**. It connects two parts of the Mediterranean Sea—the Ionian Sea and the Aegean Sea—by making a spectacular cut through the Isthmus of Corinth, between the Peloponnese peninsula and the remainder of Greece (see Figure 3-8). Designed by the ancient Greeks and started by the Roman emperor Nero, it was completed only at the end of the nineteenth century. It is used mainly by local traffic and tourist ships.

The absence of certain waterways is also detrimental to international trade and the efficient movement of goods. For example, there had been considerable talk about a canal through Nicaragua that would be "parallel" to the Panama Canal and be free of locks, an advantage that would speed up the transit time considerably.[27] In addition, the canal would be several hundred miles farther north, which would also reduce transit times. A railroad "land bridge" was also once proposed for the same region. However, both of these projects have been abandoned, and the Panama Canal is, for the foreseeable future, the only water connection between the Atlantic and the Pacific. A canal through the Isthmus of Kra in Thailand—the Malay Peninsula—which would bypass the Strait of Malacca and the Port of Singapore would speed up the transit time between Europe and the Far East as well. This project has been in the planning stages on and off for the past decade within the Thai government, and there is increased interest on the part of Malaysia, Indonesia, and particularly China.[28] No decision had been made as of summer 2009.

Figure 3-8
The Spectacular Corinth Canal in Greece
Source: Photo © David Sobeck. Used with permission.

The same lack of infrastructure is found in freshwater passages. After the Balkans war of the 1990s, there was a period during which there was no freshwater communication between the Black Sea and northern Europe, as many bridges were demolished on the Danube River[29] and barges could not pass. There is still no large-capacity freshwater communication between the Mediterranean Sea and northern Europe, as the expansion of an eighteenth-century canal between the Rhône River and the Rhine River is still being debated; however, the Europakanal, a canal between the Rhine and the Danube, was completed in 1992 and is heavily traveled.

3-2c Airport Infrastructure

Airports are a fundamental part of the transportation infrastructure. There are fewer critical issues in the management of an international airport than there are in that of a port, but they can be just as constraining.

Runways

The runways of an airport determine the type of aircraft it can serve—for instance, the lengths of the runways generally determine whether the airport can support direct flights to faraway places. Many airports in the world cannot accommodate the large jumbo jets that serve international destinations because the runways were designed mostly for smaller aircraft. As the cities around the airports grew, the airports became landlocked, unable to extend their runways. Several cities have had to build airports far from their metropolitan centers, in order to build facilities that can accommodate international flights. Whereas Charles de Gaulle Airport in Paris and Heathrow Airport in London (both built in the 1970s) are about 15 miles (25 kilometers) from the city centers they serve, the airports built in the 1990s are much farther away: Denver International is 23 miles (37 kilometers) from the city and Malpensa in Milan, Italy, is 30 miles (48 kilometers) away.

A second concern is the *number* of runways, which determines the *capacity* of the airport. Most airports have more than one runway, but the busiest airport in the world, in number of passengers—Hartsfield Airport in Atlanta, Georgia—has four runways, and both Chicago O'Hare and Dallas–Fort Worth International have seven. An airport can be quite constrained by its lack of runways. For years, Narita Airport in Tokyo had only one runway to accommodate its traffic. It was stretched to capacity, and there was no way to build a second runway, as a number of small farmers refused to sell their land to the airport. Since, by law, the Japanese government cannot expropriate them, the airport cannot build the runway on their land, and travelers and cargo shippers are inconvenienced, as the number of flights in and out of Narita is limited, increasing the landing fees. Narita has finished a second runway that avoids utilizing the reluctant farmers' land, but it is too short to accommodate jumbo jets, which constitute 90 percent of the Narita traffic, so it is used for only local traffic.

A single runway also increases the probability of delays, as the slightest accident or malfunction will immobilize the entire airport.

The Legendary Kai Tak

Kai Tak Airport in Hong Kong was one of the most unusual airports in the world. As the airplanes landed, they flew only a few hundred feet away from the high-rises and the hills that surrounded the airport (see Figure 3-9). It was an uncomfortable experience for many passengers.

In 1998, its replacement, Chek Lap Kok Airport, opened. Dubbed the most expensive construction project in the world at U.S. $20 billion—the Chunnel under the English Channel cost "only" U.S. $15 billion—it is an artificial island on the outskirts of the city, with its own

continued

The Legendary Kai Tak (Continued)

dedicated tunnel, its own suspension bridge, its own commuter railroad, and the largest cargo facility in the world. It operates twenty-four hours a day, a boon for cargo shippers involved in the Southeast Asian market, because Kai Tak closed at night.

In addition to the challenges of building such a large infrastructure, the "transfer" from one airport to the other was attempted in one night. As Kai Tak closed at midnight on July 5, 1998, all of its equipment was moved to Chek Lap Kok with 10,000 vehicle trips, seventy barge voyages, and thirty flights, and the new airport opened on July 6 at 6:30 A.M. Unfortunately, things did not go as smoothly as expected, and the first couple of weeks were hectic, especially for cargo.

Nevertheless, Chek Lap Kok has become the busiest international cargo airport in the world, handling 3.6 million tons in 2008, an increase of over 8 percent per year since its first full year of operation in 1999.[30]

Figure 3-9
The Approach at Kai Tak Airport in Hong Kong
Source: Photo © Daryl Chapman, courtesy of www.airliners.net. Used with permission.

Hours of Operation

Another concern of importance is the time frame during which airports operate. Because most airports are geographically close to large cities, their hours of operations are generally limited by noise constraints, and they operate only during "day hours." Because cargo tends to fly at night, specialized cargo airports that are located outside of large cities and can operate twenty-four hours a day, seven days a week have started to emerge, such as Prestwick in Scotland, Hahn in Germany, and Chateauroux in France.[31] To some extent, this development mirrors that of Memphis International

Airport, which has become the largest cargo airport in the world, with 3.7 million tons of freight in 2008[32] even though it is not located near a large metropolitan center.

Warehousing Space

Another concern of importance for cargo shippers at airports is the existence of appropriate warehouse space, as cargo should be protected while it is in transit and not left to the elements. This is particularly important as air cargo tends to be—erroneously—not as well packaged as cargo destined for ocean shipping.

The problem is even more acute for refrigerated warehouse space, which can be in very short supply.

3-2d Rail Infrastructure

Another element of the transportation infrastructure of a country is its railroad network. In the eighteenth and early nineteenth centuries, railroads became the most important means of long-distance land transportation. In Europe, the United States, India, Africa, and Asia, a dense network of railroads was built, sometimes under the impetus of colonizing forces that wanted to be able to move troops quickly. This historical development led to some decisions that, a century and a half later, are causing significant problems. To prevent possible invaders from using their railroad infrastructures, Spain, Brazil, and Russia developed railroad gauges (the width between the rails) that were incompatible with those in standard use in Europe. While the choice of these gauges did prevent hostile military troops from using the rail network, this decision is still causing trouble for any type of rail transportation between these countries and their neighbors. For example, most trains stop at the French-Spanish border so that cargo can be shifted to railcars that are appropriate for the gauge used in the other country; others—including passenger trains—slow down to a crawl while specially designed axles expand or contract.[33] For Brazil, the cost of the rolling stock is substantially higher, as every car and locomotive must be adapted to its unusual gauge size, whether they are purchased new or used, and trains have to travel slower because the cars are much wider than the rail was designed to handle and therefore are less stable.

Most countries have updated their railroad infrastructures as their economies grew. However, in a few countries, the economy has grown much faster than the infrastructure can keep pace. Such is the case in China, where demand for rail transportation far outstrips the supply. China's network satisfies only 60 percent of current demand.[34] The Chinese government has pledged $600 billion to develop its infrastructure in 2009, targeting specifically railroads and highways.[35] Such an investment is considerable; it represents approximately 18 percent of the total gross domestic product of the country.[36] An investment of the same magnitude would be U.S. $2,600 billion in the United States, approximately 25 times what President Obama's stimulus package is expected to spend on the U.S. infrastructure.

However, none of that stimulus package will reach railroads, as the United States has a railroad infrastructure that is atypical: All railroads are privately owned, and that fact alone limits the amount of investment that can be spent on improving the overall rail infrastructure of the country. In addition, the geography of the United States presents several large obstacles. In particular, the Rocky Mountains present challenges because of their size and climate; the amount of snow that falls in the Rockies routinely exceeds 200 inches (500 centimeters). Figure 3-10 shows the Union Pacific Railroad's rotary snowplow, used to clear the railroad after a snowfall.

Because these challenges make it very expensive to build and maintain tracks, there are several miles of important east-west railroad connections in the United States that are still "single track"; that is, traffic in both directions uses the same set of tracks. Since doubling the track often involves blasting rocks near the existing railroad,

Figure 3-10
Clearing the Railroad Path after a Snowfall
Source: Photo © Frank Keller, courtesy of railpictures.net. Used with permission.

progress is time-consuming and expensive. The "transcontinental" railway of the BNSF company will likely be completely double-tracked by 2011;[37] this alone will increase the railroad's capacity on these segments by 500 to 600 percent.

In most countries, though, as roads and trucks improve, the railroads have gradually lost their focus on shipping merchandise and have shifted their efforts to high-speed passenger transportation. Such is the case of Europe, where most merchandise is shipped by means other than railroad, but where intercity rail passenger transportation is commonplace, convenient, and fast, and competes with airlines over small distances. The best examples are the French (now European) *Trains à Grande Vitesse* (TGV), which connect Paris to London in two hours (dubbed the Eurostar) and Paris to Brussels in an hour and a half (the Thalys). There is only one TGV dedicated to merchandise transport, and it is used by the French Postal Service (*La Poste*) exclusively for mail transportation (see Figure 3-11). A similar switch from merchandise to high-speed passenger transport occurred in Japan: The Shinkansen train covers the 120 miles (192 kilometers) between Hiroshima and Kokura in less than 45 minutes, for example. These high-speed trains run on dedicated tracks that are separate from the remainder of the slower rail infrastructure.

Multimodal Emphasis

In the last two decades, three factors have contributed to the renewal of merchandise traffic on railroads: The congestion of roads has worsened, concerns about pollution and noise have increased, and the creation of the multimodal container has eliminated the need to load and unload merchandise from the traditional boxcars.

In the United States, railroads have invested heavily in the modernization of their rolling stocks; they have shifted from boxcars to piggy-back cars—allowing them to carry truck trailers—and to container cars. At the same time, they have improved their infrastructure by increasing the height clearances in tunnels and other areas, allowing trains to transport containers "double-stacked" (i.e., twice as many containers as a single-stack train would). Figures 13-8 and 13-9 in Chapter 13 illustrate these concepts. American trains tend to be exceedingly long, with at least 100 cars, allowing a crew of a few individuals to move in excess of 200 containers or truck trailers, making them particularly cost-effective. In addition, because passenger rail transport is almost

Figure 3-11
The Only "Merchandise" High-Speed Train, Used by the French Postal Service
Source: Photo © Peter Schokkenbroek. Used with permission.

nonexistent in the United States—with the minor exception of the northeastern part of the country—cargo trains have priority on the network and tend to be relatively fast.

Unfortunately, such improvements have not yet been made to the European infrastructure, which still consists mostly of aging boxcars. Moreover, the emphasis on passenger transportation gives priority to passenger trains and relegates cargo trains to second-class status, making them slow and inefficient cargo movers. Multiple attempts to create high-speed cargo railroad links from ports in northern Europe to ports in the Mediterranean have been made, but politics and administrative delays are unlikely to make this corridor a reality for some years.[38]

In the same fashion, the success of North American railroads has enticed several developments in Asia. There are plans to significantly modernize the trans-Siberian railroad, which would allow cargo to be shipped from Asia (Vladivostok) to Europe by rail.[39] There are also plans to create a trans-Asian railroad, which would connect Singapore and Seoul to Europe via Turkey.[40] However, the obstacles that remain to such a venture are substantial, including the crossing of the Bosporus in Istanbul, and its completion is far from certain.

Land Bridges

A consequence of the increased efficiency of the railroads in the United States has been the creation of **land bridges.** The concept of a land bridge is based on the idea that containerized ocean cargo needs to "cross" some landmass; for example, cargo from Southeast Asia needs to cross North America on its way to Europe. One alternative is to take the Panama Canal; however, it is a fairly long voyage south in the Pacific to reach Balboa, and a fairly long voyage north from Colón to Europe via the Caribbean Sea and the North Atlantic. Another alternative is to take the cargo around India and through the Suez Canal, which is inconvenient and expensive.

The alternative developed by the U.S. railroads is to cross North America on a land bridge; the cargo is unloaded from a large containership somewhere on the West Coast of the United States or Canada, and shipped by double-stack container train to the East Coast. The journey is faster and cheaper than by ocean. In addition, it allows shipping lines to use post-Panamax ships on their trans-Pacific and trans-Atlantic routes, which is also more efficient. A consequence of this trend is that cargo going from Taipei to Barcelona is going to transit through Chicago. Such variations from the traditional itinerary of Taipei-Panama-Barcelona are said to be "transparent" to

land bridge A term coined to describe the practice of shipping goods from Asia to Europe through the United States by using railroads.

the shipper, which means that it is unaware of them. However, such a transparent voyage may expose the shipment to lower temperatures than those the shipper expected, and a shipment may not be protected adequately enough for the extremes in temperature.

3-2e Road Infrastructure

In addition to the infrastructure of ports, airports, and railroads, a great amount of shipping moves by road, especially on the last leg of the journey, from the port, airport, or rail terminal to its final destination.

The road infrastructure of a country is evaluated somewhat differently than the rest of its transportation infrastructure. In almost no country is there a shortage of roads, for example; the exception is Russia, which still does not have a trans-Siberian road connecting the Western and Eastern parts of the country. Russians refer to a large percentage of their country's territory as *bezdorozhye*, or "place without roads."[41] However, this is the exception, and for all other countries, the issues are the quality and maintenance of the network, its congestion, and the existence of high-speed links between major metropolitan areas. The concern therefore is not one of density, but of usability.

Quality

The road infrastructure of a country is generally described in documents such as the U.S. Department of Commerce's *Country Commercial Guides*[42] or the CIA's *World Factbook*[43] in terms of total miles of road and of the percentage of these roads that are paved. For example, Argentina is listed as having 143,800 miles (231,500 kilometers) of roads, of which 43,100 miles (69,400 kilometers)—30 percent—are paved.[44] Even in the United States, paved roads represent only 65 percent of the road infrastructure.[45]

However, this is somewhat misleading, as most of the traffic obviously utilizes paved roads, and the unpaved roads serve remote rural areas. In addition, the condition of a paved road makes a substantial difference in its usefulness: An overcrowded, two-lane highway riddled with potholes is not very conducive to the safe transportation of cargo. Such is the case with the roads in the countries of Belarus, Albania, Romania, Lithuania, and Latvia. The government of Poland estimates that 80 percent of its roads are in unsatisfactory or bad condition;[46] cargo shipped under such conditions has to be particularly well packaged. Unfortunately, there is no statistical source that indicates the condition of the roads in a country, and because there are substantial variations from one region of a country to another, it is even more difficult to evaluate. China has a very good road infrastructure between Guangzhou and Shanghai, for example, but the interior of the country is plagued with deficient and outdated roads.[47]

Congestion of the road infrastructure is also endemic to certain cities: There are too many cars, trucks, and other vehicles on the road, and deliveries are difficult to make (see Figure 3-12). In Calcutta, India, the traffic is so congested that the average speed in the city is 5 miles per hour (8 kilometers per hour); most people travel by rickshaw or by public transportation rather than by car.[48] In New Delhi, the government has created a category of vehicles called VVIP—Very Very Important Persons—that are allowed to zip through traffic with blaring sirens and flashing lights.[49] The traffic in Beijing is notorious for being at a standstill for a good percentage of the day. In order to resolve congestion, many cities in developing countries have instituted a system of alternating days for traffic; vehicles with odd-numbered license plates are allowed to travel only on odd-numbered days and vehicles with even-numbered license plates can travel only on even-numbered days. Such is the case in Lagos, Nigeria, for example. The problem is not resolved, as resourceful Nigerians obtain two license plates for every vehicle from corrupt civil authorities and change the plates every morning.

Figure 3-12
Traffic Congestion in Lahore, Pakistan
Source: Photo © Usman Latif. Used with permission.

Although congestion is a problem that is extreme in developing countries, it is certainly also present in large metropolitan areas in Europe, Japan, and the United States. As the number of automobiles increases, the situation will worsen further and make deliveries to customers more problematic and inefficient. Many delivery firms are now using motorcycles and mopeds, which are more maneuverable in large cities. London enacted a very effective tax system to prevent vehicles from entering the heart of the city; vehicles' license plates are monitored and recorded through a closed-circuit television system, and commuters are charged £8.00 for each day they travel into the city. Residents receive a 90 percent discount of this daily rate. Fines for noncompliance are substantial. After it was enacted in February 2003, the program was judged to be so successful in the initial target zone (traffic decreased approximately 15 percent)[50] that it was expanded to a larger proportion of the city in February 2007. A similar system is under consideration in other cities, such as Stockholm, Manchester, Singapore, Milan, San Francisco, and New York.

Yet another issue in cities is the confusion that can be generated by the lack of signage and a different addressing system. While most North American cities have a grid of east-west and north-south streets, with a fairly logical numbering sequence of streets and buildings, European cities are plagued with a maze of different streets that change names at each—or so it seems—intersection. Mexico City has an extraordinarily confusing system of streets; there are nearly 800 streets named after Benito Juárez, 760 named for Miguel Hidalgo, and 300 streets renamed every year. To make things more interesting, 80,000 city blocks have no signage at all.[51] Japan has the tradition of numbering buildings on a street in the order in which they were built, and not in a sequential order based on location. Most of Mumbai's addresses are not based on street names but are defined by a succession of smaller and smaller areas: A person's address will include the name of the house, the name of the street, the name of the block, the name of the city, and the city code. In addition, there will be an east or a west, depending on which side of the railroad track the block is, with parallel structures on either side. Such systems make it challenging to deliver goods to a new customer. The worst situation from this perspective is on the island of Saipan in the Northern Mariana Islands, with a population of 70,000, which still has no address system at all.[52]

To decrease the congestion in cities, countries have built a network of high-speed links that avoid smaller cities while connecting the larger ones. These limited access highways speed up considerably the transportation of goods between cities. Nevertheless, these highways are subject to a number of rules and regulations, some of which limit the size of the trucks that can travel on them and the speed at which they can travel. Because these rules vary from country to country, it can be a challenge to arrange international truck transportation of merchandise. In addition, in many countries, access to high-speed highways is limited to vehicles that pay a toll, making such roads an expensive alternative. In France, for example, the private company running the high-speed highway system charges approximately €0.35 per mile (€0.21 per kilometer) for semi trucks.

Civil Engineering Structures (*Ouvrages d'Art*)

If the country is mountainous, these high-speed thoroughfares are built with numerous bridges and tunnels designed to "eliminate" the constraints of the landscape. A perfect example of such a highway is the Italian *Autostrada*, which runs along the Apennine chain and is seemingly an unending succession of tunnels and bridges. Such engineering structures are called collectively (in French) *ouvrages d'art*—art structures—and it is an apt moniker; unfortunately, there is no equivalent in English, so the French term will be used.

The dependence of international trade on such *ouvrages d'art* cannot be underestimated: Most natural borders are either water (oceans or lakes) or mountains at the watershed separation. To cross these natural borders, bridges or tunnels have to be built. The Chunnel—the tunnel built under the English Channel, between France and Great Britain—is a case in point. Until its opening in 1994, shipping goods from one country to the other was delayed by a fairly lengthy ferry voyage, which sometimes could be delayed or canceled due to bad weather. The Chunnel has substantially shortened shipping times between the two countries, although it is quite expensive; for private automobiles, the cost is £45, and for semi trucks, it can reach £500.

Another international route that has been radically changed by *ouvrages d'art* is the trade between western Europe and the Middle East, with the opening of the two suspension bridges in Istanbul, one in 1973 (Boğaziçi Bridge), the other in 1988 (Fatih Sultan Mehmet Bridge). These are the only two bridges that allow road transportation between Europe and Asia, save for an itinerary north of the Black Sea, through Bulgaria, Romania, Ukraine, and Russia. To date, there is no rail link from southern Europe to Asia, as the Orient Express ends on the European side of Istanbul, and the Baghdad Railway starts on the Asian side. No rail link is available between the two stations, and passengers and cargo cross the Bosporus by ferry.

The so-called Øresund Fixed Link between Copenhagen, Denmark, and Malmö, Sweden, is another example of an *ouvrage d'art* that has significantly altered the transportation landscape of an international border: It actually is a succession of three bridges and a tunnel, with a switchover on an artificial island in the middle of Flinte Channel. It is the first terrestrial communication between the two countries, replacing a 45-minute ferry ride with an 8-minute drive. More importantly, it is the first land link between western Europe and the Scandinavian countries.

The Millau Bridge in southern France (see Figure 3-13) opened in 2004 and is another highway bridge that significantly reduces transportation times. It links two high plateaus that are separated by a deep river gorge, over which the only crossing was in the middle of the small town of Millau. Before the construction of the bridge, vehicles had to travel down approximately 1,000 feet (300 meters) through a series a hairpin turns to the city, cross the river, and then climb up the same distance on the other plateau. The town was infamous for its traffic jams, and it was not unusual to spend two hours to go from one plateau to the other. With the bridge, it takes less than one minute. The bridge is 1,150 feet (345 meters) above the river, which is

Figure 3-13
The Millau Bridge
Source: Photo © Pierre David.

about 65 feet (20 meters) higher than the Eiffel Tower, and was built in a little over three years.[53]

Some bridges are much less architecturally noticeable but no less important to the economies of the countries they link. For example, the United States and Canada, the two largest trading partners in the world, are "connected" by only a bridge and a tunnel from Detroit, Michigan, to Windsor, Ontario, and a few bridges near Buffalo, New York, for a significant portion of their common border. At least one of those bridges, the Ambassador Bridge between Detroit and Windsor, owned by a private company, has not been updated in 50 years; it is only a four-lane bridge and carries 3.3 million trucks every year.[54] Similarly, the Peace Bridge between Buffalo and Fort Erie, Ontario, is used at its maximum capacity and has not been expanded since 1927.

Another example of the critical nature of bridges and other structures can be seen in the tiny island nation of Palau, where a 1996 bridge collapse between the capital city of Koror and the main island of Babeldaob created an economic nightmare. People on the main island used to commute to the capital via the bridge, and the bridge collapse was a major setback to the Palau people and the country's economy; while the bridge was temporarily replaced by ferry service, this was a much less efficient alternative. The bridge was not rebuilt until 2002, with a Japanese grant.[55]

It is not just in developing countries that the failure of such infrastructures can be catastrophic: All *ouvrages d'art* are vulnerable. In March 1999, a deadly fire occurred in the Mont-Blanc tunnel between France and Italy, under the Alps; the tunnel was closed until April 2002. This forced trucks to use the Fréjus Tunnel, the only other tunnel under the Alps between France and Italy, or to make a substantial detour along the Mediterranean coast, neither option being a good alternative. A fire in the Saint Gothard Tunnel—the second longest road tunnel in the world, between Switzerland and Italy—forced its closure in October 2001; while the tunnel was reopened in December 2001, it was limited to half of its traffic capacity until April 2002, as traffic was allowed in only one direction at a time. There have been several truck fires in the Chunnel as well, which reduced the Channel tunnel's capacity while it was being repaired.

The building of a bridge can also alter the character of a region. For example, Prince Edward Island is now connected to the rest of Canada by a recently-built bridge, and its residents are divided on its impact on their life and economy.[56] While the island has gained some additional tourism revenues and islanders have greater access to the amenities of the neighboring cities of Moncton and Halifax, it has also lost some of its quaint tranquility.

3-2f Warehousing Infrastructure

It is evident that transportation is dependent on an infrastructure that allows the movement of goods. However, it is equally important to realize that cargo is often stationary when it "waits" for the next transportation alternative to be available. Therefore, it is important for a shipper to obtain information about the warehousing infrastructure of the locations where a shipment will be in layover.

The issues revolving around warehousing infrastructure concern the protection of the goods when they are waiting while in transit. Will they be protected from the rain? From the sun? From possible floods? From (unusual) cold? A savvy international logistics manager will attempt to determine the conditions under which the goods will be kept, and will then determine whether they are correctly packaged, or whether they need to be shipped through a different itinerary. The Cigna Insurance Company's *Ports of the World* booklet[57] (see Table 3-2 in Section 3-2a) lists the warehouse space available in each port.

In many cases as well, shippers will use public warehouses for storage purposes, in order to deliver goods to their customers without having to resort to an international shipment. This enables the company to provide much better customer service by delivering goods with a much shorter lead time.

Unfortunately, the warehousing infrastructure of a country is difficult to evaluate, as there are no general sources of information on the availability and quality of public warehouses. Therefore, in those cases where a company is considering using a public warehouse to serve its customers, it would be best to plan an actual visit to the location considered, as the standards used in public warehousing management may be quite different than the ones expected.

3-3 Communication Infrastructure

In addition to the transportation infrastructure, the communication infrastructure is also of substantial importance to international logistics. The ability to communicate with customers and suppliers, either by mail, by phone, or through other electronic media, is very important to the smooth operation of an international transaction. Unfortunately, there are different expectations of service and performance in communication means from country to country.

3-3a Mail Services

The ability of the postal services to deliver mail on time and reliably should be a given in most developed countries. However, there is ample anecdotal evidence that it is not the case in all places. On many occasions, there are unacceptable delays and errors: While the European Union countries strive to deliver letters sent to a national address on the day after it is mailed—a so-called *D+1* policy—and on the second day if it is international mail within the European community, this is a difficult standard to achieve. Italy, especially before its national postal service was privatized, was notoriously unreliable. France has periodic strikes of its mail service and of its national railway service, both of which can substantially delay the delivery of mail. In South Africa, the mail service has become so unreliable that businesses and individuals no longer trust it enough to send payments, forcing them to make payments in person or through banks.

Another issue is the safety of the mail: Will a letter or package make it to its destination, or will it be lost, damaged, or stolen in transit? Because postal services tend to be very large employers, it is difficult to screen all employees effectively. There have been countless documented instances of postal employees stealing the contents of parcels, removing the contents of letters—especially cash, checks, and credit cards—before they reach their destinations. Developing countries have an even greater problem, as public employees' wages tend to be modest, and the temptations are many.

Many firms intent on ensuring that their postal communications are safely delivered have switched, especially for international documents' exchanges, to private services such as DHL and FedEx. While the costs of private services are much higher than the costs of traditional postal service, these companies have gained significant market share, thanks to their reputation for greater reliability. In particular, the customers' ability to track packages and documents online has increased this perception. This tracking ability is now available for some postal service products, but it is not available worldwide.

Another phenomenon is the exploitation (arbitrage) of the differences in prices and mail categories for international mail from one country to another. A direct marketer sending a substantial number of identical mail pieces internationally will determine in which country that particular mailing is going to cost the least amount; it will then ship the mailing materials in bulk to a company operating a remailing service in that country. The remailer will then place the individual items in the mail and so the overall mailing costs to the marketer will be lower. Commercial materials emanating from France have come to the author from Denmark, Great Britain, and the Netherlands; the lowest-cost provider was probably determined by the fact that the weight of the materials being sent placed them in different price categories in different countries.

3-3b Telecommunications Services

Slightly different issues are facing telecommunication services; not only has the demand for voice telecommunication increased about 10 percent a year, but the demand for data telecommunication has essentially doubled every year for the past ten years, and shows no sign of slowing down. Some countries have been able to build a sufficiently large domestic infrastructure to carry this increased load, often by using their already-existing infrastructure. Many gas and oil pipelines have been given the added responsibility of transmitting data through a fiber-optic line laid in their midst.[58] Many countries, though, have not been able to keep up with such growth, and telecommunications in those countries are slow and not very reliable.

This reliability is the primary concern in several countries where the economy has grown quickly, but the domestic communication infrastructure has not followed. Phone service is notoriously unreliable, with phone conversations disconnected, phone calls regularly connected to wrong numbers, and dial tones all but absent.[59] Table 3-4 shows the penetration rate of landline phones for selected countries; it is calculated by dividing the total number of landline phones by the population. It does not refer to the percentage of the population with access to a landline phone, because many of these phones are shared by a household.

Fortunately, in some of those countries, a phenomenon known as **leap frogging** has taken place. Because the "old" land-based telephone infrastructure is not working properly, people have switched to cellular phones very quickly and bypassed the landline-based system. This switch is facilitated by the fact that many countries quickly adopted a single operating standard (Global System for Mobile Communications, or GSM), which makes for easy portability and increased convenience. As of 2009, there were more than 40 countries in which the penetration rate for cellular phones was greater than 100 percent. Table 3-5 highlights the penetration rates for cellular telephones. Since it is calculated as the number of cellular phones divided by the population size, the rate corresponds, roughly, to the number of cell phones that an average individual owns.

leap frogging The idea that some countries will "skip" a particular technology to adopt the most recent one available.

TABLE 3-4   Landline Phone Penetration Percentages as of 2008

Rank	Country	Landline Phone Penetration
1	Monaco	103%
2	Gibraltar	87%
3	Bermuda	85%
4	Switzerland	66%
5	Germany	65%
6	Canada	63%
7	Greenland	63%
8	Taiwan	62%
9	Iceland	61%
10	Sweden	61%
11	Greece	58%
12	Liechtenstein	58%
13	France	55%
14	United Kingdom	55%
15	Hong Kong	55%
16	United States	53%
17	Montenegro	53%
18	Denmark	51%
19	Luxembourg	50%
20	Ireland	50%
21	Korea, South	49%
22	Malta	49%
	European Union	48%
23	Cyprus	47%
24	Italy	46%
25	Australia	46%
	China	27%
	World	19%

Source: CIA World Factbook.[60]

In China, there are many more cellular phones (547 million) than there are landline-based phones (365 million), and the rate of growth in cellular phones far surpasses that of the traditional technology. Countries such as the United States, which have strong landline-based infrastructures, have been slower at switching to cellular phone usage. As of 2009, the United States was not in the top fifty countries in the world when ranked by the percentage of the population that owned a cellular telephone. Although this ranking was due to the fact that the landline-based infrastructure is very good (and people have much less of an incentive to switch), it was also due to the fact that there are four different operating technologies competing for cellular phone customers and, therefore, that there are four times as many towers to be built (and paid for), making cellular phone service particularly expensive.

On the international side, telecommunications are heavily dependent on a network of underwater cables that run across the Atlantic, the Pacific, the Mediterranean Sea, or other large bodies of water. As telecommunication traffic has increased, the capacity of these cables has also increased dramatically. Altogether, though, there are still very few cables (only seven cross the North Atlantic), and their vulnerability is extraordinary. Although they are buried on the portion of their route that is located in shallow water, they are for the most part simply laid on the floor of the oceans, at the risk of being snagged by fishermen's nets and boat anchors.[61] When these cables cross land, they are just as vulnerable and at the mercy of a careless backhoe operator or

TABLE 3-5	Cellular Phone Penetration Percentages as of 2008

Rank	Country	Cell Phone Penetration
1	United Arab Emirates	158%
2	Bahrain	153%
3	Macau	153%
4	Estonia	153%
5	Qatar	152%
6	Hong Kong	150%
7	Lithuania	138%
8	Bulgaria	137%
9	Italy	135%
10	Antigua and Barbuda	129%
11	Czech Republic	128%
12	Portugal	125%
13	Israel	123%
14	Luxembourg	123%
15	Russia	121%
16	The Bahamas	121%
17	Ukraine	121%
18	Cyprus	121%
19	Singapore	121%
20	Spain	120%
21	Austria	119%
22	Germany	118%
23	United Kingdom	118%
24	Ireland	118%
25	Finland	116%
	European Union	95%
	United States	83%
	China	41%
	World	32%

Source: CIA World Factbook.[62]

other accident.[63] Whenever they are snagged or damaged, traffic on that cable seizes until it is repaired. In an outstanding article in *Wired* Magazine, Neal Stephenson followed the construction of the FLAG—Fiber-optic Link Around the Globe—and reported on the vulnerability of this network: For example, five of the major worldwide cables are routed through a single building in Alexandria, Egypt.[64]

Satellite telecommunications are no less dependent on a limited number of alternatives, and therefore are just as vulnerable; because satellites are increasingly heavily used for communications such as television programs, their capacity is entirely used, and the failure of a single satellite can wreak havoc on telecommunications. Other telecommunication infrastructures are vulnerable; the Internet, although touted as "robust," is still very dependent on so-called "root-servers" that keep the list of addresses on the Internet.

3-4 Utilities Infrastructure

Another area of concern for the manager involved in international logistics is the utilities infrastructure. While it is generally taken for granted that all utilities—electricity, water, sewage, gas—are available in most countries, experience shows that there is often a shortage of one or more of these commodities in many countries, including developed countries. And while utilities are not directly an issue in transportation, they can become critically important when a company is considering operating a warehouse or establishing a corporate office.

3-4a Electricity

The most common problem with utilities is the availability and reliability of electrical power. In countries where the rate of economic growth outpaces the rate of growth in electricity production, it is common to have blackouts for part of the day. Actually, the situation is endemic in sub-Saharan Africa, where there are scheduled blackouts because the production of electricity is much lower than the demand for it; households and businesses therefore plan their days around the availability of electricity. India, China, and Saudi Arabia are also affected by recurring blackouts. China has invested considerable amounts in electricity-generation infrastructure, including the Three River Gorge Dam (see Figure 3-14), which came online in 2008 and will eventually produce more than 10 percent of the electricity used by the country. However, there are still some disruptions in multiple areas of the country.

The availability of electricity is disrupted in many countries, as the problems tend to be regional as well as national. In the summer of 2001, there were substantial supply and demand imbalances and numerous shortages of electricity in California. However, recent evidence has shown that, even though there were infrastructural shortages at the root of the problem, the speculative behavior of the Enron Corporation was mostly responsible for the wild price fluctuations that Californians experienced. On the other hand, some countries have abundant electrical resources: Brazil and Paraguay share the Itaipu Dam, which provides 82 percent of Paraguay's electrical needs and 26 percent of Brazil's. Nevertheless, for those areas of Brazil that are geographically far from Itaipu, there are still shortages and temporary blackouts.

In addition to problems of production, utility companies are sometimes victims of theft; households and businesses bypass their meters or tap directly into the grid without the "inconvenience" of a meter, preventing utility companies from collecting

Figure 3-14
The Three River Gorge Dam
Source: Photo © Arjan Feenstra. Used with permission.

enough income to be able to invest in additional capacity. A World Bank loan to India to build additional power plants was actually made conditional on the utility getting paid for a greater percentage of its production.[65] In Russia, an endemic problem is the theft of the electrical wires for scrap, a "business" that killed 500 thieves in 1999 and forced the Russian government to replace 15,000 miles (24,140 kilometers) of high-tension wires,[66] to say nothing of the disruptions to businesses and individuals.

3-4b Water and Sewer

Water supply is also a concern in many countries in the world, leading to interruptions, rationing, and recurring water shortages. It is not uncommon for cities to ration water in the middle of a drought period, on some occasions reducing the availability of water to a few hours a day or a few days a week. As populations in cities increase, the infrastructure delivering water to the cities is often overtaxed, which can lead to potentially catastrophic problems, especially in cities with aging infrastructures. For example, New York City gets most of its water from reservoirs 125 miles (201 kilometers) away, and it is delivered by two tunnels that were built in 1917 and 1937. Neither of these tunnels has ever been shut down for repairs, as the city would not be able to function without the water they deliver.[67] A new water tunnel is currently under construction and is scheduled to start operating in 2020. Many cities have leaky pipes and lose a portion of their supply to those leaks; Manila, in the Philippines, estimates it loses *half* of its water production through leaks and illegal siphoning.[68]

The quality of the water is also a concern: In many cities, the water delivery infrastructure is not well protected, leaving a strong possibility of bacterial contamination, and forcing users to boil the water before they use it. This procedure is a common recommendation given by international travelers. The World Bank estimates that no more than 80 percent of the world population has "reasonable access" to clean water, defined as access to within one kilometer (0.62 mile) of the house.[69] For most people, that is a considerable distance.

On the other end, the infrastructure designed to remove used water is also critical. Many countries have inadequate or overburdened sewage treatment facilities, resulting in the pollution of water tables and adjacent bodies of water, or problems with sewer backups at times of heavy rains, for example. While less critical than water availability to the proper operation of a warehouse or distribution center, sewer service is still important, as it can be a nuisance to have employees deal with stench or frequent cleanups. The World Bank estimates that less than 60 percent of the world population has access to adequate sanitation.[70]

Similar observations can be made about refuse removal, a service generally provided by the municipalities, but which can be unreliable; strikes of municipal workers can take several days, during which no pickup is conducted, resulting in a problem in the operation of any type of business.

3-4c Energy Pipelines

The infrastructure of access to energy is also of importance. As most of the easily accessible oil and gas fields are near the end of their life expectancies, energy resources now come from remote areas in which it is difficult to operate and from where it is difficult to ship. Building energy pipelines from those areas is a challenge, and the obstacles include the weather—the Alaskan pipeline—natural barriers, political issues, environmental challenges, and bickering between the oil companies and the governments of the countries in which they are built.

Nevertheless, the infrastructure of pipelines is growing and allows an ever-greater percentage of the energy needs of the world to be no longer transported by ships, trucks, and railroads.

Review and Discussion Questions

1. What are the main elements of the maritime transportation infrastructure? How would the quality and dependability of the maritime transportation infrastructure affect an international shipment?

2. What are the main elements of the air transportation infrastructure? How would the quality and dependability of the air transportation infrastructure affect an international shipment?

3. What are the main elements of the land transportation and warehousing infrastructure? How would the quality and dependability of these infrastructures affect an international shipment?

4. What are the main elements of the communication and utilities infrastructure? How would the quality and dependability of these infrastructures affect an international shipment?

Endnotes

1. *American Heritage Dictionary*, 3rd ed., Boston: Houghton-Mifflin, 2000.
2. *Oxford English Dictionary*, 2nd ed., http://www.oed.com.
3. Heaney, Simon, "Top 20 container lines," *American Shipper*, September 2008, pp. 67–70.
4. *Ibid.*
5. Lipton, Eric, "Beneath the Harbor, It's Dig or Else," *New York Times*, November 23, 2004.
6. Whitman, Reg, "The Port of Prince Rupert—North America's Jewel of the Northwest," *Logistics Quarterly*, 14:5, 2008, pp. 48–49.
7. Leach, Peter, "A Bridge Too Low," *Journal of Commerce*, June 5, 2006, pp. 30–31.
8. Machalaba, Daniel, "Maersk is Ready to Start on Giant Port," *Wall Street Journal*, June 5, 2000, p. A4.
9. Ying, Wang, "Third Phase of Yangshan Port completed," *China Daily*, December 5, 2008.
10. "Waigaoqiao: The First Free Trade Zone in China," *China Economic Review*, May 12, 2009, http://www.chinaeconomicreview.com/industrial-zones/2009/05/12/waigaoqiao-free-trade-zone.html.
11. Mongelluzzo, Bill, "With Cranes, Size Is Everything," *Journal of Commerce*, December 31, 1996, p. 1B.
12. Bonney, Joseph, "Cranes to Work from Both Sides," *Journal of Commerce*, August 25, 1999, p. 1.
13. *Ports of the World*, 15th ed., Philadelphia: Cigna Insurance Corporation.
14. Mongelluzzo, Bill, "Extending Terminal Hours," *Journal of Commerce*, March 5, 1997, p. 1B.
15. "How successful is the effort to expand the hours of operations at Port shipping terminals?" FAQ page, The Port of Long Beach, http://www.polb.com/contact/qc.asp#474, accessed May 18, 2009.
16. Davies, John, "Slow Passage to Progress," *International Business*, December 1996–January 1997, pp. 14–17.
17. Casper, Bill, "The 30 Container-per-Hour Barrier," *Cargo Business News*, August 2008, pp. 24–25.
18. Smith, Jeremy N., "Breaking Through Bottlenecks at the Port," *World Trade*, June 2004, pp. 16–20.
19. Romero, Simon, "Fears Drain Support for Natural Gas Terminals," *New York Times*, May 14, 2004.
20. Beatty, Andrew, "Work Starts on Biggest-Ever Panama Canal Overhaul," *Reuters*, September 4, 2007.
21. Reagan, Brad, "The Panama Canal's Ultimate Upgrade," *Popular Mechanics*, February 2007 pp. 63–68.
22. Leach, Peter, "One Hub, Two Oceans," *Journal of Commerce*, June 2, 2008, pp. 38–40.
23. Moore, Molly, "Is the Bosporus Taking on More than It Can Handle?" *International Herald Tribune*, November 17, 2000, p. 2.
24. *Suez Canal Toll Calculator*, Leth Agencies, http://www.lethagencies.com/calculator.asp?Port=SUEZTREG, accessed June 2, 2009.
25. Carl, Traci, "Panama Wants a Bigger Canal for Bigger Ships," *Cleveland Plain Dealer*, March 31, 2002, p. G5.
26. Urquhart, John, "U.S., Canada Try to Revive Once-Grand Waterway," *Wall Street Journal*, March 12, 1998, p. A14.
27. *The Nicaraguan Canal Proposal*, Case No. 405. Washington, D.C.: The American University, May 1997, http://www.american.edu/ted/NICCANAL.HTM.
28. "China builds up Strategic Sea Lanes," *Washington Times*, January 17, 2005, http://www.washingtontimes.com/news/2005/jan/17/20050117-115550-1929r/print/.
29. Kim, Lucian, "Danube Trade Blocked by Bridges," *Christian Science Monitor*, October 6, 1999, p. 6.
30. *Hong-Kong Airport—Facts and Figures*, http://www.hongkongairport.com/eng/business/about-the-airport/facts-figures/facts-sheets.html, accessed May 20, 2009.
31. Conway, Peter, "Taking the High Road," *Air Cargo World*, January 2000, pp. 62–67.
32. "The World's Top 50 Cargo Airports," *Air Cargo World*, July 2008, p. 24.
33. "Three Routes Lead to Iberia," *SBB Cargo*, http://www.sbbcargo.ch/en/index/cargomagazin.htm, March 15, 2001.
34. Bangsberg, P. T., "One-Track Mind," *Journal of Commerce*, May 31–June 6, 2004, pp. 46A–50A.
35. Bradsher, Keith, "In downturn, China sees Path to Growth," *New York Times*, March 16, 2009, http://www.nytimes.com/2009/03/17/business/worldbusiness/17compete.html.
36. China, *World Fact Book*, Central Intelligence Agency, https://www.cia.gov/library/publications/the-world-factbook/geos/ch.html, accessed May 20, 2009.
37. Judge, Tom, "Entering the Final Stretch: BNSF's Double-tracking Project on the Transcon is nearing the Finish Line in New Mexico's Abo Canyon," *Railway Age*, February 2009, pp. 49–50.

38. "Freight—No Longer a High-Speed Poor Relation," *Railway-Technology.com*, October 2, 2007, http://www.railway-technology.com/features/feature1346.

39. Helmer, John, "Russia to Overhaul Trans-Siberian Rail," *Journal of Commerce*, April 21, 1998, p. A1.

40. Associated Press, "Asian Railway Chugging to Reality," *New York Times*, October 20, 1997.

41. Blakely, Alexander, "The Place Without Roads; Russia Paves the Trans-Siberian Gap," *Harper's*, December 2003, pp. 57–63.

42. U.S. Department of Commerce, *Country Commercial Guides for US Companies*, http://www.stat-usa.gov/tradtest.nsf, May 20, 2009.

43. *World Factbook*, Central Intelligence Agency, https://www.cia.gov/library/publications/the-world-factbook/index.html, accessed May 20, 2009.

44. Argentina, *World Factbook*, Central Intelligence Agency, https://www.cia.gov/library/publications/the-world-factbook/geos/ar.html, accessed May 20, 2009.

45. *Ibid.*

46. Feller, Gordon, "For Truckers, Polish Roads are a Deep, Dark Pothole on Route Linking EU and Russia," *Traffic World*, September 8, 1998, p. 18.

47. Field, Alan, "The Infrastructure in China's Remote Regions is Improving, but Foreign Companies Must Exercise Patience and Rely on Experienced Partners," *Journal of Commerce*, November 15, 2004, pp. 18–23.

48. Zubrzycki, John, "In City of Joy, Foot-Power Loses Pull with Rickshaw Ban," *Christian Science Monitor*, December 11, 1996, p. 1.

49. Marquand, Robert, "Driving in Delhi: Chaos of Cars, Carts and Cows," *The Journal of Commerce*, August 18, 1999, p. 1.

50. Morris, Nigel, "The Big Question: Has the Congestion Charge Been Effective in Reducing London's Traffic?" *The Independent*, February 13, 2008.

51. Dillon, Sam, "Can't Find Juárez Street? There are Hundreds!" *New York Times*, January 12, 2000.

52. Faison, Seth, "Palm Trees and Sun (and Who Needs an Address)," *New York Times*, February 23, 1999.

53. The Millau Viaduct, Web site, http://www.leviaducdemillau.com/english/index.html, accessed May 20, 2009.

54. Fitch, Stephane, and Joann Muller, "The Troll under the Bridge," *Forbes*, November 15, 2004, pp. 135–141.

55. Anonymous, "The Koror-Babeldaob Bridge," *Wikipedia*, http://en.wikipedia.org/wiki/Koror-Babeldaob_Bridge, accessed May 20, 2009.

56. De Santis, Solange, "A Long Ferry Tale Ends, to the Dismay of Some Canadians," *Wall Street Journal*, February 14, 1997, p. A1.

57. *Ports of the World*, 15th ed., Philadelphia: Cigna Insurance Corporation.

58. Ransdell, Eric, "Rolling Out the Future," *U.S. News and World Report*, August 12, 1996, pp. 47–48.

59. Goering, Laurie, "A City Hung Up by Too Many Hang-Ups," *The Chicago Tribune*, March 4, 1998.

60. *World Factbook*, Central Intelligence Agency, https://www.cia.gov/library/publications/the-world-factbook/index.html, accessed May 20, 2009.

61. *Ibid.*

62. Naik, Gautam, "Braving Sharks, Waves, to Lay Phonelines," *Wall Street Journal*, September 12, 1997, p. B1.

63. Robinson, Sara, "Cut in Fiber Cable Disrupts Internet Traffic Nationwide," *New York Times*, September 29, 1999.

64. Stephenson, Neal, "Mother Earth, Mother Board," *Wired*, December 1996, pp. 97–160.

65. Dugger, Celia W., "India Tries to Plug a Cash Drain: Its Power System," *New York Times*, February 6, 2000.

66. Tyler, Patrick E., "Power-line Thieves Loot Russia, Often Risking Death or Maiming," *New York Times*, April 18, 2000.

67. Swanson, Stevenson, "Urban Repair Bill Hard to Swallow," *Chicago Tribune*, June 20, 1997.

68. Bangsberg, P. T., "Making a Splash," *Journal of Commerce*, January 24, 1997, p. 3A.

69. *2002 World Development Indicators* database, World Bank, www.worldbank.org, April 20, 2002.

70. *Ibid.*

Methods of Entry into Foreign Markets

Chapter Four

Key Terms

agent (p. 74)
binding agent (p. 75)
contract manufacturing (p. 81)
counterfeit goods (p. 88)
distributor (p. 76)
franchisee (p. 82)
franchising (p. 82)
franchisor (p. 82)
gray market (p. 86)

intellectual property (p. 82)
joint venture (p. 83)
licensee (p. 82)
licensing (p. 52)
licensor (p. 82)
marketing subsidiary (p. 78)
principal (p. 75)
royalty (p. 82)
subsidiary (p. 84)

The first venture of most firms in the international arena is usually more the result of serendipity than of careful planning and thoughtful strategic thinking. The first few sales abroad emerge from a chance contact made at a trade show, an unexpected fax received after a prospect viewed a domestic sales brochure, or a sales inquiry resulting from an ad in a trade magazine. After a few of these haphazard transactions, the firm then realizes that there may be a substantial market—at least large enough to warrant further consideration—for its products outside their original domestic market, and management starts considering selling on a more systematic basis abroad. The pitfalls usually start at this point. Firms rarely assess correctly the market's characteristics, its potential, and, particularly, the advantages and disadvantages of a given method of entry, and instead base their entry strategy on a chance encounter at a trade show with a foreign agent or a distributor, or enter a joint venture with a partner met through casual business acquaintances. Unfortunately, some of those decisions end up being inappropriate: Countless headaches can be avoided if the correct strategy is determined early on, using as many pieces of information as possible.

4-1 Entry Strategy Factors

There are many factors that will influence a company's entry strategy into a foreign market. Some of these factors are related to the characteristics of the market that the firm is targeting, and others are related to the characteristics of the product and of the exporter.

Specifically, the exporter should analyze carefully the following determinant factors:

- **The size of the market**. While there is no easy rule, the method of entry is different for a market in which combined sales amount to €10,000,000 (U.S. $12,500,000) per year and a market that exhibits sales in billions of euros.

- **The growth of the market**. A stable market, growing at a moderate rate, will call for a different entry strategy than one in which there is a substantial potential for growth.

- **The potential market share of the exporter**. A market in which the exporter can become a major player will call for a different strategy than one in which the exporter has no chance to be much more than a niche player.

- **The type of product**. Products with technology and a need for after-sale service and parts will require a different entry strategy than a disposable consumer good.

- **The market strategy of the firm**. Although self-evident, a firm whose strategy is to provide a top-of-the-line product will have a different entry strategy than a firm that has chosen to be the lowest cost provider.

- **The willingness of the firm to get involved**. Firms that actively want to develop foreign markets should have a different entry strategy than firms that believe that their domestic market is their primary concern and consider foreign sales as "bothersome."

- **The characteristics of the country considered**. The level of development, the infrastructure of the country, the business sophistication of potential trade partners, the overall climate under which business is conducted, the culture of the market, and the culture of customers should all be considered in the decision of an entry strategy.

- **The time horizon considered**. Products that have a short life cycle, or products that are likely to generate a lot of "me-too" competitors, demand a different entry strategy than products that are patent protected or are likely to have a long life cycle or engender a long line of complementary products.

Only after all of these factors are evaluated is it possible for a firm to decide appropriately which market entry strategy to pursue. Overall, great caution should be exercised in decisions regarding entry strategies: Among all the decisions made by marketers regarding the marketing mix, the distribution decision is the one with the longest time horizon, and the least likely to be quickly adjusted. Not that product, promotion, and price can be easily adjusted, but a distribution change can be quite an undertaking, leading to ill feelings and trauma, and therefore the need for a correct initial decision is yet more critical.

The alternative entry strategies available to a casual exporter will be presented first, followed by those alternatives available to an active exporter, and then the strategies available to a company willing to manufacture abroad.

4-2 Indirect Exporting

Some firms are unwilling exporters in that they prefer to concentrate on their domestic markets and handle any foreign inquiry as a "difficult sale." As such, they do not like to handle them. Under this banner of "indirect exporting," several alternatives are possible, from the lowest level of involvement to some very moderate interest.

4-2a Export Trading Company (ETC)

In the case where a company is unwilling to undertake any of the activities of marketing abroad, the use of an export trading company is the simplest solution. An export trading company (ETC) is an intermediary that will purchase the goods in the exporting country and resell them to a customer in a foreign country.

The dominant ETCs are very large firms, with local offices in numerous countries. The trading companies operate in the following fashion: They take title to the goods in the exporting country, making this transaction a domestic transaction for the "exporter," and transfer title to the "importer" in the importing country, making that transaction a domestic transaction as well. As far as either of the parties dealing with the trading company is concerned, the product is seemingly handled by a domestic company, its foreign origin is not a concern for the buyer, and its sale abroad is not an issue for the seller.

Trading companies were first created in the Netherlands, France, and Britain for trade with India and Indochina. As these trade routes disappeared, new trading companies were founded in Spain and Portugal for commerce with South America; eventually these trade routes also disappeared in the late nineteenth century. In the twentieth century, trading companies were resurrected in Japan to handle Japan's exporting efforts after World War II. These so-called *sogo shosha* have come to mightily dominate the export trading business: Mitsubishi, Mitsui, Itochu, Marubeni, and Sumitomo. All have sales in the trillions of yen, and trade in all sorts of goods. Mitsui claims to be involved from "noodles to missiles." Because of their presence in all countries of the world, these trading companies have acquired a wealth of information on potential sellers and buyers, and they leverage this knowledge into sales. They contact sellers when they are aware of a buyer in some foreign country, and contact buyers when they become aware of a particularly motivated seller. In addition, these trading companies have come to offer a complete "package" of international logistical services; they ship, insure, and finance international trade, and, in some cases, sophisticated traders rely on their services for complex transactions rather than handle them themselves: Their expertise in handling international transactions is unmatched.

Other ETCs are in existence, but they tend to specialize in one geographical area or one product line. However, they still offer the breadth of services that a *sogo shosha* can make available to an exporter; in particular, they take title to the goods in the exporting country. In the United States, since the passage of the Export Trading

Companies Act in 1982, a number of firms have been created, all operating on this smaller scale. The United States has also created ETC cooperatives that allow trade associations to offer export services to competing companies. Most of these ETC cooperatives are involved in exports of agricultural goods.[1]

The use of an ETC makes great sense for the novice exporter or the company unwilling or unable to dabble in the complexities of an occasional international transaction. However, should the company decide to become more involved in the long run, choosing an ETC is a poor strategy, as the customers abroad are not the customers of the exporter but of the ETC, and may not be known to the exporter. It is unlikely that the ETC will relinquish this information readily if it is no longer profiting from its efforts at developing the market for the exporter's products; it is equally unlikely that the exporter could benefit from the goodwill created by the ETC with its foreign customers as well.

4-2b Export Management Corporation (EMC)

Despite the similarity in name, an export management corporation (EMC) is an altogether different type of intermediary. An EMC is typically located in the exporting country and is operating as an export-oriented manufacturer's representative (agent) for the exporter (i.e., it does not take title to the goods but earns a commission on the sale).

Most EMCs are small firms, typically with fewer than fifteen employees. The firms rarely have an office abroad, although they do have contacts with a large number of potential importers, and regularly send employees—or, more likely, the owner of the agency—abroad to visit customers and actively attend trade shows and other promotional activities. EMCs tend to restrict their sales efforts to potential customers in one country and often specialize in selling one line of products in that country. Most of them represent more than one manufacturer abroad, usually in complementary lines.[2]

Because an EMC acts as an agent, the exporter is slightly more involved in the foreign sale than with an ETC; for example, the exporter is responsible for shipping the goods, invoicing the importer, and collecting from him. The degree to which the EMC helps the exporter depends on the relationship they have established with each other and the level of sophistication of the exporter. In general, an EMC helps a lot rather than a little: it acts as the export department of the seller, handling every detail of the transaction, from freight forwarding to insurance and from invoicing to collection. The compensation of the EMC therefore varies in function of its involvement: It either earns a higher commission for handling all of the details of the sale or earns a commission on the sale and fixed fees for the remainder of its efforts. The range of alternative arrangements is such that it is difficult to generalize.

The use of an EMC makes great sense for the novice exporter; by working with an EMC, and by at least partially managing its foreign accounts, a firm gains substantial insights, which would become quite valuable should the company decide to become further involved in export sales. In practice, though, because the EMC is a small firm and has valuable contacts abroad, it is often absorbed—at least partially—and transformed into the export department of the exporter. This allows the firm to capitalize on the talent of the personnel of the EMC and the goodwill it generated abroad.

4-2c Piggy-Backing

A third alternative choice exists for a reluctant exporter: It is called "piggy-backing" and can refer to one of two possible situations:

1. A customer of a firm enters a foreign market by setting up a manufacturing facility. The customer tells its suppliers that they will need to supply parts for assembly and spare parts for customer service. The suppliers therefore end up selling

African Export Ventures

In a few areas in sub-Saharan Africa, local EMCs, such as Getrade and Fritete African Art Works in Ghana, are spurring the development of an export-led economy. They established contacts with importers in the United States and negotiated large purchases of local African artifacts for such companies as Pier 1 Imports, Cost Plus, and Body Shop International. However, none of the local companies had the capacity to handle such large orders, so the EMCs coordinated the efforts of hundreds of small artisans and, after some initial difficulties, were able to procure most of the orders placed by the U.S. firms. As the artisans realized the profitability of such export sales, they started accepting orders for artifacts that were non-traditional in their colors or shapes, to accommodate the customers' requests, creating a perfect example of international marketing.[3]

In addition, as most small businesses in sub-Saharan Africa suffer from a lack of capitalization, the EMCs also brought in "micro-lenders," or those charitable organizations that will make very small loans (U.S. $500 to $3,000) to help entrepreneurs purchase machinery or obtain working capital. As these loans allow businesses to grow, it is expected that a business infrastructure will grow, allowing greater access to financing and triggering further business development. Such micro-lending efforts, pioneered by Muhammad Yunus when he created the Grameem Bank (literally translated as "rural bank" from his native Bengali), have lifted many local economies out of abject poverty. His efforts earned him the Nobel Prize in Economics in 2006.[4]

In addition, the United States' African Growth and Opportunity Act (AGOA), passed in 2000 and renewed in 2004, allows duty-free access to the U.S. market for goods made in most sub-Saharan African countries, creating additional export growth opportunities for entrepreneurs in that part of the world.[5]

their product abroad, "piggy-backing" on the strategy of an existing customer. In some cases, the suppliers develop their own independent sales in that market. This piggy-backing also happens with franchised businesses, which require that the equipment of the franchises they establish overseas be equipped with exactly the same machinery and utilize the same supplies worldwide.

2. A successful exporter involves one of its suppliers—or a company that makes a complementary product—in the markets that this exporter has developed. This form of piggy-backing is sometimes referred to as collaborative exporting; nevertheless, there is certainly an imbalance in the ability of the two partners, with one particularly competent and the other a novice.

Piggy-backing can sometimes be seen as a passive arrangement (triggered by another firm), at which point it is difficult to call it a strategy. Nevertheless, should the opportunity present itself, it makes perfect sense for a company to seize it and acquire some knowledge about selling abroad (see Figure 4-1). If piggy-backing is initiated by a firm eager to develop its own sales in foreign markets, it is quite an appropriate strategy, as the experience gained from the experienced exporter can eventually develop into a solid export strategy with the use of agents, distributors, or even sales subsidiaries.

4-3 Active Exporting

Once a firm realizes that it wants to exploit the possibilities that sales abroad can bring and decides to become involved in export activities, a number of alternatives open up. Under the banner of "active exporting," several alternatives are possible, differing not only in the level of involvement of the exporter, but also in the strategies pursued by the exporter.[6]

4-3a Agent

agent An individual or a firm, located in an importing country, that is allowed to represent an exporter in sales negotiations. The firm being represented is called the principal.

An **agent** is usually a small firm or an individual located in the importing country who acts as a manufacturer's representative for the exporter. Therefore an agent does not

| FIGURE 4-1 | Piggy-Backing |

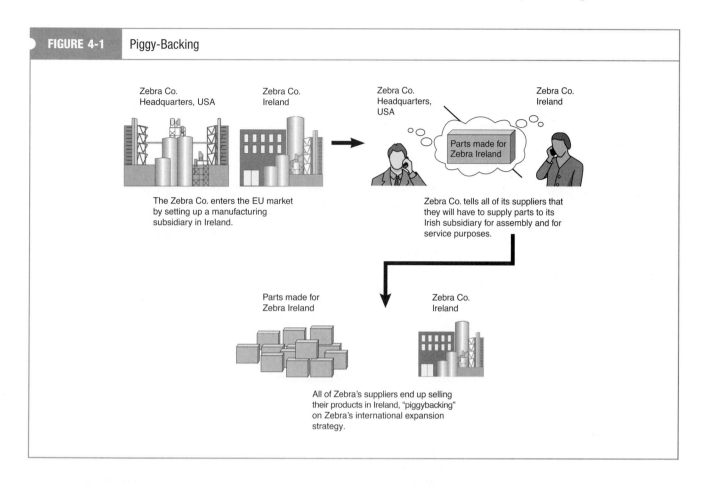

take title to the goods it sells but earns a commission on the sales it makes. In its relationship with an agent, the exporter is known as the **principal**. An agent often has several principals and generally sells a group of complementary products rather than products that compete directly with one another. The agent will handle all of the sales functions for the exporter, from the initial prospecting for customers to the close. The agent is usually given varying support by the exporter: Some exporters provide only the bare minimum of a sales brochure and a price list, while the more experienced exporters provide training on the product's characteristics, analysis on the competitors' products, information on the sales and service philosophy of the company, sales support in the form of samples, catalogs (translated or adapted), trade advertising, and financial support to attend trade shows, technical visits by corporate engineers, participation in sales incentive programs, and so on.

Agents, as a whole, like to keep control over their schedule and over their sales approach, but the exporter's support of their efforts is critical to their success and to the extent to which they expend a lot of effort selling the exporter's product. In particular, requests for quotes and *pro forma* invoices should be handled quite promptly, and negotiations on price and delivery done diligently, so as to not delay the agent's sales efforts; time differences sometimes exacerbate the perception of a lack of responsiveness on the part of the exporter.

Sometimes, there is the suggestion that, given a set of guidelines, the agent could be trusted to reach decisions and negotiate with the customer on critical aspects of the sale: price, delivery, terms of trade (see Chapter 6), terms of sale (see Chapter 7), and collection. However, it is critical that all such negotiations be handled by the principal, with the agent acting as an intermediary between the exporter and the importer. If the agent is allowed to negotiate directly with the importer, then the agent is considered by a large number of countries' governments as a **binding agent**, and the exporter is considered to have a permanent establishment in the country of import. This

principal The party represented by an agent in an international agency agreement; the exporter.

binding agent An agent who can make decisions that are binding on the principal; the principal must abide by whatever statements the representative has made.

determination has significant taxation implications; the profits realized on the sales made in that country are now considered taxable by the country of import. If there is no permanent establishment, the profits are not taxable in the country of import, although they are obviously taxable in the country of export.

After the sale is concluded between the agent and the importer, all of the other aspects of the transaction, from the *pro forma* invoice to the actual collection of payment, from packaging to shipping the goods, are handled directly and solely by the exporter. Finally, the agent does not get paid until after the exporter has been paid by the importer.

The choice of an agent should obviously be made on a large number of criteria: its ability to represent the exporter and its product accurately, its ability to sell, its contacts, its knowledge of the industry that the exporter wants to target, the compatibility of its objectives with those of the exporter, and so on. Moreover, the choice of an agent is a long-term commitment; although the contract is often based on one-year increments, the effective duration of a relationship between an exporter and its agents is much longer.

There are several alternative routes to "finding" agents in foreign countries; among the most commonly used methods are contacts made at trade shows, participations in trade missions, inquiries with the commercial attachés of the exporter's country's consulates, and contacts with other successful exporters.

The use of an agent is generally driven by several factors, one or more of which can be enough to trigger this strategic decision:

1. When the firm estimates that its potential sales in that market are small (perhaps no more than 5 or 10 percent of its domestic sales), with moderate or no growth potential
2. When the product is not a stock item, but a product specifically designed and made for a particular customer
3. When the product is a very expensive item, such as operating machinery
4. When the company expects a short product life cycle
5. When the product does not require frequent after-sale service
6. When the exporter is unlikely to ever become one of the dominant players in the market and will remain a niche player
7. When the company is reasonably well equipped to handle export sales
8. When the company is not pursuing a "top-of-the-line" strategy and does not attempt to collect premium prices
9. When the company wants to keep a reasonable amount of control over its prices and delivery policies

4-3b Distributor

Another entry strategy is to use a firm located in the importing country—or, rarely, in a neighboring country—that buys the goods from the exporter. Such an intermediary is called a **distributor**, that takes title to the goods, sells them, and earns a profit on the sales it makes. What characterizes a relationship with a distributor is that there are two sets of invoices: one set of international invoices between the exporter and the distributor, who is also the importer of record; and a set of domestic invoices between the distributor and its customers, who see these transactions as domestic sales of a foreign product. A distributor is therefore carrying inventory of the exporter's goods, and it also often carries inventory of spare parts and provides after-sale service. A distributor will carry complementary products but also may carry products that compete directly with those of the exporter.

A distributor is taking much more risk in its relationship with the exporter than does an agent, and experiences much higher costs. The distributor carries the traditional risks associated with inventory and invests a considerable sum of money in the inventory; should the goods not sell well, the distributor is saddled with the unsold

distributor An individual or a firm, located in an importing country, that purchases goods from an exporter with the idea of reselling them for a profit.

or obsolete goods. In addition, it is traditional for a distributor to participate in the costs of advertising, trade show attendance, and so on. In exchange, the distributor has much more freedom in setting prices, negotiating terms with customers, and managing all matters not directly related to the exporter's trademarks or copyrights. However, there is a large number of exporting firms that attempt to limit these freedoms, specifically on price, in order to maintain a standard strategy from country to country and to eliminate or reduce "parallel imports" (see Section 4-5).

A distributor should also be considered a long-term partner. Because it makes a substantial investment in inventory and in the training of its employees, the distributor considers itself involved for a long period of time, and great care should be taken in finding the right partner. The choice of a distributor should be made on a large number of criteria: its ability to represent the exporter and its product accurately, its ability to invest in the exporter's products, to sell them, and to provide after-sale service, as well as its employees, their contacts, its knowledge of the industry, the compatibility of its objectives with those of the exporter, and so on.

There are several alternative routes to "finding" distributors in foreign countries; among the most commonly used methods are trade shows, trade missions, the commercial attachés of the exporter's country's consulates, and contacts with other successful exporters.

The use of a distributor is generally driven by several factors,[7] one or more of which can be enough to trigger this strategic decision:

1. When the firm estimates that the market is substantial (perhaps 20 or 25 percent of its domestic sales) or when it estimates that there is substantial growth potential
2. When the product is a stock item, and generally not tailored to the needs of a specific customer
3. When the product is a rather moderately priced item
4. When the company expects a fairly long product life cycle
5. When the product requires (frequent) after-sale service and/or maintenance parts
6. When the company estimates it will not become much more than a minor player in the market
7. When the company prefers to handle export sales with only one customer
8. When the company is not pursuing a prestige pricing strategy with premium prices and service
9. When the company is comfortable relinquishing control of its price and delivery terms.

4-3c Additional Issues in the Agent–Distributorship Decision

There are two other issues to consider when determining whether an agent or a distributor would be the most appropriate partner—both issues are legal in nature. First, some countries will not allow agents at all, or will not allow agents to represent foreign manufacturers, or will mandate a physical after-sale service presence on the country's soil, all requirements that mandate the use of a distributor.

The second issue is more complicated: Many governments make a substantive differentiation in the way agents and distributors are considered by their judicial systems. Most often, because agents tend to be individuals or very small firms, many countries have decided to place them under the protection of labor law, the code of laws that deals with the relationships between employers and employees (see Chapter 5, Section 5-3a). In many countries, notably in Europe, labor law tends to be very restrictive in terms of what an employer can and cannot impose on an employee and, in those countries in which labor law applies to agents, what an exporter can and cannot require of an agent. For example, even though the principal–agent contract may call for a termination notice of thirty days and no compensation, labor law may call for a six-month notice and six-month loss-of-income compensation, overruling the terms of the contract. There are similar restrictions on the number of hours worked, the payment of taxes, the legal requirements of certifications, licenses, and so on.

In contrast, distributors, because they tend to be larger and are assumed to be more sophisticated, are covered in almost all countries by contract law. Contract law is much less restrictive, and courts tend to render judgments based upon the terms of the contract; the only restrictions are limited to contracts that are obviously biased or coerced, a situation very unlikely to be observed if one of the International Chamber of Commerce model contracts or an equivalent is used.

There is another distinction that is often made between an agent and a distributor that presents some potential for misunderstandings; it is often said that a distributor has risks (it invests in inventory), whereas the agent does not. While it is a useful distinction, it is incomplete. It is correct to understand that the distributor has substantial financial risks, because it invests in inventory and is faced with the possibility of unsold inventory. However, the agent often has considerable risks as well: It may invest time and effort in obtaining a sale for which it will not be compensated until after the product is delivered and paid. In some cases, especially if the product is custom-made for the importer, there may be a lag of several months between the sale and the receipt of the commission check.

4-3d Marketing Subsidiary

marketing subsidiary A firm, incorporated in the importing country and owned by the exporter, whose purpose is to sell the exporter's products.

Finally, a firm may decide, rather than employ an agent or a distributor (over neither of which it has much control), to create its own sales or **marketing subsidiary** in a foreign country. A marketing subsidiary is a foreign office staffed by employees of the exporting firm who will sell its goods in the foreign market. A subsidiary is incorporated in the foreign market, so it is the importer of record as far as the foreign government is concerned, and the "export" takes place between two legal entities that are part of the same company, at a transfer price. Although transfer prices can sometimes create problems in the process of clearing Customs, the process is very smooth altogether, as the traditional concerns of payment, terms of sale, and terms of trade are eliminated. All sales made by the foreign subsidiary to its customers are domestic sales and therefore are simpler to manage.

The costs of a marketing subsidiary are higher, and a good portion of them are fixed: A building must be rented, an inventory built, and employees hired and trained before measurable sales can offset these expenses. This is in stark contrast with sales through an agent, which are essentially variable cost sales (the commission is paid only if the agent sells) or sales through a distributor, where that distributor is the one bearing the costs of establishing the business in the foreign market. These investments obviously also require a long-term commitment on the part of the exporting firm (see Table 4-1).

The choice of a sales or marketing subsidiary is made when the company wants to retain control over its sales in that country, usually when the company is faced with one or more of the following situations:

1. When the firm estimates that the market potential is considerable (more than 25 percent of its domestic sales) or when it estimates that there is very substantial growth potential or very substantial profits to be made
2. When the product is technology driven, with substantial intellectual property content
3. When the product is rather complicated to sell
4. When the company expects to be involved for the long run, with additional products to be introduced later on
5. When the product requires sophisticated after-sale service and/or maintenance parts

TABLE 4-1	What Is the Correct Entry Strategy?

Match the description of these responsibilities to an *agent, distributor,* or *marketing subsidiary*.

When the company expects a short product life cycle	
When the product is not a stock item, but a product specifically designed and made for a particular customer	
When the company is not pursuing a "top-of-the-line" strategy and does not attempt to collect premium prices	
When the firm estimates that sales in the potential market are small, with moderate or no growth potential	
When the product is a rather moderately priced item	
When the company prefers to handle export sales with only one customer	
When the product requires frequent after-sale service and/or maintenance parts	
When the product is technology driven, with substantial intellectual property content	
When the company expects to become one of the major players in the market	
When the company is exacting premium prices from customers	

6. When the company expects to become one of the major players in the market
7. When the company is exacting premium prices from customers
8. When the company is uncomfortable relinquishing control of its products and prices.

4-3e Coordinating Direct Export Strategies

It should now seem self-evident that there are two types of factors included in the entry decision for an exporter: those factors that are market-driven and those that are company- or product-driven. Consequently, some firms elect to have a policy to always follow a strategy driven by their product line and always use a sales subsidiary or a distributor or an agent. However, some firms decide on a country-by-country basis which strategy is the most appropriate and juggle a combination of agents, distributors, and marketing subsidiaries. Each of these overall strategies has advantages and disadvantages.

When a company chooses to have the same entry strategy in all its export markets, it certainly simplifies the management of its exports and presents a unified front to its customers on all aspects of its marketing. In particular, if the firm uses agents or sales subsidiaries in all countries, its prices are bound to be well coordinated and its after-sale policies clearly controlled. If there are any discrepancies, they are known to the firm and can be clearly managed and understood. A firm choosing to use distributors in all of its markets can exercise the same level of control by using contracts that specify clearly which prices distributors are allowed to charge—a practice that is generally legal or, at least, tolerated—and which after-sale service they must provide. However, there are problems with this "fit-all" strategy, as inappropriate strategies may lead to a poor match with the market: A potentially very lucrative market may be given away to an agent, or a sales subsidiary may have to be established in a small market. Moreover, a firm may have to postpone entry into a lucrative market because of a lack of resources if it adheres to a strategy of building only subsidiaries.

When a firm chooses to have different entry strategies in different countries, or when it decides to sell through a series of independent distributors, the coordination of prices and after-sale service is more difficult to achieve, and the possibility of parallel imports (see Section 4-5) looms. However, the most appropriate strategy is chosen for each country, and, generally, the greatest profits can be extracted from the foreign markets.

For a firm, the decision to have a coordinated entry strategy is based on criteria that can be interpreted differently by different management teams. However, there is one significant issue to consider once a choice has been made: The costs of changing from one entry strategy where an exporter uses agents or distributors to a strategy based upon sales subsidiaries can exact a significant toll on all involved parties. The agents and distributors have generally invested a considerable amount of time, money, and talent into building a significant market for the exporter's products, for which they are rightfully compensated according to the terms of the original contract. If they are very successful, the exporter is often tempted to recover these "expenses" (the commissions paid to the agents or the profit opportunities given to the distributor) by establishing a sales subsidiary. This change of strategy should be avoided as much as possible, as it is traumatic for all involved parties and often results in reduced sales and profits for several years: The customers' loyalties usually lie more with the agent or the distributor than with the exporter, and regaining these customers' confidence can take considerable effort. The slighted distributor can also be strongly tempted to counterattack, in court or otherwise: Some companies can suffer greatly from this change of heart in strategy if the courts are sympathetic to the plight of the local firm,[8] as they often are.

4-3f Foreign Sales Corporation

Foreign sales corporations (FSCs) were created in the United States as tax breaks for exporters. It was not a method of entry at all, but rather a way for U.S.-based corporations to lower their income tax. The only conditions were that the corporation had to export products with a 50 percent U.S. content and had to incorporate a subsidiary in one of several pre-approved foreign locations, such as the U.S. Virgin Islands, Barbados, or Jamaica. By channeling its export sales through an FSC, a corporation was eligible for a reduction in its tax rate on profits earned on export sales of fifteen percentage points, from 45 percent to 30 percent.[9] It was essentially a tax incentive available to exporters, regardless of the method used for export, with the exception of sales through an ETC, because those sales are domestic in nature (see Section 4-2a).

The European Union brought a complaint to the World Trade Organization (WTO) that the FSC concept was a subsidy to exports, a practice that was prohibited by the agreement, and the WTO ruled against the United States in August 1999. Subsequently, the U.S. Congress created the Extraterritorial Income Exclusion (ETI) Act, which offered roughly the same benefits to U.S. exporters, but under a different legislation.[10] The ETI was also found to be contrary to WTO rules in 2004 under the same argument; export sales were not taxed, and therefore the ETI was considered a form of export subsidy, contrary to WTO rules. In 2005, the U.S. Congress created a new provision to counter that setback, the Domestic Production Deduction; although it is available to all companies operating in the United States,[11] it is designed to provide favorable tax treatments to exporters.[12]

Whether this latest development will be found to be nonconforming to WTO rules was not known as of May 2009. Nevertheless, the concept of a tax break to exporters is likely to stay, as the U.S. Congress has shown in previous situations that it was loathe to eliminate it: In 1984, Domestic International Sales Corporations (DISCs) were found to be in violation of the General Agreement on Tariffs and Trade, and Congress created FSCs in their place. Similarly, after the WTO ruled FSCs to be counter to free trade, the U.S. Congress passed the ETI Act. When that was found to not conform to WTO rules, the Domestic Production Deduction was created.

4-4 Production Abroad

Another alternative to exporting is for a company to start operations abroad; this strategy can be followed, for example, when the manufacturing costs are lower abroad, or when the shipping costs are prohibitive, or when domestic manufacturing capacity is reached, or when the product has a significant intangible content, such as in services. Here again, the order in which the alternatives are introduced represents an increasing level of involvement for the company interested in penetrating a foreign market.

4-4a Contract Manufacturing/Subcontracting

The first alternative is **contract manufacturing**—also called subcontracting—which occurs when a company enters an agreement with a producer in the foreign market to manufacture its goods. For example, a publishing firm may contract with a printing facility to publish its books rather than ship them from its home printing plant. Another example would be a cement manufacturer contracting with local producers to make and package cement under its brand. Yet another would be a supplier to an automobile manufacturer (often called an Original Equipment Manufacturer, or an OEM) that contracts with a company to provide subassemblies for that manufacturer's plant in a foreign country.

Contract manufacturing is not truly a method of entry—it is a way to get the product manufactured in a foreign country, and the marketing and distribution of the product remains to be organized. This distribution can be achieved through a distributor or a marketing subsidiary or, very occasionally, through the marketing channels used by the local contractor.

Contract manufacturing is often sought as a strategy to enter a market in which there are significant barriers to entry, such as high tariffs and quotas, but there is always great difficulty to find a suitable manufacturing facility in such a country: If the country has a protectionist streak, it is unlikely to have domestic firms that are operating at world standards.

4-4b Licensing

Licensing is the granting of rights to **intellectual property** owned by a company to another company for a fee. The intellectual property is either a patent on a specific

contract manufacturing A situation in which an exporter that needs to manufacture a product abroad finds a corporation in the importing country to make the product for the exporter.

licensing A process by which a firm possessing some intellectual property item grants another company the right to use the intellectual property item in exchange for a royalty.

intellectual property A type of intangible good that an individual or a firm can own; it is either a copyright, a patent, a trademark, or a trade secret.

The "Pet Shop" Bags

Firms frequently contract abroad to have a product manufactured and re-imported into their home country, taking advantage of lower production costs than at home. Nothing is particularly special about this. However, the case of the Scottish Pet Shop bags illustrates the possible unintended consequences of such an arrangement.

Back in 1990, the "Pet Shop" in Glasgow, Scotland, decided to have its plastic bags printed in China. In many ways, the bags were very traditional, with the name of the store and its address appearing on them; however, they were also adorned with a drawing of a red parrot. For some unknown reason, the printing plant where the pet store owner had had the bags printed decided to print millions more, and these additional bags found their way throughout Central Asia. They have been found by tourists and diplomats in Pakistan, China, Uzbekistan, Russia, and

Kyrgyzstan. Curious about the provenance of the bags, they sometimes contact the pet store in Glasgow to inquire about the mystery. The shop owner is as baffled as they are.

Eventually, "knock-offs" of the Pet Shop bags started emerging in these countries as well, some with two parrots, some with nonexistent names, or some with the peculiar English found on counterfeit goods all over China, to which my Chinese students refer colloquially as Chenglish: "The Plastic Bag Shop. Welcome Patronage."[1]

While it is difficult to argue that there was much intellectual property in the design of a simple shopping bag, and that the pet store actually lost much in the process—actually, this notoriety probably increased its sales—this example makes it evident that it is difficult to control what a contract manufacturer will do when the initial order is completed.

licensor The owner of an intellectual property item that grants another firm (the licensee) the right to use that intellectual property in exchange for the payment of a royalty.

licensee The party that is granted the right to use an intellectual property item owned by another party (the licensor) in exchange for payment of a royalty.

royalty The amount of money paid by the licensee to the licensor for the right to use the licensor's intellectual property.

technology, process, design, or product; a trademark; a brand; a copyright; a trade secret or other know-how, and it remains the property of the **licensor**—the firm granting the license. The company using the intellectual property—the **licensee**—has the right to use the property for a fee, or **royalty**, that it must pay for each use. Licensing is quite common in manufacturing, where companies license processes they have developed to other firms, or products such as chemical compounds and molecules.

In an international environment, the licensor is the "exporting" company and the licensee is the foreign company, and the range of intellectual property commonly licensed increases; several companies license their more visible intellectual property—trademarks, copyrights, or designs—to foreign firms. This strategy is followed when the access to the market is limited by high tariffs or nontariff barriers, when the shipping costs are prohibitive, or when the licensor is uninterested in actively pursuing the market.

Licensing, as a strategy, can be quite beneficial to a firm; it does not have to lay out any capital and can generate worldwide income from its intellectual property fairly rapidly. The downside is that intellectual property is not always well protected in some countries, that piracy is rampant in several, and that these risks can be perceived as major deterrents for the owners of intellectual property. However, these are danger associated more with the ownership of intellectual property than with the strategy of licensing. An individual who decides to violate a patent or infringe a copyright certainly does not need a licensing agreement to start: Patent information is available from all patent offices as a matter of course—the U.S. Patent Office has most of its seven million patents available online—and copyrights are by definition protecting publicly available products, such as this book and software. To a certain extent, it is probably better to have a local firm enforce its license of a copyright than to attempt to enforce the copyright from abroad.

4-4c Franchising

franchising A process by which a firm possessing an array of several intellectual property items grants another company the right to use these intellectual property items in exchange for royalties.

franchisor The owner of an array of several intellectual property items that grants another firm the rights to use that group of intellectual property items in exchange for the payment of royalties.

franchisee The party granted the right to use an array of intellectual property items owned by another party in exchange for the payment of royalties.

Franchising is, in concept, quite similar to licensing, except that the **franchisor** is granting the rights to a large number of intellectual property items, all bundled in a business package, to a **franchisee** who pays royalties for using this business model. The business model includes trademarks, copyrights, and patents, as well as know-how, training, and methods of operation. Most franchises tend to be retail establishments, because consumers tend to value a uniform product and service and like to find retail names with which they are familiar. Similarly, entrepreneurs abroad like to invest in a business concept with a proven track record, which most franchised businesses have. Finally, franchisors have the opportunity to gain market share without having to invest any capital. It has proven to be a fairly popular means of expansion both domestically and abroad.

Franchising is usually a very good option for a number of businesses seeking expansion abroad, but it certainly is inappropriate for most. The ones who can enter a market successfully are retail operations that involve a service requiring a fairly low level of employee skills, such as fast food restaurants, car repair shops, hotels, and car rental outlets. Franchising is inappropriate for high-skill consulting or advertising services, and nearly impossible for manufactured goods.

One of the consequences of the franchising strategy is that it generates a substantial amount of piggy-backing: As the franchisors demand that the franchisees use exactly the same equipment worldwide, the suppliers of those pieces of equipment end up selling worldwide as well. This is also true for items such as signage, furniture, and, in some cases, consumables: In 1997, for every dollar earned by franchisors in foreign franchising fees, U.S. $15 was spent on U.S. products by the franchisees to set up and run their franchised operations.[14] The proportion today is unlikely to be much different.

McDonald's Franchising

McDonald's Restaurants is a corporation that has used franchising as its main method of expansion in the United States and abroad. As of 2008, McDonald's had a total of 12,136 franchised restaurants in the United States, owned by about 2,400 independent franchisees. There were only 1,782 restaurants owned by the corporation, for a total of 13,918 U.S. restaurants. Abroad, the company has also followed an aggressive development policy by using franchises: In 2008, there were 18,049 McDonald's restaurants in 118 countries, with several countries having more than 1,000 restaurants (Canada, Japan, the United Kingdom, and Germany). More than 50 percent of these restaurants are franchised (13,329 units).[15]

This foreign growth was not without some hitches; for example, in 1967, McDonald's Corporation divided Canada into two franchising "territories," which it licensed to two individuals, George Tidball (Western Canada) and George Cohon (Eastern Canada). Realizing that this large market's potential could not be controlled by only two franchisees, McDonald's Corporation purchased these franchises in 1970 and 1971.[16]

Nevertheless, the company is intent on expanding the percentage of franchisees, as it believes that they are best at gauging their local markets. The franchisees have been the greatest strength of McDonald's development: Several of the company's best-selling sandwiches were developed by franchisees, notably the Big Mac (1968) and the Egg McMuffin (1973). The same was true internationally. The former franchisee in Canada, George Cohon, now head of the corporate McDonald's Restaurants of Canada, opened the first restaurant in Moscow, on Pushkin Square, in January 1990. After selling more than 30,000 meals on its first day of operations, this restaurant was still the busiest McDonald's in the world ten years later. As of May 2009, there were 103 restaurants in all of Russia.

In Japan, McDonald's used a slightly different strategy early on: It formed a 50-50 joint venture with Den Fujita in 1970, and soon opened its first restaurant on the glamorous Ginza in Tokyo. Most of Japan's 2,800 restaurants are owned by the venture, but eventually McDonald's started to add franchised operations, and today 22 percent of the restaurants are franchises.

System-wide, McDonald's restaurants' sales are roughly U.S. $71 billion, 55 percent of which is generated by outlets in foreign countries. Each of these restaurants grosses an average of approximately U.S. $2,210,000 in sales every year, the franchised restaurants being the most profitable of the lot.[17]

4-4d Joint Venture

With a **joint venture** (JV), the exporter invests in a facility abroad but finds one or more partners with which to share the costs of the venture. A joint venture is characterized by the creation of a new corporation in the foreign country, jointly owned by the venture partners in any combination of ownership percentages; most JVs involving two partners are owned 50 percent–50 percent or 51 percent–49 percent, but they can be held 97 percent–3 percent. Some JVs include three or more partners, but these are less frequent.

Entry strategies using JVs are generally created for one of several reasons:

1. The firm feels compelled to minimize its exposure in a foreign investment (i.e., the amount of money it has at stake in a foreign country), and it achieves this objective by lowering the investment costs by half or two-third.
2. The firm finds a partner with a complementary line of products to offer to the same market. Both partners feel that a joint effort, with a complete line, is the appropriate strategy, and neither of them is ready to enter the market alone.
3. The firm wants a minority local partner to teach it the local ways of business and help smooth out the many obstacles that a firm is bound to experience in a foreign venture.
4. The firm is legally required to find a local partner by the host government. This requirement was "popular" until the mid-1990s and has become less of an issue recently. Generally, the local partner was a politically connected individual rather than a partner who brought in additional capital.

The JV strategy was quite popular until the early 1990s for several reasons. First and foremost, this strategy lowered the exposure of firms to the political risk presented

joint venture (JV) A company jointly owned by two or more other firms.

by some countries. As early as the 1950s, some developing countries' governments decided that a good way to obtain means of production and create investment capital would be to "nationalize" plants owned by foreign investors. This policy also looked attractive politically, because the local perception was that the natural resources of a country should be managed and owned by its people. Libya, Egypt, Venezuela, and numerous others decided to just seize, without compensation to their actual owners, all of the petroleum production facilities within their borders. Several other countries followed the same policy, nationalizing any type of foreign-owned facility, until the late 1970s; some did it with some form of compensation, most without. The end result of these expropriation policies was clear: Not only did the countries have difficulties in running plants without the expatriate technicians of the nationalized firms, but they also scared away new foreign investors for decades. A JV with another firm was therefore a strategy developed to minimize the impact of a possible nationalization. In addition, a joint venture with a politically well-connected local partner was a good strategy for those firms that sought to minimize the probability of nationalization.

Countries that still wanted to create local ownership of capital and had not practiced nationalization found another effective strategy: Their governments asked foreign enterprises that wanted to invest in their countries to take on local businessmen as JV partners. These local businessmen were always very well connected but often largely undercapitalized and therefore did not bring anything but their contacts to the venture. In effect, the requirement was a partial nationalization of sorts, as the 100 percent investment that the foreign corporation made was quickly diluted to a 50 percent ownership of the JV. Some of these partnerships ended up being extreme examples of nepotism, such as in Indonesia, where Suharto's relatives were the only possible JV partners.[18] Obviously, the change in government and the prosecution of Suharto could have substantial consequences for these JVs. In other cases, the political partners were more of a hindrance than a help, even in dealing with the government, because they had been chosen more for their contacts than for their business acumen, and some ended up being dishonest; such was the case for the respective partners in China of Kimberly-Clark, Borg-Warner, BASF, Potain, and countless others, unfortunately.[19]

However, the greatest problem with joint ventures, and the main reason a large majority of them are unsuccessful, is that they are akin to marriages in which the spouses change over time. When the JV is first created, there is a good fit between all the partners' goals and strategies, and most JVs start well. However, as time goes on, the original management on each side changes. Some managers might retire or change positions within the firm, one of the original partners may be purchased by a conglomerate, corporate strategies can change, and gradually, the perfect strategic match that created the JV in the first place is gone and partners squabble over the JV's objectives. Eventually, they accuse each other of all ills. The JV between Ford and Volkswagen in Argentina—named Autolatina—failed because the partners' objectives changed as the venture progressed.[20]

Because of all these problems, the strategy of creating joint ventures has become less and less attractive to foreign investors. Some countries have actually retreated and no longer require foreign investors to create a JV with a local partner, at least partly because the existence of these policies deterred some highly sought investors from entering their markets: for example, Pepsico in India and 3M in China. These countries now routinely allow 100 percent ownership by a foreign entity.

4-4e Subsidiary

subsidiary A corporation entirely owned by another corporation.

A **subsidiary**, also called a wholly owned foreign enterprise (WOFE, pronounced "Woofie"), is an investment of 100 percent in a foreign venture by a firm. This strategy is followed by firms that want total control of an investment and are willing to take the risk of such a venture. A WOFE is either a "green field" operation, where a foreign firm builds a brand-new facility, or an acquisition of an existing firm, which is the preferred method of entry in most European markets, representing 56 percent of all foreign investments.

There is another alternative, which is still limited in scope but growing, particularly in the developing countries' markets: A firm will relocate an entire plant to a foreign location, usually to use cheaper labor and forgo the higher costs of a brand-new facility. The technology may not be the latest available, but the cost savings may be numerous, especially if the old plant no longer meets the environmental regulations of the exporting country. As the United States does not track export sales of used equipment—the Shipper's Export Declarations (see Chapter 9, Section 9-3c) do not distinguish between old and new equipment—the extent of this practice is not fully known, but anecdotal evidence abounds.

The WOFE strategy allows the firm to retain complete control over its investment, which has become the main reason for a firm to choose this form of entry. The firm does not have to share its trade secrets or know-how, and no one is privy to any of its strategies or policies. The firm does not have to share its profits with anyone else, does not have to rely on anyone else for information on its customers, is free to pull out from a given market if the prospective sales do not become concrete, and so forth.

The WOFE strategy is also often very beneficial to the host country—it creates jobs, for one—and many countries offer substantial incentives to foreign companies willing to establish a facility within their borders: free land, tax abatements of all sorts, training programs, and infrastructure improvements. If the foreign firm considering the investment is willing to establish itself in a rural or economically depressed area, the incentives can make a WOFE extremely attractive. For example, Ireland put in place an extensive panoply of tax incentives in the 1980s and achieved unprecedented growth and employment in the following decade. Today, Ireland is no longer perceived as an essentially rural country, but as a booming, economically prosperous country with access to the entire European market; its incentive program convinced dozens of firms to invest there.

The drawbacks of a subsidiary strategy are that there is a high cost of setting up a facility abroad, and all of it is borne by a single firm. However, the firm can use this facility to manufacture goods to be shipped back to the home country or to other markets; for example, having a facility within the European Union gives a firm duty-free access to the entire western European market and more favorable duty rates in eastern Europe than a facility in the United States. The costs can therefore be recovered fairly quickly. Similarly, a Japanese firm can get duty-free access to the United States and Canada by setting up a facility in Mexico, which also enjoys low labor costs.

A wholly owned subsidiary subjects the firm to a high exposure to the risks of investments, although it is evident that the risks that make a management team worry about its investments abroad are in decline: Political risks are becoming less prominent, with yet a greater number of countries solidly in the democratic camp, and the economic risks are in decline as well. Except for countries in which there is no real market for many products, the prospects for a stable economy, a stable government, or at least a stable transition to a new government, are very good.

A WOFE also faces the relocation costs if a decision is made to move the production facility to another country. Cost may include significant compensation to employees who will be laid off during the relocation process. The expenses vary by country and must be considered in the relocation analysis. In 2006, Kraft Foods decided to move its subsidiary from Australia to China, and this decision resulted in several substantial costs.

Finally, a WOFE presents the disadvantage of having to manage in a foreign country without a very good understanding of local customs and regulations. As a firm invests in a foreign country, it oftentimes chooses to have an expatriate manager at its helm; this manager often runs into difficulties that may have been avoided, had the firm elected to have a local partner. For example, the European countries have

Kraft Foods Australia

Kraft Foods is one of the world's largest food and beverage companies, with sales in more than 145 countries. Kraft was acquired in 1988 by Philip Morris Companies, which also purchased Miller Brewing in 1985 and Nabisco Holdings in 2000. Philip Morris changed its name to Altria Group in 2003 to reflect its more diversified business ventures.

In 2002, Kraft Foods Australia acquired a manufacturing plant in Broadmeadows, Australia, as a wholly owned subsidiary to manufacture its cookies. The Australian facility, which had been built in 1964, employed 151 people. Kraft then embarked on a strategy to improve the performance of the facility, reduce costs, and maintain quality; however, the cost reductions were not sufficient, and the older plant did not have the capacity to support an expanding market. On March 31, 2006, Kraft Foods Australia closed the cookie manufacturing facility and moved the manufacturing of cookies to a regional facility in Suzhou, China. Later in the year, Kraft Foods Australia announced that it would close its distribution center in Port Melbourne and a dairy plant in Strathmerton that manufactured cheese and Vegemite, an exclusively Australian product. All the product lines continue to be sold in Australia, with a third-party logistics provider taking responsibility for the distribution of these products there.

The employment contracts that Kraft had negotiated with its unions and the laws of Australia required the company to provide substantial support to its laid-off workers in both locations: They had to be paid a severance package that included four weeks' pay for each year worked at the plant (a benefit called an "entitlement") and given access to outplacement services for a minimum period of eight weeks (called a "redundancy package").[21]

Kraft Foods vice president and area director for Australia/New Zealand Chris Bell said, "Kraft is especially mindful of the impact this decision will have on our employees, as we greatly value the support that all our employees give to Kraft Foods Australia. We will ensure that all affected … employees are given access to every support during this difficult period, and they are guaranteed to be paid their appropriate entitlements, including a redundancy package. Employees will also have access to comprehensive career transition support services."[22]

When it purchased the Broadmeadows plant in 2002 as a wholly owned Australian subsidiary, Kraft had undoubtedly anticipated the additional costs of its legal obligations to its new workforce and had considered the employees when it decided to close the plant. Not all companies who invest abroad take those factors into consideration.

countless customs that sound peculiar or even counterproductive to any foreigner but which local managers support heavily: thirty-five-hour workweeks in France, *Mitbestimmung* (co-determination) in Germany, late-night work hours in Spain, and so on. These drawbacks can easily be overcome by hiring a competent local general manager.

All of these methods of producing products abroad are summarized in Table 4-2.

4-5 Parallel Imports

One of the greatest problems faced by a firm involved in several markets is the risk of parallel imports, which is particularly acute if the firm has relinquished some control over its goods' prices; for example, by using distributors.

gray market A process by which unauthorized intermediaries buy the products of a company in country A, export them to country B, and resell them to retailers and other intermediaries in country B.

Parallel imports—or **gray market** goods—are goods that are sold outside the regular distribution channels of a company, usually because there is a discrepancy between the price charged in one country and the price charged in another. Gray market goods are not counterfeit or shoddy goods: They are the legitimate items but are sold outside the channel chosen by the company (see Figure 4-2). For example, an item such as shampoo may sell at different prices in Germany and in Spain: For whatever reason, the Spanish version of a brand is significantly cheaper. An entrepreneur buys some shampoo in Spain, ships it to Germany, and sells it through a discount store. The price paid by a consumer in Germany for the Spanish version of the product ends up being lower than the price of the German version; since the sale is "outside" of the regular channel of distribution, it is considered a parallel import. The

TABLE 4-2	Production Abroad

Methods of Production Abroad

Licensing	Licensing is the granting of rights to intellectual property owned by a company to another company for a fee. Licensing is quite common in manufacturing, where companies license processes they have developed to other firms, or products such as chemical compounds and molecules.
Joint venture	With a joint venture, the exporter invests in a facility abroad but finds one or more partners with which to share the costs of the venture.
Contract manufacturing	Contract manufacturing occurs when a company enters an agreement with a producer in the foreign market to manufacture its goods. For example, a publishing firm may contract with a printing facility to publish its books rather than ship them from its home printing plant.
Franchising	Franchising is, in concept, quite similar to licensing, except that the franchisor is granting the rights to a large number of intellectual property items, all bundled in a business package, to a franchisee who pays royalties for using this business model. Most franchises tend to be retail establishments, like restaurants or bookshops.
Subsidiary	A subsidiary is an investment of 100 percent in a foreign venture by a firm. This strategy is followed by firms that want total control of an investment and are willing to take the risk of such a venture.

FIGURE 4-2	The Gray Market

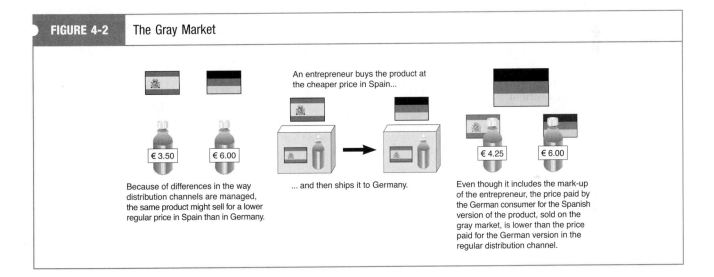

Because of differences in the way distribution channels are managed, the same product might sell for a lower regular price in Spain than in Germany.

An entrepreneur buys the product at the cheaper price in Spain...

... and then ships it to Germany.

Even though it includes the mark-up of the entrepreneur, the price paid by the German consumer for the Spanish version of the product, sold on the gray market, is lower than the price paid for the German version in the regular distribution channel.

legitimate retailer in Germany is not happy to be undersold and the shampoo manufacturer has lost some control over the marketing of its products.

Parallel imports occur in all sorts of product lines, from shampoo to cars to spare parts; however, it is a particularly sensitive issue in luxury goods, such as watches, electronics, and high-end automobiles. While there are ways to combat parallel imports, which can be found in any good textbook in international marketing, the best strategy is to avoid having discrepancies in prices from one country to another, which usually means that the firm must have a coherent entry strategy.

On a final note, there is no legal recourse possible, as the product is a legitimate product, manufactured by an authorized plant. In the United States, the Supreme Court affirmed this point recently: Once a firm has sold a product, it has no right to keep on controlling it. In Justice John Paul Stephens' words: "The whole point ... is that once the copyright owner places a copyrighted material in the stream of commerce by selling it, it has exhausted its exclusive statutory right to control its distribution."[23] The U.S. Customs Service will not stop gray market goods unless they are different from the goods sold by the traditional distribution channel in the United States—for example, products with a different chemical composition under the same brand name to satisfy foreign requirements or consumer tastes abroad.[24] Other countries have taken similar stances.

4-6 Counterfeit Goods

counterfeit goods Goods that appear to have been produced by the legitimate manufacturer, but that were actually produced by another company intent on deceiving customers and imitating the genuine goods.

One other significant issue a firm encounters when it starts to expand abroad is the increased probability that unscrupulous competitors—and sometimes partners—will manufacture and distribute counterfeits of the original product. **Counterfeit goods** are copies of the original products sold under the same (or a very similar) brand name, are generally of lower quality, and are sold at much lower prices than the original. Most of the time, the purchasers are well aware that they are not purchasing the genuine product, but do not feel that they are doing anything wrong; they are intent on saving money or are interested in obtaining the status that the brand conveys, but without paying for it.

Counterfeiting generally happen when there is a substantial discrepancy between the variable cost of manufacturing the product and the price at which it sells. Counterfeits are therefore abundant in the software and entertainment industries; a DVD of a movie or a CD of a software program can be reproduced for a few pennies but sell for much more. Counterfeit activities are also common in luxury goods (handbags, watches, clothing), pharmaceutical drugs, and cigarettes, all of which exhibit the same characteristics: low manufacturing costs and high selling prices. The probability increases further if the product is physically small and light enough that it can be sold easily and "discreetly" on the streets: Sidewalk peddlers constitute the most common "distribution channel" for counterfeit goods.

The existence of such counterfeiting activity is not dependent on the method of entry chosen. Whether a firm enters a foreign market through licensing, contract manufacturing, or a wholly owned subsidiary does not matter. Counterfeit manufacturing is generally present in countries in which government authorities have other priorities than defending the intellectual property rights of (foreign) firms. China and India are often the countries that are most commonly accused of ignoring counterfeiting activities, but they are just the most visible targets. Counterfeiting happens in just about any country in the world.[25]

Since about 2003, many countries have started to crack down seriously on counterfeiting, for several reasons. Their governments have realized that counterfeiting is not a crime that affects just the profits of foreign firms, it also affects the health of their citizens, such as when they purchase counterfeit and dangerous pharmaceutical products, it hurts their legitimate entrepreneurs who have intellectual property to protect, and it sometimes hurts the interests of the state itself. China, for example, cracked down on manufacturers of goods that use a counterfeit 2008 Beijing Olympics logo.[26] However, the task remains daunting; counterfeiting is difficult to prosecute, and most consumers—as well as local law enforcement officials who are also consumers—see counterfeiting as a crime that benefits them and hurts only the large foreign corporations, with which they do not empathize.[27]

4-7 Other Issues in Methods of Entry

4-7a Foreign Trade Zones

Foreign trade zones (FTZs) are areas of a country that have acquired a special Customs status, with the specific purpose of encouraging foreign investments and exports. Effectively, a foreign trade zone—sometimes also called a free trade zone—is an area of a country that is, for Customs purposes, still "outside" of the country;

goods can be shipped to the FTZ without being subject to duty and quotas. Once in the FTZ, the goods can be transformed, assembled, repackaged, and so on. If the goods are re-exported, they never pay duty in the host country in which the FTZ is located; if they are sold in the host country, it is only after leaving the FTZ that they have to pay duty.[28]

FTZs exist in one form or another in just about every country. Some countries use them aggressively to encourage foreign investments by allowing just about any economic activity within the zone, including manufacturing; goods come in the trade zone duty-free; are transformed in the zone into a final product, creating jobs in the host country; and the product is then re-exported abroad or into the host country. In China, for example, the Waigaoqiao Free Trade Zone is home to 104 of the world's 500 largest companies, employs 170,000 people, including 8,600 foreign workers, and adds RMB 67 billion (about U.S. $9 billion) to the Chinese economy.[29]

FTZs are particularly attractive to a manufacturer if the host country has an "inverted tariff structure" (i.e., the tariffs charged on parts are higher than the tariffs charged on the final product).[30] FTZs can also be quite advantageous to hold a good in inventory until sold, or to wait for a numerical quota to open. However, in view of the progress made in the last few years by the WTO to lead countries to lower tariffs and increase trade, FTZs may have a limited future because their advantages are dwindling. Nevertheless, they remain attractive and should be considered as a possible alternative site for a foreign investment, whether a sales subsidiary, a joint venture, or a WOFE.

4-7b *Maquiladoras*

Maquiladoras are companies in Mexico with a Customs status similar to that of an FTZ located both in Mexico and in the United States. They can import goods from the United States duty free, transform these goods by assembling them into products, and then re-export them to the United States, where the goods are assessed duty only on the value added in Mexico. Originally, *maquiladora* status could be obtained in only a geographic band located just south of Mexico's border with the United States, but it was expanded to the remainder of the country in the late 1980s. Today, with the completion of the North American Free Trade Agreement (NAFTA), maquiladoras have limited attractiveness to a foreign investor, but this alternative is still available.

4-7c Anti-Bribery Convention

One of the last aspects of significant concern in the creation of a method of entry in a foreign country is the fact that business practices in some countries tend to include corruption and bribery. The Organisation for Economic Co-operation and Development (OECD) has tried to ban such practices by developing its Anti-Bribery Convention (ABC), which 38 countries had ratified by May 2009. One aspect of the convention is that it asks the developed countries' governments to cease the practice of letting firms deduct bribery as a business expense; as of May 2009, all OECD countries prohibited the tax deduction of bribes to foreign officials.

Eleven countries (Australia, Bulgaria, Finland, France, Hungary, Iceland, Italy, Luxembourg, Mexico, Norway, and Switzerland) incorporated measures outlined in the ABC in their penal codes, and five (Canada, Germany, Greece, Korea, and the United States) passed specific separate legislation. Two of the signatory countries (Japan and the United Kingdom) wrote specific statutes penalizing companies and officers of companies involved in the bribery of foreign officials.[31]

The United States implemented in 1977 a punitive Foreign Corrupt Practices Act (FCPA), which heavily fines companies that are caught using bribery to gain access to foreign contracts. The FCPA is far-reaching and prohibits "all officers and employees and anyone else acting on behalf of the firm and its subsidiaries [from] offer[ing] any payments, direct or indirect, or through a third party, to government officials in return for getting or keeping business."[32] This includes payments made by an agent to a foreign official, or "special incentives" given to a well-connected partner in exchange for having won a contract. Anything that is not contractual is suspect. The U.S. government prosecutes any firm in the United States that it thinks has violated the law, whether it knew of the practice or not, and fines can run in the millions of U.S. dollars.

The FCPA is often understood to be aimed at preventing the bribery of high-level foreign officials; while this was originally the case, it was amended in 1998 and now targets attempts at influencing all levels of foreign officials, including such practices as asking for a favorable treatment of a Customs entry or a reduced tariff rate.[33]

The FCPA and the ABC are attempts by the developed countries' governments to "clean up" business practices abroad and prevent firms from being subject to extortion by corrupt foreign government officials. So far, there seems to be minimal evidence that these efforts have been effective, but they have taught foreign officials that it was useless to attempt to request bribes from developed countries' companies, and, in that respect, these efforts have worked. There is substantial grumbling, though, in the export community that the FCPA and the ABC have cost developed countries' exporters billions of dollars in lost business to foreign competitors that are unimpeded by these laws and can deduct bribes as a business expense.[34]

From a practical standpoint, for any exporter, the rules are fairly simple: Business abroad must be conducted aboveboard and remain within the boundaries set in the original agency or distributorship contracts.

Review and Discussion Questions

1. What are the principal differences between an agent and a distributor?

2. What are the different methods of entry regrouped under the term "indirect export"?

3. Using a product of your choice and a country of your choice, determine what would be the best method of entry for an exporter interested in that market. Justify your decision using the guidelines provided in the chapter.

4. Why would a company decide to franchise abroad?

5. What advantages would a foreign trade zone represent for an importer/exporter?

6. What are the advantages and disadvantages of using a subsidiary rather than a joint venture for a firm interested in manufacturing abroad?

Endnotes

1. Foreign Market Entry, *Breaking into the Trade Game*, Small Business Administration, 3rd ed., http://www.sba.gov/idc/groups/public/documents/sba_program_office/oit_bitg4th_chpt4.pdf, accessed May 23, 2009.

2. Root, Franklin R., *Entry Strategies for International Markets*, Revised and Expanded Edition. New York: Lexington Books, 1994.

3. Phillips, Michael M., "Carving out an Export Industry, and Hope, in Africa," *Wall Street Journal*, July 18, 1996, p. A10.

4. Dugger, Celia, "Peace Prize to Pioneer of Loans to Poor No Bank Would Touch," New York Times, October 14, 2006, http://www.nytimes.com/2006/10/14/world/asia/14nobel.html.

5. Lacey, Marc, "US Trade Law Gives Africa Hope and Hard Jobs," *New York Times*, November 14, 2003, http://www.nytimes.com/2003/11/14/world/us-trade-law-gives-africa-hope-and-hard-jobs.html.

6. Bello, Daniel C., and Ritu Lohtia, "Export Channel Design: The Use of Foreign Distributors and Agents," *Journal of the Academy of Marketing Science*, Spring 1995, pp. 83–93.

7. Root, Franklin R., *Entry Strategies for International Markets*, Revised and Expanded Edition. New York: Lexington Books, 1994.

8. Shirouzu, Norihiko, "In Japan, Breaking Up Can Be Hard to Do," *Wall Street Journal*, December 31, 1997, p. A7.

9. Tirschwell, Peter, "The ABCs of FSCs," *Journal of Commerce*, November 29, 1997, p. 1C.

10. "Overview of the Foreign Sales Corporation/Extraterritorial Income (FSC/ETI) Exclusion," The Tax Foundation, January 2, 2002, http://www.taxfoundation.org/news/show/154.html.

11. Losi, Ryan, "The Domestic Production Deduction: Does it apply to you?" Virginia International Trade, http://www.exportvirginia.org/newsletter/articles/archives/piascik.htm, accessed May 23, 2009.

12. "Comparison of Certain Provisions of H.R. 4520 as passed by the House of Representatives and as Amended by the Senate: Provisions relating to the Repeal of the Exclusion for Extraterritorial Income, Domestic Production, and the Corporate Income Tax Rates Applicable to Small Corporations," Joint Committee on Taxation, September 29, 2004, http://www.house.gov/jct/x-61-04.pdf.

13. Whalen, Jeanne, "Cool in Kyrgyzstan: a Scottish Pet Store and its Red Parrot," *Wall Street Journal*, May 2, 2000, p. A1

14. Martin, Josh, "Profitable Supply Chain," *Journal of Commerce*, March 11, 1998, p. 1C.

15. *2008 Annual Report*, McDonald's Corporation, http://www.aboutmcdonalds.com/mcd/investors/publications/2008_annual_report.html, accessed May 23, 2009.

16. Gibson, Richard, "Some Franchisees Say Moves by McDonald's Hurt Their Operations," *Wall Street Journal*, April 17, 1996, p. A1

17. *2008 Annual Report*, McDonald's Corporation, http://www.aboutmcdonalds.com/mcd/investors/publications/2008_annual_report.html, accessed May 23, 2009.

18. Engardio, Pete, and Michael Shari, "The Suharto Empire," *Business Week*, August 19, 1996, pp. 46–50.

19. Garcia-Castro, Roberto, "Governing Joint Ventures In China: Lessons from Success and Failure," *The IFCAI* [Institute of Chartered Financial Analysts of India] *University Journal of Mergers and Acquisitions*, March 2009, http://www.iupindia.org/309/IJMA_Governing_Joint_Ventures_7.html.

20. Bradsher, Keith, "After Latin Venture Fails, Volkswagen Succeeds and Ford Scrambles," *New York Times*, May 16, 1997.

21. Ross, Emily, "Sack with Care," *Business Management, Compak 2006 Supplement*, http://www.vcta.asn.au/files/2006%20files/compak06/May/BM206_2.pdf, accessed June 6, 2006.

22. *"Kraft Foods Cuts Australian Jobs, Moves to China,"* *China SCR: News & Views on Corporate Social Responsibility in China*, January 12, 2006, http://www.chinacsr.com/2006/01/12/kraft-foods-cuts-australian-jobs-moves-to-china.

23. Greenhouse, Linda, "Court Ruling Helps 'Gray Market' in U.S. Goods," *New York Times*, March 10, 1998.

24. Chester, James, "Policing and Protecting U.S. Intellectual Property Rights at the Border," Chester and Associates, March 28, 2008, http://www.tradelawfirm.com/sitebuildercontent/sitebuilderfiles/protect_ip_at_border.pdf.

25. Balfour, Frederik, "Fakes: The Global Counterfeiting Business is Out of Control, Targeting Everything from Computer Chips to Life-Saving Medicines. It's So Bad That Even China May Need to Crack Down," *Business Week*, February 7, 2005, pp. 54–64.

26. Fowler, Geoffrey A., "China's Logo Crackdown," *Wall Street Journal*, November 4, 2005, p. B1.

27. Fishman, Ted C., "Manufaketure," *New York Times*, January 9, 2005.

28. Chester, James, "Foreign Trade Zones; Creating Profits through Savings," Chester and Associates, March 28, 2008, http://www.tradelawfirm.com/sitebuildercontent/sitebuilderfiles/FTZ_ppt.pdf.

29. *"Waigaoqiao: the First Free Trade Zone in China,"* *China Economic Review*, May 12, 2009, http://www.chinaeconomicreview.com/industrial-zones/2009/05/12/waigaoqiao-free-trade-zone.html.

30. Calabrese, Dan, "Business Guide to Tax Evasion (Relax, It's Perfectly Legal)," *Inbound Logistics*, January 2009, pp. 171–179.

31. OECD Directorate for Financial and Enterprise Affairs, "Mid-Term Study of Phase 2 Reports: Application of the Convention on Combating Bribery of Foreign Public Officials in International Business Transaction," May 22, 2006, http://www.oecd.org/dataoecd/19/39/36872226.pdf, May 23, 2009.

32. "Country Descriptions of Tax Legislation on the Tax Treatment of Bribes," Organization for Economic Co-operation and Development, June 2006, http://www.oecd.org/dataoecd/42/43/37116153.pdf.

33. Chester, James, "Guide to the FCPA," Chester and Associates, April 17, 2007, http://www.tradelawfirm.com/sitebuildercontent/sitebuilderfiles/fcpa.pdf.

34. Gesteland, Richard R., "Avoiding the Bribery Trap," *Export Today*, February 1996, p. 18.

International Contracts

Chapter Five

Key Terms

acceptance (p. 95)
advertising (p. 105)
arbitration (p. 103)
arbitration panel (p. 103)
breach (p. 96)
competing lines (p. 105)
confidentiality (p. 104)
contract law (p. 97)
copyright (p. 104)
counteroffer (p. 96)
distribution contract (p. 97)
evergreen contract (p. 102)
exclusive representative (p. 100)
facilities and activities (p. 105)

force majeure (p. 100)
good faith (p. 99)
labor law (p. 98)
Lex Mercatoria (p. 93)
litigation (p. 103)
mediation (p. 103)
offer (p. 95)
ownership of the customers' list (p. 105)
patent (p. 104)
registration (p. 98)
rejection (p. 95)
termination for "convenience" (p. 107)
termination for "just cause" (p. 107)
trademark (p. 104)

Whenever a firm gets involved in international business, it enters into a substantial number of contracts, either written or implied, with a number of partners, some of which are located abroad. Examples of such contracts would be:

- The contract of sale between the exporter and the importer
- The contract of insurance between the exporter or the importer (depending on the terms of sale, which will be covered in Chapter 6) and an insurance company
- The contract of carriage between the exporter or the importer and the shipping line
- The contract between an exporter and its agent or distributor
- The contract between an exporter or an importer and its bank, regarding payment arrangements such as documentary collection or letters of credit (concepts that will be covered in Chapter 7)

All of these contracts are formed under the precepts of a multitude of traditions, local laws, multilateral governmental agreements, and international treaties that are sometimes not ratified or only partially ratified by some countries. Frequently, these contracts are further complicated by a profoundly different understanding of what a contract represents. Nevertheless, international traders and logistics managers learn to operate within this complex framework.

5-1 *Lex Mercatoria*

Whenever a contract is established between two parties in the same country, the law governing the execution of this contract is clearly determined by that country's legal system. In the United States, for example, it is the Uniform Commercial Code (UCC), and there is ample jurisprudence and expertise to determine how this contract should be executed. However, when the contract is between two parties in different countries, there is no specific law governing this contract, except what is called *Lex Mercatoria*—trade law—a multitude of international agreements and international trade customs, all of which complement domestic laws.

Lex Mercatoria is complex because it includes a multitude of different sources of law and jurisprudence. There are United Nations treaties and other decisions; international agreements, such as the General Agreement on Tariffs and Trade (GATT), which has given rise to the World Trade Organization (WTO) with its own rules and court system; multilateral agreements on specific industry issues, such as the Warsaw Convention on international air transport or the textile Multi-Fiber Agreement; regional agreements, such as the European Union and the North American Free Trade Agreement (NAFTA); bilateral agreements, such as the "Open Skies" agreement between the United States and the Netherlands (see Chapter 12) and the special status granted to Hong Kong by the People's Republic of China; International Chamber of Commerce rules, such as the Incoterms for terms of trade (see Chapter 6) and the UCP-600 for bank documentary credits (see Chapter 7); arbitration decisions and jurisprudence, established by the International Chamber of Commerce Arbitration Court or private arbitrators; and so on. In addition, many countries pick and choose which treaties they will ratify and, on occasion, which articles of the treaties they will ratify. They can also choose to become "signatories" to a treaty, which means they do not make a full commitment to a treaty, while others decide to abide by the terms of the treaty but do not ratify it. Finally, things get even more interesting when courts decide that some domestic principle cannot be violated by an international convention or custom.

The United States is an exception in many ways regarding its compliance with *Lex Mercatoria*. The courts of the United States generally do not consider that jurisprudence established in other countries, or decisions made by international

Lex Mercatoria The sum total of all the international agreements, international conventions, and other international trade customs that complement the domestic laws of any given country, and to which all international trade transactions are subject.

bodies, can be used in their decisions. The courts' position is that laws are the results of a democratic process and that neither foreign courts nor international bodies are elected by U.S. nationals, and therefore their decisions should not be binding.[1] The counter-argument is that the United States, by following such policies, is isolating itself from the rest of the world. The debate is far from settled.[2]

This chapter does not attempt to cover *Lex Mercatoria* in depth; only an overview of three of its major aspects is presented here. The first part covers the issues regarding the contract of sale between an exporter and an importer, which, for most countries, are covered by the United Nations Convention on Contracts for the International Sale of Goods (CISG), also known as the Vienna Convention. The second part of the chapter covers the issues regarding contracts between exporters and agents and contracts between exporters and distributors, as well as the resolution of eventual disputes through the arbitration system.

The specific aspects of contracts as they pertain to the terms of sale—the International Commerce Terms (Incoterms) of the International Chamber of Commerce (ICC)—will be covered in Chapter 6. Contracts relating to banking and payments will be covered in Chapter 7, insurance contracts will be covered in Chapter 10, and contracts of carriage between shippers and carriers will be covered in Chapters 11 and 12.

5-2 International Sales Contracts and the CISG

Whether or not a sales contract is "international" is not always self-evident. Courts will generally look at two criteria to decide whether a contract is international: the economic criterion, that is, whether there was a transaction that involved a transfer of merchandise from one country to another, and its mirror image of a transfer of funds; and the judicial criterion, which is based on whether the transaction has "links" to the laws of different states.[3] For example, a sale of office supplies to a French company's subsidiary located in Germany by a German supplier is not considered "international"; however, the same sale to the company's headquarters, located just across the border, would be international. Whenever there is a sales contract between two parties in two different countries, the domestic laws no longer apply, and it is governed by the Vienna Convention.[4]

The Vienna Convention, or CISG, was born in 1980 of two other conventions, the Uniform Law for the International Sale of Goods (ULIS) and the Uniform Law on the Formation of Contracts for the International Sale of Goods (ULF). Both had been written in The Hague in 1964 but were ratified by only a few countries because they were somewhat deficient.[5] In contrast, the CISG has been ratified by more than 74 countries,[6] whose export and import activities represent more than 80 percent of all world trade. The major exception to the list of developed countries that have signed the CISG is the United Kingdom, whose "[m]inisters do not see the ratification of the Convention as a legislative priority" and therefore have not taken the time to introduce legislation to ratify it in the last 20 years.[7] As often is the case, though, several countries, including the United States, have not ratified all of the Convention and have left out some provisions, some of which may have conflicted with domestic law. However, the CISG has become the law of international contracts, as traders will often elect to have their contracts governed by the laws of a contracting state, and therefore the CISG will apply.

Because the United States is not a full signatory to the CISG, transactions between United States companies and their counterparts abroad fall under the Vienna Convention only if the country of the other party is a signatory to the CISG. In addition, U.S. companies have the right to "opt in" or "opt out" of the CISG by specifying in the contract that they choose a particular law to apply to the contract. This can be deceiving, though; by choosing to have "the laws of the State of Texas" apply to a particular contract, a company would actually elect to have the CISG apply, because the State of Texas operates within the U.S. federal system, which includes all treaties in force, including the CISG.[8] This would be correct as long as the foreign company is located in a country that is a signatory, such as Poland. It would be incorrect if the foreign company were located in a non-signatory country, such as the United Kingdom.

The CISG is substantially different from the UCC—the Commercial Law of the United States—in a few of its aspects, notably the contract formation and remedies in the case of nonconforming goods or late delivery. It is likely to be different from a number of other countries' domestic laws as well, as evidenced by the number of countries that have not ratified specific articles of the CISG. Although these exclusions may make good political fodder, they may not be acceptable to the courts that will have to handle disputes between traders located in countries that have adopted different versions of the CISG or have amended it to include some other interpretation.[9]

5-2a Contract Formation

The CISG does not consider that a contract has been accepted until both parties agree to all of its terms: It is customary for a seller to make an **offer**. The buyer may respond positively but indicate that it wants a different schedule of delivery or term of payment, or some other aspect of the transaction to be handled differently. Under the UCC of the United States, such a response is construed as an **acceptance** of the offer. Under the CISG, it is understood as a **rejection** of the offer made by the seller and as a **counteroffer** by the buyer, unless the terms suggested do not materially affect the contract. The CISG specifies that changes to "price, payment, quality, and quantity of the goods, place, and time of delivery, extent of one party's liability to the other— most likely to be understood as Incoterms (see Chapter 6)—or the settlement of disputes are considered to alter the terms of the offer materially" and therefore that no acceptance is made in those cases.

offer The initial step in the formation of a contract. When one of the parties to a potential sale contacts the other party, it does so with an offer to enter into a contract. Offers are treated differently under Contracts for the International Sale of Goods (CISG) and the Uniform Commercial Code (UCC).

acceptance The second step in the formation of a contract. After an offer has been made by one of the parties, the contract is formed if the other party accepts the terms of the offer. Acceptance is determined differently under CISG and the UCC.

rejection An intermediary step in the formation of a contract. After an offer has been made by one of the parties, the other party may not agree with all of the terms of the offer, reject the original offer, and make a counteroffer.

counteroffer An intermediary step in the formation of a contract. After an offer has been made by one of the parties, the other party may not agree with all of the terms of the offer, and may want to modify them. Counteroffers are treated differently under CISG and the UCC.

Another area of difference between the UCC and the CISG regarding offer and acceptance of a sales contract is what is referred to by U.S. lawyers as the "Battle of the Forms." For most businesses, an offer or an acceptance is made on some standard business form, with a number of "small print" statements preprinted on it, designed to protect the interests of the party writing the offer (or the acceptance). In most instances, these preprinted clauses do not match. Under the UCC, the courts have determined that the differences do not matter in the formation of a contract, unless they significantly affect the terms of the contract, and regard these different terms as additions to the terms of the contract, to be sorted out by the court in case of conflict. Under the CISG, the requirement of a "mirror image" may signify a return to what, for Americans, would be the pre-UCC rules, where the terms of the contract are determined by the form of the party "firing the last shot." Then again, it may signify that there is no contract until all terms match, with little tolerance for differences.[10] There is little evidence that the second interpretation is likely to prevail, especially if both parties thought there was a contract and acted in consequence.

5-2b Creation of the Contract

The CISG treats the length of time during which the offer is considered outstanding in a significantly different manner than the UCC does. Most offers contain a clause stating that the offer is open until a certain date; under the UCC, however, the offer can be withdrawn at any time, without prejudice, for almost any reason. Under the CISG, the offer cannot be withdrawn by the seller (or the buyer) before its expiration date, and the other party can accept it at any time until that time. It is considered an irrevocable offer.

The CISG does not dictate that contracts of sale have to be written: Any agreement between a seller and a buyer can form a contract. Obviously, the issues of the proof of the existence of a contract and of the terms of the contract then become quite thorny unless there are witnesses to the discussion between seller and buyer. Even in the event where a contract of sale is signed, the written terms of the contract can be superseded by an oral exchange between the two parties, as long as there is evidence that it was the intent of both parties. In one of the jurisprudence cases contained in the United Nations Commission on International Trade Law (UNCITRAL) database—called CLOUT, for the Case Law on UNCITRAL texts— two witnesses corroborated that the written terms of the contract had been modified orally by the seller and the buyer, and the modifications were used by the court in determining the case.[11] In contrast, the UCC requires that any sales agreement above U.S. $500 be in writing.

5-2c Breach of Contract

Finally, the CISG treats nonconforming goods and delays in shipments much differently than does the UCC. Whereas the UCC applies the "perfect tender" principle (i.e., the goods must exactly conform to the goods contracted and be delivered within the framework specified in the contract), the CISG grants the seller more latitude. For example, the buyer cannot refuse delivery or cancel unless the nonconformity or the delay "substantially deprives the buyer of what it was entitled to expect under the contract and, even then, only if the seller foresaw, or a party in its position would have foreseen, such a result."[12] In other words, the buyer cannot avoid the contract unless the seller performs a fundamental **breach** of the contract. Therefore, those firms operating on a just-in-time basis should specifically notify their suppliers that they are following such a manufacturing policy, so that their suppliers can then "foresee" the problem that a delay in shipment would cause.

In counterbalance, the CISG allows the buyer to unilaterally apply a price reduction to the amount agreed upon in the contract for nonconforming goods. Such a price reduction should be proportional to the loss of value of the goods (percentage

breach In the event that one of the parties to a contract does not meet its obligation, that party can be found to have broken the terms of the contract, or to be in breach of the contract.

that is nonconforming) or to the loss of market incurred by the buyer, in the event of a delay. However, the burden placed on the buyer to notify the seller in a timely manner and to explain which remedy it will seek has a very high threshold. The notification must be made as soon as possible; it has to be clear and painstakingly detailed in the description of the problem, and it has to be extremely clear and specific in the remedies sought. Several cases in CLOUT (given by McMahon[13]) show that the burden placed on the buyer by the courts seems unduly harsh. In addition, this issue is somewhat moot for a buyer paying on a letter of credit (see Chapter 7), because it is committed to pay for the full amount in all cases. Finally, the notification by the buyer to the seller that a price reduction will unilaterally be applied must be made within two years; such a long upper limit is also of concern, because the statute of limitations for claims against a carrier may be shorter than two years in some countries, preventing the seller from recovering damages caused by a carrier.[14]

5-3 Agency versus Distributorship Legal Issues

The second type of contract of interest are the contracts between an exporter and its representatives in foreign markets; either an agent or a distributor. To briefly repeat ground covered in Chapter 4, an agent is a representative located abroad and earning a commission on the sales it makes on behalf of the exporter. An agent cannot negotiate prices, delivery, or other sales terms with the buyer, but only represents the decisions made by the exporter. In contrast, a distributor is also located abroad, but it purchases goods from the exporter, with the idea of reselling them in its country, earning a profit in the process. The distributor is setting its own prices and has an inventory of goods to sell: It is most often responsible for after-sale service as well.

It is difficult to generalize about agency and distributorship agreements: There is no international agreement on the way each of these relationships is governed. In most cases, the country of residence of the agent or of the distributor considers that it has jurisdiction over the agreement, and in many cases, despite the fact that the agreement may specify that the laws of another country apply to the contract (see Section 5-4h and Section 5-4i for specific information regarding the Choice of Law and the Choice of Forum in an international distribution contract). Because each country has its own laws and regulations regarding these agreements and because the jurisprudence of each country may differ even on similar statutes, it is very difficult to be specific without getting into tedious listings of countries. Therefore, only broader issues will be covered, to understand which aspects of a distribution contract should be examined.

5-3a Contract Law versus Labor Law

In the absence of specifics, agreements between an exporter and an agent and agreements between an exporter and a distributor will be called **distribution contracts**. One of the greatest differences among countries is whether they consider such distribution agreements as "contracts between equals" or as "contracts between unequal partners."

In the first case, courts will consider the terms of the contract when dealing in a dispute. This approach is referred to as **contract law** or case law, where the question is resolved by trying to interpret the meaning of the contract between the two parties. Both parties are considered to have equal sophistication in dealing with legal matters, and therefore neither of the parties would have entered a contract without understanding it. Most countries, but certainly not all, consider that agreements between an exporter and a distributor fall into this category. The contract between the

distribution contract An agreement between an exporter and an intermediary; it can take the form of either an agency or a distributorship agreement.

contract law A set of a country's laws that governs relationships and disputes between the parties who signed a contract. Contract law essentially dictates that the courts must settle the dispute by using the terms of the contract.

two parties is the framework that courts will consider in dealing with a dispute between the two parties. When the contract is silent about the point in contention, then the courts will use jurisprudence on what other contracts of the same type have established.

In other cases, though, countries will equate an international distribution agreement as something akin to an "employment contract," where the parties are considered unequal in their ability to interpret and understand a legal contract, and therefore where the "weaker party" has to be protected. This point of view calls for the application of **labor law** or for the application of special statutes, dealing specifically with the relationship between an exporter and an agent, or an exporter and a distributor. Such statutes cannot be overruled by the terms of the contract in any way. Therefore, the courts, in ruling in a dispute between the two contract parties, will ignore the terms of the contract and use the laws of the country in which the agent or distributor is located. Most countries that follow such an interpretation will tend to protect agents rather than distributors—Belgium being the lone country protecting its distributors but not its agents[15]—but several protect both. In addition, this point of view is often independent of the fact that the agent or the distributor is an individual or a corporation, and labor law has been used to supersede contracts between an exporter and an incorporated agent.

labor law A set of a country's laws that governs relationships and disputes between employers and employees; it assumes that one of the parties (employee) needs to be protected from the other (employer).

5-3b Home Government Restrictions

The main reason some countries use specific statutes to regulate international distribution agreements is that they feel that they need to protect agents and/or distributors against contracts that may not be fair or equitable. Specifically, they want to protect agents or distributors against wrongful or abusive termination (more specific information on this aspect of international distribution contracts can be found in Section 5-5).

In addition, those governments can also construct much more complicated systems to manage agents and distributors operating within their borders. They can require the agents and distributors to formalize and legally record their relationships with their principals. This process of **registration** is not unlike the process of joining a professional association, but it often doubles as a tax. Governments can require that the agents and distributors be nationals of the country in which they represent the exporter; such is the case in most Middle Eastern countries. They can also mandate that the terms of the contracts be inspected by their administration—in order to monitor the commissions paid to agents, for example—which they sometimes limit with a floor or a ceiling. Other governments will allow only exclusive agents or distributors—a single agent or distributor within a specific geographic area, usually the country itself—as do most South American countries. Finally, some governments will simply not allow agents at all—they mandate a distributor—or not allow any third-party representation, coercing exporters to establish a subsidiary, which they can then tax on income. Unfortunately, it is difficult to generalize about all of these different requirements, as they are very country specific—they even vary from one region of a country to another, as shown in the laws of the State of Louisiana, which are in contrast with the laws of just about any other area in the United States, or of the laws of the Alsace-Lorraine region, which are significantly different from those in the remainder of France—and can change at any time. Specific legal expertise and advice is therefore necessary before writing a distribution contract in any country.

registration A process whereby an agent or a distributor has to notify the government of the importing country that it has entered into an agency agreement or a distributorship agreement with a foreign manufacturer.

5-3c Other Issues in Agency and Partnership Agreements

There are two additional issues with which an exporter should be familiar in the context of an international distribution agreement, whether with a foreign agent or with a foreign distributor.

- The first is specific to U.S. exporters: Because the agent or the distributor acts as a representative of the U.S. exporter, the Foreign Corrupt Practices Act applies. Therefore, the exporter is liable for unlawful actions taken by the agent or distributor, even if the exporter had no knowledge of them and cannot control the agent's actions.[16] This places a particular burden on U.S. exporting companies that other countries' exporters may not have.

- The second is valid for all exporters: Whenever an exporter enters an international distributorship agreement with an agent or a distributor, it must guard against the possible perception that the parties are entering into a "partnership" agreement. If the exporter and its agent or distributor are portraying themselves as partners to other parties, then they are also communicating that they are jointly assuming each other's liabilities. This can present substantial risks for both parties.[17]

5-4 Elements of an Agency or Distributor Contract

There are a number of points that must be covered in any contract, regardless of the country of the world in which it will be used. This section explores a number of these mandatory contract elements. Some country-specific requirements can obviously still influence each one of them.

5-4a Contract Language

Because distribution agreements are usually entered into by two parties who do not share a common language, it is often necessary to have these contracts written in two languages. However, as any speaker of a foreign language can attest, it is utterly impossible to translate accurately and precisely contract terminology from one language to another. It is therefore critical to include a clause that specifies that the contract written in Language A is the original contract and that the contract written in Language B is a translation, and that in case of dispute or problems of interpretation, the original contract should prevail.

There are exceptions to this practical rule, however. Most international agreements between countries, such as the CISG or the International Chamber of Commerce's Incoterms, are written in several languages, *all of which* are given the same legal status; they are all "originals," which can sometimes present problems when translations cannot precisely duplicate the meaning of the framers of the agreement. These problems could be avoided by having one original and the others translations, but it would create political uneasiness, so it is not done.

5-4b Good Faith

Another mandatory clause in a distribution agreement states that both parties enter into the agreement in **good faith**. A contract is entered in good faith when neither of the parties has any ulterior motive about the agreement. It's probably best to understand good faith as the prerequisite for a contract to be formed: Both parties must want to fulfill the terms of the contract rather than pursue some other idea, using the contract agreement to dupe the other party into providing some necessary material toward that goal.

The same interpretation of good faith applies to the terms of the contract as well; both parties agree that they will adhere to the terms of the contract in good faith (i.e., interpret the terms without trying to distort them to their advantage). Both parties

good faith The assumption that both parties signing an agreement want to enter that agreement and have no ulterior motives.

agree to deal fairly with each other and not to try to dupe the other by attempting to find "loopholes" in the terms of the contract.

5-4c Force Majeure

force majeure An event beyond the control of any of the parties in an agreement that prevents one of the parties from fulfilling its commitment.

All contracts contain some sort of a *force majeure* clause. This is a French expression that translates loosely as "overwhelming power" but which refers to any event that cannot be avoided and for which no one is responsible, at least neither of the two parties entering the contract. Examples of such events would be a major storm that sinks the ship carrying products to the distributor, or a fire that prevents a firm from producing the goods on time, civil unrest, or a lengthy strike at a port that delays the delivery of the goods. Contracts always contain a clause that absolves either party from not fulfilling its responsibilities in case of *force majeure*, or a cause of non-performance beyond its control. Generally, there is also some statement that qualifies such exemption of liability to perform, "as long as the affected party resumes the performance of this agreement" after the *force majeure*.

Contracts may also contain another legal term, "acts of God," to address events beyond the control of the parties. However, the concept of *force majeure* is broader. "Acts of God" defines only large-scale natural disasters, such as floods or volcanic eruptions, whereas *force majeure* defines all of the events beyond the control of the parties that would prevent the fulfillment of the terms of the contract.

5-4d Scope of Appointment

The *scope of appointment* clause principally defines the function that the representative will perform; it is the clause that spells out whether the representative will be an agent or a distributor, and it is generally the first clause in the contract.

It also indicates the products to which both parties agree that the contract applies, to define the minimum product line that the agent or distributor is expected to sell, and at the same time to limit the product line the representative is allowed to sell. There is often language to the effect that the representative cannot "cherry-pick" the most profitable products and ignore the remainder of the line; this latter requirement may be expressed in quantitative terms. In addition, a list of the products that are to be sold by the representative is often placed in an Appendix and made part of the contract.

The scope-of-appointment clause also refers to the territory of the agreement and to corporate accounts, both of which are defined later in the agreement.

5-4e Territory

exclusive representative An agent or a distributor that has been granted the right of being the sole representative of the exporter in a given territory.

The territory clause defines the geographical limits within which the agent or distributor is authorized (expected) to sell. It is generally the entire country in which the representative is located, with some possible exceptions. In very large countries, there may be a regional appointment, and for countries with limited sales potential, there may be several countries included. The clause also spells out whether the agreement makes the agent or distributor an **exclusive representative** in that territory, which essentially grants a monopoly to the representative.

There are many problems associated with the definition of an exclusive territory, specifically in the European Union (EU). While it is possible to write a contract limiting a representative to a single country's territory, the EU considers that a firm operating in one EU country can also legally sell in any other. It is therefore difficult for the exporter to limit the activities of a representative to a single country—it is contrary to the laws of the EU and has been construed as an antitrust violation[18]—and it is difficult to grant exclusive rights to a territory when neighboring representatives have the right to sell there as well.

In many South American countries, the issue is different: Unless an international representation agreement specifically spells out that it is non-exclusive, it is always interpreted as an exclusive agreement in that territory.[19]

5-4f Corporate Accounts

Some agreements will specify which customers remain corporate accounts, or customers to which the representative is not allowed to sell, for whatever reason. Generally, corporate accounts are very large customers who have negotiated terms that will apply to all their purchases worldwide. The agreement always includes some provisions under which the list of corporate accounts can be amended.

It is important for an exporter to pay close attention to the number of corporate accounts that are included in a representation agreement, because too many of them may discourage the representative. An example of such a counterproductive agreement would be one that specifies that all accounts above a certain level of sales automatically become corporate accounts; consequently, a successful agent, after having developed an account and reached that critical level of sales, would see it removed from its commission basis, and therefore from its income. This is certainly not the way to reward a good representative intent on excelling and is likely to limit the sales of the exporter, as such a policy encourages the representative to limit its efforts to stay "just below" the critical threshold.

5-4g Term of Appointment

This clause determines the duration of the appointment of the representative. It must always be a definite period, with the possibility of renewal if certain performance criteria are met.

It is critical to determine the original duration of the contract appropriately. Finding the balance between a sufficiently long appointment period, so that the representative has enough time to develop the market to the point where it is a sustainable venture, and a sufficiently short period, so that an ineffective representative may be removed and replaced without too much of an opportunity cost to the exporter, is a very delicate task. Most of the time, such an initial appointment period is dictated by the market conditions and by the type of product sold. If the representative is expected to do "pioneer sales," in which it has to sell a new product with little brand awareness and unique characteristics, a longer period is necessary than for a standard product with multiple competitors and a well-known brand. If the market is characterized by personal contacts and long-term relationships between customers and suppliers, then a longer period is necessary than in a market that is more competitive and fluid.

Once the initial appointment period is completed, the clause also specifies the renewal period and, very importantly, the conditions under which the contract will be renewed for that duration. Renewal periods can be similar in duration to the initial appointment period or can be shorter; there are no specific recommendations either way. What is important is to specify clearly the performance criteria for renewal: level of sales reached, market share obtained, number of customers contacted, amount spent on advertising, number of sales calls made, and so forth. The issue is to make sure that the contract is not renewed as a matter of course.

Should the representative not meet the criteria for renewal set in the contract at the end of the initial appointment period, then the principal has two alternatives. It certainly can terminate the contract, which is often a bad solution, unless the representative has done particularly poorly, as the exporter is now confronted with the task of finding another representative. This decision also creates ill will: The slighted representative can always retaliate and create problems for the next appointed representative and alienate existing customers by giving them the impression that the firm is not committed to that market.

The other alternative is to renew the contract anyhow. The representative may have been unable to achieve the objectives set in the original agreement because of circumstances beyond its control, or because the difficulties of entering the market had been underestimated, or because the market potential had been overestimated. In any case, what is important is to renew the contract but to make clear to the representative, in a carefully worded communication, that the terms of the renewal had not been met, although the exporter was willing to renew because of the circumstances.

Should such a communication be omitted and the contract be renewed anyhow, it could then be construed by a court as an **evergreen contract**, that is, a contract with no determined duration, and a contract that can no longer be terminated for non-performance, as there was a precedent of non-performance and simultaneous renewal. Although generally a couple of instances are necessary before such a conclusion is reached, some overprotective court may not see it that way.

5-4h Choice of Law

Because an international contract is a contract that has links to the laws of two different countries, some different interpretations of specific clauses are quite possible. To avoid these problems of interpretation, every contract includes a clause that determines which of the two sets of laws should be used by a court or by an arbitration panel when a conflict arises between the parties. In general, the choice of law is made by the exporter rather than the agent or distributor; however, this does not preclude a possible resolution in the courts of the importing country, which may assume jurisdiction over the contract because of the country's statutes regarding agents or distributors, despite the clause.

In a well-publicized case, individual American investors in Lloyd's of London insurance syndicates tried to sue the company in U.S. courts to circumvent an exemption from liability from negligence that the company enjoys in the United Kingdom. However, because the contract between the investors and Lloyd's clearly stated that the laws of the United Kingdom would prevail in case of dispute— the choice of law—the Supreme Court ruled that the U.S. courts had no jurisdiction over the dispute,[20] even though such an exemption is contrary to generally accepted principles of law in the United States. The peculiarities of Lloyd's insurance market and its functioning, as well as its problems with investors, are covered in Chapter 10.

The International Chamber of Commerce (ICC) model contracts for agency[21] and for distributorship[22] approach the issue of choice of law innovatively, by giving the contract writer two possibilities, the first being the traditional choice of a specific country's laws, and the second being the "principles of law generally recognized in international trade as applicable to international agency [distribution] contracts,"[23] or those principles that constitute the *Lex Mercatoria* mentioned earlier in this chapter. As more and more arbitration jurisprudence accumulates, this alternative may become the preferred way of wording choice of law clauses, as it shields both parties from unexpected outcomes.

5-4i Choice of Forum or Venue

Strongly linked to the choice of law is the choice of forum—or choice of venue— clause. In it, both parties agree on the location of the court that will rule on an eventual dispute, using the laws chosen in the choice of law clause. In most instances, the choice of law somewhat dictates the choice of forum, as it makes logical sense to link both and benefit from a court experienced in the jurisprudence of the laws governing the contract.

One of the preferences of exporters—and of their legal representatives—is to choose courts with which they are familiar, and that generally means a court in the

evergreen contract A contract that, by design or by default, does not have a specific term of appointment, thus being likened to an "evergreen" plant.

exporting country. While this has obvious advantages of convenience for the exporter, it may present more difficulties when it comes time to ask a foreign court to enforce the decision. It should be noted that in general, foreign courts will look more favorably upon enforcing the resolution of a dispute in another court if the terms of the contract are clearly "international," that is, if the contract uses terminology and concepts that are specifically international—for example, the CISG, the ICC's Incoterms, and/or arbitration under ICC rules.

5-4j Arbitration Clause

An increasing number of contracts include a clause which does not call for a court to settle disputes, but for an **arbitration panel**. Either the arbitration panel is decided upon at the outset of the contract or a mention is made of the "Rules of Conciliation and Arbitration of the International Chamber of Commerce" to outline how the panel should be chosen. Generally speaking, the panel is made up of three arbitrators, with each of the parties choosing one and the third being chosen by the arbitration organization, such as the ICC. In many instances, the clause states that the dispute will be "finally settled"[24] by the panel (i.e., that the panel's decision is binding on both parties). If the country in which the **arbitration** takes place is one of the 130 signatory countries to the Convention on the Recognition and Enforcement of Foreign Arbitral Awards, also known as the New York Convention, then the ruling can be enforced just about anywhere;[25] unfortunately, China, although a signatory, has stood out as the only country where arbitration awards have not been enforced.[26] There are several specific advantages to settling a dispute through arbitration, most of which are outlined in Section 5-6.

arbitration panel A group of (generally) three arbitrators who are empowered by the parties involved in a contract dispute to reach a decision on the facts of the dispute and whose decision is binding on all parties.

arbitration A process by which the parties to a contract can settle a dispute, involving a panel of arbitrators who will render a decision in a short period of time.

5-4k Mediation Clause

In some contracts, the possibility of **mediation** or conciliation is encouraged before arbitration or **litigation** is undertaken. A mediator is an individual who will encourage and facilitate the communication between both parties in a dispute so that they can reach a compromise satisfactory to both. A mediator will not reach a decision for the parties but will lead the parties toward a compromise. Mediation is not binding, which means that the decision cannot be enforced and has to be agreed upon by both parties. Because mediation is also done in private, there are no public records of mediation, and it is an appropriate alternative to settling disputes when one of the parties is concerned about "saving face."[27] Mediation is sometimes initiated by the arbitration panel or the court for resolutions of disputes where both parties seem open to conciliation. (The advantages of mediation over arbitration and litigation are outlined in Section 5-7.)

mediation A process by which the parties to a contract can attempt to settle a dispute, generally involving a third, independent party who can suggest a compromise solution, acceptable to all concerned parties.

litigation A process by which the parties to a contract can settle a dispute, involving the courts of the country chosen in the "Choice of Forum" clause of an international contract.

5-4l Profitability or Commission

This clause is worded quite differently if it spells out the amount of commission that the agent will earn or, reciprocally, the price at which the distributor is expected to sell the product, or the margin that it is expected to add to its costs.

For agency agreements, the exporter spells out the commission that the agent will earn for sales in its territory. It may vary from product to product, so that the agent is given a financial incentive to sell a specific product, but it generally is around 5 percent of the selling price of a product, obviously depending on the type of industry in which the agreement takes place. A savvy exporter sometimes adds the possibility of negotiating the commission with its agent, in order to win a contract for which the price is critical. Agents usually go along with such reduced commissions on the philosophy that "a lower commission is better than no commission at all," if the sale is not successful. For sales outside of the territory that the agent may generate accidentally—for example, by attending a trade show and meeting some prospect from a different country—the contract will often call for a lower commission.

Finally, the exporter will also spell out when the commission will be paid to the agent. As a matter of course, the commission is never paid until after the customer to which the agent sold the product has paid the exporter. Commissions can then be paid as they are earned, or monthly, quarterly, or even semi-annually or annually.

For distributorship agreements, the issue of price can be thorny; if the distributor is completely free to set its own prices, then there is always the possibility of having substantially different prices for the same product in different countries, thereby creating the possibility of parallel imports (see Chapter 4, Section 4-5) and risking the aggravation of customers and distributors alike.

However, if an exporter is attempting to limit the probability of parallel imports, for example by trying to control the price at which the distributor sells the product or the margin—markup— that the distributor can add to the product, then there is always the possibility that such a clause will be construed as "price fixing" and therefore an attempt at reducing competition. Nevertheless, several versions of such clauses exist: Some companies bluntly set exactly the same price worldwide and argue that they do not want their distributors to compete on price, but rather on such other attributes as service, assortment, and repair facilities. Others make advertising support and other sales help conditional upon the distributor keeping the price in line with the exporter's guidelines. Some others do not contractually state anything but make explicit "threats" of possible delays in delivery for those distributors who do not respect guidelines. Obviously, all of these attempts can be struck down by courts as collusion, but such agreements evidently exist worldwide. Obtaining advice from an experienced lawyer in drafting such clauses would be money well spent.

5-4m Intellectual Property

trademark An intangible good (intellectual property) that an individual or a firm can own. A trademark represents the rights to a commercial name or slogan.

patent An intangible good (intellectual property) that an individual or a firm can own. A patent is the term used to refer to the rights to a process, material, or design.

copyright An intangible good (intellectual property) that an individual or a firm can own. A copyright entitles the holder to the rights to a work of art, a musical piece, or a written article.

confidentiality In a contract between two parties, the promise by each of the parties to not divulge what it has learned about the other party's customers, manufacturing processes, and business practices.

Exporters who benefit from substantial advantages due to intellectual property items will also want to specify the handling of **trademarks**, **patents**, and **copyrights** particularly carefully when a contract between an exporter and an agent or a distributor is drawn.

While the exporter can protect its intellectual property by making sure that it follows the proper registration procedures in the importing country, it is often useful to specify and define the intellectual property issues in the contract, especially in countries where intellectual property protection is lax. By including an intellectual property clause in the contract, the exporter transforms the protection of patents, trademarks, and copyrights into contractual issues, which are more likely to be enforced by a court. There are countless instances, unfortunately, of distributors or agents who violate intellectual property items, but a good contract can dissuade them from attempting to do so.

The contract should also include a **confidentiality** clause to determine how trade secrets and other strategic advantages are handled. The International Chamber of Commerce provides a model agreement for the international protection of confidential information.[28]

Finally, the contract should specify how improvements to existing products made by the agent or the distributor are handled. Although they traditionally become the property of the exporter, the compensation to which the agency or the distributor is entitled should be outlined. This is an important aspect of contracts for all parties involved. Chapter 4 shows that two of the most popular products sold by McDonald's Corporation were first created by franchisees: the Big Mac and the Egg McMuffin.

5-4n Miscellaneous Other Clauses

There are evidently many more clauses in a foreign distribution contract, whether with an agent or with a distributor, most of which are more "managerial" in nature and become much more specific to the industry, the strategy of the exporter, and its representatives than can be generalized.

For example, the **facilities and activities** clause spells out what the exporter and the agent or distributor have agreed with respect to the type of establishment that the representative will maintain, the size of retail establishments and of inventory they will carry, the type of training that employees will receive, and the expectations of managerial policies toward customer complaints, all of which are specific to an industry or a corporate strategy. McDonald's has much more stringent requirements in that respect than would an exporter of agricultural by-products.

The same is true regarding the **advertising** clause, which spells out the obligations of both parties regarding promotional activities such as advertising, trade show attendance, ownership of ideas for advertising campaigns and sales promotion items, and, very importantly, how the costs of such promotional activities will be paid for. For many consumer products, advertising costs are shared by the exporter and the representative in some varying percentages, but for industrial products, the spectrum can go from "entirely the responsibility of the exporter" to "entirely the responsibility of the representative." This may also vary as a function of the country in which the representative operates. A word of caution, though: If there are large discrepancies among the cost burden of distributors in different countries, the sale price may be affected and parallel imports triggered, which is something that an exporter should attempt to avoid.

The clause regarding **competing lines** spells out how an agent or distributor will be allowed to handle products manufactured by competitors. In most instances, an agent is not allowed to represent firms that are competing with the exporter's products, but a distributor is allowed to do so. Both are encouraged to carry products that complement the product line of the exporter, with the understanding that they would increase the attractiveness of the agent or the distributor's assortment. Some exporters, though, prefer that the agent or the distributor sell their products at the exclusion of all others, to ensure that the representative is concentrating its efforts on their products. Such decisions are made generally as a function of the bargaining strength of the parties: A Japanese *sogo shosha* will carry whatever it pleases, whereas a small dealer involved in distributing products manufactured by a large firm, such as Caterpillar, will have to abide by whatever its principal dictates.

Finally, the issue of the **ownership of the customers' list** has to be resolved for distributors. Because they sell for their own account, the exporter is usually not privy to the identity of these customers. In some cases, the exporter may find out who the distributor's customers are when they are requested to fill out some sort of warranty registration form, but in general, they are unknown to the exporter. Some exporters demand that the distributor report the names of its customers, while others prefer to leave this issue alone. Except for warranty issues, the only reasons an exporter would want to know the names of the distributor's customers are in expectation of poor performance of the distributor or in expectation of the creation of a sales subsidiary in the future, neither of which represent a good basis on which to start a contract. As far as agents are concerned, because the exporter is shipping and billing directly to the customers to whom the agent sold, the exporter is aware of the customers' identities, and therefore the issue is of much less significance.

Table 5-1 illustrates what a company, Michigan Marmalades, Inc. (MMI), must review before entering into contract negotiations with a distributor, Confitures de France. The table shows the checklist of decisions and issues that Michigan Marmalades must cover in its contract with Confitures.

5-5 Termination

Most definitely, the most sensitive issue in an international distribution contract is the issue of termination, or the act of ending the relationship between the exporter and the agent or the exporter and the distributor. All contracts will

facilities and activities In a contract between a principal and an agent or distributor, a clause that spells out what specific facilities each will maintain and what specific activities each will engage in.

advertising A marketing term that includes all of the techniques that a firm uses to promote its products by using communication media, such as television, radio, and print.

competing lines In a contract between a principal and an agent or distributor, competing lines are products manufactured by a company other than the principal that compete with the products manufactured by the principal.

ownership of the customers' list The list of the customers of a particular company is considered a business asset.

TABLE 5-1	Contract Checklist

Michigan Marmalades, Inc. contract negotiations with a distributor, Confitures de France

Contract language	Because the two parties in the contract speak different languages, MMI drafted the contract in English and had it translated into French. They included a clause stating that the English contract was the original and the French one a translation, in case of a dispute.
Good faith	MMI and Confitures agreed to do business fairly and honorably with one another.
Force majeure	This standard clause covers any unforeseen and unpreventable incidents that might disrupt the normal course of business. For instance, if a shipment of MMI Lemon Spread sinks during a storm, MMI can't be held responsible by Confitures.
Scope of appointment	The scope of appointment specifies which products Confitures must sell and what other responsibilities Confitures has as a distributor.
Territory	The territory clause defines the geographical areas in which Confitures is to work as the distributor for MMI. MMI and Confitures decide that Confitures will be responsible for the entire area of France and Belgium.
Corporate accounts	This clause states that Confitures cannot sell to certain customers, who will remain corporate accounts. These customers are the two supermarket chains that buy directly from MMI: Carrefour and Auchan.
Term of appointment	The term of appointment is the definite length of time Confitures will serve as distributor for MMI. MMI and Confitures agree to an initial term of three years. After three years, MMI will renew its contract for another year if it is satisfied with Confitures' performance. The contract will be renewed yearly thereafter.
Choice of law	Usually, the exporter makes the choice of law decision. In the event of a dispute, MMI decides that all legal issues will be settled in the United States. Confitures de France agrees.
Choice of forum, mediation, and arbitration	MMI and Confitures de France agree that they want to avoid going to court in case of a dispute. Therefore, they include in the contract a chosen mediator whom they will involve to work out disagreements. The clause in the contract also specifies an arbitration panel that will be used in the event that mediation fails.
Profitability and commission	If Confitures were acting as an agent for MMI, this part of the contract would spell out the price at which Confitures is expected to sell MMI's products and what commission Confitures would earn by doing so. Because Confitures is used as a distributor, MMI has less control over pricing; however, MMI includes the minimum and maximum prices at which Confitures must sell the products in order to avoid parallel import problems.
Miscellaneous other clauses	The facilities and activities clause states that Confitures will maintain a specific level of inventory of MMI's products and clarifies how the employees will be trained and how Confitures will handle customer service. The advertising clause specifies how Confitures will promote MMI's spreads, how the costs of promotion will be shared, and what public relations activities Confitures will undertake. In the competition clause, MMI and Confitures agree that Confitures may carry other products that will enhance sales of MMI's products. Confitures also is granted the right to carry products that compete with MMI's marmalades. The trademarks, patents, and copyrights clause specifies how Confitures can use MMI's logo and other protected information, and the confidentiality clause allows Confitures' access to MMI's production secrets. Finally, the ownership-of-customer-lists clause resolves that Confitures will share its customer list with MMI.

contain a termination clause, which will include a pre-termination notice and specify termination compensation.

- A pre-termination notice spells out how many days the exporter must give to the agent or the distributor before the termination becomes effective. This duration usually is shorter for agents than it is for distributors, but country statutes can extend it far beyond the contractual agreement. Some contracts call for no pre-termination notice—the contract is canceled immediately upon notice[29]— and some go as high as a year.

- Termination compensation, often called a "goodwill compensation," would be equivalent to the amount of income the agent or distributor would have earned for a certain period. This compensation can be as low as none, and as high as two years' worth of income. Again, this provision of the contract may also be rendered null by the importing country's statutes, which may mandate a specific compensation.

Both of these issues are dependent upon the reason behind the termination of the contract, which can be for either just cause or convenience.

5-5a Just Cause

Termination for "just cause" is triggered when either of the parties (exporter, agent, or distributor) is not honoring the terms of the contract. Generally, the representative is not doing something that it is contractually obligated to do, such as meet the sales performance objectives, spend a certain percentage of sales on advertising, or maintain the type of establishment spelled out in the contract; or the representative is doing something that it is contractually not allowed to do: for example, selling competitors' products, applying for patent protection on the improvements it has made to the products, or keeping the list of customers a secret. Only in a few cases is just-cause termination due to the exporter not performing its obligations, such as not providing the agent with prompt *pro forma* invoices—quotes—or not shipping diligently. Most terminations for just cause are triggered by a problem with the representative's performance.

In any case, it is relatively easy to terminate a contract for just cause, as there is a reason to terminate it. In most instances, the party "guilty" of not fulfilling its part of the agreement is not entitled to compensation or even any notice. Nevertheless, statutes may still supersede the agreement in such cases, and mandate a minimum notice period and a minimum compensation, even though there is breach of the contract.

5-5b Convenience

Termination for "convenience" can occur for any other reason than non-performance. It can be triggered by any of the parties, but generally, it is the exporter that is seeking to terminate the contract. One of the most egregious—but unfortunately very common—reasons is that the representative is very successful and the exporter realizes that it is earning "too much" and wants to replace it with a sales subsidiary. Another cause for termination is a change in the exporter's strategy that modifies how the exporter intends to penetrate foreign markets, or, worse, necessitates a complete retrenchment on the domestic market. In any case, the problem is that the termination is not linked to the contract—or the lack of fulfillment of the contract—but due to some extraneous reason.

A termination for convenience should be handled with the greatest care, as the potential for damages to the spurned party can be substantial; in those cases, a lengthy termination notice, as well as a generous goodwill compensation package, is the only way to ensure no litigation and a smooth(er) termination. In particular, if there are issues to resolve, such as inventories of unsold merchandise or outstanding orders, every effort should be made by the exporter to compensate the distributor or the agent. If it is not done, the representatives can very easily ask courts to intervene. In most instances, courts look upon terminations for convenience very harshly, sometimes assimilating distributors to agents so as to give them the advantages that the statutes of their country give agents. These statutes usually mandate long notice periods and generous compensation packages. Belgian courts granted three months of income to a distributor in compensation for a contract that lasted only four months, and *three years* of profits in compensation to a distributor who was associated with a manufacturer for 22 years but had been fairly unsuccessful, with yearly sales of BFr. 1,400,000 or roughly U.S. $28,000 at that time.[30]

Unfortunately, going to court may even be perceived as one of the best-case scenarios, as several injured representatives took upon themselves to sabotage the efforts of the exporter later on, through all sorts of means, from mentioning to all of their customers the callous treatment they suffered at the hands of the exporter to attracting new competitors in the market.

termination for "just cause" The unilateral decision, by one of the parties to a contract, to end a contract before its term of appointment expires, because the other party has not met some of the terms of the contract that it had agreed to perform.

termination for "convenience" The unilateral decision, by one of the parties to a contract, to end a contract before its term of appointment expires, for reasons unrelated to the performance of the contract by the other party(ies).

5-6 Arbitration

Arbitration is fast becoming the preferred way of resolving disputes between international partners. In 1960, the ICC received about 50 requests for arbitration; in 1999, it received 529 requests. In order to accommodate such growth, the ICC developed its "Rules of Conciliation and Arbitration," as did UNCITRAL, both of which are the most commonly used frameworks under which arbitration takes place.[31] However, there are many alternative venues for arbitration: the London Court of International Arbitration, the Stockholm Chamber of Commerce, the World Intellectual Property Organization, the American Arbitration Association, and countless individual law firms that specialize in this function, a number of which are located in Switzerland.[32]

The advantages presented by arbitration over litigation in court are many:

- Arbitration tends to be perceived as fair. Arbitration panels are not a court in either of the parties' countries and therefore are perceived as being more independent and even-handed. This is, of course, only a perception, because courts in any developed country using a modern commercial code are fair, but it is often a perception of importance in dealing with sensitive litigants.

- Arbitration tends to be much more expeditious than litigation. Arbitration panels are numerous and do not have the same backlog as traditional courts, which are generally understaffed and overworked. In some countries, commercial disputes can drag on for years: In India, probably one of the worst cases, there are more than three million backlogged civil cases—by the government's own admission—12 percent of which have gone on for more than ten years![33]

- Arbitration tends to be much more efficient. Because arbitration panels do not have to follow the same rules of evidence as courts, proceedings go much faster, and testimony can be given much more efficiently. Because other procedures are also simplified—there is no pretrial discovery—an arbitration meeting generally lasts a few days, whereas a lawsuit can take weeks.

- Arbitration tends to be much more "creative." Arbitrators seek to resolve the dispute to the satisfaction of both parties and can find compromises that are impossible in a formal court, where one of the parties has to win, while the other loses. There is also the possibility of iterative negotiations between the parties and the arbitration panel, a process that can lead to an acceptable compromise. Courts do not have this freedom.

- Arbitration tends to be more effective. Arbitrators generally have a wealth of experience in international business matters and can very quickly understand the issues at stake, draw on their experience and knowledge of arbitration jurisprudence, and settle the dispute to the satisfaction of both parties more effectively than can a court with limited experience in international business matters.

- Arbitration is not open to the public. Whereas court decisions are generally published and available to all, arbitration decisions are private, and only the parties involved in the dispute know what steps were taken to resolve it.

- Probably most importantly, arbitration is cheaper. All of the advantages previously presented tend to lower the costs of the litigation. In addition, these lower costs are generally shared by the parties in dispute, whereas court costs are usually borne by the loser, a custom called "European rules"; however, in court disputes adjudicated in the United States, both parties pay their own costs.

The only step to ensure arbitration in the case of disputes between the exporter and its representatives abroad is to include a clause directing that "any dispute … shall be finally settled in accordance with the Rules of Conciliation and Arbitration of the International Chamber of Commerce."[34]

5-7 Mediation

Mediation is a process by which a third party attempts to find a middle ground between the parties that are having a dispute. The mediator will often "shuttle" between the two companies and seek to find a commonly acceptable solution to both parties. Most mediators are people with a legal background or who have knowledge of the particulars of an industry; they can be found through referrals and within the trade associations of most industries.

Mediation presents several advantages over litigation or arbitration in several cases:

- Mediation is less formal. The parties in a dispute are often concerned about arbitration because it is a fairly formal process, taking place over a few days, involving meetings in a neutral venue, and restricted to a few individual managers. Litigation is even more formal. Mediation is often achieved over a longer period of time, each party has the opportunity to meet with the mediator in its own corporate environment, and the mediator can meet with many different people in both organizations, in order to get a better idea of the issue.

- Mediation is nonbinding. It can be the first step in resolving a dispute and can help both parties assess how their positions are perceived by unrelated parties. In other words, it is an indicator for both litigants of the strength of their respective positions and of their probabilities of winning an arbitration hearing or a court case.

- Mediation is more practical for smaller disputes or when parties are interested in keeping a business relationship. Unfortunately, arbitration is commonly perceived as resulting in the formal severing of all commercial relationships between both parties. Mediation allows both parties to resolve a dispute without affecting the remainder of their business.

- Mediation is often best for disputes that have arisen from misunderstandings. Both parties are unable to reach a compromise because they do not understand what the other was trying to accomplish, and the mediator can help them reach that middle ground.

Mediation is often the best approach when there is a genuine interest on the part of both parties to resolve the dispute in a manner that is fair to both parties and when both parties are interested in resuming normal business relationships as quickly as possible.

Review and Discussion Questions

1. What are the general provisions of the United Nations Convention on Contracts for the International Sale of Goods?

2. What are the issues brought about by the concept of "labor law" in an international distribution agreement?

3. Describe three of the elements generally found in an agency or distributorship agreement.

4. What are the differences between the "choice of law" and "choice of forum" clauses? How are they related?

5. What two possible forms of termination are there? How differently will they be handled by a court of law?

6. What are the differences between mediation and arbitration? How different are they from a proceeding in a court of law?

Endnotes

1. Feldman, Noah, "When Judges Make Foreign Policy," *New York Times*, September 25, 2008, http://www.nytimes.com/2008/09/28/magazine/28law-t.html.

2. Associated Press, "Supreme Court Justices Spar over International Law," *Law.com*, January 18, 2005, http://www.law.com/jsp/article.jsp?id=1105364112559.

3. Gourion, Pierre-Alain, and Georges Peyrard, *Droit du Commerce International*, 1997, Librairie Générale de Droit et de Jurisprudence, 14, rue Pierre et Marie Curie, 75005 Paris, France.

4. JBC International, "Think You Understand the Vienna Convention? Then Read This Sad Tale," *Journal of Commerce*, June 24, 1998, p. 12C.

5. Lookofsky, Joseph M., *Understanding the CIGS in the USA: A Compact Guide to the 1980 United Nations Convention on Contracts for the International Sale of Goods*, 1995, Klumer Law International, Boston, The Hague, London.

6. Kritzer, Albert, "CISG: Table of Contracting States," Pace Law School Institute of International Commercial Law, http://www.cisg.law.pace.edu/cisg/countries/cntries.html, accessed May 19, 2009.

7. Moss, Sally, "Why the United Kingdom has not ratified the CISG," *Journal of Law and Business*, 25, 2005–2006, pp. 483–485.

8. Chester, James, personal e-mail communication, January 19, 2009.

9. Ziegler, Jacob, "Canada Prepares to Adopt the International Sales Convention," *Canadian Business Law Journal*, vol. 18, issue 3, Fall 1991.

10. Gellman, Gila E., "Forming International Sales Pacts," *Marketing Management*, Winter 1994, pp. 60–62.

11. Ferrari, Franco, "What Sources of Law for Contracts for the International Sale of Goods; Why One has to Look Beyond the CISG," *International Review of Law and Economics*, 25, September 2005, pp. 314–341.

12. Walt, Steven, "The CISG Expansion Bias: A Comment on Franco Ferrari," *International Review of Law and Economics*, 25, September 2005, pp. 342–349.

13. McMahon, John P., "Applying the CISG: Guide for Business Managers and Counsels," Pace Law School Institute of International Law, http://www.cisg.law.pace.edu/cisg/guides.html, accessed May 23, 2009.

14. Huber, Peter, and Alastair Mullis, *The CISG: A New Textbook for Students and Practioners.* Munich: Sellier European Law Publisher, 2007.

15. Heron, Karl G., and David D. Knoll, "Negotiating and Drafting International Distribution, Agency, and Representative Agreements: The United States Exporter's Perspective," *The International Lawyer*, Fall 1987, pp. 939–983.

16. Deming, Stuart, *The Foreign Corrupt Practices Act and the New International Norms.* Chicago: American Bar Association, 2005.

17. Chester, James, personal e-mail communication, January 19, 2009.

18. Heron, Karl G., and David D. Knoll, "Negotiating and Drafting International Distribution, Agency, and Representative Agreements: The United States Exporter's Perspective," *The International Lawyer*, Fall 1987, pp. 939–983.

19. Dubberly, David E., "When Giving Your Rep the Boot: In Latin America, Labor Laws May Prove Surprisingly Costly, Unless You Plan Ahead," *Export Today*, May 1998, p. 26.

20. "Lloyd's Revamp Won't Be Challenged," Associated Press News Release, June 23, 1997.

21. *The ICC Model Commercial Agency Contract*, 2nd ed., 2002, publication No. 644 of the International Chamber of Commerce, ICC Publishing, 156 Fifth Avenue, New York, NY 10010, USA and ICC Publishing SA, 38, Cours Albert 1er, 75008 Paris, France.

22. *The ICC Model Distributorship Contract*, 2002 ed., publication No. 646 of the International Chamber of Commerce, ICC Publishing, 156 Fifth Avenue, New York, NY 10010, USA and ICC Publishing SA, 38, Cours Albert 1er, 75008 Paris, France.

23. *The ICC Model Commercial Agency Contract*, 2nd ed., 2002, publication No. 644 of the International Chamber of Commerce, ICC Publishing, 156 Fifth Avenue, New York, NY 10010, USA and ICC Publishing SA, 38, Cours Albert 1er, 75008 Paris, France.

24. *The ICC Model Distributorship Contract*, 2002 ed., publication No. 646 of the International Chamber of Commerce, ICC Publishing, 156 Fifth Avenue, New York, NY 10010, USA and ICC Publishing SA, 38, Cours Albert 1er, 75008 Paris, France.

25. Ulmer, Nicolas C., "Bullet-proofing Your International Arbitration: Part 2 of 2," *World Trade*, August 2000, p. 68.

26. Zirin, James D., "Confucian Confusion," *Forbes*, February 24, 1997, p. 136.

27. Connors, Kathleen, "Arbitration Taking Hold in Asia with Help of International Chamber," *Journal of Commerce*, April 2, 1997, p. 8A.

28. *The ICC Model Confidentiality Agreement*, 2006 ed., publication No. 664 of the International Chamber of Commerce, ICC Publishing, 156 Fifth Avenue, New York, NY 10010, USA and ICC Publishing SA, 38, Cours Albert 1er, 75008 Paris, France.

29. Puelinckx, A. H., , and H. A. Tielemans, "The Termination of Agency and Distributorship Agreements: A Comparative Survey," *Northwestern Journal of International Law and Business*, Fall 1981, 3:542, pp. 452–495.

30. *Ibid.*

31. Ulmer, Nicolas C., "Bullet-proofing Your International Arbitration: Part 2 of 2," *World Trade*, August 2000, p. 68.

32. *Ibid.*

33. Karp, Jonathan, "India's Laws a Mixed Blessing for Investors," *Wall Street Journal*, July 11, 1997, p. A10.

34. *The ICC Model Distributorship Contract*, 2002 ed., publication No. 646 of the International Chamber of Commerce, ICC Publishing, 156 Fifth Avenue, New York, NY 10010, USA and ICC Publishing SA, 38, Cours Albert 1er, 75008 Paris, France.

Terms of Trade or Incoterms

Chapter Six

Chapter Outline

Key Terms

Whenever an exporter sells goods to a foreign company, whether through an intermediary such as an agent or a distributor or directly to an importer, there are a large number of steps involved in getting the goods to the customer:

- Clearing the goods for export
- Organizing the transport of the goods between the exporter and the importer, often using several means of transportation
- Clearing Customs in the importing country

The terms of trade used in the contract of sale determine which of these steps are the responsibility of the exporter and which are the responsibility of the importer. Often, the number of issues involved in an international shipment is substantial, and specifically dividing all of these tasks between the exporter and the importer for each shipment would be a daunting task. In addition, it would be virtually impossible to anticipate everything that could go "wrong" during transit and determine at the time of the contract which of the parties should be responsible for each incident.[1]

6-1 International Commerce Terms

Fortunately, a set of standardized terms of trade was created in 1936 by the International Chamber of Commerce (ICC). They have evolved into thirteen International Commerce Terms, from which the acronym **Incoterms** is derived. These Incoterms were revised in 1953, 1967, 1976, 1980, 1990, and most recently in 2000, the latter revision bringing only moderate changes to a few terms.[2] It is of significant benefit to both parties to use one of these Incoterms, because ample information is available for each, and substantial jurisprudence has accumulated for each through the ICC arbitration system. For example, a *pro forma* invoice would read: "FCA Milwaukee, Wisconsin, USA" to indicate which tasks the exporter would be willing to perform and which tasks would remain the responsibility of the importer.[3] If a standard contract is used, the same clarification should be made.

Incoterm An International Commerce Term, or a formalized international term of trade which specifies the responsibilities of the exporter and the importer in an international transaction.

6-2 Understanding Incoterms

The terms of trade, or Incoterms, that the exporter and the importer agree to use in a given transaction (see Table 6-1 for a complete list) define several aspects of an international sale:

- Which tasks will be performed by the exporter
- Which tasks will be performed by the importer
- Which activities will be paid by the exporter
- Which activities will be paid by the importer
- When the transfer of responsibility for the goods will take place

 *Incoterms 3000*

The latest revisions of Incoterms were made in 1980, 1990, and 2000, bringing a large number of people to speculate that there would be a new version—"Incoterms 2010"—introduced on January 1, 2010. However, the International Chamber of Commerce, along with the representatives of all of the national chambers of commerce who participate in the revision of the Incoterms, did not want to create Incoterms 2010, as it would then increase the expectation that Incoterms "had" to be revised every ten years.

An international committee nevertheless started working on a revision of Incoterms 2000 sometime in 2008; they created a draft that was circulated in early 2009 for further comments but which was not made public. The international committee met at the end of May 2009 in Helsinki, Finland, and in December 2009 in London, U.K., to discuss those comments that had been generated on the first draft. As of January 2010, little had transpired of their efforts, except for a few things:

- The new Incoterms will be named "Incoterms 3000" to squelch the anticipation that the terms would be revised every ten years.
- The new Incoterms should be released in the Fall of 2010, with a scheduled implementation date of January 1, 2011. However, those target dates may eventually be changed.
- Incoterms 3000 will be more "user friendly" than Incoterms 2000. Each will include a preamble that will inform users of its intended use.
- A new Incoterm will be created to facilitate trade in domestic transactions as well as in international transactions for which no export or import clearance obligations exist, such as within a Customs Union.
- The Institute Cargo Clauses will be referenced when appropriate.

As progress is made on these Incoterms, additional information will be posted on the international-logistics.info website.

TABLE 6-1	Incoterms
Incoterm	**Description**
EXW	Ex-Works
FCA	Free Carrier
FAS	Free Alongside Ship
FOB	Free On Board
CFR	Cost and Freight
CIF	Cost, Insurance and Freight
CPT	Carriage Paid To
CIP	Carriage and Insurance Paid To
DAF	Delivered At Frontier
DES	Delivered Ex-Ship
DEQ	Delivered Ex-Quay
DDU	Delivered Duty Unpaid
DDP	Delivery Duty Paid

This last point is complicated: It is conceptually difficult to make the distinction between (1) the transfer of responsibility for the goods between the exporter and the importer and (2) the transfer of title between the exporter and the importer. The transfer of responsibility (transfer of risk) is dictated by the choice of the Incoterm. The transfer of title (transfer of ownership) is usually done when the importer has either paid the exporter (and obtained the original bill of lading), accepted to sign a draft (see Chapter 7), or performed some other event specifically outlined in the contract of sale between both parties. The transfer of responsibility happens at the delivery of the goods, a point that is clearly outlined in each of the Incoterms, and in most cases, a point that occurs chronologically much earlier than the transfer of title.

The transfer of responsibility of the exporter never extends beyond the services for which that company has paid. There are several Incoterms, however, where the exporter is obligated to pre-pay a portion of the transportation costs, even though it is no longer responsible for the goods. Such is the case for the so-called C-terms, the ones whose acronyms start with the letter C.

6-3 Incoterm Strategy

The proper choice of an Incoterm is therefore contingent upon the strategy followed by the exporting firm, but is also somewhat constrained by the following parameters:

- The type of product sold. Several industries (commodities in particular) prefer using some specific terms of trade rather than others.
- The method of shipment. Goods shipped by ocean or barge will be sold under different Incoterms than containerized goods using several transportation modes.
- The ability of either of the parties to perform the tasks involved in the shipment.
- The amount of trust placed by either of the parties in the other.

Nevertheless, the greatest criterion to be used is the willingness of both parties to perform and pay for some of the tasks involved in the shipment. In some cases, a strategic advantage can be gained by an exporter willing to facilitate the sale of its products by assisting the importer in the shipment. In others, a price advantage may be obtained by an importer willing to perform all or most of the tasks involved in the shipment. A company generally does not determine which Incoterm to use on a case-by-case basis, but will determine which strategy it would like to pursue and will determine which term of trade should be used regularly, given its product line, its customers' expectations, and its trade volume.

Another issue to understand clearly in this decision is that regardless of the Incoterm chosen, the importer is always paying for the transportation and other costs of shipping internationally. The fact that the exporter is pre-paying and arranging for certain aspects of the shipment is reflected in the invoice price; therefore, the importer ends up paying for it. In addition, it is likely, although not always the case, that the exporter's invoice is going to include a charge that is higher than the actual cost of the service. Some exporters add a premium to these costs to reflect the fact that it took some time and effort for the exporter to arrange for those services.

Nevertheless, the choice of Incoterm is often the exporter's decision. It is difficult for an exporter to "adapt" its Incoterm strategy to accommodate the requirements of an importer, as it may require the exporter to be responsible for tasks that it has decided it would rather not perform. Should the importer feel that the exporter is not providing a service that is adequate, it can always purchase from another source. However, should the importer want to perform more tasks than the exporter prefers, it is certainly possible for the exporter to do *less* than expected and use a different Incoterm on that transaction, one for which it is responsible for less.

TABLE 6-2	Responsibilities of the Exporter and Importer under Incoterms

The responsibilities of the exporter are denoted with an "X," those of the importer with an "I." Wherever there is no obligation on either party, or wherever there is ambiguity as to whether the activity is the responsibility of the exporter or the importer, the spot is left blank. Please refer to the appropriate section for further details.

Task	EXW	FCA	FAS	FOB	CFR	CIF	CPT	CIP	DES	DEQ	DAF	DDU	DDP
Export Packing	X	X	X	X	X	X	X	X	X	X	X	X	X
Inland Freight	I		X	X	X	X	X	X	X	X	X	X	X
Export Clearance	I	X	X	X	X	X	X	X	X	X	X	X	X
Arrange Carrier	I	I	I	I	X	X	X	X	X	X	X	X	X
Load onto Carrier	I	I	I	X	X	X	X	X	X	X	X	X	X
Pay Carrier	I	I	I	I	X	X	X	X	X	X	X	X	X
Unload Carrier	I	I	I	I			I	I	I	X	I	I	X
Pay Insurance						X		X					
Import Clearance	I	I	I	I	I	I	I	I	I	I	I	I	X
Pay Duty	I	I	I	I	I	I	I	I	I	I	I	I	X
Pay Inland Freight	I	I	I	I	I	I	I	I	I	I	I	X	X

Finally, the choice of the proper Incoterm is a critical decision for a firm, as it is an integral part of its export strategy and is linked to the level of customer service it is aiming to provide.[4] The thirteen Incoterms are reviewed in a progressive order of service provided by the exporter (see Table 6-2).

6-4 Ex-Works (EXW)

The EXW Incoterm can be used for any merchandise and for any means of transportation. It should be used with the following syntax:

EXW Poughkeepsie, New York, USA

where Poughkeepsie is the town in which the exporter will hold the merchandise available to the importer. It is usually located in the exporting country.

Ex-Works is the "easiest" of the Incoterms for the exporter, and the most difficult for the importer. In an Ex-Works transaction, the exporter has only the obligation to "place the goods at the disposal of the buyer" and "render every assistance . . . in obtaining . . . any export license or other official authorization necessary for the export of the goods."[5] In addition, the exporter has to package the goods for export, but the exporter does not even have to load the goods onto the importer's prearranged vehicle. It should be evident that this is not an advantageous Incoterm from the importer's perspective. Arranging to pick up goods in a foreign country is not easy, and neither is providing domestic transportation or clearing goods for export in a foreign country.

In the case where the exporter and the importer agree that the expense and responsibility of loading the goods should fall on the exporter, it is possible to amend the Incoterm to include this condition, usually by what the ICC refers to as a **variant** of an Incoterm. This is usually accomplished by including "EXW loaded" to the *pro forma* invoice. Because variants of Incoterms are not defined by the ICC, the correct syntax for such a modification should be:

EXW Poughkeepsie, New York, USA, loaded

The choice of an EXW Incoterm should be made only when the exporter knows that the importer is extremely savvy; otherwise, there is a strong possibility that the

variant A modification to one of the Incoterms codified by the International Chamber of Commerce. Variants are generally used to further clarify the responsibilities of the exporter and of the importer in a given transaction.

quote will not be turned into a sale, as the exporter's competitors are likely to offer better (more importer friendly) terms of trade.

6-4a Delivery under EXW

There is nothing specified in this Incoterm regarding delivery. It occurs at the time that the importer (or the importer's agent) picks up the goods at the exporter's plant. This delivery has to take place at a mutually convenient time. The exporter has the obligation to notify the importer that the goods are available for pickup, and the importer has the obligation to notify the exporter of the time at which the goods will be picked up.

There is no specific transportation document corresponding to the delivery of the goods under this Incoterm, although, if a transportation company is picking up the goods, the exporter will generally be given a copy of the bill of lading or some form of receipt for the goods.

6-4b Exporter's and Importer's Responsibilities under EXW

The exporter's responsibilities are limited to the most basic functions: make the goods available to the buyer, package the goods for export shipment, assist in the export clearance procedures, and provide the documents to the importer so that the goods can clear Customs in the importing country or be insured. None of these requirements are trivial, though.

The exporter has to package the goods in such a way that the goods are protected during their international voyage. That requirement means that the exporter should find out what the means of transportation will be and make sure that the goods are adequately packaged to make sure that they are not damaged. If the goods are damaged in transit due to "improper packaging," the exporter is responsible, and the insurance coverage contracted by the importer will not cover the costs of the damage.

The exporter also has to provide all of the documents necessary for the importer to clear Customs in the importing country; this means that the invoice has to be a good international invoice and include product description, Harmonized System numbers, weights, volume measures, unit price, total price, and so on (see Chapter 9 for further details and examples); that the other documents are prepared carefully and accurately (certificate of origin, packing list, and so on); and that the correct number of originals and copies are included. Because the importer is also the one in charge of exporting the products, the exporter should provide the documents necessary to clear the exporting requirements of the exporting country.

As far as the documents necessary for export are concerned, the United States has relatively recently made a change in the Shipper's Export Declaration (SED) (an export document explained in Chapter 9), specifically to record correctly who the exporter is in the case of a sale under an EXW Incoterm. Until 2000, the exporter of record was the importer (or the importer's freight forwarder). Under rules put in place on July 10, 2000, the importer is no longer listed as the exporter of record, and the seller-exporter is listed as the "U.S. principal party in interest." This terminology was specifically created to allow the U.S. Census Bureau to record who the exporter of specific merchandise is under an EXW sale, rather than record the importer of the goods. The term "exporter" has been stricken from the SED. Because of this requirement, the U.S. government has placed the responsibility for providing the correct Export Commodity Classification Number (ECCN) and any information that could affect an export license on the exporter in the case of an EXW transaction.[6]

The importer is responsible for all other aspects of the shipment in an EXW transaction. It has to clear the goods for export, arrange for transportation, clear Customs in the importing country, purchase insurance, and provide domestic transportation in the importing country.

6-5 Free Carrier (FCA)

The FCA Incoterm can be used for any merchandise and for any means of transportation, but it was specifically created for goods shipped through multimodal transportation (i.e., merchandise shipped through multiple means of transportation without being "handled" because it is containerized). This Incoterm can be used for shipments of either full-container loads (FCL) or less-than-container loads (LCL). FCA is expected to become one of the most popular Incoterms as the number of multimodal shipments increases. This Incoterm should be used with the following syntax:

FCA Castres, France

where Castres is the city in which delivery takes place. It is usually located in the exporting country or in a neighboring country.

In a Free Carrier transaction, the exporter delivers the goods to a carrier selected by the importer. Because FCA is a fairly recent Incoterm—created in 1990—great care has been taken to define specifically what responsibilities are borne by the exporter and the importer, respectively. There are no known variants to this Incoterm.

The FCA Incoterm replaced three other Incoterms, which were abandoned in 1990: Free on Rail (FOR), Free on Truck (FOT), and Free on Board-Airport (FOB-Airport).

6-5a Delivery under FCA

Under FCA, the delivery takes place when either of two conditions is met:

- If the named point in the Incoterm refers to the exporter's plant, then delivery takes place when the goods are loaded, by the exporter and at its expense, onto the carrier's truck.

- If the named point in the Incoterm refers to the carrier's premises, then delivery takes place when the goods are made available to the carrier (i.e., when the goods have arrived at the carrier's dock). The goods are unloaded from the exporter's truck by the carrier and at the carrier's expense (i.e., at the importer's expense).

The document that corresponds clearly to the transfer of responsibility for an FCA shipment is the receipt given by the carrier to the exporter; it can be a bill of lading, a sea waybill, an air waybill, or a multimodal bill of lading (see Chapter 9 for an explanation of each of these terms).

6-5b Exporter's and Importer's Responsibilities under FCA

The exporter is still in charge of packing the merchandise for export, as it is under EXW. However, its responsibilities increase to include loading the merchandise into a container provided by the carrier and loading the container onto the carrier's truck, or delivering the merchandise to the carrier's facilities. In addition, the exporter is responsible for clearing the merchandise for export, and has to provide whatever information is needed by the importer to clear Customs in the importing country and to obtain insurance. In the United States, the exporter fills out the SED and is the "U.S. principal party in interest." In countries where export authorities require a pre-shipment inspection (see Chapter 16), the exporter has to pay for it.

The importer is responsible for arranging the contract of carriage (i.e., finding a carrier between the exporter's town and the final destination) and communicating to the exporter which carrier it is. The importer is also responsible for arranging for insurance and for clearing Customs in the importing country. If the importing country requires a pre-shipment inspection, the importer has to pay for it.

6-6 Free Alongside Ship (FAS)

Although the FAS Incoterm can be used for any merchandise, it is specifically designed for ocean transportation, and is not meant for any other means of transportation or for merchandise that is not destined to be handed to an ocean shipping line at the port of departure. This Incoterm should be used with the following syntax:

FAS Santos, Brazil

where Santos is the port in which the delivery takes place. This port is usually located in the exporting country or a neighboring country.

In a Free Alongside Ship transaction, the exporter is responsible for bringing the goods to the port, "alongside" a ship designated by the importer, at which time the responsibility shifts to the importer. One major change was made in the 2000 version of the FAS Incoterm: The exporter is now responsible for clearing the merchandise for export, leaving EXW as the only Incoterm for which the importer has to perform this task.

6-6a Delivery under FAS

The delivery officially takes place when the exporter has delivered the goods "alongside" a ship designated by the importer. The problem with this Incoterm is that ports rarely keep merchandise "alongside" a ship, or keep merchandise on a quay waiting for a ship. There is always delivery to a holding area, then cartage (transportation within the port area) from the holding area to the ship before the **stevedoring** (loading onto the ship) takes place. When and where the delivery does take place is sometimes difficult to determine.

Compounding this difficulty is the fact that there is no transport document that clearly corresponds to a delivery to a holding area or to the quay alongside the ship. The suggestion by the ICC that the exporter should obtain "a transport document (for example, a negotiable bill of lading, a non-negotiable sea waybill")[7] is contradicted by the fact that no ocean carrier will issue a bill of lading until the goods have been received in good condition on board the vessel. The ICC further comments that the seller "may not always receive a receipt or a transport document from the carrier"[8] and adds that the exporter must then "provide some other document to prove that the goods have been delivered"[9] but does not suggest what it may be. A dock receipt from the port authorities may be sufficient; however, this lack of clear physical evidence of delivery could be a substantial deterrent to the use of the FAS Incoterm. However, the use of Electronic Data Interchange (EDI) by the parties involved can remedy this problem: The exporter can notify the importer that the delivery has been made in the port of departure, and the terminal operator can do the same.

6-6b Exporter's and Importer's Responsibilities under FAS

The exporter is responsible for packing the goods for export, transporting them to the port, and unloading them onto the quay or holding area in the port. With the advent of the 2000 version of the Incoterms, another duty was added to the responsibilities of the exporter under an FAS transaction. The exporter is responsible for clearing the goods for export as well as providing whatever documents and assistance the importer may need to clear Customs in the importing country and obtain insurance. In the United States, the exporter fills out the SED and is the "U.S. principal party in interest" or the exporter of record. In countries where export authorities require a pre-shipment inspection, the exporter has to pay for it.

The importer is responsible for the shipment starting from the point of delivery. Therefore, the importer is responsible for port handling charges, stevedoring (loading the goods in the vessel), and ocean transportation costs, as well as insurance,

stevedore A company or a person whose responsibility is to load and unload ships in a port.

unloading in the port of arrival, and Customs duties in the importing country. If the importing country requires a pre-shipment inspection, the importer has to pay for it.

6-7 Free on Board (FOB) Port of Departure

Although the FOB Incoterm can be used for any merchandise, it is specifically designed for ocean transportation and is not meant for any other means of transportation or for merchandise that is not destined to then be handed to an ocean shipping line at the port of departure. This Incoterm should be used with the following syntax:

FOB Cape Town, South Africa

where Cape Town is the port in which the delivery takes place. This port is generally located in the exporting country or a neighboring country.

The Free On Board term, sometimes called Freight On Board, is one of the oldest maritime terms of trade. The exporter is responsible for the goods until they are placed on the ship. The importer is responsible for them after that.

Unfortunately, because FOB is such an old term of trade, its meaning is somewhat dependent on the practices of the port in which the goods are loaded. These differences matter specifically in the way the loading costs are billed. Some ports have the tradition of including loading, stowing, and securing of the goods in the hold of the ship as part of the stevedoring costs. Other ports will customarily bill for these services as part of the ocean cargo costs. The shipping line contracted by the importer obviously would be able to communicate what the practice is at a given port of departure. However, these differences in practices have triggered the need for a variant to the FOB Incoterm to reflect which of the trade partners is responsible for handling costs on the ship: Either "FOB stowed" or "FOB stowed, trimmed, and secured"[10] can be used to denote that the exporter is responsible for those specific costs. Here again, because the ICC does not regulate Incoterm variants, the correct syntax should be:

FOB Cape Town, South Africa, stowed

6-7a Delivery under FOB

In an FOB transaction, the point of delivery is extremely clear and has been governed by centuries of maritime tradition. The "FOB point," the point at which the responsibility shifts from the exporter to the importer, is the **ship's rail**. Until the merchandise has cleared the ship's rail, it is the responsibility of the exporter. After that, it is the responsibility of the importer. What happens if the merchandise falls and is damaged as it crosses the ship's rail depends on whether it remains on the ship or falls back toward the quay.[11]

ship's rail An imaginary line that circles the entire hull of a ship.

The document associated with the FOB term is also quite clear: The proof of delivery is an ocean bill of lading or a sea waybill. Only after receiving the goods will the shipping line issue this document, giving a copy to the exporter.

6-7b Exporter's and Importer's Responsibilities under FOB

The exporter is responsible for packaging the goods for export, shipping them to the port of departure, and loading them onto the ship. The exporter is responsible for clearing the goods for export and has the obligation of providing whatever documents and assistance the importer may need to clear Customs in the importing country and obtain insurance. In the United States, the exporter fills out the SED and is the "U.S. principal party in interest" or the exporter of record. In countries where export authorities require a pre-shipment inspection, the exporter has to pay for it.

FIGURE 6-1 | EXW, FCA, FAS, and FOB Incoterms

EXW Ex-Works	FCA Free Carrier	FAS Free Alongside Ship	FOB Free on Board

ANY	MULTI-MODAL	OCEAN	OCEAN
The exporter only has the obligation to place the goods at the disposal of the buyer.	The exporter delivers the goods to a carrier selected by the importer.	The exporter is responsible for bringing the goods to the port, "alongside" a ship designated by the importer, at which time the responsibility shifts to the importer.	The exporter is responsible for the goods until they are placed on the ship. The importer is responsible for them after that.

The importer is responsible for arranging and paying for ocean transportation from the port of departure to the goods' destination, Customs clearance in the importing country, and eventually arranging and paying for insurance. If the importing country requires a pre-shipment inspection, the importer has to pay for it.

Figure 6-1 provides a summary for the EXW, FCA, FAS, and FOB Incoterms.

6-8 Cost and Freight (CFR)

Although the CFR Incoterm can be used for any merchandise, it is specifically designed for ocean transportation and is not meant for any other means of transportation or for merchandise that is not destined to then be handed to an ocean shipping line at the port of departure. This Incoterm should be used with the following syntax:

CFR Lagos, Nigeria

where Lagos is the port of destination in which the importer takes physical control of the goods. This port is usually located in the importing country or in a neighboring country.

In a Cost and Freight transaction, the delivery (the transfer or responsibility or the transfer of risk) does not take place in the port of destination, but in the port of departure. The CFR term is also one of the oldest maritime terms of trade, and it was known until the 1990 Incoterms as C&F or C+F, abbreviations which are now obsolete. The exporter is responsible for the goods until they are placed on the ship, and the importer is responsible for them after that, but the exporter pre-pays the ocean freight.

Unfortunately, because CFR is such an old term of trade, its meaning is somewhat dependent on the practices of the port in which the goods are unloaded. These differences matter specifically in the way the unloading costs are billed. Some ports have the tradition of billing separately for the unloading of the goods as stevedoring costs, and others will ask shipping lines to bill for these services as part of the ocean cargo costs. The shipping line contracted by the exporter obviously would be able to communicate what the practice is at a given port of discharge.

Nevertheless, in order to account for these differences in practices, variants to the CFR Incoterm were created to reflect which of the trade partners is responsible for unloading costs. "CFR landed" explicitly states that the costs of unloading are borne by the exporter, and "CFR undischarged" notes that unloading costs are borne by the importer.[12] In these cases, the correct syntax should be:

CFR Lagos, Nigeria, landed

6-8a Delivery under CFR

In a CFR transaction, the point of delivery is the "FOB point," the point at which the responsibility shifts from the exporter to the importer: the ship's rail. Until the merchandise has cleared the ship's rail, it is the responsibility of the exporter; after that, the responsibility shifts to the importer.

The document associated with the CFR term is also quite clear. The proof of delivery is an ocean bill of lading or a sea waybill. Only after receiving the goods will the shipping line issue this document, giving one of the originals to the exporter.

6-8b Exporter's and Importer's Responsibilities under CFR

The exporter is responsible for packaging the goods, shipping them to the port of departure, loading them onto a ship "of the type normally used for the transport of goods of the contract description,"[13] and pre-paying for the shipment. Depending on the practices at the port of destination, this pre-paid contract of carriage may include the costs of unloading the goods. If it does not, then the importer has to pay for unloading the ship. The exporter is also responsible for clearing the goods for export, and assisting the importer by providing the documentation necessary to clear Customs in the importing country and to obtain insurance. In the United States, the exporter fills out the SED and is the "U.S. principal party in interest" or the exporter of record. In countries where export authorities require a pre-shipment inspection, the exporter has to pay for it.

The importer takes responsibility for the goods at the delivery point (i.e., at the ship's rail in the port of departure), even though the exporter is the one who contracts for the ocean shipping of the goods. Depending on the practice at the port of destination, and the possible Incoterm variant used, the importer may also have to pay for the unloading costs. It is also responsible for clearing Customs in the importing country and for inland transportation after that. If the importing country requires a pre-shipment inspection, the importer has to pay for it.

6-9 Cost, Insurance, and Freight (CIF)

Although the CIF Incoterm can be used for any merchandise, it is specifically designed for ocean transportation and is not meant for any other means of transportation or for merchandise that is not destined to then be handed to an ocean shipping line at the port of departure. This Incoterm should be used with the following syntax:

CIF Kobe, Japan

where Kobe is the port of destination in the importing country in which the importer takes control of the goods.

In a Cost, Insurance, and Freight transaction, the delivery does not take place in the port of destination, but in the port of departure. The CIF Incoterm is quite similar to the CFR term, with the exception that the exporter has the additional responsibility to pre-pay for marine cargo insurance until the port of destination. Unfortunately, the mandate of the ICC is for "minimum cover," that is, the so-called Coverage C of the

Institute Cargo Clauses (see Chapter 10, Section 10-8d), resulting in yet another Incoterm variant.[14] CIF maximum cover—mandating Coverage A of the Institute Cargo Clauses—exists in addition to the predictable CIF undischarged and CIF landed, which are mirrors of their CFR equivalents. The syntax again must accommodate the fact that Incoterm variants are not regulated by the ICC and should read:

CIF Kobe, Japan, maximum cover, landed

Finally, under the CIF Incoterm, the amount insured must be at least 110 percent of the value of the goods, a custom that dates back to 1906, when Great Britain instituted the Marine Insurance Act.[15]

One aspect of CIF is unusual: Certain countries (see Table 6-3) do not allow their importers to purchase insurance abroad, and therefore prevent any import on a CIF basis. This restriction is in place to conserve foreign currency—it obligates importers to purchase insurance locally in local currency—and to subsidize the national insurance industry; all of the countries practicing this restriction are relatively small traders.

6-9a Delivery under CIF

In a CIF transaction, the point of delivery is again the "FOB point," the point at which the responsibility shifts from the exporter to the importer: the ship's rail. Until the merchandise has cleared the ship's rail, it is the responsibility of the exporter; after that, the responsibility shifts to the importer.

The document associated with the CIF term is also quite clear. The proof of delivery is an ocean bill of lading or a sea waybill. Only after receiving the goods will the shipping line issue this document, giving one of the originals to the exporter.

6-9b Exporter's and Importer's Responsibilities under CIF

The exporter has to package the goods for export and has to pay for shipping costs and minimum insurance costs to the port of destination. It is also responsible for clearing the goods for export. In the United States, the exporter fills out the SED and is the "U.S. principal party in interest" or the exporter of record. In countries where export authorities require a pre-shipment inspection, the exporter has to pay for it.

The importer is taking responsibility for the goods at the ship's rail in the port of departure, even though the contract of carriage is between the seller and the ocean shipping line. The importer is responsible for clearing Customs in the importing country and for inland transportation after that. If the importing country requires a pre-shipment inspection, the importer has to pay for it.

6-10 Carriage Paid To (CPT)

Conceptually, the CPT Incoterm is the same as the CFR Incoterm, except that it applies to goods shipped by means other than ocean transport, or shipped by sea without being handed over the ship's rail (i.e., in the case of roll-on/roll-off cargo), or containerized cargo using multiple modes of transportation, including ocean transport as one of the modes. This Incoterm should be used with the following syntax:

CPT Köln, Germany

where Köln is the city of destination in which the importer takes control of the goods. This city is generally located in the importing country or a neighboring country.

In a Carriage Paid To transaction, the delivery does not take place in the city of destination, but in the city where the exporter delivers the goods to the carrier. The

TABLE 6-3	Countries with Restrictions on Incoterms

The following countries place restrictions on the purchase of insurance and therefore on the Incoterms that can be used by their exporters or importers. These restrictions are current as of August 2008.[a]

Country	Restrictions Import	Export	Country	Restrictions Import	Export
Algeria	■		Laos	■	■
Angola	■		Libya	■	
Bangladesh	■		Malaysia	■	
Barbados	■		Mali	■	
Benin	■		Mauritania	■	
Burkina Faso	■		Morocco	■	
Burundi	■	■	Myanmar	■	■
Cameroon	■		Nicaragua	■	
Central African Republic	■		Niger	■	
Chad	■		Nigeria	■	
Congo (Brazzaville)	■		Oman	■	■
Congo (Kinshasa)	■	■	Pakistan	■	
Cuba	■		Papua–New Guinea		■
Djibouti	■		Qatar	■	■
Dominican Republic	■		Russia	■	
Ecuador	■		Rwanda	■	■
Ethiopia	■		Senegal	■	■
Gabon	■		Serbia	■	■
Georgia	■		Sierra Leone	■	
Ghana	■		Solomon Islands	■	
Guatemala		■	Sudan	■	
Guinea	■		Syria	■	
Haiti	■		Tanzania	■	
Indonesia	■		Thailand	■	■
Iran	■		Togo	■	
Iraq	■		Tunisia	■	
Ivory Coast	■		Uganda	■	
Jordan		■	Venezuela	■	■
Kenya	■		Yemen	■	■

The definitions of these restrictions are summarized as follows:

Import restrictions: An importer in that country is not allowed to purchase insurance abroad (it is therefore presumably impossible to sell to an importer in that country on CIP or CIF terms).
Export restrictions: An exporter from that country is not allowed to purchase insurance abroad (it is therefore possibly more difficult for an exporter from that country to offer CIP, CIF, DDU, and DDP terms, as the restrictions limit the exporter's access to some insurance providers).

Most of the countries in this list tend to be fairly small trade partners: if further information is specifically necessary for any of them, the commercial attaché of any embassy to this country would be the best source of information on the exact implementations of these restrictions.

[a] "Restrictive Laws and Regulations," International Union of Marine Insurance, as quoted by the American Institute of Marine Underwriters, http://www.aimu.org/brochures.html, May 24, 2009.

exporter pre-pays shipping charges until the city of destination. Unless unusual circumstances prevail, shipping charges do not include the unloading of the merchandise in the destination city.

6-10a Delivery under CPT

Delivery takes place when the exporter hands over the goods to the carrier in the exporting country and the exporter is given a bill of lading or equivalent document (air waybill, sea waybill, multimodal bill of lading), which acts as the proof of delivery.

6-10b Exporter's and Importer's Responsibilities under CPT

The exporter is responsible for packaging the goods for export, shipping them to the carrier, and pre-paying the shipping costs to the city of destination. In the United States, the exporter fills out the SED and is the "U.S. principal party in interest" or the exporter of record. In countries where export authorities require a pre-shipment inspection, the exporter has to pay for it.

The importer assumes responsibility for the goods at the time the seller delivers them to the carrier. The importer is responsible for unloading the goods from the carrier's truck, clearing Customs, and paying inland transportation (if any) beyond the city of destination. If the importing country requires a pre-shipment inspection, the importer has to pay for it.

6-11 Carriage and Insurance Paid To (CIP)

Conceptually, the CIP Incoterm is the same as the CIF Incoterm, except it applies to goods shipped by means other than ocean transport, or shipped by sea without being handed over the ship's rail (i.e., in the case of roll-on/roll-off cargo), or containerized cargo using multiple modes of transportation, including ocean transport as one of the modes. This Incoterm should be used with the following syntax:

CIP Sofia, Bulgaria

where Sofia is the city of destination in which the importer takes control of the goods. This city is located in the importing country or a neighboring country.

In a Carriage and Insurance Paid To transaction, the delivery does not take place in the city of destination, but in the city where the exporter delivers the goods to the carrier. Unlike the CPT Incoterm, the exporter has the added responsibility of pre-paying for minimum-cover insurance (Coverage C of Institute Cargo Clauses) until the city of destination. Therefore, an additional variant of the CIP Incoterm has emerged, "CIP maximum cover," to request that the exporter take on the responsibility of providing Coverage A of the Institute Cargo Clauses. The syntax again must accommodate the fact that Incoterm variants are not regulated by the ICC and should read:

CIP Sofia, Bulgaria, maximum cover

Finally, under the CIP Incoterm, the amount insured must be at least 110 percent of the value of the goods, a custom that dates back to 1906, when Great Britain instituted the Marine Insurance Act.[16]

6-11a Delivery under CIP

Delivery takes place when the exporter hands over the goods to the carrier in the exporting country and the exporter is given a bill of lading or equivalent document (air waybill, sea waybill, multimodal bill of lading), which acts as the proof of delivery.

6-11b Exporter's and Importer's Responsibilities under CIP

The exporter is responsible for export packing, transportation costs to the city of destination, and minimum insurance costs. In addition, the exporter is responsible for

FIGURE 6-2 | CFR, CIF, CPT, and CIP Incoterms

CFR Cost and Freight	CIF Cost, Insurance, and Freight	CPT Carriage Paid To	CIP Carriage and Insurance Paid To
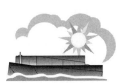			
OCEAN	OCEAN	MULTI-MODAL	MULTI-MODAL
The exporter is responsible for the goods until they are placed on the ship and the importer is responsible for them after that, but the exporter prepays the ocean freight.	Until the merchandise has cleared the ship's rail, it is the responsibility of the exporter; after that, the responsibility shifts to the importer.	The importer assumes responsibility for the goods at the time the seller delivers them to the carrier.	The importer's responsibility starts when the exporter delivers the goods to the carrier, even though the exporter is the party that contracted with the carrier to get the goods delivered.

clearing the goods for export. In the United States, the exporter fills out the SED and is the "U.S. principal party in interest" or the exporter of record. In countries where export authorities require a pre-shipment inspection, the exporter has to pay for it.

The importer's responsibility starts when the exporter delivers the goods to the carrier, even though the exporter is the party that contracted with the carrier to get the goods delivered. The importer is responsible for unloading the carrier's truck, clearing Customs in the importing country, and paying transportation costs beyond the city of destination. If the importing country requires a pre-shipment inspection, the importer has to pay for it.

Figure 6-2 provides a summary for the CFR, CIF, CPT, and CIP Incoterms.

6-12 Delivered Ex-Ship (DES)

Although the DES Incoterm can be used for any merchandise, it is specifically designed for ocean transportation and is not meant for any other means of transportation or for merchandise that is not destined to be delivered by an ocean shipping line at the port of destination. In practice, the DES Incoterm is mostly used for bulk shipments of commodities where the parties wish to have the importer pay for the unloading of the ship. This Incoterm should be used with the following syntax:

DES Istanbul, Turkey

where Istanbul is the port of destination in which the importer takes responsibility for the goods. That port is usually located in the importing country or in a neighboring country.

In a Delivered Ex-Ship transaction, the exporter is responsible for the goods until they are placed at the disposal of the importer in the port of destination.

6-12a Delivery under DES

The delivery takes place in the port of destination, once the ship has reached port and makes the merchandise available to the importer.

There is no specific document that conveys the transfer of responsibility between the exporter and the importer at the point of delivery. It is common practice to have the exporter provide the ocean bill of lading as evidence of delivery in the port of destination, although it is only proof of delivery at the port of departure. Should something happen to the goods during the ocean voyage, while under the responsibility of the exporter, the bill of lading is unaffected, even though delivery has certainly not been made, because the goods have not been made available to the importer. Nevertheless, this is not as major an issue as with the EXW or FAS Incoterms, as the importer is often represented in the port of destination, and delivery problems can easily be uncovered.

6-12b Exporter's and Importer's Responsibilities under DES

The responsibilities of the exporter include the handling of the goods until their arrival in the port of destination; however, the exporter does not handle (or pay for) unloading the ship. In addition, the exporter must clear the goods for export. In the United States, the exporter fills out the SED and is the "U.S. principal party in interest" or the exporter of record. In countries where export authorities require a pre-shipment inspection, the exporter has to pay for it.

The importer is responsible for unloading the ship, clearing Customs in the importing country, and paying for whatever shipment costs there may be beyond the port of destination. If the importing country mandates a pre-shipment inspection, the importer has to pay for it.

6-13 Delivered Ex-Quay (DEQ)

Although the DEQ Incoterm can be used for any merchandise, it is specifically designed for ocean transportation and is not meant for any other means of transportation or for merchandise that is not destined to then be handed to an ocean shipping line at the port of departure. In practice, the DEQ Incoterm is used mostly for bulk shipments of commodities where the parties wish to have the exporter pay for the unloading of the ship. This Incoterm should be used with the following syntax:

DEQ Valparaiso, Chile

where Valparaiso is the port of destination in which the importer takes control of the goods. This port is generally located in the importing country or in a neighboring country.

In a Delivered Ex-Quay transaction, the exporter is responsible for the goods until they are unloaded from the ship in the port of destination. The only difference between the DES and DEQ Incoterms is that the unloading costs are borne by the exporter in the DEQ transaction.

6-13a Delivery under DEQ

The delivery for a DEQ shipment takes place when the goods are placed, once they have been unloaded ("landed"), at the disposal of the importer. There is no specific document that conveys the transfer of responsibility between the exporter and the importer at the point of delivery. It is common practice to have the exporter provide the ocean bill of lading as evidence of delivery in the port of destination.

6-13b Exporter's and Importer's Responsibilities under DEQ

Under a DEQ shipment, the exporter has the same responsibility as in a DES shipment, with the following exception: The exporter has to pay for the unloading of the ship in the port of destination.

6-14 Delivered at Frontier (DAF)

The DAF Incoterm can be used for any merchandise, but it is specifically designed for land transportation and should not be used for ocean transportation, where the DES or DEQ Incoterms fulfill the same function. This Incoterm should be used with the following syntax:

DAF Nogales, Arizona, USA

where Nogales is the border city in which the importer takes physical control of the goods. This city is usually located at the border between the exporting country and the importing country or a neighboring country.

In a Delivered at Frontier transaction, the delivery (the transfer or responsibility or the transfer of risk) takes place in the city named in the Incoterm, but with the merchandise still loaded on the vehicle or the railroad car on which it arrived in that city. Common practice calls for the merchandise to remain on the truck or the railroad car until its final destination, but the responsibility of getting it there shifts to the importer who must contract for carriage. When carriage is done by railroad, it is not unusual for the term to read "DAF Poland-Belarus border" and for the goods to remain on the same train until their destination, with no exact location mentioned; the final crossing point is left to the discretion of the railroad company. In trade within the North American Free Trade Area, this Incoterm is very commonly used between the United States (or Canada) and Mexico, and usually specifies a town. There is still some political uneasiness about letting Mexican trucks and trailers on U.S. and Canadian highways, but it should subside.

The DAF Incoterm was almost eliminated from the 2000 Incoterm revisions for several reasons: It is rarely used, it can be easily replaced with a DDU (see Section 6-15) or possibly a DDP (see Section 6-16), and no specific documents mark the transfer of responsibility between the exporter and the importer.[17] Nevertheless, with the advent of EDI, it is possible for the carrier to notify both the exporter and the importer that the goods are at the border and that they have been delivered by the carrier to the importer.

6-14a Delivery under DAF

In a DAF transaction, the delivery takes place when the merchandise, still on the truck or the railroad car, is placed at the disposal of the importer at the border city.

There is no specific transportation document that conveys the transfer of responsibility between the exporter and the importer, but some carriers provide a "through document of transport" that fulfills that role.[18]

6-14b Exporter's and Importer's Responsibilities under DAF

In a DAF shipment, the exporter is responsible for packing the goods for export and paying for transportation until the border city. The exporter is responsible for clearing the goods for export and providing information to the importer so that the merchandise can be insured and can clear Customs in the importing country. In the United States, the exporter fills out the SED and is the "U.S. principal party in interest" or the exporter of record. In countries where export authorities require a pre-shipment inspection, the exporter has to pay for it.

The importer is responsible for the costs of transportation from the border city to the final destination and for the costs of clearing Customs. If the importing country requires a pre-shipment inspection, the importer has to pay for it.

6-15 Delivered Duty Unpaid (DDU)

The DDU Incoterm can be used for any merchandise and can be used for any means of transportation, including goods that are meant to be carried by ocean. However, this Incoterm is not meant for ocean goods to be delivered to a port of destination, for which the DES and DEQ Incoterms were specifically designed. The DDU Incoterm is meant to be used when the exporter is willing to perform most of the tasks involved in a shipment, up to the city named in the Incoterm, with the exclusion of Customs clearance and duty payment. This Incoterm should be used with the following syntax:

DDU Xi'an, China

where Xi'an is the city of destination in which the importer takes control of the goods. This city is generally the place of business of the importer, but can be any city located in the importing country or in a neighboring country.

In a Delivered Duty Unpaid transaction, the exporter is responsible for the goods until they arrive, still loaded on a truck or a railroad car, in the city of destination. The unloading costs are borne by the importer.

In most cases, the DDU Incoterm is used in those cases where the exporter wants to offer the greatest level of customer service, but where it is impossible for a foreign company to be the importer of record; it may be illegal for a foreign company to apply for an import license, the Customs official may want to deal only with local firms, or some other compelling reason exists to prevent the exporter from providing a Delivered Duty Paid (DDP) shipment.

6-15a Delivery under DDU

Under the DDU Incoterm, delivery takes place when the exporter places the goods at the disposal of the importer in the city of delivery mentioned in the Incoterm. The goods are delivered unloaded (i.e., it is the responsibility of the importer to arrange and pay for unloading the goods). However, this is often a very minor point, as the point of delivery is often the importer's plant, which obviously has the ability to unload a truck.

Although there is no transportation document that corresponds to this delivery, it is common for the exporter to provide the bill of lading at the time of delivery.

6-15b Exporter's and Importer's Responsibilities under DDU

The exporter is responsible for arranging and paying for all shipping issues until the goods are delivered to the importer, with the exception of paying duty and clearing Customs. The exporter is therefore responsible for export packing, export clearance, domestic transportation in the exporting country, international transportation, domestic transportation in the importing country, and insurance. In the United States, the exporter fills out the SED and is the "U.S. principal party in interest" or the exporter of record. In countries where export authorities require a pre-shipment inspection, the exporter has to pay for it.

The importer is responsible for Customs clearance and for paying duty. If the importing country mandates a pre-shipment inspection, the importer is responsible for that cost.

6-16 Delivered Duty Paid (DDP)

The DDP Incoterm can be used for any merchandise and for any means of transportation. However, if the goods are carried by ocean and delivered in the port of destination, then the correct Incoterms to use are DES and DEQ. This Incoterm should be used with the following syntax:

DDP Karlsruhe, Germany

where Karlsruhe is the city of destination in which the importer takes control of the goods. This city is generally the place of business of the importer, but can be any city located in the importing country or in a neighboring country.

Choosing the DDP Incoterm is the ultimate in customer service on the part of the exporter. The exporter handles everything for the importer, including shipment to the customer's plant and Customs clearance. For the importer, this type of transaction is exactly equivalent to receiving a domestic shipment from a domestic supplier. The only thing left to the importer's care is the unloading of the merchandise, something that is usually its responsibility under a domestic shipment.

In some cases, it may be advantageous for pragmatic reasons to use a variant of the DDP Incoterm. In a number of countries, the Customs authorities collect not only duty on the goods imported but also Value Added Tax (VAT) on the value of the goods. Because of the peculiarities of VAT accounting, it is often much more convenient for the importer to pay for the VAT than it is for the exporter. In those circumstances, the "DDP VAT unpaid" Incoterm variant may be used. The syntax should be:

DDP Karlsruhe, Germany, VAT unpaid

to reflect the fact that the variant is not officially sanctioned by the ICC.

6-16a Delivery under DDP

Under the DDP Incoterm, delivery takes place when the exporter places the goods at the disposal of the importer in the city of delivery mentioned in the Incoterm. The goods are delivered unloaded (i.e., it is the responsibility of the importer to arrange and pay for unloading the goods). However, this is often a very minor point, as the destination of the delivery is often the importer's plant, which obviously has the ability to unload a truck.

Although there is no transportation document that corresponds to this delivery, a commonly used alternative is for the exporter to provide the bill of lading at the time of delivery.

6-16b Exporter's and Importer's Responsibilities under DDP

The exporter assumes all responsibilities in a DDP shipment: clearing the goods for export, transporting them to the importer's facilities, and clearing Customs in the importing country. All costs and responsibilities are for the exporter.

The importer has only the responsibility to receive the goods at delivery and unload them. Figure 6-3 provides a summary for the DES, DEQ, DAF, DDU, and DDP Incoterms.

6-17 Electronic Data Interchange

Electronic Data Interchange (see Chapter 9) has somewhat changed one of the main issues in Incoterms: the documentation of the delivery.

For a number of Incoterms, there is no transport document that is issued at the point where the responsibility shifts from the exporter to the importer (i.e., when the delivery takes place). For example, in an EXW transaction, the delivery takes place when the merchandise is placed "at the importer's disposal," and a similar situation is

---

FIGURE 6-3   DES, DEQ, DAF, DDU, and DDP Incoterms

DES Delivery Ex-Ship	DEQ Delivered Ex-Quay	DAF Delivered at Frontier	DDU Delivered Duty Unpaid	DDP Delivered Duty Paid

OCEAN	OCEAN	LAND	ANY	ANY
The responsibilities of the exporter include the handling of the goods until their arrival in the port of destination; the importer is responsible for unloading the ship, clearing Customs in the importing country, and paying for whatever shipment costs there may be beyond the port of destination.	The exporter has the same responsibility as in a DES shipment, with the following exception: the exporter has to pay for the unloading of the ship in the port of destination.	The exporter is responsible for packing the goods for export and paying for transportation until the border city.	The exporter is responsible for arranging and paying for all shipping issues until the goods are delivered to the importer, with the exception of paying duty and clearing Customs.	The exporter assumes all responsibilities in a DDP shipment: clearing the goods for export, transporting them to the importer's facilities and clearing Customs in the importing country.

---

present with the use of the FAS Incoterm and, to a lesser degree, the DES, DEQ, DAF, DDU, and DDP Incoterms.

EDI has, to a considerable extent, solved this problem: Whenever there is no transport document possible, the exporter can still send an EDI "notice" to the importer, which acts as a document for both parties. The exporter has a record of the notification sent, and the importer knows unambiguously when the goods were delivered to the quay (FAS shipment) or when they arrived in port (DES and DEQ shipments). Therefore, one of the problems associated with the use of Incoterms is likely to abate substantially over the next few years, as the use of EDI increases. Unfortunately, EDI usage is still fairly new and limited to developed countries.

6-18 Common Errors in Incoterm Usage

Despite the wide use of Incoterms in international trade, the complexity of the relationships that they help delineate makes them often misunderstood and used incorrectly for a myriad of reasons.

6-18a Incoterm Confusion with Domestic Terms

Probably the most commonly made error in international terms of trade is the substitution of domestic terms of trade for international terms of trade. An inexperienced exporter will use "FOB factory" rather than the correct corresponding Ex-Works (EXW) Incoterm; similarly, rather than the correct Delivered Duty Paid (DDP) Incoterm, the same inexperienced exporter would use "FOB destination."

"FOB factory" (also known as "FOB origin") is a term of trade used in the United States for domestic sales that limits the responsibility of the seller to the loading of the merchandise onto a vehicle owned or hired by the buyer. At the time at which the merchandise is loaded onto the vehicle, the title of the merchandise transfers to the buyer. There are therefore several differences between the "FOB factory" concept and its closest Incoterm equivalent, which is EXW. Firstly, it shows a transfer of title, which none of the Incoterms do, rather than a transfer of responsibility, the only concept to which the Incoterms refer. Secondly, it specifically includes the loading of merchandise onto the vehicle provided by the buyer, which EXW does not explicitly do, except in the variant called EXW-loaded. Thirdly, "FOB factory" does not make reference to any form of documentation, which is critical to the international buyer, because these documents are needed to clear Customs. Fourthly, it applies to any form of transportation, and not only to ocean transportation, as the FOB Incoterm does. Finally, "FOB factory" does not have any specific requirements regarding packaging, whereas EXW clearly requires packaging sufficient to withstand the international voyage.

"FOB destination" (also known as "FOB delivered") is also a term used in the United States for domestic sales that extends the responsibility of the seller to the delivery point, at the buyer's place of business; the seller pays for the carriage cost to the point of delivery. At the time at which the merchandise is unloaded from the vehicle, the title transfers to the buyer. The "FOB destination" term of sale is not equivalent to the DDP Incoterm. For one, it also refers to the transfer of title, whereas the DDP Incoterm does not. Second, it makes no reference to Customs clearance, which DDP requires.

Other terms that are used incorrectly in international trade are "Freight Pre-Paid" and "Freight Collect," which are generally used for small packages (less than truckload, or LTL) and refer to the fact that the seller either includes or excludes the cost of shipment in the invoice. These terms do not work in an international environment for essentially the same reasons that "FOB factory" and "FOB destination" do not.

On occasion, there are some terms used in international trade that have their roots in domestic trade, although they have become obsolete. For example, some invoices will reflect a "franco" price, which is conceptually equivalent to the "FOB factory" term; however, it does not specifically require the loading of the merchandise onto the vehicle provided by the buyer. There are no reasons to use this term of trade domestically, and a multitude of reasons not to use it internationally.

6-18b Incoterm Confusion with Older Incoterm Versions

The International Chamber of Commerce modified the Incoterms in 1980, 1990, and 2000. It eliminated some Incoterms, modified others, and created some new ones. For a number of reasons, several exporters have failed to adapt to these changes.

Older ICC versions included several Incoterms that eventually disappeared: FOB rail (which eventually changed to FOR, "Free on Rail" in 1980, then was abandoned altogether in 1990), FOB truck (which became FOT, "Free on Truck" in 1980 and was also abandoned in 1990), and FOB airport (eliminated in 1990). On occasion, though, such older Incoterms are still used on invoices. Although this is a practice that is allowed under ICC rules, it is most likely that the use of such obsolete Incoterms is more due to carelessness than to a deliberate attempt at using an Incoterm that has advantages over the current version. It is therefore preferable to use the 1990 creation of "Free Carrier," FCA, instead of the previous similar Incoterms, as fewer and fewer people are familiar with the specific requirements of the former Incoterms.

Less of a problem is the use of C&F or C+F rather than CFR to communicate that an ocean shipment is made under a Cost and Freight Incoterm, because only the abbreviation changed. However, it should be avoided. Because the CFR abbreviation was created in the 1990 version of Incoterms, it is possible that the use of another abbreviation could confuse the importer and present challenges, should the shipment experience a mishap.

TABLE 6-4   Appropriate Incoterms by Mode of Transportation

The possible alternative Incoterms for a given means of transportation are marked with a "YES." Those that would be improper or likely to present problems are clearly marked as such.

Mode of transport	EXW	FCA	FAS	FOB	CFR	CIF	CPT	CIP	DES	DEQ	DAF	DDU	DDP
Ocean cargo	YES	NO	YES	YES	YES	YES	NO	NO	YES	YES	NO	YES	YES
Multimodal (FCL)	YES	YES	NO	NO	NO	NO	YES	YES	NO	NO	YES	YES	YES
Multimodal (LCL)	YES	YES	NO	NO	NO	NO	YES	YES	NO	NO	YES	YES	YES
Rail	YES	YES	NO	NO	NO	NO	YES	YES	NO	NO	YES	YES	YES
Road	YES	YES	NO	NO	NO	NO	YES	YES	NO	NO	YES	YES	YES
Air	YES	YES	NO	NO	NO	NO	YES	YES	NO	NO	NO	YES	YES

Another obsolete term is "Free Domicile," although there is no evidence that such a term was ever part of the recognized Incoterms. This pricing term is used when the exporter pays all the applicable duties and all the transportation and other charges until the shipment is delivered to the importer's premises. Because this term is not recognized by the ICC Arbitration Panel, it should be replaced by the Incoterm DDP.

6-18c Improper Use of Correct Incoterms

Another cause of possible problems is the misuse of correct Incoterms. Probably the most frequent misuse occurrence is when FOB is used with an air shipment, whereas FOB is designed to be used only with an ocean shipment term. The correct Incoterm to use for an air shipment should be Free Carrier (FCA), to clearly outline the responsibilities of the exporter and of the importer.

Table 6-4 outlines the proper use of Incoterms by mode of transportation.

Another issue is the use of correct Incoterms but for the incorrect commodity. Table 6-5 outlines the proper use of Incoterms for specific commodities. For example, a containerized shipment would not be shipped DES, but could easily be shipped CIF or CFR.

TABLE 6-5   Appropriate Incoterms by Type of Commodity

Incoterm	Bulk	Break-Bulk	Roll-on/Roll-off	Container	Small Packet
EXW	Yes	Yes	Yes	Yes	Yes
FAS	Yes	Yes	Yes	Yes	No
FCA	No	Yes	Yes	Yes	Yes
FOB	Yes	Yes	Yes	Yes	No
CIF	Yes	Yes	Yes	Yes	No
CIP	No	Yes	Yes	Yes	Yes
CFR	Yes	Yes	Yes	Yes	No
CPT	No	Yes	Yes	Yes	Yes
DES	Yes	No	No	No	No
DEQ	Yes	No	No	No	No
DDP	Yes	Yes	Yes	Yes	Yes
DDU	Yes	Yes	Yes	Yes	Yes
DAF	Yes	Yes	Yes	Yes	No

6-19 Incoterms as a Marketing Tool

As mentioned earlier, the greatest criterion to be used in the choice of a particular Incoterm is the willingness of both parties to perform and pay for some of the tasks involved in the shipment. In some cases, a strategic advantage can be gained by an exporter willing to facilitate the sale of its products by assisting a novice importer in the handling of a shipment. In other cases, a price advantage may be obtained by an experienced importer willing to perform all or most of the tasks involved in the shipment.

Generally speaking, an exporter does not determine which Incoterm to use on a case-by-case basis. It adopts a "policy" to include in international quotes those services that it feels competent providing. As noted in Section 6-3, it is difficult for an exporter to adapt its Incoterm strategy to accommodate the requirements of each importer. However, an exporter can determine the maximum level of services it is willing to provide in an export sale. It is then certainly possible for the exporter to do *less* than expected should the importer want to perform those tasks, and to simply use a different Incoterm on that transaction, allowing the importer to do more.

The choice of the proper Incoterm is a critical decision for a firm and should be an integral part of its export strategy, linked to the level of customer service it wants to provide. It therefore makes sense for an exporter to become as well versed as possible in international logistics and be prepared to include as many of the transportation functions as possible in its quote.

An exporter intent on increasing its sales should offer to provide the importer with the most customer-friendly Incoterm quotes (either DDU or DDP), if only by using the services of a competent freight forwarder. Should the importer want to shoulder more responsibilities, it is always possible for the exporter to reduce its involvement and quote FCA or even EXW. The best type of quote would be one in which the exporter lists different prices for different Incoterms, leaving the importer with the decision to choose which is best for its specific case.

For example, a quote could read:

- EXW Cleveland, Ohio: $10,000
- FCA Cincinnati Airport: Covington, Kentucky: $11,000
- CIP Paris, France: $15,500
- DDU Clermont-Ferrand, France: $16,500
- DDP Clermont-Ferrand, France: $17,800

and leave the customer to decide which of the Incoterms it would like to choose.

Review and Discussion Questions

1. Describe two Incoterms of your choice.
2. What is the Incoterm that is most importer friendly? The least importer friendly? Justify your answer.
3. Which of the Incoterms include a requirement of "insurance" by the exporter?
4. The "Delivered" Incoterms (DEQ, DES, DDP, and DDU) do not include insurance. Why not?
5. Using a product of your choice as well as an importer and an exporter of your choice, determine what would be the ideal Incoterm for a transaction. Make as many assumptions as necessary to justify your decision.
6. Explain why a developing country would want to prevent its importers from purchasing CIF or CIP and instead require CFR or CPT shipments.
7. A certain *sogo shosha* (a Japanese trading company) always requests its suppliers to provide an EXW quote. Knowing what you know about trading companies, why do you think this is the case?

Endnotes

1. Debattista, Charles, ed., *Incoterms in Practice*, 1995, International Chamber of Commerce Publication No. 505(E), ICC Publishing S.A., 38 Cours Albert 1er, 75008 Paris, France and ICC Publishing, Inc., 156 Fifth Avenue, Suite 417, New York, NY 10010, USA (refers to 1990 Incoterms).

2. Gooley, Toby B., "Incoterms 2000: What the Changes Mean to You," *Logistics Management Distribution Report*, January 31, 2000, p. 49.

3. Reynolds, Frank, "Implications of Incoterms 2000," *Journal of Commerce*, September 15, 1999, p. 10.

4. Freudmann, Aviva, "Traders Get a Brand-new Bible," *Journal of Commerce*, September 9, 1999, p. 1.

5. *Incoterms 2000*, 1999, International Chamber of Commerce Publication No. 560, ICC Publishing S.A., 38 Cours Albert 1er, 75008 Paris, France and ICC Publishing, Inc., 156 Fifth Avenue, Suite 417, New York, NY 10010, USA.

6. Biederman, David, "New Rules for Exports," *JoC Week*, July 24–30, 2000, pp. 10–12.

7. *Incoterms 2000*, 1999, International Chamber of Commerce Publication No. 560, ICC Publishing S.A., 38 Cours Albert 1er, 75008 Paris, France and ICC Publishing, Inc., 156 Fifth Avenue, Suite 417, New York, NY 10010, USA.

8. Ramberg, Jan, *ICC Guide to Incoterms 2000*, 1999, International Chamber of Commerce Publication No. 620, ICC Publishing S.A., 38 Cours Albert 1er, 75008 Paris, France and ICC Publishing, Inc., 156 Fifth Avenue, Suite 417, New York, NY 10010, USA.

9. *Ibid.*

10. Raty, Asko, "Variants on Incoterms (Part 2)," in Debattista, Charles, ed., *Incoterms in Practice*, 1995, International Chamber of Commerce Publication No. 505(E), ICC Publishing S.A., 38 Cours Albert 1er, 75008 Paris, France and ICC Publishing, Inc., 156 Fifth Avenue, Suite 417, New York, NY 10010, USA (refers to 1990 Incoterms).

11. Reynolds, Frank, "Tale of a Rail and Other Nuances of the Marine Cargo Insurance Experience," *Journal of Commerce*, November 18, 1998, p. 10A.

12. Raty, Asko, "Variants on Incoterms (Part 2)," in Debattista, Charles, ed., *Incoterms in Practice*, 1995, International Chamber of Commerce Publication No. 505(E), ICC Publishing S.A., 38 Cours Albert 1er, 75008 Paris, France and ICC Publishing, Inc., 156 Fifth Avenue, Suite 417, New York, NY 10010, USA (refers to 1990 Incoterms).

13. *Incoterms 2000*, 1999, International Chamber of Commerce Publication No. 560, ICC Publishing S.A., 38 Cours Albert 1er, 75008 Paris, France and ICC Publishing, Inc., 156 Fifth Avenue, Suite 417, New York, NY 10010, USA.

14. Mikkola, Kainu, "Variants on Incoterms (Part 1)," in Debattista, Charles, ed., *Incoterms in Practice*, 1995, International Chamber of Commerce Publication No. 505(E), ICC Publishing S.A., 38 Cours Albert 1er, 75008 Paris, France and ICC Publishing, Inc., 156 Fifth Avenue, Suite 417, New York, NY 10010, USA (refers to 1990 Incoterms).

15. Reynolds, Frank, "Seminar in Paris Yields Answers to Widely Asked Questions on Incoterms," *Journal of Commerce*, April 22, 1998, p. 2C.

16. *Ibid.*

17. Reynolds, Frank, *Incoterms for Americans*, 1999, published by International Projects, Inc., P.O. Box 352650, Toledo, Ohio 43635-2650, USA.

18. Ramberg, Jan, *ICC Guide to Incoterms 2000*, 1999, International Chamber of Commerce Publication No. 620, ICC Publishing S.A., 38 Cours Albert 1er, 75008 Paris, France and ICC Publishing, Inc., 156 Fifth Avenue, Suite 417, New York, NY 10010, USA.

Terms of Payment

Chapter Outline

Key Terms

advising bank   (p. 145)
amendment   (p. 150)
applicant   (p. 145)
aval   (p. 154)
bank guarantee   (p. 157)
banker's acceptance   (p. 154)
beneficiary   (p. 144)
bill of exchange   (p. 151)
commercial risk   (p. 139)
confirmed letter of credit   (p. 148)
confirming bank   (p. 148)
contractor   (p. 157)
correspondent bank   (p. 148)
country risk   (p. 139)
credit insurance   (p. 142)
date draft   (p. 153)

discrepancy   (p. 149)
exposure   (p. 139)
guarantor   (p. 157)
instruction letter   (p. 153)
international factoring   (p. 143)
international forfaiting   (p. 155)
irrevocable letter of credit   (p. 148)
issuing bank   (p. 144)
political risk   (p. 139)
presenting bank   (p. 152)
protest   (p. 152)
remitting bank   (p. 151)
sight draft   (p. 153)
stand-by letter of credit   (p. 150)
time draft   (p. 153)
trade acceptance   (p. 154)

One of the greatest concerns an exporting company has is to make sure that it will be able to collect payment from its foreign customers. Although this is also a legitimate concern domestically, an international transaction is generally perceived to involve a much greater nonpayment risk than a strictly domestic sale, for many reasons.

There are a number of ways in which an exporting company can ensure that it will get paid and be paid on time; a company can always tailor its international terms of payment to the characteristics of its customers, the countries in which it does business, and its own tolerance for risk. Although these methods are more complex than the open account arrangements traditionally found in all domestic sales, they are universally accepted, and there is ample jurisprudence to buttress them. It is therefore relatively simple to arrive at a choice of international terms of trade that will secure the interests of the exporter.

What is difficult in choosing an international term of trade is managing the delicate balance between protecting the interests of the exporter and offering good marketing practices that will engender good customer relations.

7-1 Characteristics of International Payment Issues

Exporters tend to prefer conservative measures in handling their foreign receivables. They tend to err on the side of caution for several reasons:

- **Credit information**. There is generally much less information available on the creditworthiness of a creditor in a foreign market than there is for a domestic customer. Although a few credit reporting agencies, accounting firms, and factoring houses do keep information, it is not always readily obtainable or is not always in existence for a specific customer, especially if the customer is a recently created firm or is in a developing country. Some improvements have been made recently, though, with the creation of centralized credit information portals, which offer links to access foreign countries' credit agencies. The task, though, is usually much more complicated for a foreign customer than for a domestic one, if only because the identity of a domestic firm is usually easier to establish. The paucity of information about certain countries is often coupled with an unfamiliarity with the diverse business organizations (different types of partnership and corporations) of a foreign country's legal system and with an inability to decipher businesses' names.

- **Lack of personal contact**. International transactions tend to be conducted in a more impersonal fashion (through fax, telex) than are domestic transactions, which tend to be conducted at least initially with some sort of personal contact (in person or over the phone). This lack of contact tends to lead to a climate in which the exporter has no way to evaluate the "character" of the importer, and where the possibility of a greater risk is often assumed. Where there is personal contact, it is often between people who are not always well versed in intercultural communication and can substantially misunderstand each other. This can foster the perception of a greater risk and encourages a more cautious approach.

- **Difficult and expensive collections**. Should a foreign customer renege on a payment, the collection of such a past-due account can be particularly difficult. Although there is a generally well structured system on the domestic side, there are few firms that have the capability of offering international collection services. Those that do tend to offer the service at a very high price. In some cases, relying on a foreign collection agency can lead a company to unwillingly employ some pretty unsavory characters, a situation that can eventually taint the image of the exporter, as Citibank discovered to its detriment when it used a "strong-arm" collection company in India.[1]

- **No easy legal recourse**. Unlike in a domestic setting, in which there is often a commercial code (of laws) and abundant jurisprudence, there is little of either in international trade. In addition, there is no court with jurisdiction over international disputes, and therefore a ruling by a court in the exporter's country cannot be easily enforced in the importer's country. The reciprocal is also true.

  The creation of the United Nations Convention on Contracts for the International Sale of Goods (CISG) and its implementation in 1980 have helped establish a body of legal principles for the sale of goods between companies located in two different sovereign countries. As of 2009, 74 countries had ratified this treaty, representing about 80 percent of the world's trade, but some countries, such as the United States, have ratified only part of it,[2] presumably those articles that do not conflict with their own code law (Uniform Commercial Code [UCC] for the United States). The United Kingdom has yet to ratify this convention at all. The enforcement of the convention is left to the domestic courts' interpretation, and although there is some jurisprudence in this area, it is still fairly scant (all of the available jurisprudence is made accessible through a database created by the United Nations Commission on International Trade Law [UNCITRAL] called CLOUT, for Case Law On UNCITRAL Texts). There are always concerns on the part of exporters that conflicts of law between domestic laws and the CISG and differences in interpretation by the courts make the prospect of a court battle much more daunting. Chapter 5, Section 5-2 outlined several of the differences between the CISG and the United States UCC.

  It is a common misconception that there is some sort of an international court of justice; although the International Court in The Hague, Netherlands, arbitrates disputes between governments and between governments and multinational corporations, it never interferes in disputes between corporations. In addition, its rulings are non-binding, as the International Court does not have the executive authority to enforce them.

- **Higher litigation costs**. The costs of international litigation, arbitration, or mediation are generally much greater than those of domestic litigation. Seeking a ruling against an importer in the importer's country is time-consuming, can involve several trips abroad, and necessitates the hiring of foreign law specialists, a process that involves greater expenses than domestic disputes. In some countries, the backlog of civil and commercial cases in the court system is such as to render impossible the probability of a swift decision. In India, for example, a judgment is generally not rendered for at least five years, with cases meandering through the system for much longer periods than that. Other countries, such as China, Russia, Indonesia, and Ukraine, are not much different.[3,4]

Suing a foreign customer for non-payment in the courts of the exporter's country could be perceived as a means to speed this process up and eventually lower its costs; however, it is followed only by the prospect of having to file suit in the importing country's courts as well, just to enforce the judgment rendered against the importer. Most exporters perceive that litigation should be an absolute last resort.

- **Mistrust**. Finally, there is the perception that the importing company is well aware of all these factors and knows that the exporter is unlikely to aggressively pursue an uncollected foreign receivable. This creates a climate of distrust on the part of the exporter, who could assume the worst intentions on the part of the importer.

7-2 Alternative Terms of Payment

There are essentially four "traditional" methods to handle the issue of payment in foreign transactions, all involving a different level of risk: cash in advance, open account, documentary collection, and letters of credit. Although there are variations in each of these methods, each designed to mitigate one or another aspect of the risks involved in the transaction, they have not changed much in the past thirty years. However, in the past fifteen years, an interesting fifth alternative has emerged, called "TradeCard," and it promises to become a particularly effective means of securing payment from a customer abroad without involving as many fees or intermediaries as do some of the more secure traditional alternatives. However interesting this alternative is, though, it has not been particularly successful in gaining market share.

Each of these five general alternatives presents advantages and disadvantages and can be generally seen as a trade-off between the risk of non-payment and the risk of losing the business to a more aggressive competitor who is willing to accept a greater risk and therefore present the customer with a "simpler" alternative form of payment. Table 7-1 gives an example of the most common perceptions in terms of this trade-off.

Table 7-1 is an overly simplified summary of the different alternatives. The ultimate choice of a term of sale should be carefully determined as a function of several objective and subjective factors, and each variant of the preferred method should be given careful consideration. Unfortunately, if only for the obvious reason of simplification of the process of selling, several exporting firms do not have the inclination—nor do they have the time and personnel—to tailor terms of payment to specific customers or countries, and these firms have designed a "foreign sales policy" to deal with all orders from importers, regardless of where these customers are located or who they are. Such a lack of flexibility tends to lead to exceedingly conservative policies. One exporter confessed to the author that it considered only cash-in-advance sales

TABLE 7-1	Advantages and Disadvantages of Several Terms of Payment	
Term of Payment	**Probability of Losing the Business Because of the Choice of Method of Payment**	**Probability of Loss due to Non-payment**
Cash in advance	High	Nil
Letter of credit	Fairly high	Almost nil
Documentary collection	Low	Low
Open account	Nil	Relatively high
TradeCard	Low	Almost nil

orders; undoubtedly this conservative stance never got the company into trouble, but it very likely yielded much lower sales than a slightly more aggressive approach. Ideally, the terms of sale of a particular transaction should be evaluated according to the risks attached to the transaction.

7-3 Risks in International Trade

There are three sources of risk in international trade that need to be considered. First is obviously the **commercial risk**, which is also encountered in domestic transactions and relates to the ability (and the willingness) of the importer to pay the invoice in time. However, there is also the **country risk** that encompasses all of the issues related to the country to which an exporter is shipping and that may affect payment, regardless of the creditworthiness of the importer. Finally, exporters also associate risk with **exposure**, which is the potential financial impact of non-payment or reduced payment on the exporter's business.

7-3a Country Risk

Country risk is made up of an aggregate of different issues, some political, and some strictly economic.

On the political side, the government's stability should be considered. For example, the possibility that a government may be changed (with a new election) may influence import policies, which, in turn, could mean that goods cannot clear Customs as easily, or that tariffs increase, or that other policies are changed to such an extent that the importer will refuse delivery. In a country in which such a **political risk** is perceived, the exporter would prefer a term of payment that is more secure. Similarly, a government that is in a weak position could also see its policies challenged by a strong public opposition, a situation that can lead to strong political unrest, as was the case in the French Caribbean islands of Martinique and Guadeloupe, where there was a massive general strike early in 2009.[5,6] When such general strikes take place, just about all economic activity stops, and therefore importers do not pay their creditors until the situation is stabilized. The strike in Guadeloupe lasted more than a month.

Port personnel or other personnel critical to the timeliness of a shipment—such as Customs officers—strike often in some countries, and this fact should be factored into the decision of the terms of payment. A strike in U.S. West Coast ports lasted only a day in May 2008,[7] but a similar action in 2002 lasted ten days and disrupted many shipments. Sometimes, social movements are so commonplace that businesses have to learn to plan around them. The French government tallies an average of at least 2 million worker-days of strike every year, and many more are lost because of the strikes (when nonstriking employees cannot make it to work, for example).[8]

Finally, in some cases, the government chooses to delay payment of international obligations, including trade obligations, whenever it is found to make sense politically. However, although a few governments have reneged on their public debt, there has been no recent evidence of governments reneging on their commercial (trade) debt.

Secondly, the overall health of the economy should also be considered. If there is high unemployment, policies against "job-stealing imports" could be implemented. If there is high inflation, price controls may be initiated. Moreover, the balance of payments of the importing country may also be relevant: If it is badly in a deficit position, imports of "non-essential" goods could be curtailed. Such would be the case when the "import cover," or the amount of foreign currency that the country has to cover its imports, starts to become low; generally, the import cover is expressed in months (i.e., foreign currency reserves can cover the next X months of imports).

Finally, a quick survey of the social system of the country could be conducted. Some countries' societies foster a climate where fraud is commonplace, sometimes

commercial risk The probability of not getting paid by a certain creditor, because this creditor does not have the funds to pay the debt, or because the creditor refuses to pay the debt.

country risk (or political risk) The probability of not getting paid by a certain creditor because the creditor's country does not have the funds to pay the debt (insufficient foreign exchange reserves) or because the creditor is not legally allowed to pay the debt (political embargo).

exposure The relative consequences of a particular risk for an exporter; the risk of a $50,000 loss would represent a greater exposure for a small exporter than for a large exporter.

TABLE 7-2	Ease of Conforming to Administrative Requirements and of Enforcing Contracts in Selected Countries (May 2009)

| | Days Needed To | | | |
Country	Import a Product	Export a Product	Settle a Lawsuit	Get a Construction Permit
Brazil	19	14	616	411
France	11	9	331	137
India	20	17	1420	224
Japan	11	10	316	187
Singapore	3	5	150	38
United States	5	6	300	40
Zimbabwe	73	53	410	1,426

Source: The World Bank.

prevalent (e.g., Nigeria),[9] a situation that is conducive to much caution on the part of an exporter. The fairness of the legal system should also be considered. An importer located in a country in which claims are handled professionally should be offered more lenient terms of payment than one located in a country where the administrative and justice systems are notoriously biased, inadequate, or agonizingly slow. Table 7-2 outlines the number of days that it takes an importer to clear a product for import (once all documents are received), the number of days it takes to export a product, and the average duration of a commercial lawsuit. The World Bank has information on all countries of the world.[10]

The magazine *WT100*—formerly called *World Trade*—provides in each of its issues a summary report of a region of the world and of the situation in each country of that region. It also provides recommended terms of payment and credit terms generally expected in that country. The data are consolidated from several reliable sources: Dun & Bradstreet and *The Economist*'s Intelligence Unit. Table 7-3 is an excerpt of the information published in Dun & Bradstreet's *Exporters' Encyclopaedia*.[11]

Finally, it is important to note that expectations of currency exchange rate fluctuations do not affect the choice of the term of payment but will affect the choice of the currency of quote (see Chapter 8) and the strategy used to minimize this risk.

7-3b Commercial Risk

This is the area in which it is more difficult to obtain accurate and reliable information. If the potential customer is a distributor who does business with other exporting

TABLE 7-3	Recommended Credit Terms and Terms of Payment for Selected Countries (May 2009)

Country	Credit Terms	Recommended Terms of Payment
Finland	30 days	Open account
Bolivia	30-60 days	Confirmed letter of credit
Japan	30-90 days	Open account
Czech Republic	15-30 days	Sight draft (documentary collection)
Singapore	30-60 days	Open account
Nicaragua	30-60 days	Confirmed letter of credit
United Kingdom	30-60 days	Open account

Source: Exporters' Encyclopedia, 2008.

TABLE 7-4	Several Credit Reporting Services

Company	Web Address
COFACE	www.cofacerating.com
Dun & Bradstreet	www.dnb.com
International Company Profile (UK)	www.icpcredit.com
Latin American Business Credit Reporting Association	www.alaic.com
Estimo Reports (Italy)	www.estimoreports.com
Arab Business Information	www.cedar-rose.com
Unicredit Beijing (China)	www.unicredit.com.cn
Graydon International (UK)	www.graydon-group.com
Rencom International (France)	www.rencom.fr
Owens Online	www.owens.com
AMS Inform Private Limited (India)	www.amsinform.com

firms, it is often possible to obtain firsthand information from these other exporters. Actually, it is considered good commercial practice in the United States to share information on the creditworthiness of a common customer—and in some cases to monitor this customer's payments—with other suppliers.

Commercial risk can also be evaluated from private sources, including credit report companies, factoring houses, some accounting firms, insurance companies, and banks. However, these are usually fee-based services and tend to be focused on larger established firms in developed countries. These sources are reliable and unbiased, though they tend to be conservative in their evaluations.

Table 7-4 lists several companies offering foreign credit reports on overseas customers. Each of these firms usually issues a report on a foreign customer for about U.S. $150.[12]

7-3c Exposure

The risk of non-payment is the *probability* of not getting paid or of getting paid late, and it therefore dictates the terms of payment chosen by the exporter.

However, another issue to be considered is the consequence of that loss on a company, or the exposure of a company. At equal probabilities of loss, a small business would be much more careful in handling a U.S. $50,000 export transaction than a large company would be. The amount is a much greater percentage of its business, and the loss of this amount could be very significant. The greater the exposure, the more secure the terms of payment should be.

7-4 Cash in Advance

7-4a Definition

In a cash-in-advance transaction, the exporter requests that the customer provide payment in advance, before shipment of the goods can take place. Payment is usually made with an electronic SWIFT (Society for Worldwide Interbank Financial Tele-communication) fund transfer from the customer's bank to the exporter's bank.

This is the ultimate "risk-free" alternative for the exporter. The importer has to pay before the goods are released; therefore, there are no collection worries, no foreign exchange fluctuation exposure, no cash-flow problem, and only nominal fees to pay to banks.

In a cash-in-advance transaction, the risk is completely transferred to the importer. It sends cash to the exporter with the expectation that the exporter will ship the goods that were requested, in the quantity that was ordered, in due time, and with the documents necessary to clear Customs in the importing country. In addition, this takes place in an atmosphere in which the exporter just demonstrated that it has no trust whatsoever in the importer because it is requesting "cash in advance."

7-4b Applicability

Cash in advance is a recommended way of conducting international transactions in countries in which fraud is rampant, in which there is a substantial risk of political instability or the possibility of foreign exchange freezes, and in which there is no convertible currency. Transactions conducted in the republics of the former Soviet Union and eastern Europe, with the possible exceptions of Hungary and the Czech Republic, would probably best be conducted on a cash-in-advance basis.

However, this method is unsound for business conducted in developed countries and in countries in which there is a significant level of sophistication in international business. In these countries, the probability that an importer will place a cash-in-advance purchase is infinitesimally small if there are other comparable suppliers available, and insisting on this method of payment is likely to create resentment on the part of the importer rather than initiate an amicable business relationship. It should be avoided at all costs.

7-5 Open Account

7-5a Definition

In an open-account transaction, the exporter conducts international business in a manner similar to the way it conducts business domestically. The exporter just sends an invoice to the importer along with the shipment and trusts the customer to pay within a reasonable amount of time, commensurate with the credit usually granted in the country in which the importer operates, usually 30 to 90 days. It is essentially the conceptual opposite of cash in advance, as the exporter shows complete trust in the importer and ships the merchandise without any guarantee that it will be paid. The only recourse in case of non-payment is legal action in the importing country, a time-consuming and expensive process that exporters rarely undertake.

7-5b Applicability

This term of payment should be reserved to established customers, or customers with whom the exporter expects to have an ongoing relationship. It could possibly be extended to new orders from large companies and/or companies for which commercial credit data is available, and whose credit rating is excellent. At least, that's theoretically the way that this term of payment should be used.

In practice, however, this term of sale has become almost necessary in some markets if the exporter is to expect any sales. For example, in the European Union, it has become very difficult to conduct business on any other basis. It is to be expected that the trend will continue and expand to other markets as well. For example, European Union companies offer open-account terms of payment to 80 percent of their customers[13] outside of the EU. The main reason is that, historically, European exporters have often benefited from their government's support, and were often offered free (or substantially discounted) commercial insurance on their foreign receivables. Until 1994, for example, a French exporter could obtain insurance from COFACE (*Compagnie Française d'Assurance pour le Commerce Extérieur*), a government-run insurance company, at a greatly reduced cost; its risk of non-payment had therefore essentially been assumed by the government. Today, COFACE and other European-based companies constitute the largest providers of international commercial **credit insurance** and are present in many different countries, a position reached through many consolidations.

credit insurance An insurance policy under which commercial risk is covered; in exchange for a premium paid by the exporter, the insurance company will bear the risk of nonpayment by the importer, deducting a slight percentage of the receivable.

7-5c Commercial Credit Insurance

In order to compete in those markets in which open-account has become the rule, companies must offer this term of payment in their quotes to new customers. However, the risks associated with an open-account transaction should entice an exporter to acquire credit insurance on those sales.

Therefore a commercial policy covering credit risks should be contracted either on a "blanket" basis (i.e., covering all export transactions, up to a certain overall amount) or on a per-sale basis (i.e., each individual transaction is covered by a separate commercial insurance contract). Chapter 10, Section 10-12 gives more detailed information on these types of coverage.

7-5d Factoring

Factoring is a process used most frequently domestically (between two parties in the same country) by which the creditor uses an intermediary, called a factor or a factoring house, to finance a receivable. There are two cases: In the first, called factoring "without recourse," the creditor sells the receivable to the factor, who is then responsible for collecting from the debtor. If the latter does not pay, the factor assumes that responsibility, and the creditor keeps the proceeds of the sale of the receivable. In the second case, called factoring "with recourse," the factor attempts to collect the funds from the debtor but, if it is unsuccessful, can turn to the creditor for assistance. Ultimately, in a factoring transaction with recourse, the creditor is responsible for collecting the funds.

In an international transaction, it is possible that the importer wants credit terms that are beyond what the exporter is comfortable giving—for example, a 90-day credit is requested when the exporter can afford only a 30-day credit—there is the possibility of using **international factoring** as a means to extend this credit. When it involves two countries, factoring is much more complicated than in a domestic sale: The exporter would contact a factor in the exporting country that would in turn contact a factoring house in the importing country. Once both factors agree to the transaction, the sale is completed on an open-account basis. The exporter, once the invoice is sent, sells the receivable to the exporting country's factor and collects its face value, from which are deducted the fees and interest charges covering the period of time during which credit is extended.[14]

> **international factoring**
> A means of financing international receivable accounts, by which a firm can ask a factoring company to advance funds on a receivable account.

In an international transaction, the factoring is generally done without recourse (i.e., the factoring house is responsible for collecting the receivable and cannot turn to the exporter if it is unable to collect). This is the main reason for which factoring houses often involve a second factoring company located in the importing country; its responsibility is to check the creditworthiness of the importer and, in some cases, to act as a collection agent for the factoring company in the exporting country.[15]

If the exporter is unable to provide the importer with the type of credit terms that the importer requests, the importer can, on its end, find financing for its purchase by asking a financial institution to lend it funds based upon this incoming "inventory." In the United States, for example, the United Parcel Service offers "capital cargo finance," which allows an importer to borrow money against an incoming in-transit shipment.[16]

7-6 Letter of Credit

7-6a Definition

A letter of credit is a document in which the importer's bank essentially promises to pay the exporter if the importer does not pay. The creditworthiness of the bank is substituted for the creditworthiness of the importer. However, the concept is substantially more complex than this. The promise is not made upon the exporter meeting certain conditions (or the importer not meeting certain conditions), but it is made on the *documents* of the transaction. This is the reason why a letter of credit is often called a *documentary* letter of credit and the process is called *documentary credit*.

It is fundamental to understand that the *documents* are the critical elements to a letter of credit. The bank is under no obligation to pay if the documents do not conform to the letter of credit's requirements, even though delivery has been made and the importer has obtained control of the merchandise. Similarly, the bank is obligated to pay if the documents are in order, even though the merchandise may be shoddy or not fit for sale.

The letter of credit is a contractual agreement between the **issuing bank** and the **beneficiary** that is undertaken on behalf of the importer. This agreement is independent of the underlying business relationship between the exporter and the importer; only the documents relating to a particular transaction between the exporter and the importer matter.[17] This obviously means that extreme care must be taken in handling the documents related to a letter of credit; otherwise, it triggers a very time-consuming and expensive process of amendments and corrections.

A transaction conducted on a letter-of-credit basis is almost as good as one made on a cash-in-advance basis in that the exporter will be paid, but it involves going through a lot more steps and paying a lot more banking fees. Figures 7-1 through 7-3 in Section 7-6b explain the process followed by a letter of credit transaction from issuance to payment.

issuing bank The bank providing the letter of credit to the importer. It is that bank that, should the importer be unable to pay and should the exporter provide all the necessary documents, has the contractual obligation to pay the beneficiary.

beneficiary The firm named in a letter of credit as the firm to which the bank is insuring payment if the importer does not pay. Usually, the beneficiary of a letter of credit is the exporter.

7-6b Process

Issuance

- The first step in the process (see Figure 7-1) is the negotiation, which takes place between the exporter and the importer, in which it is agreed that the terms of payment will be by letter of credit. The exporter then sends a *pro forma* invoice to the importer, which estimates the terms of the transaction as closely as

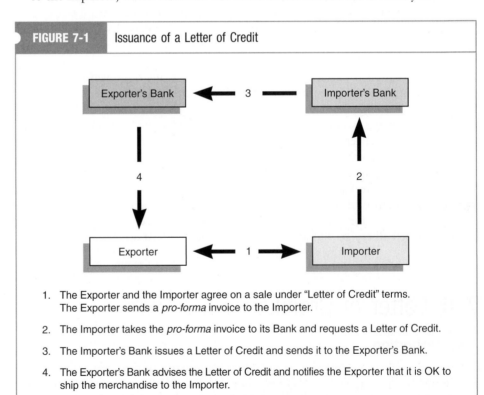

FIGURE 7-1   Issuance of a Letter of Credit

1. The Exporter and the Importer agree on a sale under "Letter of Credit" terms. The Exporter sends a *pro-forma* invoice to the Importer.

2. The Importer takes the *pro-forma* invoice to its Bank and requests a Letter of Credit.

3. The Importer's Bank issues a Letter of Credit and sends it to the Exporter's Bank.

4. The Exporter's Bank advises the Letter of Credit and notifies the Exporter that it is OK to ship the merchandise to the Importer.

possible (see Chapter 9, Section 9-2b for further details on the elements of a *pro forma* invoice). The exporter also provides a series of instructions to the importer, detailing the terms of the transaction.

- The second step takes place when the importer (the **applicant**) requests its bank (the issuing bank) to open a letter of credit on the importer's behalf, naming the exporter as the beneficiary. The importer follows the instructions of the exporter regarding the terms of the sale and makes sure to include in the application all of the documents that it will need to clear Customs in the importing country. The importer may also send a copy of the application to the exporter, to ensure that the terms listed on the application are acceptable to the exporter.

  Because it is promising that it will pay if the importer does not pay, the issuing bank may request that the importer "freeze" a certain percentage (from 0 to 100 percent) of the amount of the letter of credit in an account or on a line of credit, essentially ensuring that the importer will pay the bank by obtaining the funds before the letter of credit is issued. This constraint on cash flow is one of the reasons why importers prefer other terms of payment to a letter of credit. Another is the fact that the issuing bank will request a fee that will vary between 0.5 and 3 percent of the amount of the letter of credit, although most of them request about 1.5 percent.

- In the third step, the issuing bank sends the letter of credit (generally electronically, using the SWIFT network; or by fax; or, rarely, by mail) to the exporter's bank, which acts as the **advising bank** (in this simplified example). The advising bank checks a number of things: first, that the letter of credit is drawn on a legitimate bank and that its content meets the requirements of the exporter. It also wants to make sure that the letter of credit is irrevocable: An irrevocable letter of credit cannot be modified without the express consent of both the issuer and the beneficiary. All letters of credit issued under the Universal Customs and Practice for Documentary Credit of the International Chamber of Commerce (UCP 600) are irrevocable unless specifically marked as "revocable." The advising bank finally confirms that the letter of credit's information matches the *pro forma* invoice exactly and that the expiration date is appropriate for the transaction.

- The advising bank notifies the beneficiary that the letter of credit is acceptable from the bank's perspective. By reviewing the letter of credit, the bank is not engaging its responsibility; it is only acting as an adviser to the exporter and will have no liability (will not have to pay) if the issuing bank does not honor its commitment.

- The bank then forwards the letter of credit to the exporter (the beneficiary), who then determines that the terms of the letter of credit are consistent with what was agreed upon between the exporter and the importer. Once the exporter has determined that the letter of credit is acceptable, the exporter can then start the shipping process.

Shipment

- The fifth step in the process of a letter of credit (see Figure 7-2) takes place when the exporter ships the merchandise. Most of the time, the exporter ships directly to the importer, but in some cases, it may be to another party; in any case, the exporter ships the goods according to the terms outlined in the letter of credit.

- In this process, the exporter generates a lot of paperwork (an invoice, a certificate of origin, an export license, a packing list, a Shipper's Export Declaration [U.S.], and so on) and collects a lot of paperwork, such as a bill of lading or an air waybill from the shipping company and miscellaneous certificates (insurance, inspection, and so on) from different suppliers (for more information on all of these terms, please see Chapter 9). Extreme care must be given to make sure

applicant The firm asking the issuing bank for a letter a credit. Usually, the applicant is the importer.

advising bank The bank that determines whether the issuing bank is a legitimate bank and whether the terms of the letter of credit offered by the issuing bank on behalf of the importer are appropriate.

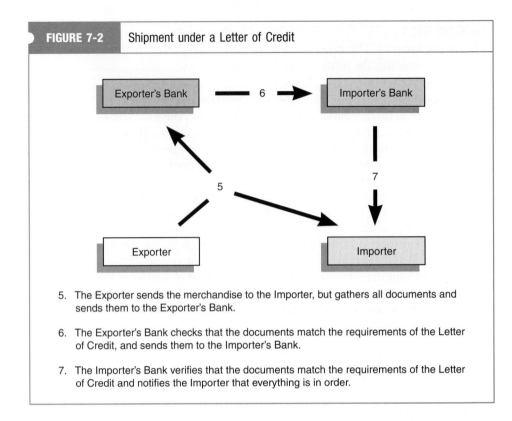

FIGURE 7-2   Shipment under a Letter of Credit

5. The Exporter sends the merchandise to the Importer, but gathers all documents and sends them to the Exporter's Bank.

6. The Exporter's Bank checks that the documents match the requirements of the Letter of Credit, and sends them to the Importer's Bank.

7. The Importer's Bank verifies that the documents match the requirements of the Letter of Credit and notifies the Importer that everything is in order.

that the paperwork matches precisely the requirements of the letter of credit, as the issuing bank's promise to pay is contingent upon presenting the proper documents. Any error or omission in the documents will trigger a discrepancy and will delay payment (see Section 7-6c).

- After these documents are collected, the exporter will send them to its bank (the advising bank), which will check them against the terms of the letter of credit. If the documents conform, the bank will then send the documents (sixth step) to the importer's bank (the issuing bank). In some cases, depending on the working relationship between the issuing bank and the advising bank, the advising bank could issue a credit (payment) to the exporter at that point. However, this payment is not final and is dependent on the issuing bank honoring the letter of credit. The simplest example illustrated in Figure 7-2 does not presume such a relationship and assumes that the advising bank will wait until it is actually paid by the issuing bank before it credits the exporter's bank account.

- After receiving the documents sent by the exporter's bank, the issuing bank will check them, and determine whether they conform to the requirements of the letter of credit. If the documents conform, the issuing bank notifies the importer that the documents are in order and it exchanges them (concentrating on the bill of lading or the air waybill, which acts as the certificate of title to the goods) against payment by the importer. The importer can then clear Customs in the importing country.

Payment

- The payment of a letter of credit is a fairly simple process: Payment is first made by the importer to its bank, then the importing bank wires the payment to the exporter's bank, and finally the exporter's account is credited (see Figure 7-3).

The entire process of a letter of credit is shown in Figure 7-4. The reason the process is labeled "simplified" is because a number of additional parties can get involved in the process, as will be seen in the following section.

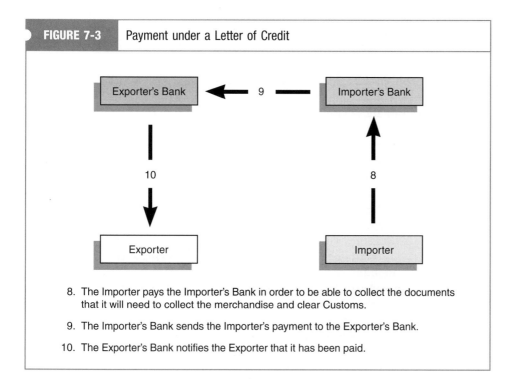

FIGURE 7-3   Payment under a Letter of Credit

8. The Importer pays the Importer's Bank in order to be able to collect the documents that it will need to collect the merchandise and clear Customs.

9. The Importer's Bank sends the Importer's payment to the Exporter's Bank.

10. The Exporter's Bank notifies the Exporter that it has been paid.

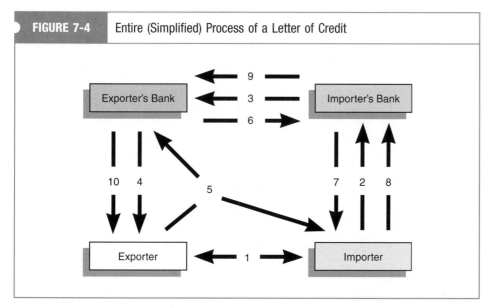

FIGURE 7-4   Entire (Simplified) Process of a Letter of Credit

7-6c Additional Information

Advising Bank

It is not unusual for an exporter's bank to determine that it does not have the expertise to advise a particular letter of credit. It is the case when the letter of credit comes from a country with which the exporter's bank rarely conducts business, or when the letter of credit is issued by a bank with which the exporter's bank is unfamiliar.

In those cases, the exporter's bank will decline advising the letter of credit and will ask another bank to become the advising bank for that transaction. For that responsibility, the exporter's bank will generally seek the expertise of a large bank located in one of the world's international financial centers (New York, London, or Hong Kong). Figure 7-4 would then include an additional bank, the advising bank, separate from the exporter's and the importer's banks.

Confirming Bank

In some cases, the exporting company may not be comfortable doing business with the issuing bank, which, after all, is an unknown foreign entity. It may not know the bank's creditworthiness, it may feel that the risk of relying on a foreign bank is too high, or it may simply be quite risk averse or new to the export business. In any case, the exporter can ask the advising bank to confirm the letter of credit; it then becomes a **confirmed letter of credit**.

In the event the issuing bank does not honor its letter of credit, then the **confirming bank** will pay the exporter, as long as the documents submitted conform to the terms of the letter of credit. It is a way to substitute the creditworthiness of the domestic bank for that of the issuing bank. Because the confirming bank is often also the advising bank, the practice is that the confirming bank will issue a credit to the exporter upon presentation of the documents at the time of shipment. It therefore speeds up the process of collection by a week or so.

In most cases, confirming a letter of credit is not a wise choice, as banks are creditworthy. In addition, confirming a letter of credit is expensive, costing 0.5 to 1.5 percent of the amount of the letter of credit, a substantial cost considering that foreign banks rarely fail. Some U.S. companies have a policy of always confirming letters of credit, generally because they prefer dealing with U.S. banks should there be difficulties in collection; nevertheless, this leads companies to confirm letter of credit drawn on extraordinarily solid banks, such as Crédit Suisse, with less-than-stellar U.S. banks. Then again, venerable banks have been known to fail; Barings did in 1995.

Correspondent Bank

In some cases, yet another bank can get involved in the process. Most banks enter agreements with other banks in which they act as **correspondent banks** for each other. The purpose of these agreements is for each bank to have a "representation" in a foreign market. The consequence of these agreements is that the banks favor their correspondent banks in financial transactions, and will generally direct some of the business they conduct in the correspondent bank's country to that bank.

For the sake of example, let's pretend that Bank A in Germany has an agreement with Bank Z in Thailand in which they are each other's correspondent bank. An exporter in Germany, doing business with Bank B, requests a letter of credit from its Thai customer, which itself has an account with Bank Z. It is quite likely for Bank A to be part of the transaction and act as the "courier" between Bank Z and Bank B, or even for Bank Z to request that Bank A become the advising bank. In most cases, it would be advantageous for the German exporter to have Bank A involved, as Bank A may release the funds *on behalf of* the issuing bank, Bank Z (under the International Chamber of Commerce's URR 725 regulations). Payment would then be collected earlier.

Irrevocable Letter of Credit

An **irrevocable letter of credit** cannot be canceled by the issuing bank for any reason, unless the beneficiary agrees to it. A *revocable* letter of credit can be changed by the importer (or the issuing bank) without prior approval of the beneficiary. In very few cases does it make sense for a beneficiary to accept a revocable letter of credit. Almost all letters of credit are irrevocable.

A letter of credit issued under UCP 600—and almost all of them are—is assumed to be irrevocable unless otherwise specified. Under the previous guidelines (UCP 500), this was also true. However, before 1993, under the UCP 400 rules, the opposite was true. There seems to still be some confusion regarding this important distinction, even though it is more than 15 years old, and exporters are still told to make sure that Letters of Credit are irrevocable. If they are issued under UCP 600, they are irrevocable.

UCP 600

UCP 600[18] is the *Universal Customs and Practice for Documentary Credit*, 2007 revision, Publication 600 of the International Chamber of Commerce. It is a

---

confirmed letter of credit A payment alternative in which the exporter asks a bank to provide an additional level of payment security to a letter of credit: Should the importer not pay and should the issuing bank not pay, the confirming bank will pay.

confirming bank The bank providing an additional level of payment security to the beneficiary of a letter of credit; the confirming bank certifies that it will pay the letter of credit if the importer and the issuing bank do not pay.

correspondent bank A foreign bank with which a domestic bank has a preferred business relationship.

irrevocable letter of credit A letter of credit is said to be irrevocable if it cannot be changed without the express approval of the issuing bank and of the beneficiary.

publication that details the responsibilities of the banks involved in letter of credit, as well as the responsibilities of the applicant and the beneficiary. It also attempts to address most of the areas in which there could be misunderstandings between the issuing bank, the advising bank, the applicant, and the beneficiary. Because of the jurisprudence that has accumulated with the almost universal usage of UCP 600 (and its predecessor, UCP 500), it is greatly preferable to always follow its guidelines and to request that the letter of credit be issued "subject to" UCP 600.[19]

Whenever a letter of credit is issued through the SWIFT network, it is by convention issued under UCP 600 guidelines unless otherwise noted. Because most banks belong to the SWIFT network, almost all letter of credit are therefore issued under UCP 600.

URR 725

The International Chamber of Commerce has also published a document entitled *Uniform Rules for Bank-to-Bank Reimbursements under Documentary Credits*, which is called URR 725 and was implemented in October 2008.[20]

These rules outline the responsibilities of the banks involved in an international transaction conducted under UCP 600 and in which payment to the exporter is made directly by the advising bank (or by the correspondent bank of the issuing bank). The paying bank is then reimbursed by the issuing bank. This practice is becoming more and more common as a means to expedite the process of a letter of credit. The International Chamber of Commerce felt that uniform rules were necessary in this matter and created URR 525 to accompany UCP 500. It upgraded the rules with URR 725 to reflect the changes made in UCP 600. Although these rules apply to banks rather than exporters, it might be advisable to refer to them before requesting payment from the advising or the correspondent bank of the issuing bank.

Discrepancies and Amendments

Unfortunately, and for a number of reasons, there are often discrepancies between the requirements outlined in the letter of credit and the documents presented by the exporter. Since no payment will be made to the exporter (and no document will be released to the importer) if they do not match, the exporter and the importer must resolve any **discrepancy** that arises so that the transaction can be completed.

Such discrepancies can be on shipping dates, changes in the number of packages, changes in part numbers, suppliers' costs (insurance, shipping charges), and a host of different reasons (see Table 7-5)[21]. It is estimated that around 50 percent of all letters of credit have some sort of discrepancy. Given these potential problems, it is crucial

discrepancy A difference between the documents required by a letter of credit and the documents provided by the exporter.

TABLE 7-5	Leading Causes of Discrepancies in Letters of Credit (as a percentage of all discrepancies)

Source of Discrepancy	Percent (%) of All Discrepancies
Inconsistent data	25.1
Absence of documents	8.4
Late presentation	7.9
Carrier not named	8.8
Incorrect goods description	4.1
Incorrect data	7.1
Incorrect BOL* endorsement	3.8
Incorrect insurance cover	1.8
Other discrepancies	33.0

*BOL=bill of lading.

Source: Sitpro.

for the exporter to pay close attention to the terms of the letter of credit and to attempt to adhere to them as closely as possible.

For example, great care should be given to the preparation of the *pro forma* invoice, as this is the document upon which the issuing bank relies to issue the letter of credit. In those few cases in which the letter of credit does not reflect exactly the *pro forma* invoice (misspellings, for example), it is wise to issue an invoice that matches the letter of credit. While this is obviously difficult to do with an automated invoice processing system, it may save a considerable amount of aggravation later on. Actually, many bankers have "horror stories" of issuing banks refusing payment on a letter of credit because there was a typo on it—an error on their part as they miscopied the *pro forma* invoice—which obviously does not appear on the commercial invoice. In their defense, though, a letter of credit issued by a bank in a third-world country may have been typed by a clerk with no knowledge whatsoever of the exporter's language.

amendment A change to a letter of credit to which all parties to a letter of credit agree: the exporter, the importer, the issuing bank, and the advising bank.

In those cases in which there is a discrepancy between the requirements of the letter of credit and the documents presented by the exporter, the exporter and the importer must request their respective banks to negotiate an **amendment** to the letter of credit. The process is initiated by the advising bank, which requests an amendment to the letter of credit from the issuing bank. Since the amendment is a change to an irrevocable letter of credit, it must be authorized by both parties; the beneficiary and the importer (through the issuing bank) must agree to it. There is usually a fee attached to an amendment, and in some cases it can be difficult to obtain because the importing country's government gets involved (the import license may have to be changed) or because the change is not to the advantage of the importer (a delay in shipping date, for example). In the overwhelming majority of cases, though, the problem can be solved to the satisfaction of both parties; one personal banking acquaintance could recall only one deal "gone bad" in 20 years of letter of credit management.

Yet More Complications

Things can get a lot more complicated in a letter of credit transaction, as yet more parties can get involved. For example, the exporter's bank may feel that it is unqualified to advise the letter of credit and will request that another, larger or more experienced bank become the advising bank. In those cases, there would then be at least three banks involved; the importer's bank, the exporter's bank, and the advising bank.

In the "worst" case, there are six banks involved: the exporter's bank, the importer's bank, an advising bank (to help the exporter's bank), a confirming bank (to reassure the exporter), and the correspondent banks of the latter two (to "simplify" the exchange of documents). When so many banks are involved, it can quickly become quite confusing, and it may be difficult to ascertain where the documents are at any point in time.

Drafts

It is possible to add a draft (see Section 7-7c) to a letter of credit. The draft is an instrument that legally binds the importer to pay within a certain period of time. This allows the exporter to grant commercial credit to the importer whenever it is deemed necessary. If no draft is attached to a letter of credit, the assumption is that the importer is not granted any credit (i.e., that the letter of credit is payable at sight; in other words, immediately). The different types of drafts are presented in Section 7-7c.

7-6d Stand-By Letters of Credit

stand-by letter of credit A type of letter of credit that covers more than one shipment; a stand-by letter of credit allows for multiple bills of lading, issued on different dates.

A **stand-by letter of credit** is similar to a "simple" letter of credit, with a few exceptions. First, it generally has a much longer validity period, sometimes longer than a year. Second, it usually applies to more than one shipment from the exporter to the importer. Under such a system, the exporter will make shipments on an open-account basis and will "call" on the letter of credit only if the importer is not meeting its obligations;[22] for example, if it is not paying on time. These qualities make stand-by letters of credit a tool of choice for handling business with a distributor, for example, or making a series of shipments to a customer.

The stand-by letter of credit is an instrument that was created by U.S. banks as a substitute for bank guarantees, because U.S. banks are prohibited from offering them.[23] Therefore, stand-by letters of credit are often also used to secure the obligations of the seller/exporter (as in a performance bond) (see Section 7-11). The sums secured by stand-by letters of credit are vastly superior to the amount secured by traditional letters of credit, as they involve long, large-scale contracts.

The rules for stand-by letters of credit are regulated by the International Stand-By Practices ISP98, a series of 89 rules governing the language, documentation, and practices of these letters of credit.[24]

7-6e Applicability

A letter of credit used to be the instrument of choice in international transactions, especially in those cases in which the exporter had no pre-existing business relationship with the importer, or when the importer was located in a country that was considered to be risky. It still is an outstanding means of making sure that the exporter will be paid, and is recommended in situations in which the exporter is risk averse, new to the business of exporting, has substantial exposure in the transaction in question, or has some uneasiness regarding the creditworthiness of the importer.

However, it is often a disadvantage to request a letter of credit because of the costs (and the cumbersome process) associated with it. It is also unwise to demand payment on such restrictive terms when other competitors can offer open-account terms. Therefore, it may be a more sensible alternative, especially in western Europe, to offer terms that are more favorable to the importer and to use commercial insurance to cover the commercial risk.

7-7 Documentary Collection

7-7a Definition

Documentary collection is a process by which an exporter asks a bank located in the importer's country to "safeguard" the exporter's interests. The exporter asks the bank not to release the documents—specifically the bill of lading, which is the certificate of title to the goods (see Chapter 9)—until the importer satisfies certain requirements, most often paying the exporter or signing a financial document (called a draft or a **bill of exchange**) promising that it will pay the exporter within a given amount of time. This allows the exporter, should the importer decide not to take delivery of the goods, to have them shipped back to the exporting country and to lose only the costs of shipment rather than the total value of the goods. Another possibility is to find another customer for these goods.

bill of exchange In a documentary collection transaction, another term for a draft.

7-7b Process

Although the process can conceivably be done with the exporter sending the documents directly to the bank in the importer's country, the process generally starts (see Figure 7-5) with the exporter sending the documents to its own bank, which acts as a conduit for sending the documents to the importer's bank. The exporter's bank is the **remitting bank**, and it acts only as an intermediary; it has no responsibility in the process but the safe transmittal of the documents. The reason a remitting bank is used is to help the foreign bank ascertain the legitimacy of the exporter; the bank is not dealing with an unknown exporter, it is dealing with a bank with which it has dealt in the past, and which it trusts.

remitting bank In a documentary collection transaction, the bank that interacts with the exporter and with the presenting bank in the importing country. The remitting bank is the one that receives the documents from the exporter and then sends them to the presenting bank.

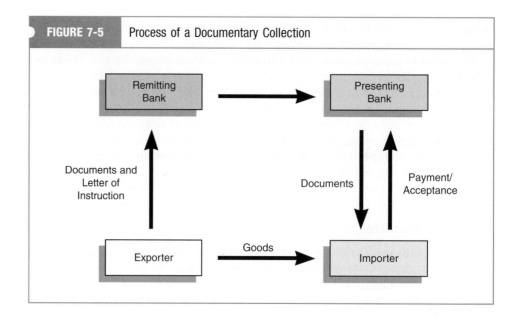

FIGURE 7-5   Process of a Documentary Collection

presenting bank In a documentary collection transaction, the bank that interacts with the importer on behalf of the exporter. The presenting bank is the one receiving the documents from the exporter or from the remitting bank and that holds them until the importer either signs a draft or pays the exporter.

The remitting bank then forwards the documents, as well as an instruction letter from the exporter (see Section 7-7d), to the **presenting bank**. The presenting bank can be the importer's bank or another bank in the importing country, but it is most often the correspondent bank of the remitting bank in the importer's country. The presenting bank then follows the instruction letter and alerts the importer that the documents have arrived. It notifies the importer that it will have to either pay for the goods or sign a draft (see Section 7-7c) in order to obtain the documents. Since the importer needs the documents in order to clear Customs in the importing country, it complies with the requirements of the presenting bank. If the importer decides not to collect the documents, the bank retains them and follows the exporter's instruction letter to determine what its next steps should be.

Once the presenting bank has obtained payment from the importer, it forwards the funds to the remitting bank, which then notifies the exporter that the funds have arrived.

7-7c Drafts

The exporter has several alternatives in deciding what it wants the presenting bank to request in exchange for delivering the documents to the importer. It can request immediate payment or it can grant the importer some time to make the payment, and uses a draft in order to do so. A draft is a promissory note, signed by the importer in the presence of a representative of the presenting bank, in which the importer commits to pay the invoice amount to the exporter on a given date.

A draft (or a bill of exchange) is a legal document in the importing country in which the importer officially recognizes a commercial debt toward the exporter. This makes it easier to collect payment if the importer decides not to honor its commitment, as the default is now a *domestic* issue rather than an international one—a dispute over which a domestic court would have no problem ruling. Specifically, in the instructions to the presenting bank, it is possible to request a **protest** in case of non-payment on a draft, which is a legal process that can have serious consequences for an importer; it may be difficult (if not impossible) for the importer to obtain credit after it has been recorded that it does not honor its debt. In some countries, such defaults are even published prominently in the local business press, tarnishing the reputation of a business.

protest In a documentary collection transaction, if the drawee (importer) does not pay a draft that it has signed, the presenting bank will file a protest, a legal document that notifies other parties that the drawee is not honoring its debts.

Although drafts are introduced in the section dealing with documentary collections, it is not unusual for a draft to accompany a letter of credit as well. When they accompany a letter of credit, they fulfill exactly the same role; the documents held by the issuing bank are not given to the importer until the importer signs the draft.

Sight Draft

The exporter can request that the presenting bank release the documents only upon payment of the invoice by the importer. Such a transaction is called "documents against payment" (D/P) or a **sight draft** transaction, meaning that the draft (a promissory note) is payable "at sight" (i.e., immediately). In this case, the exporter retains the title to the goods, embodied in the bill of lading or air waybill, until payment is made and the bill of lading or air waybill is given to the importer.

sight draft In a documentary collection or a letter of credit transaction, a sight draft is a promise by the importer that it will pay immediately, "at sight."

Time Draft

In some cases, the exporter may want to grant some credit terms to the importer but still want some means to ensure it will be paid. In that case, it can request that the bank exchange the documents against a **time draft**: The importer has to sign (endorse) a document promising it will pay within a certain time (generally multiples of thirty days: 30, 60, 90, and 180 days are the most common credit terms) after the draft is endorsed. The presenting bank should specifically be instructed to remit the documents when the draft is signed ("documents against acceptance" [D/A]), or to remit them against payment (D/P), in which case the importer will not take title to the goods until after payment is made, a requirement that mostly defeats the purpose of granting credit. Specifically because of problems associated with the custody of the goods between their arrival in the importing country and the time they become the property of the importer, the International Chamber of Commerce advises that "[c]ollections should not contain bills of exchange payable at a future date with instructions that commercial documents are to be delivered against payment."[25]

time draft In a documentary collection transaction, a time draft is a promissory note that the importer has to pay a number of days (30, 60, 90, or 180 days) after it accepts the draft by signing it.

Date Draft

A **date draft** is another way of granting credit to the importer. The difference is that the credit is extended to the importer for 30, 60, or 90 days from the *shipment date* rather than from the endorsement of the draft. The shipment date is determined by the main contract of carriage, generally the date at which the ocean bill of lading or the air waybill is issued.[26] The advantage of the date draft over the time draft is that the exporter has control over the date at which shipment is initiated (and therefore over the date at which the payment is due), whereas it has no control over the date at which the importer will endorse the draft.

A date draft transaction therefore alleviates one of the problems of documentary collection in general: the date at which the importer will endorse the draft. Under the Uniform Rules for Collection of the ICC,[27] the bank must notify the importer as soon as it receives the documents. However, the importer has no incentive to come to the bank to collect them—if the draft is a sight or time draft—because delaying endorsement delays payment as well.

date draft In a documentary collection transaction, a date draft is a promissory note that the importer has to pay a number of days (30, 60, 90, or 180 days) after the exporter ships the goods.

7-7d Instruction Letter

In addition to the "normal" documents (e.g., invoice, bill of lading, certificates, licenses) and the draft, each documentary collection includes an **instruction letter** in which the exporter—through the remitting bank—tells the presenting bank what it is expected to accomplish.

The instruction letter is a document in which the remitting bank instructs the presenting bank on the procedures it should follow in its dealings with the importer—for example, whether the documents should be exchanged against payment (D/P) or against an acceptance of the draft (D/A)—but also what the procedures should be if the importer refuses to sign the draft, if the importer refuses to pay for the fees (if any), or if the importer does not honor its signature. The presenting bank could be asked to file a protest, for example.

instruction letter A document sent by an exporter to a presenting bank in which the exporter spells out its instructions regarding how it expects the bank to handle the documents and how it expects the bank to handle an importer that does not accept the draft sent.

This instruction letter is the only document that the presenting bank will follow in a documentary collection. The bank does not need to find its instructions among the other documents that accompany the documentary collection. The International Chamber of Commerce is quite clear about this issue in its new Uniform Rules for Collections (URC 522) (see Section 7-7f). It is also preferable to mention in the instruction letter that the collection is subject to URC 522.

7-7e Acceptance

Trade Acceptance

The responsibilities of the presenting bank generally stop at notifying the importer that the documents have arrived and at requesting that the importer endorse the draft (D/A) or at requesting payment (D/P) before releasing the documents. In those cases, this process is called **trade acceptance**—sometimes "trader's acceptance"—as the importer has control over the decision to accept or reject the draft and over the timing of the endorsement.

This could be somewhat inconvenient for the exporter, as the importer could delay acceptance of the draft for an inordinate amount of time—a problem that can be solved with a date draft—or even refuse to sign the draft. In such a case, the exporter still has title but over merchandise that is warehoused in a foreign country. The costs associated with warehousing goods in an unknown location, as well as the risks of pilferage and the exporter's difficulties in arranging for such storage, can lead unscrupulous importers to take advantage of the situation by extorting better terms from the exporter (e.g., a discounted price, given the costs of repatriating the goods) before signing the draft. This is a strategy that would work only once, but an unscrupulous importer could attempt to follow it.

Banker's Acceptance and Aval

The problems presented by a trade acceptance can be solved by requesting a **banker's acceptance**. In this case, it is the presenting bank that endorses the draft on behalf of the importer. The bank will usually endorse the draft immediately upon receipt of the documents, and the endorsement of the bank engages the responsibility of the importer: It signs on behalf of the importer. The presenting bank is unlikely to offer a banker's acceptance unless it feels in a position to "aval" the draft.

An **aval** is a promise by the presenting bank that the importer will honor the draft and that, should the importer default, the bank will make the payment. The bank therefore acts as a "co-signer" of the draft.

Although an aval is theoretically independent and different from a banker's acceptance, in practice the latter is often used as a substitute for aval. Therefore the remitting bank will often offer credit to an exporter based upon a "banker's acceptance," as it understands that the credit risk is now based upon the creditworthiness of the presenting bank, which is a situation almost as good as that of a letter of credit, but at a lower cost.

7-7f URC 522

The International Chamber of Commerce publishes guidelines for documentary collections in its Uniform Rules for Collections (URC 522).[28]

The main benefit of these rules is that they outline specifically the responsibilities of the remitting bank and the responsibilities of the presenting bank, as well as the limits of their responsibilities. For example, the presenting bank has to make sure that it promptly notifies the importer to come in to sign the draft (D/A) and is responsible for making sure that the draft is signed properly (according to local laws), but it has no obligation to determine that the person has the authority to sign. All of these obligations (and limitations) are very well described and explained in the Commentary on URC 522.[29]

---

trade acceptance In a documentary collection transaction, the alternative whereby the exporter expects the importer to readily accept signing a draft after being notified by the presenting bank that the documents have arrived.

banker's acceptance In a documentary collection transaction, the alternative whereby the exporter is not certain that the importer will readily accept signing a draft after being notified by the presenting bank that the documents have arrived. It therefore asks the presenting bank to "accept" the draft on behalf of the importer.

aval In a documentary collection transaction, the fact that a presenting bank is willing to sign the draft on behalf of the importer.

One issue that is quite clear (and a change from the previous Uniform Rules for Collections [URC 322]) is the inclusion of an obligatory instruction letter to the presenting bank, which clarifies what the presenting bank has to do with the documents. Because URC 522 is becoming the international standard for documentary collection—although it has not reached the universal nature of UCP 600—it is advisable to always state in the instruction letter that the collection is subject to the Uniform Rules for Collections (URC 522) of the International Chamber of Commerce.

7-7g Applicability

Documentary collections are a good way to conduct international sales because they are clearly less cumbersome (and less expensive) than letters of credit and provide a good amount of safety. The title remains in the hands of the exporter until the importer accepts the draft (D/A) or makes payment (D/P). This risk is further reduced if a banker's acceptance is requested.

However, documentary collections represent more risk for the exporter than a letter of credit because payment is dependent upon the primary transaction (the contract of sale); the importer could refuse to sign the draft (invoking poor-quality merchandise, for example) or delay signing the draft (until it has resold the merchandise), in which case the exporter retains title but does not get paid. A letter of credit, however, is not dependent on the primary transaction, but only on the documents; it will ensure payment as long as the documents are in the proper form.

A documentary collection could be used for customers in which there is a fair amount of trust but for which an open-account transaction is out of the question for whatever reason. A banker's acceptance could be used for customers who refuse to conduct business on a letter of credit basis and about whose creditworthiness the exporter is uncertain.

7-8 Forfaiting

In those cases where the importer wants credit terms that are beyond what the exporter is comfortable giving—for example, a five-year term is requested on a piece of machinery when the exporter can extend only a 180-day credit—there is the possibility of using **international forfaiting** as a means to extend this credit. In an international transaction, forfaiting is generally achieved with the help of a series of drafts from the importer, which have been given an aval by the importer's bank. Forfaiting is used for longer credit terms than factoring, which tends to be used for credit terms of up to 180 days. In contrast, forfaiting can be used for terms as long as seven years.

international forfaiting
A means of financing an international transaction in which an exporter collects a series of drafts from the importer and sells them to a forfaiting firm who buys them without recourse.

The exporter, once it has obtained an agreement from the forfaiting firm, will obtain this series of drafts, all with different due dates from the importer. It will then sell this series of drafts to the forfaiting firm at a discount. The forfaiting firm purchases them without recourse, which means it cannot hold the exporter responsible for non-payment by the importer. Forfaiting is an arrangement that usually satisfies the credit requirements of the importer at no risk—and at a fairly moderate cost—to the exporter.

7-9 Procurement Cards

A number of banks are offering a system of credit cards for their corporate accounts. The product originates from the observation that companies purchase myriad small items, from office supplies to small maintenance parts. In most instances, the traditional process to purchase these parts is through a centralized purchasing department that issues a purchase order, processes a significant amount of paperwork, and then pays an invoice. The idea of a procurement card is to allow a department to make certain purchases directly from a vendor, which is a much more expedient process. The procurement card is similar in concept to a consumer's credit card; it has a certain credit limit, it is billed directly to the department (or at least can provide an itemized billing statement showing which department is responsible for a specific purchase), and most importantly, it allows transactions to be conducted extremely rapidly. Moreover, the supplier is paid immediately—minus a certain transaction percentage, in the neighborhood of 2 percent—and the customer is billed at the end of the month.

Most procurement cards are used for domestic purchases, but there are several advantages to using a procurement card for international purchases. The first is that the exporter is essentially paid "in advance," because it is paid almost immediately after the goods have been shipped. The second is that the exchange rate on the transaction is essentially the best one can get: Because the banks process many transactions worth millions of dollars on the same date, the exchange rate is the one that such large transactions can earn. Finally, the importer has some sort of recourse (in a way similar to a consumer using a Visa or American Express card) if the merchandise is defective. It should be expected that this type of transaction will increasingly take place in international business, particularly for small items (maintenance parts) and will facilitate the handling of rush orders, which will increase the level of customer service a company can offer from its home country.

This product seems to present only advantages, and the number of banks currently offering such a service is increasing rapidly. However, one issue that has recently affected negatively the use of procurement cards is the way that banks have modified their foreign exchange procedures. In 2005, many of the banks that offer procurement cards changed their policies on currency exchange and added a fee on foreign currency transactions that can vary from 1 to 3 percent of the value of the transaction. This additional cost negates the advantageous exchange rates that procurement cards can offer. Another slight disadvantage is that the exchange rate in effect on the processing date may differ from the rate on the date used for the transaction, resulting in a slightly different currency exchange rate than was initially anticipated. As of May 2009, there was still one notable exception: Capital One in the United States and Britain did not charge a foreign transaction fee.

7-10 TradeCard

Created by the World Trade Centers Association in 1994, TradeCard is a proprietary electronic system that is gaining greater acceptance in the trade community and is an alternative that combines the advantages of letters of credit and of procurement cards:

- No payment is made until all the documents are in order and there are no discrepancies.
- The buyer is obligated to pay if the documents are in order.
- The system is expedient (payment is received quickly).

TradeCard also has two advantages over both of these methods of payment in that it is extremely inexpensive—charging only $150 for a transaction up to $100,000, in contrast to 1 to 3 percent for letters of credit and 2 to 3 percent for procurement cards—and combines document handling as well as payments.

TradeCard encompasses several electronic tools. First, it has a secure system for the transmission of documents, from the *pro forma* invoice to the bill of lading, packing list, and other transportation documents. It also has a system that checks the credit-worthiness of the customer and, should the importer be deemed creditworthy, guarantees payment to the exporter if the documents conform. This service is offered through a partnership with COFACE. Finally, TradeCard has a system that automatically settles invoices once the documents have been found to be in order and without discrepancies.

Unfortunately, TradeCard has still not achieved "critical mass" (a significant enough number of customers), and therefore, as of 2009, despite its gains, it remains an unusual form of payment in international trade, far behind letters of credit, documentary collections, and open accounts. When an exporter suggests a payment on TradeCard, it is unlikely that the importer already has an account with TradeCard, and therefore it is unlikely that the transaction will be completed under this term of sale. The reciprocal is also true: A savvy importer may have a TradeCard account, but the exporter may not have one. Add to this issue the fact that importers and exporters often ask their bankers for advice in such matters, and that the latter are generally quite conservative in their recommendations, and it becomes clear why this method of payment has not gained as much momentum as was originally anticipated. Nevertheless, TradeCard presents such advantages over the other forms of international payment that it should be expected to become the dominant method of payment in the 2010s.

7-11 Bank Guarantees

7-11a Definition

A **bank guarantee** is another instrument used in international trade, but in different situations. A bank guarantee is usually requested to secure the performance of the seller (exporter), rather than to ensure that payment will be made by the buyer (importer). This requirement happens in cases in which the exporter is a company contracting to build a plant, establish a drilling platform, or install a sewer system; for example, companies like Bechtel and Bouygues. A bank guarantee is applicable to all long-term contracts in which the importer wants to ensure that the work will be brought to completion. Frequently, the bank guarantee is offered by a group of banks rather than a single bank, because of the amounts involved. Finally, a bank guarantee is usually for an amount that is only a fraction of the total amount of the contract.

Like a letter of credit, a bank guarantee is an independent contract between the bank giving the guarantee (**guarantor**) and the beneficiary.

7-11b Guarantee Payable on First Demand (at First Request)

A bank guarantee payable at first request is one in which the beneficiary does not have to provide any evidence that the terms of the underlying contract between the **contractor** and the beneficiary have not been met; the issuing bank has to pay at the first request of the beneficiary, solely upon the presentation of a request for payment, sometimes accompanied by a statement from the beneficiary stating that the contractor is not meeting its obligations. No other proof is necessary. This type of bank guarantee is the most common one.

7-11c Guarantees Based upon Documents—Cautions

In some cases, a guarantee can be made conditional upon presentation of certain documents rather than "on first demand." The beneficiary must present documents that demonstrate that the contractor is not meeting its obligations; such a document may be a ruling by a court, or some other evidence as agreed upon in the terms of the guarantee.

The International Chamber of Commerce has issued a series of conventions regarding documentary bank guarantees in Publication No. 325, *Uniform Rules for*

bank guarantee A contract from a bank whereby the bank guarantees that an exporter will perform as required by its contract with the importer. If the exporter does not perform, the bank pays a compensation to the importer. Bank guarantees are illegal in the United States.

guarantor The bank that provides a bank guarantee. If the party to which it provides a guarantee does not perform, the bank pays a compensation to the injured party.

contractor When used in the context of a bank guarantee, a company fulfilling a large construction contract, usually the construction of a substantial infrastructure work or a major project.

Contract Guarantees. These rules are not widely used,[30] primarily because documentary guarantees are rarely used.

7-11d Stand-By Letters of Credit

Because U.S. law prohibits bank guarantees, American banks instead offer the same type of financial instrument through stand-by letters of credit. The only difference between a stand-by letter of credit and a bank guarantee is that the stand-by letter of credit is always *documentary* (i.e., the beneficiary must present a document before collecting from the bank). A simple statement that the contractor is not performing is usually considered sufficient.[31]

7-11e Types of Bank Guarantees

Several types of bank guarantees—or stand-by letters of credit—are available:

- The tender guarantee or bid guarantee is one that is requested by a beneficiary to ensure that the contractor is bidding in good faith and will enter the contract if awarded.
- The performance guarantee is the most commonly used type of guarantee and is used to ensure that the contractor finishes the project.
- The maintenance guarantee is used to ensure that the contractor performs the services necessitated by the contract after the completion of the project (i.e., maintenance and after-sale service).
- The advance payment guarantee or repayment guarantee is used to ensure that payments made by the beneficiary in advance of the work (to enable the contractor to purchase supplies or machinery) would be reimbursed if the contractor fails to start the project.
- The payment guarantee is used in a very different context. It covers the obligations of the buyer (often a distributor) toward the exporter, and is presented in Section 7-6d.

7-12 Terms of Payment as a Marketing Tool

An exporter has several alternatives from which to choose in negotiating terms of payment with the importer. Although the choice of the term of sale is dependent on the level of experience of both the exporter and the importer and on the level of confidence that the exporter has in the ability of the importer to make the payment, there are some alternatives that are definitely preferable and will increase an exporter's probability to clinch the sale.

An importer, in most situations, is getting several possible quotes from several exporters located in different countries. For example, a Brazilian newspaper looking to replace a printing press will seek bids from a number of suppliers, who could very well be located in the United States, Germany, Japan, Switzerland, Taiwan, and Canada. Although the alternative bids are likely to be evaluated on a large combination of criteria (price, specific capabilities, after-sale service, delivery terms, credit terms, financing, and so on), one of the issues will be the ease with which the purchase transaction will take place. From the importer's perspective, the easiest alternative—and the one that does not demand that cash flow be affected—is to purchase on an open-account basis. It is likely that at least one of the potential suppliers will offer such terms, and that others will ask for a letter of credit. Therefore, the supplier offering an open-account transaction has an advantage over the others and, if it has purchased credit insurance, has not affected its probability of getting paid.

A quick review of Table 7-6[32] shows that, even if there are some regions of the world in which letters of credit are still playing a significant role, in just about all cases,

TABLE 7-6	Percentage (%) of Transactions Conducted on a Letter of Credit (given the location of the importer)	
	European Union [15]	9
	Rest of Europe	20
	North America	11
	Latin America	27
	Middle East	52
	Asia-Pacific	43
	Africa	49
	Asia	46
	Australia-New Zealand	17
	Source: Sitpro.	

more than half of all transactions and more than 90 percent of the transactions in which the importer is located in the fifteen original European Union countries or North America are conducted using some other means of payment. Although no specific information is known, it is likely that the rank order of the other methods of payment are:

1. Open account (with or without credit insurance)
2. Documentary collection
3. Procurement cards (for smaller purchases)
4. TradeCard (for larger purchases)
5. Cash in advance

An exporter intent on increasing its sales should choose to display that it is confident in the ability of the importer to pay for the goods by using an open account. After all, this is the way its domestic sales are conducted—and generally the way many other competing exporters are intent on selling. If the exporter is unsure about the ability of the importer to pay, it should consider purchasing a credit insurance policy.

Review and Discussion Questions

1. Why is it more difficult and riskier to collect receivables from a foreign purchaser?

2. What are the differences between political risks and commercial risks of non-payment?

3. Describe the concept of cash in advance.

4. Describe the process of documentary collection.

5. Describe the mechanism of a letter of credit, from the exchange of the *pro forma* invoice to final payment.

6. What is credit insurance? Why is it associated with open-account transactions?

7. Several people claim that letters of credit will soon be replaced by the concept of TradeCard. What is this product, and why do those people think it has such a bright future?

8. Describe the concept of bank guarantees. What are the different types of bank guarantees?

Endnotes

1. Stecklow, Steve, and Jonathan Karp, "Citibank in India Used Collectors Accused of Strong-Arm Tactics," *Wall Street Journal*, May 5, 1999, p. A1.
2. Kritzer, Albert, "CISG: Table of Contracting States," Pace Law School Institute of International Commercial Law, http://www.cisg.law.pace.edu/cisg/countries/cntries.html, accessed May 19, 2009.
3. Freedman, Michael, "Judgment Day: U.S. Companies Complain They Can't Get a Fair Shake from America's Plaintiff-Friendly Juries. Try Resolving a Dispute in Russia, Indonesia, or Ukraine," *Forbes*, June 7, 2004, pp. 97–98.
4. Dolven, Ben, "Foreign Investors Find that China's Legal System Resolves Few Disputes," *Wall Street Journal*, April 7, 2003, p. A14.

5. Chrisafis, Angelique, "France faces revolt over poverty in its Caribbean Islands," *The Guardian*, February 12, 2009, http://www.guardian.co.uk/world/2009/feb/12/france-revolts-guadeloupe-martinique.

6. Bremner, Charles, "Sarkozy in Iraq as his woes pile up in France," *The Times*, February 10, 2009, http://timescorrespondents.typepad.com/charles_bremner/2009/02/sarkozy-in-iraq-as-his-woes-pile-up-in-france.html.

7. Yardley, William, "Union's War Protest Shuts Down West Coast Ports," *New York Times*, May 2, 2008, http://www.nytimes.com/2008/05/02/us/02port.html.

8. Ministère du Budget, des Comptes Publics et de la Fonction Publique, *Rapport Annuel sur l'Etat de la Fonction Publique: Faits et Chiffres 2007–2008*, Volume 1, p. 591, http://lesrapports.ladocumentationfrancaise.fr/BRP/084000616/0000.pdf, accessed May 24, 2009.

9. Shoenmakers, Y. M. M., E. De Vries Robbé, and Anton Van Vijk, *Mountains of Gold: An Exploratory Research on Nigerian 419 Fraud: Backgrounds.* SWP Publishers, Amsterdam: SWP Publishers, 2009.

10. *Business Planet: Mapping the Business Environment*, The World Bank Group, http://rru.worldbank.org/businessplanet.

11. *Exporters' Encyclopaedia*, Dun & Bradstreet, May 2009.

12. Kansas Department of Commerce—Trade Development, "International Credit Reports," http://kdoch.state.ks.us/KDOCHdocs/TD/CofaceInternationalCreditReportsFlier.pdf, accessed May 24, 2009.

13. Banham, Russ, "Credit Clout: Export Credit Insurance Offers Low-Cost Insurance that Protects Shippers from Non-Payment," *International Business*, March 1997, pp. 8–44.

14. Pereira, Ray, "International Factoring: The Viable Financing Alternative," *World Trade*, December 1999, pp. 68–69.

15. *Trade Finance Guide: a Quick Reference for U.S. Exporters*, U.S. Department of Commerce, International Trade Administration, April 2008, http://www.ita.doc.gov/media/Publications/pdf/tfg2008.pdf.

16. "UPS Capital Cargo Finance," United Parcel Service, http://www.upscapital.com/solutions/cargo_finance.html, accessed October 13, 2008.

17. Wood, Jeffrey, "Drafting Letters of Credit; Basic Issues under Article 5 of the Uniform Commercial Code, UCP 600 and ISP 98," *Banking Law Journal*, February 2008, pp. 103–149.

18. *Uniform Customs and Practices for Documentary Credits*, 2007 Revision, Publication No. 600 of the International Chamber of Commerce, ICC Publishing S.A., 38 Cours Albert 1er, 75008 Paris, France and ICC Publishing, 156 Fifth Avenue, New York, NY 10010.

19. *User's Handbook for Documentary Credits under UCP 600*, Publication No. 694 of the International Chamber of Commerce, ICC Publishing S.A., 38 Cours Albert 1er, 75008 Paris, France and ICC Publishing, 156 Fifth Avenue, New York, NY 10010.

20. *Uniform Rules for Bank-to-Bank Reimbursements under Documentary Credits* [URR 725], 2008, publication No. 725 of the International Chamber of Commerce, ICC Publishing S.A., 38 Cours Albert 1er, 75008 Paris, France and ICC Publishing, 156 Fifth Avenue, New York, NY 10010.

21. Adapted from "Report on the Use of Export Letters of Credit 2001/2002," dated April 11, 2003, Sitpro, *Simplifying International Trade*, http://sitpro.org.uk/reports/lettcredr, accessed May 25, 2009.

22. Tyler, Joseph W., "Financing Exports," in *Export Practice: Customs and International Trade Law*, Terence P. Stewart, ed., Practicing Law Institute, New York: Practicing Law Institute, 1994.

23. Bertrams, R. I. V. F., *Bank Guarantees in International Trade*, Kluwer Law and Taxation Publishers, Deventer, The Netherlands, 1990.

24. *International Standby Practices, ISP98*, Institute of International Banking Law and Practice, Inc., Publication No. 590 of the International Chamber of Commerce, ICC Publishing S.A., 38 Cours Albert 1er, 75008 Paris, France and ICC Publishing, 156 Fifth Avenue, New York, NY 10010.

25. *Uniform Rules for Collection [URC 522]*, 1995, publication No. 522 of the International Chamber of Commerce, ICC Publishing S.A., 38 Cours Albert 1er, 75008 Paris, France and ICC Publishing, 156 Fifth Avenue, New York, NY 10010.

26. Reynolds, Frank, "Use Caution with Semi-Secured Terms," *The Journal of Commerce*, October 20, 1999, p. 10.

27. *Uniform Rules for Collection [URC 522]*, 1995, publication No. 522 of the International Chamber of Commerce, ICC Publishing S.A., 38 Cours Albert 1er, 75008 Paris, France and ICC Publishing, 156 Fifth Avenue, New York, NY 10010.

28. *Ibid.*

29. *Commentary on the ICC Uniform Rules for Collections*, 1995, Publication No. 550 of the International Chamber of Commerce, ICC Publishing S.A., 38 Cours Albert 1er, 75008 Paris, France and ICC Publishing, 156 Fifth Avenue, New York, NY 10010.

30. Bertrams, R. I. V. F., *Bank Guarantees in International Trade*, Kluwer Law and Taxation Publishers, Deventer, The Netherlands, 1990.

31. *Ibid.*

32. "Ninth Survey of International Services Provided to Exporters," commissioned by the Institute of Exporters, and reproduced in the *"Report on the Use of Export Letters of Credit 2001/2002,"* dated April 11, 2003, Sitpro, Simplifying International Trade, http://sitpro.org.uk/reports/lettcredr, accessed June 1, 2006.

Currency of Payment (Managing Transaction Risks)*

Chapter Outline

Key Terms

* The authors would like to thank Earl Peck, Ph.D, Baldwin-Wallace College, for his assistance in preparing this chapter.

The previous chapters have shown that, for each international sale, the exporter and the importer must agree on two particular points:

term of trade An element in a contract of sale that specifies the responsibilities of the exporter and of the importer.

- The **terms of trade** under which the sale is conducted (i.e., the costs the exporter should pay, the costs the importer should pay, and the point at which the responsibility for the cargo shifts from one to the other). These responsibilities are determined by the Incoterm chosen.

term of sale An element in a contract of sale that specifies the method of payment to which an exporter and an importer have agreed.

- The **terms of sale** under which the transaction is performed (i.e., at what point in the transaction the exporter wants to be paid, and what its level of confidence is in the ability of the importer to pay). The exporter and the importer can choose any number of alternatives, from cash in advance to an open-account transaction to a TradeCard.

currency The monetary unit used in a particular country for economic transactions.

However, there is still one more issue for the exporter and the importer to consider: the **currency** under which this transaction is undertaken. There are three alternatives possible: the exporter country's currency, the importer country's currency, or a third country's currency.

Figure 8-1
Banknotes of the World
Source: Photo © Pierre David.

Choice of Currency: When the Exporter Carries the Exchange Rate Risk

The choice of a currency is a fundamental aspect of the sale. It can substantially affect the profitability of a sale for an exporter. Take for example a sale for $1,000,000 on which an exporter was expecting to generate a 10 percent profit margin; its total costs are therefore $900,000 and its expected profits are $100,000.

Suppose the exporter and importer agree to conduct this transaction in the importer's currency, the European euro. The exporter will then be the one assuming the exchange rate risk. Assuming that the exchange rate at the time of the sale is U.S. $1.2761/€; the exporter bills the importer for €783,637.65.

If the value of the euro declines by 2 percent by the time the actual payment is made, about a month later, then the exchange rate at that time will be $1.2506/€. When the customer pays the invoice for €783,637.65, the U.S. exporter converts that amount of money into U.S. dollars and collects $980,017.24, assuming, for the sake of this example, that there are no banking fees collected. The importer pays exactly what had been agreed, and carries no currency fluctuation risk whatsoever.

The $100,000 profit that the exporter was anticipating has been reduced to $80,017.24 ($980,017.24 – 900,000), which is about 20 percent less than what it had anticipated.

The reverse can also happen: The profitability of the exporter can be drastically affected by an increase in the value of the currency that it uses to pay for its merchandise. For example, if the exchange rate had changed the "other way," and the euro had increased in value by 2 percent, the new exchange rate would have been $1.3016, which means that the U.S. exporter, after collecting his €783,637.65, would have been able to convert the currency into $1,019,982.77, for a profit of $119,982.77, an increase of roughly 20 percent.

8-1 Sales Contract's Currency of Quote

In the choice of a currency for a given transaction, two factors should be considered:

- **The risk of currency fluctuation**. This is a speculative risk, that is, one for which there is the possibility of a gain or a loss, depending on which "way" the exchange rate fluctuates and on who, of the exporter or the importer, is holding the currency risk. If the transaction is conducted in the exporter's currency, then the importer is the one who is carrying the **exchange rate risk**. If the transaction is conducted in the importer's currency, it is the exporter who is assuming the exchange rate risk. The two vignettes illustrate this point.

- **The convertibility of the currency**. This is a pure risk that reflects the degree to which a currency can be converted into other currencies. Major countries' currencies are fully convertible—they are called **hard currencies**—and these currencies can be freely exchanged, at a moment's notice: They are also called **convertible currencies**.

  However, some developing countries' currencies are not readily convertible into hard currencies, because the country has few exports and its government controls which imports get paid first. The ability to convert a currency into hard currency is generally measured in "months of foreign exchange cover," or an approximation of the size of the hard currency stock a given country has, expressed in months of import activities this stock can cover. In most cases, the lack of convertibility of the currency just delays the date at which it can be exchanged for hard currency. All currencies that are difficult to convert into hard currencies are called **soft currencies**.

  In some rare cases, the currency is not convertible at all (i.e., the currency cannot be exchanged for any other currency, at any time), or more commonly, the currency has a different exchange rate for purchases and for sales. Finally, some currencies can be purchased but not sold. All of these currencies are collectively called **inconvertible currencies**.

exchange rate risk The risk represented by the fluctuation in exchange rates between the time at which two companies entered in an international contract and the time at which that contract is paid.

hard currency A currency that can easily be converted into another currency.

convertible currency A currency that can be converted into another currency.

soft currency A currency that cannot be easily converted into another currency.

inconvertible currency A currency that cannot be converted into another currency.

Choice of Currency: When the Importer Carries the Exchange Rate Risk

The first textbox was an example of a sale for which the exporter assumed the currency fluctuation risk. If the exporter and the importer had agreed to conduct the transaction in the exporter's currency (U.S. dollars) rather than in the importer's currency (euros), then the importer would have assumed the exchange rate risk.

For the sake of simplification, take the same sale on which the exporter is expecting to generate a 10 percent profit margin. Its selling price is $1,000,000, its total costs are $900,000, and its expected profits are $100,000.

Suppose also that the exchange rate at the time of the sale is still $1.2761/€, the same as it was in the previous example. The exporter bills the importer for $1,000,000 and the importer equates this amount to a payment of €783,637.65.

If, as in the previous example, the value of the euro declines 2 percent by the time the actual payment is made,

about a month later, the exchange rate will be $1.2506/€. When the customer pays the invoice for $1,000,000, the U.S. exporter collects exactly what it had anticipated, but the importer needs to supply its bank with €799,616.18, assuming, for the sake of this example, that there are no banking fees collected.

The importer had anticipated to pay €783,637.65 for these goods, but it actually has to pay €799,616.18, which is about 2 percent more.

The reverse can also happen: The cost for the importer can be lower if the value of the importing country's currency increases. For example, if the euro had increased 2 percent, the exchange rate would have been $1.3016, which means that the importer, in order to pay the $1,000,000 that it owes the exporter, would have needed to convert only €768,285.19, a 2 percent decrease.

Figure 8-2a
The Euro Currency
Source: Photo © European Central Bank. Used with permission.

The three alternative currency possibilities for an international transaction—exporter, importer, and third-country currency—are summarized in the following sections.

8-1a Exporter's Currency

In this first case, the exporter and the importer agree that the currency of the transaction will be the currency of the exporter's country. For example, if the exporter is located in Germany and the importer is located in Colombia, then the transaction takes place in euros, the currency of (most of) the European Union.

In this case, the exchange rate risk is nil for the exporter; all of the risks are borne by the importer, and it has to determine how it will handle its transaction risks. In addition, the possible convertibility problems of the currency are to be resolved by the importer. In this particular case, because the Colombian peso is fully convertible, this is not an issue.

8-1b Importer's Currency

In this case, the exporter and the importer determine that the currency of the transaction will be the currency of the importer's country. For example, if the exporter is located in Jordan and the importer is located in the United States, then the transaction takes place in U.S. dollars, the currency of the United States.

In this case, the exchange rate risk is nil for the importer; all of the risks are borne by the exporter, and it has to determine how it will handle its transaction risks. It is also ultimately responsible for converting the currency so that any convertibility problem will have to be resolved by the exporter. In this particular case, there is no issue, as the Jordanian dinar is fully convertible.

8-1c Third Country's Currency

Finally, the exporter and the importer can agree that the currency of the transaction will be a third country's currency. For example, if the exporter is located in Thailand

and the importer is located in India, they may decide to use the U.S. dollar as the currency of the transaction.

This alternative presents several advantages for both the exporter and the importer. For example, they each bear the risks of currency fluctuation of their respective country's currency against the currency of the transaction. In this example, the exporter is responsible for the fluctuations of the baht against the dollar, and the importer is responsible for the fluctuations of the rupee against the dollar.

In some cases, the exporter and the importer choose an artificial currency (a non-circulating currency) for a transaction, such as the **Special Drawing Rights (SDRs)** of the International Monetary Fund (IMF), which are sometimes used for international contracts; such is the case of the liability conventions of the ocean shipping industry (see Chapter 11, Section 11-5).

All three of these alternatives present challenges and call for some form of management of the risks presented by exchange rates.

8-1d The Special Status of the Euro

The **euro** was first created as an artificial currency; in its early years, when it was known as the European Currency Unit (ECU), its value was determined by the value of a basket consisting of the various currencies of the European Union. When it was officially unveiled as the euro in 1999, its value was fixed in terms of each of the 11 (later 12) currencies of the participating EU countries. Only in January 2002 did it become a circulating currency, losing its status as an artificial currency. When four other countries adopted the euro, their legacy currency's value was also translated using a fixed currency exchange rate with the euro.

The euro is a unique case as a truly international currency; not only has it become the official domestic currency of 16 of the European Union countries, but it is also used for all of the intra-European trade in the Eurozone and is therefore a currency used extensively to settle international debts. The stated goal of the European Union is to eventually transform the euro into a challenger to the U.S. dollar as the preferred third-country currency.

Table 8-1 lists the rates at which the legacy currencies of the European Union countries were converted to the dollar, and Table 8-2[1] lists the status of the conversion for the 11 countries of the European Union that have not yet adopted the euro.

Special Drawing Right (SDR) An artificial currency of the International Monetary Fund. Its value is determined by the value of a basket of four currencies: the euro, the Japanese yen, the U.S. dollar, and the British pound.

euro The common currency of 16 of the 27 countries of the European Union.

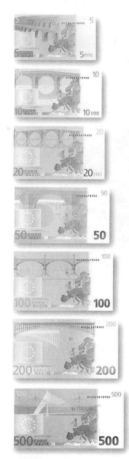

Figure 8-2b
The Euro Currency
Source: Photo © European Central Bank. Used with permission.

TABLE 8-1	Value of the Euro to Legacy National Currencies	
Currency	**Fixed Exchange Rate**	**Date of Determination**
Belgium (franc)	40.3399 BEF	December 31, 1998
Germany (mark)	1.95583 DEM	December 31, 1998
Spain (peseta)	166.386 ESP	December 31, 1998
France (franc)	6.55957 FRF	December 31, 1998
Ireland (punt)	0.787564 IEP	December 31, 1998
Italy (lira)	1936.27 ITL	December 31, 1998
Luxembourg (franc)	40.3399 LUF	December 31, 1998
The Netherlands (guilder)	2.20371 NLG	December 31, 1998
Austria (schilling)	13.7603 ATS	December 31, 1998
Portugal (escudo)	200.482 PTE	December 31, 1998
Finland (markka)	5.94573 FIM	December 31, 1998
Greece (drachma)	340.750 GRD	June 19, 2000
Slovenia (tolar)	239.640 SIT	July 11, 2006
Cyprus (pound)	0.585274 CYP	July 10, 2007
Malta (lira)	0.4293 MTL	July 10, 2007
Slovakia (koruna)	30.126 SKK	July 8, 2008

| TABLE 8-2 | European Countries That Have Not (Yet) Adopted the Euro |

Country (currency)	Status
Bulgaria (lev)	Bulgaria plans to adopt the euro on January 1, 2012. The lev is pegged to the euro.
Czech Republic (koruna)	The Czech Republic will probably not adopt the euro until 2015. The Czech koruna does not participate in the ERM-II system.
Denmark (markka)	Denmark rejected the euro by referendum on September 28, 2002. Another vote is expected in 2010–2011. The markka is part of the ERM-II system (semi-pegged to the euro).
Estonia (kroon)	Estonia will adopt the euro on January 1, 2011. The kroon is pegged to the euro.
Hungary (forint)	Hungary plans to adopt the euro on January 1, 2011. The forint is not part of the ERM-II system.
Latvia (latvian)	Latvia plans to adopt the euro on January 1, 2012. The latvian is part of the ERM-II system (semi-pegged to the euro).
Lithuania (litas)	Lithuania will adopt the euro on January 1, 2010. The litas is part of the ERM-II system (semi-pegged to the euro).
Poland (zloty)	Poland has plans to introduce the euro as of January 1, 2011. The zloty is not part of the ERM-II system, so this introduction is likely to be delayed.
Romania (leu)	Romania will adopt the euro on January 1, 2014. The leu is not part of the ERM-II system.
Sweden (krona)	Sweden rejected the euro by referendum on September 13, 2003. The krona is not part of the ERM-II system.
United Kingdom (pound)	The United Kingdom is officially in favor of adopting the euro, but there are five economic tests that the UK economy must meet before the UK government decides on a change-over date.

ERM = Exchange Rate Mechanism

8-2 The System of Currency Exchange Rates

In order to manage exchange rate risks (the risks presented by currency exchange rate fluctuations), it is necessary to have a good understanding of the functioning of the system of exchange rates. Unfortunately, this section can only be a cursory review of the current knowledge in this area; the reader interested in obtaining a greater understanding of the field of international corporate finance should refer to any number of excellent textbooks in this field.[2,3,4,5]

8-2a Types of Exchange Rate Quotes

The exchange rate of two currencies is the value of one currency expressed in units of the second. For example, on May 25, 2009, the exchange rate for the euro against the U.S. dollar was \$1.4011/€ (i.e., one euro was worth U.S. \$1.4011).[6] As the *Wall Street Journal* defines it, the exchange rate is the midpoint between the bid and offer rates for exchanges of a value greater than \$1,000,000 between banks. The *Financial Times* published the midpoint, as well as the bid-offer spread.[7] The actual exchange rate offered to a company seeking to purchase euros would be different: It would have to pay more, say \$1.415, for every euro purchased. Reciprocally, the exchange rate offered to a company seeking to sell euros would be lower: It would collect less, say \$1.385, for every euro sold.

Traders in foreign exchange consider two ways to quote a currency:

direct quote The value of a foreign currency expressed in units of the domestic currency.

- The first way to value a currency is the **direct quote**, in which the value of the foreign currency is expressed in units of the domestic currency. For example, the direct quote for the euro in U.S. dollar terms would be \$1.4011/€ as of May 25, 2009. This is the preferred way of quoting the euro, the British pound, the Australian dollar, and the New Zealand dollar.

indirect quote The value of the domestic currency expressed in units of the foreign currency.

- The second way to value a currency is the **indirect quote**, in which the value of the domestic currency is expressed in units of foreign currency. For example, the indirect quote for the yen against the U.S. dollar would be ¥94.82/\$ as of May 25, 2009. Most currencies are traditionally expressed as indirect quotes—the Canadian dollar, the Swiss franc, and the Japanese yen, for example.

It should be self-evident that there is an inverse relationship between the two ways of quoting a currency exchange rate between two currencies:

$$\text{Direct quote} = \frac{1}{\text{Indirect quote}}$$

Spot Exchange Rate

The first type of exchange rate is the **spot exchange rate**, or the exchange rate for a foreign currency for immediate delivery. This "immediate delivery" is somewhat subject to interpretations that vary from country to country and, within one country, from one currency to another; however, it is (roughly) the price of a foreign currency to be delivered within 48 hours.

This is the exchange rate with which most international travelers are familiar. It is the one used by foreign exchange kiosks and banks all over the world (see Table 8-3).[8] Comprehensive spot currency exchange rates are published daily in the *Wall Street Journal* and many dailies; however, the *Financial Times* is the most comprehensive of all periodicals in that respect, and it quotes daily the spot currency exchange rates for more than 150 currencies against the U.S. dollar, the British pound, the European euro, and the Japanese yen.[9] These quotes are available for free.

Forward Exchange Rates

The second type of exchange rate is the **forward exchange rate**, or the exchange rate for a foreign currency to be delivered any number of days in the future. Financial newspapers such as the *Wall Street Journal* often publish forward exchange rate quotes for 30 days, 90 days, 180 days, or one year in the future. The party entering into a forward currency contract is committing to purchasing one currency with another at a certain price on a certain date. The exchange rate quotes given are the mid-points for transactions of U.S. $1,000,000 or more that take place between banks; the actual exchange rate obtainable by a company involved in international trade would be less favorable.

In the United States, the *Wall Street Journal* publishes only the forward rates for four currencies: the British pound, the Japanese yen, the Swiss franc, and the Canadian dollar. Surprisingly, as of May 2009, it was still not publishing forward rates for the European euro. However, there is a forward market for almost all currencies, and most forward rate quotes are published in the *Financial Times*, including the forward exchange rates for the Czech krona, the Indian rupee, and the Thai baht. Another difference between these two periodicals is that the *Wall Street Journal* publishes rates for 30, 90, and 180 days, but does not publish a one-year forward rate, whereas the *Financial Times* publishes 30- and 90-day and one-year rates, but not a 180-day rate (see Table 8-4).[10,11]

The **outright rate** is the rate at which a commercial customer purchases or sells a foreign currency forward. It is the exchange rate quote shown in Table 8-4.

However, in the interbank market, there is another way of quoting forward exchange rates, called the **swap rate**. Such a forward rate is expressed in **points** that must be subtracted or added to the spot rate in order to arrive at the forward exchange rate. A point is the unit of the last digit quoted: For example, if the spot exchange rate for the Japanese yen was $0.010546/¥ on a given date, and the forward swap rate for 180 days was expressed at a 22-point premium on the same day, then the 180-day forward exchange rate would be $0.010546 plus 0.000022, for a forward exchange rate quote of $0.010568/¥ for a delivery 180 days from that date.

A foreign currency swap refers to the practice of a simultaneous purchase of one currency on the spot market and the sale of the same currency, in the same amount, on the forward market. A foreign currency swap can also refer to the practice of purchasing and selling the same currency forward, but with two different maturity dates. That is, a swap transaction is either a spot transaction and a forward transaction,

spot exchange rate The exchange rate of a foreign currency for immediate delivery (within 48 hours).

forward exchange rate The exchange rate of a foreign currency for delivery in 30, 90, or 180 days from the date of the quote.

outright rate The exchange rate of a foreign currency for delivery in 30, 90, or 180 days from the date of the quote. The outright rate is the rate at which a commercial customer would purchase the currency.

swap rate The exchange rate of a foreign currency for delivery in 30, 90, or 180 days from the date of the quote. The swap rate is the difference between the current spot rate and the rate at which a commercial customer would purchase the currency. It is expressed in points that must be subtracted or added to the spot rate.

points In a forward exchange rate, the difference between the outright rate and the swap rate. Points are not fixed units; their value depends on the way a currency is expressed, but is the smallest decimal value in which that currency is traded.

TABLE 8-3   Selected Spot Rates for Foreign Currencies, May 25, 2009

Country	Currency	U.S. $ Equivalent (direct quote)	Currency per U.S. $ (indirect quote)
Argentina	Peso	0.2677	3.7355
Australia	Dollar	0.7820	1.2788
Brazil	Real	0.4945	2.0222
Canada	Dollar	0.8900	1.1236
Chile	Peso	0.001772	564.33
China	Renminbi/Yuan	0.1465	6.8239
Czech Republic	Koruna	0.05252	19.040
Denmark	Krone	0.1882	5.3135
Hong Kong	Dollar	0.1290	7.7512
Hungary	Forint	0.005001	199.96
India	Rupee	0.02115	47.281
Indonesia	Rupiah	0.0000972	10288
Israel	Shekel	0.2525	3.9604
Japan	Yen	0.01546	94.82
Jordan	Dinar	1.4114	0.7085
Kuwait	Dinar	3.4710	0.2881
Lebanon	Pound	0.000666	1501.50
Malaysia	Ringgit	0.2866	3.4892
Mexico	Peso	0.0761	13.1423
New Zealand	Dollar	0.6208	1.6108
Norway	Krone	0.1579	6.3331
Pakistan	Rupee	0.01246	80.257
Peru	New Sol	0.3324	3.008
Philippines	Peso	0.0212	47.081
Russia	Ruble	0.03225	31.008
Saudi Arabia	Riyal	0.2666	3.7509
Singapore	Dollar	0.6909	1.4474
South Africa	Rand	0.1214	8.2372
South Korea	Won	0.0008031	1245.17
Sweden	Krona	0.1335	7.4906
Switzerland	Franc	0.9233	1.0831
Taiwan	Dollar	0.03068	32.595
Thailand	Bhat	0.02909	34.376
Turkey	New Lira	0.6503	1.5379
United Kingdom	Pound	1.5913	0.6284
Venezuela	Bolivar fuerte	0.465701	2.1473
Special Drawing Rights	SDR	1.5401	0.6493
European Union	Euro	1.4011	0.7137

Source: The Wall Street Journal.

or two forward transactions.[12] The swap market is much larger than either the spot market or the forward market. This technique is used by banks and companies that have funds readily available in one currency and temporary needs in another currency; they exchange the currencies on the spot market and know at what exchange rate they will be able to change them back, at some pre-determined time in the future.

Currency Futures

Finally, some currencies are also traded in the **currency futures'** market as commodities. In the United States, futures for six currencies are traded on the Chicago Mercantile Exchange. A futures contract is an agreement between two parties: the seller (called the "short"), who promises to deliver the currency on a certain date, and

currency futures A method used to trade currencies; the value of a fixed quantity of foreign currency for delivery at a fixed point in the future is determined by market forces.

TABLE 8-4	Selected Forward Exchange Rates for Foreign Currency, May 25, 2009

Country	Currency	Delivery	U.S. $ Equivalent (direct quote)	Currency per U.S. $ (indirect quote)
Canada	Dollar	Spot	0.8900	1.1236
		Forward 30 days	0.8902	1.1233
		Forward 90 days	0.8906	1.1228
		Forward 180 days	0.8911	1.1222
Japan	Yen	Spot	0.010546	94.82
		Forward 30 days	0.010550	94.79
		Forward 90 days	0.010558	94.71
		Forward 180 days	0.010568	94.63
Switzerland	Franc	Spot	0.9233	1.0831
		Forward 30 days	0.9236	1.0827
		Forward 90 days	0.9243	1.0819
		Forward 180 days	0.9258	1.0801
United Kingdom	Pound	Spot	1.5913	0.6284
		Forward 30 days	1.5911	0.6285
		Forward 90 days	1.5907	0.6287
		Forward 180 days	1.5901	0.6289
European Union	Euro	Spot	1.4011	0.7137
		Forward 30 days	1.3982	0.7152
		Forward 90 days	1.3975	0.7156
		Forward 180 days	1.3959	0.7164

Source: The Wall Street Journal and Financial Times.

the buyer (called the "long"), who agrees to buy the currency at a price that is agreed upon ahead of time.

Futures contracts were first created for commodities other than currencies (such as corn or wheat) and fulfill very different purposes for the parties that use them. Generally, the contract takes place between a party that wants to limit its risk and a party that is speculating. For example, a farmer knows that he will be able to harvest a certain amount of corn; in order to limit his uncertainty regarding the price at which he will be able to sell this commodity, he enters into a futures contract, which obligates him to deliver a specified amount of corn on a certain date, at a set price. The other party to the contract is a speculator who is not interested in the corn at all but is intent on reselling it immediately to another party and speculates that the corn, on that date, will fetch a higher price than what he promised to pay the farmer.

Similarly, a company that uses wheat for a particular purpose may enter into a futures contract to make sure it can purchase a certain amount of that commodity on that date at a set price. The other party to the futures contract is a speculator who thinks that he can obtain the wheat on that date for less than what he can sell it to the company.

In the first case, the farmer is intent on minimizing his risk (for example, a bumper crop lowers the value of his corn), and in the second case, the company is looking to minimize its uncertainty regarding the price of one of its raw materials. In both cases, the speculator is taking the risk: If the corn supply is lower than what the market anticipated, he will be able to take delivery from the farmer at a price lower than the spot price and make money. In the second case, he makes money if the supply of wheat is larger than what the market anticipated, and he will make money. If he is incorrect, he loses money, but must make good on his promise to purchase the corn or sell the wheat.

There are two major differences between a forward contract and a futures contract as they apply to currency exchange rates:

1. The amount of the foreign currency for which a company can purchase futures is fixed; in the United States, they are only available in increments of 100,000

Australian dollars, 62,500 British pounds, 100,000 Canadian dollars, 125,000 euros, 5 million Japanese yen, and 500,000 Mexican pesos. This is in contrast with the forward market, in which any given amount can be purchased or sold.

2. The date at which the future has to be settled (purchased or sold) is fixed. In the United States, it is always the third Wednesday of the months of March, June, September, and December. This is in contrast with the forward market, in which any given date can be chosen in advance.

Because of this lack of flexibility, futures contracts for currencies are not used as frequently as forward contracts.

Currency Options

currency options A method used to speculate on the value of a currency in the future. A firm can purchase options to buy (called call options) or options to sell (called put options) a particular currency at a particular price, called the strike price, on a given date.

call options A currency option in which a firm agrees to buy a particular currency at a particular price, called the strike price, on a given date.

put options A currency option in which a firm agrees to sell a particular currency at a particular price, called the strike price, on a given date.

strike price The price at which a currency option is exercised.

In addition to the futures market, there is also a **currency options'** market, which takes place, in the United States, at the Philadelphia Stock Exchange's United Currency Options Market.

An option contract is quite different from a futures contract. In a futures contract, both parties are obligated to deliver (or buy) the currency on the date at which the futures contract is settled. In contrast, in the options market, the buyer of the option is purchasing the right (the option) to buy or sell a particular currency at a predetermined price. However, the buyer of the option does not have the obligation to exercise that option; it can decline to purchase or sell at that price. If the buyer of the option elects to exercise the option, however, the seller of the option is obligated to comply.

There are two types of options: **call options** and **put options**. A call option is the right to buy—but not the obligation to buy—a predetermined amount of foreign currency at a predetermined price (called the **strike price**) on a predetermined date. A put option is the right to sell—but not the obligation to sell—the same. If the buyer of the option decides not to exercise its option, it loses only the amount that it paid for that option. The seller of the option keeps the amount that it charged for the option, regardless of what the buyer decides to do.

To add to the complexity, there are two styles of options: The U.S.-style option gives a company the right to exercise its option at any time until the expiration date, while a European-style option allows it to exercise that option only on that date.

How Does the Options Market Work?

Call Options

A U.S. firm purchases a call option—the right to buy—British pounds on November 1 at a predetermined exchange rate of £1.00/U.S. $1.88; that price is called the strike price. The firm has to pay U.S. $4,000 for that option.

On November 1, it can exercise its call option and tell the seller of the option that it wants delivery of the currency, and the seller of the option has to comply. The buyer of the option does that only if the spot exchange rate of that currency on November 1 is higher than the agreed-upon strike price, say £1.00/U.S. $1.90, because buying British pounds on the spot market on that date would be more expensive than exercising the option. If the spot exchange rate were lower, say £1.00/U.S. $1.84, the buyer of the option would not exercise its option and would purchase the currency on the spot market instead; it would willingly forego what it had paid for the option, or U.S. $4,000.

Put Options

A German firm purchases a put option—the right to sell—European euros on December 1 at a predetermined exchange rate of €1.00/U.S. $1.26; that price is called the strike price. The firm has to pay €3,000 for that option.

On December 1, it can exercise its put option and tell the seller of the option that it wants the money for the currency, and the seller of the option has to comply (buy the currency from the German firm). The buyer of the option does that only if the spot exchange rate of that currency on December 1 is lower than the agreed-upon strike price, say €1.00/U.S. $1.24, because selling the euros on the spot market on that date would be more attractive than exercising the option. If the spot exchange rate were higher, say €1.00/U.S. $1.30, the buyer of the option would not exercise its option and would sell the currency on the spot market instead; it would willingly forego what it had paid for the option, or €3,000.

An option is priced by the "market" between companies wanting to purchase options and speculators and other companies that are selling options. Several mathematical models can be used in determining the pricing of options, but their complexity is beyond the scope of this textbook.

8-2b Types of Currencies

In determining the exchange rate risks carried by a specific transaction, it is helpful to determine the type of currency with which the exporter (or importer) is dealing. There are three types of currencies.

Floating Currencies

Floating currencies are foreign currencies whose value changes (or *can* change) continuously against other currencies. For example, the U.S. dollar continuously changes in value as it is traded between companies having dollars and companies wanting dollars; only the market determines its value. Figure 8-3 illustrates the exchange rate between the U.S. dollar and the European euro since the latter's creation in January 1999.[13] The countries representing the greatest percentage of world trade all have floating currencies.

The fact that a currency is floating does not always represent unpredictability for a company involved in international trade. Most currencies are relatively stable in their values in the short term. However, those currencies that are considered "volatile" (i.e., currencies that can experience a great deal of variation in their exchange rates from one day to the next) can present significant risk. Even though the euro has fluctuated substantially against the U.S. dollar—almost 100 percent, from a low of €1.00/U.S. $0.8270 on October 25, 2000, to a high of €1.00/U.S. $1.601 on April 22, 2008[14]—in the ten years since the euro's inception, neither the euro nor the U.S. dollar have been considered volatile currencies.

In order to squelch some of this volatility, currencies are sometimes "assisted" by their country's government, which intervenes in the foreign exchange markets in order to sustain the value of a currency. Such policies can be quite onerous for countries. In order to support the value of a currency, the government must purchase it in the market, and that is achieved only by selling foreign exchange, or the proceeds

floating currency A currency whose value is determined by market forces. The exchange rate of a floating currency varies frequently.

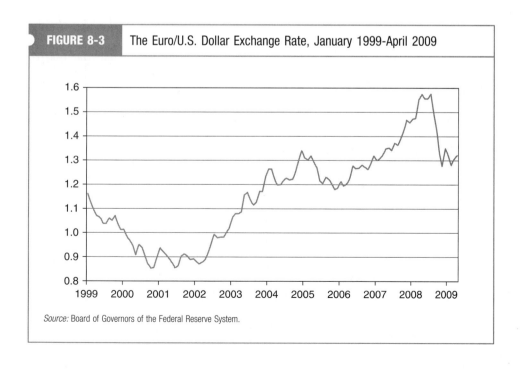

| FIGURE 8-3 | The Euro/U.S. Dollar Exchange Rate, January 1999–April 2009 |

Source: Board of Governors of the Federal Reserve System.

of export sales. George Soros made a fortune (more than $1 billion) by betting against the British pound in September 1992, at a time when the British government was intent on shoring up its value.

Most of the developed countries have currencies that are stable, that is, currencies for which it is reasonable to expect a predictable exchange rate. It's only under those conditions that an international firm will accept payment—or agree to pay—in that country's currency.

Pegged Currencies

pegged currency A currency whose value is determined by a fixed exchange rate with another, more widely traded currency.

A number of countries have been plagued with very volatile currencies. There are several reasons for this situation, most notably the lack of a sustained level of trade, giving rise to substantially varying demands on the currency from one month to the next. **Pegging a currency** makes it worth a fixed exchange rate relative to another, stronger currency. The exchange rate is therefore entirely predictable at any time. In most instances, the currency chosen is that of the greatest trading partner, and therefore it is often the U.S. dollar; such was the case of the Argentinean peso, which, until February 2002, was pegged to the U.S. dollar. It is now a floating currency.

dollarization A phenomenon whereby other countries decide to adopt the U.S. dollar as their circulating currency.

In some rare cases, the country can elect to completely eliminate its currency and replace it with the currency of another country altogether. This occurred in Panama and Ecuador, which both have adopted the U.S. dollar as their currency, a phenomenon dubbed the **dollarization** of these economies.

currency bloc A group of currencies whose values fluctuate in parallel fashion. The currencies within the group have a fixed exchange rate, but their exchange rates with currencies outside of the group float.

Floating Currency Blocs—European Monetary System

Finally, there is the case of countries that trade so much with each other that they decide to create a **currency bloc**. Such was the case of the European Monetary System (EMS), which eventually gave rise to the creation of the common currency of the European Union, the euro.

The EMS was designed in such a way that the currencies of the member countries would have to stay within a few percentage points of each other's value, a policy that was called the Exchange Rate Mechanism (ERM). In the beginning of this experiment, the maximum percentage variation allowed was 5 percent, and toward the end of the system, it was as low as 1 percent. Such variations were continuously controlled by the governments of the European countries, which intervened routinely in the foreign exchange markets. Such a system allowed the EMS currencies to float as a "bloc" against other non-EMS currencies, while maintaining a very stable foreign exchange environment within the European Union, a situation that greatly promoted trade among the Union members.

artificial currency A currency that is not in circulation. After the euro was changed into a circulating currency on January 1, 2002, the only artificial currency left was the Special Drawing Rights of the International Monetary Fund.

Eventually such a bloc can evolve into a fixed exchange rate between all the internal currencies. In Europe, the fixed exchange rates were established in terms of an **artificial currency**, the European Currency Unit (ECU), which was created in January 1999 and whose value was determined by the values of a basket of the internal currencies. The ECU was named the euro soon thereafter. Finally, on January 1, 2002, all internal currencies were eliminated and the European euro became the only circulating currency for 12 of the European countries (see Table 8-1). When the European Union was expanded on June 1, 2004, the original ERM was resurrected as ERM-II, and many of the new countries' currencies will eventually be replaced by the euro (see Table 8-2) after they meet certain requirements for admission and have been part of the ERM-II system for at least two years.

There are other currency blocs and common currencies in the planning stages as of May 2009. The Gulf Cooperation Council (GCC), encompassing Bahrain, Kuwait, Oman, Qatar, Saudi Arabia, and the United Arab Emirates, has proposed the creation of a common currency, tentatively called the "khaleeji," but Oman withdrew from the project in 2006 and the U.A.E. in 2009, threatening the most advanced of these projects.[15] In addition, since the GCC countries' currencies are all pegged to the U.S. dollar (with the exception of Kuwait's), this new currency was more symbolic than substantial.

The Chinese Conundrum

From the 1980s until the recession years of 2008–2009, the Chinese ran a very large yearly trade surplus with the United States, reaching two consecutive record-high years, with U.S. $262 billion in 2007 and U.S. $290 billion in 2008. This recurring trade deficit allowed the Chinese government to accumulate as much as U.S. $2.5 trillion in foreign currency reserves, 82 percent of which it invested in U.S. Treasury bonds.[16] Part of the reason behind such large trade deficits is that the Chinese government refused to let the value of the yuan "float" during the 1990s. If it had, the large deficit would have shrunk as the value of the yuan increased, erasing some of the competitive position of the country's manufacturers.

The Chinese are earning a very modest income on these bonds, as the interest rates in the United States are relatively low, but the Chinese government seems relatively satisfied with the arrangement, because the investment is safe. However, the 2007–2009 fall of the value of the dollar against all major world currencies presents the Chinese with a major challenge: As the value of the dollar goes down, so does the value of their investments in U.S. dollars;[17] if the value of the dollar decreases by 5 percent, so does the value of their investments. For the Chinese, a decrease of 5 percent equates to a capital loss equivalent to U.S. $102 billion, or one-third of the trade surplus it earned in 2008, and about half of what it earned in 2009.

The conundrum is that, in order to protect this investment, the Chinese could diversify into other currencies, including the euro and the British pound, but doing so would further depress the value of the dollar, as any large influx of dollars on the world markets would affect its value.

In March 2009, at the G20 meeting in London, the governor of the Chinese Central Bank, Zhou Xiachuan, proposed the creation of a "super-sovereign reserve currency,"[18] not unlike the Special Drawing Rights (SDR) of the International Monetary Fund, which would be independent of a particular country's currency. This new currency would wean the world economies from their dependence on the dollar and its exchange rate fluctuations, many of which are due to domestic political choices (the huge government deficits of 2008–2010, for example). It would also make the international currency system more stable and more predictable, leading a number of U.S. economists to cautiously endorse the proposal.

There was, however, hostility in the United States regarding this particular idea, with much of the opposition stemming from the realization that the dollar would lose its dominant role in international governmental reserves.[19] Nevertheless, the proposal has some definite advantages, and the creation of a worldwide new currency is no more unrealistic than the creation of a pan-European currency; the euro was first greeted with the same type of concerns.

8-3 Theories of Exchange Rate Determinations

In order for a company to determine what its risks are in an international currency transaction, it is imperative to understand how exchange rates are determined. Once a company's management understands the theories behind the exchange rate fluctuations, it can then forecast them, and therefore determine what would be its best strategy for a specific transaction.

There are a total of five different, complementary theories that help explain the variations between two countries' exchange rates. After each one is presented, Section 8-3f and Figure 8-9 will summarize how these theories interact and influence the change in the spot exchange rate of two currencies.

8-3a Purchasing Power Parity

In its absolute form, the **Purchasing Power Parity** theory holds that exchange rates should reflect the price differences of each and every product between countries. The idea is that exchange rates should fluctuate in such a way as to "equalize" the price differences of similar products between countries, so that a set amount of currency would purchase the same goods in any country of the world.

Purchasing Power Parity
An economic theory that holds that exchange rates should reflect the price differences of each and every product between countries.

However, this is essentially impossible to achieve (and measure), given the disparity of goods and services that are purchased worldwide. Even for a perfectly uniform good, there are wide discrepancies in its price from one country to the next. This inconsistency is illustrated very well with the Big Mac Index, published by *The Economist* (see Table 8-5),[20] which observes that the price of one of McDonald's Big Mac sandwiches can vary from 43 percent (in Malaysia) to 163 percent (in Norway) of the U.S. price. In effect, the price of a Big Mac is 3.8 *times* as much in Norway as it is in Malaysia.

TABLE 8-5	The Big Mac Index

In this famous study from *The Economist*, the Purchasing Power Parity of worldwide currencies is shown by using the cost of a McDonald's Big Mac.

Country	In Local Currency	In U.S. Dollars	As % of U.S. Price
United States	$ 3.54	3.54	100%
Argentina	Peso 11.50	3.30	93%
Australia	A$ 3.45	2.19	62%
Brazil	Real 8.02	3.45	98%
Bulgaria	Lev 2.99	1.95	78%
Canada	C$ 4.16	3.36	95%
Chile	Peso 1,550	2.51	71%
China	Yuan 12.50	1.83	52%
Czech Republic	Koruna 65.94	3.02	85%
Denmark	DKr 29.5	5.07	143%
Egypt	Pound 13	2.34	66%
Eurozone	€3.42	4.38	124%
Hong Kong	HK$ 13.3	1.72	48%
Hungary	Forint 680	2.92	82%
Iceland	Krónur 469	2.08	59%
Indonesia	Rupiah 19,800	1.74	49%
Israel	Shekel 15.00	3.69	104%
Japan	¥ 290	3.23	91%
Malaysia	Ringgit 5.50	**1.52**	**43%**
Mexico	Peso 33.00	2.30	65%
New Zealand	NZ$ 4.90	2.48	70%
Norway	Kroner 40.00	**5.79**	**163%**
Pakistan	Rupee 150	1.87	53%
Peru	New Sol 8.06	2.54	72%
The Philippines	Peso 98.00	2.07	58%
Poland	Zloty 7.00	2.01	57%
Russia	Rouble 62.00	1.73	49%
Saudi Arabia	Riyal 10.00	2.66	75%
Singapore	S$ 3.95	2.61	74%
South Africa	Rand 16.95	1.66	47%
South Korea	Won 3,300	2.39	68%
Sweden	SKr 38.00	4.58	129%
Switzerland	SFr 6.50	5.60	158%
Taiwan	NT$ 75.00	2.23	63%
Thailand	Bhat 62.00	1.77	50%
Turkey	Lira 5.15	3.13	88%
United Kingdom	£2.29	3.30	93%
Venezuela	Bolivar Fuerte 6.20	2.89	82%

Source: The Economist

Practically speaking, Purchasing Power Parity is determined by using a "basket of goods" and calculating how much domestic currency an average person would have to spend to purchase it. The World Bank uses this version of the Purchasing Power Parity to determine the gross domestic product *per capita* (Purchasing Power Parity adjusted) of all the nations of the world.

In its relative form, as used in international finance as a determinant of changes in exchange rates, Purchasing Power Parity is calculated using inflation rates, which is only a slightly different methodology, because in each country, inflation rates are determined by taking the level of prices of a basket of goods. Therefore, the only differences between the Purchasing Power Parity determined by the World Bank and that determined through inflation rates is that the basket of goods of the World Bank attempts to be identical in each country (whereas the inflation rate is calculated using different baskets of goods in most countries) and that the basket of goods used for inflation determination tends to include a wider number of items.

Purchasing Power Parity theory holds that exchange rates should reflect the differences in inflation rates between countries. In other words, if the inflation rate is higher in one country, then its currency should decrease in value relative to other currencies. This can be illustrated mathematically as:[21]

$$\frac{\text{Spot value of Currency F at time } t \text{ in Country D}}{\text{Spot value of Currency F at time } 0 \text{ in Country D}} = \frac{(1 + \text{inflation rate in Country D})^t}{(1 + \text{inflation rate in Country F})^t}$$

or

$$\frac{S(e_t)}{S(e_0)} = \frac{(1 + inf_{\text{D}})^t}{(1 + inf_{\text{F}})^t}$$

and schematically as shown in Figure 8-4.

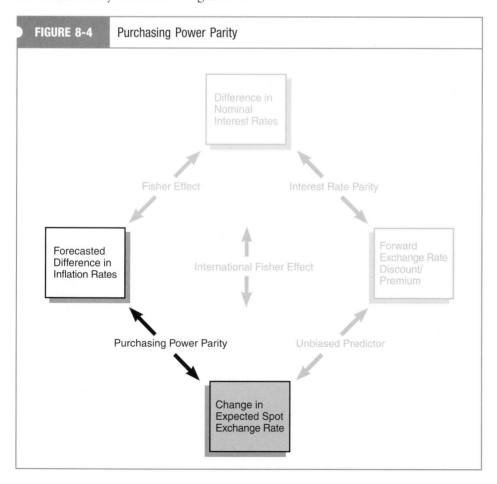

FIGURE 8-4 Purchasing Power Parity

Fisher effect An economic theory that holds that the interest rates that businesses and individuals pay to borrow money should be uniform throughout the world and that the nominal interest rates that they actually pay in a given country are composed of this common interest rate and the inflation rate of that country.

8-3b Fisher Effect

The **Fisher effect** is the observation that a country's nominal interest rate (what a borrower actually has to pay for a loan) comprises both the inflation rate in that country and the real interest rate that borrowers are paying. This real interest rate is expected to be "uniform" throughout the world. In other words, the theory holds that people expect to pay the same real interest rate in every country, at all points in time. Therefore, countries with high inflation rates should be expected to have high nominal interest rates. The mathematical representation of this phenomenon is:

$$(1 + \text{real interest rate}) \times (1 + \text{inflation rate}) = 1 + \text{nominal interest rate}$$

or

$$(1 + \text{rir})(1 + \text{inf}) = 1 + \text{nir} \quad \text{or} \quad \text{nir} = \text{inf} + \text{rir} + (\text{inf} \times \text{rir}) \approx \text{inf} + \text{rir}$$

and schematically as shown in Figure 8-5.

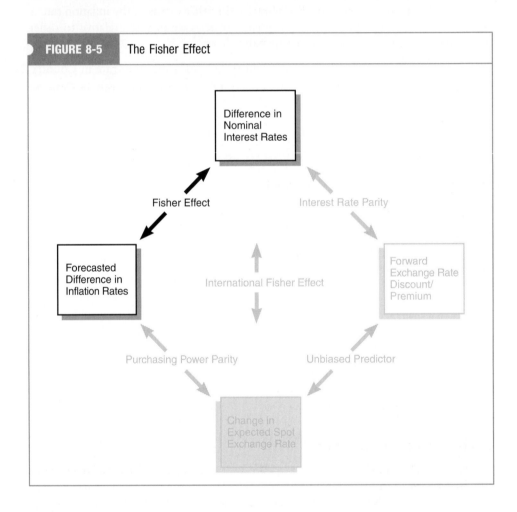

FIGURE 8-5   The Fisher Effect

8-3c International Fisher Effect

International Fisher effect An economic theory that holds that the spot exchange rates between two countries' currencies should change in function of the differences between these two countries' nominal interest rates.

The **International Fisher effect** is the observation that exchange rates reflect the differences between nominal interest rates in different countries. It posits that, if nominal interest rates are higher in Country F than in Country D, then Country F's currency should be expected to decrease in value relative to Country D's currency.

Conceptually, the expected spot rate reflects the fact that an investor would get the same yield on an investment, whether it is made in Country D or Country F.

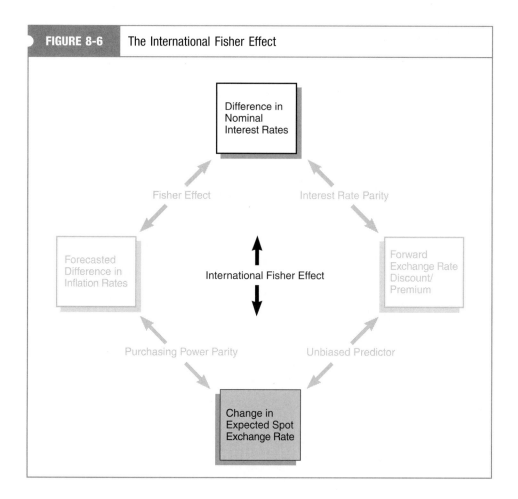

FIGURE 8-6 The International Fisher Effect

Mathematically, this can be described as:

$$\frac{\text{Spot value of Currency F at time } (t+1) \text{ in Country D}}{\text{Spot value of Currency F at time } t \text{ in Country D}} = \frac{(1 + \text{nominal interest rate in Country D})}{(1 + \text{nominal interest rate in Country F})}$$

or

$$\frac{S(e_{t+1})}{S(e_t)} = \frac{(1 + \text{nir}_D)}{(1 + \text{nir}_F)}$$

and schematically as shown in Figure 8-6.

8-3d Interest Rate Parity

The **Interest Rate Parity** theory links the forward exchange rate of a foreign currency to its spot rate, using the differences in nominal interest rates between the foreign country and the domestic country. The principle is that the forward exchange rate should be expressed as a discount if the foreign country is experiencing higher nominal interest rates than the domestic country, and should reflect a premium if the foreign nominal interest rates are lower.

In other words, at time t, the forward exchange rate F $\{t+1\}(e_t)$ for delivering Currency F n days from t—that is, at time $t+1$—reflects the difference between the nominal interest rate in Country D and the nominal interest rate in Country F, adjusted for the length of n days. This relationship always holds in the real world unless prevented by government action.

Interest Rate Parity An economic theory that holds that the forward exchange rate between two currencies should reflect the differences in the interest rates in those two countries.

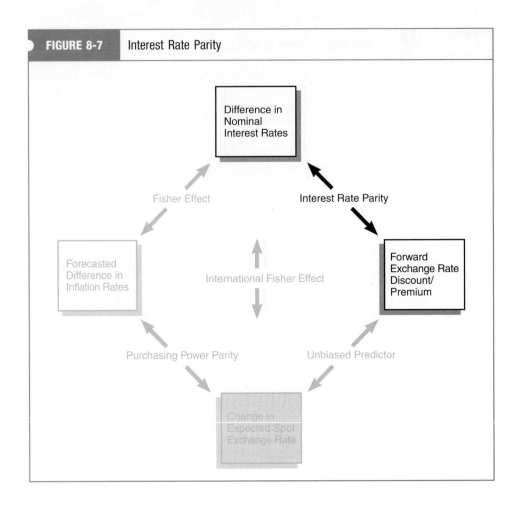

FIGURE 8-7   Interest Rate Parity

This relationship translates mathematically as:

$$\frac{F_n(e_t) - S(e_t)}{S(e_t)} \times \frac{360}{n} = nir_D - nir_F$$

and schematically as shown in Figure 8-7.

8-3e Forward Rate as Unbiased Predictor of Spot Rate

This theory holds that forward exchange rates for currencies are good predictors of the future spot exchange rates of that currency. In other words, if the forward rate for a currency shows a discount of 2 percent for a maturity date of n days, then the spot rate in n days should be 2 percent lower than it is today.

Conceptually, the relationship is that the forward exchange rate of currency F at time t in country D for delivery at time $t+1$ is the expected (average) spot value of currency F at time $t+1$ in country D.

This can be expressed mathematically as:

$$F_{t+1}(e_t) = S(e_{t+1})$$

and schematically as shown in Figure 8-8.

8-3f Entire Predictive Model

The five relationships can be combined to understand how each can be used to forecast expected spot exchange rates, as shown in Figure 8-9.[22]

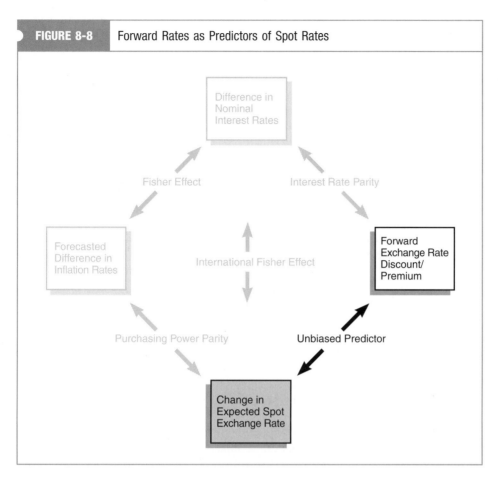

FIGURE 8-8   Forward Rates as Predictors of Spot Rates

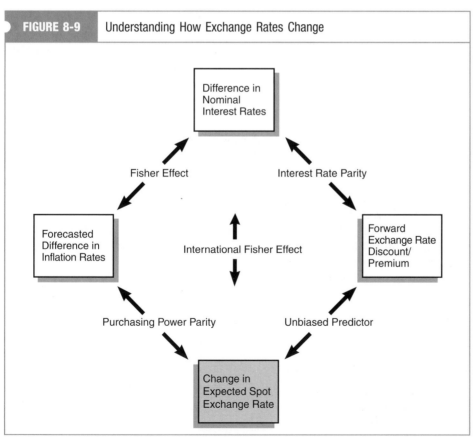

FIGURE 8-9   Understanding How Exchange Rates Change

8-4 Exchange Rate Forecasting

It should now be evident that forecasting exchange rates is difficult. In addition to the five theories mentioned in the preceding section, there are always political changes, unpredictable economic variations, and the occasional natural catastrophe that influence the exchange rate of a given currency. Figure 8-10 illustrates the exchange rate of the Japanese yen versus the U.S. dollar over the past 35 years;[23] it has been altogether very unpredictable, although reasonably stable in the short run. Historical exchange rates can easily be obtained, for any currency, from the Bank of Canada[24] and from the Pacific Exchange Rate Service at the University of British Columbia.[25]

There are three general methods that can be utilized for forecasting exchange rates, and, again, the reader should refer to textbooks dealing with forecasting specifically in order to understand these techniques better. Only a cursory review is made here.

8-4a Technical Forecasting

The so-called technical forecasting methods are essentially all based upon time-series analysis, from simple moving averages (something that can be done easily on a spreadsheet) to sophisticated ARIMA (auto-regressive integrated moving average; also called Box-Jenkins) methods and neural-network models that require dedicated software packages and powerful computers. Several possible sources on technical forecasting exist.[26,27,28,29]

Technical forecasting is based on the premise that future movements in the value of a currency are "mathematically" linked to its past movements, and use techniques that extract patterns in the historical data. These patterns are then duplicated with very recent data to forecast the future exchange rates of the currency.

Such technical forecasts are valuable in determining the possible variations of a currency's exchange rate in the short run. In the long run, they tend to accumulate

FIGURE 8-10   The Yen/U.S. Dollar Exchange Rate, February 1971-April 2009

Source: Board of Governors of the Federal Reserve System.

errors fairly quickly, as they ignore the economic fundamentals of exchange rate determination.

8-4b Fundamental Forecasting

The idea behind fundamental forecasting is to integrate all of the theories presented in Section 8-3 into a mathematical, causal model that would use the exchange rate of a specific currency as the dependent variable and the expected inflation rates, nominal interest rates, forward interest rates, and real interest rates as the independent variables. Fundamental forecasting is "just" the use of a large multiple linear regression and of ANOVA—analysis of variance—techniques, and it can be done with any good spreadsheet program, such as Excel. However, there are several pitfalls with causal models, and a good survey of such models should be undertaken before they are used. A large number of sources can be consulted to learn about these linear models.[30],[31],[32]

The problem with causal models in general, and especially in the case of foreign exchange forecasting, is the difficulty in accounting for all of the possible influences on a given currency's exchange rate—it is impossible to isolate its movements to a single pair of currencies—and at the same time limit the inevitable collinearity of the independent variables. Novices tend to increase the number of independent variables, which increases the coefficient of determination (R^2), but they often overlook the problem of collinearity that this strategy brings along.

8-4c Market-Based Forecasting

Market-based forecasting is based on the premise that "the market knows best" and that, therefore, the forward exchange rate of a given currency is the best unbiased predictor of the future spot rate of a particular currency.

Because it is very likely that speculators have conducted their own analytical and mathematical forecasts for a given currency, it is quite logical to conclude that the forward exchange rate includes the entire wisdom of the market and that, therefore, it is the best predictor of the future value of a currency. This observation is called the Efficient Market Hypothesis.

However, this assumption may be incorrect, as forward rates often reflect the futures contract rates, which are set by speculators who may include people driven by entirely different motives than the actual purchase and delivery of a currency. Such was the case with George Soros in 1992 when he decided to "bet" against the British pound, driving the government of the United Kingdom to spend a large amount of foreign currency to sustain its value, and eventually forcing the pound out of the Exchange Rate Mechanism (ERM) of the European Union.[33]

Moreover, the forward rates do not account for government interventions, which can wreak havoc on the actual spot rates of currencies. For example, in the spring of 2002, the Japanese government consistently kept the value of the yen down, in order to boost the Japanese economy through undervalued exports. The forward rates also do not reflect the possibility of an unexpected change or a currency crisis; such was the case when the Argentinean peso, which was pegged to the U.S. dollar at the rate of $1.00 per peso, suddenly was allowed to float on January 6, 2002, and reached $0.25 on March 25, 2002. It stabilized relatively quickly at around U.S. $0.35, and stood at U.S. $0.27 in May 2009.[34] The Chinese currency, the renminbi (also known as the RMB or the yuan), was also artificially kept at a pegged rate against the U.S. dollar at the rate of RMB 8.28/$ from 1994 until July 2005, when it was changed to "better reflect market conditions" and appreciated to RMB 8.11/$. The the yuan progressively appreciated, reaching RMB 7.50/$ in October 2007, and RMB 7.00/$ in May 2008;[35] it stood at RMB 6.83/$ in May 2009. Nevertheless, the yuan is still considered undervalued, helping Chinese exports and making imports to China more expensive.

8-5 Managing Transaction Exposure

transaction exposure The risk represented by the financial impact of fluctuations in exchange rates in an international transaction. A small exposure means that the firm is likely to be largely unaffected by a change in exchange rates, because the amount of the transaction is small relative to the company's size.

Whenever a company is engaged in an international transaction and agrees to use a foreign currency to conduct this transaction, it is then exposed to a certain amount of risk, due to possible fluctuations in currency exchange rates. Such risk is called **transaction exposure** and can be handled in one of two ways: It can be retained by the firm, or it can be "hedged," or reduced, by using one of three possible techniques, which are presented in Sections 8-5b, 8-5c, and 8-5d.

Under these general guidelines, firms can pursue one of two strategies:

1. Determine what its decision should be on an invoice-by-invoice basis, depending on the currency at stake, the amount of the invoice, and its forecast of the currency's exchange rate.
2. Set a policy that the firm follows for all of its foreign currency receivables and payables.

In either case, the choice of the strategy should be dependent on the forecast that the company makes of the exchange rate at stake; it also depends on the size of the firm and its ability to weather a currency risk, on the size of the invoice relative to the total sales of the firm (called the exposure), and on the company's degree of sophistication in terms of international finance. In general terms, it is almost always better for a firm to hedge its foreign exchange risks, with only a few exceptions; however, certain firms choose to retain their exchange rate risks instead.

8-5a Risk Retention

risk retention A risk management strategy in which a company elects to retain a certain type of risk and decides not to insure that risk.

The strategy of **risk retention** is fairly simple: The company decides that it is best to retain the risk of currency fluctuation. There are three different types of companies that will decide to systematically retain their currency risks:

- Very large traders—importers and exporters, often in the same currency—that simultaneously carry risks on the "up" side, which means they can earn additional income because of a favorable exchange rate change, and on the "down" side, which means they can lose money for exactly the same reason. Overall, for these firms, transaction exchange rate risks are a zero-sum game, and it is not necessary to hedge, as the positions they hold offset each other. Nevertheless, those firms tend to be very sophisticated in international finance, and they would actually hedge their positions, and even speculate in the currency markets.

- Exporters or importers that have little exposure (i.e., that are shipping or buying goods of relatively small value, in fairly small shipments, and therefore for which a currency loss would not have substantial financial consequences). Often, for these firms, the costs of hedging, or of determining whether they should hedge, exceed the benefits that they would accrue.

- Firms that do not evaluate the international currency transaction risks clearly; they are not following a specific policy; they just have no policy, or have a management that is not well versed in the intricacies of international trade. Those firms are also often the ones that cannot afford not to hedge, as they tend to be smaller, and therefore more susceptible to a partial loss due to exchange rate fluctuations.

8-5b Forward Market Hedges

forward market hedge A financial technique designed to reduce exchange rate fluctuation risks in which a business agrees to purchase (or sell) a particular currency at a predetermined exchange rate at some future time (generally 30, 60, 90, 180, or 360 days later).

The first of the strategies that a company can follow to protect itself from currency fluctuations is a **forward market hedge**. This strategy involves selling forward a future receivable in a foreign currency, or purchasing forward the currency necessary to cover a foreign payable. This strategy varies in its implementation for each situation.

Two examples will make this strategy much clearer:

- A U.S.-based company is selling a product to an Italian firm on March 1, 2009; the invoice is payable in euros on June 2, 2009 (90-day credit). The amount that the firm would like to collect is U.S. $200,000. If it used the spot exchange rate—U.S. $1.2661/€—the firm could then bill the customer for €157,965.00.[36] However, as of March 1, 2009, the 90-day forward exchange rate for the euro is U.S. $1.2530/€, indicating that the market is expecting a decrease in the value of the euro against the U.S. dollar. The firm therefore decides to invoice its customer for $200,000/1.2530 = €159,617.00. A forward market hedge, in this case, would consist of the U.S. firm entering a forward contract with a bank, in which it would promise to sell €159,617.00 to the bank on June 2, 2009, at the predetermined (forward) exchange rate of U.S. $1.2530/€. On that date, the U.S. company presents €159,617.00 to the bank and collects the U.S. $200,000 it wanted to collect. The U.S. firm is unconcerned about the spot exchange rate of the euro on June 2, 2009.

- A German firm is purchasing a machine from a British firm for £250,000.00. The machine is delivered on April 4, 2009, and payment is expected (in pounds) on July 6, 2009. On April 4, 2009, this amount was equivalent to €272,200.00 because the spot exchange rate between the U.K. pound and the euro was €1.1008/£.[37] However, on April 30, 2009, the pound was expected to rise in value, and the 90-day forward exchange rate with the euro was €1.1220/£. The German firm wants to make sure it knows how much it will spend on the machine, and can use a forward market hedge by entering into a contract with a bank from which it promises to purchase £250,000 on July 6, 2009, at a predetermined (forward) exchange rate of €1.1220/£. On that date, the German firm hands €280,500.00 to the bank and obtains in exchange the £250,000 that it needs to pay its British supplier. The German firm could determine on April 4, 2009, exactly how much it had to pay for the machine and is unconcerned about the spot exchange rate of the British pound on July 6, 2009.

In either of these cases, the firm has eliminated its exchange rate risk by using a forward market hedge; it knew, with total certainty, at the time it entered the forward contract with the bank how much it would collect (U.S. firm) or how much it would have to pay (German firm). The hedge, for both of those firms, removed the exchange rate risk.

8-5c Money Market Hedges

A **money market hedge** consists of using the banking system of the country of the currency in which the receivable or the payable is going to be paid. The firm hedging its exposure either borrows from a bank in the foreign country or deposits money in a bank in the foreign country.

This can again be explained best with two illustrations:

- A firm located in Switzerland sells a piece of machinery to a firm located in Japan for the equivalent of SwF 150,000.00; in order to be competitive with Japanese competitors, though, it decided to bill the customer in Japanese yen. The transaction takes place on January 16, 2009, with a payment date of March 15, 2009. The transaction amount is expressed in Japanese yen, for a total of ¥12,115,545.00 because the exchange rate on January 16, 2009, is ¥80.7703/SwF.[38] To protect itself from currency fluctuations, the Swiss firm can use a money market hedge, by borrowing from a Japanese bank the present value (as of January 16, 2009) of ¥12,115,545.00 on March 15, 2009. Supposing that the commercial lending rate in Japan on January 16, 2009, was 3 percent *per annum*, or about 0.5 percent for two months. The amount the Swiss firm would borrow would be then be ¥ (1−0.005) × 12,115,545.00 = 12,054,967.28;

money market hedge
A financial technique designed to reduce exchange rate fluctuation risks in which a business invests funds in an interest-bearing account abroad or borrows funds from a bank abroad.

it will pay the bank back on March 15, 2009, using the payment of
¥12,115,545.00 made by its customer. On January 16, 2009, the Swiss firm would
exchange the proceeds from the loan (¥12,054,967.28) for SwF 149,250.00 (the
exchange rate on January 16, 2009 is ¥80.7703/SwF), and get an amount roughly
equal to the payment of SwF 150,000.00 it had expected, although decreased by
the cost of getting the money two months earlier. The Swiss firm is unconcerned
about the spot exchange rate of the yen on March 15, 2009.

- On May 2, 2009, a firm located in Denmark purchases raw materials from a
firm located in Australia, which asks to be paid in Australian dollars. The
amount of the invoice is A$20,000,000, payable on November 1, 2009. The
Danish firm can eliminate its exposure to exchange rate fluctuations by using a
money market hedge. It can invest a sum in an Australian bank that will mature
to A$20,000,000 on November 1, 2009. Assuming an annual interest rate of
4 percent paid on deposits in Australia, the Danish firm would have to invest
A$20,000,000/(1 + 0.02) = 19,607,845 to have enough to cover its obliga-
tion on November 1, 2009. On May 2, 2009, the Danish firm then converts
DKr 80,288,498.36 into Australian dollars (the exchange rate is A$0.2444/
DKr on May 2, 2009).[39] The Danish firm is unconcerned about the spot
exchange rate of the Australian dollar on November 1, 2009.

The money market hedging strategy is effective because it allows the firm to use the
exchange rate as of the date of the transaction rather than speculate on the value of
the exchange rate at the date of payment. In that respect, it is a strategy that eliminates
the risks of currency fluctuations; the only cost to the Swiss firm is the interest it has to
pay to the Japanese bank, in addition to the fees that will be charged for the foreign
exchange transactions. However, the amount of interest it pays should be the same as
what it would have paid by borrowing the same amount in Switzerland, at least if the
Interest Rate Parity holds. Similarly, the only cost to the Danish firm—in addition
to the fees—is the opportunity cost of the investment, from which the interest earned
in Australia must be deducted. Both of these should offset each other approximately
as well.

8-5d Options Market Hedges

options market hedge
A financial technique designed
to reduce exchange rate
fluctuation risks in which a
business purchases (or sells)
options in a particular currency.

It is also possible to hedge a foreign currency fluctuation risk with options. An
options market hedge is yet a more sophisticated alternative, because it amounts to
remaining unhedged—retaining the risk—if the exchange rate turns favorable and to
purchasing an insurance policy to protect against unfavorable exchange rate
fluctuations. If the exchange rate turns unfavorable, the firm can exercise its option—
its insurance policy—and is covered. If the exchange rate turns favorable, the firm can
still benefit from this situation by not exercising its option, even though it will lose the
cost of the option.

This strategy involves purchasing put or call options, or the option to sell or
purchase certain currencies at a certain exchange rate on (European-style options) or
before (U.S.-style options) a certain date. This agreed-upon exchange rate is called
the strike price. Here again, two examples will illustrate the concepts better than an
abstract description:

- A company located in the United States sells a large piece of equipment to a
firm located in the United Kingdom and agrees to be paid in pounds. The
invoice, for £1,000,000, is issued on December 10, 2008, but is not payable until
March 10, 2009. The exporting firm can minimize its currency fluctuation risk by
using an option hedge; on December 10, 2008, it purchases a put option—the
right to sell £1,000,000 on March 10, 2009—at an agreed-upon exchange rate of
U.S. $1.3615/£. If the spot exchange rate on March 10, 2009, is lower than
U.S. $1.3615/£, then the American firm will exercise its option and sell the

currency at that price. If the spot rate is higher than U.S. $1.3615/£, the firm will let its option lapse and will sell the currency it received at the spot market rate. Because the exchange rate on March 10, 2009, is U.S. $1.3842/£,[40] the firm sells its pounds without using its option. The firm still incurs the cost of the option, which is approximately 1.25 percent of the contract amount, or about U.S. $17,018.75; however, this cost is offset by the fact that it sells its British pounds for U.S. $22,700 more than it had anticipated. The net profits on this financial transaction are U.S. $5,681.25.

• A company located in Spain purchases a plant located in Canada. The contract is signed on June 28, 2008, and the firm has agreed to make three installment payments of Can$1,000,000 each on December 28, 2008, March 28, 2009, and June 28, 2009 (6 months, 9 months, and 12 months after purchase). In order to minimize its currency risks, the Spanish firm can use an option hedge by purchasing call options—the right to buy Can$1,000,000—at exchange rates of Can$1.6522/€ for December 28, 2008, Can$1.7081/€ for March 28, 2009, and Can$1.7452/€ for June 28, 2009. Because the spot exchange rate for the Canadian dollar was Can$1.7316/€ on December 28, 2009,[41] the Spanish firm did not exercise its option, purchased the Canadian dollars on the spot market, and sent them to the Canadian supplier. On March 28, 2009, the spot market was Can$1.6488/€,[42] and therefore the Spanish firm exercised its option and purchased the Canadian dollars at Can$1.7081/€ (the strike price of its option), because it was a more favorable exchange rate than the spot market. As for its future June 28, 2009, payment, the firm still has the possibility of saving money if the spot rate is more favorable than its option rate; if not, it will exercise its option. The cost of these successive options for the Spanish firm was approximately 1.25 percent, 1.5 percent, and 2 percent of the contract amounts for December, March, and June, respectively, for a total of approximately €29,000.00. However, the costs were reduced by the fact that the firm saved €27,753.00 in December by not having to spend as many euros as it had anticipated.

The main problem with option hedging is that options are very expensive, which is somewhat understandable, as they are only covering the "down side." The second issue is that options are commonly traded for only a limited number of currencies, and that the amounts are not as flexible as in forward markets. Nevertheless, some banks will write options that are tailored to their customers' needs. For the sophisticated firm involved in international trade, this strategy has great potential.

For further information on this hedging strategy, the other hedging strategies described in this section, and additional strategies, the reader is referred to a number of textbooks in international finance[43] or to textbooks on options and futures.[44]

8-6 International Banking Institutions

There are several institutions that are involved in international banking; however, only a few of these have a function that is linked to international payments. A brief synopsis of each of these institutions is given in this section. The reader interested in gaining more information on these institutions should consult a textbook in international economics or international banking.[45,46]

8-6a Central National Banks

In every country in the world, there is a central bank, or some institution that acts as a central bank: Great Britain has its Bank of England, the European Union has its European Central Bank (ECB), and the United States has the Federal Reserve System, which, although not technically a central bank, fulfills the role of one. Each of the countries of the European Union has also retained its central bank, because only the control of the monetary supply is in the hands of the ECB; France has its Banque de France and Germany has its cherished Bundesbank.

Central banks provide several services to the domestic banks of their respective countries. Their first role is the creation and control of the monetary supply, through market operations and the control of currency. This role can be one of maintenance or a more active role, such as executing monetary policy operations. Their second role is their function as a check clearinghouse where accounts regarding checks written on different domestic banks' accounts are settled. In some countries, they also "manage"—if conceivable—the exchange rate of the national currency and the national foreign exchange reserves.

8-6b International Monetary Fund

The International Monetary Fund (IMF) was created in 1944 at the Bretton Woods Conference. It was designed to oversee the fixed exchange rate system that the conference had started. When exchange rates started to float in 1971—the end of the gold standard—the IMF changed its focus to helping countries manage their balance of payments. In particular, the IMF lends money to countries that experience difficulties with their balance of payments. These loans are usually accompanied by a number of conditions to which the country has to agree; inflation control and money supply growth are often on the list. The funds necessary for those loans are collected from the countries that become members of the IMF; they are assessed a "quota" that is determined by the country's economic size.

The IMF is also the curator of an artificial currency, the "Special Drawing Rights" (SDRs), which was designed to supplement the U.S. dollar in its role as the international currency. The SDR's value is determined by a basket of four currencies (U.S. dollar, European euro, British pound, and Japanese yen). Although the SDR is not often used by businesses, it is often used by governments to settle their debts with each other. It is also used in the settlement of disputes under the liability conventions of ocean cargo shipping (see Chapter 11, Section 11-5).

8-6c Bank for International Settlements

The Bank for International Settlements was created after World War I to manage Germany's war reparation payments. Since then it has evolved into a major international institution, providing support to central banks—which constitute its membership—and particularly recently providing guidance to the new central banks of the former Eastern Bloc countries. Although membership was originally limited to European central banks, the U.S. Federal Reserve System joined in 1994.

8-6d International Bank for Reconstruction and Development—World Bank

The International Bank for Reconstruction and Development—known as the World Bank—was created in 1945 after the Bretton Woods Conference. Its purpose was to help countries rebuild their infrastructures after World War II, and it has slowly changed to become the bank in charge of financing large infrastructure projects. The government borrowing the funds must be a member of the IMF and the loan is usually repaid as a long-term loan.

8-6e Export-Import Bank

The Export-Import (Ex-Im) Bank is a federal agency of the U.S. government. Its purpose is to provide assistance to U.S. exporters in the form of loans (available only to large exporters), loan guarantees (available to banks that finance exporters), or political-risk insurance policies available through the Foreign Credit Insurance Association (FCIA). See Chapter 10, Section 10-12c for further details.

8-6f Society for Worldwide Interbank Financial Telecommunication

The Society for Worldwide Interbank Financial Telecommunication (SWIFT) is a corporation supporting an Electronic Data Interchange network, which was created by banks to obtain a secure and reliable means of transferring financial information internationally. In particular, it allows the communication of letters of credit and miscellaneous fund transfers. Because of the high level of security that the network enjoys, documents transferred through the network have the same value as original paper documents.

8-7 Currency of Payment as a Marketing Tool

In an international transaction, the choice of the currency exposes the exporter (or the importer) to the risk of currency exchange rate fluctuation. Rather than consider this risk to be a drawback in an international sale, a good exporter should consider it an opportunity.

There are four main tactics that the exporter can pursue to eliminate this foreign exchange risk:

- Elect to quote in the exporter's currency. Although this is the easiest of the alternatives for the exporter, it only shifts the risk onto the importer, who is just as likely to consider this risk to be a burden. In addition, if the exporter's quote is being evaluated against other quotes, including some domestic proposals, a quote that is presented in a foreign currency is going to be less attractive to the importer.

- Elect to quote in the importer's currency and minimize the risk of exchange rate fluctuation with a forward market hedge. In that case, the importer has no currency fluctuation risk and the exporter knows exactly what its foreign exchange "cost" is going to be at the time of the transaction. The only drawback is that the exporter may not have easy access to the forward market of some currencies that are not commonly traded in the forward markets (a currency other than the European euro, the Japanese yen, the British pound, or the Canadian dollar). Nevertheless, these other currencies are traded in the forward market in London, and with some help from a savvy international banker, an exporter can hedge just about any receivable in any currency.

- Elect to quote in the importer's currency and minimize the exchange rate risk with a money market hedge. In that case, the importer has no currency fluctuation risk; the exporter also knows exactly what its foreign exchange cost is going to be, although it requires knowing what the interest rates are in the importing country. However, the exporter has to be quite experienced—and have an international presence—to be able to borrow from a bank in a foreign market; only a few companies have this option available, although a savvy international banker can provide substantial help in this regard.

- Elect to quote in the importer's currency and minimize the exchange rate risk with an options market hedge. In that case, the importer has no currency fluctuation risk and the exporter benefits in two ways. If the exchange rate fluctuation is favorable, the exporter benefits from it. If the exchange rate fluctuation is unfavorable, the exporter has minimized its risk. The main issue with options market hedges is the same as with the forward market hedges: Not all currencies are readily available in the home country of the exporter, and the help of a savvy international banker may be required to purchase options on the London market, for example.

Because of the intense competition that an exporter faces in international markets, it is very likely that a significant percentage of its competitors will offer quotes in the importer's currency. Because it is easier for the importer to handle a purchase in its own currency, it would place an exporter at a strategic disadvantage not to quote in that currency.

An exporter intent on increasing its sales abroad should therefore consider very seriously offering quotes in the importer's currency and discuss with its banker which of the three hedging tactics would be most appropriate.

Review and Discussion Questions

1. What are three of the possible choices that an exporter can make (in terms of currency) for a specific transaction?

2. Explain the three different types of exchange rates. Find the three exchange rates for a currency of your choice and explain the values you find.

3. Explain the three different types of currencies. Give an example of each.

4. Choose two of the theories of exchange rate determination and explain them.

5. What does it mean for a firm to retain its currency fluctuation risk in a transaction?

6. There are three types of hedges that a firm can use to protect itself against transaction exposure. Choose one of them and explain it.

Endnotes

1. Multiple sources, but *Wikipedia* has generally an instant update of the status of all of these countries toward their accession to the euro.

2. Sercu, Piet, *International Finance: Theory into Practice*. Princeton, NJ: Princeton University Press, 2009.

3. Eiteman, David K., Arthur I. Stonehill, and Michael H. Moffett, *Multinational Business Finance*. 11th ed. Reading, MA: Pearson-Addison-Wesley Publishing Company, 2007.

4. Madura, Jeff, *International Financial Management*. 9th ed. Cincinnati: South-Western Publishing, 2008.

5. Shapiro, Alan C., *Multinational Financial Management*. 8th ed. Upper Saddle River, NJ: Prentice-Hall, 2006.

6. "Currencies," *Wall Street Journal*, May 26, 2009, p. C2.

7. "Currencies," *Financial Times*, http://markets.ft.com/ft/markets/currencies.asp, accessed May 26, 2009.

8. "Currencies," *Wall Street Journal*, May 26, 2009, p. C2.

9. "Currencies," *Financial Times*, http://markets.ft.com/ft/markets/currencies.asp, accessed May 26, 2009.

10. "Currencies," *Wall Street Journal*, May 26, 2009, p. C2.

11. "Currencies," *Financial Times*, http://markets.ft.com/ft/markets/currencies.asp, accessed May 26, 2009.

12. "Foreign Exchange Swap Transactions," The Learning Center, Allied Irish Bank, http://www.fxcenterusa.com/us/learning/FX%20Swaps.pdf, accessed May 30, 2009.

13. "U.S./Euro Exchange Rate," Economic Research, Board of Governors of the Federal Reserve System, http://research.stlouisfed.org/fred2/series/EXUSEU/downloaddata, accessed May 26, 2009.

14. "U.S./Euro Exchange Rate," Economic Research, Federal Reserve Bank of St. Louis, http://research.stlouisfed.org/fred2/data/DEXUSEU.txt, accessed May 26, 2009.

15. Reuters, "U.A.E. Quits Gulf Monetary Union," *Wall Street Journal*, May 21, 2009, p. C2.

16. Bradsher, Keith, "China Grows More Picky About Debt," *New York Times*, May 21, 2009, http://www.nytimes.com/2009/05/21/business/global/21reserves.html.

17. Krugman, Paul, "China's Dollar Trap," *New York Times*, April 3, 2009, http://www.nytimes.com/2009/04/03/opinion/03krugman.html.

18. Batson, Andrew, "China Takes Aim at the Dollar," *Wall Street Journal*, March 24, 2009, p. A1.

19. Slater, JoAnna, "Beijing Facess Big Barriers in Effort to Supplant Dollar," *Wall Street Journal*, March 24, 2009, p. A10.

20. "Big Mac Index," *The Economist*, February 4, 2009, http://www.economist.com/markets/indicators/displaystory.cfm?story_id=13055650.

21. Shapiro, Alan C., *Multinational Financial Management*. 8th ed. Upper Saddle River, NJ: Prentice-Hall, 2006.

22. Peck, Earl, "Prices, Interest Rates, and Exchange Rates in Equilibrium," unpublished research paper, Baldwin-Wallace College, Berea, Ohio.

23. Board of Governors of the Federal Reserve System, http://research.stlouisfed.org/fred2/series/EXJPUS/downloaddata, accessed May 26, 2009.

24. "10-Year Currency Converter," Bank of Canada, http://www.bankofcanada.ca/en/rates/exchform.html, accessed May 26, 2009.

25. Antweiler, Werner, "Pacific Exchange Rate Service," http://fx.sauder.ubc.ca/, accessed May 27, 2009.

26. Bowerman, Bruce L., Richard L. O'Connell, and Anne Koehler, *Forecasting, Time Series, and Regression*. 4th ed. Cincinnati: Southwestern Publishing, 2005.

27. Box, George E., Gwilym M. Jenkins, and Gregory C. Reinsel, *Time Series Analysis: Forecasting and Control*. 4th ed. Hoboken, NJ: John Wiley, 2008.

28. Makridakis, Spyros, Steven C. Wheelwright, and Rob Hyndman, *Forecasting: Methods and Applications*. 3rd ed. New York: John Wiley and Sons, Inc., 1998.

29. McNelis, Paul, *Neural Networks in Finance: Gaining Predictive Edge in the Market*. New York: Elsevier Academic Press Advanced Series in Finance, 2005.

30. Neter, John, Michael H. Kutner, William Wasserman, and Christopher Nachtsheim, *Applied Linear Statistical Models*. 4th ed. New York: McGraw-Hill, 1996.

31. Seber, George, and Alan Lee, *Linear Regression Analysis*. Hoboken, NJ: John Wiley, 2003.

32. Weisberg, Sanford, *Applied Linear Regression*. 3rd ed. Hoboken, NJ: John Wiley, 2005.

33. Weiss, Gary, "George Soros, All Warm and Cuddly," *Business Week*, March 4, 2002, p. 68, reporting on Michael T. Kaufmann's *Soros: The Life and Times of a Messianic Billionaire*. New York: Alfred A. Knopf, 2002.

34. "Currencies," *Wall Street Journal*, May 26, 2009, p. C2.

35. "10-Year Currency Converter," Bank of Canada, http://www. bankofcanada.ca/en/rates/exchform.html, accessed May 26, 2009.

36. *Ibid.*

37. *Ibid.*

38. *Ibid.*

39. *Ibid.*

40. *Ibid.*

41. *Ibid.*

42. *Ibid.*

43. Eiteman, David K., Arthur I. Stonehill, and Michael H. Moffett, *Multinational Business Finance*. 11th ed. Reading, MA: Pearson-Addison-Wesley Publishing Company, 2007.

44. Hull, John C., *Fundamentals of Futures and Options*. Englewood, NJ: Prentice-Hall, 2008.

45. Krugman, Paul, and Maurice Obstfeld, *International Economics: Theory and Policy*, 8th ed. New York: Addison-Wesley, 2008.

46. Smith, Roy, and Ingo Walter, *Global Banking*, 2nd ed. New York: Oxford University Press, 2003.

International Commercial Documents

Chapter Nine

Key Terms

A very large number of documents are involved in international transactions, many more than in a purely domestic exchange. Some of these documents are required by the exporting country, some by the importing country, some by the banks involved (especially if the shipment is made under a letter of credit), some by the shipping (transportation) company, and some by the importer of the goods.

Under each of the Incoterms outlined in Chapter 6, the exporter is responsible for generating and collecting all—or almost all—of the documents linked to an international transaction. Any error or omission in the creation of these documents can create difficulties for both the exporter and the importer, as the goods will be detained by Customs in the importing country, the bank will request amendments in order to process payment, or the carrier will load the goods improperly.

It is therefore imperative for international logistics managers to exert special care and follow "best practices" in generating the documents linked to every international transaction.

9-1 Documentation Requirements

Most international trade transactions require numerous documents, each of which must be filled out in a very specific fashion, depending on the country of destination for the goods, the type of goods, the method of transportation, the method of payment chosen by the exporter and importer, the bank(s) involved, and so on. Each of these documents must also contain very detailed information and specific statements, and must often be filed in a certain time frame with a specific administration. Such are the difficulties of generating these documents that a multitude of software packages exist to help the international logistics manager complete the task. Most of them promise that they can help an exporter complete an entire set in "as little as two hours."

In addition, it is a common requirement to issue more than one *original* for some of these documents, as well as a multitude of copies—one for just about every possible intermediary involved. For some transactions, the number of originals and copies can be staggering: A particularly egregious case was a letter of credit from Ethiopia for $1,067 that called for "15 original invoices, five of them certified by a chamber of commerce."[1] In most cases, therefore, the thickness of the export documentation necessary for an international transaction reaches more than 1.5 centimeters (0.5 inch), even for a simple export.

Finally, most countries still require all of these documents to be issued on paper. Although there has been a recent increase in the number of countries that *accept* electronic submissions of paperwork, most still prefer paper. For many of them, it is required to file everything on paper; for others, only documents that are in paper form have legal status. This is the case in countries that have a legal system based on the old Napoleonic Code and have not updated their laws. Italy, for example, formally started to give an equivalent legal status to electronic documents only in February 2002.[2]

9-2 Invoices

One of the documents common to both international and domestic transactions is the bill (invoice) that the exporter sends to the importer. However, the content of an international invoice is more complex and should be prepared substantially differently for a foreign customer than for a domestic one.

9-2a Commercial Invoice

commercial invoice The invoice sent by the seller to the buyer, detailing the goods purchased and the amount due. A bill. In international trade, a commercial invoice should be quite detailed and include all of the pertinent information.

The invoice that accompanies the shipment is called the **commercial invoice**. Depending on the terms of payment to which the exporter and the importer agreed (see Chapter 7), the commercial invoice may be sent directly to the importer (with the merchandise) or indirectly, through the banking channels.

This invoice should present precisely what the importer is being billed for. This seems obvious, but it is a much greater challenge to fulfill this requirement for an international transaction than it is for a domestic transaction. Several areas of the invoice must be very carefully written in order to avoid problems later on (see Figure 9-1):

- A very precise description of the product should be given. In domestic marketing, it is common to just print a part number, a number of units, a per-piece price, and a total. This is highly insufficient in international trade, as the invoice is one of the documents that will be used by the importer (or the exporter, depending on the terms of trade or Incoterm; see Chapter 6) to clear Customs in the importing country. Because the tariff paid is a function of the classification (type) of the product imported (see Chapter 16, Section 16-1), a clear and accurate description of the product should be written on the invoice, including the Harmonized System Number. In addition, because tariff rates are determined using a multiplicity of criteria—the number of units in the shipment, their dimensions, weight, and total value—such information should also be included. It is not possible to assume that tariffs will be calculated on the same basis everywhere; Switzerland, for example, uses weight to calculate duty for a number of products, including computers.

- The terms of trade (or Incoterms) should be made quite clear and should indicate that the seller intends to follow the guidelines proposed by the International Chamber of Commerce (see Chapter 6). This information is crucial to clarify whether the exporter or the importer is responsible for the payment of a number of ancillary services and fees: shipping, stevedoring, insurance, dock fees, duty, and so on. A misunderstanding in this area can cause countless problems and cost a substantial amount of money. The use of nontraditional terms of trade or the use of domestic terms of trade in an international transaction, which no one understands, should be avoided at all costs.

- A detailed list of the items that the exporter has prepaid for the importer should be noted; for example, the amount paid by the exporter for international insurance should be clearly indicated in the case of a CIF or CIP shipment, as some importing countries—such as the United States—will exclude this amount from the amount on which duty is calculated. Stevedoring charges in the port of departure should be spelled out for the same reason. There are probably countries for which it would make sense to spell out what amounts were prepaid for domestic transportation in the exporting country as well.

> **FIGURE 9-1**   A Good Example of an International Invoice

EBERT PIPE ORGANS, INC.

INVOICE: 072309-001

Date: July 23, 2009

Sold By:
Ebert Pipe Organs, Inc.
1234 Carnegie Avenue
Cleveland, OH 44111
USA

Shipped By:
Ebert Inc. Warehouse
7200 Industrial Parkway
Cleveland, OH 44111
USA

Sold To:
Australian Importers
4/2 Wilson Avenue
Brunswick, Victoria 3089
Australia

Shipped To:
St. John's Methodist Church
76 Ewing Road
Brunswick, Victoria 3095
Australia

Crates: 3   **Weight:** 57.55 kg net each
65.00 kg gross each
195.00 kg total

Volume: 1.2 x 0.6 x 0.4 m each
0.288 m³ each
0.864 m³ total

Purchase Order: 062083

Quantity	Description	Unit Price	Total
3	Catalog Item # 095673. Pipe organ blower. HS 8414.59.1000	USD 975.00	USD 2,925.00
	Insurance paid to Brunswick, Australia Airfreight Costs to Brunswick, Australia US Domestic Transportation Costs	USD 128.70 USD 585.00 USD 87.00	
	Total:		USD 3,725.70

Shipped via: Trans-Air   CIP Brunswick, Australia, Incoterms 2000

Country of Origin: USA

Terms: 1.5% 10 days / net 30 days

- The terms of payment (see Chapter 7) should also be clearly detailed; they are the conditions under which the invoice should be paid. The invoice may be accompanied by a letter of credit or a bank draft. It could also indicate that the merchandise has already been paid for (as in a cash-in-advance, a "procurement card," or TradeCard purchase) or just show a due date (as in the case of a sale conducted on an open-account basis).

- The currency in which the payment is to be made should be clear. The issues regarding the choice of the currency and ways to manage the risk of currency fluctuations are presented in Chapter 8.

- The shipping information should also be presented; it includes the ports of departure and destination, the name of the shipping company(ies), the dates of the shipment, the number of boxes or containers, their weight (gross and net), and their size.

- Finally, the customary information should be provided: the name of the seller-exporter, the name of the buyer-importer, the persons to be contacted, addresses, and so forth. The telephone access codes should be eliminated, so as to not confuse the foreign customer.*

9-2b *Pro forma* Invoice

pro forma invoice A quote provided by the exporter to the importer for the purpose of the importer obtaining a Letter of Credit.

A *pro forma* invoice is a very common international document; despite its name, it is not an invoice at all, but a quote.

An international transaction includes so many variables that it is sometimes difficult for an importer to have a good grasp of what its final costs will be; for example, the cost of the goods is increased by the costs of shipping, insurance, and so forth. In order to determine these costs, the importer may request a *pro forma* invoice, literally an invoice "as a matter of form" (i.e., an invoice in advance—an accurate and precise preview of what the actual invoice would be like if the transaction were to take place). The importer can then compare this invoice to the other quotes it receives.

In those cases in which the exporter requests payment on a letter of credit basis, the information contained on the *pro forma* invoice is used by the issuing bank to open the letter of credit. Because the letter of credit dictates that the documents submitted for payment must match exactly those outlined in the letter of credit, whatever information is included in the *pro forma* invoice will be present in the letter of credit. Therefore, it is actually against the information contained in the *pro forma* invoice that the actual documents will be reviewed. Extreme care should therefore be given to the writing of a *pro forma* invoice, as the final commercial invoice should not vary from it. If it does, it is likely that this situation will be considered a discrepancy between the letter of credit and the actual documents, and amendments will have to be made, and paid for. It is therefore imperative for the exporter to have a very accurate *pro forma* invoice, including exactly the same type of information as the final commercial invoice would have, in the same amount, with exact quotes from the other suppliers involved (shipping, insurance, and the like).

It also should include an expiration date, or the date after which the quote is no longer valid. The expiration date in an international transaction is treated very differently than in a domestic transaction. Whereas under the Uniform Commercial Code of the United States (UCC) and under the domestic laws of many other countries, where the offer can be withdrawn at any time, without prejudice, for almost whatever reason, it is not the case in an international transaction conducted under the United Nations Convention on the International Sale of Goods (CISG). Under the CISG, the offer cannot be withdrawn by the seller (or the buyer) before its expiration date, and the other party can accept it at any time until then; it is an irrevocable offer. Most countries have now adopted this convention for international sales contracts (see Chapter 5, Section 5-2 for further details).

Casual handling of a *pro forma* invoice may cause countless problems later on. As *A Basic Guide to Exporting* wisely points out, "problems … are more easily avoided than rectified after they occur."[3]

9-2c Consular Invoice

consular invoice A commercial invoice that is printed on stationery provided by the consulate of the country in which the goods will be imported.

For exports to some countries—specifically a decreasing number of Latin American countries—a **consular invoice** may be necessary. A consular invoice is nothing more

---

* In the United States, it is necessary to dial "1" before making a phone call to another state. In Great Britain and in France, it is necessary to dial "0" before making a domestic call. These access digits should be omitted from the letterhead.

than a regular commercial invoice, but printed on stationery (paper) provided by the importing country's consulate, and *visa*-ed (stamped, embossed, or whatever other procedure is used to legalize it) by the consulate before the invoice can be sent to the importer. The process of obtaining a consular invoice is often time-consuming, as it involves at least one exchange (by mail or in person) with the consulate. Because consulates for most countries are rarely located in a city convenient to the exporter, there are a number of messenger service companies that provide couriers who will pick up the invoice, wait in line at the consulate, have it legalized, and return it to the exporting company.

This process is usually favored by countries that want to accurately forecast their needs for foreign currency. From these consular invoices, they can determine their foreign currency outflows and therefore accurately manage their needs for foreign currency. However, this process also has the added "benefit" of generating additional revenues, as the stationery sold by the consulate and the **visa** procedure are usually quite expensive. All of these fees are also obviously generated in "hard currency," another added benefit to the importing country.

Fortunately, this type of requirement is slowly disappearing, as it is often viewed as a nontrade barrier by exporters. As of May 2009, consular invoices were still required in a dozen countries, mostly in Latin America.

visa A process by which the consulate of the country in which the goods will be imported reviews and approves the consular invoice for a fee. A visa shows on the consular invoice as a rubber stamp or a seal.

9-2d Specialized Commercial Invoices

Some countries require that all commercial invoices be printed on a standard form, which is usually easily available at a low cost from specialized printers of international stationery, such as Unz & Co. These countries include Canada, Mexico, New Zealand, Brazil, and Israel.[4] In general, these requirements are not considered trade barriers, and it is understood that their purpose is to simplify the work of Customs employees.

9-3 Export Documents

A country's government may require a number of documents before a product can be exported. These requirements are primarily motivated by the desire to keep accurate data on what is exported from that country—such is the case for the **Shipper's Export Declaration (SED)** in the United States, for example. In some cases, though, the government also wants to control the outflow of certain types of merchandise, or does not want to trade with certain countries for political reasons (embargoes). In those cases, the country will require the exporter to obtain an export license.

Shipper's Export Declaration (SED) A document collected by U.S. Customs designed to keep track of the type of goods exported from the United States, as well as their destination and their value.

9-3a Export Licenses

An export license is an express authorization by a given country's government to export a specific product before it is shipped. There are many reasons for a government to require an export license, but they are usually triggered by one of the following two viewpoints:

- The government is attempting to control the export of national treasures or antiques. This is the case in India, which prohibits the export of any object older than 100 years old; with Britain and with France, which both control the export of antiques and works of art; with Russia, which prohibits the export of cultural artifacts;[5] and with Turkey, which was recently involved in a high-stakes fight over a trove of antique coins that were discovered in 1984 and eventually smuggled into the United States, and which Turkey wants back.[6] Several countries have been successful in repatriating such artifacts: Italy convinced the Metropolitan Museum of Art in New York City to return some 15 objects,[7] and Greece repatriated several objects from the Getty Museum in Los Angeles.[8] Other countries are attempting their own restrictions: China is considering limiting the export of artifacts made before 1911.[9]

- The government is trying to exert some control over foreign trade for political or military reasons: This is mostly the way the United States government manages its export licensing program; the process it follows is described further in the next section. Some other countries also pursue similar objectives: China seized and prohibited from export a book published by an American firm but printed in China, as it depicted opinions with which the Chinese government was at odds.[10] The European Union prohibits the export of personal data gathered on customers or consumers.[11]

9-3b U.S. Export Controls

Commerce Control List A list, maintained by the Bureau of Industry and Security, which details which commodities and products cannot be exported from the United States without the express authorization of the U.S. government.

The U.S. government's policy regarding export controls is anchored in several milestones: the existence of a (once secret) agreement between Western countries to deny access to certain military technologies (nicknamed CoCom), which ceased to exist in 1994;[12] the Export Administration Act, which controlled the type of goods that could be exported to certain "unfriendly" countries, but that lapsed in 1992; the Fenwick Anti-Terrorist Amendment of the Export Administration Act, written to prevent exports to nations supportive of international terrorism; and the Comprehensive Anti-Apartheid Act, which created a number of regulations for exports to South Africa. These documents brought into existence the current **Commerce Control List**, which details which commodities and products can and cannot be shipped to certain countries. The list is updated regularly and published in the U.S. Export Administration Regulations (EAR).[13] In 1996, the EAR was completely revised to reflect a major shift from a policy of "everything that is not explicitly authorized needs an export license" to a policy of "everything is authorized unless specifically prohibited." Finally, in April 2002, the Bureau of Export Administration, which was in charge of administering the EAR, changed its name to the Bureau of Industry and Security.

For some products, therefore, the U.S. government wants to ascertain that the goods are purchased for a legitimate commercial purpose (and not a military or a

Internet Business and Security

The Internet is a growing area of interest for companies that expect to be able to conduct business by using this international network. However, conducting business transactions through a computer network necessitates a means to keep certain data, such as credit card information, confidential.

It is quite possible to keep data secure with encryption software, a type of computer program that scrambles data in such a way that it cannot be read intelligibly by anyone but the intended recipient equipped with the same software. However, the United States government has long regarded encryption technology as "sensitive"—it could be used for military purposes—and therefore has kept it on its Commerce Control List.[14] For years, it steadfastly refused to allow companies to use encryption

software on the Internet, as it considered its use to be an export because the network is essentially borderless. Only banks, subsidiaries of U.S. firms, health and medical facilities, and online merchants were allowed to have access to U.S. encryption technology abroad.

It is only recently that the Bureau of Industry and Security (BIS) has allowed "low level" encryption to be sold freely outside of the United States; the terminology used by BIS is "mass market" encryption, or encryption items available to the public that cannot be easily modified beyond their original intent. However, software products containing high-level encryption are still listed in the Commerce Control List, and each and every potential export must be reviewed by the BIS.[15]

criminal one) and that there is no risk of diversion (sale to another, unfriendly company or country). This is particularly true of products that have a dual use (i.e., that can be used for several purposes, one of which is commercial, the other military in nature). For example, Polaroid employees need to use night-vision goggles to assemble some instant cameras. When sales of the product surged in Japan, the company tried to expand its manufacturing facility in Mexico and attempted to ship more night-vision goggles there, but was rebuffed by the Bureau of Export Administration (BXA), the predecessor of the BIS, because these instruments have a dual use.[16]

The U.S. export control policies are focusing on three elements: the product considered for export, the entity abroad that is buying the product or an intermediary (abroad or in the United States) involved in the sale of the product, and finally, the ultimate country of destination for the product.

The Product Exported

To determine which products fall under the possible control of the EAR, the BIS publishes a Commerce Control List (CCL) on which it lists all products for which the BIS has deemed that exports should be of concern to the United States. Each product on the CCL is given an Export Control Classification Number (ECCN)—which is different from the Harmonized System Number used by Customs—and determines whether it will necessitate an export license.

All of the products that do not fall on the CCL list are given the classification "EAR99" by the BIS. However, a few of the EAR99 products can still require an export license, if they fall under the jurisdiction of another government entity that controls export. For example, the Drug Enforcement Administration controls the export of pharmaceuticals under the authority of the Controlled Substances Act and can require an export license for some products.

The BIS gives the reason for the inclusion of all products listed on the CCL. Items are listed for reasons of national security, anti-terrorism, crime control, chemical and biological weapons control, nuclear nonproliferation, regional stability, encryption, short supply, United Nations embargo, or "significant item."

Depending on the reason for which they were listed, ECCN commodities do not require a license for some countries, but do for others. The BIS maintains a Product/Country License Determination Matrix to help the exporter in determining its obligations.[17]

The Purchaser of the Product

In those cases where the ECCN classification does not require a license, or when the product is classified as EAR99, the exporter is still required to determine whether the importer or an intermediary involved in the sale is on one of several lists:

- **The Entity List**. This list identifies people, companies, and organizations engaged in weapon proliferation, drug smuggling, or terrorism, and to which the U.S. government wants to control exports. Sales to persons or organizations on the Entity List require an export license. That list is maintained by the BIS.

- **The Unverified List**. This list identifies individuals, companies, and organizations that are suspected of engaging in activities that the BIS considers illegal. Before making a sale to a person on that list, the exporter is required to inquire with the BIS about possible issues. That list is also maintained by the BIS. In addition, the exporter is required to report a suspect transaction when the transaction has elements that the BIS considers "red flags," such as when a cash sale is made for a product that is generally purchased on credit terms, or when a product is sold to a company that does not appear to be in the exporter's main line of business.

- **The Specially Designated Nationals and Blocked Persons List**. On this list are the names of persons located abroad with whom exporters are expressly warned not to do business. These persons have been deemed to represent countries to which the United States does not want to export, or they represent companies or organizations engaged in terrorism or trafficking. That list is maintained by the Department of the Treasury.

- **The Denied Persons List**. This list identifies U.S. persons, companies, or organizations "whose export privileges have been revoked." Some of these companies are located in the United States. That list is maintained by the BIS. An exporter is expressly prohibited to sell to a person on that list, and a company that is contacted (even for a domestic sale) by one of these companies must notify the BIS.

The Country of Import

The Commerce Control List determines whether a given product, for which an ECCN exists, can be sold to a specific country. There are substantial differences in an exporter's ability to export to countries that the United States considers "friendly" and to countries that it considers "unfriendly."

In addition, though, the United States has embargoes on sales of certain products to several countries. Exporters cannot sell any of these products and will never be able to obtain an export license. Finally, the United States has a total embargo on seven countries; no products whatsoever can be exported to Cuba, Iran, Myanmar, North Korea, the Republic of Congo, Sudan, and Syria. It has limited embargoes on a number of other countries, including the Ivory Coast, Liberia, and Zimbabwe.[18]

In any of the cases in which a license is deemed necessary, the U.S. government requires an exporter to obtain an **Individual Validated Export License**, or an express authorization to ship that particular product to a particular country, and to write the following **Destination Control Statement** on the commercial invoice and the SED: *This merchandise licensed by U.S. for ultimate destination [country]. Diversion contrary to U.S. law prohibited*. An Individual Validated Export License is generally granted with very specific terms and conditions to which the exporter is required to adhere.

A product not on the CCL or whose ECCN does not call for an export license is classified as "EAR99," a classification that needs to be included on the Shipper's Export Declaration.

Deemed Export

The U.S. Bureau of Industry and Security determines that the export of products that could be used against the United States must be controlled. However, the BIS also considers that products that are sold to foreign nationals in the United States are "deemed" exports, and therefore fall under its jurisdiction. For example, companies should carefully monitor the access of their foreign employees to technology (computers that have access to certain databases, or hold certain programs) and apply for an export license to allow them access. All foreign employees are subject to this rule, except those who are "permanent residents" of the United States.[19]

Fines

The fines levied by the BIS can be staggering and are meant to strongly enforce compliance. Here are a few cases from a BIS booklet called *Don't Let This Happen to You! Actual Investigations of Export Controls and Anti-Boycott Regulations*:[20]

- The Hittite Microwave Corporation exported microwave solid state amplifiers to Russia, China, and Latvia without a Validated Export License. The company was fined $221,250.

- The Aviacsa Airlines company sold aircraft parts to Mexico without proper Validated Export Licenses. It was fined $450,000.

Individual Validated Export License The express authorization, granted by the government of the exporting country, to export a particular product, or to export to a particular country or particular individual.

Destination Control Statement A formal statement, which an exporter has to print on its invoice and on the Shipper's Export Declaration if the goods shipped are subject to a validated export license: "This merchandise licensed by U.S. for ultimate destination [country]; diversion contrary to U.S. law prohibited."

- The Metric Equipment Sales company was fined $200,000 for selling digital oscilloscopes to Israel without a Validated Export License.
- The president of Sirchie Fingerprint Laboratories was held criminally responsible for the sale of crime control equipment to China through intermediaries in Italy and Hong Kong. For a sale that totaled $1.2 million, the fine was $850,000.
- The Bass Pro company exported gun sights to several countries without Validated Export Licenses. It was fined $510,000.

9-3c Shipper's Export Declaration

The Shipper's Export Declaration (SED) is a data collection document required by the U.S. government for all exports valued at more than $2,500 per item category, as determined by the Harmonized System Number ($500 for parcels sent through the postal system), and for all shipments that require an Individual Validated Export License. The SED is not required for exports to Canada, but it is required for shipments to Puerto Rico, the U.S. Virgin Islands, and Guam, even though those shipments are not exports. The SED must be sent electronically to the U.S. Customs Service.

This form (see Figure 9-2) allows the U.S. government to tabulate what products are exported from the United States and to determine where these products are sold. The data are available for all commodities and for all countries in the National Trade Data Bank, available on the Internet at www.stat-usa.gov with a subscription. However, when the procedure was done in paper form, it did not ensure that all exports were properly counted. As late as 1998, it was estimated that up to 50 percent of the SEDs had defective entries, from the value of the goods to their classification.[21] In addition, many SEDs were filed very late, and several shipments that would have been inspected or seized had already left the United States. The results were fines for the shipping lines that accepted such shipments.[22] For that reason, the SED must now be submitted to Customs before the shipment is allowed to leave the United States.

In 1999, the U.S. Census Bureau, the entity that eventually collects all of this information through Customs, decided to fight another issue with SEDs; many of them were filled out by hand, and then faxed, and some of those were literally illegible. The Census Bureau started to entice exporters to use a new electronic system for filing SEDs, one that would no longer allow errors or incomplete entries as the old system did. The Automated Export System (AES) became the only way exporters could submit SEDs on September 30, 2008.[23]

Several other recent changes in the SED include its definition of "exporter." Because errors in classifications can sometimes be attributable to a lack of understanding of the products being shipped, the exporter of record—now called euphemistically "U.S. principal party in interest"—is now always the manufacturer of the goods, even on an EXW shipment, where the goods are actually owned by the importer when they leave the United States. With this move, the Census Bureau has effectively forced the seller to provide accurate and timely information to the importer, who is still responsible for filling out and filing an SED. Both of these policy changes are likely to increase the reliability of the export statistics of the United States.

9-3d End-Use Certificates

In some cases, and in particular for shipments of military equipment, an importer will be required to provide the exporter with an **End-Use Certificate**, or a document that certifies that the product is going to be used for a legitimate purpose—such as military training—and that the product will not be diverted to another, less acceptable task—such as police ammunition against a civil unrest. Most of these certificates are provided by the governments of the importing country.

End-Use Certificate A document required by some governments in the case of sensitive exports, such as ammunition, to ensure that the product is used for purposes that are acceptable to the exporting country's government.

FIGURE 9-2   The U.S. Shipper's Export Declaration

U.S. DEPARTMENT OF COMMERCE – U.S. CENSUS BUREAU – Economics and Statistics Administration – BUREAU OF EXPORT ADMINISTRATION

FORM 7525-V (7-25-2009)   **SHIPPER'S EXPORT DECLARATION**   OMB No. 0607-0152

1a. U.S. PRINCIPAL PARTY IN INTEREST (USPPI) (Complete name and address)

ZIP CODE   **2.** DATE OF EXPORTAION   **3.** TRANSPORTATION REFERENCE NO.

b. USPII EIN (IRS) OR ID NO.   **c.** PARTIES TO TRANSACTION

___Related   ___Non-related

4a. ULTIMATE CONSIGNEE (Complete name and address)

b. INTERMEDIATE CONSIGNEE (Complete name and address)

5. FORWARDING AGENT (Complete name and address)

6. POINT (STATE) OF ORIGIN OR FTZ NO.   **7.** COUNTRY OF ULTIMATE DESTINATION

8. LOADING PIER (Vessel only)   **9.** METHOD OF TRANSPORTATION (Specify)   **14.** CARRIER IDENTIFICATION CODE   **15.** SHIPMENT REFERENCE NO.

10. EXPORTING CARRIER   **11.** PORT OF EXPORT   **16.** ENTRY NUMBER   **17.** HAZARDOUS MATERIALS _____YES _____NO

12. PORT OF UNLOADING (Vessel and air only)   **13.** CONTAINERIZED (Vessel only) _____YES _____NO   **18.** IN BOND CODE   **19.** ROUTED EXPORT TRANSACTION _____YES _____NO

20. SCHEDULE B DESCRIPTION OF COMMODITIES (Use columns 22–24)

D?F or M (21)	SCHEDULE B NUMBER (22)	QUANTITY – SCHEDULE B UNIT(S) (23)	SHIPPING WEIGHT (Kilograms) (24)	VIN/PRODUCT NUMBER/ VEHICLE TITLE NUMBER (25)	VALUE (U.S. dollars, omit cents) (Selling price of cost if not sold) (26)

27. LICENSE NO./LICENSE EXCEPTION SYMBOL/AUTHORIZATION   **28.** ECCN (When required)

29. Duly authorized   The USPPI authorizes the forwarder named above to act as forwarding agent for export control and customs purposes.

30. I certify that all statement made and all information contained herein are true and correct and that I have read and understand the instructions for preparation of this document, set forth in the **"CORRECT WAY TO FILL OUT THE SHIPPER'S EXPORT DECLARATION."** I understand that civil and criminal penalties, including forfeiture and sale, may be imposed for making false or fraudulent statements herein, failing to provide the requested information or for violation of U.S. laws on exportation (13 U.S.C. Sec. 305; 22 U.S.C. Sec. 401; 18 U.S.C. Sec. 1001; 50 U.S.C. App. 2410)

Signature   **Confidential** – For use solely for official purposes authorized by the Secretary of Commerce (13 U.S.C. 301(g)).

Title   Export shipments are subject to inspection by U.S. Customs Service and/or Office of Export Enforcement.

Date   **31.** AUTHENTICATION (When required)

Telephone No. (Include Area Code)   E-mail address

This form may be printed by private parties provided it conforms to the official form. For sale by the Superintendent of Documents, Government Pricing Office, Washington, DC 20402, and local Customs District Directors. The **"Correct Way to Fill Out the Shipper's Export Declaration"** is available from the U.S. Census Bureau, Washington, DC 20233.

Source: United States Department of Commerce.

9-3e Export Taxes

Several countries require exporters to pay an export tax on certain commodities. While this appears at first sight to be quite counterproductive—discouraging exports prevents a country from earning foreign currency with which it could import other products, and is likely to affect negatively its balance of trade—it can make sense in the case where the goods are minerals in short supply, or when the product has been heavily subsidized by the government. This was the case for the European Union when it decided to tax the export of wheat in 1996.[24] However, although export taxes may seem attractive to some governments to raise funds quickly, they can be politically difficult to implement: In 2008, after the Kirchner government in Argentina implemented an export tax increase on agricultural products from a fixed 35 percent to a floating rate as high as 44 percent, farmers rebelled and the measure was defeated in the Argentinean Parliament.[25]

9-3f Export Quotas

In the same spirit, several countries have **export quotas**, which physically limit the amount of a certain category of goods that can be exported from the country. This strategy can be followed in an attempt to control scarce resources, such as in Vietnam, which has had an export quota of 5 million metric tonnes of rice, which it increased to 5.2 million metric tonnes in 2009 because of a large crop.[26] An export quota can also be used to attempt to control the prices of a commodity on which the country has a monopoly. Such was the case with Russia, which imposed strict export quotas on platinum, palladium, rhodium, and ruthenium—commodities for which it is one of the very few world suppliers. After its application to join the World Trade Organization (WTO) was denied in part because of these export quotas, Russia lifted them in 2008.[27] As of May 2009, Russia was still seeking WTO membership.

export quota A limit, set by the exporting country's government, on the quantity of a specific commodity that can be exported in a given year.

9-4 Import Documents

A very large number of documents are required by countries in which goods are imported. There are several reasons for these requirements. These documents:

- ensure that no goods of shoddy quality are imported,
- help determine the appropriate tariff classification,
- help determine the correct value of the imported goods,
- protect importers from fraudulent exporters, and
- limit (or eliminate) imports of products that the government finds inappropriate for whatever reason.

However, there is also the possibility that the country is trying—not so subtly—to hinder imports and therefore adopt a protectionist stance. In Russia, for example, it takes an average of 36 days to clear Customs, and shipments require 13 documents before clearance is given. The *Business Planet* of the World Bank gives this information for all countries of the world, and Russia is far from being the worst offender; it takes 18 documents to enter the Central African Republic and 104 days to clear Customs in Uzbekistan. In contrast, it takes 2 documents for France and 3 days in Singapore.[28]

9-4a Certificate of Origin

The most common type of required document is a **Certificate of Origin**, which the exporter must have signed by its chamber of commerce (see Figure 9-3). In most instances, the chamber of commerce delegates that responsibility to the exporter and allows the exporter to sign the Certificate of Origin on its behalf.

Certificate of Origin A document provided by the exporter's chamber of commerce that attests that the goods originated in the country in which the exporter is located.

FIGURE 9-3   A U.S. Certificate of Origin

Certificate of Origin

The undersigned _____ Robert E. Ebert _____
(Owner or Agent)

for _____ Ebert Pipe Organs, Inc. _____ **declares**
(Shipper's Name and Address)

the following listed goods shipped on _____ Trans-Air _____
(Name of Carrier)

on ___ July 25, 2009 ___ **consigned to** ___ Australian Importers, ___
(Shipment Date)

Brunswick, Australia _____ **are the products of the United States of America.**

Marks and Numbers	No. of Pkgs Boxes or Cases	Weight in Kilos Full		Description of Item
		Gross	Net	
095673	3	195	173	Pipe Organ Blowers

State of _____ Ohio _____

Country of _____ United States of America _____

Sworn to me _____ Ronald Ehresman _____

This ___ 25th ___ **day of** ___ July ___ **2006** _____
(Signature of Owner or Agent)

The Greater Cleveland Partnership, a recognized Chamber of Commerce under the laws of the State of Ohio, has examined the manufacturer's invoice or shipper's affidavit concerning the origin of the merchandise and, according to the best of its knowledge and belief, finds the products named originated in the United States of America.

Secretary _____

Source: Courtesy of Jamie Serenko. Used with permission.

The Certificate of Origin is a statement that the goods *originated* in a particular country; it is important to note that it does not attest to the location where the product was manufactured, but only that the goods were shipped from a specific locale. This situation sometimes leads to abuses (fraud), in which merchandise is shipped from a different country than the one in which it was manufactured, often to avoid numerical quotas or higher tariffs. In order to prevent these practices, the Certificate of Manufacture was instituted (see Section 9-4b).

The Certificate of Origin is often used by importing countries to determine the tariff applied to the goods, as most countries apply a multi-column tariff system— different groups of countries pay different tariffs (see Chapter 16)—and to compile trade statistics. As in the case of commercial invoices, some countries require a specialized Certificate of Origin; for example, there is a specific Certificate of Origin for the North American Free Trade Area (see Figure 9-4).

In most countries, more than one original copy of the Certificate of Origin must be provided; in the countries that were formerly part of the Soviet Union, three

FIGURE 9-4 A NAFTA Certificate of Origin, U.S. Version

DEPARTMENT OF THE TREASURY
UNITED STATES CUSTOMS SERVICE

OMB No. 1515-2040
See back of form for
Paperwork Reduction
Act Notice.

NORTH AMERICAN TRADE AGREEMENT
CERTIFICATE OF ORIGIN

1. EXPORTER NAME AND ADDRESS TAX IDENTIFICATION NUMBER:	2. BLANKET PERIOD (DD//MM//YY) FROM TO
3. PRODUCER NAME AND ADDRESS TAX IDENTIFICATION NUMBER:	4. IMPORTER NAME AND ADRESS TAX IDENTIFICATION NUMBER:

5. DESCRIPTION OF GOODS	6. HS TARIFF CLASSIFICATION NUMBER	7. PREFERENCE CRITERION	8. PRODUCER	9. NET COST	10. COUNTRY OF ORIGIN

I CERTIFY THAT:

-THE INFORMATION ON THIS DOCUMENT IS TRUE AND ACCURATE AND I ASSUME THE RESPONSIBILTY FOR PROVING SUCH REPRESENTATIONS. I UNDERSTAND THAT I AM LIABLE FOR ANY FALSE STATEMENTS OR MATERIAL OMISSIONS MADE ON OR IN CONNECTION WITH THIS DOCCUMENT;

-I AGREE TO MAINTAIN, AND PRESENT UPON REQUEST, DOCUMENTATION NECESSARY TO SUPPORT THIS CERTIFICATE, AND TO INFORM, IN WRITING, ALL PERSONS TO WHOM THE CERTIFICATE WAS GIVEN OF ANY CHANGES THAT COULD AFFECT THE ACCURACY OF VALIDITY OF THIS CERTIFICATE;

-THE GOODS PRIGINATED IN THE TERRITORY OF ONE OR MORE OF THE PARTIES, AND COMPLY WITH THE ORIGIN REQUIREMENTS SPECIFIED FOR THOSE GOODS IN THE NORTH AMERICAN FREE TRADE AGREEMENT, AND UNLESS SPECIFICALLY EXEMPTED IN ARTICLE 411 OR ANEX 401, THERE HAS BEEN NO FURTHER PRODUCTION OR ANY OTHER OPERATION OUTSIDE THE TERRITORIES OF THE PARTIES; AND

-THIS CERTIFICATE CONSISTS OF -------------- PAGES, INCLUDING ALL ATTACHMENTS.

11.				
	11a. AUTHORIZED SIGNATURE		11b. COMPANY	
	11c. NAME (Print or Type)		11d. TITLE	
	11e. DATE (DD/MM/YY)	11f. TELEPHONE> NUMBER	(Voice)	(Facsimile)

Customs Form 434 (040397)

Source: United States Department of the Treasury.

copies are required, but, in addition, all of these copies must be notarized—embossed—and signed.[29]

9-4b Certificate of Manufacture

Certificate of Manufacture A document provided by the exporter's chamber of commerce that attests that the goods were manufactured in the country in which the exporter is located.

A **Certificate of Manufacture** is quite similar to a Certificate of Origin, except that it attests to the location of manufacture of the exporting products. The Certificate of Manufacture must also be signed by the chamber of commerce of the exporter.

9-4c Certificate of Inspection

Certificate of Inspection A document provided by an independent inspection company that attests that the goods conform to the description contained in the invoice provided by the exporter.

In some cases, an importer will request a **Certificate of Inspection**, which is a document signed by an independent company—a third party—which attests to the authenticity and accuracy of the shipment. The company determines that the product being shipped is actually the product shown on the invoice, that the quantity shipped is actually the one for which the importer is invoiced, that the product is in the same condition as the importer expects (new rather than used, for example), and so forth (see Figure 9-5).

A Certificate of Inspection is useful to the importer in several situations; for example, in a purchase conducted on the basis of documentary collection, or with a letter of credit, the documents are the only items that the bank will inspect before making payment on behalf of the importer, or before committing the importer to pay (see Chapter 7). There is no possible way of withdrawing payment if there is a problem with the merchandise, and often no way to inspect the merchandise without first taking delivery. A Certificate of Inspection provides evidence that there are no problems with the merchandise.

pre-shipment inspection (PSI) An inspection conducted by an independent inspection company before the goods are shipped internationally. A Pre-Shipment Inspection generates a Certificate of Inspection.

Some countries require **pre-shipment inspections** (PSIs) and the submission of a Certificate of Inspection for all or some of their imports (see Table 9-1[30]), and they generally have this requirement for reasons similar to the motivations of the importers. They want to protect their importers from unscrupulous exporters, but they also find it a convenient way to ensure the correct classification and valuation of the goods upon entry. Once classification and valuation are established by an independent inspection company in the exporting country, it prevents the potential corruption of local Customs officials and generally speeds up the process of Customs clearance and the collection of duties.[31]

There are several companies that provide PSI services; the largest—with an estimated 60 to 70 percent of the world's business—is the *Société Générale de Surveillance* (SGS) of Switzerland.[32] In some cases, the SGS has an agreement with a country that all shipments made to that country must have a Certificate of Inspection signed by SGS (this is the case, for example, for Indonesia).

PSIs are often considered by exporters as a major annoyance, because inspection companies delve into information that exporters feel should not be divulged to a third party. In addition, because the inspection companies have the responsibility to make sure that the shipment is valued correctly, they can—and sometimes do—recommend a change in the value of the merchandise on the invoice. This generally infuriates sellers, justifiably, especially when they feel that the inspection company inflates the value of the goods to increase tariff revenues in the importing country.[33]

Nevertheless, the inspection companies provide a valuable service to the importer; had Daewoo used their services, it would have discovered that its Chinese supplier shipped 15 containers of cement blocks rather than the expected plastic videocassette holders. Because the shipment was made on a letter of credit and because the documents were in perfect order, Daewoo had to pay for the goods.[34]

9-4d Certificate of Certification

A number of countries have industrial standards that define quite clearly the technical characteristics that a part or product must possess before being allowed for sale in that

FIGURE 9-5   A Certificate of Inspection

CSI
Control Services, Inc.
Certificate of Inspection

1234 Broadway Avenue
New York, N.Y. 10004
Tel: (212) 555-4500
Fax: (212) 555-4501

July 29, 2009

MATEXIM COMPANY
HOANG QUOC VIET STR.,CAU GIAY DIST.,
HA NOI CITY, VIETNAM

REFERENCE: invoice 987654

INSPECTION, TESTWEIGHING AND SAMPLING CARRIED OUT AT:

Warehouse No. 1, City Docks, Hai Phong City, Vietnam

ON: July 23, 2009

ON A SHIPMENT OF:

30,000 cartons of roasted peanuts marked "Roasted Peanuts with coconut oil", each carton containing 50 cellophane packages of 500g each.

PACKING: In cellophane bags and corrugated cardboard cartons in good condition, loaded on plastic pallets, in 30 containers. All containers clean and dry.

WEIGHT: Testweighing of 600 cartons (or 2%), selected at random, and test taring of 5 empty cartons indicated:

Average per carton   26 kg gross
1 kg tare
25 kg net

On this basis 30,000 cartons would weigh:
780.000 kg gross
30.000 kg tare
750.000 kg net

SAMPLING & ANALYSIS: Representative sampling of 600 cartons (or 2%) selected at random yielded 10 kilos, a composite of which was analyzed by our Laboratory with these results, which meet contract specifications:

(18% Moisture Basis)
Protein   27.84%
Ash   0.46%
Moisture   16.30%

LOADING: Shipment loaded aboard MV "Shining Star," in 30 containers, Lower Hold and Tweendeck No. 1, July 23, 2009 under our supervision.

ALL INSPECTIONS ARE CARRIED OUT TO THE BEST OF OUR KNOWLEDGE AND ABILITY
AND OUR RESPONSIBILITY IS LIMITED TO THE EXERCISE OF REASONABLE CARE

Source: Courtesy of Jamie Serenko. Used with permission.

country. For example, Germany has the *Deutsche Industrie Normen* (DIN), Japan has the *Japanese Industrial Standards* (JIS), and France has the *Normes Françaises* (NF). The United States has several of its own as well, including the *American National Standard Institute* (ANSI).

An importer may require a Certificate of Certification in order to ascertain that the product purchased meets the requirements of the standard and that the product can "pass" whatever certification procedures are required by the standard. In some countries, this certificate is called a **Certificate of Conformity**.

Certificate of Conformity
Another term for a Certificate of Certification.

TABLE 9-1	Countries for Which PSIs Are Mandatory

Angola	Indonesia (steel, waste products, and rice)
Bangladesh	Iran
Benin	Kenya (under review as of 05/2009)
Burkina Faso	Kuwait (a few products)
Burundi	Liberia
Cambodia	Madagascar
Cameroon	Malawi
Central African Republic	Mali
Comoros	Mauritania
Republic of Congo (Brazzaville)	Mexico (a few non-NAFTA products)
Democratic Republic of Congo (Kinshasa)	Mozambique
Cote d'Ivoire	Niger
Ecuador	Senegal
Ethiopia	Sierra Leone
Guinea	Togo
India (steel and steel scrap products)	Uzbekistan

Certificate of Certification A document provided by an independent inspection company that attests that the goods conform to the manufacturing standards of the importing country.

Phyto-Sanitary Certificate A document provided by an independent inspection company, or by the agricultural department of the exporting country's government, that attests that the goods conform to the agricultural standards of the importing country.

Certificate of Analysis A document provided by an independent inspection company that attests that the goods conform to the chemical description and purity levels contained in the invoice provided by the exporter.

Certificate of Free Sale A certificate that attests that the product that is exported conforms to all of the regulations in place in the exporting country and that it can be sold freely in the exporting country.

Although there are no well-defined procedures for a **Certificate of Certification**, it is often assumed that it is written by an independent company or by a trade association's representative. However, there are some cases in which the exporter writes and signs the certificate and has it countersigned by its chamber of commerce, in a way similar to the manner a Certificate of Origin is obtained.

9-4e Phyto-Sanitary Certificate

In the cases of transactions involving agricultural products and foodstuffs, the importing country often requires a **Phyto-Sanitary Certificate** along with the paperwork (see Figure 9-6). Such a certificate is used to ensure that the product being shipped is free of (certain) diseases, that it is fit for human (or animal) consumption, that it is free of pests, and so forth.

This certificate is often written by the governmental agency in charge of agricultural and food services in the exporting country (such as the U.S. Department of Agriculture [USDA] or the U.S. Food and Drug Administration [FDA]), but it also can be obtained from a commercial third party.

9-4f Certificate of Analysis

A **Certificate of Analysis** is a document attesting to the composition of certain products; for example, it is used to determine the purity of certain chemicals (for example, the exact percentage of alcohol in a "pure alcohol" shipment, which always has some amount of water) or the exact composition of certain mixtures (cement, steel alloys, plastic polymers).

A Certificate of Analysis is usually provided by an independent laboratory or another independent inspection company, such as SGS.

9-4g Certificate of Free Sale

A **Certificate of Free Sale** attests that the product sold by the exporter can be sold legally in the country of export. Such a certificate is usually written and signed by the exporter and is countersigned by the local chamber of commerce or the regulatory

FIGURE 9-6   A Phyto-Sanitary Certificate from Vietnam

Source: Courtesy of Marrisa Newsom. Used with permission.

agency that is responsible for this type of product. In the United States, that could be the USDA or the FDA.

A government or an importer concerned that the exporter might attempt to send some "defective" or "second-rate" products that it could not sell in its home country might require a Certificate of Free Sale to protect itself from this possibility. Neither the importing government nor the importer wants to be perceived as possible dumping grounds for products that are not legally sellable in the exporting country.

This is a common fear if the requirements of the importing country are in some way less stringent than the ones of the exporting country.

This type of certificate has become relatively common for pharmaceutical imports. Because of stringent regulations, medical supplies have a relatively short shelf life in most developed countries, and some pharmaceutical firms sell or donate expired or soon-to-expire drugs to relief agencies in order to generate tax write-offs and generate goodwill.[35] While some may perceive this behavior as unethical, the companies argue that most drugs are equally useful beyond their artificially determined expiration dates. Nevertheless, the governments of countries where these products are sold are requiring Certificates of Free Sale with increasing frequency.

In commercial transactions, a possible example of the use of a Certificate of Free Sale would have been when Coca-Cola introduced its Dasani purified water in the United Kingdom. By adding calcium to its purified water, the company also inadvertently added bromates, at a level that exceeded the standards of the United Kingdom, but not those of the remainder of the European Union and of the United States.[36] A concerned importer may have wanted to get a Certificate of Free Sale to make sure that it was not sold these "sub-standard" products.

9-4h Import License

import license The express authorization, granted by the government of the importing country, to import a particular product in a given quantity.

Some countries, notably developing countries, will require the importer to obtain an **import license**, or an express authorization to import a given product or commodity. Often, this requirement is instituted to prevent the import of items considered luxurious or nonessential, especially in countries in which there is a short supply of foreign currency, which the government would rather spend on imports that enhance the country's economic position.

The process by which an importer obtains an import license varies from country to country, but it is often assumed that it is the responsibility of the importer. In that regard, the importer will probably need a *pro forma* invoice before requesting an import license.

9-4i Consular Invoice

In some cases, an importing country can require the exporter to provide a consular invoice. A consular invoice is a regular commercial invoice, but printed on stationery provided by the country of import and *visa*-ed by its consulate in the exporter's country. For more details, see Section 9-2c.

9-4j Certificate of Insurance

Certificate of Insurance A document provided by the insurance company of the exporter that attests that the goods are insured during their international voyage.

Depending on the terms of trade of a specific shipment—and particularly on whether contracting insurance for the shipment is the responsibility of the exporter or of the importer, a responsibility determined by the Incoterm chosen—the importer or the importing country can require a **Certificate of Insurance** with the shipment. This certificate is easily obtainable from the insurance company that insures the cargo. The insurance policy can be contracted for a single shipment or can be an umbrella policy, covering all of the shipments of a particular exporter. Figure 9-7 shows an example of umbrella coverage. For further details on the content of insurance policies in international shipments, see Chapter 10, Section 10-7.

bill of lading A generic term used to describe the contract of carriage issued by the carrier to the shipper.

ocean bill of lading A bill of lading used in international transportation of goods on oceangoing vessels.

9-5 Transportation Documents

9-5a Bill of Lading

air waybill A bill of lading used in the transportation of goods by air, domestically or internationally.

A **bill of lading** is a fundamental international shipping document used in ocean transportation. It is also referred to as the **ocean bill of lading**; its (almost) equivalent for shipments by air is called the **air waybill** (see Section 9-5d). A bill of lading (see

> **FIGURE 9-7**   An Umbrella Insurance Certificate

Universal Insurance Company of America

"We got You covered"

Campbell Brake Manufacturing Company
2009 Marine Cargo Insurance Summary

Insurance Company: Universal Insurance Company of America

Policy Period: January 1, 2009 – December 31, 2009

Goods Insured: All lawful goods and/or merchandise of every description consisting principally of car and truck brake assemblies and parts, samples, machines and apparatus, household goods (HHG) and personal effects (PE), and similar merchandise incidental to the business of the insured.

Geographical Scope: From all ports and places in the world to and at ports and/or all places in the world, excluding shipments to or from those countries with which the Government of the United States of America currently prohibits trade, and including foreign and domestic inland transit.

Valuation: CIF + 10 percent

Household Goods (HHG) and Personal Effects (PE) are valued in accordance with a valued packing list submitted prior to shipment showing the value of any and all items where the value of the item is US$ 500 or more.

Limits: US$ 2,500,000 on any one vessel at any one time
US$ 2,500,000 on any one aircraft at any one time
US$ 1,000,000 on any one inland transit conveyance
US$ 25,000 for HHG and PE

Deductible: US$ 10,000 per each occurrence, except
Nil per each occurrence for HHG and PE of employees.

Terms and Conditions: All Risks of physical loss or damage from any external cause
American Institute War Clauses
Extended Radioactive Contamination Exclusion Clause
Economic and Trade Sanctions Clause
Chemical, Biological, Bio-Chemical and Electromagnetic Exclusion Clause

Universal Insurance Company of America, 275 Eastland Road, Hartford, CT 06103, USA.
A member of the American Insurance Association

Source: Courtesy of Marrisa Newsom. Used with permission.

Figure 9-8) is the contract of carriage used for the shipment of containers, automobiles, crates, and any form of cargo that does not requisition the capacity of the entire ship; when a shipment requires the use of the entire capacity of a ship— generally a bulk shipment of oil or other commodities, another document, called a charter party, is used (see Section 9-5e).

The ocean bill of lading when issued by an ocean carrier (a steamship company) is also frequently called a master bill of lading. When the bill of lading is issued by a **Non-Vessel-Operating Common Carrier**, it is often called a house bill of lading.

Non-Vessel-Operating Common Carrier A shipment consolidator or freight forwarder that does not own any means of transportation, but issues its own bills of lading and therefore acts as a carrier.

FIGURE 9-8	A Bill of Lading

Shipper MATEXIM COMPANY HOANG QUOC VIET STR., CAU GIAY DIST., HA NOI CITY, VIETNAM	Document No. VN/ 02459	Bill of Lading No. **SHINING LINES** VN 919242
	Export references Shipper's Ref. 987654	

Consignee (not negotiable unless consigned to order) OOO "KORVET TEKHKOR" LIT. A 10 BLDG, GONCHARNAYA STR. 193036 SAINT PETERSBURG RUSSIAN FEDERATION	Forwarding agent - references (complete names and addresses) Shining Ocean Lines 345 Strumond Street Hong Kong
Notify party (see Clause 19) OOO "KORVET TEKHKOR" LIT. A 10 BLDG, GONCHARNAYA STR. 193036 SAINT PETERSBURG RUSSIAN FEDERATION	Unless marked "NON NEGOTIABLE/EXPRESS BILL", one original BILL of Lading must be surrendered endorsed in exchange in for the goods or delivery order. For the release of goods apply to: Shining Ocean Lines Warehouse Complex No. 3 Port of Saint Petersburg 193036 Saint Petersburg Russian Federation Tel. : 00132 628990 Fax : 00132 628991

Pre-carriage by	Place of receipt by pre-carrier Hai Phong Vietnam	
Vessel/Voy. No. V.90 MV Shining Star	Port of loading Hai Phong	On carriage to
Port of discharge Saint Petersburg	Place of delivery by on-carrier Saint Petersburg	

Marks and Numbers	Number of Container(s) or pkgs	Kind of packages - description of goods	Gross weight (kilos)	Measurement (cubic metres)
See attached list	30	Containers	26,000 net each 27,000 gross 810,000 total	72.5 each 2175 total

Total number of Container(s) or Pkgs 30	Freight payable by Origin	Excess Value Declaration: Refer to Clause 13 and 14 on reverse side. N/A				
Freight and charges		Quantity based on	Rate	Per	Prepaid	Collect
USD 25,500 Stevedoring		30	850	Cont.	X	
USD 6,000 Document Prep.		30	200	Cont.	X	
USD 350 Storage Fees						
USD 2,000						
TOTAL: USD 33,850						

RECEIVED by the carrier from the shipper in apparent good order and condition (unless otherwise noted herein) the total number or quantity of containers or other packages or units indicated stated by the shipper to comprise the goods specified for carriage subject to all the terms hereof (INCLUDING THE TERMS ON PAGE ! HEREOF AND THE TERMS OF THE CARRIER'S APPLICATION TARIFF) from the place of receipt or the port of loading, whichever is applicable to the port of discharge or the place of the delivery, whichever is applicable. In accepting the Bill of Lading the merchant expressly accepts and agrees to all its terms, conditions and exceptions whether printed, stamped or written, or otherwise incorporated, notwithstanding the non-signing of this Bill of Lading by the merchant	IN WITNESS whereof the number of the original Bills of Lading stated below all of this tenor and date has been signed, one of which being accomplished, the other(s) to stand void. Number of original B(S)/L These commodities, technology or software were exported from the U.S in Accordance with the Export Administration Regulations. Diversion contrary to U.S. law Prohibited.	Place of B(S)/L issue DATE Cleveland 07/24/09 SHINING OCEAN SERVICES *As Agents for the Carrier* SHINING OCEAN LINES COPY Not Negotiable

Source: Courtesy of Jeff Halaparda. Used with permission.

A house bill of lading should indicate the name of the underlying ocean carrier and the master bill of lading.

The bill of lading is extremely important because it fulfills three roles in an international transaction:

shipper The party to an international transaction that is responsible for arranging the transportation of the goods.

- **It is a contract**. The shipping company agrees with the **shipper**—either the exporter or the importer, depending on the terms of trade (or Incoterms), see

Chapter 6—to transport the merchandise from one port to another for a given amount of money; it is a contract of carriage.

- **It is a receipt for the goods**. When the shipping company signs the bill of lading, it is acknowledging that it has received the goods in good condition and that everything seems in proper order. The document acts as a receipt for the goods; the shipping company accepts responsibility for the goods until their port of destination. However, in some cases, the shipping company finds that something is "wrong" with the merchandise it is picking up (e.g., the drums in which the merchandise is contained are rusty, there are some damaged crates, the merchandise was loaded when it was raining, the merchandise was packaged in crates that are too weak to sustain an ocean voyage) and it does not want to assume responsibility for that condition. In those cases, the shipping company will make a note about the issue or write an exception on the bill of lading of what it has observed. The bill of lading then becomes a **soiled bill of lading** or a **foul bill of lading**. In the opposite situation (i.e., when the shipping company finds everything in proper order at the time of loading and does not record any reservations at the receipt of the goods), the bill of lading is considered clean. In general, letters of credit and documentary collection transactions require a **clean bill of lading**; should the bill of lading be soiled, it would require an amendment to the letter of credit. Carriers may not accept goods for transportation if loading them would result in a soiled bill of lading.

- **It is a certificate of title**. The document that the shipping company will need to see to authorize the release of the goods in the port of destination will also be the bill of lading. It is commonly considered that the company that has the *original* of the bill of lading is the one to which the goods belong, or that the bill of lading is a certificate of title.[37] There are two types of bills of lading in this respect: The **straight bill of lading** is one on which the name of the **consignee** (the person or company that will pick up the goods at the port of destination) is specified. The **to order bill of lading** is one in which the name of the consignee is left blank or the term "to order" is written. This means that the bill of lading is **negotiable**; in other words, it allows the sale of the cargo while it is at sea. This is a common occurrence in certain industries, notably in the oil business, in which it is not unusual to see a specific cargo change hands several times during a given voyage. In some cases, the cargo is sold to a company that wants it delivered to a different port, and the shipping company is asked to arrange for that alternative.

9-5b Uniform Bill of Lading

The **uniform bill of lading** is a document that fulfills the same functions as an ocean bill of lading but is used either for inland transportation between the exporter's place of business and the port of departure, or for land transportation (rail or road) between the exporter and a foreign customer. In the immense majority of cases, the uniform bill of lading is a straight bill of lading. The uniform bill of lading also acts as a receipt for the goods and as a contract between the shipper and the carrier.

9-5c Intermodal Bill of Lading

The **intermodal bill of lading** is a fairly recent document that has emerged because of the substantial increase in the number of international shipments in which the exporter delivers the goods to a **carrier** who will arrange for the transportation and delivery of the shipment until its final destination. Because the shipment is likely to take more than one mode of transportation, it is called an **intermodal shipment**. Intermodal bills of lading, therefore, cover several legs of an international shipment. They are straight bills of lading in the majority of cases. Intermodal bills of lading are

---

soiled bill of lading A bill of lading that reflects the fact that the carrier received the goods in anything other than good condition.

foul bill of lading Another term for a *soiled bill of lading*.

clean bill of lading A bill of lading that reflects the fact that the carrier received the goods in good condition.

straight bill of lading A bill of lading on which the name of the consignee has been entered.

consignee The party named on a bill of lading as the owner of the goods, or, at least, as the party to whom the goods should be surrendered at their destination.

to order bill of lading Another term for a *negotiable bill of lading*.

negotiable bill of lading A bill of lading on which the name of the consignee has been left blank, or where the words "to order" have been entered.

uniform bill of lading A bill of lading used in the transportation of goods on trucks and trains, either domestically or internationally.

intermodal bill of lading A bill of lading used in the intermodal transportation of goods, domestically or internationally.

carrier The transportation company that will provide transportation services to the shipper.

intermodal shipment An international shipment that will use several means of transportation under a single bill of lading.

also receipts for the goods and evidence of a contract of carriage between the shipper and the carrier.

9-5d Air Waybill

An air waybill is a document that fulfills the same function as an ocean bill of lading, but applies only to airfreight (see Figure 9-9). An air waybill is always a straight air waybill and is therefore non-negotiable. This can be easily understood because, in most cases, the documents and the merchandise arrive approximately at the same time in the country of destination, and there is literally no time to sell the cargo while it is in shipment. As the other bills of lading, it is also a receipt for the goods and a contract between the shipper and the air carrier.

FIGURE 9-9   An Air Waybill

Source: Courtesy of Jeff Halaparda. Used with permission.

9-5e Charter Parties

Whenever it is shipping bulk commodities (oil, ores, grains, polymers, sand, cement, sugar, and so on), an exporter does so in such large quantities that an entire ship is often necessary to accommodate the goods. In those cases, the ocean bill of lading is not the document used as the contract of carriage; the contract between the carrier and the shipper is called a **charter party**.

Charter parties are fairly complex, as they can be negotiated for a single shipment (a voyage charter party) or for a period of time (a time charter party); charter parties that cover more than one voyage but do not demand the exclusive use of the ship for a specific period of time (for example, one shipment every other month) are called contracts of affreightment. Moreover, some shippers negotiate charter parties that only include the use of the ship, exclusive of the boat's crew, as the shipper provides the captain and the crew (a bareboat charter party). Finally, because there are different requirements for different commodities, most charter parties are industry specific (oil, grain, gas, and so forth).

Similarly, the owner of a freight aircraft can lease its equipment under three types of charter agreements, whether for a single voyage or for a duration of time. A **wet lease** agreement is one under which the owner of the aircraft provides the airplane, insurance, maintenance services, fuel, and a flight crew to the lessor, who has to cover all of the other variable costs: airport fees, for example. A **dry lease** is one under which the owner provides only the aircraft, and the lessor has to secure a crew and insurance and has to provide maintenance. A **damp lease** is yet another type of agreement, under which the owner provides fewer services than in a wet lease, but more than in a dry lease. For example, a damp lease could include the aircraft, maintenance, and insurance, but not the crew, which would need to be hired by the lessee.

9-5f Packing List

A **packing list** always accompanies the shipment. It is a detailed document provided by the exporter that spells out how many containers there are in the shipment and which merchandise is packaged in each container (see Figure 9-10 for an example). Because of the recent emphasis placed by the International Maritime Organization and world governments on security, packing lists have become more precise; while at one time it was acceptable to mention "freight all kinds," often abbreviated FAK, it is now necessary to clearly list all items in a shipment, in as detailed a manner as possible. Whenever authorities determine that a shipment presents some risks and should be inspected, a detailed packing list can prevent the inspection and avoid further delays.

9-5g Shipper's Letter of Instruction

A **Shipper's Letter of Instruction** is delivered to the shipping company when the shipper—again, either the exporter or the importer, depending on the terms of trade, or Incoterms—wants specific steps taken during the transport of the merchandise. For example, the shipper may request that the cargo be stowed below deck (if there's a problem if the cargo became wet) or stowed at the "water line" (i.e., the location in the ship that experiences the least movement), or even above deck (if the cargo is dangerous). When the cargo is livestock, the Shipper's Letter of Instruction explains what to do in most situations.

9-5h Shipments of Dangerous Goods

International shipments of dangerous goods are regulated by either the International Maritime Organization's *International Maritime Dangerous Goods Code*,[43] by the International Air Transport Association's *Dangerous Goods Regulations*,[44] by the International Civil Aviation Organization's *Technical Instructions for the Safe*

charter party A type of contract of carriage between a carrier and a shipper, in which the shipper uses all or most of the carrying capacity of the ship to transport commodities.

wet lease An agreement under which the owner (lessor) of an aircraft provides the airplane, insurance, maintenance services, fuel, and a flight crew to the lessee, who has to cover all of the other variable costs, such as airport fees.

dry lease An agreement between the owner (lessor) of an aircraft and a lessor, in which the owner provides only the aircraft and no other services.

damp lease An agreement between the owner (lessor) of an aircraft and the lessee, under which the owner provides some services in addition to the aircraft itself.

packing list A detailed list of what is contained in a shipment.

Shipper's Letter of Instruction A document in which the shipper spells out how it wants the carrier to handle the goods while they are in transit.

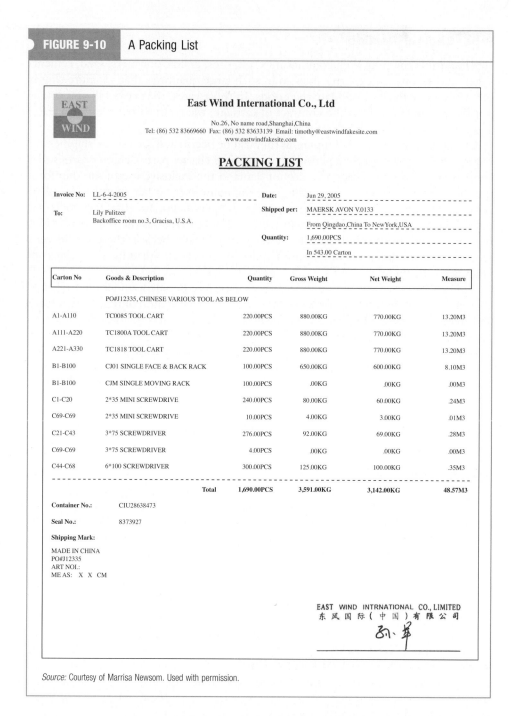

FIGURE 9-10 | A Packing List

East Wind International Co., Ltd

No.26, No name road,Shanghai,China
Tel: (86) 532 83669660 Fax: (86) 532 83633139 Email: timothy@eastwindfakesite.com
www.eastwindfakesite.com

PACKING LIST

Invoice No:	LL-6-4-2005		Date:	Jun 29, 2005
			Shipped per:	MAERSK AVON V.0133
To:	Lily Pulitzer Backoffice room no.3, Gracisa, U.S.A.			From Qingdao,China To New York,USA
			Quantity:	1,690.00PCS
				In 543.00 Carton

Carton No	Goods & Description	Quantity	Gross Weight	Net Weight	Measure
	PO#J12335, CHINESE VARIOUS TOOL AS BELOW				
A1-A110	TC0085 TOOL CART	220.00PCS	880.00KG	770.00KG	13.20M3
A111-A220	TC1800A TOOL CART	220.00PCS	880.00KG	770.00KG	13.20M3
A221-A330	TC1818 TOOL CART	220.00PCS	880.00KG	770.00KG	13.20M3
B1-B100	CJ01 SINGLE FACE & BACK RACK	100.00PCS	650.00KG	600.00KG	8.10M3
B1-B100	CJM SINGLE MOVING RACK	100.00PCS	.00KG	.00KG	.00M3
C1-C20	2*35 MINI SCREWDRIVE	240.00PCS	80.00KG	60.00KG	.24M3
C69-C69	2*35 MINI SCREWDRIVE	10.00PCS	4.00KG	3.00KG	.01M3
C21-C43	3*75 SCREWDRIVER	276.00PCS	92.00KG	69.00KG	.28M3
C69-C69	3*75 SCREWDRIVER	4.00PCS	.00KG	.00KG	.00M3
C44-C68	6*100 SCREWDRIVER	300.00PCS	125.00KG	100.00KG	.35M3
	Total	**1,690.00PCS**	**3,591.00KG**	**3,142.00KG**	**48.57M3**

Container No.:   CIU28638473

Seal No.:   8373927

Shipping Mark:

MADE IN CHINA
PO#J12335
ART NOI.:
ME AS: X X CM

EAST WIND INTRNATIONAL CO., LIMITED
东 风 国 际 (中 国) 有 限 公 司

Source: Courtesy of Marrisa Newsom. Used with permission.

Transport of Dangerous Goods by Air, or by local shipment codes, such as the United States Code of Federal Regulations, Title 49 (abbreviated 49CFR).[45]

There are such an extensive number of regulations that can affect a shipment of hazardous goods that it is always best to entrust a specialized shipper to handle the paperwork associated with such a shipment—this statement is also true for the packing and the labeling of the goods. There are often very specific forms to be filled out; in the case of an air shipment, a Shipper's Declaration for Dangerous Goods must be provided, and a specific mention must be made on the air waybill that the shipment contains dangerous goods. In some cases, the air waybill must also specify that the cargo cannot be shipped on a passenger airplane, but only on a cargo airplane. Similar restrictions must also be observed for ocean, road, and railroad cargos.

The complexity of the rules is such that in an audit conducted by the Canadian Coast Guard in 1995, 66 percent of hazardous shipments inspected were found to

A Whale of a Shipment

The business of shipping live animals is quite substantial: the value of such shipments reached more than $900 million in 2005.[38] It is also the part of international shipping in which the Shipper's Letter of Instruction is critical, as every shipment is somewhat different because every animal has its own requirements regarding temperature, humidity, and its tolerance for shipment delays.

As he related it in a lengthy article,[39] Barry Lopez spent days accompanying airfreight cargo pilots on 40 flights, totaling 110,000 nautical miles, to report on this part of international lore. In some legs of his journey, the cargo included Vietnamese potbelly pigs, a killer whale, racehorses, and ostriches. In these situations, the shipper can ask for very specific considerations. Lopez reports that on his flight from Chicago to Tokyo, during which he traveled with sixteen horses, "[t]he pilot made a shallow climb out of Chicago to lessen the strain on the horses'

back legs." (It has since become common practice to ship horses facing the rear of the plane to lessen the strain on their necks and front legs.) When the plane hit some turbulence, the pilot changed altitude and a handler went in the cargo hold to soothe the animals.

Shipments of live animals cannot be mixed with shipments of frozen goods kept in dry ice, because dry ice is carbon dioxide and the gas would kill the animals.[40] Cattle require handlers to feed them and clean their stalls, especially on long ocean voyages.[41] However, it is "exotic animals," such as elephants, rhinoceroses, and the like, that place the greatest number of constraints on the shipper, with numerous instructions, including climate control in the airports. Consider that a firm shipping salmon embryos from Alaska to Chile managed to lower its mortality rate by 66 percent by improving the way the airlines handled the fish.[42]

have some rule violation: 41 percent did not have the correct markings, 31 percent did not have the correct documentation, 19 percent were incorrectly stowed (secured in the containers or on the ship), and so on.[46]

9-5i Manifest

The **manifest** is a shipping document that is quite dissimilar to the documents seen so far in this chapter. The manifest is a document created by the shipping company (the operator of the ship or the aircraft) that lists the exact makeup of the cargo, its ownership, its port of origin and its port of destination, whether there are specific handling instructions, and so forth. Although officially an internal document of the shipping company, it is often used by public authorities to verify that rules and regulations are respected. The following example may clarify this point.

A number of Middle Eastern countries—Jordan, Saudi Arabia, United Arab Emirates, Syria, Kuwait, Iraq, Iran, and Libya—engage in what is referred to as the Arab embargo of Israel; no ship that delivers goods to these Arab nations can have stopped (or be planning to stop) in any Israeli port or have cargo coming from or going to Israel. The manifest is used by authorities in those countries to determine whether the ship or its cargo has had any "unlawful" contact with Israel.[47] American firms dealing in that region are prohibited from honoring this embargo, a situation that makes for complicated arrangements, which both Israel and its neighbors conveniently choose to ignore—business is business, after all.

> **manifest** A document, internal to the shipping company (the carrier), that lists all cargo onboard the transportation vehicle.

9-6 Electronic Data Interchange

9-6a Proprietary Commercial Electronic Data Interchange

The alternative way to send documents overseas is through **Electronic Data Interchange (EDI)** rather than by airmail. The best way to define EDI is to determine what it is not: First, it is not a fax, which transmits only a reproduction of a paper document. A fax is essentially a copy machine where the original is in one location and the copy is in another location. Second, EDI is not e-mail (electronic mail). E-mail is only the electronic transmission of text, as in a letter or a memo, for which there is no need to have a specified format ahead of time.

> **Electronic Data Interchange (EDI)** A method to send documents (invoice, certificates, packing list, and so on) from one company to another, using electronic means.

FIGURE 9-11   Tons of Paperwork

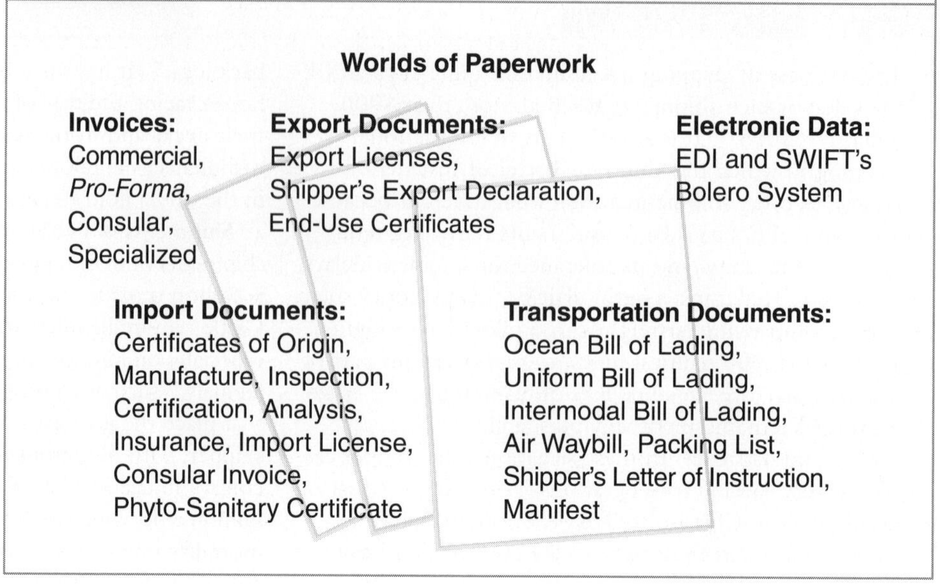

Worlds of Paperwork

Invoices:
Commercial,
Pro-Forma,
Consular,
Specialized

Export Documents:
Export Licenses,
Shipper's Export Declaration,
End-Use Certificates

Electronic Data:
EDI and SWIFT's
Bolero System

Import Documents:
Certificates of Origin,
Manufacture, Inspection,
Certification, Analysis,
Insurance, Import License,
Consular Invoice,
Phyto-Sanitary Certificate

Transportation Documents:
Ocean Bill of Lading,
Uniform Bill of Lading,
Intermodal Bill of Lading,
Air Waybill, Packing List,
Shipper's Letter of Instruction,
Manifest

EDI is an electronic exchange of documents, from computer to computer, following a format to which both the sending and the receiving parties have agreed. There are two areas in which the agreement to a common format is crucial:

- First, the sender and the recipient have to agree to a *technical* EDI understanding; for example, the choice of a computer protocol, the determination of a standard outline—which electronic field corresponds to which information on the document (sender, consignee, product description, purchase order number, invoice number, and so forth)—and the possible use of a third-party intermediary to "translate" one electronic format into another or archive the transmissions between the parties. Such translating service providers are called Value-Added Networks (VANs). They also archive whatever transmission takes place between the two parties.

  Currently, there are only a few international agreements on EDI formats; they tend to be company, industry, or country specific. The most likely to prevail internationally is the standard developed by the United Nations Working Party on the Facilitation of International Trade Procedures of the Committee on Trade of the Economic Commission for Europe (nicknamed WP4, for short), called the United Nations Electronic Data Interchange for Administration, Commerce, and Transport (UN-EDIFACT), which has been accepted by a significant number of countries, including the United States. Actually some U.S. firms have adopted EDIFACT for all of their EDI communications with their suppliers. General Motors is one of them.[48]

- The second issue is the existence of a *legal* agreement between the parties; not only should the definition of responsibilities (acknowledgment of an EDI transmission, procedure to follow when there is a "garbled" transmission, confidentiality of the data) be specified, but legal issues have to be addressed, such as the timing of the contract formation, liability for errors in the communication, and the "evidentiary value" of messages—whether they can be introduced in a court proceeding.

To date, there have been several efforts made to create a universal EDI agreement; the International Chamber of Commerce has Uniform Rules of Conduct for Interchange of Trade Data by Teletransmission (UNCID), and several EDI associations have created their own versions.[49] Nevertheless, there is yet no agreement that has international acceptance, and courts tend to rely on laws designed for written documents whenever there are problems.

9-6b Network Electronic Data Interchange: SWIFT's Bolero System

Another well-developed EDI system is the one that was developed by the Society for Worldwide Interbank Financial Telecommunication (SWIFT) to facilitate the exchange of banking documents such as letters of credit. As banks become members of the SWIFT system, they can exchange secure messages with each other. Because of a large number of safeguards in the network,[50] banks can rely on the data transmitted over the network, and a letter of credit transmitted by SWIFT is considered genuine (as good as a paper original). In addition, the SWIFT network adds new services regularly, such as Interbank File Transfers (in free form such as database files, graphs, spreadsheets) over a secure network, a requirement that is of paramount importance to the banks. The security and reliability of the network is ascertained by the protocols that the computers in the network must follow. Each login is recorded and must be cleared, messages must first be stored before they are sent, there must be positive confirmation of each message by the recipient, there are redundant links, there is a double backup of each file, and so forth.

Because of the reliability of its system—and its experience in that area—SWIFT created the Bolero network. Bolero is similar to the SWIFT banking network, but it allows the transmission of all sorts of documents (specifically logistics documents) such as invoices, bills of lading, certificates, and so on; however, Bolero does not support payment through the network. Bolero became active in September 1999.

Such an EDI network is "shared" by several hundreds of customers worldwide, which makes it very different from proprietary EDI systems because communications between member parties are authenticated and there is a common standard. Therefore, both of the issues of proprietary EDI are overcome. It is a much more efficient way of exchanging information.

Bolero is currently competing with TradeCard on many points; Bolero has the distinct advantage that it is supported by a company with which bankers have dealt for a long time and trust. TradeCard has the advantage of offering payment options through its network; time will tell whether both of these systems will remain or whether one will start dominating the business. One thing is certain, though: Paper documents are in jeopardy, and they will undoubtedly disappear by 2015.

9-7 Document Preparation as a Marketing Tool

It should be relatively clear by now that accurate and timely documents are an essential part of international logistics and of the smooth transfer of goods from an exporter to an importer:

- The *pro forma* invoice must be a perfect preview of the actual invoice. Otherwise, payment through the letter of credit can be affected—i.e., the actual invoice does not match the requirements of the letter of credit and both parties have to pay for amendments—or Customs clearance can be delayed because the actual invoice does not match the import license.

- The commercial invoice must be clear, detailed, and precise. It must include all the information that is necessary for the importer to clear Customs and minimize the duty that it has to pay (i.e., description, Harmonized System number, weight, size, number of packages, domestic transportation costs, insurance costs, stevedoring charges, international transportation costs, and so on). It also minimizes the probability of an inspection.

- Certificates of many kinds have to be provided. They have to be properly prepared, signed, and occasionally stamped and notarized to facilitate the goods' Customs clearance in the importing country.

- The correct number of originals and copies of a multitude of documents must be prepared (invoices, certificates, and so on) or collected (bill of lading). A discrepancy in the number of originals can delay Customs clearance until another original is mailed to the importer.

- The packing list must be prepared carefully and precisely. An incomplete or imprecise packing list increases the probability of a Customs inspection.

- The export paperwork must be prepared and filed correctly and in a timely manner. Several countries, including the United States, will not allow goods to be loaded if there are issues with the export paperwork (SED).

Any failure to provide these documents or to provide complete and accurate documents in a timely manner is likely to delay a shipment, generate additional costs by requiring last-minute mailings of critical documents, or create "headaches" for one or more of the parties involved in the transaction. Unfortunately, problems with documents are common, although they are clearly avoidable in most instances.

Because the responsibility of proper document preparation falls mostly on the exporter, regardless of the Incoterm used in a transaction, an exporter can turn its ability to do a good and thorough job in this aspect of international logistics into a marketing advantage.

An exporter intent on increasing its sales should therefore be thorough and meticulous in the way it prepares the documents that it provides to the importer. This should be reflected in the first contact, the *pro forma* invoice, and be communicated to the importer by emphasizing the experience of the company at providing accurate and thorough documents.

Review and Discussion Questions

1. There are three types of "invoices" mentioned in this chapter. Explain each one of them and tell which is truly an "invoice" and which is not.

2. Explain why a country could consider having no deficit in its balance of trade even though the value of its exports represents only 98 percent of the value of its imports.

3. What documents are necessary for exporting from the United States?

4. There are many different types of certificates that can be requested by the importing country or the importer. Describe three of them.

5. A pre-shipment inspection certificate can be requested by the importing country or by the importer. Why would a country request one? Why would an importer request one?

6. The ocean bill of lading has three general functions. Explain each one in detail and tell what alternative "types" of ocean bills of lading there are.

7. What are the advantages of conducting international trade using electronic document transmissions, such as EDI, Bolero, and TradeCard?

Endnotes

1. Mehta, Ravi R. Singh, "Freak and Faulty L/C's from Third World and Eastern Europe," *The Exporter*, September 1997, pp. 15–17.

2. Scannicchio, Tommaso, "Important Decision of the Italian Supreme Court of Cassazione in the Matter of Electronic Documents," *Electronic Law Journals*, JILT 2002, http://www2.warwick.ac.uk/fac/soc/law/elj/jilt/2002_2/scannicchio/#a3, accessed May 27, 2009.

3. *A Basic Guide to Exporting*, U.S. Department of Commerce, 10th ed. Washington, DC: U.S. Government Printing Office, 2008.

4. *The UNZ & Co. Sourcebook: A How-to Guide for Exporters and Importers*, Unz & Co., 190 Baldwin Avenue, P.O. Box 308, Jersey City, NJ 07303.

5. Schwirtz, Michael, "Tourist in Russia Stumbles into Legal Predicament," *New York Times*, August 27, 2007, http://www.nytimes.com/2007/08/27/world/europe/27soviet.html.

6. Meier, Barry, "The Costly, Bitter Case of the Coins of Elmali," *New York Times*, September 24, 1998.

7. Eakin, Hugh, and Elizabetta Povoledo, "Ceding Art to Italy, Met Avoids Showdown," *New York Times*, February 21, 2006.

8. Eakin, Hugh, "Getty Museum Will Return 2 Antiquities to Greece," *New York Times*, July 10, 2006, http://www.nytimes.com/2006/07/10/arts/design/10cnd-getty.htm.

9. Kahn, Jeremy, "Art: Is the U.S. Protecting Foreign Artifacts? Don't Ask," *New York Times*, April 8, 2007.

10. Kirkpatrick, David, "China Seizure Halts Delivery of U.S. Book," *New York Times*, August 28, 2000.

11. Clayton, Gary E., "Eurocrats Try to Stop Data at Border," *Wall Street Journal*, November 2, 1998, p. A34.

12. Litman, Gary V., and John M. Breen, "Overview of Federal Export Restriction Programs," in *Export Practice: Customs and International Trade Law*. Terence P. Stewart, ed. New York: Practicing Law Institute.

13. *U.S. Export Administration Regulations Database*, Bureau of Export Administration, http://www.access.gpo.gov/bis/ear/ear_data.html, accessed May 28, 2009.

14. Gallacher, David, "Encryption Export Restrictions Loosened under New Rules that Reduce Pre-Review and Reporting Requirements," *Government Contracts Blog–Sheppard-Mullin*, November 17, 2008, http://www.governmentcontractslawblog.com/2008/11/articles/export-controls/encryption-export-restrictions-loosened-under-new-rules-that-reduce-prereview-and-reporting-requirements/.

15. *U.S. Export Administration Regulations Database*, Bureau of Export Administration, http://www.access.gpo.gov/bis/ear/ear_data.html, accessed May 28, 2009.

16. Klein, Alec, "The Techies Grumbled, but Polaroid's Pocket Turned into a Huge Hit," *Wall Street Journal*, May 2, 2000, p. A1.

17. "Introduction to Commerce Department Export Controls," March 2007, Bureau of Industry and Security, http://www.bis.doc.gov/licensing/bis_exports2.pdf, accessed May 28, 2009.

18. "OFAC Country Sanctions Programs," U.S. Department of the Treasury, Office of Foreign Asset Control, http://www.treas.gov/offices/enforcement/ofac/programs/index.shtml, accessed May 28, 2009.

19. "Deemed Exports: Questions and Answers," Bureau of Industry and Security, United States Department of Commerce, http://www.bis.doc.gov/deemedexports/deemedexportsfaqs.html#1, accessed May 28, 2009.

20. *Don't Let This Happen to You! Actual Investigations of Export Controls and Anti-Boycott Regulations*, July 2008 Edition, Bureau of Industry and Security, United States Department of Commerce, http://www.bis.doc.gov/complianceandenforcement/dontletthishappentoyou-2008.pdf.

21. Lelyveld, Michael S., "Electronic Export Filings Triple, Boosting Census," *Journal of Commerce*, April 20, 1998, p. 6A.

22. Tirschwell, Peter, "The New Cost of Exporting," *JoC Week*, August 14–20, 2000, p. 4.

23. Kulish, Eric, "Mandatory AES debuts," *American Shipper*, July 2008, pp. 38–45.

24. Wilson, William, D., Demcey Johnson, and Bruce L. Dahl, "Transparency and Export Subsidies in International Wheat Competition," *Agricultural Economic Reports No. 415*, May 1999, http://ageconsearch.umn.edu/bitstream/23208/1/aer415.pdf.

25. Barrionuevo, Alexei, "Argentina Blocks Farm Export Tax," *New York Times*, July 18, 2008, http://www.nytimes.com/2008/07/18/world/americas/18argentina.html.

26. "Vietnamese Exporters Urge Hike in Export Quotas," *Oryza*, May 20, 2009, http://oryza.com/Asia-Pacific/Vietnam-Market/10225.html.

27. "Quota Removal Secures Russia Platinum Exports," *Reuters*, January 17, 2007, http://uk.reuters.com/article/businessIndustry/idUKL1532931620070117.

28. *Business Planet: Mapping the Business Environment*, The World Bank Group, http://rru.worldbank.org/businessplanet.

29. Rao, N. Vasuki, "Indian Customs System Stuck in Miles of Thick, Red Tape," *The Journal of Commerce*, January 7, 1998, p. 4A.

30. "When Is Pre-Shipment Inspection Required?" http://www.export.gov/logistics/eg_main_018120.asp, accessed May 28, 2009.

31. Wilmott, Peter, "Pre-Shipment Inspection—A Force for Good?" *American Shipper*, November 2006, pp. 24–27.

32. Freudmann, Aviva, "Top Provider Alters Its Approach," *Journal of Commerce*, April 7, 2000, p. 1.

33. Green, Paula, "U.S. Exporters Slam Inspection Companies," *Journal of Commerce*, December 31, 1997, p. 1A.

34. Mottley, Robert, "Shippers' Case Law: Consignee, Nvos Clash Over Sealed Shipments," *American Shipper*, April 2000, p. 69.

35. Russell, Timothy E., "The Humanitarian Relief Supply Chain: Analysis of the 2004 South-East Asia Earthquake and Tsunami," Master's of Engineering in Logistics thesis, Massachusetts Institute of Technology, June 2005, http://ctl.mit.edu, August 1, 2006.

36. Jones, Chris, "Coke Admits Defeat in Dasani Rollout," *Food and Drink Europe*, March 26, 2003, http://www.foodanddrinkeurope.com/Products-Marketing/Coke-admits-defeat-in-Dasani-rollout. "Dasani UK Delay Cans Europe Sales," BBC News, March 24, 2004, http://news.bbc.co.uk/1/hi/business/3566233.stm.

37. Reynolds, Frank, "Debating the Rights (and Wrongs) of Consignees of Various Bills of Lading," *Journal of Commerce*, December 24, 1997, p. 2C.

38. *International Maritime Dangerous Goods Code*, 1994, Consolidated Edition, International Maritime Organization, 4 Albert Embankment, London SE1 7SR, United Kingdom, http://www.imo.org.

39. *Dangerous Goods Regulations*, 1996, 37th Edition, International Air Transport Association, 33 Route de l'Aéroport, Case Postale 672, CH-1215 Genève 15 Aéroport, Switzerland and 2000 Peel Street, Montréal, Québec, Canada H3A 2R4.

40. *Code of Federal Regulations, Title 49*. Washington, DC: U.S. Government Printing Office, 1995.

41. *First Quarter 2006 Newsletter*, Animal Air Transportation Association, http://www.aata-animaltransport.org/Publications/newsletters/AATA_1stQtr2006_Newsletter.pdf.

42. Lopez, Barry, "On the Wings of Commerce," *Harper's*, October 1995, pp. 39–54.

43. Putzger, Ian, "Live Seafood Takes to the Skies as Northeast Cargo Market Evolves," *Journal of Commerce*, February 2, 1999, p. 6A.

44. Tower, Courtney, "Canned Cattle," *The Journal of Commerce*, September 2, 1997, p. 1A.

45. Banham, Russ, "Fish Embryos Take to the Sky like Ducks to Water," *Journal of Commerce*, June 6, 1997, p. 8C.

46. Compton, Mike, "Saying and Doing," *Cargo Systems*, March 1996, pp. 77–78.

47. Lelyveld, Michael S., "Peace Dividend: Easing in Arab Boycott of Israel," *Journal of Commerce*, February 17, 1997.

48. Zuckerman, Amy, "Edifact Gaining in Acceptance," *Journal of Commerce*, November 10, 1999, p. 16.

49. Boss, Amelia H., and Jeffrey B. Ritter, *Electronic Data Interchange Agreements*, 1993, International Chamber of Commerce, ICC Publishing, 156 Fifth Avenue, New York, NY 10010.

50. Isobe, Asahiko, Kevin J. Kerney, and Shirley Kearney-Stevens, editors, *Payment Systems: Strategic Choices for the Future*, 1993, Hitachi Research Institute, Institute of Advanced Business Systems Hitachi, Ltd., published by F.I.A. Financial Publishing Co.

International Insurance

Chapter Ten

Key Terms

One of the most complex issues in international logistics is the field of international insurance. Not only is the topic difficult to understand, but it also involves a plethora of vocabulary exclusively used in the marine cargo insurance field and nowhere else, such as "jettison," "barratry," and "Inchmaree." In addition, in an international insurance contract, the term "average" denotes something else entirely than the arithmetic mean. The difficulty is compounded by the fact that there are centuries-old traditions and concepts, some of which have essentially not changed for that long and that can be interpreted either the British way or the United States way.

Nevertheless, the topic is of utmost importance: Shipping goods abroad is fraught with perils. A company has to knowingly accept these risks or transfer them onto an insurance company. This chapter will first present some of the terms used in international insurance, then explain the risks associated with shipping goods internationally by ocean and by air and introduce possible strategies for dealing with those risks, and finally conclude with more details on the elements of a marine cargo insurance policy, which is the name used for this type of policy, whether the goods actually travel by ocean or by air.

Eventually, another form of insurance will be presented: commercial credit insurance, which is one of the alternatives available to cover one of the other great risks of international trade: the possibility that the importer will default on an open-account transaction. For details on this and other terms of payment, see Chapter 7.

10-1 Pitfalls of International Insurance

One of the greatest concerns in international insurance is to make sure that the coverage of the shipment is the coverage that the exporting firm prefers. All too often, the fact that the firm is improperly insured is discovered only after a loss. This is due to several reasons:

- The complexity of the field is substantial. Not only is there a minimum of six different standard insurance policies, but there are also countless variations in the specific clauses that can be included or excluded. Section 10-8 explains these different policies in detail.

- Many of the risks are misunderstood. Historically, international shippers were located in ports or near ports and had a good understanding of the risks of the sea. Today's international shippers are located mostly inland, and have a hard time comprehending the damage that a "bad storm" can inflict on cargo. Sections 10-3 and 10-4 present some of the many risks an international shipment faces.

- The Incoterms are somewhat misleading. Although both CIF (Cost, Insurance, and Freight) and CIP (Carriage and Insurance Paid) both mention insurance, they refer to the most basic coverage available, which is inadequate for many goods (see Section 10-8).

- The carriers offer very limited coverage. Under the various international liability conventions, carriers offer very basic coverage, with very low limits, and are exempt from liability in many cases. Chapter 11, Section 11-5 covers that aspect.

The international logistics manager should therefore become familiar with all of the peculiarities of this field in order to reach the best decisions.

10-2 Insurance Glossary

Insurance uses a precise terminology linked to risks, and it makes sense to understand this terminology before using it to develop risk management strategy.

Average: A loss incurred on an ocean voyage by a cargo owner. It can be further qualified as a particular average or as a general average.

General average: A loss incurred on an ocean voyage that is "general," in the sense that it involves all of the cargo owners on board. A general average can occur when there is a fire on board a ship, when a vessel is grounded, or when a ship capsizes. Insurance companies also consider it a general average when the captain of the ship takes an action to save the ship, the crew, and the remainder of the cargo; for example, the captain may decide to throw some cargo overboard to save the ship or to ground the ship to prevent it from sinking. The owners of the cargo that was saved by this action are indebted to the owners of the cargo that was sacrificed and to the owners of the damaged ship. The marine insurance industry recognizes that responsibility, and the owners of the cargo that was saved have to indemnify the owners of the cargo that was lost and/or the owners of the ship that was damaged. This complex concept is explained in Section 10-3h.

Particular average: A partial loss incurred by a cargo owner on an ocean voyage; the cargo may have become wet from seawater or may have been damaged by rough seas. Unlike a general average, the costs of a particular average fall exclusively on the owner of the cargo or its insurance company.

Barratry: An act of disobedience or willful misconduct by the captain or the crew of a ship that causes damage to the ship or the cargo.

Hazard: A situation that increases the probability of a peril and therefore of a loss. For example, a hazard would be a storm, which increases the probability of the peril of water damage, or a poorly-trained crew, which increases the probability of improper stowing.

Jettison: The act of throwing overboard part of the cargo of a ship (or the fuel of an airplane) in an attempt to lighten the ship. The purpose of such an action is to save the ship, the remainder of the cargo, and the crew.

Peril: The event that brings about a loss. For example, a fire, a collision, and a flood are perils.

Risk: The chance or the probability of a loss. There are different ways to categorize risks:

Speculative risk: The chance or probability of a loss as well as the chance or probability of a gain (i.e., the risk sustained in a foreign exchange transaction, as described in Chapter 8).

Pure risk: The chance or the probability of a loss only. Pure risks can be insured against (i.e., transferred to an insurance company).

Objective risk: The chance of a loss that can be accurately calculated, because ample empirical data are available (probability of a fire causing a total loss on a residence) or because a good mathematical model has been developed.

Subjective risk: The perceived risk of a loss by an individual or company. Whether this perception is correct can only be settled by calculating the objective risk. Many psychological studies demonstrate that individual managers regularly underestimate the probability of a peril that has a high actual probability, and overestimate the probability of a peril that has low actual probability.[1]

10-3 Perils of the Sea

A shipment by ocean is subject to a large number of risks, most of which are only vaguely familiar to a land-based exporter accustomed to shipping by truck or rail to its domestic customers. However, these risks are frequent, with losses in the billions of U.S. dollars every year. The trade magazine *Marine Digest Marine Transportation News* lists incidents occurring every month in the territorial waters of the United States, and it is rare that there are fewer than 15 reports per month of fires, groundings, or capsizings, although not all are cargo-carrying vessels. Because the United States has pretty stringent policies for safety and seaworthiness, it is not an exaggeration to estimate that it experiences relatively fewer incidents than the rest of the world. Assuming a 5 percent "market share" of incidents worldwide, there are conservatively 300 maritime losses every month. The *Shipping Statistics and Market Review* of the Institute for Shipping Economics and Logistics lists 98 large merchant

Web Exercise

There are several sources that detail some of the incidents that happen at sea and even include photographs. There are two Web sites in particular that list accidents at sea and provide photographs when they are available.

- www.cargolaw.com
- www.containershipping.nl

This Web site provides a comprehensive list of all the incidents that occur at sea worldwide.

- www.wkwebster.com/general/recent0.asp

ships completely lost in 2005 (through grounding, "foundering," fire, and collisions), the last year for which complete information was available.[2]

The perils of transporting cargo by ocean—and to a lesser extent by road, rail, and air—evidently have implications for insurance coverage. However, they also influence the way a company packages its products for export and the way it packs them in containers. Chapter 14 specifically addresses the packing choices available to a shipper.

10-3a Cargo Movements

A shipment by ocean is subjected to numerous cargo movements, many more than during a strictly land-based domestic shipment. In the case of containerized cargo, the goods are placed in the container at the exporter's facility and loaded onto a truck. Generally, this is done carefully, as the employees of the exporter are aware of the contents and of their value. However, once it has left the exporter's shipping dock, the goods are in the care of less experienced hands. The goods are unloaded in the port, placed in a holding area, tilted when handled by a forklift, possibly pushed and dragged, then subjected to rapid accelerations and decelerations when loaded onto the ship, handled again several times in the same manner in the port of arrival, then loaded onto a truck for final delivery. A typical container will be handled four to six times in each of the ports of departure and destination. In some cases, the goods transit through another port before being sent to their final destination. In some cases, the container is damaged in these multiple handlings and the cargo can be damaged (see Figure 10-1).

However, it is on the ship that the cargo is subjected to the greatest number of shocks and movements. A ship can move in six directions, often in an irregular fashion, and repetitively, even during a voyage with good weather. If the weather is stormy, the cargo is shaken in often inconceivable ways: "Boxes [containers] stowed on the outside, on either side of the bows, endure sixty-foot elevator drops. Plus, they are tossed in an arc, up and over, as the ship tilts to starboard. Up and down, over and back, side to side," relates Tom Baldwin, a respected journalist, when he

Figure 10-1
Container Damaged During Loading Operations in the Port of Departure and Awaiting Unloading in the Port of Rotterdam

Source: Photo © Danny Cornelissen. Used with permission.

Figure 10-2
Cargo Movements on Ships
Source: Photo © Jamie Serenko. Used with permission.

visited a containership in a near gale.[3] The different types of movement are shown in Figure 10-2 and can cause severe damage to all but the most carefully packed cargo.

Ship motions can reach 30 degrees from side to side (roll) and 10 degrees front to back (pitch). These regular movements are accompanied by drops (heave) that can reach 30 feet (10 meters), as well as brief movements forward (surge) or sideways (sway) that end in a violent shock when the ship hits another wave. When a sea voyage lasts two to three weeks, and the motions are repeated every 30 seconds or so, the cargo is subjected to more than 100,000 movements, and it better be well packaged to endure this very long "roller coaster" ride.

10-3b Water Damage

Obviously, bad weather also affects the cargo in another way. As the ship tosses and shakes in a stormy sea, waves wash overboard and can slowly infiltrate the cargo containers or the break-bulk cargo on board (see Figure 10-3).

Pacific Ocean storms produce 70-foot swells several times a year, which submerge the decks of many containerships. At times, the ship can avoid such storms, but at other times, because they are on tight schedules, they choose not to, or because the storm is moving too fast, they cannot. The end results are that there is a strong possibility of water damage to the cargo on those ships unless the cargo is very well packed and protected. In some instances, the pounding of the waves is such that it deforms the container walls and crushes the cargo inside (see Figure 10-4).

While it is traditional for a shipper of higher-value merchandise to request that the cargo be stored "under deck" (i.e., inside the ship) rather than "on deck" (outside, exposed to the elements), the way a container or cargo is actually stowed is mostly out of the control of the shipper. In addition, on very modern containerships equipped with stack bars (see Figure 11-9 in Chapter 11), the concept of deck has disappeared, making the distinction moot and increasing the possibility that a cargo will be exposed to serious quantities of sea- and rainwater.

Another possibility is that the storm will cause cargo to shift on board and to damage the ship to the point where water seeps in the hull: "At some point in the storm, a bulldozer fell off its carriage [a flat container, called a half-rack], and punched a hole in a fuel tank … [and] split a seam in the hull. Some 15 feet [4.5 meters] of water and fuel oil subsequently flooded a container-laden hold."[4]

Figure 10-3
Stormy Seas Washing Over the Deck of a Ship
Source: Photo © Cpt. Robert Johnson, Columbia River Bar Pilot. Used with permission.

Figure 10-4
Containers Damaged by Wave Action During a Storm
Source: Photo © Danny Cornelissen. Used with permission.

Yet another peril is water damage from the rain, as well as water damage caused by having a container sit in a low area in a port that floods during a rainstorm. During Hurricane Katrina in August 2005, several ports reported substantial flooding: All of the ports in the states of Mississippi and Louisiana were extensively flooded, particularly in the container staging areas. When southern Brazil experienced unusually heavy rains in December 2008, several ports were flooded and their facilities damaged. Cargo stored on the docks was also under water (see Figure 3-4 in Chapter 3).

Finally, cargo can be damaged by container "sweat." Most containers are pretty tightly closed, and no air circulation takes place. If some of the cargo inside the container has a high moisture content (agricultural or forestry products, for example), or if the cargo was loaded in a hot and humid area, then the humidity can condense on the inside walls of the container and damage the remainder of the cargo. A similar problem can happen for break-bulk merchandise placed in a tight cargo hold, as the ship "sweats" as well. These humidity problems can be solved by proper packaging and the use of desiccants. Figure 10-5 shows the variations in temperature and humidity for a container shipped from Houjie, near Guangzhou (Canton) in the province of Guangdong in the south of China, to Glenwillow, a suburb of Cleveland, Ohio, in the Midwestern United States. For a shipment that traveled in March 2006, the temperatures ranged from a high of 122 degrees Fahrenheit (50 degrees Celsius) to a low of 30 degrees Fahrenheit (–1 degree Celsius), and humidity levels ranged from a high of 91 percent to a low of 13 percent.

10-3c Overboard Losses

Another common problem for cargo is the fact that it can be lost overboard in a storm. It is not uncommon for ships to lose containers overboard—actually,

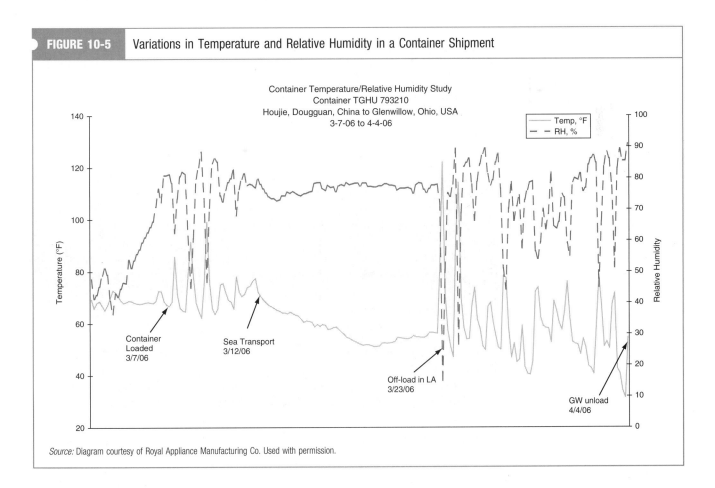

FIGURE 10-5 Variations in Temperature and Relative Humidity in a Container Shipment

Container Temperature/Relative Humidity Study
Container TGHU 793210
Houjie, Dougguan, China to Glenwillow, Ohio, USA
3-7-06 to 4-4-06

Source: Diagram courtesy of Royal Appliance Manufacturing Co. Used with permission.

Figure 10-6
A Deck Stow Collapse after a Storm
Source: Photo © Tim Schwabedissen, Courtesy of Cargolaw.com. Used with permission.

worldwide, it is a daily occurrence. The containers placed on top of the ship's deck are lashed down with bars holding them to the deck and to each other (see Figure 11-8 in Chapter 11). However, the cargo inside a container can shift, causing the container's balance to change. The container can also be improperly tied down, or the cleats holding the container can be damaged, and therefore the lash bars break or become loose, allowing some containers to fall overboard. The remainder of the container stack usually collapses as well, a situation that is called a deck stow collapse and leads to crushed and damaged cargo (see Figure 10-6).

Sometimes, the containers that fall overboard float for weeks on end, and end up being hazards to other ships; such "flotsam" (cargo that accidentally falls overboard) and "jetsam" (cargo that was deliberately jettisoned, or thrown overboard by the crew, an action described in Section 10-3d) can still be the responsibility of the carrier if they cause damage. If they present a risk of environmental damage because they contain hazardous cargo, the carrier is often obligated to retrieve them, especially in U.S. or European waters. Most eventually sink or wash up on some shore.

10-3d Jettison

In some cases, a container lost overboard is not an accident. The captain of a ship—who thinks that this action will save the ship and the remainder of the cargo—is allowed to toss containers or cargo overboard to lighten the ship, to remove a container that may have become dangerous because it became loose, or to throw overboard some cargo to free a stranded ship. Such acts are called "jettison" (or jettisoning) and they are a fairly common occurrence. When this is the case, an old maritime tradition, called "general average," dictates how the owners of the jettisoned cargo are compensated (see Section 10-3h). All parties on board pay for this loss.

Legendary Container Losses

Although a major loss for any company whose container falls into the sea, two container spills in the trade lanes of the North Pacific have allowed geo-scientists to develop better models of currents in the North Pacific.

The way geo-scientists traditionally trace currents is by releasing drift bottles at certain points in the ocean and noting where these bottles land on beaches. Generally, these releases are small in number: For example, Project North Pacific released 34,000 bottles between 1956 and 1959 in increments of 500 to 1,000 bottles.

A container spill in May 1990 included 80,000 Nike shoes, most of which were eventually recovered by beachcombers on the Northwest coast of the United States and West coast of Canada. Scientists asked beachcombers—who were holding swap meets to find matching pairs—to report where they had found these shoes. From these data, and using models of the North

Pacific, scientists were able to improve their knowledge of ocean currents in that region of the world.

However, the most notorious of all spills used for scientific purposes was the loss of 12 containers, one of which was owned by a company shipping plastic bathtub animals, or "rubber duckies." Some 29,000 toys spilled in the ocean in January 1992, and some ten months later, they landed on the beaches of Alaska. Scientists were able to develop a model to simulate the currents that brought these toys back to shore, so some good came out of this loss. There also were quite a few grins about the methodology, including an article in the *Journal of Irreproducible Results*, but it has now become accepted and is called "flotsam science." Newer research efforts in glacier movements are now using rubber duckies, because their resilience allows scientists to dump them in glacier crevasses and wait until they resurface a few miles farther down.[5]

10-3e Fire

Fire is also a fairly significant peril of shipping by ocean cargo containers. Because all dangerous cargo can legally travel internationally only by ocean—and not by air—such cargo is often present on board. Fireworks, explosives, compressed gases, ammunition, and chemicals of all sorts are crowded on deck. If these items happen to be poorly stowed, or are damaged in a storm, they can leak and mix with one another, resulting in fires or explosions. According to John Waite, chief surveyor of the Salvage Association, the most pressing issue for container vessels is fire, because "there is no effective measure by which crews can fight a deck fire on a modern container ship." Moreover, he notes that almost all cargo carried above deck is flammable and that chemical products account for 10 to 25 percent of it.[6]

For example, the containership *Harmony* was the victim of an explosion on November 16, 1998, which triggered a fire that was not extinguished until four days later. The ship lost 85 to 90 percent of its cargo in this fire, or approximately 1,100 containers.[7] The shipping line declared a general average, which is to say that this incident's costs were borne by the owners of all of the cargo on board.

In March of 2006, the containership *Hyundai Fortune* (built in 1996) suffered a major explosion and massive fire in stacks of containers that were stowed on-deck while in the Gulf of Aden (see Figure 10-7). The entire aft end (rear part) of the ship was completely engulfed in fire. Multiple explosions ensued, as the ship was carrying fireworks. Containers were blown over the side, and the area around the vessel was covered with flotsam. The crew abandoned ship. It is estimated that 500 containers were lost. On April 17, 2006, the ship was safely towed into Port Salalah, Oman, where the remaining 2,249 containers were discharged. General average was declared for the vessel and cargo losses. Marine cargo experts at insurance brokerage group Aon estimated at the time that total losses would amount to at least U.S. $300 million.[8]

10-3f Sinking

One of the other consequences of bad weather is the possibility of sinking. While not common for modern containerships, the possibility of sinking is always present. While

Figure 10-7
Fire Aboard the Containership *Hyundai Fortune*
Source: Photo © Royal Netherland Navy. Used with permission.

most of the ships lost every year to sinking are older bulk ships flying flags of Third World countries (i.e., not always very well maintained), even the most modern ships can fall prey to a rogue wave and be lost or seriously damaged at sea. The International Union of Marine Insurance reports on the number of ships lost at sea, as well as the human casualties. In 2008, there were 75 ships lost at sea, a substantial decrease over the 106 casualties of 2007 and the high of 225 vessels lost in 1984.[9]

10-3g Stranding

Another peril facing cargo is the possibility of stranding, which also happens fairly frequently. Mechanical breakdown, stormy weather, and sometimes incompetent crews are responsible for a significant number of grounded ships every year. The improvements made in navigational technologies, such as the Global Positioning System, have improved the precision with which ships operate. However, they cannot rely on precise maps. Only about 35 percent of the world's oceans have been accurately mapped, and many charts rely on data that were collected—somewhat inaccurately—some 50 to 100 years ago. In addition, currents, coastal rivers, and strong storms modify the relief of coastal areas frequently; this is why many ports employ pilots to guide ships in their approach to port.

For example, a combination of bad luck and a partially inaccurate map caused the stranding of the *Queen Elizabeth 2* ocean liner in August 1992 in Martha's Vineyard Sound, off the coast of Massachusetts. It shows that strandings can still occur in well-traveled shipping lanes and with exceptional crews. She damaged part of her hull, passengers had to be evacuated, and Cunard Lines had to put the ship in dry dock for repairs.[13] The four-year-old cruise ship *Royal Caribbean Monarch of the Seas*, equipped with the most modern technologies, struck a reef in Saint-Maarten in December 1998 and had to be beached to avoid sinking.[14]

Direct damage to the cargo is not very likely when a ship is stranded. Nevertheless, because stranded vessels can take days or weeks to be freed, the cargo on board can be

The MSC Carla's Christmas Cargo Loss

On November 24, 1997, the containership *MSC Carla*, designed to hold approximately 3,300 containers, was traveling from Le Havre, France, to Boston. About 200 miles (300 kilometers) north of the Azores Islands, the ship was caught in a storm and hit with a very large "rogue" wave, estimated to be 100 feet (30 meters) high, which split the ship's hull in half. The bow section of the ship, while it stayed afloat for a few days, finally sank with 1,000 containers on board. The stern, after being heroically kept afloat by its crew, was eventually towed by a high-sea tugboat to the Canary Islands, a few weeks later. Fortunately, there was no loss of life.[10]

The cargo losses included a lot of goods destined for American consumers for Christmas. In particular, several hundred cases of rare wines, old and irreplaceable Cognac and Armagnac bottles, some of them valued at $700 per bottle. Unfortunately, the goods sank in such deep

waters of about 10,000 feet (3,000 meters) that they could not be recovered. Even for those goods that were "safe" in the Canaries, a lot of them were damaged and unsellable: Frozen foods had thawed—all the electrical power on board had been used to operate the pumps—and other cargo was heavily water damaged. "High-quality slabs of architectural stone were reduced to a 'pile of shattered granite and small lumps of marble'."[11]

The task of sorting out the responsibilities and settling the insurance claims was a job that took more than three years (it was settled in 2001) because the Mediterranean Shipping Company had declared a general average, which meant that the U.S. $170 million cost of the accident was shared by all the cargo owners on the ship. The final dispute between the insurers and the builders of the ship was settled by the U.S. Court of Appeals in 2005.[12]

damaged while it waits; it is obviously the case for refrigerated or produce cargo. In addition, when the ship is freed, cargo is often "lightered" onto another ship, with all the perils associated with a transfer of cargo in less than ideal conditions. If the ship's hull is damaged, there can also be significant water infiltration, and the cargo can be flooded. In other cases, part of the cargo is simply jettisoned to lighten the ship. This is more often the case with bulk cargo of low value rather than with cargo of higher value or containerized cargo.

On December 25, 2005, the *APL Panama* (built in 2001) grounded itself on sand while inbound to the port of Ensenada, Mexico. The vessel had 1,805 containers aboard when it became stranded. It wasn't until after 74 days that salvors were able to get it afloat after discharging approximately 1,300 containers using helicopters and a shore crane operating from a makeshift jetty and removing sand from around the hull with dredging equipment. General average was declared. After being refloated, the vessel was towed to a shipyard due to the damage to its propeller.[15]

On January 18, 2008, the *MSC Napoli*, a Panamax containership, ran into rough weather in the English Channel and the ship started to take on water. The ship was then towed toward a British port, but on the way, it started to list substantially and was eventually grounded purposefully to prevent it from sinking (see Figure 10-8). Overnight, the ship lost over a hundred containers overboard, all of which eventually washed onto the beach, where local residents scavenged motorcycles, car parts, and cosmetics.[16]

10-3h General Average

The concept of general average is used exclusively in marine insurance. It predates the concept of insurance and was the idea that, when there is an "average"—a term derived from the French word *avarie*, which means "damage to a ship or its cargo"—or a major loss on a ship, all cargo owners and the ship owner share in the loss. In other words, a general average is a general loss, or a loss affecting all the parties involved in an ocean voyage. It is based on the principle that the owner of the ship and the cargo owners all share the goal of a successful completion of the voyage and that therefore all share in the risks and the costs of the venture.

Figure 10-8
The Stranded *MSC Napoli* Near the Coast of Britain
Source: Photo © Gary Tanner. Used with permission.

The concept is applied in a very unusual fashion: When a portion of the cargo is lost in bad weather, or when there is a major fire on board (see the case of the *Hyundai Fortune* in Section 10-3e), or when a portion of the cargo is jettisoned to save the ship, all of the owners of the cargo and the owner of the ship (or their insurers) pay for the lost cargo if a general average is declared by the ship owner.

It's probably best to explain how this works with a specific example: Assume a bulk cargo ship, valued at $1,070,000 loses power to its rudder and becomes stranded in shallow waters. It is carrying a shipment of iron ore in its fore holds (front of the ship) valued at $100,000, and a shipment of coal in its aft holds, valued at $80,000. In order to free the ship, the captain calls on a tug, and the decision is made that a portion of the ore will have to be jettisoned to allow the bow of the ship to get free. The ship is then towed to a port where several repairs are made to make the ship seaworthy again. After this adventure, the owner of the ship declares a general average, and an adjuster is called to settle the claims.

First, the adjuster calculates the market value of the jettisoned cargo; in this case, the ore that was jettisoned would have been sold for $10,000. Second, the cost of the salvage operation, including the damage done to the ship while freeing it, is added up: The tug charged $45,000, and damage to the hull, engine, and propeller shaft ended up costing $20,000. Finally, the ratio of the losses to the combined value of the cargo and the ship is calculated:

$$\frac{(10,000 + 45,000 + 20,000)}{(1,070,000 + 100,000 + 80,000)} = \frac{75,000}{1,250,000} = 0.06 = 6 \text{ percent}$$

The adjuster then uses this ratio to calculate the liabilities of the cargo owners and of the ship owner:

- The company shipping the iron ore cargo has a liability of $100,000 × 6 percent = $6,000. However, because it had a loss of $10,000 for the jettisoned cargo, it collects the difference of $10,000 − $6,000 = $4,000 from the adjuster. Realistically, if the cargo owner is insured, it will collect $10,000 from its insurer, and eventually, the latter will collect $4,000 from the adjuster.

- The company shipping the coal has a liability of $80,000 × 6 percent = $4,800, which it (or its insurance company) pays to the adjuster.

- The company owning the ship has a liability of $1,070,000 \times 6$ percent = $64,200. Once the direct costs for tug and damages are deducted, though, it ends up collecting $65,000 - $64,200 = $800. Most likely, its hull insurance coverage would have covered the remainder.

For at least a portion of the owners of cargo on board, general average means that the owners of the goods that arrive safely have a liability to the owners of the goods that did not arrive. Companies that had sufficient insurance have only their goods to worry about; companies with no insurance will have to place a cash deposit with the adjuster of roughly one-third of the value of the goods on the ship.[17] Because of its complexity—imagine a ship such as the *Carla* with 3,000 containers aboard, most likely owned by a similar number of different owners—the settlement of a general average situation can take years to complete. Every year, there are approximately five situations in which a shipping company declares a general average involving cargo from U.S. shippers.[18]

10-3i Theft

Cargo theft is yet another concern for companies shipping by ocean. While the risks are much greater on shore, or specifically in transit to the port of departure and from the port of arrival, it is becoming a major concern of exporters and importers of cargo that is easy to resell, such as athletic shoes, cellular telephones, consumer electronics, and computer equipment. The total value of cargo thefts is difficult to pinpoint, for two reasons: The police often tally these data together with other types of thefts, and companies are reluctant to report cargo theft out of concern for their reputations and fear of increased insurance premiums. The U.S. Federal Bureau of Investigation estimates cargo theft to represent at least U.S. $15 billion per year in the United States,[19] and multiple sources estimate cargo theft to represent more than U.S. $50 billion worldwide.[20]

Cargo theft can be classified in three basic ways:

- **Pilferage** occurs where individuals steal cargo when they see an opportunity; such crimes are not planned and usually happen at random. They are more frequent for cargo that can be identified by its markings or packaging, because it makes a more tempting target. Containerization has reduced pilferage because it makes the cargo much more difficult to identify and more difficult to steal in small quantities.

- **Organized theft** refers to carefully planned operations that are directed at the entire container. Organized theft usually targets high-value cargo and often includes a group of individuals, some of whom may be "insiders" in the supply chain and provide information about the content of the container.

- **System's theft** uses the information system of the supply chain to change paperwork, substitute paperwork, or delete files so that cargo can be removed without immediate detection. This type of theft requires either inside accomplices or the ability to gain access to a company's computer system.

Depending on a company's operating profitability, it can take from $10 to $15 in increased revenues to make up every dollar lost through theft. Corporations should be guided by a strong preventive security and loss prevention program. An effective security and loss prevention program is therefore money well spent for most companies whose cargo can be tempting to thieves. Chapter 15 addresses how companies can minimize their security risks.

10-3j Piracy

Piracy is the last of the major risks associated with shipping by ocean. Although the mention of this term always raises a chuckle in any audience, it is a serious risk in several parts of the world. Consider that the International Chamber of Commerce

pilferage Theft of part of a cargo shipment due to opportunity. The thief did not plan the crime; the circumstances were such that it was possible to commit it.

organized theft Theft of a cargo shipment (or part of a cargo shipment) that is due to organized criminal activity, in which one or more individuals plan and eventually commit the theft.

system's theft Theft that is perpetrated by someone who also gains access to a computer in the information system of the supply chain and deletes the files related to that shipment to make the theft undetectable.

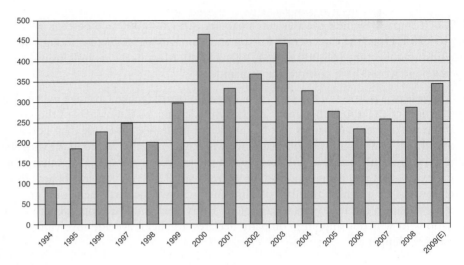

Figure 10-9
Number of Piracy and Armed Robbery Attacks Against Ships
Source: ICC International Maritime Bureau.

(ICC) reported a total of 469 attacks for 2000, the worst year since accurate records have been kept. Figure 10-9 shows the number of attacks and armed robberies against ships from 1994 to 2009. The problem is so significant that the ICC created the Piracy Reporting Centre in Kuala Lumpur, Malaysia, in October 1992, which allows the ICC to issue a monthly piracy report.[21]

The areas of the world in which piracy is most active are the Indonesian archipelago, Bangladesh, Somalia, Nigeria, and the Gulf of Aden. The greatest number of ships that are attacked are bulk or tanker ships carrying commodities that can be relatively easily sold in some loosely-policed countries; these two categories combined represented 40 percent of all ships attacked. However, general merchandise ships and containerships represented about 15 percent of all victims in these categories, and are generally held for ransom rather than captured to sell the cargo or the ship.

Most of the piracy incidents involve thugs attacking a ship and stealing the crew's possessions. However, on a number of occasions, the ship's crew is transferred to a small boat and left adrift, while the pirates take the ship and its cargo. Still at sea, the ship is renamed, all evidence of its former identity is destroyed, a complete makeover is executed—including a new paint job—and a new set of paperwork is created. Although it may sound impossible to "pull this off," the reality is that it is a strong possibility, especially for bulk cargo shipped on relatively small ships; there are roughly 40,000 such ships, none of which are particularly distinct from one another, and which change legal ownership fairly frequently. In addition, in those parts of the world where most of these attacks occur, the police are either too busy with other pressing matters or cannot be bothered. Despite those odds, the Piracy Reporting Centre has helped recover many of the hijacked ships that were reported.[22]

10-3k Other Risks

Numerous other risks exist in shipping by sea:

- The risk of collision at sea is not substantial but is still present. Collisions usually happen in crowded shipping lanes, such as the English Channel or the Strait of Gibraltar. Thanks to radar equipment, this risk has been minimized, but it still happens. In August 1999, the *Ever Decent*, a modern containership, collided in the English Channel with the *Norwegian Dream*, a newly built cruise ship.[33] In February 2003, just east of the Port of Singapore, the liquefied-petroleum-gas

Somali Pirates

For centuries, pirates have been exploiting the lawlessness of the sea, and since they "operate" outside the reach of courts and governments, there is little that governments can do to deter or prevent piracy. While for most people, the word "pirate" conjures up comical images of a man with an eye patch and a parrot on his shoulder, for those sailing ships in certain parts of the world, the image is very different.

The Gulf of Aden is one such area which has seen an alarmingly high increase in pirate attacks. This body of water between North Africa and the Arabian Peninsula is one of the world's busiest shipping lanes, and the attacks are causing major problems for international commerce. The waterway is "an important thoroughfare for goods heading to Europe and the U.S. from Asia," and carries about "4% of [the] daily global demand" for crude oil.[23]

Most of the pirates roaming the Gulf come from Somalia, a country which is currently without an effective government. "Working in small, fast boats, the pirates typically speed up alongside target ships, fire on them with small arms and then board them with simple ladders and grappling hooks."[24] The ships' crew and cargo are usually held for ransom and later released. Three particular attacks attracted much attention in 2008–2009, among the more than 50 that took place in that period.

The *Faina* was taken hostage on September 25, 2008. The Ukrainian ship, bound for Kenya, was carrying "33 T-72 Soviet-era tanks, 150 grenade launchers, 6 antiaircraft guns and heaps of ammunition,"[25] a fact that was likely unknown to the pirates, but which brought much attention to the incident. The pirates initially demanded a $35 million ransom. For four months, the ship was tracked by American warships determined to prevent the arms from being unloaded, during which time the captain mysteriously died. The ship was finally released after the owners paid a ransom of $3.2 million to the pirates. The cash was literally dropped from a helicopter into the sea, next to the pirates' ship.

The hijacking of the *Sirius Star* on November 15, 2008, showed the increasing boldness and resources of the pirates. The modern Liberian ship (it was built in 2008) was attacked in an area far outside what was assumed to be

the pirates' normal operating zone—it was 400 miles off the coast—and was much larger than any of the ships attacked until then. It was carrying a cargo of 2.2 million barrels of crude oil, valued at over $100 million.[26] The pirates sailed the ship to the Somali port of Harardhere and a ransom of $25 million was demanded. After nearly two months of negotiation, the ship and its crew were released for $3 million. Upon releasing the ship, the pirates escaped on a small speedboat which capsized, and at least one of the pirates drowned. His body was found later washed ashore with $153,000 in cash in a plastic bag.[27]

Finally, the *Maersk Alabama*, with a cargo of 17,000 metric tonnes of U.N. relief supplies and a crew of 21 Americans, was hijacked on April 8, 2009. The captain was held hostage and the pirates demanded a ransom. Because it was a U.S.-flagged ship, the U.S. Navy intervened (to protect a U.S. asset and U.S. lives), surrounding the vessel and the pirates' boat, and the Somali pirates were eventually killed.[28] This episode was reportedly the first pirate attack on a U.S. ship since the early nineteenth century.

With the threat of increased violence, ship owners are beginning to seriously consider their options in combating pirates, even though these options are limited. Officials at Maersk have said that they "will divert some of [their] oil tankers around the Cape of Good Hope and transfer some cargo to faster ships amid the rise in piracy in the Gulf of Aden."[29] This is a poor option, however, as it does nothing to curb piracy and causes an increase in insurance, payroll costs, and shipping fuel bills, "and it will mean goods take weeks longer to reach their destinations."[30] Other ship owners are hiring armed guards to ride along on ships, and navies from around the world are helping to patrol shipping channels. However, those measures are not very attractive, as an exchange of fire aboard a cargo ship laden with flammable cargo could lead to a much greater loss than the price of the ransom.

Therefore, despite all the technological and political advances made over the past 20 centuries, pirates are proving just as big a threat to ships as they were in Roman times. It is still a huge lawless sea.[31,32]

carrier *Gas Roman* collided with the *Springbok*, a small cargo ship. The collision was of such force that the vessels were not separated until they had drifted to more sheltered waters, in order to prevent both of them from sinking[34] (see Figure 10-10).

- There is also the risk of collision with non-vessels; floating or sunken containers or debris are present in shipping lanes as well, and represent some degree of risk for ships, but little for cargo. Oddly enough, there is still the possibility of collision with icebergs, including very large ones from Antarctica. Icebergs drift

Figure 10-10
Collision between the *Gas Roman* and the *Springbok*
Source: Photo © International Salvage Union. Used with permission.

continuously in the Antarctic Ocean, and these massive blocks of ice can reach 27 by 36 nautical miles (50 kilometers by 67 kilometers). The position and progress of all very large Antarctic icebergs is monitored by the National Ice Center.[35]

- Other collisions can happen as well. In May 1980, a freighter hit the Skyway Bridge in Tampa, Florida, and caused the collapse of a 1,400-foot (420-meter) span of the bridge,[36] damaging part of the ship and its cargo. In February 1997, in the Port of San Francisco, an indisposed pilot left the bridge of the *Orion* for a few minutes and the ship ended up crashing into the pier, causing U.S. $250,000 worth of damage to a gantry crane.[37]

- The risk of having a cargo contaminated or affected by other cargo is also present. It is always possible for a cargo to be contaminated by residues of the cargo that was previously in the same container or in the same ship, particularly foodstuffs contaminated by chemical products. A shipper importing rice found that it was unsellable due to the smell it acquired in the cargo hold of the ship.[38] Another found that its cargo of 2,500 metric tonnes of vinyl pellets was contaminated by a few pounds of styrene left in the hold. Refining costs amounted to $188,000.[39]

- In some cases, other cargo on board can be a hindrance to a shipper. For example, a ship was carrying a cargo of wheat to the Dominican Republic and stopped in Dakar, Senegal, to pick up an additional load of groundnuts. The nuts eventually proved to be infested with khapra beetles. After the beetles were discovered in the port of destination, the ship was fumigated twice, which nonetheless failed to rid the cargo of the pests. The ship was then ordered to dump all of its cargo—including the wheat—into the sea.[40] The owners of the wheat cargo had done nothing improper; they just happened to have loaded it onto the "wrong" ship.

- For some ships sailing out of impoverished countries, another increasing problem is stowaways. Young men sneak into the cargo holds or into containers, and hide until they are discovered at sea. In most cases, the stowaways become a larger problem at the port of destination, where police and immigration officials fine the ship and question the crew. In 2008, there were 436 stowaways found in the ports of the United States.[41] Many more were not discovered. U.S. Immigration and Customs Enforcement estimates that about 3,000 stowaways enter the United States every year.[42] In most countries, the responsibility to repatriate the discovered stowaways falls on the carrier that brought them into the country. The expense of repatriating stowaways, who frequently are in small groups of two or three and have no identifying papers, runs into the thousands of dollars. In a few instances, the fear of these delays, expenses, and fines leads the crews to engage in criminal behavior, such as killing the stowaways or setting them adrift at sea on makeshift rafts.[43]

The consequences for the cargo beyond the delay are many; most of the time, the cargo is damaged by the stowaways while they are living with the merchandise from a few days to a few weeks. Approximately 2 percent of all vehicles going from Mexico to the United States by rail are damaged by stowaways who sleep, eat, and defecate in the cars.[44] Sometimes, the stowaways hide in cargo holds that are closed and where the cargo is often laden with toxic chemicals or fumigated with insecticides. The stowaways die and the cargo is then considered unfit for consumption and destroyed in the country of destination.[45] There are unfortunately no practical ways to prevent this type of occurrence.

- In some cases, and for whatever reason, a government may decide to arrest a ship (i.e., keep it in port rather than let it sail away). Such was the case for five Yugoslavian ships that were held in U.S. ports for more than five years, when the U.S. government seized all Yugoslavian assets during the Bosnian civil war.[46] The cargo destined for the United States had been unloaded, but the cargo loaded for the return trip was on board for the entire duration of the ordeal.

- In other cases, the owners of a ship declare bankruptcy while the ship is away, or they just decide to abandon the ship and its crew for economic reasons. In 1998, there were a substantial number of ships, most of them from the former Soviet Union and Eastern Bloc or flying flags of convenience, that had been abandoned by their owners. The crew of the *Delta Pride* was abandoned by its Karachi owners in the waters of Mexico; 14 months later, the men finally made it to the United States and were flown home after a Pakistani charity got involved and the ship and its cargo were sold at auction.[47] The *Oituz*, one of 22 Romanian ships abandoned by its owners, waited with its cargo of 14,000 metric tonnes of sugar for 9 months off the coast of Mexico.[48] The eventual whereabouts of the ship, its crew, and its cargo are unknown. There were a total of 18 ships abandoned by ship owners in 2005, according to the International Transport Workers Federation.[49]

- In ports where the equipment is inadequate or in short supply, some of the cargo may be unloaded from the ship by taking apart the crates and the merchandise, and reconstructing the goods and the crates on the quay. This can be quite damaging to the cargo. In Chapter 14, this issue, as it relates to packaging and packing the goods, is discussed. Cigna, the insurance corporation, publishes a guide to the equipment in place in all the ports worldwide, called *Ports of the World*,[50] so that a firm may plan the size of its shipment accordingly.

- Some ports have a history of social unrest and are shut down for several days by strikes or other civil disturbances. During the summer of 2000, French fishermen and French truckers blockaded the ports and then the refineries of the country to protest high diesel fuel prices. The government eventually lowered taxes on that fuel. Soon, their counterparts in Spain, Britain, Italy, and Germany followed suit, and for about a month, all cargo traffic in Europe was affected. Time-sensitive cargo was delayed, and transportation costs increased. Such strikes occur with much frequency in France and other southern European countries. Strikes in the ports of Japan occur almost annually to force negotiations for higher wages for dockworkers. All of these actions affect cargo movements in many ways; even if cargo going from Cairo to Bombay is not specifically caught in an Italian strike, it is delayed because the containership on which it was supposed to sail is delayed.

The possible perils that cargo can encounter at sea and on its way to and from a seaport are many; this list illustrates the point that many of the risks that are associated with a sea voyage may be easily underestimated by an exporter or an importer arranging for ocean cargo services. The importer or the exporter, whichever is responsible for the cargo, must be quite alert in its management of these risks.

10-4 Perils Associated with Air Shipments

Compared to what can happen to an ocean shipment, the perils to which an air shipment is exposed are minimal, a situation due mostly to the fact that air transport is, by nature, less perilous than ocean transportation. In addition, the airline industry is still dominated by companies located in, and therefore regulated by, developed countries' governments, which tend to have stringent rules regarding safety, pilot training, and maintenance. Despite the large number of aircraft in operation—in 2009, there were approximately 14,000 commercial airplanes in the world, including 1,948 freighters[51]—and the correspondingly high number of voyages, the number of accidents per year is very small, reflecting the emphasis on safety of the entire industry.

The risks of fire and explosion are greatly diminished, mostly because regulations by the International Civil Aviation Organization and the International Air Transport Association prohibit shipments of dangerous goods by air. The risk of total loss of cargo due to aircraft crashes is essentially nil, as is the risk of loss while the aircraft is aloft. The three biggest concerns for shippers should be:

- **Cargo movement**. While in the aircraft, the cargo is subjected to rough weather and sudden and quick accelerations and decelerations. Because freighter airplanes do not have to worry about passenger comfort, their pilots do not fly around turbulences the way passenger airline pilots do, and the cargo on board can be subjected to sudden and fairly violent bumps. In a similar fashion, the aircraft will brake faster on landing, bank at a wider angle on approach, and altogether be less gentle than if passengers were on board. However, a good percentage of cargo moves in passenger airplanes, which do not experience such conditions; that percentage is expected to decrease in 2010, though, as U.S. legislation demands that 100 percent of all cargo be screened before it can travel on a passenger aircraft, a cost-prohibitive and cumbersome measure.

  For air cargo, the greatest hazards are still in the shipping and handling that precede the flight. In the truck on the way to the airport, in the warehouse, on the tarmac, and during their counterpart activities in the transit airport and the airport of arrival (forklift truck damage, for example).

- **Theft and pilferage**. While airports tend to have a fairly good handle on controlling theft while the goods are on the airport premises, it is not often the case in the vicinity of the airports, where problems abound in warehouses, truck terminals, and other satellite locations. Because most cargo sent by air has a high value, it is interesting to thieves, and because it tends to be packaged in cardboard boxes and not palletized, it is somewhat more easily pilfered and stolen (sometimes the brands are displayed on the packaging, inciting pilferage). The key to controlling losses in these instances is to make sure that the cargo documents are handled by as few people as possible and that the boxes are not marked in any way to indicate their content.

- **Exposure to inclement weather**. Although it seems counterintuitive, goods in transit from a warm place to another warm place may be subjected to very cold weather. For example, the third largest freight airport in the world is Anchorage, Alaska (after Memphis and Hong Kong), where the average high temperature is below freezing from mid-October to early April. Reciprocally, cargo moving from a cold climate to another cold climate may stop at a tropical airport. Such was the case for salmon fry shipped from Alaska to southern Chile, which routinely stopped in Miami, Florida. Cargo is commonly left on the tarmac for a couple of hours between flights, and the shipper should anticipate that the cargo will be exposed to atmospheric conditions that are different from the ones in the airports of departure and destination.

There are a number of other risks associated with air shipment: particularly the cold and the changes in air pressure that can be found in some freighters. Cargo tends to be kept at lower temperatures and operated at lower air pressure during the flight than what is practiced in passenger airplanes, for obvious reasons of cost. For most cargo, these slight differences may not be significant, but for some cargo, it can be a problem. Because, by definition, sensitive cargo moves by air, care should be exerted in making sure that perishable cargo is not kept at temperatures that it cannot handle or that live cargo and sensitive mechanical instruments are not subjected to air pressures that are too low. However, because such a large percentage of air cargo demands controlled temperatures and pressures, the remainder of the cargo on board benefits from these requirements. Again, therefore, the greatest risk is usually not while the freighter is in flight, but while the cargo is on the tarmac, waiting to be loaded, or already loaded and waiting to take off; it can be exposed to extreme temperatures as well as rain and snow.

10-5 Insurable Interest

There are several parties interested in the safe arrival of an international cargo shipment. The first, obviously, is the owner of the goods. Whether the owner is the exporter or the importer is dependent on a number of factors, principally the terms of payment of the transaction (see Chapter 7). However, there are many cases in which non-owners are interested in making sure that the goods arrive safely at their destination. The terms of trade, or Incoterms, used in the transaction between the exporter and the importer (see Chapter 6) indicate the cases in which the exporter is responsible for the goods before the title transfers to the importer. However, even if the importer is not responsible for the goods while they are in transit, it still has an interest in making sure that the goods arrive safely to their destination.

All of these situations illustrate the concept of insurable interest:

An insurance contract is legally binding only if the insured has an interest in the subject matter of the insurance and this interest is in fact *insurable*. In most instances, an insurable interest exists only if the insured [were to] suffer a financial loss in the event of damage to, or destruction of, the subject matter of the insurance.[52]

The use of Incoterms helps the exporter and the importer determine where their respective responsibilities start and end. It should therefore follow that the insurable interest of the exporter ends when possession shifts to the importer, at which time the importer is the party with an insurable interest; unfortunately, while this is correct, it is not that simple.

The issue is, once again, muddied by several factors. Several examples can be used to illustrate them:

- **Foreign exchange exposure**. An exporter in a developing country sells to an importer in a developed country on a CIF basis. Responsibility transfers once the merchandise crosses the ship's rail (see Chapter 6, Section 6-9), but the exporter is responsible for providing minimum cover insurance (i.e., Coverage C of the Institute Marine Cargo Clauses—see Section 10-8d). Assuming that the importer is in agreement with such minimum coverage, there is still the problem that, should there be a loss, the importer would have to file a claim with the insurer in the developing country, or, at least, an insurer not chosen by the importer. It is possible that the claim processing will take a few months, leaving the importer with the risk of foreign exchange devaluation. Because the terms are CIF, the exporter delivers the goods as agreed—when the goods cross the ship's rail—and therefore the invoice has to be paid by the importer, causing a cash-flow problem as well. In this case, the importer has an insurable interest and can obtain coverage in its country to minimize its foreign exchange risk exposure; it would be covered against a loss that happens in transportation and would be able to pay the exporter the amount owed. A similar situation can arise in a CIP shipment.

- **Trust**. An exporter may sell FCA to an importer in a country that mandates that the importer buy insurance in the importing country. The exporter usually ships without evidence of coverage, and correctly so, because the responsibility shifts to the importer as soon as the goods are in the carrier's care. However, should they be damaged in transit, the importer may refuse payment, despite the fact that the accident happened under its responsibility. The exporter has therefore an insurable interest in the completion of the trip. Note that the problem would be avoided if the exporter sold on a letter of credit basis, as the *documents* for the shipment, including the intermodal bill of lading, would be in order, and the issuing bank would have to pay (see Chapter 7, Section 7-6a). The same situation would arise in FAS, FOB, CFR, CPT, and DAF shipments; it could also happen in an EXW transaction.

- **Insufficient coverage**. An exporter agrees to sell to an importer on a CIF basis. The importer requests that the terms be modified to "CIF maximum cover" (i.e., Coverage A of the Institute Marine Cargo Clauses—see Section 10-8a) but, because it is an open-account shipment, it does not obtain evidence of this coverage. The goods are slightly damaged in transit by condensation, and the importer seeks to collect compensation under the terms of the insurance policy provided by the exporter. However, the claim is turned down because the exporter did not contract for Coverage A, but for Coverage B or C, which do not allow claims for such damage. Clearly, the importer has an insurable interest in this cargo and can obtain coverage in its country to protect itself from such losses.

While the owner of the goods has a clear insurable interest in the merchandise while it is in transit, non-owners, such as the buyers in the first and third examples above, have an insurable interest that is less direct: It is usually qualified as a "contingent" insurable interest.[53]

10-6 Risk Management

There are three ways in which a company can manage its risks, whether they are international cargo insurance or any other type of risk: It can retain the risk, transfer the risk, or take a mixed approach, retaining some risks and transferring others.[54] This section will concentrate on the management of international logistics risks, mainly the risks associated with transporting goods from one country to another.

10-6a Risk Retention

The strategy of risk retention is fairly clear: The company decides that it is more economical to not purchase insurance for those risks. In general, there are four reasons for which a company will decide to retain its international logistics risks:

- **Very large international traders—importers or exporters**. They already act somewhat as an insurance company in some respects: They have a lot of merchandise in transit, and therefore would have to pay large insurance premiums, but would only occasionally collect on a loss. Therefore, the many savings incurred by not paying premiums end up covering the few losses they do experience. Those firms have decided to "self-insure," which is the euphemism for not contracting with an insurance company and for deciding to pay all risks with current cash flow.

- **Exporters or importers that have little exposure**. They are shipping or buying goods of fairly small value, in fairly small shipments, and therefore a loss would not have substantial financial or cash-flow consequences for those companies.

- **Exporters or importers that have little relative exposure**. Their international transactions represent a very small percentage of their business. The individual amount may be large, but relative to the size of their domestic sales, it is not significant.

- **Firms that did not evaluate the international transaction risks clearly**. They are not insuring because they do not insure their domestic transactions or, for whatever reasons, think that the risks of shipping internationally are not very high. Generally, the firms that choose to retain these risks by ignorance are also the ones that are more likely to incur losses because of improper packing or improper security measures for the same reasons. Relying upon the liability coverage provided by the shipping line is also imprudent; the current liability for shipping lines under U.S. law—the Carriage of Goods by Sea Act (COGSA)—provides a maximum coverage of U.S. $500 per package, which is often interpreted as a "container," and the shipping lines have 17 specified defenses they can invoke, essentially shielding them from liability except in the most egregious cases.

10-6b Risk Transfer

The strategy of risk transfer is also fairly clear: The firm decides to transfer all of its risks to an insurance company. In exchange for paying a premium for an insurance policy, the firm is certain to be covered against losses experienced during international shipments. This strategy is followed for three reasons:

- **Firms with a lot of exposure**. The value of the goods they ship or import is high, and the loss of some or all of these shipments would be a substantial financial blow to their operations. In those cases where goods are expensive, though, the insurance companies often request, in cooperation with the firms, to restrict the total amount at risk on any single shipment. Usually this is achieved by having the shipment split over several carriers.

- **Firms with a relatively high exposure**. Even though the amount may be small, it ends up being relatively high for the firms. A perfect example of such a situation is found in personal effects shipments, which generally are worth fairly small sums, but are relatively quite valuable to their owners.

- **Firms with little experience**. Companies that lack experience in international trade will insure because they are uncomfortable with the risks involved or because they are unable to properly assess their exposure.

10-6c Mixed Approach

The mixed approach is one where the firm decides to retain some of the risk and transfer the rest. This strategy can be achieved in two different ways:

- The decision is made based upon the maximum amount of exposure that a firm is willing to risk: This objective is traditionally achieved with the use of a deductible. A deductible can be managed on a per-claim basis—the insurance company is responsible for the portion of a given loss that is greater than the deductible and the firm is responsible for the amount of the deductible, as well as all losses that have a value lower than the deductible. It can also be a cumulative deductible, where the firm pays for losses until the cumulative deductible amount is reached, and the insurance company pays for the losses incurred beyond the amount of the deductible.

- The decision is made based on the types of risks that the firm is willing to take, and those that it would rather transfer to an insurance company. For example, a firm may choose to insure using Coverage B of the Institute Marine Cargo Clauses (see Section 10-8c) and retain the risks not covered by this policy, among which are condensation, pilferage, leakage, and breakage.

Either of these strategies can be followed for a number of reasons. However, while the choice of a monetary deductible is based essentially upon the maximum amount of exposure that a firm is willing to bear, the strategy of splitting risks between the firm and an insurance company is a much more difficult strategy to implement, as it involves identifying risks, determining whether they are significant enough to transfer, and negotiating with an insurance company a specific contract of insurance, taking advantage of the fact that "customized cargo policies are limited only by the imagination of the carriers offering them."[55]

10-7 Marine Insurance Policies

An international trading firm—exporter or importer—intent on transferring all or part of its international shipping risks is generally interested only in purchasing marine cargo insurance, because it just needs to protect itself from damage to the cargo as well as from its liability toward the ship owners and the rest of the cargo in a general average case. However, there are a couple of additional insurance coverages available in international shipping that should be mentioned: They pertain mainly to vessel or aircraft owners, but, on rare occasions, those policies matter to an exporter or importer chartering an entire ship for a bulk shipment.

10-7a Marine Cargo Insurance

Marine cargo insurance can be purchased either under an open ocean cargo policy or under a special cargo policy.

Open Policy
An open policy is an insurance contract with which a firm insures every international shipment it makes for a fixed period of time. Such a policy is formally known as an *open ocean cargo policy* and it automatically covers all the shipments of the insured, as long as the firm reports every shipment to the insurance company. This reporting is done using a set of declaration forms, either every time an export shipment is made—or an import shipment is received—or on a monthly basis. There is a presumption of goodwill on the part of the firm in that the insurance company will cover damage to an undeclared shipment, as long as the firm intended to notify the insurance company.[56] Because the premiums are based upon the value of the shipments made under such a policy, it presents one great advantage: The firm knows the costs of its insurance coverage and can easily incorporate it in its *pro forma* invoices without having to request a quote for each shipment.

Special Cargo Policy
The second alternative is for the exporter or importer to purchase an individual policy, called a *special cargo policy*, for each of its shipments. This alternative allows a firm to

specifically purchase coverage that pertains best to a shipment. However, it tends to be cumbersome to enter a contract every time the firm gets involved in an international transaction, and this method is not very commonly used.

Obtaining Insurance Certificates

On a large number of occasions, the exporter is requested to provide a Certificate of Insurance to the importer and its bank, often because this certificate is required by the letter of credit. This requirement is usually not a problem under a special cargo policy, because there is evidence from the insurance company that a specific shipment is insured.

Under an open ocean cargo policy, however, this requirement used to present some difficulties until recently. The practice used to be that the insurance company would provide the exporter with a Certificate of Open Insurance (see Figure 9-7 in Chapter 9); however, this certificate did not specifically address the insurance status of a given shipment, and some (few) banks did not accept evidence of an open policy as a proof of insurance for a specific shipment as required in the terms of the letter of credit.[57] Therefore, the practice is now for the insurance company to give the insured a supply of blank special cargo policy forms, which are then filled out by the exporter to show that a specific shipment is covered. These forms appear—to the issuing bank—as if a special cargo policy has been contracted for the shipment, even though it is covered under an open policy.[58]

Purchasing Marine Cargo Insurance

Marine cargo insurance can be purchased from two sources:

- An insurance agent, who can assist the firm in obtaining the most appropriate coverage, given its product mix and its risk management strategy. Agents sell most open ocean cargo policies.

- A freight forwarder, who can provide "generic" coverage for a given shipment almost immediately. Freight forwarders sell a lot of special cargo policies.

10-7b Hull Insurance

Hull insurance is contracted by the ship owners to cover the risk of damage to their ship when it is involved in a peril, such as grounding or fire. It also covers the owners in case of a complete loss, such as a sinking. This policy also covers the ship owners' liability toward the cargo owners in the case of a general average and its damages in the event of a collision with another ship. An equivalent hull insurance is available to owners of aircrafts.

Hull insurance rates are dependent on the seaworthiness of a ship, the way it is maintained, and the equipment it has on board, all three of which are appraised by **classification societies**. Ships are placed in different classes, and hull insurance rates are dependent on the class of a ship. The Lloyd's Register of Ships—in its 244th year and now available on CD-ROM[59]—keeps information on almost all ships in the world and their classification. Hull insurance is effectively paid indirectly by the cargo owners, as the cost of the insurance is included in the freight rates quoted.

10-7c Protection and Indemnity

Protection and Indemnity is yet another form of insurance for ship owners; it is a protection against liability to other parties when a ship sinks or is damaged. In the last few decades, it has meant liability for oil spills—specifically cargo spills, but also ship fuel spills—on beaches, and their extensive clean-up costs. However, it also includes the ship owners' liability toward the crew (injury, death) or in repatriating stowaways.

Protection and Indemnity insurance is not a traditional insurance, but a mutual **P&I club** to which ship owners contribute, and which absorbs the costs of one of the owners' mishaps. The liability of a single P&I club is limited to U.S. $7 million;

classification society
A company that is responsible for determining the seaworthiness of a particular vessel. It places a ship in a specific "class" as a function of its age, maintenance records, and the availability of on-board equipment.

Protection and Indemnity club (P&I) A group of ship owners who agree to mutually share the costs of a member's liabilities to other parties; for example, the club members would be individually responsible for the costs of a single member's liability in the event of an oil spill.

for claims that are higher than that, the 13 P&I clubs form an alliance and mutually insure each other, up to a limit of U.S. $30 million. The P&I clubs are then covered by an additional re-insurance policy, to a maximum of U.S. $2.05 billion.[60] Claims involving cargoes of crude oil are covered by a series of international agreements to which 103 countries are signatories, called the International Funds for Oil Pollution Compensation, which has limits that vary in function of the size of the ship. As of May 2009, the maximum cover is SDR 953 million, or U.S. $1,125 million.[61] The United States is not a signatory to this fund.

10-8 Coverages Under a Marine Cargo Insurance Policy

There are two major groups of policies that can be purchased in order to protect cargo during an ocean or air shipment. The first group is governed by British law and was completely rewritten in 1982. This group of insurance policies seems to have become the standard for other countries as well. They are known as the Institute Marine Cargo Clauses, Coverage A, B, or C.

The second group is older, with some antiquated clauses and more modern ones, and is mostly written by U.S.-based insurance companies, although some of the coverage can be written using older British clauses. These traditional policies are known as "All Risks," "General Average," and "Free of Particular Average."

To make things more interesting, these six general policies can be modified to add coverage that is not included in the original contract, such as the risks of strikes and civil unrest. However, none of the policies will cover five specific risks, against which it is impossible to find insurance:

- **Improper packing**. The goods must be adequately packed for an ocean voyage and be well protected against shocks and water damage, as well as be well secured in the container or the crate. Chapter 14 discusses this issue in depth.

- **Inherent vice**. The goods shipped have a natural propensity to be affected in a certain way; for example, steel will exhibit surface rust after being exposed for some time to air and moisture, agricultural product shipments will foster insects and rodents, and wood will warp and split. None of these "inherent vices" are insurable.

- **Ordinary leakage**. Also known as "ordinary loss in weight and volume" and "ordinary wear and tear," this states that several products, when shipped, will leak or lose weight; for example, any agricultural product, such as wool, will lose some weight as its moisture content decreases; petroleum oil transported in bulk will partially evaporate; and an automobile carried on a roll-on/roll-off ship will show additional mileage. Again, none of these risks are insurable.

- **Unseaworthy vessel**. This exclusion is not a problem for goods shipped by regularly scheduled container or break-bulk ships; however, it puts a burden of care on the shipper in the case of a shipment going by bulk ship, as the shipper must make certain that the ship is classified by a classification society as seaworthy. In addition, a vessel can depart for a voyage in seaworthy condition and then become unseaworthy due to the perils it encounters. When a ship becomes unseaworthy during a voyage, most policies include a statement that "an unreasonable delay in repairing the ship exonerates the insurer from liability on any loss arising from the defect."

- **Nuclear war**. This risk is always specifically excluded from policies. Note that the risk not covered is the direct result of nuclear war, such as irradiation or destruction. However, should a shipment be damaged by a fire caused by nuclear war, the shipment is covered—if the risk of fire is covered in the policy—because the fire was the peril that caused the loss.

10-8a Institute Marine Cargo Clauses—Coverage A

The first general policy is referred to as Coverage A of the Institute Marine Cargo Clauses. Coverage A is quite similar to a traditional All Risks policy (see Section 10-8b), in that it covers "all risks of loss or damage to the subject-matter insured,"[62] yet it is not identical to one. For one, it is written in plain English, which makes it much simpler to decipher. Moreover, unlike traditional All Risks policies, which can be written with U.S. or British clauses—and the different interpretations they imply—a policy written with Coverage A of the Institute Marine Cargo Clauses is identical in all countries.

Despite its name, a Coverage A policy—and an All Risks policy itself—does not cover literally all risks, as it does not cover the perils mentioned earlier (improper packing, inherent vice, ordinary leakage, unseaworthy vessel, and nuclear war), as well as a number of risks for which specific additional coverage must be purchased separately as endorsements to the main policy: strikes and other civil disturbances (see the Strikes, Riots, and Civil Commotions clause in Section 10-8g) and acts of war and seizure by a government (see the Free of Capture and Seizure clause in Section 10-8h).

Nevertheless, Coverage A of the Institute Marine Cargo Clauses is the maximum coverage that an exporter or an importer would need to purchase in the case of a shipment for most trade lanes in the world, specifically from a developed country to another, as long as the route does not cross a particular "hot spot" of the world.

10-8b All Risks Coverage

An All Risks policy is an older—but still very commonly used, particularly in the United States—type of policy. Because an All Risks policy can be written as an American contract or as a British contract, it will contain different wordings of the clauses and other relatively minor changes, which will make an American policy differ from a British policy on a few points; therefore, careful reading of such policies should always be done to ensure that there is a proper match between the risks that the shipper—exporter or importer—is willing to assume and the ones that the policy excludes.

For a U.S. All Risks policy to be enforceable, the goods have to be shipped "under deck," which means that the goods must be stowed inside the ship, for the obvious reason that goods inside a ship are exposed to fewer perils than goods stowed "on deck." However, this presents a practical problem because the shipper usually is unaware of the way the goods are stowed in a ship, and because some containerships no longer have a deck and are instead equipped with stack bars. The problem is solved by requesting that the insurance company cover the goods based upon the Shipper's Letter of Instruction, which requests that the goods be shipped under deck, and not based upon the way the goods are actually stowed by the steamship line. Such coverage can be obtained as an endorsement to the main policy, usually at no additional charge.[63] Once this endorsement has been granted, the All Risks policy is even more similar to a Coverage A policy, and therefore an All Risks policy is also quite appropriate for shipments of any nature between two developed countries.

10-8c Institute Marine Cargo Clauses—Coverage B

Another general policy is referred to as Coverage B of the Institute Marine Cargo Clauses. It is also called a named-perils policy, as it lists specifically the risks that it will cover. The list of covered perils includes fire, stranding, sinking, collision, jettisoning, washing overboard, water damage, and *total* losses during loading and unloading;

however, losses due to bad weather are not covered, and neither are partial losses happening during loading and unloading of the ship.[64] For a complete list, refer to Table 10-1, where a comparison is given for all six standard coverages.

Coverage B of the Institute Marine Cargo Clauses is appropriate for goods that have a good tolerance for bad weather, such as bulk raw materials, including coal, iron ore, polymer pellets, and lumber. It would not be appropriate for machinery, paper, and any type of finished goods, unless they were particularly resilient.

10-8d Institute Marine Cargo Clauses—Coverage C

The last of the general Institute Marine Cargo Clauses is Coverage C. It is also a named-perils policy, as it lists specifically the risks that it will cover. The list of covered perils is limited to fire, stranding, sinking, collision, and jettisoning; it does not include washing overboard, rough weather damage, or water damage and losses during loading and unloading.[65] For a complete list, refer to Table 10-1, where a comparison is given for all six standard coverages.

Coverage C is the minimum coverage required by the Incoterms CIF and CIP. It is minimal enough as to be inappropriate for most goods, and companies doing business on CIF or CIP terms should definitely extend this coverage to "maximum cover" (i.e., Coverage A of the Institute Marine Cargo Clauses), or, if they are importing on those Incoterms, purchase Difference in Condition coverage (see Section 10-8j).

TABLE 10-1   Marine Insurance Coverage Summary

Perils Covered Against	A	B	C	AR	WA	FPA
Fire	X	X	X	X	X	X
Explosion	X	X	X	X	X	X
Stranding	X	X	X	X	X	X
Sinking	X	X	X	X	X	X
Collision	X	X	X	X	X	X
General average	X	X	X	X	X	X
Jettison	X	X	X	X	X	(*)
Loss overboard	X	X		X	X	(*)
Seawater damage	X	X		X	X	(*)
Lightening	X	X		X	X	(*)
Condensation	X			X		
Improper stowage by carrier	X			X		
Theft	X			X		
Pilferage	X			X		
Leakage	X			X		
Breakage	X			X		
Damage while loading/unloading	X	X		X	X	
Damage on land before loading	X	X	X	X	X	X

(*) Under an FPA policy, any partial loss incurred would not be covered unless it is due to a ship sinking, burning, becoming stranded, or being involved in a collision; a total loss would be covered.
A Coverage A of the Institute Marine Cargo Clauses
B Coverage B of the Institute Marine Cargo Clauses
C Coverage C of the Institute Marine Cargo Clauses
AR All Risks coverage
WA With Average (typical coverage)
FPA Free of Particular Average (typical coverage)

Note: Because so many different types of WA and FPA policies exist, the table is only indicative. Please refer to the actual policy for definitive coverage.

Coverage C is generally insufficient for most containerized goods, with the possible exception of goods that are unlikely to be affected by an international voyage in any way and, if lost overboard, would not be a major loss. There are few cargoes that fit this description, with the possible exception of scrap merchandise, such as scrap metal or recyclable paper. Coverage C is appropriate for bulk cargo, as it is unlikely to experience a loss unless there is major damage to the ship.[66]

10-8e With Average Coverage

The "With Average" policy is generally written to include coverage in-between an All Risks policy and a policy with Coverage B of the Institute Marine Cargo Clauses. A With Average policy is a named-perils policy, as it lists specifically the risks that it will cover. Again, because a With Average policy can also be written as an American contract or as a British contract, care should be given to ensure that the shipper is not unwillingly accepting a risk that it does not want to retain.

A With Average policy covers risks such as fire, explosion, stranding, collision, and so on (see Table 10-1), but covers damage to cargo from heavy weather, as well as partial losses while loading and unloading the vessel, and the bursting of boilers, none of which Coverage B provides.

The way a With Average policy insures partial losses is through the use of a **franchise**, which is to say that for partial damage below a certain percentage—say 3 percent—of the value of the merchandise, the goods are not covered. For partial losses greater than this franchise, the entire loss to the insured is covered. A franchise is therefore different from a deductible, which would consider that if a loss of 10 percent of the value of the merchandise occurred, the insured would be responsible for the first 3 percent and the insurance company would be responsible for the remaining 7 percent. In a With Average policy with a franchise of 3 percent, the insurance company would cover the entire 10 percent.

A standard With Average policy is appropriate for some percentage of the merchandise shipped internationally; however, because some other coverages such as freshwater damage, condensation, or breakage and pilferage are often added,[67] it seems that shippers use a With Average policy to tailor their coverage to include those perils to which the merchandise they export or import is sensitive.

franchise The portion of a loss, expressed as a percentage, below which a "With Average" insurance policy will not cover a partial loss. If the amount of the partial loss exceeds the franchise, then the entire costs of the partial loss are covered.

10-8f Free of Particular Average Coverage

The last general policy is referred to as a "Free of Particular Average," a named-perils policy. A Free of Particular Average policy covers total losses, but covers only partial losses in some circumstances. The major issue is whether the policy is a Free of Particular Average—English Conditions policy or a Free of Particular Average—American Conditions policy. Under an American Conditions policy, partial losses are covered only if they result *directly* from a fire, a stranding, a sinking, or a collision. Under an English Conditions policy, the partial losses are covered if they occur on the same voyage that a fire, a stranding, a sinking, or a collision occurs, without these perils having directly caused the loss.

A Free of Particular Average policy is even more restrictive than Coverage C of the Institute Marine Cargo Clauses. It does not cover many of the risks associated with an international shipment and it is rarely sufficient or appropriate for an international shipment of containerized or break-bulk cargo, unless the cargo considered is particularly inexpensive and a loss would be no substantial problem for the shipper. It would be appropriate (with some reservation, because no partial losses are covered) for some bulk cargo of minimal value.

Finally, a Free of Particular Average policy would not be enough to cover the minimum insurance requirements of a CIF or CIP shipment, which both require the "minimum cover" of Coverage C of the Institute Marine Cargo Clauses.[68]

10-8g Strikes Coverage

All the previous standard policies include a clause, called the "Strikes, Riots, and Civil Commotions" (S.R. & C.C.) clause in the American policies and the "Strikes Exclusion" clause in the Institute Marine Cargo Clauses policies, which excludes coverage of damage to cargo due to strikes and other civil disturbances.

Should a shipper be concerned about the possibility of such problems in a specific port or during a specific period, a possible amendment to include such coverage can always be added, generally called an S.R. & C.C. Endorsement. However, the coverage would include only direct physical damage to the goods or the additional costs incurred in storing the goods during the strike, but would not include incidental damage caused by delay to market, nor the financial losses that accompany a delay in the sale of a cargo.

10-8h War and Seizure Coverage

All the previous standard policies also include a clause, called "Free of Capture and Seizure" (F.C. & S.) in the American policies and "War Exclusion" in the Institute Marine Cargo Clauses policies, which excludes coverage of damage to cargo due to war and warlike situations, such as the seizure of a ship by a foreign government or the accidental collision of a ship with a mine.

It is possible for a shipper to insure its cargo against war damages, but it is through an additional policy, called the "War Risks Only" policy, which would cover hostile acts by a foreign government or by an organized power. For obvious reasons, a War Risks policy is cancelable by the insurance company with a 48-hour notice; however, it cannot be canceled for cargo that is in transit (i.e., that has already left the port of departure), which is really the coverage that any shipper would want. Most open cargo policies are accompanied by a separate War Risks policy, according to Cigna Insurance Companies.[72] In times of naval warfare against merchant ships, war risk insurance may be obtainable through only a government-backed policy. This was the case for most Allied vessels and cargoes during World War II.

Lemongate

On July 30, 2004, the United States Coast Guard (USCG), acting upon an "unconfirmed anonymous report" received by e-mail, seized the *Rio Puelo*, a containership bound for Canada that was transporting 120 metric tonnes of lemons from Argentina to Montreal. The Coast Guard was concerned that the lemons could contain a biological agent that would be released when the ship stopped in Port Elizabeth, New Jersey.[69]

The ship was ordered at anchor seven nautical miles from shore, and the ship was boarded by USCG agents. They located the containers aboard the ship and lowered their refrigeration temperature from 40 degrees Fahrenheit (4.5 degrees Celsius) to below 32 degrees Fahrenheit (less than 0 degrees Celsius) to slow down or kill all biological activity in the containers, but also essentially destroying the fruits. After six days, the ship was allowed to enter the port and unload the containers bound for the United States. The lemon containers were also discharged, and immediately isolated. Access holes were cut in the containers and the cargo fumigated with chlorine dioxide gas and eventually incinerated.[70] No biological agent was ever found to be present.

There were many costs associated with this seizure.[71] Cargo aboard the ship was delayed seven days, the ship had to "skip" some ports of call to get back on schedule, and the shipping line was forced to find other carriers for some of the cargo that it could not load; and the load of lemons, estimated to be worth about U.S. $70,000, was completely lost. None of these costs were covered by the insurance companies of the shippers (exporters or importers), unless they had "Free of Capture and Seizure" coverage, which is highly unlikely, as they would not have anticipated such a risk for a shipment from Argentina to Canada.

10-8i Warehouse-to-Warehouse Coverage

Another common additional coverage to an open cargo policy is the "Warehouse–to-Warehouse" coverage, which covers the goods from the time they leave the exporter's warehouse until the time they arrive at the importer's warehouse, or 15 days after they arrive in the port of destination, whichever occurs first.

The Warehouse-to-Warehouse coverage grew from the demands of shippers who were tired of finding coverage for only the ocean portion of the voyage. First, the All Risks and With Average insurance policies added a "Shore Perils" endorsement to include the perils occurring while loading and unloading ships; this clause was also made part of the Institute Marine Cargo Clauses. Finally, a true Warehouse to-Warehouse clause was added to most open cargo policies. In addition, in some policies, there is a "Marine Extension" clause, which essentially expands the Warehouse-to-Warehouse coverage to ensure unforeseen changes in the voyage and unexpected transshipments. Such a clause was developed during World War II to account for unusual and unknown transshipments, because all shipping data were classified.[73] It fulfills few practical purposes today.

Warehouse-to-Warehouse coverage is an extension of the traditional All Risks, With Average, and Free of Particular Average policies, but it is an integral part of the Institute Marine Cargo Clauses policies for Coverages A, B, and C, in which it is called a "Transit" clause.

10-8j Difference in Conditions

Another addition of significance to open cargo policies would be "Difference in Conditions" coverage. Difference in Conditions coverage is designed to fill the gap between what an importer would like to have covered under its open cargo policy and what is covered under its supplier's CIF or CIP coverage.

Because the International Chamber of Commerce requires only Coverage C of the Institute Marine Cargo Clauses for a CIF or CIP shipment, it can be difficult to ensure that a supplier will actually cover the shipment more fully, even though the importer may request maximum cover. In those cases, it is simpler for the importer to purchase a Difference in Conditions endorsement and not have to worry about what the supplier will provide.

10-8k Other Clauses of a Marine Insurance Policy

There are many other clauses in a marine insurance policy, either as a part of the general policy or as an endorsement to the general policy. This section will give a brief overview of some of them.

General Average Clause
All insurance policies contain a general average clause, which specifies that the insurer will cover the general average responsibilities of a shipper.

Constructive Total Loss Coverage Clause
All insurance policies contain a "Constructive Total Loss Coverage" clause, which essentially specifies that the insurer will reimburse the shipper for goods that have been abandoned after a stranding or a sinking, as long as the costs of recovering the goods and making them marketable is greater than their value. If it is possible to recover the goods at a cost lower than their value, then the insurance company pays for these costs.

Sue and Labor
All traditional insurance policies—All Risks, With Average, and Free of Particular Average—have a clause called "Sue and Labor" (policies written under the Institute

Marine Cargo Clauses have similar wording but do not use this clause name), which directs the shipper to act in the best interest of the insurance company when a loss occurs. The principle is that, after a loss, the insured should protect the cargo from further damage, as it would if it had not been insured, in order to keep the loss to a minimum.

Inchmaree Clause

One of the quaint vestiges of the old marine insurance policies is the *Inchmaree* clause, so named after a lawsuit between the owners of the *Inchmaree*, a vessel, and the insurers of its cargo, which determined that damage caused by a burst boiler (steamship engine) was not covered by the traditional marine insurance policy of the time. Insurers quickly added this coverage to their policy, and it has remained to this day in the All Risks, With Average, and Free of Particular Average policies. The *Inchmaree* clause also covers cargo owners in the event that the ship owner is guilty of errors in navigation and seamanship.

Coverages A through C of the Institute Marine Cargo Clauses do not include the *Inchmaree* clause and do not mention coverage of poor navigation. An analysis of the American Carriage of Goods by Sea Act (COGSA), in Chapter 11, Section 11-5, covers this issue of seamanship further.

10-9 Elements of an Airfreight Policy

Fortunately, airfreight policies tend to be much less complicated than ocean marine cargo insurance policies. They are all written as All Risks policies, with the exclusions already described in Section 10-8:

- **Improper packing**. The goods must be adequately packed for an air shipment and be reasonably protected against shocks and rainwater damage, as well as well secured in the container or the crate. The standards for airfreight packing are much less stringent than for an ocean shipment.

- **Inherent vice**. This problem is essentially moot in an air shipment, as the goods are in transit for a much shorter period of time. Nevertheless the risk is specifically excluded from coverage.

- **Ordinary leakage**. Also known as "ordinary loss in weight and volume" and "ordinary wear and tear," this is also much less of a concern for air shipments, as transit times are much shorter.

- **Unairworthy aircraft**. This exclusion is not a problem for goods shipped by air; governments do extend much greater efforts to the oversight of aircraft than they do for ships. The absence of "flags of convenience" is also a positive factor.

- **Nuclear war**. This is a traditional exclusion.

In addition, policies will also exclude war coverage and S.R. & C.C. coverage, like an ocean cargo policy, as well as two risks inherent to air travel: damage caused by cold and changes in atmospheric pressure. All of these risks can be covered, however, by purchasing additional coverage.

Practically speaking, most air cargo policies are included as a clause in the open cargo policy of a firm, which allows the firm to manage its shipping risks with a single document, whether its goods are moving by ocean or by air.

10-10 Filing an Insurance Claim

Unfortunately, any company that engages in international business faces the prospect of cargo loss or damage, and with that occurrence follows the need to file an insurance claim. Proper handling of an insurance claim is paramount to making sure that the company recovers its loss. There are several steps that must be taken by the insured.

10-10a Notification

The first and most important step is to promptly notify both the carrier and the insurance company of the loss. The best practice is to notify the carrier or the carrier's agent and the insurance company immediately if the damage is visible at the time the goods are discharged—for instance, if the packaging shows signs of damage, the container seal show signs of tampering, or the shipment shows some other outward sign of damage. If there is no apparent exterior damage, there are different requirements for the timely notification and eventual filing of a claim, depending on the mode of transportation. If the cargo was transported by ocean, the carrier should be notified within three days. For international air shipments, the carrier must be notified within seven days. For international and domestic land transportation, and for domestic shipments, the notification requirements vary and are spelled out in the air waybill or the (intermodal) bill of lading; however, such a notification will likely be within, at most, seven days as well.

It is therefore quite important to inspect cargo as quickly as possible after it has been received, even if it shows no sign of damage or pilferage, so that, should the cargo be damaged, a notification and eventual claim can be filed within the contractual time limits.

This notification has to be made in writing in all cases; it should include a description of the damage and a record of the seal number and of its condition. The notification should be sent to the insurance company, to the insurance agent, and to the carriers involved in the shipment, even if they are "agents" of the main carrier, if they are known; for example, the trucking company hired by the shipping line to make the final delivery should be notified. Notification should be made by certified mail, with return receipt requested, to provide evidence of a timely notification. Even in cases where the damage is apparent, it is not sufficient, although it is definitely necessary, to make an annotation on the delivery receipt for the goods. In addition, the more precise the annotation on the delivery receipt, the greater the level of protection for the insured.

Once damage is discovered, the insured should hire a **surveyor**, an independent company that is not affiliated with the insurance company and whose responsibility is to evaluate and assess the damage to the cargo. The insured may use any surveyor who is approved by Lloyd's of London or the American Institute of Marine Underwriters. In most cases, the insurance company can recommend a surveyor. The surveyor is directly paid by the insurance company in most cases, although in some cases, the insured pays the surveyor and is then reimbursed by the insurance company. A surveyor may not be necessary if the damage is minor.

surveyor An individual or company whose responsibility it is to determine the extent and the circumstances of a marine cargo loss.

10-10b Protection of the Damaged Cargo

Once an insured has identified that the cargo has been damaged, it has several responsibilities. As much as possible, it should stop unloading the goods from the container and leave the cargo as it was found; if that is not possible, an extensive number of photographs should be taken to document the problem thoroughly. In all cases, the insured should segregate the damaged cargo from other cargo, appropriately mark the damaged cargo so that it is not inadvertently mixed with other shipments, and protect it so that there will be no further damage. There are several reasons for these recommendations.

The first reason, one of the important tenets of insurance, is that the insured must protect the property "as if it were not insured," as the insured has an "onus of good faith" and must protect the interests of the insurance company. For example, further damage, resulting from lack of care after the goods have been damaged, is not covered. If a shipment of cement arrives with several torn bags, the insured must make sure that the cement is protected from rain, even if the torn bags are no longer usable. The damage (tearing) to the cement bags that occurred during the voyage would likely be paid by the insurance company as long as it falls within the coverage of the policy, but the water damage after the shipment arrived would not be covered, because it was due to the negligence of the insured. Actually, in cases where the insured has to incur additional costs in order to prevent further loss, the insurance company will cover such costs under the Sue and Labor clause of the ocean cargo policy.

The second reason is to make sure that the cause of the damage is correctly determined. Such procedures facilitate the work of the surveyor, who is responsible for inspecting the cargo and determining the party responsible for the damage. For example, the surveyor may want to determine the type of bracing that was used in the container. Because improper packing is the responsibility neither of the carrier nor of the insurance company, but of the exporter, the surveyor will want to see how the cargo was stowed in the container. If that evidence is no longer there, it affects its ability to assess responsibility accurately. Finally, following these guidelines will also allow the carrier(s) to inspect the goods and protect its interests.

10-10c Filing of a Claim

Two fundamental requirements drive the system in properly filing a claim for recovery of losses. The first requirement is the timeliness of the filing of the claim, and the second is the submission of proper documentation for the claim. The logistics manager should review the insurance policy to see that all requirements in the event of a claim are met.

As mentioned earlier, there are very strict time limits for notifying carriers and insurance companies of the filing of a claim. Three days for ocean cargo, seven days for international air transport, and an estimated seven days for other forms of transportation. The formal filing of the claim may take somewhat longer, so that the documents required to complete the claim can be collected. The filing of a claim should also be made by certified mail, with return receipt requested.

The claim must be in writing and follow a format that is acceptable to the insurance company. For example, claims filed electronically (by e-mail or Internet) may not be acceptable to some carriers and in some jurisdictions. The claim must contain information to identify the shipment, must assert liability against the carrier, and must be for a specific or determinable amount.

Filing an insurance claim also necessitates collecting and copying a large number of documents, most of which should be submitted with the claim; however, the specific documents should be determined from the contractual language on the back of the bills of lading, on the insurance certificate, and in consultation with the insurance company. Generally speaking, the following documents should be included:

- Insurance policy or Certificate of Insurance
- All bills of lading from origin to final destination
- All invoices (from the exporter and from all carriers and service providers)
- Cargo surveyor's report
- Complete packing lists and manifests
- Seal numbers and reports
- Any and all documents generated during the voyage of the cargo; depending on the type of shipment, the country of origin and the country of destination, and the mode of transportation, a shipment can generate a very large number of possible reports, all of which should be included with the claim. Such reports include pre-shipment inspection reports, monitoring tapes and logs (especially for refrigerated cargo), delivery receipts, transportation interchange reports,

equipment interchange reports, exception reports, dock receipts, warehouse and container freight station receipts, survey requests, loading surveys, mate's receipts, vessel stowage plan, ship's bridge log, deck reefer log, bilge and engineer's log, vessel hatch survey, discharge survey, and so on

- Product destroyed or thrown away (such as perishable products) will need a Certificate of Destruction filed with the claim.
- Cargo that can be salvaged at a cost should include salvage bids and receipts.

10-10d Carrier Liability Limits

A shipment that is not insured by a specific marine cargo insurance policy can still be covered by the insurance policy of the carrier. However, carriers, as noted earlier in this chapter and explained in greater depth in Chapters 11 and 12, have limits on their liability. When a claim is filed against marine cargo insurance, it becomes the responsibility of the insurance company to pursue its own claim against the carrier.

To that effect, the controlling law noted in the bill of lading must be reviewed. Usually it is the COGSA, or the so-called Hague, Hague-Visby, Hamburg, or Rotterdam Rules for ocean shipments, and the Warsaw Convention for international air shipments. However the bill of lading may cite different laws that are applicable. Therefore, the contractual portion of the bill of lading should be reviewed in terms of the stated damage limit and the controlling law; that contractual language is usually found on the reverse of the bill of lading.

In the case of an intermodal shipment, because a through or combined bill of lading was issued, the company needs to determine which carrier is "principal" and which carrier is "agent."[74] When filing a claim for an intermodal shipment, the principal carrier should be notified; however, as noted earlier, notifying agent carriers at the same time is a prudent course.

Freight forwarders, Non-Vessel-Operating Common Carriers, and other third-party logistics providers (called 3PLs in the United States and the United Kingdom) frequently limit their liability and also set their own statute of limitations on the submission of a claim.[75] The 3PL may obtain insurance coverage only on specific instructions from the shipper. The 3PLs will normally accept claims only for damages from their own actions, not those of carriers, even though the 3PL may have issued a combined or intermodal bill of lading. The 3PLs may be required by regulatory bodies to have a bond for insurance purposes, and there may be additional regulations regarding filing claim against the bond.[76]

Unfortunately, even though a claim may have been filed with all the proper documentation and in a timely manner, there is no guarantee that the claim will be honored; there is also the possibility that the insurance company will only partially cover the losses. In those cases, it may become necessary for the shipper to file a lawsuit against the carrier; this action should be undertaken by an attorney who practices cargo law and, if appropriate, admiralty law and is licensed to practice in the court that has jurisdiction.

10-11 Lloyd's

Lloyd's of London is the oldest insurance *market* in the history of shipping, having started in Edward Lloyd's coffee house as early as 1688. Although it is commonly perceived as an insurance company, that perception is incorrect. Since its humble beginnings in Lloyd's coffee shop, the company has acted as an intermediary between people who want insurance and those willing to provide it. Lloyd's does not provide insurance coverage; when one hears of an athlete whose legs are insured "by Lloyd's of London," it is an inaccurate statement: The athlete's legs are insured *through* Lloyd's.

10-11a Principles

Before explaining how the functioning of Lloyd's is different from the functioning of an insurance company, it seems relevant to explain how the latter works. An insurance company attempts to strike a balance between the collection of a large number of premiums, each of a moderate monetary amount, and the payment of a few claims, each of a large monetary amount. The correct calculation of a premium relies upon the determination of the expected monetary value of claims (their probability multiplied by their expected costs) divided by the number of policyholders. Over time, the law of (arithmetic) averages allows an insurance company to be profitable. In order to determine the probability of a loss, insurance companies rely on **actuarial tables** of statistical data collected over a significant period of time.

In contrast, Lloyd's of London acts as a market through which unusual risks are insured; unusual risks are those that a traditional insurance company would not consider covering because there is no way to collect a large number of premiums, and therefore the law of averages does not apply. For example, consider a firm that would like to insure the launching of its communication satellite. Although there may be as many as 50 satellite launches worldwide every year, the number of companies launching a satellite—the possible number of premiums to collect—is too small to spread the high expected monetary value of a single loss. Therefore, the firm would be faced with a series of years in which it would collect premiums without a loss, and then would have one or two losses in a single year, which would have a substantial adverse effect on its income.

Lloyd's of London is the place where companies and people wanting to have such risks insured find a group of "members" willing to assume (insure) this risk. These members are either individual persons, who are called **Bespoke Names** in Lloyd's particular vernacular, or corporations, which are called Corporate Members. All members are organized in a **syndicate**. Each member is actually "wagering" that the loss will not happen, and collects a portion of the premium that the member shares with the remainder of the syndicate. This share of the premium is therefore income to the member. Should a loss occur, the member is then asked to pay its share of the loss, along with every other member in the remainder of the syndicate. This payment comes out of the member's income or assets. The members, organized in a syndicate, are the **underwriters** of the insurance.

Historically, all members of Lloyd's were "Names," and very wealthy individuals; this is still the case for current Names. For Names, participation in a syndicate can be quite a profitable venture. It is not truly an investment, because the Name only collects premiums (additional income) while a portion of his or her assets can continue to be invested in other vehicles on which he or she collects market rates. However, because each Name has unlimited liability on his or her personal assets, this can also be an extremely risky venture. Because of this risk, each Name must have substantial personal assets—as of June 2009, the required net wealth was £400,000 (U.S. $650,000), only 50 percent of which has to be invested with Lloyd's—in order to be allowed to participate in a Syndicate. Joining a specific syndicate can cost an additional £200,000 (U.S. $325,000).[77] Names cannot ever "retire" from Lloyd's; they can stop underwriting new risks, but they have to remain in the syndicate until all of their liabilities have been settled.

In 1994, Lloyd's decided to allow Corporate Members. These members were given the advantage of having limited liability, and joined syndicates in which individual Names retained unlimited liability. This decision, which allowed the syndicates to have more capitalization, also created some friction, as individual Names resented the creation of two classes of members and responsibilities. Today, most of Lloyd's underwriting capability is provided by corporations. In 2009, the number of individual unlimited liability Names had dropped to 773, with 1,238 corporate members.[78]

Over the years, the type of insurance coverage provided through Lloyd's has increased to include more traditional risks, such as automobile and home insurance.

actuarial tables Tables used by insurance companies that illustrate the exact probability, based upon historical data, of a particular peril.

Bespoke Names In the Lloyd's of London vernacular, the individuals who take on the risks insured by syndicates and who have unlimited liability for those risks on their personal assets.

syndicate Under the Lloyd's concept of an insurance market, a group of Names who agree to insure a certain type of loss. The risks are shared by all the members of the syndicate.

underwriter The company, syndicate, or Name that assumes the risk of a loss for another party, in exchange for a premium.

However, most of the Lloyd's syndicates will cover risks that a traditional insurance company will not consider. As of 2009, there were 93 underwriting syndicates.[79]

Some of the risks that Lloyd's syndicates covered in the last few decades included the risk of asbestos product liability. Such was the extent of the liability, though, that many Names were brought to personal bankruptcy, despite efforts by Lloyd's to spread the risk to more syndicates than had originally been involved. The number of Names soared from 14,000 in 1978 to 34,000 by the end of the 1980s. Some of the Names who joined in the 1980s claim to not have been informed of the extent of the liabilities that Lloyd's syndicates faced, and filed lawsuits alleging fraud.[80] In November 2000, Lloyd's was found not guilty of fraud by the British courts, but the language used by the judge in the decision was quite strong, calling Lloyd's "grossly negligent."[81] Some lawsuits against Lloyd's are still pending as of June 2009.

10-11b Lloyd's in International Logistics

From the perspective of an exporter or importer, the Lloyd's market would only be used for some of what is referred to as "project cargo," or cargo of exceptional dimensions that would not fit in a traditional container or would need special arrangements with the shipping line. An example of such extraordinary project cargo would be a firm shipping several large pieces of equipment to a customer or a subsidiary overseas. Because such cargo may not be insurable by a traditional insurance company, it could be insured through Lloyd's.

Lloyd's is also used substantially by carriers in insuring their transportation assets, such as ships, aircrafts, and pipelines.

10-12 Commercial Credit Insurance

Another area where a firm involved in international matters can transfer some of its risks is in the commercial credit area.

Increasingly, competitive pressures are pushing firms to sell on an open-account basis, as customers try to acquire the best possible payment alternatives. Several countries used to offer subsidized terms on export insurance to their exporters and, although these practices have officially ended with the creation of the World Trade Organization (WTO), which prohibits export subsidies, the mindset was established. In France, for example, nearly 25 percent of all export sales are insured by the *Compagnie Française d'Assurance pour le Commerce Extérieur* (COFACE), which was privatized in May 1994 but was still heavily subsidized by the French government, to the tune of FFr. 2.5 billion (U.S. $500 million) in 1996.[82]

A firm may have to cover several types of transactions for which it feels uncomfortable:

- A sale to a foreign customer on an open-account basis, where the firm is concerned about its exposure, or the amount of money it has at stake in the sale.

- A sale to a foreign customer on credit terms. The customer has requested that payments be extended over a period of several months. The terms are also open account because the sellers' competitors have offered this alternative to the customer. The exporter is concerned about its exposure to this stream of payment.

- A construction firm retained by a foreign customer to build a plant; however, in order to earn the contract, it must post a number of performance bank guarantees (or performance bonds). It is concerned about its exposure in the case of unexpected delays, such as if the customer calls on the bank guarantee. For more information on bank guarantees, refer to Chapter 7, Section 7-11.

10-12a Risks Involved

In each of these transactions, there are two components to the risk of non-payment:

- **Political risk**. This is the risk presented by the country in which the transaction takes place. This risk can take many forms. The country's government can decide to increase tariffs on certain imports while the customer refuses delivery; the country's government can decide to freeze accounts held in foreign currencies while the customer cannot pay; the country's government can decide to prohibit the sale of a particular product; the country's government can commit a political *faux pas* and an embargo is declared by the remainder of the world, which means that no payments can be forwarded by the customer; and so on.

- **Commercial risk**. This is the risk presented by the customer defaulting on its obligation to pay, for whatever reason. Generally, the customer encounters financial difficulties or the customer has a complaint about the product that it cannot resolve any other way—in its management's mind, at least—than by withholding payment to the exporter.

10-12b Risk Management Alternatives

As in the case of international cargo insurance, the firm exposed to these risks has three alternatives available to manage them: It can decide to retain the risks, it can decide to transfer the risk to an insurance company, or it can follow a mixed strategy of retaining some of the risks and transferring others. There are many different reasons for choosing one strategy or another, most of which are covered in Section 10-6.

10-12c Insurance Policies Available

Should a company decide to cover its receivable risks with insurance coverage, there are many alternatives available, which can be obtained from a large number of insurance companies and governmental or quasi-governmental agencies. Most of these sources have multiple programs, presenting a dizzying array of possible contracts. Most companies interested in such programs should contact an insurance agency specializing in these types of policies, as well as contact their banks or governmental export support agencies in their country for further and more specific information.

A quick summary of the programs available in the United States gives an example of what is possible.

Government Programs

There are three government-related organizations in the United States that provide exporters with commercial and political insurance coverage:

- **The Ex-Im Bank**. The Export-Import (Ex-Im) Bank was created as an independent government agency in 1934. Its mission is to help create jobs in the United States by supporting export sales. It has a very large number of programs, from political and commercial credit insurance to loan guarantees (for banks lending money to exporters) and loans extended to foreign purchasers of American products. For years, the Ex-Im Bank was the only provider of political risk insurance in the United States.

  There are two difficulties in dealing with the Ex-Im Bank. The first is the lengthy delays that usually accompany an application—which means that an exporter involved in a negotiation with a foreign customer should attempt to secure coverage very early. The second is that it is an arm of the U.S. government and therefore subject to political pressures, such as abrupt cancellation of coverage for certain countries of the world. In addition, the product sold abroad must have at least 50 percent American content. Nevertheless, the Ex-Im Bank provides programs that are extremely popular with exporters and their bankers, such as the

Ex-Im Bank Guarantee, which covers loan repayments by foreign purchasers. The complete program of the Ex-Im Bank is available at its Web site (www.exim.gov).

- **OPIC**. The Overseas Private Investment Corporation is also a governmental agency, created in 1971 with the purpose of encouraging private investments in developing countries. Its purpose is quite political, as it seeks to further U.S. values overseas, but it offers several programs of loans, political insurance, and private equity investment funds, all quite advantageous to corporations interested in investing in developing countries. As of October 2006, there were more than 140 countries eligible for its programs, details of which can be found at its Web site (www.opic.gov).

  Unfortunately, OPIC presents the same challenge as the Ex-Im Bank—long processing times—but because the products it offers cover long-term investments owned by U.S. firms, these delays are less critical.

- **SBA**. The Small Business Administration has created two programs designed to help exporters finance their sales abroad: working capital loans and long-term loans for capital investments. However, the SBA does not provide insurance of any sort for exporters.

All of these programs, even if not used, present substantial value to an exporter. For example, the Ex-Im Bank has established exposure fees for medium- and long-term loans. Its cost of guarantees and insurance vary according to, among other factors, the political and commercial risks of non-repayment in a given country and for a particular creditor. The Ex-Im Bank assigns exposure fee levels and transaction risk increments to transactions on the basis of this risk, and calculates them relying upon:[83]

- credit ratings and market spreads,
- credit agency and bank references,
- historical financial statements, and
- the Ex-Im Bank's credit experience with the borrower/guarantor and its industry.

Because banks involved in foreign trade often use a process similar to the Ex-Im Bank's process as their model for establishing transaction risk, it would be useful to an exporter to assess quickly a risk with which it may be unfamiliar.

Private Insurance Companies

In the United States, there has recently been a substantial increase in the number of programs offered by private insurance companies, but it is still a business restricted to a few players, because the practice of insuring a company's foreign receivables is not as well established as it is in many European countries. In the United States, there are few insurance agencies specializing in this field, with approximately 20 of them underwriting most of the business.[84]

The insurance companies that dominate the market are:

- **FCIA**. The Foreign Credit Insurance Association was created in 1961, primarily to offer products that combined the Ex-Im Bank's political insurance coverage and commercial credit insurance products. Today, many of the Ex-Im Bank products that contain credit insurance are using the FCIA for that portion of the coverage. The FCIA, though, is not a government agency but is owned by Great American Insurance Company, a conglomerate of insurance companies. The FCIA products are mostly commercial credit insurance products, ranging from short-term to medium-term coverage for receivables. More information on the company's products can be found on its Web site (www.fcia.com).

- **Euler-ACI**. American Credit Indemnity is the other large player in the field, offering a similar array of commercial credit insurance products. It was recently purchased by the Euler Group, a French insurance conglomerate. More information on ACI's products can be found on its Web site (www.eulerhermes. com/en).

- **American International Group**. American International Group (AIG) is the largest U.S.-based provider of commercial credit insurance, a product it calls Trade Credit Insurance; more information is available on its Web site (www.aig.com).

- **Lloyd's**. Certain Lloyd's syndicates have added coverage of political risks to their underwriting portfolio and present the advantage of offering insurance for countries for which the U.S. government will not provide any, such as Afghanistan, Albania, and Belarus. Although the U.S. government allows trade with any of these countries, it will not provide political insurance coverage; however, a Lloyd's syndicate will.

Review and Discussion Questions

1. Describe some of the risks that an ocean shipment faces.

2. Describe some of the risks that an air shipment faces.

3. Explain the concept of general average, and explain, with a numerical example, how it is utilized.

4. Explain the concept of "insurable interest." Explain who has an insurable interest in three different transactions conducted under three different Incoterms.

5. What possible risk management strategies can an exporter/importer follow? Explain each strategy's advantages and disadvantages from the perspective of a small exporter.

6. What insurance coverage is required under CIF or CIP Incoterms? Explain which risks are not covered, and how an importer can still protect itself against them.

7. Choose three possible marine insurance clauses and describe their usefulness.

8. Explain the concept of international credit insurance and explain how it is possible to contract a policy covering commercial and political risks.

Endnotes

1. March, James, and Zur Shapira, "Managerial Perspectives on Risk and Risk Taking," *Management Science*, November 1987 (33) 11, pp. 1404–1418.

2. ISL Market Analysis 2006, World Shipbuilding and Marine Casualties, *Shipping Statistics and Market Review*, August/September 2006, pp. 3–8.

3. Baldwin, Tom, "It's Time to Inspect the Containers ... (Don't Attempt This One at Home, Folks)," *Journal of Commerce*, November 13, 1997, p. 2B.

4. Baldwin, Tom, "Container Industry Braces for Lawsuits," *Journal of Commerce*, November 12, 1998, p. 1A.

5. Holtz, Robert Lee, "The Sober Science of Migrating Rubber Duckies," *Wall Street Journal*, November 14, 2008, p. A13.

6. Journal of Commerce Staff, "Complexity, Speed of Modern Ships Increases Risks," *Journal of Commerce*, November 19, 1999, p. 9.

7. Baldwin, Tom, "Ship Hit by Fire and Explosion Has Lost 85% to 90% of Its Cargo," *Journal of Commerce*, November 25, 1998, p. 16A.

8. "Impact on Insurance Market of M/V Hyundai Fortune," *Lloyd's Press*, March 31, 2006.

9. Graham, Philip, "Casualty and World Fleet Statistics as of 31.12.2008," International Union of Marine Insurance, http://www.iumi.com/index.cfm?rub=782, accessed June 21, 2009.

10. Baldwin, Tom, "Salvors Struggle to Stabilize the Carla in Stormy Atlantic," *Journal of Commerce*, December 2, 1997, p. 12A.

11. Baldwin, Tom, "Storm-Tossed Boxship Splits: Crew Rescued," *Journal of Commerce*, November 26, 1997, p. 14A.

12. Rible, Stephen, *Rationis Enterprises, Inc. of Panama, vs. Hyundai Mipo Dockyard Co., Ltd*, 2005, U.S. App. Lexis 22323 (2nd Cir. 2005), http://www.usaverageadjusters.org/Rationis.pdf.

13. Baldwin, Tom, "The Case of the Reappearing Rock, and Other Unchartered Navigational Hazards," *Journal of Commerce*, April 30, 1998, p. 2B.

14. Associated Press, "Cruise Ship Hits Caribbean Reef," December 15, 1998.

15. Dibble, Sandra, "German Container Ship Sticks Around for Easter," *San Diego Union-Tribune*, April 12, 2006.

16. BBC News, "Scavengers Take Washed-up Goods," January 22, 2007, http://news.bbc.co.uk/2/hi/uk_news/england/devon/6287457.stm.

17. Hastings, Warren, *Marine Insurance Compendium*, 1999, General Management Services, Inc., Publisher, 76 Mamaroneck Avenue, Suite 6, White Plains, NY 10601, USA.

18. Fabey, Michael, "Remember the Titanic? Your Business Does Not Have to Sink, Even If Your Cargo Does," *World Trade*, January 1998, p. 54.

19. Killcarr, Sean, "Dealing with Cargo Theft," *FleetOwner*, November 24, 2008, http://fleetowner.com/management/transportation_cargo_theft_1124.

20. Hoffman, William, "Cargo Theft: $50 Billion in Annual Losses Worldwide," *Gulf Shipper*, December 31, 2007, http://www.accessmylibrary.com/coms2/summary_0286-33630832_ITM.

21. ICC International Maritime Bureau, *Piracy and Armed Robbery Against Ships: 2008 Annual Report*, http://www.icc-ccs.org, accessed June 24, 2009.

22. "Piracy Reporting Centre Foils Another Hijack on the High Seas," press release of the Piracy Reporting Centre, June 16, 2000, http://www.iccwbo.org, October 5, 2000.

23. Cummins, Chip, "Piracy Grips Gulf of Aden," *Wall Street Journal*, September 8, 2008, A10.

24. Cummins, Chip, "Oil Tanker Waylaid by Pirates," *Wall Street Journal*, November 18, 2008, A1.

25. Gettleman, Jeffrey, and Mohammed Ibrahim, "Somali Pirates Get Ransom and Leave Arms Freighter," *New York Times*, February 6, 2009.

26. Cummins, Chip, "Oil Tanker Waylaid By Pirates," *Wall Street Journal*, November 18, 2008, A1.

27. "Somali Pirate Drowns," *Wall Street Journal*, January 11, 2009.

28. McFadden, Robert, and Scott Shane, "In Rescue of Captain, Navy Kills Three Pirates," *New York Times*, April 13, 2009, http://www.nytimes.com/2009/04/13/world/africa/13pirates.html.

29. Cowley, Elizabeth, "Tankers Rerouted Away from Pirates," *Wall Street Journal*, November 11, 2008, B2.

30. *Ibid.*

31. Langewiesche, William, *The Outlaw Sea: A World of Freedom, Chaos and Crime*. New York: North Point Press 2004.

32. Burnett, John, *Dangerous Waters: Modern Piracy and Terror on the High Seas*. New York: Penguin Books, 2002.

33. BBC News, "UK Liner Damaged in Collision," August 24, 1999, http://news.bbc.co.uk/2/hi/uk_news/428545.stm.

34. "Gas Roman Collision," *Fortunes de Mer*, February 27, 2003, http://www.fortunes-de-mer.com/rubriques/liens%20et%20contacts/detailsactualites/GasRoman2003ru.htm.

35. "Southern Hemisphere Icebergs," National Ice Center, http://www.natice.noaa.gov, accessed June 19, 2009.

36. Associated Press, "Skyway Disaster Lives Remembered," May 8, 2000.

37. Tirschwell, Peter, "Pilot's Trip to Restroom Leads to Expensive Damage to Crane," *Journal of Commerce*, February 19, 1997, p. 3B.

38. Motley, Robert, "Shippers' Case Law," *American Shipper*, February 1999, p. 36.

39. Motley, Robert, "Shippers' Case Law," *American Shipper*, March 2000, p. 46.

40. Motley, Robert, "Shippers' Case Law," *American Shipper*, June 1998, p. 40.

41. Human Rights Watch, "Forced Apart (by the Numbers): Non-Citizens Deported Mostly for Nonviolent Offenses," April 2009, http://www.unhcr.org/refworld/pdfid/49e6dccd0.pdf.

42. Department of Homeland Security, Office of Inspector General, "A Review of CBP and ICE Responses to Recent Incidents of Chinese Human Smuggling in Maritime Cargo Containers," May 2007, http://www.dhs.gov/xoig/assets/mgmtrpts/OIG_07-40_Apr07.pdf.

43. Malcomson, Scott L., "The Unquiet Ship," *New Yorker*, January 20, 1997, pp. 72–81.

44. Hall, Kevin G., "Free Rides Have Big Price Tags," *Journal of Commerce*, March 11, 1997, p. 1A.

45. Bunce, Matthew, "Stowaway Deaths Haunt Ship Industry in Africa," *Journal of Commerce*, March 13, 1997, p. 3B.

46. Associated Press, "Yugoslav Ship May Be Set Free," *Journal of Commerce*, March 31, 1997, p. 4B.

47. Scherer, Ron, "Abandon Ship: New Law of Sea," *Christian Science Monitor*, December 29, 1998, p. 2.

48. Associated Press, "Romanian Sailors Abandoned on Decaying Ship," April 8, 1998.

49. International Transport Workers' Federation, "Out of Sight, Out of Mind: Seafarers, Fishers and Human Rights," June 2006, http://www.itfglobal.org/files/extranet/-1/2259/HumanRights.pdf.

50. *Ports of the World*, 15th ed., Cigna Insurance Corporation, available from publisher, *Ports of the World*, Cigna Companies, P.O. Box 7716, Philadelphia, Pennsylvania 19192, USA.

51. Crabtree, Thomas, Thomas Hoang, James Edgar, and Kai Heinicke, *The World Air Cargo Forecast 2008–2009*, Boeing Corporation, http://www.boeing.com/commercial/cargo, accessed June 21, 2009.

52. Vaughan, Emmett J., and Therese M. Vaughan, *Fundamentals of Risk and Insurance*, 10th ed. John Wiley and Sons New York: John Wiley and Sons 2008.

53. *Marine Insurance: Notes and Comments on Ocean Cargo Insurance*, Cigna Property and Casualty Specialty Insurance, P.O. Box 7716, Philadelphia, Pennsylvania 19192, USA.

54. Vaughan, Emmett J., and Therese M. Vaughan, *Fundamentals of Risk and Insurance*, 10th ed. John Wiley and Sons New York: John Wiley and Sons 2008.

55. Banham, Russ, "They've Got Them Covered," *Journal of Commerce*, February 23, 1998, p. 6A.

56. *Marine Insurance: Notes and Comments on Ocean Cargo Insurance*, Cigna Property and Casualty Specialty Insurance, P.O. Box 7716, Philadelphia, Pennsylvania 19192, USA.

57. *Ibid.*

58. *Ocean Cargo Handbook*, Chubb Group of Insurance Companies, Warren, New Jersey 07059, USA.

59. *The Register of Ships 2008–2009*, Lloyd's Register, available at http://www.lrfairplay.com/Maritime_data/Register_Of_Ships/Register_Of_Ships.html, accessed June 22, 2009.

60. Thomas Miller, Ltd., "UK P&I Circular Reference 04/09," February 2009, http://www.ukpandi.com/ukpandi/infopool.nsf/HTML/ClubCircular0409.

61. International Oil Pollution Compensation Funds, "Facts and Figures," http://www.iopcfund.org/facts.htm, accessed June 22, 2009.

62. "Institute Marine Cargo Clauses–A," http://www.natlaw.com/treaties/global/global/global31.htm, accessed June 22, 2009.

63. Bogart, Susan, "Loss to Cargo," *Marine Insurance and General Average*, Maritime Law Association of the United States, January 1, 2001, http://www.mlaus.org/article.ihtml?id=558&committee=160.

64. "Institute Marine Cargo Clauses–B," http://www.jus.uio.no/lm/institute.marine.cargo.clauses.b.1982/doc.html, accessed June 22, 2009.

65. "Institute Marine Cargo Clauses–C," http://www.jus.uio.no/lm/institute.marine.cargo.clauses.c.1982/doc.html, accessed June 22, 2009.

66. Ramberg, Jan, *ICC Guide to Incoterms 2000*, 1999, International Chamber of Commerce Publication No. 620, ICC Publishing S.A., 38 Cours Albert 1er, 75008 Paris, France and

ICC Publishing, Inc., 156 Fifth Avenue, Suite 417, New York, NY 10010, USA.

67. *Marine Insurance: Notes and Comments on Ocean Cargo Insurance*, Cigna Property and Casualty Specialty Insurance, P.O. Box 7716, Philadelphia, Pennsylvania 19192, USA.

68. Ramberg, Jan, *ICC Guide to Incoterms 2000*, 1999, International Chamber of Commerce Publication No. 620, ICC Publishing S.A., 38 Cours Albert 1er, 75008 Paris, France and ICC Publishing, Inc., 156 Fifth Avenue, Suite 417, New York, NY 10010, USA.

69. Blustein, Paul, and Brian Byrnes, "Lemons Caught in Homeland Security Squeeze," *Washington Post*, September 10, 2004.

70. Ramirez, Anthony, "Sour Surprise for Officers who Raided Container Ship," *New York Times*, August 7, 2004.

71. Jones, Eric, *International Economic Effects of Halting the Voyage of the CSAV Rio Puelo*, Master of Business Administration Thesis, 2005, Massachusetts Institute of Technology, http://dspace.mit.edu/bitstream/handle/1721.1/32115/63201956.pdf, accessed June 22, 2009.

72. *Marine Insurance: Notes and Comments on Ocean Cargo Insurance*, Cigna Property and Casualty Specialty Insurance, P.O. Box 7716, Philadelphia, Pennsylvania 19192, USA.

73. *Ocean Cargo Handbook*, Chubb Group of Insurance Companies, Warren, New Jersey 07059, USA.

74. Faber, Diana, et al., *Multimodal Transport: Avoiding Legal Problems*. LLP London: LLP 1997.

75. Clark Worldwide Transport, Inc. *Terms and Conditions of Service*, revised 6/94, http://www.clarkworldwide.com/terms.jsp.

76. U.S. Federal Maritime Commission, Subchapter B—Regulations Affecting Ocean Shipping in Foreign Commerce Part 515—Licensing, Financial Responsibility Requirements, and General Duties for Ocean Transportation Intermediaries, http://www.fmc.gov/home/515Licensingandsurety-requirementsforoceantransportationintermediaries.asp accessed April 30, 2006.

77. Stevenson, David, "How to Become a Lloyd's Name," *Money Week*, March 22, 2009, http://www.moneyweek.com/investment-advice/how-to-invest/how-to-become-a-lloyds-name-42723.aspx.

78. "Members," Lloyd's Market, http://www.lloyds.com/Lloyds_Market/Capacity/Overview.htm, accessed June 22, 2009.

79. *Ibid.*

80. McClintick, David, "The Decline and Fall of Lloyd's of London," *Time*, European Edition, February 21, 2000.

81. Redman, Christopher, "For Whom the Bell Tolls," *Time*, European Edition, November 13, 2000, p. 42.

82. Laurent, "COFACE: Les Outils pour Équilibrer vos Risques," *Le MOCI [Moniteur du Commerce International]*, September 28, 1995, pp. 116–125.

83. "Exposure Fee Table and Calculator," Export-Import Bank of the United States, revised April 10, 2009, http://www.exim.gov/tools/fee_calc.html.

84. Barovick, Richard, "Brokers Sit in Catbird Seat," *Journal of Commerce*, September 24, 1997, p. 1C.

International Ocean
Transportation

Chapter Outline

Key Terms

In order to manage international logistics, it is fundamental to have a good understanding of the transportation alternatives open to an international shipper. The next three chapters provide an overview of the many options given to an exporter or an importer interested in making transportation arrangements for a given shipment.

The first chapter (Chapter 11) deals with the alternatives available in ocean transportation and the complexities of the international framework of rules that enable shipping lines to operate. The second chapter (Chapter 12) deals with air transportation and its rules and regulations. The third chapter (Chapter 13) deals with land transportation—rail and road—but also covers multimodal transportation, which is not really a mode of transportation, but a shipping alternative that simplifies the work of the shipper—exporter or importer—by allowing it to send its freight with only one carrier (shipping company). It also covers pipelines and several other unusual modes of transportation, mostly used in very limited domestic markets.

The world's merchant fleet is registered in over 150 nations and is manned by over a million seafarers of virtually every nationality. The international shipping industry is responsible for the carriage of 90 percent of world trade (by weight). Ocean shipping is key to the global economy. Without shipping, the transport of raw materials and the import/export of affordable food and manufactured goods would be impossible. Modern ships are technically sophisticated, high-value assets: Large ships have a capital cost of well over U.S. $100 million. Merchant ship operations generate an estimated annual revenue of over U.S. $380 billion in freight within the global economy, and transport over 7.7 billion tons of cargo.[1]

11-1 Types of Service

liner A ship that operates on a regular schedule, traveling from a group of ports to another group of ports.

tramp A ship that does not operate on a regular schedule and is available to be chartered for any voyage, from any port to any port.

The first differentiation to be made is between **liner** ships and **tramp** ships.

Liner ships travel on a regular voyage, following a pre-established schedule, and with determined ports of call. A scheduled voyage may include only two ports (Santos, Brazil, to Miami, USA, and back) or, more commonly, a series of ports in one region of the world (e.g., Bremerhaven, Germany; Rotterdam, Netherlands; Felixstowe, Great Britain) to another (e.g., Boston, USA; Baltimore, USA; Nassau, Bahamas). Quite a few liners follow "round the world" (RTW) schedules, either eastbound or westbound, passing through the Panama Canal and/or the Suez Canal. There are many types of liner ships, a large number of which are adapted to specific routes, their size and equipment dependent on the ports of call they visit and on the specific types of cargo that their trade route entails. Liners are common carriers in that they offer their services to any company that will pay the freight rate.

Unlike liners, tramp ships operate wherever and whenever the market dictates. They do not operate on a regular schedule but travel wherever the company that has contracted (chartered) the vessel wants the cargo delivered. Because of the way they operate, tramp ships usually carry only one type of cargo at a time, for one exporter or importer. Most tramp ships therefore are designed for one type of cargo exclusively, even if they carry several "dry" cargoes or several grades of petroleum products. A possible analogy is that a tramp vessel is a taxicab, whereas a liner ship is a public bus.

11-2 Size of Vessels

The second principal differentiation to be made is the size of the vessel. Vessel size dictates trade routes, economies of scale, and ports of entry.

Ships are often categorized by their size, which is expressed in "tons." Unfortunately, there are several types of tons and several ways of evaluating the tonnage of a vessel, and the "tonnage" of a vessel can be used for very different purposes, a situation that can lead to some substantial confusion.

Under the English system of measurements, tons are generally used as units of weight and may be "short," or equal to 2,000 pounds (907 kilograms), or "long," equal to 2,240 pounds (1,016 kilograms). However, tons can also be units of volume, equal to 100 cubic feet (2.83 cubic meters), and vessel size can be expressed in those units. Under the metric system, a tonne is only a measure of mass (weight), equal to 1,000 kilograms (2,204.6 pounds).

11-2a Deadweight Tonnage and Cubic Capacity

The **deadweight tonnage (dwt)** is the total capacity of the ship (i.e., the maximum weight of the cargo that a vessel can carry) expressed in long tons (2,240 pounds) or in metric tonnes (2204.6 pounds). It is the measurement used by companies interested in shipping cargo and is often just called "tonnage." It is measured using the weight of the difference in water displacement when the ship is empty and when it is fully loaded to its maximum. The deadweight tonnage of a ship includes the fuel that the ship needs to travel—called **bunker**—and the supplies that it needs to function—called **stores**—and any ballast that the vessel may carry. Therefore, it is the theoretical capacity of the ship more than its actual capacity.

Vessels also have volumetric capacity for cargo that is called **grain** or **bale** cubic capacity. The grain cubic capacity is the cargo space available for loading a flowing cargo such as grain. The bale cubic capacity represents the total volume of space available for loading solid cargoes such as bales or boxes. The grain cubic capacity is always a larger figure. A vessel, when loaded with a very dense material—such as iron ore—can utilize its weight capacity before it reaches its cubic (volume) capacity; conversely, it can reach its volume capacity before it reaches its weight capacity if it is loaded with a light but voluminous cargo, such as timber or corn. A vessel that uses all of its cubic capacity and is also loaded down to its maximum draft is said to be "full and down."

11-2b Gross and Net Tonnage

The **gross tonnage** is the total *volume* capacity of the ship, expressed in tons, which are in this case equal to hundreds of cubic feet (2.83 cubic meters). The gross tonnage measures only the capacity of the ship below its deck, so this measurement is not appropriate for determining the cargo-carrying capacity of a ship, because a good number of vessels also carry cargo above deck, particularly containerships. This measurement is used to determine how much a ship owner will have to pay in taxes to the country in which the ship is registered, or tolls to the authorities of the ports it visits or the canals it uses; that measure is also used for regulatory purposes. In that case, gross tonnage is referred to as **gross registered tonnage (GRT)**, which takes into account the specific way a canal authority (such as Suez or Panama) determines gross tonnage. Once the volume occupied by the engine room, the crew, and other space necessary for the good operation of the ship is removed, the **net tonnage** is obtained.

Gross tonnage is commonly used when assessing the size of fleets for statistical purposes. Because different organizations set the cutoff for ship size at different gross tonnage levels (for example, in increments of 300 or 1,000 gross tons), this difference in base line often is the principal cause of fleet size discrepancy between reports.

11-2c Displacement

The **displacement tonnage** is the total weight of the ship, when fully loaded, measured by the weight of the volume of water it displaces. The **light tonnage** is the weight of the ship, measured the same way, but when the vessel is empty, which means that it is the displacement of the vessel after it was built but before any ballast, cargo, fuel, or supplies were put aboard. Both are generally measured in long tons and are used for naval architecture purposes in order to determine the vessel's stability, the stress it endures, and other engineering issues.

deadweight tonnage (dwt) The maximum weight that a ship can carry.

bunker The amount of fuel that a ship carries on board and that it needs to travel.

stores All the supplies that a ship carries and that it needs to function.

grain An agricultural commodity, such as corn, wheat, oats, or soybeans.

bale The end result of a packaging technique which consists of taking a commodity and unitizing it by compressing it and placing it into a bag or encircling it with string, metal, or plastic bands.

gross tonnage The total volume of a ship's carrying capacity, measured as the space available below deck, and expressed in hundreds of cubic feet.

gross registered tonnage (GRT) The volume capacity of a ship (see *gross tonnage*), calculated in a way that meets the requirements of a specific authority, such as the Panama Canal Authority or the Suez Canal Authority.

net tonnage Obtained by subtracting the volume occupied by the engine room and the spaces necessary for the operation of the ship (crew quarters, bridge) from the gross tonnage.

displacement tonnage The total weight of the ship, when fully loaded, measured by using the weight of the water displaced.

light tonnage The total weight of the ship, when empty, measured by using the weight of the water displaced.

Vessel Tonnage

The relationship between vessel tonnages can be expressed mathematically, and the following is an example of an actual 35,000 dwt (deadweight tonnage) Handysize bulk vessel ready for a 3,500-nautical-mile voyage (6,500 kilometers):

Length overall (LOA)	611 feet, 3 inches	(186.31 meters)
Beam (width)	93 feet, 2 inches	(28.40 meters)
Summer draft (amount of water needed to float)	35 feet, 2.5 inches	(10.73 meters)
Freeboard (distance between the water line and deck)	15 feet, 0.75 inches	(4.59 meters)
Winter draft	34 feet, 5.75 inches	(10.50 meters)
Freshwater draft	35 feet, 11.5 inches	(10.96 meters)
Net tonnage (NT)	19,513 tons	(55,222 cubic meters)
Gross tonnage (GT)	24,384 tons	(69,007 cubic meters)
Suez gross registered tonnage (GRT)	24,596 tons	(69,607 cubic meters)
Displacement	44,122 long tons	(44,828 metric tonnes)
Light ship displacement	7,646 long tons	(7,768 metric tonnes)
Deadweight tonnage (dwt) at summer loadline	36,476 long tons	(37,059 metric tonnes)
Bunker capacity (varies with voyage length)	600 long tons	(610 metric tonnes)
Potable drinking water (varies with voyage length)	240 long tons	(244 metric tonnes)
Constant (allowance for crew and consumable stores)	150 long tons	(152 metric tonnes)
Ballast (carried for trim if needed)	100 long tons	(102 metric tonnes)
Cargo deadweight (deadweight available for cargo)	35,386 long tons	(35,952 metric tonnes)

11-2d Plimsoll Mark and Load Lines

One more difficulty arises when one understands that ships are considered "fully loaded" at different drafts (how deep they sit in the water) in function of the season in which they are operating, of the latitudes under which they ply their trade, and of the density of the water. The deepest draft a ship can sit in is called the "tropical line" (T), followed by the "summer line" (S), the "winter line" (W), and the "winter North Atlantic line" (WNA). A "freshwater line" (F) is also present, as freshwater density is lower—a ship will sit lower in freshwater than it would in saltwater with the same quantity of cargo. At the same height as the vessel's summer deadweight draft, there is another diagram called the Plimsoll mark: a circle bisected by a horizontal line, which identifies the classification society that determined the vessel's load lines. Figure 11-1 shows the Plimsoll mark and load lines for a ship classified by the Chinese Classification Society. The Plimsoll mark and load lines are located on the hull of a ship and amidships (halfway between the bow and the stern) and are marked with a bead welded onto the hull and painted.

The deadweight tonnage is generally determined at the summer line or at the line that represents accurately the conditions under which a ship is used. For example, a vessel used consistently in the Caribbean would have its deadweight tonnage calculated with the tropical load line. The load lines correspond to geographical regions of the globe, and a vessel must be at the appropriate load line when it arrives in the geographical region. For instance, a vessel that loads in Matadi, Congo, in January and sails for Antwerp will load to the tropical load line (T) but must consume enough fuel to be at the winter North Atlantic load line (WNA) when the vessel arrives in that geographical region. A vessel that exceeds appropriate load lines is subject to heavy fines and may also be considered to be in an unseaworthy state.

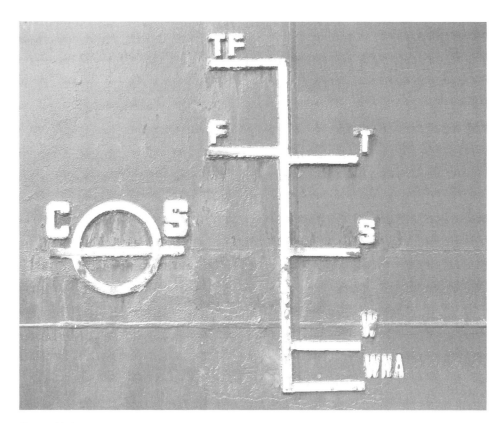

Figure 11-1
The Plimsoll Mark and Load Lines
Source: Photo © Jamie Serenko. Used with permission.

11-2e Size Categories

One of the biggest distinctions made in ships' sizes is between the ships that can travel through the locks of the Panama Canal and the ones that cannot. A ship of the maximum size that can possibly fit through these locks is called a **Panamax** ship; such a ship can have up to 75,000 long tons of deadweight tonnage, and its outside dimensions allow it to barely fit within the locks, with only a few inches of clearance between the locks' walls and the ship (see Figure 11-2). The locks are 1,000 feet long (304 meters) and 110 feet wide (33 meters). The longest ship to cross the Panama Canal is the *Marcona Prospector*, which is 973 feet long (296 meters) and 106 feet wide (32 meters), and the widest is the *USS New Jersey*, which is 108 feet wide (33 meters).[2] All ships built that are larger than this size are called **post-Panamax** ships. Other terminologies used are:

Panamax A ship of the maximum size that can enter the locks of the Panama Canal.

post-Panamax A ship whose size is too large to enter the locks of the Panama Canal.

- **Handysize ship**. A term commonly used in the dry-bulk trade and which refers to ships in the 10,000 to 50,000 deadweight ton range. Such ships tend to be used for tramp service.

- **Suez-Max ships**. This term is used to describe ships sized at roughly 150,000 deadweight tons and which are of the maximum size that can fit through the Suez Canal (about 285 meters long, 35 meters wide, and 23 meters of draft; that is 935 feet long, 115 feet wide, and 75 feet of draft). In 1996, the Suez Canal was deepened and widened, so the Suez-Max terminology is losing some of its validity.

- **Capesize ships**. This term is used to describe large dry-bulk carriers of a capacity greater than 80,000 deadweight tons.

- **Very large crude carrier**. This term is used to describe an oil tanker of up to 300,000 deadweight tonnage, which is about 350 meters long and 55 meters

Figure 11-2
A Panamax Containership, the *CMA-CGM Berlioz*

Source: Photo © Kelvin Davies. Used with permission.

wide and has 28 meters of draft. That's 1,150 feet long, 180 feet wide, and 92 feet of draft.

- **Ultra-large crude carrier (ULCC).** This term describes an oil tanker of more than 300,000 deadweight tonnage. The largest ULCC built, the *Knock Nevis*, formerly called the *Seawise Giant* and the *Jahre Viking*, has a deadweight tonnage of 565,000 metric tonnes, is 458 meters long and 69 meters wide and has a draft of 26.4 meters.[3] That represents a surface of 2.5 hectares and translates to 1,527 feet long, 230 feet wide, a draft of 88 feet, and an area of 6.25 acres. Such ships generally are unable to go into traditional ports, and they remain in deep sea at all times. Their cargo is removed using a process called "lightering," which consists of transferring the cargo onto smaller ships (see Section 11-3f), or using offshore oil terminals (see Figure 11-3).

For comparison purposes, the largest containership as of 2009, the *Emma Maersk*, is 397 meters long and 56 meters wide, has a draft of 15.5 meters (1,302 feet long, 184 feet wide, and a draft of 51 feet), and has a deadweight tonnage of 156,900 metric tonnes (154,430 long tons). It can carry 13,500 twenty-foot equivalent units (TEUs) (i.e., 20-foot containers).[4] There were 85 containerships of this approximate size (larger than 13,000 TEUs) on order as of August 2008 (see Table 3-1 in Chapter 3).

11-3 Types of Vessels

The third principal differentiation to be made is based on the type of cargo carried by the vessels, and those cargoes are used to classify merchant ships into many different categories (see Figure 11-4).[5] First, a distinction is made between cargo ships that carry **wet-bulk (liquid) cargoes** and those vessels that carry **dry-bulk cargoes**. Second, wet and dry cargoes can either be shipped in bulk or unitized (shipped in units that are unloaded one at a time, such as boxes, crates, or containers).

There are more than 46,000 commercial vessels worldwide with an individual capacity greater than 500 gross tonnes. The total cargo carrying capacity of the world's

wet-bulk (liquid) cargo Liquid cargo that is loaded directly into the hold of a ship, without any form of unitization.

dry-bulk cargo Dry cargo that is loaded directly into the hold of a ship, without any form of unitization. Although dry, the cargo exhibits the properties of a liquid, in that it takes the shape of the hold.

Figure 11-3
The Ultra-Large Crude Carrier *Ab Qaiq* Loading at the Mina-Al-Bakr Oil Terminal in Iraq
Source: Photo © Andrew Meyers, United States Navy. Used with permission.

commercial fleet exceeded 1 billion deadweight tons in 2008 (see Figure 11-5).[6] Almost every single one of these ships is designed differently. It is therefore difficult to classify them much better than in broad-based groups, with many ships not fitting neatly into one category.

11-3a Containerships

The containerized trade is growing rapidly. Approximately 60 percent of world trade (in value) is containerized, and container transportation volume has been growing

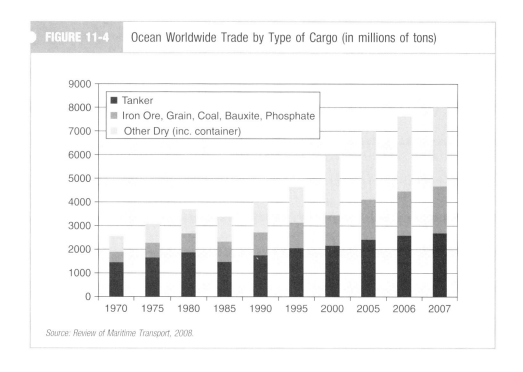

FIGURE 11-4   Ocean Worldwide Trade by Type of Cargo (in millions of tons)

Source: Review of Maritime Transport, 2008.

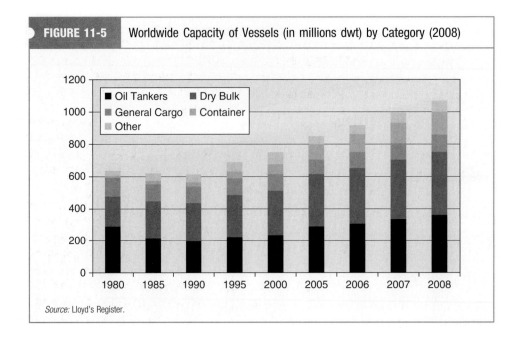

FIGURE 11-5   Worldwide Capacity of Vessels (in millions dwt) by Category (2008)

Source: Lloyd's Register.

by 9.8 percent per year since 1990 (see Figure 11-6). Even in trade lanes where containers are solidly implanted, such as Asia–North America or Europe–North America, the growth in the volume of shipment is estimated at 5 percent.[7] Given the fact that goods that traditionally traveled in bulk are now shipped using containers—for example, forestry products and grain—and given the fact that intermodal transportation is responding well to customer needs, it seems that the container, which was created in 1956, will dominate international trade yet further.

Containerships, also known as "box ships," carry containerized cargo on a scheduled voyage. Vessels dedicated to the container trade can carry up to 13,000 TEUs—20-foot equivalent units, or the space equivalent of a 20-foot container—but there are many mixed-cargo ships that can also carry containers, sometimes as few as 100 TEUs. Most containerships rely upon the port cranes to unload their cargo, but

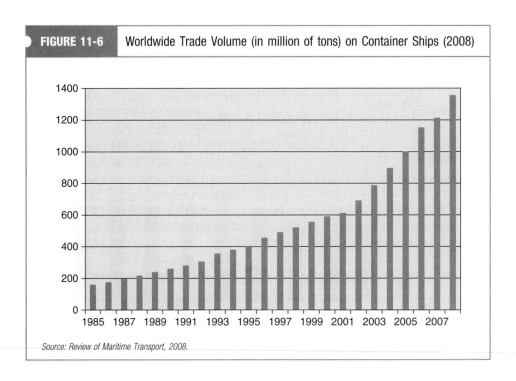

FIGURE 11-6   Worldwide Trade Volume (in million of tons) on Container Ships (2008)

Source: Review of Maritime Transport, 2008.

Figure 11-7
A Post-Panamax Containership
Source: Photo © Volker Kreinacke. Used with permission.

some do have cranes on board. All containerships used to be capable of going through the Panama Canal and carried around 4,500 TEUs. When the first post-Panamax containerships were delivered, they carried more than 6,000 TEUs and forced some substantial changes in ports. For example, they were so wide and so high (see Figure 11-7) that some ports had to upgrade their crane equipment. Moreover, some ports became entirely inaccessible; some of the post-Panamax ships cannot enter some of the ports on the East Coast of the United States, because their air drafts do not allow them to "fit" under the bridges, or their water drafts do not allow them to float in the port channels, since they are not deep enough (for example, Port Elizabeth of the Port of New York–New Jersey).

As there are plans to build yet larger ships, as big as 18,000 TEUs, there will be additional demands made on port infrastructure, and it will certainly reduce the number of ports in which these giant ships can berth to a handful worldwide. The trend in the industry is therefore seen as the creation of a system of large "hubs," to and from which the mega-ships would travel, coupled with a number of smaller ships, called "feeder ships," which would travel between these giant hub ports and smaller ports. Those feeder ships would essentially be the existing fleet of traditional containerships. Although this would cause transshipments to occur, it is estimated that it would lower transportation costs.

Traditional containerships hold containers "under deck" as well as "on deck." Some containers are first loaded in the holds of the ship, then the hatch covers (the deck) are put in place, and the remainder of the containers are placed on top of them. Containers placed under deck are usually held in place by vertical guides, along which the crane operator slides them. On-deck containers are usually stacked on top of each other and latched to each other with metal bars and twistlocks (see Figure 11-8). Since the early 1990s, several shipping lines have tried to speed up the process of loading containers by equipping their ships with vertical guides for on-deck containers as well, and some have eliminated the deck hatches altogether (see Figure 11-9), simply choosing to equip the vessel with much larger bilge pumps (the pumps that remove the water from the inside of a ship). Eventually, it is conceivable that the concept of "deck" will no longer exist in the container trade.

Figure 11-8
Containers Lashed on the Deck of a Containership
Source: Photo © Ole Tange. Used with permission.

Another possible change in the container industry would be the creation of fast ships, or ships capable of crossing the Atlantic Ocean in three and a half days, a project pursued by a company aptly named FastShip. Those ships would carry 1,500 TEUs and travel between two specifically equipped ports—Philadelphia, U.S.A., and Cherbourg, France—reducing the transit time from supplier to customer to seven days, or somewhat similar to the six days that an airline can achieve. While the costs of shipping would be 60 percent higher than for a traditional trans-Atlantic crossing, they would be lower than for an air shipment, and there would be no restriction on the type of cargo that could be shipped. The founders of the venture estimate that some time-sensitive cargo could benefit from their service, expected to start in 2011.[8] Skeptics abound, but there is certainly a trend toward faster transportation and reduced inventory costs. In addition, it is likely that such competition will reduce the costs of airfreight, so most shippers should benefit.

The principal problem for such a service will be to make high-speed, low-drag hull forms and fuel-efficient propulsion systems cost-effective enough for a business model to work. A 2003 RAND study pointed out that today's "fast ships are not generally considered to be commercially viable because of their very high operating costs."[9] However, as fuel costs increase, fast ships are becoming increasingly more attractive, as they consume 60 percent less fuel (per ton of cargo transported) than airfreighters.

11-3b Roll-On/Roll-Off Ships

Roll-on/roll-off (RORO) ships were created to accommodate cargo that was self-propelled, such as automobiles or trucks, or cargo that could be wheeled into a ship, such as railroad cars or excavation equipment. They are essentially floating parking garages (see Figure 11-10).

The concept is fairly straightforward. Because it takes a long time to load such vehicles "over the rail" (i.e., by using a crane), it is preferable to load them by rolling them onto the ship. RORO ships therefore have a portion of their hulls that opens up

Figure 11-9
Containers on a Hatchless Containership
Source: Photo © Danny Cornelissen. Used with permission.

and acts as a ramp on which the vehicles are driven before being parked on the many decks of the ship and secured with chains. The hull opening is either on the side of the ship or on its stern (rear).

RORO ships have an advantage in that specialized lifting equipment is not required, even for the heaviest of loads, because the cargo rolls under its own power or is pulled by a tractor. It therefore needs only some docking space and a substantial number of dock workers to load or unload its cargo. There are distinctions between a pure car-carrier (PCC) ship, which loads only cars and has decks with only 5 feet (1.5 meters) of overhead clearance, and other, more versatile, "true" RORO ships that can accommodate larger cargo. Many RORO ships are equipped with adjustable decks, which allow them to transport any sort of rolling cargo.

As the number of cars manufactured worldwide increases, it seems that the future of the RORO concept is secure. However, there are several companies that are selling specialized equipment that can be used in traditional 40-foot containers and can handle six automobiles (on two levels) at once with equipment that can be collapsed and placed into another container for the return trip. This concept is attractive, as it overcomes some of the drawbacks of the RORO ships. There is no need to hire expensive stevedore labor to drive the vehicles onto the ship—it is replaced with cheaper "inland" labor to load and unload the containers—and it makes the loading and unloading faster, as it requires only one cargo movement for every six vehicles. This alternative also eliminates the cost of modifying the configuration of the decks so

Figure 11-10
A Roll-On/Roll-Off Ship, the *Asian Emperor*
Source: Photo © Kelvin Davies. Used with permission.

that regular bulk cargo can be loaded in the now-empty RORO ship on the return trip. The latter issue is significant for trades with countries that import a lot of vehicles but export far fewer, such as the United States.

The concept of RORO has been expanded to another variation, designed for the transport of livestock, which are led aboard the ship rather than hoisted over its rail. Therefore, the ships are given the moniker of **trot-on/trot-off** ships. Such ships are used mainly to transport sheep between Australia or New Zealand and the Middle East. The TOTO ships also return empty to their ports of origin.

11-3c Break-Bulk or General-Merchandise Ships

Break-bulk ships (also called general-merchandise ships) constitute the least homogeneous category of vessels. There are all sorts of break-bulk ships, which were often created for a specialized trade or a given shipping lane. Altogether, though, break-bulk cargo ships are multipurpose ships that can transport shipments of unusual sizes, unitized on pallets, in bags, or in crates (see Figure 11-11). Because of the increase in the percentage of international cargo shipments that are containerized, including the "containerization" of some goods that are larger than what can "normally" fit in a regular container (see Chapter 13, Section 13-3a), and because of the increasing role of RORO ships, break-bulk ships' share of international trade is decreasing but is still the single largest fleet in number of ships.

The main problem with general-merchandise ships stems from their labor-intensive loading and unloading; each unitized piece must be handled separately, with several stevedores in the hull of the ship and several stevedores on the quay, in addition to the crane operators. Because the cargo is of different sizes, each piece may require different equipment (a different number of hooks, shorter or longer slings, and so on) and in some cases demand "problem solving," which may involve a few attempts before it is loaded or unloaded successfully. In addition, the securing of the loads on the decks is just as labor intensive, because pieces of cargo have odd sizes. Consequently, break-bulk ships stay in port much longer, especially because they cannot load or unload in the rain, and their schedules can be erratic.

trot-on/trot-off A ship designed to carry livestock. It possesses a ramp that the animals can use to walk on-board and exit the vessel.

Figure 11-11
A Break-Bulk Ship
Source: Photo © Dan Barnes. Used with permission.

Since a large percentage of break-bulk ships are equipped with an onboard crane, which allows them to load and unload without relying on port equipment, they can call at just about any port to load different kinds of cargo loads, giving them a flexibility that containerships do not have. Although decreasing in percentage, the break-bulk trade has a significant future in that it will always carry odd-sized shipments and always carry heavy cargoes that cannot be containerized. Nevertheless, it is likely that there will be fewer general-merchandise ships in the future—almost no new break-bulk ships have been built in the last 15 years—although it is likely that there will be a corresponding increase in the number of "combination ships," which will carry break-bulk cargo, but also some bulk, some RORO cargo, and a few containers.

11-3d Combination Ships

The ultimate multipurpose ships are combination ships, which are designed to carry all sorts of different loads in a single voyage. A typical combination ship has several holds in which bulk cargo, such as timber or grain, can be placed. Those holds can also be used for break-bulk cargo, especially oversized and heavy cargo, such as machinery, and sometimes containers. It also has a **tweendeck**, or a deck below the main deck, which accommodates smaller break-bulk cargo as well as vehicles that are loaded through the RORO access door. On its main deck, the typical combination ship can carry several containers as well. Finally, a combination ship has one or more onboard cranes, to increase its versatility and allow it to unload its cargo in any port (see Figure 11-12).

Combination ships thrive in shipping lanes that have a low volume of trade, such as the trade between developed countries and developing countries, or the trade to and from small island nations, such as those in the South Pacific or the Caribbean.

11-3e LASH Ships

LASH (lighter-aboard-ship) ships represent yet another type of ship that is quite versatile. The concept is similar to that of a containership, in that the LASH ship carries

tweendeck In a combination ship, a deck located below the main deck that is used to carry smaller-size break-bulk cargo, such as vehicles.

Figure 11-12
A Combination Ship
Source: Photo © Losinjska Plovidba. Used with permission.

LASH barges Floating containers measuring 18 by 9 by 3 meters that can be loaded and unloaded from a lighter-aboard-ship (LASH) mothership and can be tugged to their destination in a port or to an area without port facilities.

LASH mothership A ship equipped with cranes that is designed to carry approximately 80 lighter-aboard-ship (LASH) barges and can load and unload them at anchor (i.e., without having to be in port).

standardized units of cargo, but with the difference that the units of cargo are much larger, each with a capacity of 385 metric tonnes of deadweight tonnage. Because these units can also float, they are called **LASH barges**. Their dimensions are 59 feet, 30 feet, and 10 feet (18 meters long, 9 meters wide, and 3 meters deep). Each barge is covered with a hatch cover and is watertight. The capacity of the average LASH ship, also called the **LASH mothership**, is about 80 barges. The concept of LASH was created in 1969 to carry forest products from the United States to northern Europe,[10] and this trade is still one of the concept's mainstays (see Figure 11-13).

Just like containers, LASH barges present the advantage of allowing the shipper to pack and unpack the barge independently of the ship's schedule, and it allows for a very fast loading and unloading of the vessel carrying the LASH barges. In addition, the LASH system also has an advantage in that the barges can be floated to the mothership, then loaded on board using the crane of the vessel. This allows the ship to call on ports that have very little lifting equipment or that are very shallow. It actually allows the LASH vessel to load and unload at anchor (i.e., without having to be docked). Many project cargo barges can then be delivered to remote areas of the world, either in coastal areas or at the mouths of rivers, or to areas where oceangoing ships cannot go, such as inland ports. The barges can then be unpacked after the mothership has unloaded them.

The innovative LASH ship concept never really took hold in maritime commerce. This was in part due to the poor maneuverability of the LASH barges in river transit and the large number of high cost barges needed for an operating system, which required two barges off the vessel for every one onboard. Also, the 500-ton lot size of a LASH barge did not suit the needs of most shippers. There was a short-lived attempt to increase economies of scale with the 2,000-ton SEABEE barge system, but it was less successful than LASH operations. The container proved to be more versatile without the very high capital costs inherent in a LASH operation.

11-3f Product, Chemical, and Crude Carriers

Petroleum products transported in bulk by ships are broken down into three principal trades: product, chemical, and crude.

Product vessels transport refined products such as gasoline, diesel oil, or other refined products. These products need to be carefully segregated and kept from contamination. The vessels range in size from small coastal vessels (about 1,000 dwt) to large product carriers, roughly 60,000 dwt in size. The vessels may carry up to six different products if the vessel's tank and piping system allow segregation.

Figure 11-13
LASH Barges and Their LASH Mothership
Source: Photo © Donn Young, Port of New Orleans. Used with permission.

Chemical carriers are specially designed ships in the 1,000 to 40,000 dwt range that carry chemicals (see Figure 11-14). Some may transport as many as 40 different chemicals and are referred to as "drugstore" ships. The hazardous nature of some chemicals, such as benzene, and the handling requirements of other chemicals that require special tanks, dedicated piping systems, and complex safeguards limit the vessels to the chemical trade.

Crude carriers are the bulk ships dedicated to the transport of unrefined (crude) oil. The largest ships in the world are crude carriers; there is a distinction made between crude carriers of up to 80,000 dwt, which are called AfraMax; very large crude carriers (VLCC), of up to 300,000 dwt; and ultra-large crude carriers (ULCC) beyond this tonnage. There were approximately 450 VLCCs and ULCCs in 1997, a figure that is unlikely to have changed in 2009, even though the international oil trade is growing; the only change being that older ships are replaced with more modern ships, equipped with double hulls, which makes them less likely to spill their cargoes if they accidentally run aground.

VLCCs and ULCCs are such large ships (see Figure 11-15) that they can call on only a few ports in the world; because their draft, when loaded, can reach 115 feet (35 meters), they need very deep ports and, because they are so long and wide, a very large docking area. In a number of cases, the VLCCs and ULCCs do not enter a port but stay at anchor outside of the port in deep waters. The oil cargo of the large crude carrier is then transferred into smaller crude carriers that subsequently transport it and unload it into the port. This process is called **lightering** and is also occasionally used for traditional break-bulk or dry-bulk ships. On other occasions, the VLCCs and ULCCs are connected to an artificial island, or a "floating island," which is a pipeline terminal in deep waters. Some countries have transformed natural islands into deepwater oil terminals for such ships, such as in the case of the Mina-al-Bakr oil terminal in Iraq (see Figure 11-3).

lightering The process by which a large vessel's cargo is unloaded offshore into smaller vessels that then take the cargo to nearby ports.

Figure 11-14
A Chemical Carrier
Source: Photo © Zennie. Used with permission.

After the oil spill from the VLCC *Exxon Valdez* into Alaskan waters in March 1989, the United States enacted the Oil Pollution Act of 1990, which requires that all oil tankers entering U.S. waters be double-hulled. The additional hull (and the space between the hull of the ship and the part of the ship that contains the

Figure 11-15
A Very Large Crude Carrier, the *Sirius Star*
Source: Photo © William Stevens, United States Navy. Used with permission.

Becoming a "Master Unlimited"

Maneuvering an ultra-large crude carrier (ULCC) is a job that few people can handle, but it is the daily responsibility of captains who have reached the prestigious title of *master unlimited*. There are only about 3,000 of them worldwide and they are the only ones accredited to command ships of more than 5,000 tons GRT.[11] Handling such large ships can be quite a hair-raising experience. Consider that a ULCC can be as long as four football fields and that, at cruising speed and fully loaded, it stops in a mere six miles if its engine is stopped. If put in full reverse, the distance "shrinks" to two miles.[12]

In order to learn how to pilot these behemoths, captains either practice on computer simulations or travel to the unusual training camp of Port Revel in the foothills of the Alps in France, where they are placed in models of large ships. A similar model training program is operated by the Massachusetts Maritime Academy in Buzzards Bay, Massachusetts. Like their real-life equivalent, these model ships are extremely underpowered: A ship of this size is "like a large lorry [truck] with a moped engine and no brakes," says an instructor at Port Revel, noting that the 40-foot-long model *Europe*, weighing 41,000 pounds, has a motor of less than one horsepower with which the skipper has to maneuver it.[13] After a few days on the pond at Port Revel, these gifted sailors are capable of maneuvering these ships so well that they can squeeze a 700-foot behemoth into the 750-foot space left between two other ships in port without the help of a tug. In other words, simple parallel parking.

petroleum oil) is believed to provide some protection in the case of groundings, but the design reduces the carrying capacity of vessels by as much as 15 percent and adds to the cost of construction and maintenance. This unilateral requirement impacted all tankers worldwide, as most will eventually travel to the United States because it has the highest oil consumption. This act requires a phasing in of the technology, and its first phase was completed in 2005; more recent tankers can wait until 2015.

11-3g Dry-Bulk Carriers

Dry-bulk carriers operate on the same basis as oil tankers in that they are chartered for a whole voyage. Dry-bulk ships (see Figure 11-16) have several holds in their hull, in which non-unitized cargo is loaded through hatches (openings on deck). There are many types of dry-bulk ships, and because of the trade in which they are engaged—the type of merchandise that they carry and the ports on which they call—dry-bulk ships can have specialized configurations or equipment. Generally speaking, dry-bulk ships carry agricultural products, such as cereals, as well as coal, ores, scrap iron, dry chemicals, and other bulk commodities. Some of those ships, because of the versatility of the cargoes that they can carry, are called oil-bulk-ore (O-B-O) carriers, as they can transport oil during one leg of the voyage and then on the next leg, after cleaning the tanks/holds, carry dry-bulk products.

In terms of size, dry-bulk ships are generally classified into three types: Capesize, which are ships that are too large to fit through the Suez Canal and must go around the Cape of Good Hope on the southern tip of Africa; Panamax ships, which are small enough to fit through the Panama Canal; and Handysize bulkers, which are from 10,000 to 45,000 deadweight tons. Many of these Handysize tramp bulkers are somewhat older vessels.

A good portion of the trade in commodities in the world transits through a myriad of these Handysize vessels, carrying cargoes of sugar, rice, and other staples from small ports to other small ports. These ships are chartered primarily through the **Baltic Exchange**, which is a meeting place for brokers representing the ship owners and the cargo owners to meet and conduct business. The business is initially done verbally, and the word of the brokers is their bond.[14]

Baltic Exchange The world market for maritime cargo transportation, located in London, where cargo owners and ship owners negotiate the cost of moving cargo. It publishes multiple indices reflecting the market conditions for particular cargos and types of ship.

Figure 11-16
A Dry-Bulk Carrier with Its Hatches Open
Source: Photo © Dan Prat. Used with permission.

voyage charter A lease agreement between the owner (lessor) of a bulk cargo ship and a lessee, in which the owner provides the lessee with the ship, the crew, and all other services or supplies, for a single voyage.

time charter A lease agreement between the owner (lessor) of a bulk cargo ship and a lessee in which the owner provides the lessee with the ship, the crew, and all other services or supplies, for an agreed-upon period of time.

bareboat (or demise) charter A lease agreement between the owner (lessor) of a bulk cargo ship and a lessee, in which the owner provides the lessee with only the ship, without any other services or supplies.

laker A cargo ship designed for the Great Lakes of the United States and Canada. Its maximum size is dictated by the size of the locks through which it will travel.

As seen in Chapter 9, Section 9-5e, three types of charters are typically used for bulk vessels. A **voyage charter** hires the ship with all functions provided by the ship owner, such as crew, management, and fuel, to deliver cargo to one or more ports in the world. A **time charter** is a vessel hired to deliver cargo with the ship owner providing all services over a fixed period of time, which may vary from a few months to several years. A **bareboat** or **demise charter** is a vessel hired and run by another party. The ship owner provides a vessel that is bare of crew and supplies. The vessel charterer operates the vessel in all respects and returns the bareboat to the ship owner after the end of the demise charter, which can last months or years. Both dry and wet trade vessels are chartered.

There is a specific group of dry-bulk carriers that serve the ports of the Great Lakes, between the United States and Canada, called **lakers** (see Figure 11-17). Their characteristics are determined by the size of the canal locks of the Welland Canal, which gives them long and narrow hulls. Lakers trade mostly in three commodities: iron ore and iron ore pellets, coal, and finished steel. They are not ocean-going vessels, but they fit the general description of dry-bulk carriers. These vessels have self-unloading gear that allows for the rapid (10,000 short tons per hour) unloading of bulk cargoes. The design of the self-unloading booms allows the vessels to place cargo up to 150 feet (45 meters) off the side of the vessel. A number of the self-unloading

The Baltic Exchange and the Indices

Located in London, the Baltic Exchange was once the location where traders and ship owners would meet to arrange for the maritime transportation of commodities. Through a process not unlike that of a commodities exchange, the cargo owners and the ship owners would negotiate the cost of moving bulk cargo from one port to another. Today, the Baltic Exchange is the world's only independent source of maritime market information, obtained through the same process of negotiation. Its more than 550 members, representing the vast majority of the world's shipping companies, help determine the costs of shipping cargo through a series of indices, called the Baltic Exchange Indices, which are published daily.

The indices reflect the average costs per day (expressed in U.S. dollars) for an end customer to have a shipping company transport a certain commodity in a certain type of ship. The exchange calculates the indices by averaging the daily costs of shipping dry-bulk cargo on different routes. The most frequently used indices are the Baltic Exchange Capesize Index (BCI), which is the average daily cost of utilizing a vessel capable of carrying 172,000 metric tonnes of cargo, calculated over ten routes; the Baltic Exchange Panamax Index (BPI), which is the daily cost of utilizing a Panamax ship capable of carrying 74,000 metric tonnes of cargo, averaged over four routes; the Baltic Exchange Supramax Index (BSI) for ships capable of carrying 52,454 metric tonnes averaged over six routes; and the Baltic Exchange Handysize Index (BHSI) for ships capable of carrying 28,000 metric tonnes calculated over six routes. These indices are then combined to form the Baltic Exchange Dry Index (BDI).[15]

For oil-related cargoes, the Baltic Exchange publishes the Baltic Exchange Dirty Tanker Index (BDTI), which reflects the costs of shipping unrefined petroleum oil, calculated on the average costs of 17 different routes, and the Baltic Exchange Clean Tanker Index (BCTI), which reflects the costs of shipping oil-based refined products, such as gasoline or naphtha, averaged over seven routes. Both of these indices are combined into the Baltic Exchange International Tanker Route Index (BITR). Finally, there is a Baltic Exchange Palm Oil Route Index (BPOIL) and a Baltic Exchange Liquefied Petroleum Gas Index (BLPG).[16]

The Baltic Exchange Dry Bulk Index is widely considered a leading economic indicator. Since ships are hired (chartered) only when there is a cargo to be moved as a result of primary demand, the costs of shipping reflect the derived demand of transportation services. The worldwide demand for raw materials drove the Baltic Exchange Dry Index to reach a record high level of 11,793 points on May 20, 2008. On December 5, 2008, less than six months later, the index had dropped by 94 percent, to 663 points, the lowest since 1986.[17]

The component indices of the BDI have experienced similar fluctuations. In April 2008, a Capesize vessel chartered for U.S. $106,289 per day, while a Panamax vessel chartered for an average of U.S. $47,100 per day. In early February 2009, a Capesize vessel had dropped to a daily hire rate of U.S. $17,410 and a Panamax to U.S. $6,357 a day. For many shipowners, the daily hire rates had sunk below operating costs. By June 26, 2009, the rates had recovered to U.S. $77,968 and U.S. $22,992 respectively.[18]

lakers are over 1,000 feet in length (304 meters) and can trade only in four of the five Great Lakes, as they cannot fit through the Welland Canal into Lake Ontario.

Although not altogether the same as dry-bulk carriers, there are also a large number of ships that carry specialized cargoes that can be considered as dry bulk. Examples are refrigerated ships—also called "reefer ships"—which are slowly being replaced by refrigerated containers aboard containerships, with the possible exception of specialized refrigerated ships called banana ships; liquid food carriers, which therefore carry liquid bulk cargoes such as molasses, orange juice, and vegetable oils; lumber carriers; and cement carriers.

11-3h Gas Carriers

Another important bulk trade is the transportation of liquefied natural gas (LNG) and of liquefied petroleum gas (LPG). These types of carriers have a very distinctive shape. These ships hold several spheres of compressed gasses, only part of which are visible above their main deck (see Figure 11-18). The LNG and LPG trades tend to be

Figure 11-17
A Laker with Its Characteristic Bridge in the Fore of the Ship
Source: Photo © Earl Minnis. Used with permission.

slightly different than the average bulk transport, as they are used in a particular trade for long periods of time, on long-term contracts—called time charter parties (see Chapter 9, Section 9-5e)—and therefore nearly have a sailing schedule, not unlike liner ships. They carry cargo on only half of their voyage and return empty.

11-4 Flag

By international convention, each vessel engaged in international trade must be registered in a specific country, and therefore "flies" a specific country's flag. In many ways, the vessel is an extension of the territory of this country, and all its laws and regulations apply on board the ship. In exchange, the naval forces of the flag of registry will protect those flagged merchant ships in time of conflict. In addition, the vessel must pay the taxes that this country imposes. There is one significant caveat to this situation: With very few exceptions, a ship owner can *choose* the country in which its ship is registered, or choose the flag that it flies.

The flags of developed countries tend to impose very substantial regulations on the way a ship is operated, in such areas as the composition of the crew on board, its minimum training requirement, its nationality (because it is a country's extension of its territory, its immigration rules apply), the work rules on board (such as the number of hours worked per day and week before overtime pay is earned), the vacation time earned by the crew, and so on. In addition, taxation can be significantly higher. In contrast, regulations and taxes for some developing countries are minimal. It is estimated that flying an American flag rather than a developing country's flag can add at least 30 percent to the operating costs of a vessel. A 1997 Maritime Administration study showed that a break-bulk ship flying the U.S. flag required a crew of 34 and cost U.S. $13,300 per day, whereas the same ship flying a developing country's flag would require a crew of 24 and cost U.S. $1,400 per day.[22]

The National Defense Transportation Administration determined that the taxes that a U.S.-flagged ship would have to pay would be approximately U.S. $700,000

Figure 11-18
A Liquefied Natural Gas Carrier
Source: Photo © Oleksandr Kalinichenko. Used with permission.

per year. In contrast, the same vessel, operating under the flag of Panama would have to pay U.S. $10,497, and under the flag of the Isle of Man, only U.S. $680.[23]

To take advantage of their much lower fiscal costs, a small number of countries have created what is called an **open registry**, which means that any ship owner can choose to have its vessel fly this country's flag. There are no requirements regarding the citizenship of the owners of the ship. Because these countries tend to have minimal onboard requirements and taxes, many ship owners decide to fly such countries' flags, which have been derisively called **flags of convenience**. Most of these open registries emanate from developing countries, but, fairly recently, some developed countries established their own versions of open registries, which are called **secondary registries**, with much less stringent requirements than their "normal" registries in order to prevent their merchant fleets from being entirely registered under flags of convenience. Norway, Denmark, and France are three notorious examples. Table 11-1[24] shows the 25 largest open registry fleets in the world, and Table 11-2[25] shows the true nationality of the ships flying these open registries, as well as the percentages of the largest fleets in the world that are registered under a flag of convenience.

It should be noted that the choice of a flag regulates the qualifications of the crew, its compensation, and the amount of taxes that the ship owners pay. It does not

open registry A country that allows vessels owned by companies having no business relations in its territory to be registered in that country and carry its flag.

flag of convenience Designation of the open registry of a country that has lower taxes and more lenient on-board regulations than other countries with open registries. A derogatory term.

secondary registry A response by developed countries to the threat of open registries and flags of convenience: These developed countries created a secondary registry with lower on-board standards and taxes to entice ship owners to carry their flags and not defect to flag-of-convenience countries.

The End of the Shipping Line

Most ships, after a mere 20 to 25 years at sea, end up so damaged by the sea and the elements that they are no longer economically viable vessels (it costs too much to maintain them). In addition, as the size of ships increases, shipping lines have a surplus of capacity that they are loathe to sell, as they do not want to encourage new competitors.[19]

Where do all of these old ships end their lives?

Many of them end up on the beaches of Pakistan, Bangladesh, or India, where they are dismantled, by hand, into sellable chunks of scrap steel and other metals. At the present time, 90 percent of older ships end their lives in

these three countries, and half of them die in Alang, a beach in the Indian state of Gujarat, where 600 or so scrap businesses dismantle 400 ships every year.[20] These are dangerous and poorly paid jobs, but it is estimated that they provide direct and indirect employment for at least 200,000 workers.

Despite governmental protests about the impact of this business on India's image and its workers' health, more and more ships are dismantled in this area of the world and, as the world fleet ages and is replaced with more modern and technologically advanced ships, this trend shows no sign of abating.[21]

TABLE 11-1	Number of Ships and Tonnage in the Top National Fleets (2008)	

Country	Number of Ships	Tonnage (000s of dwt)
Panama	7,616	252,564
Liberia	2,173	117,519
Greece	1,477	61,384
Bahamas	1,422	59,744
Marshall Islands	1,097	59,600
Hong Kong	1,238	59,310
Singapore	2,243	55,500
Malta	1,442	45,218
China	3,816	37,124
Cyprus	982	29,431
South Korea	2,962	21,141
Norway	595	20,501
India	1,420	15,041
Germany	881	15,031
Japan	6,447	14,810
Isle of Man	339	13,850
United Kingdom	1,631	13,840
Italy	1,559	13,267
United States	6,419	12,139
Antigua and Barbuda	1,124	11,183
Denmark	438	10,904
Bermuda	153	9,870
Malaysia	1,150	9,448
Saint Vincent and the Grenadines	1,043	8,503
France	164	7,413

Source: *Review of Maritime Transport 2008.*

influence the seaworthiness of the vessel, which is evaluated by classification societies and determines the insurance premiums (hull insurance and P&I insurance) that the vessel owners have to pay (see Chapter 10, Section 10-7). A competent crew and a seaworthy vessel are guaranteed if the vessel is registered in a developed country, if it is operated by a reputable shipping company, or if it is classed with one of the major classification societies; however, problems are more likely to arise with vessels registered under a flag of convenience.

Countries attempt to influence, as much as possible, the flags of the ships that enter their ports. Although they cannot outright ban certain nationalities, they can prevent ships not registered in the country from carrying certain freight. For example, the Cargo Preference Act of the United States requires that at least 50 percent of U.S. government cargo be carried by U.S.-flagged ships. The Jones Act requires that cargo transported from one port in the United States to another port in the United States—a trade called **cabotage** (from the French verb *caboter*, which means "sail along the coast")—must be carried exclusively on U.S.-flagged ships. This is the case for cargo going from the West Coast to Hawaii, for example. Finally, all cargo in trades supported by the Ex-Im Bank must be shipped through U.S.-flagged ships. A study by the Maritime Administration of the United States found that over 50 maritime countries had some form of cabotage or flag protection laws of one form or another.[26]

cabotage An ocean trade consisting of shipping between ports located in the same country.

| TABLE 11-2 | True Nationality of Ships Registered in the Top Ten Open Registries (2008) |

| | Panama | Liberia | Bahamas | Marshall Islands | Malta | Cyprus | Isle of Man | Antigua and Barbuda | Bermuda | St. Vincent and the Grenadines | Percentage of National Fleet | |
											In Foreign Registries	In Own Registry
Greece	8.8	20.2	23.0	26.7	57.5	50.0	31.5	0.0	2.7	30.8	62.7	37.3
Japan	54.4	6.2	7.8	1.0	0.3	1.9	0.1	0.0	2.9	0.0	83.7	16.3
Germany	2.2	32.5	5.1	19.6	6.7	17.4	6.1	93.8	13.4	0.2	77.0	23.0
China	9.0	0.3	1.7	0.0	0.5	0.8	0.0	0.0	28.1	34.7	27.9	72.1
Norway	0.7	2.2	11.8	11.4	1.9	2.8	14.7	0.5	1.0	1.4	42.2	57.8
United States	1.3	3.8	8.6	20.3	0.4	0.2	2.2	0.3	5.8	2.3	58.4	41.6
Korea	7.3	0.4	0.0	0.9	1.6	0.1	0.0	0.0	0.0	0.0	48.2	41.8
Hong Kong	2.9	3.4	0.4	0.1	0.1	0.1	0.0	0.0	10.4	1.3	33.5	66.5
Singapore	1.6	4.0	0.7	1.7	0.0	0.5	0.0	0.0	0.0	2.0	32.4	67.6
Denmark	0.4	0.4	1.7	1.3	0.8	0.2	3.2	1.1	0.0	0.6	14.0	84.0
Taiwan	4.5	5.8	0.0	0.5	0.0	0.0	0.0	0.0	0.0	0.1	64.2	35.8
United Kingdom	0.8	0.7	3.7	1.6	0.8	3.2	40.8	1.3	9.8	2.5	49.4	50.6
Canada	1.2	0.6	14.4	0.6	0.0	0.2	0.0	0.0	0.0	0.0	61.2	38.8
Others	4.9	19.5	21.1	14.3	30.0	22.6	1.4	3.0	25.9	22.1		
	100%	100%	100%	100%	100%	100%	100%	100%	100%	100%		

Source: Review of Maritime Transport 2008.

The U.S. situation is yet more complicated. It compensates the ship owners who elect to flag their vessels with the stars-and-stripes to the tune of several million per year per vessel,[32] but not just because it is more expensive to run a U.S.-flagged ship. The reason is purely military. Because of its geographical situation, the United States would need a lot of ship transport capacity to ship troops and military materials abroad in the case of a conflict such as the 1990 Persian Gulf War, and the current program was developed in response to military sealift issues.[33] In that eventuality, the U.S. government can then requisition all merchant ships registered with the U.S. flag that are under the subsidy program. In order to ensure that it does have some ships to requisition, the U.S. government subsidizes ship owners who choose this alternative. In 1997, two large shipping companies re-flagged some of their ships with the U.S. flag—Maersk[34] and APL[35]—because of this incentive.

11-5 Liability Conventions

In 1924, the International Convention for the Unification of Certain Rules of Law Relating to Bills of Lading was adopted by 26 participating countries. This convention, known as the **Hague Rules**, limited the liability of a ship owner to the cargo owners to U.S. $500 per package "or customary freight unit," and it allowed ship owners to escape liability in 17 specified cases—called the 17 "defenses"— including the infamous **nautical fault**, or errors of the crew of a ship in its management or navigation. In 1936, the United States adopted the Hague Rules by incorporating them into the Carriage of Goods by Sea Act (COGSA).

The U.S. $500 limit per package became a problem with the advent of containers, when shipping lines began claiming that they were "freight units" and attempted to limit their liability to U.S. $500 per container. The Hague Rules were therefore revised in 1968 to clarify the definition of "package" to the units listed on the bill of

Hague Rules An international liability convention for ocean-going carriers that limits their liability to U.S. $500 per package. The liability convention followed by U.S. carriers until the *Rotterdam Rules* enter into force.

nautical fault An error in navigation made by the crew of a ship.

Flying the Flag

The choice of a flag has many consequences beyond the crew's training and the taxes that the ship owners have to pay:

- Cabotage rules require that American flags and crews be used for ships traveling from one port in the United States to another port in the United States. Cruise ships, not one of which flies the U.S. flag, therefore cannot travel between two U.S. ports. Cruise ships destined for Alaska leave from Vancouver, Canada, and cruise ships destined for Hawaii leave from Ensenada, Mexico.

- Most of the cruise ships fly flags of convenience, such as that of the Bahamas, or secondary registries, such as that of Norway. Because those registries do not exert much oversight over working conditions on their vessels, working cruise ship crews are generally employed for substandard wages and in miserable jobs. Very low wages are commonplace, and so are 12- to 15-hour days. Passengers are usually oblivious to the discrepancies between their lifestyle on board and that of the crew around them. U.S. court decisions have determined that because these cruise vessels are based in U.S. ports, select U.S. labor laws apply.[27] There may be a growing trend to extending port state control over labor issues aboard vessels.

- When Hong Kong became part of the People's Republic of China (PRC) in July 1997, a flag issue surfaced. Because it is common courtesy to fly a host port's flag on a ship, it meant that the ships of the Taiwanese shipping company Evergreen would have had to fly the PRC's flag when they called on the port of Hong Kong, and that Hong Kong ships would have had to fly the Taiwanese flag when they were in Taipei. Neither alternative was welcome; the issue was finally resolved when both sides decided not to fly any flag in each other's ports.[28]

- During the conflict between Iran and Iraq in the Persian Gulf, several Kuwaiti ships were temporarily placed under the U.S. flag so that they could gain the protection of the U.S. Navy, a protection refused to U.S. owners of tankers flying flags of convenience.[29] The U.S. Navy finally relented, and all crude carriers were temporarily re-flagged as American while they were in the Persian Gulf.[30]

- When more than a hundred merchant ships were attacked by pirates in the Gulf of Aden in 2008–2009, the U.S. Navy was empowered to intervene to protect only the *Maersk Alabama*, because it was the only ship that was flying the U.S. flag.[31] It was flying the U.S. flag because it was carrying a cargo of relief supplies for USAID, which mandates that its cargo be carried on U.S.-flagged ships.

Hague-Visby Rules An international liability convention for ocean-going carriers that limits their liability to SDR 667 per package or SDR 2 per kilogram, whichever is higher. This liability convention is the most commonly used in the world; however, the United States did not ratify this convention and therefore still abides by the Hague Rules.

Hamburg Rules An international liability convention for ocean-going carriers that limits their liability to SDR 835 per package or SDR 2.50 per kilogram, whichever is higher, and eliminates most of the "defenses" a carrier could use to discharge itself of liability. The Hamburg Rules have not been ratified by many countries.

lading. It also increased the liability of the carrier to U.S. $666.67 or U.S. $2 per kilogram, whichever was higher. These revised rules are known as **Hague-Visby Rules**. The United States has not ratified this treaty, although it has been ratified by all of its major trading partners. In 1979, the Hague-Visby Rules were amended to reflect the declining value of the U.S. dollar, and the liability limits were expressed in Special Drawing Rights (SDRs), the artificial currency of the International Monetary Fund, and set at SDR 666.67 per package or SDR 2 per kilogram, whichever was higher.

The advent of better navigational equipment and the annoyance of shippers at the continuous existence of the nautical fault defense triggered yet another round of international negotiations led by the United Nations Commission on International Trade Law (UNCITRAL), which abolished the 17 defenses of the Hague and Hague-Visby Rules and replaced them with only three: damage that the carrier took all reasonable steps to avoid, damage by fire, and damage due to an attempt by the carrier to save life or property at sea. It also increased liability limits to SDR 835 per package and SDR 2.5 per kilogram. These rules are known as the **Hamburg Rules** and have been ratified by only a small number of countries, only a handful of which are significant international traders. A complete list of which countries have adopted which rules is available on the Internet.[36]

Because the United States has not ratified either the Hague-Visby Rules or the Hamburg Rules, the COGSA is still in effect, even though it is grossly outdated with its limit of U.S. $500. Several efforts have been made to attempt to revise COGSA, but none of them have been successful to date. In 1999, with the creation of the Ocean Shipping Reform Act (OSRA), the United States brought one additional level of complexity to the conventions regulating the liability of shipping lines by allowing private, confidential contracts between shippers and shipping lines, where traditional liability constraints are replaced by negotiated ones. OSRA allowed private contracts between shippers and shipping lines, and it is likely that the liability limit of carriers was lifted in many of these agreements and that all but a handful of defenses have been eliminated. Therefore, the revision of COGSA may become moot in the near future.

There is still a problem with liability in intermodal freight; that is, freight that is shipped through several means of transportation using only one bill of lading and for which one of the legs is carriage by sea. The liability limits are different for domestic transport in the exporting country, international transport by ocean (and depend further on the nationality of the carrier, which governs which liability convention will apply), and domestic transport in the importing country. When cargo is damaged in transit without the possibility of tracing where specifically in the voyage the peril occurred, which liability limit is applicable? This is a question that the United Nations Conference on Trade and Development (UNCTAD) answered in 1980, in a treaty that was proposed but never ratified. These rules, though, form the basis for the guidelines developed by the International Chamber of Commerce.

In June 2000, the United Nations Commission on International Trade Law (UNCITRAL) started the process of creating a formal multimodal liability framework. UNCITRAL finished its work in July 2008, and the General Assembly of the United Nations voted to accept the **Rotterdam Rules** in February 2009. In September 2009, the United States and 15 other countries ratified the convention, heeding the recommendations of the International Chamber of Commerce, which had strongly advocated its ratification.[37] Each of the countries still has to complete its own legislation to implement the rules, and the Rotterdam Rules will not enter into force until one year after the twentieth country ratifies the treaty;[38] nevertheless, there is optimism that a single liability convention may finally govern international shipments of goods, regardless of the method of transportation. The Rotterdam Rules have their critics, though, who are concerned that they are too complex, allow too many exceptions, and are just trying to cover too much under one agreement.[39]

The main aspects of the Rotterdam Rules are that it is a convention with higher liability limits for the carrier: SDR 875 per package and SDR 4 per kilogram for items that are not considered packages, such as automobiles and machinery. The convention eliminates several of the 17 defenses of the Hague Rules, including the "errors in navigation" defense, which has become unsupportable in an era of inexpensive Global Positioning System devices. Finally, the convention applies "door-to-door," which subjects the legs of the voyage that are in the exporting and importing countries to the same liability limits. In order to mirror the private agreements of the U.S. Ocean Shipping Reform Act, it allows private contracts between shippers and carriers—contracts that could raise or lower the liability limits. While large shippers are likely to be able to negotiate higher liability limits, small shippers are concerned that they will be subjected to lower liability limits by "boilerplate" bills of lading offered by the carriers.[40]

Not only are these issues of interest to insurance companies, but they also are of interest to any shipper that decides to retain its shipping risks and decline insurance coverage. As the liability of the carrier is very difficult to engage, even in the case of navigational errors or negligence, it may make more sense to purchase insurance coverage (see Chapter 10, Section 10-6) and let the insurance company interact with the carrier in determining the carrier's responsibility under these international conventions.

Rotterdam Rules A liability convention for intermodal shipments, implemented by the United Nations, but which only fifteen countries (including the United States) had ratified as of September 2009.

11-6 Non-Vessel-Operating Common Carriers

Non-Vessel-Operating Common Carriers (NVOCCs) make up another type of shipping company, but with the caveat that they do not own and operate ships. Nevertheless, NVOCCs are regulated by the Federal Maritime Commission (FMC). The way an NVOCC operates is by purchasing space on a ship on a given voyage and by selling this space to companies that need to ship cargo. The shipping line gets paid for the space—and weight—whether or not the NVOCC fills its allocation. The NVOCC makes money only by reselling the space at a higher rate than the one at which it purchased it. In most instances, an NVOCC also acts as a freight consolidator and aggregates less-than-container-load (LCL) freight from several customers into a full container. This allows small shippers to benefit from the protection of a container and allows them to ship without the extra packing protection that break-bulk demands.

The NVOCC system was the basis for the model followed by consolidators in the air passenger business. These consolidators purchase blocks of seats on airplanes and resell them to individuals, generally through discount travel agencies.

11-7 Security Requirements

After the terrorist attacks in New York on September 11, 2001, a number of measures were taken worldwide to limit the probability of terrorist attacks carried out by sea. The countries that felt that they could be targets reasoned that an "easy" way for a terrorist organization to smuggle a dangerous weapon was to bring it in using the traditional import channels, mixed with traditional ocean cargo. Several initiatives to limit the probability of a terrorist attack through ocean imports were started within a few years, most by the United States, but several others by other countries and the International Maritime Organization. More information on these different approaches can be found in Chapter 15, but there are two main measures that affect ocean cargo.

11-7a Cargo Inspections

Most countries have a program under which their Customs Service inspects cargo when it arrives in the port of importation. For example, a percentage of all shipments entering the United States are inspected upon arrival; this percentage varies from 1 to 5 percent, depending on the port. Such inspections have traditionally been conducted to prevent fraud (the import of products that were not correctly identified or valued on the import documentation), but they are now much more focused on terrorism prevention.

For the past decade, inspections have also happened in the port of exportation, either through non-invasive measures, such as a X-rays, or through physical investigation of the contents of a shipment. For example, the United States has implemented a **Container Security Initiative**, through which Customs and Border Protection (CBP) inspectors are temporarily assigned to foreign ports where they inspect containers bound for the United States. Such containers are either pulled at random or are flagged as suspicious because of their specific characteristics. A World Customs Organization initiative encourages ports abroad to purchase container-scanning equipment and agree to inspect cargo when such inspection is requested by the country of importation. In exchange, cargo shipped from these ports get preferential treatment when they enter the country that requested the inspection.

Container Security Initiative A program instituted by the U.S. Customs and Border Protection agency, through which Customs agents are sent to the port of departure to inspect containers bound for the United States.

Freight Charges

Shipping lines will charge for container shipping either by following published tariff rates or by negotiating contract rates with large volume shippers. All tariff rates can be negotiated, and shipping lines will negotiate rates for as few as 12 containers shipped at once. Rates are determined per package or by weight, including cargo shipped in containers on a less-than-container-load (LCL) basis. In addition to the freight rate, there are additional charges of which the international logistics professional must be aware:[41]

ARB—Arbitrary charge. This charge is for added expenses, such as transshipment in an intermediary port, ice-breaking, cleaning of returned containers that are not ready for the next cargo, electrical power to refrigerated containers, and monitoring of refrigerated containers.

BAF or FAF—Bunker adjustment factor, also known as fuel adjustment factor or surcharge. This is an extra charge applied by shipping to reflect fluctuations in the cost of bunker fuel. This surcharge is expressed either as an amount per freight ton or as a percentage of the freight charge.

CAF—Currency adjustment factor. This is a surcharge applied to freight rates by shipping lines. It is to ensure that the revenue of the shipping lines is unaffected by movements in the currencies in which transactions are carried out by the lines in relation to the freight rate currency. It is normally expressed as a percentage of the freight and may be negative as well as positive.

CY/CY—Container yard to container yard movement of cargo. This is a charge added to the freight rate to reflect the cost of moving cargo from one yard in the port to another yard, a function that is fulfilled by a cartage company.

CFS/CY—Container freight stations to container yard movement of cargo. This is a charge added to the freight rate to reflect the cost of moving cargo

from outside of the port to a yard inside the port, a function that is fulfilled by a cartage company.

Chassis charge. This is a charge imposed by container shipping lines for providing customers with a truck chassis at the harbor terminals. A chassis is a truck trailer on which the container will be placed before it is loaded onto the ship or after it is unloaded from the ship.

THC—Terminal handling charge, also known as container yard charge. This is a charge payable to a shipping line either for receiving a full container load at the container terminal, storing it, and delivering it to the ship at the load port or for receiving it from the ship at the discharge port, storing it, and delivering it to the consignee.

Determining the correct charge for a container can be challenging and can amount to much more than the published or negotiated freight rate. Here is an example of the calculation of the cost of a full container shipment from Oakland, California, to Singapore. The container is filled with paper products.

Base Container rate	U.S. $2,000
Additional charges:	
CAF—Currency adjustment factor	5%
BAF—Bunker adjustment factor	15%
THC—Terminal handling charge	U.S. $125
ARB—Arbitrary charge: cleaning fee	U.S. $40
Total container freight cost: container rate	$2,000
[container rate×(CAF+BAF)]+THC+ARB= [$2,000×(0.05+0.15)]+$125+$40	$565
	$2,565

Note: Container-based rates may at times be calculated by weight or by package, especially if the shipment is less-than-container load (LCL).

11-7b Advance Shipping Notifications

Many countries have implemented a process by which shippers have to notify the importing country's Customs authorities of the particulars of a shipment before cargo is loaded onto the carrier's ship. Such notification has to be made at least 24 hours in advance, and must include information on the shipper, the type of cargo, the consignee, and the carrier.

The first program that required such advanced notification was the **24-hour rule** implemented by the United States and administered by the CBP of the Department of Homeland Security. That rule required that all importers (and carriers) provide a copy of the manifest of an ocean shipment bound for the United States, including

24-hour rule A rule first instituted by the U.S. Customs and Border Protection agency, which requires that carriers send Customs the manifest of all cargo destined for the United States 24 hours prior to the cargo being loaded in the port of departure.

Importer Security Filing A set of required pieces of information that the shipper is required to provide to the U.S. Customs and Border Protection agency at least 24 hours prior to loading a shipment in the port of origin. Also known as the *10+2 rule*.

10+2 rule Another term for the documents required by the *Importer Security Filing*.

shipments that were just transiting through a U.S. port and were bound for another country, 24 hours before that shipment was loaded onto the vessel bound for the United States.

The U.S. program has been superseded since January 26, 2010, by a program called the **Importer Security Filing**, which follows the guidelines of the World Customs Organization's SAFE initiative of June 2007 (see Chapter 15, Section 15-2), which mandates that importing countries make uniform the type of information that can be required of shippers. The requirements of the Importer Security Filing expand the number of points of information that the shipper must provide, and it has become better known in the United States as the **10+2 rule**, which somewhat mirrors the number of items required.

The purpose of these advanced notification rules is that the importing country's Customs authorities are able to inspect the paperwork, and eventually warn the carrier that something may be inappropriate with the shipment. When a shipment is identified as problematic, it is not loaded, and is inspected in the port of departure before it is loaded onto the next available ship. In some cases, the inspection is conducted by Customs inspectors from the importing country assigned to the foreign port.

Review and Discussion Questions

1. What two different types of ocean cargo services are there?
2. Describe three different types of ships used in international ocean transportation. What type of cargoes are they used for?
3. Explain the concept of a "flag." Why does a ship need a flag? Why would an owner choose to fly a "flag of convenience"?
4. What is the Baltic Exchange? What is the purpose of publishing the Baltic Exchange indices?
5. What are the differences between the Hague Rules, the Hague-Visby Rules, the Hamburg Rules, and the Rotterdam Rules?
6. What are the major initiatives of the world governments in terms of cargo security?

Endnotes

1. Shipping Key Facts, Maritime International Secretariat Services, http://www.marisec.org/shippingfacts/worldtrade/volume-world-trade-sea.php, accessed June 22, 2009.
2. *The Panama Canal*, November 1996, a publication of the Panama Canal Commission Office of Public Affairs, APO Miami 34011-5000.
3. "Knock Nevis," http://www.ships-info.info/mer-Knock-nevis.htm, accessed June 24, 2009.
4. "Emma Maersk," http://www.ships-info.info/mer-emma-maersk.htm, accessed June 24, 2009.
5. *Review of Maritime Transport 2008*, United Nations Conference on Trade and Development, UNCTAD/RMT/2008, New York, USA and Geneva Switzerland, 2009, http://www.unctad.org/en/docs/rmt2008_en.pdf, accessed June 24, 2009.
6. Lloyd's Register, *Fairplay*, multiple dates, compiled by UNCTAD.
7. *Review of Maritime Transport 2008*, United Nations Conference on Trade and Development, UNCTAD/RMT/2008, New York, USA and Geneva Switzerland, 2009, http://www.unctad.org/en/docs/rmt2008_en.pdf, accessed June 24, 2009.
8. FastShip, Inc., "About FastShip," http://www.fastshipatlantic.com/aboutfastship.html, accessed June 24, 2009.
9. Gordon, John, and David Orletsky, *Chap. 9, Moving Rapidly to the Fight*, U.S. Army and the New National Security Strategy, RAND Corporation, 2003.
10. Plume, Janet, "LASH Vessels Still Providing Snappy Service," *Journal of Commerce*, September 22, 1997, p. 7C.
11. Sullivan, Allanna, "A 700-ft Tanker Just Does Not Handle Quite Like a Honda," *Wall Street Journal*, April 14, 1989, p. 1.
12. Wells, Ken, "Captain's Course: Life on a Supertanker Mixes Tedium, Stress for Kenneth Campbell," *Wall Street Journal*, September 11, 1986, p. 1.
13. McPhee, John, "The Ships of Port Revel," *The Atlantic Monthly*, October 1998, pp. 67–80.
14. The Baltic Exchange, "The Baltic Code," http://www.balticexchange.com/default.asp?action=article&ID=4, accessed June 27, 2009.

15. The Baltic Exchange, *A History of Baltic Indices*, accessed June 1, 2009, http://www.balticexchange.com/media/pdf/a%20history%20of%20baltic%20indices%20160909.pdf.

16. Sykes, Janet, "Third Annual Invest in International Shipping," *Capital Link Forum*, March 26, 2009, http://www.capitallinkforum.com/shipping/2009/profiles/baltic.htm.

17. Wright, Robert, "Collapse in Dry Bulk Shipping Rates Unprecedented in Its Severity," *Financial Times*, December 01, 2008.

18. Dry Ships, Inc., "Baltic Dry Index," http://www.dryships.com/pages/report.asp, accessed June 27, 2009.

19. Knee, Richard, "Many Owners of Aging Vessels Would Rather Scrap than Sell," *Journal of Commerce*, May 7, 1998, p. 13A.

20. Langewiesche, William, "The Shipbreakers," *The Atlantic Monthly*, August 2000, pp. 31–49.

21. "India Bars Dismantling of U.S. Ships that Held Hazardous Materials," *Journal of Commerce*, Reuters News Release, August 7, 1997, p. 2B.

22. Lesher, Dave, "Sailing Through the School of Experience," *Los Angeles Times*, July 30, 1997.

23. Gillis, Chris, "Changing U.S.-Flag Vessel Economics," *American Shipper*, October 2004, pp. 72–76.

24. *Review of Maritime Transport 2008*, United Nations Conference on Trade and Development, UNCTAD/RMT/2008, New York, USA and Geneva Switzerland, 2009, http://www.unctad.org/en/docs/rmt2008_en.pdf, accessed June 24, 2009.

25. *Ibid*.

26. MARAD publication, *By the Capes Around the World: A Summary of World Cabotage Practices*, U.S. Maritime Administration, 1995.

27. *Dahingo v. Royal Caribbean Cruises, Ltd.*, 99 CIV 12774, 312 F. Supp. 2d 440 442 S.D.N.Y. 2004, United States District Court Southern District of New York.

28. Bangsberg, P. T., "Shipowners Tackle Asia Flag Question," *Journal of Commerce*, May 29, 1997, p. 8B.

29. Carrington, Tim, "U.S. Owners of Foreign-Registry Ships Want Navy to Rally Round the Flag their Vessels Don't Fly," *Wall Street Journal*, December 29, 1987, p. 44.

30. O'Rourke, Ronald, "Gulf Ops," *Proceedings, U.S. Naval Institute*, May 1989, pp. 42–43.

31. McFadden, Robert, and Scott Shane, "In Rescue of Captain, Navy Kills Three Pirates," *New York Times*, April 13, 2009, http://www.nytimes.com/2009/04/13/world/africa/13pirates.html.

32. Bloom, Murray, "Notice of Open Season for Enrollment in the Voluntary Intermodal Sealift Agrement (VISA) Program," *Federal Register*, October 15, 2009, http://www.gpo.gov/fdsys/pkg/FR-2009-10-15/html/E9-24788.htm.

33. David G. Harris, and Richard D. Stewart, "U.S. Surge Sealift Capabilities: A Question of Sufficiency," *Parameters U.S. Army War College Quarterly*, Spring 1998.

34. Baldwin, Tom, "Maersk Reflags Four More Ships," *Journal of Commerce*, February 11, 1997, p. 1A.

35. Mongelluzzo, Bill, "Boxships Buck Currents," *Journal of Commerce*, December 15, 1997, p. 1B.

36. "International Conventions Membership List," *InforMARE*, www.informare.it/dbase/convuk.htm, accessed June 27, 2009.

37. Edmonson, R. G., "ICC Endorses Rotterdam Rules," *Journal of Commerce*, June 2, 2009, http://www.joc.com/node/411658.

38. O'Reilly, Joseph, "Rotterdam Rules Inch Forward," *Inbound Logistics*, October 2009, pp. 17–18.

39. Tetley, William, "Summary of Some General Criticisms of the UNCITRAL Convention (The Rotterdam Rules)," McGill University School of Law Internal Document, http://www.mcgill.ca/files/maritimelaw/Tetley_Criticism_of_Rotterdam_Rules.pdf, November 5, 2008, accessed June 27, 2009.

40. Hailey, Roger, "Freight Forwarders Step Up Attacks on Rotterdam Rules," *Lloyd's List*, June 2, 2009, http://www.lloydslist.com/ll/news/freight-forwarders-step-up-attack-on-rotterdam-rules/1243872041051.htm.

41. Brodie, P., *Dictionary of Shipping Terms*. London: Lloyd's of London Press, Ltd. 1994.

International Air Transportation*

Chapter Twelve

Key Terms

ACMI (p. 296)

airfreighter (p. 299)

charter airfreight (p. 295)

combi aircraft (p. 298)

dry lease (p. 296)

express cargo (p. 294)

freight tonne kilometer (FTK) (p. 291)

integrator (p. 295)

International Air Transport Association (IATA) (p. 305)

International Civil Aviation Organization (ICAO) (p. 306)

onboard courier (OBC) (p. 298)

open-skies agreement (p. 306)

quick-change aircraft (p. 299)

revenue tonne kilometer (RTK) (p. 291)

roller deck (p. 301)

sustainability (p. 306)

time-definite shipment (p. 291)

volume-weight (dimensional weight) (p. 305)

wet lease (p. 296)

Chapter Outline

* The authors would like to thank Robert Materna, Ph.D, Embry-Riddle Aeronautical University Worldwide, for his assistance in preparing this chapter. Dr. Materna is a certified professional logistician and a certified airline transport pilot.

The scale and scope of international air cargo transportation has grown steadily over the past three decades, driven by globalization and the increasing expectations of business and consumers worldwide. Today, even though airfreight may represent only 1 percent of world trade by weight, it accounts for approximately 40 percent of world trade by value. The demand for airfreight is also highly correlated with world GDP, and more than 70 percent of the world's airfreight is carried by non-U.S. airlines.[1] The slow but steady growth in this premium mode of transportation has been driven, in part, by the advent of **time-definite shipments**, a concept that was implemented with military-like precision by Federal Express in the United States market in the 1970s, and which has been adopted by just about all cargo airlines in the international arena. Figure 12-1 illustrates the growth in airfreight in **revenue tonne kilometers (RTKs)** from 1997 through 2007.[2]

Prior to 2007, many experts felt that the airfreight industry had no alternative but to grow further.[3] However, high fuel prices and financial turmoil took a toll on air cargo traffic in 2008, resulting in a drop in airfreight that had not been seen since the terrorists' attacks on the United States in September 2001.[4] At the end of 2008, both Boeing and Airbus were still optimistic on the long-term prospects for airfreight,[5] but by mid-2009, both manufacturers and most carriers were less certain about the demand for airfreight over the next two to three years.[6]

12-1 Cargo Airlines, Airports, and Markets

FedEx (previously called Federal Express) is the largest airfreight company in the world, serving more than 375 airports worldwide.[7] As can be seen in Table 12-1, FedEx also won the top spot for international cargo volume in 2007 with 15.7 billion **freight tonne kilometers (FTKs)**, followed by UPS (United Parcel Service) and Korean Air (see Table 12-1).[8] The top ten cargo carriers in the world account for almost half of the world's freight transportation revenues.

The top ten cargo airports in the world for 2007 are listed in Table 12-2.[9] Each of the largest cargo airports is dominated by one or several large cargo airlines, either because it is headquartered in that city or it uses that airport as a major base for its operations. In the United States, Memphis is FedEx's main hub and headquarters;

time-definite shipment Cargo or package shipments that must be delivered by a guaranteed, predetermined time and day.

revenue tonne kilometer (RTK) Unit used to express the volume of cargo transported by an airline; it is the number of metric tonnes of freight, mail, passengers, and baggage carried multiplied by the distance they have been carried, in kilometers. This measure is often used interchangeably with the *freight tonne kilometer (FTK)*.

freight tonne kilometer (FTK) Unit used to express the volume of cargo transported by an airline; it is the number of metric tonnes of freight, mail, passenger, and baggage carried multiplied by the distance they have been carried, in kilometers. This measure is often used interchangeably with the *revenue tonne kilometer (RTK)*.

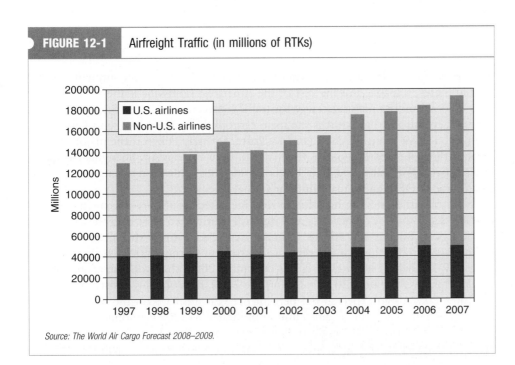

FIGURE 12-1   Airfreight Traffic (in millions of RTKs)

Source: The World Air Cargo Forecast 2008–2009.

TABLE 12-1	Top Ten Cargo Airlines, 2007 (in millions of FTKs)	
Rank	**Airline**	**Millions of FTKs**
1	FedEx	15,710
2	UPS	10,961
3	Korean Air	9,568
4	Lufthansa	8,348
5	Cathay Pacific	8,225
6	Singapore Airlines	7,945
7	China Airlines	6,301
8	Air France	6,126
9	Emirates	5,497
10	Cargolux	5,482

Source: Air Cargo World.

TABLE 12-2	Top Ten Cargo Airports, 2007 (in metric tonnes)	
Rank	**Airport**	**Total Tonnes**
1	Memphis	3,840,491
2	Hong Kong	3,773,964
3	Anchorage	2,825,511
4	Shanghai	2,559,310
5	Incheon/Seoul	2,555,580
6	Paris	2,297,896
7	Tokyo	2,254,421
8	Frankfurt	2,127,646
9	Louisville	2,078,947
10	Miami	1,922,985

Source: Airports Council International.

Anchorage is a major trans-Pacific transit point between the Asian continent and the United States, Canada, and the rest of the Americas; Louisville is the main hub for UPS; and Miami is a major gateway for traffic between the United States and Latin America. In Europe, Frankfurt is the main cargo hub for Lufthansa, and Paris is the main hub for Air France, FedEx, and La Poste. In Asia, Tokyo is the major hub for Japan Airlines; Incheon (Seoul) is the major hub for Korean Air; Shanghai is a major hub for Great Wall Airlines, China Eastern, and UPS; while Hong Kong is the major Asian hub for DHL and a main hub for Cathay Pacific.

As stated earlier, despite high fuel prices, increased security requirements, and an unstable economy, the demand for air cargo will continue to grow over the long term. In fact, both Boeing and Airbus estimate strong growth in the international air cargo market in the range of 5.8 percent to 6 percent through 2027. As illustrated in Figure 12-2, Boeing estimates, as late as December 2008, that world air cargo volume would triple over the next 20 years.[10] In June 2009, the company revised its forecast for 2009–2027 to an expected 5.4 percent per year, rather than the 5.8 percent of Figure 12-2, reflecting the negative impact of the 2008–2009 economic downturn.[11]

According to Airbus, airfreight traffic over the next 20 years will be dominated by flows between the People's Republic of China and North America, and the People's

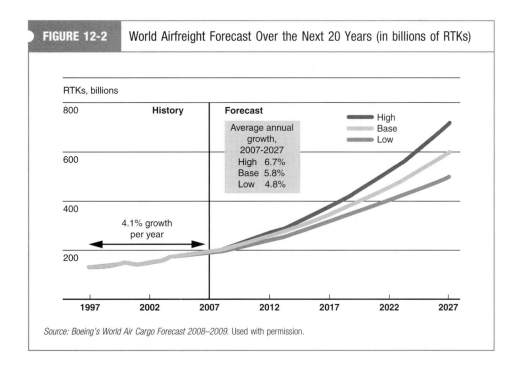

FIGURE 12-2   World Airfreight Forecast Over the Next 20 Years (in billions of RTKs)

Source: Boeing's World Air Cargo Forecast 2008–2009. Used with permission.

Republic of China and Europe. Airfreight traffic between Europe and North America is expected to grow as well, but at a more moderate pace. The primary markets for airfreight for 2009 through 2028 are illustrated in Figure 12-3.[12]

12-2 Types of Service

The types of service offered by the airfreight industry are defined by the nature of the demand and type of commodity. Airfreight is particularly well suited for commodities that have a high value-to-weight ratio, or are perishable, quickly obsolete, required on short notice, or expensive to handle or store. Shipping by air is also attractive when

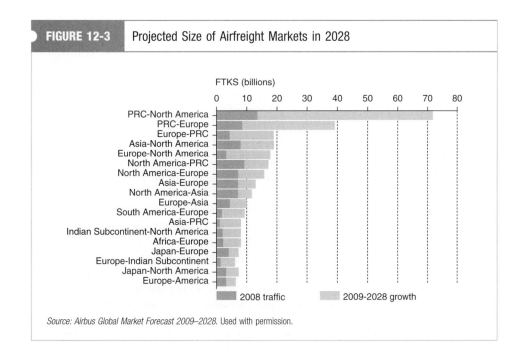

FIGURE 12-3   Projected Size of Airfreight Markets in 2028

Source: Airbus Global Market Forecast 2009–2028. Used with permission.

demand is unpredictable, infrequent, exceeds local supply, or is seasonal. Shippers also choose air when the risk of pilferage, breakage, or deterioration is great, when the cost of insurance is high for long periods of transit, when heavy packaging is required for surface transportation, or when there is need for special handling. In some circumstances, shipping by air can be used to avoid warehousing costs that would otherwise be required if other, slower modes of transportation were used, such as ocean transportation.[13] Difficult terrain or the lack of rail, port, or road infrastructure are also valid reasons for shipping by air. Finally, the risk of losing a customer or halting production due to the lack of an urgently-needed repair part can also justify the expense of moving goods by air.[14]

Although the types of products shipped vary by region, in general, air transportation lends itself to the movement of industrial equipment, computers and office machines, consumer products, work-in-process goods, apparel, perishables, small packages, documents, and other manufactured goods. To meet the demand for these products, various types of service have evolved, including air mail services, express airfreight services, scheduled airfreight services, charter airfreight services, leasing, and airfreight forwarder services.

12-2a Air Mail Services

Air mail was the first type of cargo service offered and "an important factor in the formation of air transportation in the United States."[15] Today, air mail services are still important but represent a little under 3 percent of airline revenue and about 4 percent of air cargo carried, measured by RTKs.

12-2b Express Airfreight Services

express cargo Cargo shipped with a guaranteed pre-determined delivery date and time.

Although DHL, FedEx, and UPS were not the first carriers to offer express air cargo services, these carriers and their services have continued to grow ever since FedEx deployed 14 small aircraft to deliver its first 186 packages on the night of April 17, 1973.[16] Within the United States, FedEx and UPS now dominate the air **express cargo** market and are still competing for DHL's share following its withdrawal from the U.S. market in late 2008. As the volume of domestic express services has grown, international express air cargo services have also continued to grow and now represent over 13 percent of international air cargo traffic, even as the distinction between express air cargo and regularly-scheduled air cargo services continues to blur.[17]

Today, FedEx employs over 148,000 people and maintains the world's largest all-cargo airline, operating over 650 aircraft in more than 220 countries. Through its

Web-Enabled Tools Enhance Self-Service Shipping

For those who ship packages internationally, two of the newest and most impressive services offered by FedEx and UPS are their Web-enabled self-service international shipping capabilities. FedEx now offers *Global Trade Manager*, which provides customers with instant access to the information, tools, and documents they need to readily complete an international shipment.

Global Trade Manager also allows customers to access profiles on the countries to which items are being shipped, estimate duties and taxes that must be paid, review important advisories that may be relevant to their shipments, and

identify individuals, companies, and other parties that have been placed on official denied-party screening lists. This tool also includes an International Resource Center, which provides customers with shipping checklists and links to other external resources that may be important to the shipper.

UPS offers a similar capability called UPS *TradeAbility*. TradeAbility allows customers to access international forms, check export licenses and import requirements, find Harmonized System codes, screen for denied parties, and estimate landed costs through a single Web interface and user-friendly tools.

Super Hub in Memphis, Tennessee, FedEx Express operates more than 5,000 flights a month and serves 95 percent of the global economy on a 24- to 48-hour basis.[18] In addition to multiple hubs in the United States, FedEx operates major hubs in Paris (France), Subic Bay (The Philippines), Toronto (Canada), Guangzhou (China), and Cologne/Bonn (Germany).

While FedEx entered the market with a new and distinct business model, UPS evolved over time from a messenger service and common carrier into a leader in global supply chain management. Today, UPS owns 268 aircraft (and leases another 307) to provide express airfreight service to over 200 countries. In addition to its major hub at Worldport in Louisville, Kentucky, UPS operates major hubs in Cologne/Bonn (Germany), Taipei (Taiwan), Pampanga (The Philippines), Ontario (California), Hong Kong, Singapore, and Shanghai (China)—and is developing an intra-Asia hub in Shenzhen (China). Worldport has been expanded several times and now occupies a 4 million square feet distribution center (approximately 40 hectares) with the capacity to sort over 300,000 packages per hour.[19]

Outside the United States, Belgium-based DHL, a subsidiary of Deutsche Post, is the leader in many European and Asian markets, claiming 24 percent of the European market for courier, express, and parcel services, 34 percent of the Asian express market, and 40 percent of the eastern European, Middle Eastern, and African express market in 2006.[20] As of 2008, DHL operated a fleet of 350 aircraft serving over 220 countries. Another Belgium-based airline is TNT Airways, the fourth largest consolidator in the world, and a very strong presence in Europe and China.

One of the major factors leading to the continued growth and long-term success of the express air cargo industry has been the shift in focus from carrying cargo to providing a bundle of services to meet the needs of customers who are willing to pay for the convenience of one-stop shopping. Over time, FedEx, UPS, DHL, TNT, and others have continued to expand their services to the point of offering supply chain solutions versus package delivery. As a result, these firms are often referred to as **integrators**, where the scope of integrated services has been continuously expanding.

integrator An air cargo carrier that offers its customers complete door-to-door services. Such services usually include pickup, transportation, delivery, processing, and numerous related tasks.

12-2c Scheduled Airfreight Services

As the name implies, this category of service refers to flights that are offered on a published schedule. Scheduled airfreight services have many advantages. Since these services are offered on a routine basis, they tend to be highly reliable and efficient, resulting in relatively low cost airfreight delivery. Scheduled airfreight services also make up the bulk of international air cargo traffic. However, it is interesting to note that, even though the overall volume of international air cargo has increased over the years, the percent of world air cargo carried by U.S. carriers has declined as the U.S. domestic market has matured.[21]

Today, passenger airlines, integrators, and airfreight companies offer scheduled airfreight services. Although passenger airliners hold cargo in the belly of the aircraft, such cargo is often considered secondary to their focus on serving passengers. As a result, many of the all-cargo airliners and integrators, such as Cargolux and FedEx respectively, operate airfreighters on both a scheduled and non-scheduled basis. Some of the leading international scheduled airfreight service providers include Korean Air, Lufthansa, Cathay Pacific, Singapore Airlines, FedEx, China Airlines, Air France, Emirates, Cargolux, JAL, UPS, British Airways, KLM, United Airlines, Quanta, El Al, and DHL.

12-2d Charter Airfreight Services

Charter airfreight services are those that are based on demand and do not operate on a published schedule. Although this alternative can be more expensive than scheduled service, charter airfreight services offer shippers more flexibility. Charter services can

charter airfreight A type of freight that is shipped on a dedicated aircraft, either because it cannot be shipped on an airliner because of its weight or size, or because of its destination.

be tailored to meet the individual shipper's needs for specialized cargo, emergencies, or delivery to destinations that are not normally served by scheduled airlines or freight carriers. For example, charter aircraft can be used to meet the demands of seasonal traffic, such as the shipment of cherries from the Northwest of the United States to Japan in July, or roses from Colombia to the United States in February. A large increase in demand for a new product, such as the shipment of a spectacular new *Beaujolais Nouveau* from France to the United States and Japan in November, can also cause a carrier to supplement its capacity through the use of charter airfreight services. Some of the world's largest air charter cargo providers include Air Charter Services, Lufthansa Cargo Charter, and Polar Air Cargo.

In addition to meeting emergency needs or the demand for products that exceed plans, there are also times when shippers need to ship products that do not fit in the cargo bay of a traditional cargo aircraft. Often referred to as "project cargo" (see Chapter 13, Section 13-5), such items exceed the volume or weight restrictions of traditional aircraft and require special handling and carriage by aircraft designed to meet these special needs. Airbus's A-300 *Beluga* (see Figure 12-14), Boeing's 747 *Dreamlifter* (see Figure 12-15), and the Antonov 124 *Ruslan* (see Figure 12-12) and its even larger cousin, the Antonov 225 *Mriya* (see Figure 12-13) certainly fit that category. It is also interesting to note that, in at least three of these cases, these aircraft were originally developed to meet the outsize cargo needs of the aviation and aerospace industry itself. For example, the *Beluga* was originally designed to meet the complex logistics challenges of shipping parts across Europe to support the production and assembly of the Airbus series of aircrafts from Hamburg, Germany, to Toulouse, France. Similarly, the *Dreamlifter* was designed to meet the just-in-time assembly needs of Boeing's worldwide network of suppliers for the 787 *Dreamliner*. Finally, the *Mriya* was originally designed to transport the Russian space shuttle.

12-2e Leased Cargo Aircraft Services

As in other industries which involve large capital expenditures, leasing is also an option for the major carriers and other providers of airfreight services. There are a variety of leasing options available, but most leases take the form of a "dry" lease, "damp" lease, "wet" lease, or "aircraft, crew, maintenance, and insurance" lease.

In the past, a **wet lease** referred to a short-term lease which usually included the aircraft, crew, maintenance, insurance, and fuel. Today, the most common cargo aircraft leases include only the aircraft, crew, maintenance, and insurance (ACMI) and are therefore called **ACMI** leases. Damp leasing is similar to ACMI, but without the aircrew. Finally, a **dry lease** is a form of leasing where the lessor provides an aircraft without any crew, maintenance, insurance, services, or fuel.

According to Boeing's World Air Cargo Forecast for 2008–2009, about 6 percent of the world's air cargo is now transported by ACMI providers.[22] Although the demand for ACMI services does tend to vary with the economy, the market for large, long-haul international airfreight aircraft has increased over the years, since the new wide-body freighters are more efficient than most conversions—a passenger aircraft converted into a freighter aircraft—and older airfreight aircraft.

Both UPS and FedEx lease aircraft to supplement their core capacity, especially during the November–December holidays. FedEx, for example, leases almost 100 large jets to supplement its own fleet and approximately 50 smaller piston-driven and turbo-prop aircraft to deliver packages to and from airports served by its larger aircraft.[23]

12-2f Airfreight Forwarder Services

Like other modes of transportation, airfreight forwarders provide the link between shippers of airfreight and consignees at the destination. Freight forwarders contract

---

wet lease An agreement under which the owner (lessor) of an aircraft provides the airplane, insurance, maintenance services, fuel, and a flight crew to the lessee, who has to cover all of the other variable costs, such as airport fees.

ACMI *A*ircraft, *C*rew, *M*aintenance, and *I*nsurance. A type of aircraft lease, where the owner is responsible for providing the aircraft, the crew, maintenance, and insurance, but not the fuel.

dry lease An agreement between the owner (lessor) of an aircraft and a lessee in which the owner provides only the aircraft, without other services.

with air carriers, consolidate shipments, buy space on flights, and arrange intermodal surface transportation needs. Some freight forwarders provide a full range of supply chain management services, while others specialize in performing specific tasks. Today, many of the integrators, such as DHL, UPS, and FedEx, offer international freight forwarding services and compete directly with traditional freight forwarders such as Schenker, Kuehne + Nagel, Panalpina, and numerous others.

12-3 Types of Aircraft

Although many types of aircraft are used to meet the growing demand for fast and efficient air transportation, in general these aircraft can be broken down into four categories: passenger aircraft, combination or "combi" aircraft, quick-change aircraft, and large cargo aircraft that are designed to serve as airfreighters.

12-3a Passenger Aircraft

Just about every passenger aircraft transports cargo in addition to the passengers carried on its main deck. The "belly" of the aircraft is designed to accommodate the passengers' luggage and additional airfreight. Some of this airfreight cargo is loose freight (i.e., not palletized or containerized) and is shipped piece by piece; the packages are not secured to the aircraft and are shipped in a manner that is similar to passenger luggage. In larger, wide-body aircraft (see Figure 12-4), the freight is containerized (see Figure 12-5) and secured to the aircraft. International cargo services on passenger aircraft are somewhat unreliable, as airlines sometimes "bump" freight, creating more capacity to carry additional passengers and their luggage. Therefore, only the most urgent of cargo makes it on passenger aircraft, and it is often made up of machine or computer parts necessary for the repair of a critical piece of equipment, or small shipments of fresh produce, such as vegetables or fish.

Figure 12-4
The Largest Passenger Aircraft in the World, the Airbus A-380
Source: Photo © Konstantin von Wedelstaedt, courtesy of www.jetphotos.net. Used with permission.

Figure 12-5
A Container Placed in the Belly of a Passenger Aircraft
Source: Photo © Pierfabrizio Di Marco, Aeroporto FVG SpA. Used with permission.

The biggest constraint on a shipper regarding the use of passenger airplanes for shipping freight is the maximum weight or volume of the shipment. The issues to consider are the size of the hold, the weight capacity of the floor of the cargo hold, the overall weight limitations of the aircraft, and the size of the door used to access the cargo hold. Most freight forwarders have a good grasp of the maximum sizes of packages that can be shipped in passenger airplanes and are quite helpful in determining whether or not the cargo will be allowed on a passenger flight. The second constraint is that there are some items that are not allowed on passenger aircraft but may be transported on cargo aircraft. Such hazardous material must be labeled Cargo Aircraft Only (CAO) and can be shipped only in airfreighters.

Another alternative way of using passenger airplanes for cargo is to use an **onboard courier (OBC)** service. A courier is often a student or a retiree who will fly to a city and take cargo as his or her luggage. This is often the fastest way for cargo to get anywhere and is a service used for delivery of critical parts and documents. It also presents the advantage of the cargo always "making" the plane, as passengers' luggage has priority over all other freight. The OBC business is substantial, but unfortunately there are no aggregate statistics for this activity. One OBC company in San Francisco shipped 2,000 metric tonnes of freight by courier.[24] That's a lot of document pouches.

onboard courier (OBC) A passenger on a regularly scheduled flight who relinquishes his or her baggage allocation, allowing companies to ship extremely urgent cargo.

12-3b Combination Aircraft

Combination aircraft, or "**combis,**" are passenger airplanes that are designed to carry freight on the main deck as well as in the belly hold. The main deck is "split" at some point in the middle of the aircraft, with one portion of the plane reserved for passengers and the other portion reserved for freight. Some aircraft are designed in such a way that this partition is somewhat mobile, depending on the demand for passenger seats (a decision usually based on seasonal fluctuations).

combi aircraft A type of airplane that is designed to carry both passengers and cargo on the main deck of the plane.

Some of the more common combi aircraft include the Airbus 330 and 340; the DC-10; and the Boeing 737, 747, and 757. Many of the larger wide-body combis, such as the Boeing 747 and DC-10, are used to fly passengers and cargo nonstop to remote areas of the world, such as the islands of the South Pacific, where the volume of passenger traffic by itself is not sufficient to justify such flights. In another example, Alaskan Airlines recently started using modified Boeing 737-400 combis to meet the needs of the seafood industry, as well as to transport passengers to and from the northern and western parts of Alaska.[25] Canadian North (see Figure 12-6) operates similar flights.

For shippers, combis present an advantage over passenger aircraft. The main deck has a greater weight capacity and a much larger door, and can accommodate palletized and containerized cargo. Moreover, the cargo can be secured to the plane to prevent damage caused by movement within the aircraft. However, the restrictions on what is allowed to be shipped with passengers aboard remain.

12-3c Quick-Change Aircraft

As the name implies, **quick-change aircraft** are those which can be reconfigured from passenger to cargo configurations and vice-versa in a matter of hours. Airlines that operate quick-change aircraft use palletized sections of seats that can be easily added or removed from the main deck. Although limited in demand, the Boeing 737 200/300 series aircraft have been popular in that configuration, especially in Europe and Asia. Of the 1,731 airfreighters included in Airbus's computation of the world's airfreighter size, 59 are quick-change aircraft.[26]

quick-change aircraft An aircraft that can very quickly be converted between passenger and freight operations through the use of palletized sections of seats.

12-3d Airfreighters

Over the past decade, the amount of cargo carried on **airfreighters** versus the lower decks of passenger aircraft has been about equally split, with slightly more than half of all air cargo carried by airfreighters. However, both Boeing and Airbus project that

airfreighter An aircraft entirely dedicated to the transport of cargo.

Figure 12-6
A Canadian North Boeing 737 Combi Aircraft, with Passengers Aft and Cargo Fore
Source: Photo © Kevin Wachter, courtesy of www.airliners.net. Used with permission.

Figure 12-7
A Large Cargo Airliner: The Boeing 747-400F
Source: Photo © Mark Abbott, courtesy of www.airliners.net. Used with permission.

the demand for new freighters is going to grow. There are several reasons for this, including the increasing demand for air cargo, a decreased number of wide-body passenger aircraft available for conversion, and the fact that older airfreighters are reaching the end of their useful lives. In addition, the new airfreighters (see Figure 12-7) are much more fuel efficient, larger, and have lower maintenance costs.[27]

Figure 12-8
The "Roller Deck" of a Freighter Aircraft
Source: Photo © EDDL Photography, courtesy of www.airliners.net. Used with permission.

Most airfreighters are "liners" (i.e., they operate on a regular schedule) traveling between two airports, one of which is usually a "hub," the location at which the cargo will be transferred to another flight. Most airfreighters are also variations of aircraft used for passenger service, with the exception that the freighter is equipped with a **roller deck** (see Figure 12-8). A roller deck is a main deck equipped with rollers that allows the palletized or containerized cargo to be pushed into or off the aircraft, either through an oversize side door or through the nose of the airplane, which, in some cases, can be lifted (see Figure 12-9). The cargo is then secured to the aircraft floor and walls using locks, hooks, and slings.

In the past, most airfreighters were older passenger airplanes that were retrofitted for cargo service by specialized firms.[28] Today, passenger-to-freighter (P-F) conversions are still popular, but both Boeing and Airbus now offer freighter versions for almost every aircraft they build. For example, Boeing's 777-200F has done quite well as a new-built airfreighter, and Airbus plans to launch its new-build A330-200F in 2010.[29] The Airbus A-380 (see Figure 12-4) is also planned to be made into a freighter version. The A380-800F would present the advantage of having two main decks which can be loaded simultaneously, a fact that overcomes one of the pitfalls of a single-deck freighter, for which the loading sequence must be done very carefully, so as to not upset the balance of the aircraft on the ground. It is such a problem that most airfreight companies add a tail stand to prevent "nose up" situations during loading operations (see Figure 12-10).

Just as the ocean shipping industry has its own way of characterizing vessels, the air cargo industry has its own way of classifying freighters. The airfreighter fleet, for example, is often described in terms of standard body, medium wide-body, and large wide-body. The standard body category includes aircraft such as the McDonell-Douglas DC-8 and DC-9, the Boeing 727, 737, and 757, and the Airbus 320. The medium wide-body category includes the McDonell-Douglas DC-10, the Boeing 767 and 787, and the Airbus 300, 310, 330, and 340. The large wide-body category includes aircraft like the McDonell-Douglas MD-11, the Boeing 747 and 777, the

roller deck The configuration of the deck of an aircraft when it is designed to accept cargo shipments; the deck is equipped with rollers and bearings that allow cargo to be moved in any direction without much friction.

Figure 12-9
Some Freighters Can Be Loaded Through the Nose
Source: Photo © Ronén Björkquist, courtesy of www.jetphotos.net. Used with permission.

Figure 12-10
The Tailstand for a Cargo Aircraft
Source: Photo © Ben Wang, courtesy of www.airliners.net. Used with permission.

Airbus 340-600SF, 350, and 380, and the Antonov 124.[30] Each of these aircraft was designed to meet specific air transportation needs. Figure 12-11[31] illustrates how they vary by payload and range. As can be seen in this diagram, a Boeing 757 freighter would be well suited to carry 30 metric tonnes (66,140 pounds) over 2,500 nautical miles (4,630 kilometers), while a Boeing 777-200 could carry three times that payload twice as far. As of 2009, the largest airline freighter is the Boeing 747-400F, but the introduction of the freighter version of the Airbus 380 will jeopardize this

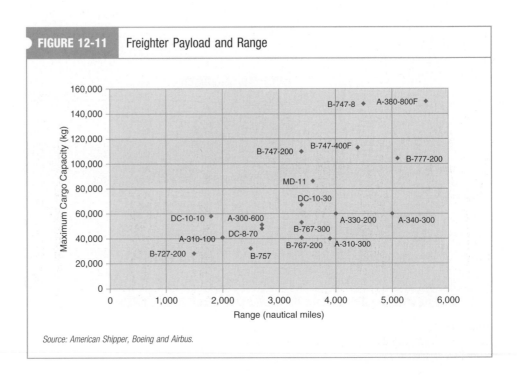

FIGURE 12-11   Freighter Payload and Range

Source: American Shipper, Boeing and Airbus.

standing, since it is designed to carry 150 metric tonnes (330,693 pounds) over 5,600 nautical miles (10,371 kilometers).[32]

Airfreighters can also be aircraft that do not have passenger versions and are constructed exclusively for the purpose of moving freight. The Antonov 124 *Ruslan* (see Figure 12-12) was built primarily for military use, but has found a niche in the civilian transport of cargo. The Antonov 124 can take off and land from poorly-maintained and short runways, despite a payload of 150 metric tonnes (330,693 pounds) and a range of 2,900 nautical miles (5,370 kilometers). It was the largest aircraft ever built until the Antonov 225 *Mriya* (see Figure 12-13) took that distinction, with a payload of 250 metric tonnes and a range of 8,500 nautical miles (15,742 kilometers). The Antonov 225 was designed to transport the Russian Space Shuttle. It now specializes in the transport of very heavy airfreight.

Other aircraft designed exclusively for the purpose of transporting freight include the Airbus 300-600 ST *Beluga* (see Figure 12-14) and the Boeing 747-400 *Dreamlifter* (see Figure 12-15), both of which were transformations of traditional aircraft, designed to transport pieces of other aircraft from one assembly plant to another. The *Beluga* is used by Airbus to shuttle fuselage and wings from its plants in the U.K., Spain, and Germany to their final assembly location in Toulouse, France, and the *Dreamlifter* fulfills the same function for Boeing, transporting parts from Japan and Italy to Everett, Washington.

Figure 12-12
Project Cargo Being Loaded on an Antonov 124 *Ruslan*
Source: Photo © Air America Fuel and Services, Inc., by Larry Godden, CEO. Used with permission.

Figure 12-13
The Largest Airfreighter in the World, the Antonov 225 *Mriya*
Source: Photo © Dennis Muller, courtesy of www.airlines.net. Used with permission.

Figure 12-14
The A 300-600 ST *Beluga* Operated by Airbus
Source: Photo © Michael Lutz, courtesy of airliners.com. Used with permission.

12-4 Airfreight Tariffs

The tariff structure of international air cargo is not nearly as complicated as that of the ocean cargo industry, with its innumerable categories. Airfreight is priced as a function of two things: weight and volume.

Figure 12-15
The B747-400 *Dreamlifter* Operated by Boeing
Source: Photo © S.L. Tsai, courtesy of www.airlines.net. Used with permission.

Carnations and Cherries

In 2007, exports of cut flowers from Colombia totaled 231,943 metric tonnes, and 85 percent of these flowers were shipped to the United States,[33] utilizing the air services of FedEx and UPS, which slowly have replaced the specialized airfreight services that once dominated this trade route, such as Aeroflora. Improvements in the techniques used to chill and handle the flowers allow them to stay fresh for more than a week, until they are delivered to flower retailers. Most of the exports enter the United States through the Miami airport. Roses account for 25 percent of that volume, with carnations and chrysanthemums another 14 percent each. A normal day will see from seven to ten flights from Bogotá to Miami, loaded with flowers.[34]

However, it is during the week preceding the Valentine's Day holiday that this business becomes crazy, with U.S. sales of roses reaching 11 million dozens.[35] In 2008, in the week preceding the holiday, there were 158 daily flights from Colombia to Miami, each a large wide-body, packed tightly with literally millions of flowers. A Boeing 747, packed to the gills, can hold 3.6 million roses.[36]

Cut flowers are not the only unusually seasonal business handled by airfreighters, though. From late May until late June, it is "cherry season" on the West Coast of the United States. More than 1.1 million cartons (cardboard boxes of 18 pounds [8.2 kilograms]) of cherries leave the United States for the Japanese market. That is more than 9,000 metric tonnes of cherries, all traveling by airfreighters or in the bellies of passenger flights, at sometimes prohibitive rates because all West-bound capacity at that time is taken by these fruits (U.S. $1.95 per kilogram, whereas cargo normally fetches no more than U.S. $1.00 per kilogram on that route). It is the most profitable period of the year for the airlines involved in that trade because Narita Airport operates at full capacity and cannot accommodate any more flights.

In order to arrive at the freight cost of a particular shipment, airlines calculate two alternatives: The first is based on the actual weight of the shipment, and the other is based on its volume, a computation that uses the volume of the cargo to determine its "equivalent" weight, which is called either the **volume-weight** of a shipment or its **dimensional weight**. The airline will then charge the higher of the volume-weight or the actual weight of the cargo. On international shipments, the volume-weight conversion traditionally uses 166 cubic inches per pound (6,000 cubic centimeters per kilogram), although some airlines may calculate this ratio slightly differently. To illustrate, using one international airfreight calculator in February 2009, the cost to fly a cargo of 200 pounds (91 kilograms) would vary greatly depending on its volume. If the shipment consisted of five containers, each measuring 60 × 60 × 48 inches (152 × 152 × 122 centimeters), the cost from Atlanta to Abu Dhabi was approximately U.S. $7,400. However, the cost to ship the same weight in five larger containers with four times the volume (five 120 × 120 × 48 inch containers [305 × 305 × 122 centimeters]) was over U.S. $29,000. Thus, one can readily see how the volume of an air shipment can vastly affect the price.

volume-weight (dimensional weight) A weight, calculated based upon the dimensions of a shipment, used by airlines to determine the tariff to be charged to a shipper, when a shipment is not very dense.

The difficulty for a shipper using airfreight for lightweight products—products for which the volume-weight of the shipment exceeds their actual weight—is to make sure that it does not pay too much for shipping by using packaging that is too voluminous. The trade-off is relatively simple. The shipper must decide between using packaging that satisfactorily protects but reduces the overall dimensions of the cargo and therefore reduces its volume-weight, and using more traditional packaging, which is likely to be less expensive but increases the freight costs by increasing the volume weight. The decision to decrease packaging should never be made without a thorough analysis, since improper packaging is one of the primary reasons insurance companies deny claims.

12-5 International Regulations

In terms of regulations, the international airfreight business is dominated by the **International Air Transport Association (IATA)** and the **International Civil**

International Air Transport Association (IATA) A trade association comprising almost 230 airlines, representing 93 percent of all scheduled air traffic.

International Civil Aviation Organization (ICAO) An agency of the United Nations whose mission is to establish safety and security standards for international civil aviation.

open-skies agreement An agreement between two or more countries whereby air carriers from one of the countries are allowed to serve any of the other countries' airports.

sustainability A deliberate attempt at using resources, including aircraft, in such a way as to preserve and protect the environment and meet the needs of future generations.

Aviation Organization (ICAO). International regulation of air traffic started with the Paris Convention of 1919, which established the concept of sovereignty of a country over its airspace. In 1929, the Warsaw Convention was signed, limiting the liability of international airlines to passengers and freight in case of accidents. Both liability limits were eventually increased in 1955 with the Hague Protocol; in 1966 with the Montréal Agreement; in 1971 with the Guatemala City Protocol; in 1995 with the IATA Intercarrier Agreement on Passenger Liability; and the Montréal Protocol No. 4. As of 2009, for those countries that had ratified the Montréal Protocol, the liability limits for death or bodily injury had been removed, and the liability for lost cargo was limited to 17 Special Drawing Rights (SDRs) per kilogram.

Under IATA and ICAO rules, a country can restrict the number of airline flights in and out of its airspace. Generally, the limit is set to favor national airline companies; however, in 1992, the United States and the Netherlands agreed to remove limits on the number of flights that each country's airlines could fly into the other's territory, creating an **"open-skies" agreement**. Since 1992, numerous additional bilateral agreements have been signed. By late 2008, the United States had 94 open-skies partners, including agreements with the 27 European countries that are part of the U.S.–European Union Trade Agreement that was signed on April 30, 2007.[37] Open-sky provisions apply to passenger and cargo flights as well as scheduled and charter air transportation services.

Even though open-skies agreements have removed many of the restrictions placed on international routes and carriers, flights in and out of specific airports are still restricted by the number of "landing slots" available at that airport. For example, the United States and Japan have an open-skies agreement, but Narita Airport cannot accommodate any more flights than it already handles.[38]

Both the IATA and ICAO are also starting to assume a more active role in establishing industry standards for environmental protection. In 1983, ICAO established the Committee on Aviation Environmental Protection (CAEP). This committee now includes a number of groups that focus on both the technical and operational aspects of noise reduction and aircraft emissions.[39] The IATA has been equally aggressive and has established a vision of becoming a carbon-free mode of transportation in the next 50 years.[40]

12-6 Environmental Issues and Sustainability

Over the past five years, the aviation industry has seen an enormous increase in concern for the environment and the adoption of **sustainability** practices. This shift is affecting the design and operation of passenger and cargo aircraft, as well as the airports and infrastructure that support them. The IATA, for example, is attempting to reduce greenhouse emissions by focusing on new technologies, changes in operations, infrastructure changes, and various economic incentives to encourage the industry to adopt more environmentally-friendly and sustainable aviation-related standards. Innovations in technology have already led to more fuel efficient aircraft engines, lighter airframes, more efficient wing designs, and new biofuels; while changes in operations have led to reduced toxins and waste in ground operations.[41] In fact, today's aircraft are 75 percent cleaner and 70 percent quieter than they were 40 years ago.[42]

In 2008, Virgin Atlantic conducted the world's first commercial aircraft flight, powered in part by biofuel, to demonstrate the potential of clean jet fuels.[43] Other more extensive tests have since been conducted using various blends and types of biofuels, suggesting that there are, in fact, environmentally-friendly alternatives to traditional jet fuels.[44]

The major aircraft manufacturers are equally committed to producing eco-friendly and more efficient aircraft. As stated in Airbus's Global Market Forecast for 2007–2026, "the need for an increasingly eco-efficient industry, which creates economic and social value with less environmental impact, is well understood by the millions of people involved in aviation. Aircraft manufacturers have an intrinsic requirement to be technological pioneers and to develop increasingly eco-efficient aircraft."[45]

Changes in air traffic control routing and other technology-enabled process changes are also expected to reduce fuel consumption, emissions, and noise pollution. Airfreighters, for example, often operate at off-hours, as their noise can create problems with airport neighbors. Some airports have considered banning night flights altogether. Brussels (Belgium) and the European Union have enacted some very stringent noise regulations, mostly aimed at older airfreighters.[46] The future is likely to hold yet more regulations for other heavily-used metropolitan airports, leaving room for the creation of other hubs in less urbanized centers, such as Prestwick in Scotland, Hahn in Germany, and Chateauroux in France.[47] To some extent, this development mirrors that of the Memphis airport, which has become the largest cargo airport in the world, even though it is not located in a large metropolitan center. The same motivation was behind the development of the Mid-America Airport near St Louis, Missouri, although it has not been as successful.

In addition to the actions noted above, two relatively new approaches have recently been introduced to reduce the impact of aviation carbon emissions on the environment: carbon trading and voluntary carbon offset programs. These two unique programs allow owners and operators to purchase credits in organizations that absorb or offset carbon in an effort to mitigate total emissions.[48]

12-7 International Air Cargo Security

Beyond fuel prices and the overall state of the world's economy, security requirements represent the biggest challenge to the air cargo industry today, and the challenge is overwhelming.[49] Within the United States, for example, over 700 million people travel on commercial aircraft each year,[50] and more than 150 million travel from the United States to foreign destinations.[51] That represents more than 700 million pieces of baggage screened for explosives every year. There are also approximately 13 million tons of cargo transported by air domestically, and 3 million shipped internationally.[52] Of the 13 million tons of cargo transported domestically by air, 3 million are shipped on passenger aircraft and the remaining 10 million are moved on cargo aircraft.

One of the difficulties is that the security requirements are different for cargo shipped on passenger aircraft and for cargo shipped on freighters. In addition, because of the evolving state of technology and the dynamic and unpredictable nature of terrorism, the security guidelines and safety processes followed in the air cargo industry are continuously changing.

12-7a Transportation Security Administration

Within the United States, the Transportation Security Administration (TSA) has overall responsibility for transportation security for the air cargo industry. To meet this challenge, TSA, with the help of Customs and Border Protection (CBP), relies on several methods to enhance security.[53] For air cargo transportation, the TSA uses:

- Advance information on shipments by demanding the electronic submission of manifests before a flight is allowed to leave the airport of departure or before the flight is allowed to land in the United States
- An Automated Targeting System (ATS) that screens U.S.-bound shipments prior to their arrival to determine the level of risk they represent, using a risk-analysis algorithm

- Mandatory security inspections using non-intrusive inspection technology (NII) for all high-risk shipments. These efforts include large-scale imaging and radiation technologies, as well as canine detection teams.
- A partnership with the trade community designed to strengthen air cargo security by giving shippers an incentive to strengthen their internal security systems. One example of such cooperation is the Customs-Trade Partnership against Terrorism (C-TPAT) (see Chapter 15, Section 15-3a).

12-7b Advance Manifest Rules for Air Carriers

The Trade Act of 2002 requires that cargo manifests for all freight shipments that transit the United States be submitted electronically prior to arrival to Customs and Border Protection through its Automated Manifest System (AMS). For flights originating outside North America, electronic manifests must be received at least four hours prior to arrival at their first U.S. airport. For Mexico, Canada, and other locations that are less than four hours away, manifests must be transmitted to CBP prior to the time of the aircraft's departure.

CBP has launched a Web-based Automated Commercial Environment (ACE) that enables multimodal manifest processing and allows importers, exporters, brokers, and transportation providers to use one single integrated system to expedite shipping.[54]

12-7c Certified Cargo Screening Program

Another key component in TSA's approach to security is the Certified Cargo Screening Program (CCSP). The CCSP mandates 100 percent screening of all air cargo transported by passenger aircraft by August 2010, whether shipped within the United States or coming from abroad into the United States. This inspection is to be conducted at the "piece level," which means that every item in a shipment needs to be inspected.[55]

The Certified Cargo Screening Program selects and approves Certified Cargo Screening Facilities (CCSFs) and monitors and maintains the security of shipments throughout the supply chain. The concept is that security is achieved with an inspection at the CCSF and with the continuous monitoring of the goods between the time they are inspected and the time at which they are loaded onto the aircraft. Such efforts are called "chain-of-custody" security methods. Once approved, a CCSF must adhere to increased TSA-directed security standards, share responsibility for supply chain security, employ chain-of-custody methods, permit onsite validations, submit a facility security plan, and be subject to transportation security inspections.[56]

It should also be noted that the United States built its air cargo Certified Cargo Screening Program based, in part, on best practices adopted from other countries such as the United Kingdom and Ireland.[57] It is also clear that many of the concepts now associated with the CCSP are being adopted by other foreign entities, in partnership with TSA, to validate and maintain the security of airfreight across international boundaries.

12-7d Air Carriers and C-TPAT

As is the case for all companies involved in international logistics, the CBP is looking for air carriers to join C-TPAT to enhance existing security practices and reduce the threat of terrorism to international air shipments. As of 2009, air carriers wishing to enroll in C-TPAT are required to meet minimum-security criteria in order to achieve certification. To be eligible, air carriers must meet the following requirements:[58]

- Be an active air carrier transporting cargo shipments to the United States
- Have an active IATA code
- Possess a valid continuous international carrier bond registered with CBP

- Have a designated company officer who will be the primary cargo security officer responsible for C-TPAT
- Commit to maintaining the C-TPAT security criteria for air carriers
- Create and provide CBP with a C-TPAT supply chain security profile, which identifies how the air carrier will meet, maintain, and enhance internal policy to meet the C-TPAT security criteria for air carriers.

As indicated above, air carriers must conduct a comprehensive assessment of their security practices using C-TPAT criteria. These criteria include meeting business partner requirements, as well as the requirements for container or unit load devices (ULD) security, physical access controls, personnel security, procedural security, security training and threat awareness, physical security, and information technology security.[59]

12-7e Air Cargo Security Requirements for Other Countries

By mid-2009, numerous countries were in the process of developing and applying air cargo security standards similar to those established by the United States following 9/11. The United States and the European Union (EU), for example, signed an agreement in late 2008 to harmonize cargo screening standards for passenger aircraft. This agreement, signed between the TSA and the EU's Directorate General for Energy and Transport, is expected to provide a foundation for other bilateral security agreements based largely on the standards set by the 9/11 Commission Act of 2007.[60] There is still room for greater harmonization between countries, however, and substantial concern among practitioners about multiple conflicting standards. As stated by Harald Zielinski, director of security for Lufthansa Cargo, "It is not possible to have 15 processes for 15 different security standards," and there is much work to be done.[61]

Review and Discussion Questions

1. Briefly describe the different types of air cargo services available.

2. Do you think that the demand for air cargo will increase or decrease over the next three years? Why?

3. How does an air carrier determine how much a shipment will cost? What can a shipper do to reduce the costs of shipping a light but voluminous package?

4. What is project cargo? Use the Internet to find and describe at least one example of the use of air transportation to ship project cargo internationally.

5. Using the freighter/payload range chart (Figure 12-11), what type of airfreighter would you expect to use to ship 60,000 kilograms over 3,500 nautical miles?

6. What is the purpose of an open-skies agreement?

7. What are some of the environmental challenges facing the air cargo industry today? What is the industry doing to deal with these issues?

8. What is the purpose of the Certified Cargo Screening Program?

9. What are the Advance Manifest Rules and how do they apply to air shipments bound for the U.S.?

Endnotes

1. Crabtree, Thomas, Thomas Hoang, James Edgar, and Kai Heinicke, *World Air Cargo Forecast 2008-2009*, Boeing Corporation, http://www.boeing.com/commercial/cargo, accessed June 21, 2009.

2. *Ibid.*

3. Thuermer, Karen, "2007 State of Logistics Report/Air Cargo: No Where to Go but Up," *Logistics Management*, July 1, 2007, http://www.logisticsmgmt.com/article/CA6457613.html.

4. "Air Cargo Plunges 17.2 Percent," *Traffic World Online*, January 6, 2009, http://www.joc.com/node/354428, January 15, 2009.

5. Parmalee, Patricia, "Boeing Is Bullish on Freight," *Aviation Week & Space Technology*, November 10, 2008, p. 16.

6. Dahl, Robert, "Market Outlook for Cargo Aircraft," *Aviation Week & Space Technology*, January 26, 2009, p. 53.

7. FedEx, "About FedEx," http://about.fedex.designcdt.com/our_company/company_information/fedex_corporation, accessed January 15, 2009.

8. "The World's Top 50 Cargo Airlines," *Air Cargo World*, http://www.aircargoworld.com/Magazine/Features/Archive-2009/September-2009/IATA-s-Top-50-Cargo-Carriers/IATA-Top-50-Stats-2A, accessed October 30, 2009.

9. "Top 30 World Airports by Cargo," *Airports Council International*, July 2008, http://www.aci.aero/aci/aci/file/Press%20Releases/2008/TOP30_Cargo_2007.pdf.

10. Crabtree, Thomas, Thomas Hoang, James Edgar, and Kai Heinicke, *World Air Cargo Forecast 2008-2009*, Boeing Corporation, http://www.boeing.com/commercial/cargo, accessed June 21, 2009.

11. "Current Market Outlook 2009–2028," Boeing Corporation, http://www.boeing.com/commercial/cmo/index.html, accessed July 6, 2009.

12. *Airbus Global Market Forecast 2009–2028*, Airbus Industrie, September 2009, http://www.airbus.com/en/gmf2009/data/catalogue.pdf, accessed October 29, 2009.

13. Wensveen, John, *Air Transportation: A Management Perspective*. 6th ed. Burlington, VT: Ashgate Publishing 2007.

14. *Airbus Global Market Forecast 2007–2026*, Airbus Industrie, December 2007, http://www.airbus.com/fileadmin/documents/gmf/PDF_dl/00-all-gmf_2007.pdf, accessed June 29, 2009.

15. Wensveen, John, *Air Transportation: A Management Perspective*. 6th ed. Burlington, VT: Ashgate Publishing, 2007.

16. "The FedEx Express Super Hub in Memphis, TN," *FedEx Corporation*, http://news.van.fedex.com/files/FedEx%20Express%20Super%20Hub%20in%20Memphis.pdf, accessed January 27, 2009.

17. Crabtree, Thomas, Thomas Hoang, James Edgar, and Kai Heinicke, *World Air Cargo Forecast 2008-2009*, Boeing Corporation, http://www.boeing.com/commercial/cargo, accessed June 21, 2009.

18. "The FedEx Express Super Hub in Memphis, TN," *FedEx Corporation*, http://news.van.fedex.com/files/FedEx%20Express%20Super%20Hub%20in%20Memphis.pdf, accessed January 27, 2009.

19. "Overview – UPS Worldport Fact Sheet," UPS Inc., http://pressroom.ups.com/Fact+Sheets/UPS+Worldport+Facts, accessed January 27, 2009.

20. *Deutsche Post World Net Annual Report 2007*, Bonn, Germany: Deutsche Post, 2007, 56–58.

21. Crabtree, Thomas, Thomas Hoang, James Edgar, and Kai Heinicke, *World Air Cargo Forecast 2008-2009*, Boeing Corporation, http://www.boeing.com/commercial/cargo, accessed June 21, 2009.

22. *Ibid*.

23. "FedEx Corporation Annual Report (10K), Item 2. Properties," FedEx Corporation, http://fedex.com/us/investorrelations/financialinfo/2008annualreport/corp_info.html, accessed February 16, 2009.

24. Kayal, Michele. "Couriers on Board: Crucial Links Between You and Your Packages," *Journal of Commerce*, November 3, 1997, p. 1A.

25. "Alaska Airlines Introduces Two 737-400 'Combi' Aircraft to Fleet," *RedOrbit News*, February 1, 2007, http://www.redorbit.com/news/business/823041/alaska_airlines_introduces_two_737400_combi_aircraft_to_fleet/index.html.

26. *Airbus Global Market Forecast 2009–2028*, Airbus Industrie, September 2009, http://www.airbus.com/en/gmf2009/data/catalogue.pdf, accessed October 29, 2009.

27. Dahl, Robert, "Market Outlook for Cargo Aircraft," *Aviation Week & Space Technology*, January 26, 2009, p. 53.

28. Davies, John, "Boeing Creates Unit for Jet Conversion," *The Journal of Commerce*, November 17, 1998.

29. Wall, Robert, "Heavy Lifting," *Aviation Week & Space Technology*, February 23, 2009, p. 48–49.

30. Crabtree, Thomas, Thomas Hoang, James Edgar, and Kai Heinicke, *World Air Cargo Forecast 2008-2009*, Boeing Corporation, http://www.boeing.com/commercial/cargo, accessed June 21, 2009.

31. "Merge Global. End of an Era?" *American Shipper*, August 2008, p. 45.

32. "Airbus 380-800F Wide-Bodied Freighter, Europe," *Aerospace Technology*, http://www.aerospace-technology.com/projects/airbus_a380/specs.html, accessed July 1, 2009.

33. Eyerdam, Rick, "Flower Exports Drive Colombian Economy," *Cool Cargoes*, February 23, 2009, http://www.coolcargoes.com/content/?p=46.

34. "Roses are … brown? Flower imports showcase international logistics," *Compass Online*, UPS, http://compass.ups.com/goingglobal/article.aspx?id=1649, accessed July 2, 2009.

35. Mathews, Don, "The Economics of the Rose Market," Ludwig von Mises Institute, February 11, 2003, http://mises.org/story/1164.

36. Sharpe, Rochelle, "Hearts of Gold: All Romance Aside, Valentine's Day Can Be Frantic—and Lucrative," *Wall Street Journal*, February 15, 1996, p. A1.

37. "Open Skies Partners," *U.S. Department of State*, http://www.state.gov/e/eeb/rls/othr/ata/114805.htm, accessed March 14, 2009.

38. Wald, Matthew L., "U.S., Japan to Remove Air-Traffic Restrictions," *New York Times*, January 31, 1998.

39. "Committee on Aviation Environmental Protection," International Civil Aviation Organization, http://www.icao.int/env/caep.htm, accessed March 12, 2009.

40. *Building a Greener Future*, 3rd ed., International Air Transport Association, October 2008, http://www.iata.org/nr/rdonlyres/c5840acd-71ac-4faa-8fee-00b21e9961b3/0/building_greener_future_oct08.pdf.

41. Gardner , T., "Aviation Goes Green from the Ground on Up," *Chicago Tribune*, March 9, 2008, p. 2.

42. *Airbus Global Market Forecast 2007–2026*, Airbus Industrie, December 2007, http://www.airbus.com/fileadmin/documents/gmf/PDF_dl/00-all-gmf_2007.pdf, accessed June 29, 2009.

43. "Virgin Atlantic Flies Biofuel-Powered Jumbo Jet," *MSNBC News*, February 24, 2008, http://www.msnbc.msn.com/id/23321510.

44. Warwick, Graham, "Bio-fueled Jet Flies Cross-Country," *Aviation Week*, November 10, 2008, http://www.aviationweek.com/aw/generic/story_channel.jsp?channel=comm&id=news/BIO11108.xml.

45. *Airbus Global Market Forecast 2009–2028*, Airbus Industrie, September 2009, http://www.airbus.com/en/gmf2009/data/catalogue.pdf ,accessed October 29, 2009.

46. Barnard, Bruce, "Night flights to be banned in Brussels," *Journal of Commerce*, January 5, 2000, p. 3.

47. *Ibid*.

48. Essler, David, "The Greening of Business Aviation, Part III," *Aviation Week*, July 22, 2008, http://www.aviationweek.com/aw/generic/story_channel.jsp?channel=busav&id=news/bca0708p1.xml.

49. Ott, James, "Cargo Fleet Evolves Under the Demand of World Trade," *Aviation Week*, May 7, 2007, http://www.aviationweek.com/aw/generic/story_channel.jsp?channel=comm&id=news/aw050707p1.xml.

50. Bureau of Transportation Statistics, "U.S. Air Carrier Traffic Statistics Through July 2009," http://www.bts.gov/xml/air_traffic/src/index.xml#CustomizeTable, accessed October 30, 2009.

51. Office of the Assistant Secretary for Aviation and International Affairs, *U.S. International Air Passenger and Freight Statistics*, March 2009, http://ostpxweb.dot.gov/aviation/international-series/mar2009.pdf.

52. *Ibid.*

53. "TSA/CBP Air Cargo Security Workshop," *U.S. Customs and Border Protection*, http://www.cbp.gov/linkhandler/cgov/trade/trade_outreach/symposium08/event_materials/air_cargo_ccsp.ctt/air_cargo_ccsp.pdf, accessed March 16, 2009.

54. U.S. Customs and Border Protection, "CBP Approves Design for ACE Air e-Manifest Capabilities," http://www.cbp.gov/xp/cgov/trade/automated/modernization/whats_new/whats_new_ace_archives/2008/feb_march08_archive/ace_air_emanifest.xml, accessed March 17, 2009.

55. Transportation Safety Administration, "TSA is Concerned About Lack of U.S. Shippers' Impact Awareness About 100% Screening Issues (August 2010)," June 5, 2009, http://www.tsa.gov/assets/pdf/ccsp_at_a_glance.pdf.

56. "TSA/CBP Air Cargo Security Workshop," *U.S. Customs and Border Protection*, http://www.cbp.gov/linkhandler/cgov/trade/trade_outreach/symposium08/event_materials/air_cargo_ccsp.ctt/air_cargo_ccsp.pdf, accessed March 16, 2009.

57. *Ibid.*

58. U.S. Customs and Border Protection, "Air Carrier Eligibility Requirements," http://www.cbp.gov/xp/cgov/trade/cargo_security/ctpat/security_criteria/air_carrier_criteria/air_carriers_criteria.xml, accessed March 1, 2009.

59. U.S. Customs and Border Protection, "Air Carrier Criteria," http://www.cbp.gov/xp/cgov/trade/cargo_security/ctpat/security_criteria/air_carrier_criteria/, accessed October 28, 2009.

60. Fiorino, Frances, "Improving Cargo Screening," *Aviation Week & Space Technology*, November 10, 2008, p. 17.

61. Conway, Peter. "Air Cargo Security Screening Deadline Draw Near," *Airline Business*, October 29, 2008, http://www.flightglobal.com/articles/2008/10/29/318023/air-cargo-security-screening-deadlines-draw-near.html.

International Land and Multimodal Transportation

Key Terms

This chapter is the last of a series of three covering the means of transportation available to an international shipper. The preceding two chapters covered ocean and air transportation. This chapter presents the remaining alternatives.

First, it will present the two main land-based shipping methods available to an international shipper: road and rail transportation. Both are much more frequently used in Europe for international freight, where they represent a majority of the total intra-European freight traffic (see Figure 13-1),[1] than they are in Asia and North America. However, practices differ, and a savvy international logistics manager should be familiar with the issues presented by road and rail transportation.

In its second part, the chapter will cover the specifics of international intermodal transportation, which is not a transportation alternative properly speaking, but is the practice of shipping a product under a single bill of lading that covers more than one mode of transportation. For many shippers, that practice is often associated with container shipping.

Finally, two additional alternative methods of transportation are covered: inland waterway barges and pipelines. Although both represent a large percentage of the volume of the international shipments of some specific commodities (agricultural raw materials and crude oil), they are quite limited in their capabilities.

13-1 Truck Transportation

Trucking, from a North American perspective, is primarily a domestic means of transportation, with the exception of the significant amount of trade between Canada and the United States and some limited trade between the United States and Mexico. However, the latter is still mostly trade to and from the U.S.-Mexico border, as a large percentage of the trade is done on a DAF (Delivered at Frontier) basis (see Chapter 6) and because Mexican trucks are, for all intents and purposes, not yet authorized on American highways.

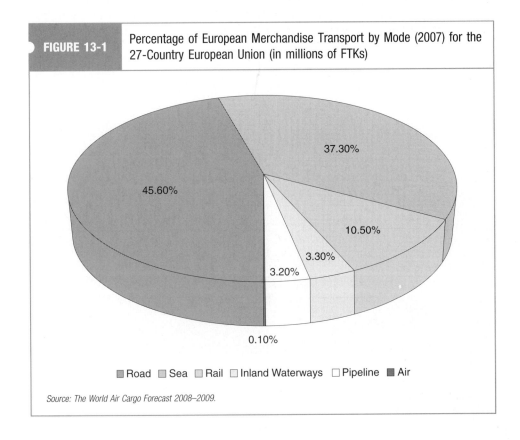

FIGURE 13-1 Percentage of European Merchandise Transport by Mode (2007) for the 27-Country European Union (in millions of FTKs)

37.30%

45.60%

10.50%

3.30%

3.20%

0.10%

■ Road ■ Sea ■ Rail □ Inland Waterways □ Pipeline ■ Air

Source: The World Air Cargo Forecast 2008–2009.

tractor The part of an articulated semi truck that is in the front and whose engine pulls the trailer.

trailer The part of an articulated semi truck that is in the rear and is pulled by the tractor.

piggy-back A technique, developed by railroad and trucking companies, that consists of placing truck trailers on specially designed railroad cars, so that the trailers can be carried over long distances economically.

For the rest of the world, though, trucking is a vital way of shipping goods internationally. More than 82 percent of merchandise shipped by truck within the European Union is shipped to a destination in a foreign country,[2] and this share is increasing.

Worldwide, trucking is still dominated by a patchwork of domestic rules and regulations, which greatly influence the way the industry is organized. There are limits on the number of axles a truck may have, on the weight it can carry per axle, on its total weight, on its length and width, as well as requirements regarding its mandatory equipment, and the training of drivers and the number of consecutive hours they can drive. All of these constraints generate fleets of trucks that are different from country to country. Altogether, though, trucks carrying international cargo tend to be semi trucks. These are made up of two distinct units: a **tractor** pulling a **trailer**, both of which take on characteristics that are country specific (see Figures 13-2 and 13-3).

The biggest challenge in shipping goods internationally by trucks is to abide by all these rules and regulations, the complexity of which should not be underestimated. Case in point: European countries, even the smallest ones, like Luxembourg, have driving bans on certain days—generally Sundays—but none of these bans are coordinated or harmonized. There are hundreds of different driving bans or restrictions in the European Union, if the special holiday restrictions are included,[3] which can create havoc on a company's ability to ship goods just-in-time, or for a shipper to reach a port before a sailing. Poland, for example, prohibits trucks from driving when temperatures reach 30 degrees Celsius (86 degrees Fahrenheit), and Switzerland prohibits trucks weighing more than 28 metric tonnes from going farther into Switzerland than 10 kilometers (6 miles), relegating all large trucks crossing the country to **piggy-back** on railroad cars[4] (see Figure 13-4); in 2008, the *Rollende Landstrasse* (rolling highway) carried a total of 330,000 tractor-trailers through the Alps.[5] The Freight Transport Association publishes an annual *Yearbook of Road Transport Law* to keep its members informed of all of the different laws and road regulations within the European Union.[6]

Such constraints often have the effect of creating giant "parking lots" of trucks at the entry points into a country and at highway exits. The enforcement of this myriad of rules and regulations also creates delays. Although there are officially no longer any

Figure 13-2
A European Semi Truck
Its overall length is limited to 61.5 feet (18.75 meters).
Source: Photo © Pierre David.

Figure 13-3
A North American Semi Truck
Limited to a 53-foot-long trailer (16.1 meters), but there is no limit on the length of the tractor.
Source: Photo © Denis Desmond. Used with Permission.

Figure 13-4
The Swiss "Rolling Highway"
Source: Photo © Josef Petrák. Used with permission.

border controls for trucks within the European Union, police routinely stop truckers in order to enforce rules regarding driving times, speed limits, and so on, none of which are the same from one country to the next.

The second challenge regarding shipping by truck is the state of the infrastructure. Load limits, height limits, and speed limits (road conditions) hinder the smooth transportation of goods and have an impact on packing. For example, the E-30 highway, one of the key links between western Europe (Berlin) and Russia, is so crowded and in such a state of disrepair that traffic is very slow, making it one of the most dangerous highways in Europe. Its replacement is under construction, but only about 40 percent of it is completed and usable, leaving long stretches of the East-West itinerary to be completed under less than ideal conditions.[7]

However, that is not all: The prohibitive taxation of diesel fuel in some countries influences the power of trucks, the size of the trailers, and the speeds at which cargo moves. The high tolls of some European highways lure truckers into driving on secondary roads that are not as cargo friendly. Some companies are "flagging out" their trucks—registering them in other countries—to take advantage of lower taxation and regulations,[8] bringing the same kind of concerns that "flags of convenience" have triggered for the marine industry (see Chapter 11, Section 11-4). Another factor is the "cultural" aspect of the industry. While **overloaded** trucks are rare in North America and Europe, they are strikingly commonplace in Africa and in some parts of Asia, where, seemingly, a truck is not full until one more piece of cargo will fit (see Figure 13-5).

Finally, the complementary infrastructure of railroads influences the way that some goods are shipped. In North America, for example, a large fleet of railroad cars capable of carrying truck trailers enables trucking companies to load trailers onto trains rather than drive them across the country. In Australia, however, the seemingly complete lack of railroads has pushed trucking companies to develop **road-trains**, which are tractors pulling three to five full-size semi trailers (see Figure 13-6).

The last challenge regarding trucking, specifically in Europe, is the fact that road transport is often delayed by social unrest. In the first six months of 2009, there were no fewer than ten instances during which some group or another blocked truck traffic somewhere in the European Union. Farmers protesting high gas prices, truckers protesting low wages, ecologists worried about pollution—just about every pretext was used to block entrances to highways, harbors, refineries, Alpine routes, or whatever else, causing lengthy delays, up to seven days, for truck shipments. Because governments routinely cave in to these demands, it is unlikely that the number of such protests will diminish in the future.

overloaded A mode of transportation that carries cargo of a greater weight or greater volume than it is designed to carry.

road-train An Australian trucking technique, consisting of having one tractor pulling multiple trailers. Road-trains are the conceptual equivalent of trains, but operating on a road.

Figure 13-5
An Overloaded Truck in Mali, Africa
Source: Photo © Roberto Neumiller. Used with permission.

Figure 13-6
An Australian Road-Train
Its maximum overall length is 175.5 feet (53.5 meters).
Source: Photo © Ryan and Nada Clontz. Used with permission.

13-2 Rail Transportation

Another contrast between North America and the rest of the world is the extent that railroads are used for freight movements. In the United States, for example, 1.85 trillion ton-miles (2.71 trillion freight tonne kilometers [FTKs]) were shipped by rail in 2007, or a "market share" of more than 40 percent of all ton-miles shipped long-distance in the country.[9] The growth of intermodal freight accounted for more than one-third of the total number of carloads transported, a total of more than 12 million trailers or containers. Although there are no figures available for international freight within North America, it is likely that the percentages are similar.

In contrast, European railroads carried only about 436.8 billion FTKs of freight traffic (about 300 billion ton-miles) in 2007,[10] even though the 27 countries of the European Union have a cumulative economy and territorial size that are larger than those of the United States—representing a "market share" of less than 18 percent of all FTKs shipped within the European Union.[11] In addition, only a small percentage of those were intermodal, with a great percentage of the cargo transported in traditional railroad cars (see Figure 13-7). **Intermodal** transport (or **co-modality**, as it is called within the European Union) grew from 28.5 billion FTKs in 1999 to 46 billion FTKs in 2008 (about 10 percent of the total rail traffic), and the number of trailers transported grew from 1.8 million to 3 million units during the same period.[12]

The railroad infrastructure in Europe is still focused mostly on passenger traffic, and freight traffic is mostly neglected, with almost no investments in railroad cars and facilities designed to facilitate intermodal cargo. For example, all European intermodal cargo is transported on single-stack railroad cars (cars carrying a single **container**, see Figure 13-8), whereas most of the United States infrastructure has been modified to accommodate double-stack cars (see Figure 13-9).

In the last few years, the European Community has introduced the idea of "freight corridors" that would carry freight from northern Europe's major ports (Antwerp, Belgium, and Amsterdam, the Netherlands) to Milan, Italy, and Vienna, Austria—and eventually to other cities as well—bypassing the requirements to change to a national locomotive and a national crew at every border crossing and allowing private freight companies to compete with the state-owned enterprises.[13]

Nevertheless, as these "rail freight freeways" are going to utilize currently existing lines, and because passenger trains have priority over all other traffic, there are widespread doubts about the feasibility of this politically motivated initiative.[14] Two

intermodal A shipment that takes several different means of transportation from its point of departure (seller/exporter) to its point of destination (buyer/importer).

co-modality Another term for *intermodal.*

container A large metal box used in international shipments that can be loaded directly onto a truck, a railroad car, or an ocean-going vessel.

Figure 13-7
A Traditional European Freight Box Car
Source: Photo © Anton Kendall, courtesy of http:/www.continentalwagons1.fotopic.net. Used with permission.

Figure 13-8
A European Single-Stack Container Train
Source: Photo © Anton Kendall, courtesy of http:/www.continentalwagons1.fotopic.net. Used with permission.

of these corridors have been implemented. The *Société Nationale des Chemins de Fer Français* (SNCF), the French national railroad company, boasts on its Web site that Belgium can be linked to northern Italy in a mere 33 hours, or at an average of 35 kilometers per hour (less than 25 miles per hour). Combine that with the fact that there are only two departures per day, except Saturdays, Sundays, and holidays, when

Figure 13-9
A U.S. Double-Stack Container Train
Source: Photo © Chad Hewitt. Used with permission.

there are none, and the conclusion is that rail transportation in Europe is far from being a viable alternative for all but the least time-sensitive cargo.

To date, a single rail project involving a new rail corridor has been built, from the port of Rotterdam to the Netherlands-Germany border: It is called the *Betuweroute*. It carries only freight trains and has a capacity of ten trains in either direction every hour. It connects to the network of the Dutch and German railways and relieves congestion in the port.

In contrast, in the U.S. railroads have traditionally had three business activities:

1. Bulk freight, not only grain, coal, lumber, steel, ores, chemicals, and oil, but also molasses, vegetable oils, and other heavy items. Each of these bulk cargoes tends to have its own type of railroad car.
2. Break-bulk freight placed in boxcars, either palletized or simply in its packaging
3. Automobile freight, placed on specialized car carriers

In the last two decades, the advent of intermodal transportation has radically changed this mix and dramatically altered the railroad business. Railroads are now carrying an increasing number of containers placed on container carriers (see Figure 13-9) and of truck trailers on piggy-back cars (see Figure 13-10).

First, these container carriers were designed to be only one container high, but then double-stacks were introduced, which eventually doubled the capacity of each train but forced railroads to update their infrastructures—tunnels in particular—so that these cars would "fit." In 2008, the U.S. railroads carried a total of 12 million trailers or containers,[15] an estimated 25 percent of which were transiting on a "land bridge" between Asia and Europe (see Section 13-3b).

The discrepancy between North American and European railroads is striking. As much as the future of rail transportation in the United States was bleak in the 1970s, it has transformed itself into a customer-oriented vibrant industry—despite some serious disturbances when Union Pacific bought Southern Pacific—with substantial expected growth emerging from its traditional cargoes, such as grain and automobiles, moving to containers. The European railroads appear to have noticed this trend and are attempting to embrace it; however, the national railroads are such bloated bureaucracies that progress is slow and success is elusive. In November 2000, EU railroad companies passed a resolution that they will open their networks to each other's crews

Figure 13-10
A U.S. Piggy-Back Train
Source: Photo © Chad Hewitt. Used with permission.

and engines; however, as of 2009, little progress had been made. Moreover, France opposes opening its network despite the agreement, so a large, geographically necessary swath of the network may not be available at all. Add to this information the discrepancies of at least two railroad gauges, five electrical systems, and 16 signaling systems, and the task seems daunting. The creation of the European Association for Railway Interoperability in 1996, charged with creating a trans-European network of high-speed passenger trains, has spurred cooperation between the national railroad companies, and such effort should eventually be extended to freight transport.

Another possible development is the replacement of some ocean trade with rail transportation, notably between the Far East (China, Korea) and Europe; such a possibility would seriously shorten transit times between the two areas and relieve some of the congestion in southern China's ports. Such a land bridge has been extensively studied,[16] but, despite its attractiveness, it is still more in conceptual stages than ready for implementation as of September 2009.

13-3 Intermodal Transportation

Probably the best way to introduce intermodal transportation is to define the concept:

> Intermodal describes a shipment that takes several different means of transportation—road, rail, ocean, air—from its point of departure (seller/exporter) to its point of destination (buyer/importer). The meaning has evolved recently to limit the use of this term to freight for which a single bill of lading covering more than one of these alternatives is issued.

Intermodal transportation is therefore not a means of transportation *per se*, but instead is the practice of utilizing a single bill of lading to cover several means of transportation for a single shipment. For that reason, it is also called **multimodal** transportation or co-modality. To use a recent cliché, the changes in means of transportation are "transparent" to the user, which means that the shipper does not have to worry about them, but only needs to be aware of them, so as to pack accordingly. The responsibility of arranging for all of the means of transportation falls onto the shipping company.

multimodal A shipment that takes several different means of transportation from its point of departure (seller/exporter) to its point of destination (buyer/importer).

Shipping companies have had to change their perspectives from that of simple transportation providers to that of providers of a multiplicity of services, one of which is transportation in their core competency, such as ocean shipping. However, they also have to provide transportation services in other modes, such as trucking or rail. In addition, shipping companies now interact with their customers directly and offer such ancillary services as tracking of shipments online. Most important of all, intermodal service created the possibility for an exporter (or an importer) to have a single interlocutor in a complex international shipment involving more than one mode of transportation. This "one-stop" shopping is probably what has made intermodal transportation so popular with shippers.

Because of the ubiquitous use of the seagoing container in multimodal shipments, the term *intermodal* has also been strongly associated with this transportation concept. The container idea is fairly recent. It was created in 1956 by Malcom McLean in an attempt to eliminate the large number of handlings to which ocean cargo was subjected, and to speed up the loading and unloading of ships. This concept of container has been a smashing success, with more than 10.7 million TEUs (20-foot equivalent units) in use worldwide.[17]

Certainly, the use of containers allowed the concept of intermodality to develop, but the two concepts are not entwined. It is quite possible to have an intermodal shipment that is not packaged in a container, and it is possible to use only one mode of transportation to ship containerized cargo. Nevertheless, the two are strongly tied together, and probably 95 percent of all intermodal cargo is shipped in containers, of which there are many different types. In addition, that percentage is growing, as more container types have been created to allow nonstandard cargo to be containerized.

Movable Boxes

International commerce was completely changed by the arrival of the container.[18]

Before containers, the traditional method for loading and unloading a ship was a very time-consuming and labor-intensive process. Goods, in boxes small enough to be handled by humans, were loaded by cranes onto break-bulk ships. Gangs of longshoremen were responsible for stowing them into the ship and making sure that they would not be damaged during the ocean voyage. They had to make sure that heavy goods were lower in the hold than lighter goods, that the weight of the cargo was distributed correctly through the ship, and that every piece of cargo was wedged solidly against the others. It was back-breaking, dangerous work. Because a ship could not be loaded until it had completely been unloaded, it took days to perform both operations. As trade increased, there was evermore gridlock in the ports, and ocean shipping was agonizingly slow.

Containers revolutionized this system; containers would be loaded, once, in the plant that manufactured the product, and unloaded, once, in the plant of the customer. There was no intermediary handling, no chance for pilferage, no possible damage from mishandling.

The labor costs would be lower, as the laborers loading the containers would be inland and not part of the strong (and costly) longshoremen's unions.

Containers of different sizes had been proposed several times before, but it was Malcom McLean, the owner of a trucking company, who eventually made the first investment in movable boxes of a size similar to a truck trailer and shipped them from Newark to Houston in April 1956. He eventually expanded this concept to other U.S. routes: the West Coast to Hawaii, Miami to Puerto Rico.

McLean's greatest challenges were with the unions of the ports in which he set up his operations; while West Coast ports' unions embraced the system, the East Coast unions were more difficult to convince. He also had difficulties convincing port authorities to invest in cranes and docks; in particular the Port of New York was unwilling to invest in docks that were wide enough to allow trucks to come alongside ships. Eventually, the movable container prevailed, as all began to understand the benefits of the concept.

In the late 1950s, containers were everywhere in the United States, except that they were of different sizes;

continued

Movable Boxes (Continued)

as McLean had expanded its concept, others had copied him and chosen different standard sizes. The incompatibility of these sizes made for a cumbersome system. It was eventually determined, after long negotiations between truckers, ship owners, railroads, and port authorities, both in the United States and in Europe, that containers should be 8 feet wide, 8 feet high (2.44 meters), and either 10, 20, or 40 feet long (3, 6, or 12 meters). This standardization effort took the better part of a decade. Today, seagoing containers are only 20 or 40 feet long, so that they can fit in the holds of containerships. A few exceptions to these sizes exist, but they are rare; the composition of the 2009 worldwide fleet of containers is described in Figure 13-11.

FIGURE 13-11 | The 2009 Worldwide Fleet of Containers (in TEUs)

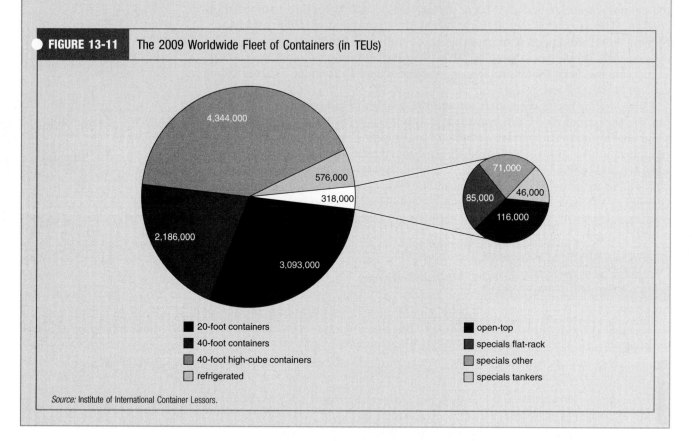

- 20-foot containers
- 40-foot containers
- 40-foot high-cube containers
- refrigerated
- open-top
- specials flat-rack
- specials other
- specials tankers

Source: Institute of International Container Lessors.

13-3a Types of Seagoing Containers

The greatest number of containers in the seagoing trade are the "standard" 20-foot and 40-foot units (6.1 and 12.2 meters, respectively), called "boxes"; these containers are 8 feet wide, 8 feet tall (2.44 meters), and fully enclosed in steel (see Figure 13-12). They are equipped with a double door at one end (called the front of the container) and have a wooden floor; some have wooden sides as well. Seagoing containers can be stacked up to 9 high, and in some cases, they can be stacked higher (under deck, in the holds of the larger containerships). Whenever the capacity of a containership is measured, it is given in TEUs, or the number of 20-foot equivalent units it can transport.

There are a large number of variants that were designed around this common "platform" measuring 8 × 8 × 40 feet. Each of these alternatives is called a "special," and its availability may be limited to certain routes and/or shipping lines.

- **The liquid-bulk container** (see Figure 13-13). In this container, a tank designed to hold liquids is placed inside a frame that has the same outside dimensions as a 20-foot unit. Containers holding liquid bulk actually have

Figure 13-12
A Forty-Foot Container Being Unloaded from a Truck in the Port of Santos
Source: Photo © Pierre David.

Figure 13-13
A Liquid-Bulk Container
Source: Photo © Zhongshan Zhoughua Tank Containers Limited. Used with permission.

different designs depending on the type of cargo carried and can be made of a variety of materials as well. Nevertheless, the frame is built to standards of the International Organization for Standardization (ISO), and liquid-bulk containers can be stacked with traditional containers.

- **The dry-bulk container.** This container is designed to hold dry-bulk products, such as grain or polymer pellets. This method of shipping dry bulk is becoming more common, as it allows for fewer handlings than when the cargo is strictly

Figure 13-14
An Open-Top Container
Source: Photo © Korean National Railroad. Used with permission.

bulk or packaged in drums or bags (see Chapter 14, Section 14-3c). Because some bulk cargo is quite heavy (grain, for example), a shorter container was created—about 5 feet tall—so that three containers can "fit" where two traditional ones normally do. This design greatly facilitates rail transport, as three containers fit on a double-stack train. Those containers can also be stacked with traditional ISO boxes as well.

- **The open-top container** (see Figure 13-14). This container is designed to hold cargo that is too large to fit through the door of a regular container and therefore must be loaded from the top. The container is then covered with a tarpaulin. Open-top containers can also be used to hold cargo that is taller than 8 feet, and the cargo then protrudes through the top of the container. Because it is then impossible to stack another container on top of that tall cargo, these containers are always considered "top of stack," whether placed under deck or on deck.

- **The extended-length container** (see Figure 13-15). This container is designed to hold cargo that does not fit in a 40-foot container. Designed so that the cargo "sticks out," they are fairly difficult to pack and load onto the ship, as the center of gravity still has to be within the box itself. They are generally placed on top of stacks, but must have the next stack's slot empty as well, so that the cargo is not damaged. These containers probably represent an extreme utilization of containers for what otherwise would be break-bulk cargo.

- **The flat rack** (see Figure 13-16). This container is designed to hold cargo that is less than 8 feet wide but would not fit in a standard container, which has inside dimensions of 92.5 inches (2.35 meters). Sometimes the flat rack has corners or two end walls, giving it a shape that allows a flat rack to be part of a stack. Sometimes it does not, which then forces it to be a top of stack as well. Flat racks are used for shipments of pleasure boats, trucks, and military vehicles.

Figure 13-15
An Extended-Length Container
Source: Photo © Chad Hewitt. Used with permission.

Figure 13-16
A Flat Rack Container
Source: Photo © Robert Crallé, Chick Packaging. Used with permission.

- **The refrigerated container** (see Figure 13-17). This container is designed to hold cargo at a constant temperature during the voyage. It needs an outside power source (electricity) to function and must be plugged in during all the legs of its intermodal journey. Most containerships can accommodate a few refrigerated container units. These containers are also called "reefers."

Figure 13-17
A Refrigerated Container or "Reefer"
Source: Photo © Tank Yard Corporation. Used with permission.

- **The high cube container**. This container is 9.5 feet (3 meters) tall and therefore can hold slightly more cargo. Such containers are designed to hold cargo that "cubes out" before it "weighs out"—i.e., it fills the volume of the container before it reaches the maximum weight limit of a container, which is 52,910 pounds (24 metric tonnes) for a 20-foot container and 67,200 pounds (30.5 metric tonnes) for a 40-foot container.

- **The hanger container**. This container is designed to hold garments "on hanger" (i.e., it is equipped with steel bars on which clothes are hung). The hanger container is a relatively new device, but it seems to fulfill the need for a more convenient way to ship hanging clothes, which may be damaged when they are shipped flat in boxes or may be difficult to fold. Garment containers seem to be all high cube containers as well.

A myriad of other "specials" are available. Several have been designed to ship automobiles, several to ship livestock, and others to ship ever-different cargo that could not otherwise be shipped in a standard ISO box. One aspect of importance in these modifications made to the standard, though, is that they all can accommodate the rigors of ocean shipping and fit within the existing ocean vessel and port infrastructure. In that, they are still all intermodal containers.

One of the difficulties of the development of "specials" is the fact that they are not multipurpose: While a traditional ISO box that holds a cargo of automobile parts from the United States bound for Malaysia can be used on the way back to ship garments or toys, such is not the case with a livestock container. If it is designed for cattle, it is unlikely that it can be used for anything else but cattle, and will come back empty, forcing its owner to pay for the return trip.

To a much lesser extent, a similar problem exists with all ISO boxes because of the imbalance of trade between ports. For example, much more trade arrives in the Ports of Los Angeles and Long Beach in the United States from Asia than leaves the ports for Asian destinations. There is therefore an accumulation of "empties" in the United States, while there is a shortage of boxes in most Asian ports. For some trade routes, there is another reason for the shortage of boxes in one direction: A substantial portion of empty containers shipped to some destinations "disappear," as they are used for storage or housing. Such is the case in some of the republics of the former Soviet Union and some African countries.

Shippers returning empty containers are charged freight for transport. Empty containers entering the United States are considered "implements of international trade" and do not require a Customs Entry Processing form. However, U.S. Customs requires that empty containers be manifested and clears them as entry-exempt items. Empty containers must be completely empty: No blocking, bracing, or securing equipment, materials, or residual products of any kind can be found inside them. Because they can be inspected by U.S. Customs, the shipper is subject to being fined for illegal entry of goods if they are not completely empty.

13-3b Land Bridges

The intermodal environment created several new ways of shipping goods internationally. One of the striking changes made was the concept of "land bridges." Via a land bridge, cargo traveling on ocean liners can cross a land obstacle by being unloaded in one port, transferred to a train, carried across the land obstacle by rail, and reloaded onto another ship.

The use of a typical **land bridge** would involve cargo going from the Far East to Europe. A few years ago, break-bulk cargo loaded onto a ship would have crossed the Pacific, gone through the Panama Canal, and crossed the Atlantic before reaching its destination. (It could also have gone westward, through the Suez Canal, but then it would be a different story.) Today, the same cargo would be containerized and could use a land bridge: The cargo is shipped by ocean from the Far East to the West Coast of the United States, after which it is unloaded and placed on a train that takes it to the East Coast of the United States. It is then reloaded onto another ship and sent to its destination in Europe. Using a land bridge is the penultimate in "intermodal shipment"; such changes in modes of transportation are so transparent to the shipper that it generally has no idea that its international cargo traveled through the Arizona desert on its way from Kobe, Japan, to Rotterdam, the Netherlands.

Such land bridges emerged because of several factors. The first is that the time spent by a ship traveling the Panama Canal route was greater than the time necessary to unload the cargo, cross the United States, and reload the cargo. The second is that it was equivalent in cost, or cheaper. The third was that economies of scale could be achieved with larger ships, which would not fit through the Canal. The fourth was the concern, expressed by a few shipping lines, regarding the reliability of the Canal when it became the responsibility of the Panamanian government, a concern that fortunately did not materialize.

There are several possible other locations for land bridges outside of the United States. The African continent is an obvious one, but at this time land bridges do not exist and are not planned. Another is the traffic from the Far East to eastern Europe, which can transit faster through Russia than by vessel: The port of Vostochny on the eastern shore of Russia was developed in the mid-1970s using Japanese funds to provide such a service. From having conveyed a high of 143,000 containers in 1983 to only 55,000 in 2000, this land bridge is but a speck in the transit from Japan and Korea to Europe.[19] However, the development of a seriously important land bridge is possible if North Korea were to re-open its railway system, which would allow cargo from South Korea to link with the Russian trans-Siberian railway and Europe. A 2007 conference in Canada outlined the possibility of a Eurasian land bridge, which would be quite ambitious, with a crossing of the Bering Strait into Canada and the North American continent.[20]

land bridge A term coined to describe the practice of shipping goods from Asia to Europe through the United States by using railroads.

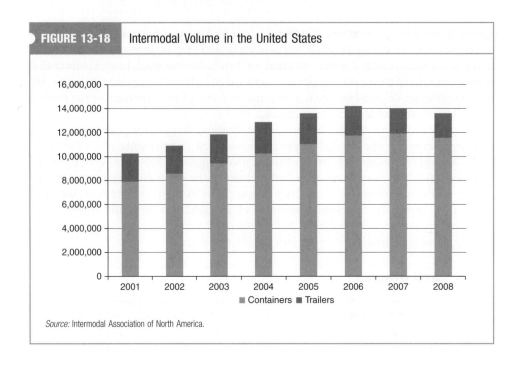

FIGURE 13-18 | Intermodal Volume in the United States

Source: Intermodal Association of North America.

A growing problem with land bridge use in the United States is the increasing demand for domestic intermodal service, which competes for capacity with international container service (see Figure 13-18).[21] Specially designed 53-foot-long, high-capacity containers have been built and put into use by Schneider National, the largest private trucking company in the United States. The company expects to have 30 percent or more of its trucks going intermodal by 2010. These domestic intermodal movements add strain to a rail system that is already at or near capacity on key corridors, the primary routes for international intermodal cargo, some of which are still single-track (see Chapter 3, Section 3-2d). Therefore, the potential for higher freight rates exists.

13-3c Liability Issues

One aspect of intermodal shipping that has yet to be resolved is the liability of the carrier toward the shipper when the goods are damaged while in the carrier's care. As goods travel from one mode of transportation to another, the legal or regulatory liability limits change. The limits are different for the trucking leg of the trip, the rail leg, and the ocean leg. In many cases, they are also different from one carrier to another, if such carrier has negotiated a different limit under the U.S. Ocean Shipping Reform Act (OSRA). To add further complexity, the flag under which the carrier operates also matters. This issue is relevant mostly for shippers who elect to not insure their cargoes and for insurance companies. Nevertheless, it is one of the few issues left to be determined in intermodal transportation.

As mentioned in Chapter 11, Section 11-5, the United Nations Commission on International Trade Law (UNCITRAL) has designed a multimodal liability framework, called the Rotterdam Rules, that govern the liability of carriers when a multimodal bill of lading is used. The General Assembly of the United Nations voted to accept the Rotterdam Rules in February 2009, and in September 2009, the United States and 15 other countries ratified it, heeding the recommendations of the International Chamber of Commerce, which had strongly supported the new convention.[22] Each of the countries still has to complete its own legislation to implement the rules, and the Rotterdam Rules will not enter into force until one year after the twentieth country ratifies the treaty; nevertheless, there is optimism that a single liability convention may finally govern international shipments of goods, regardless of the method of transportation. The fact that the Convention applies "door-to-door," which subjects all of the legs of a multimodal voyage to the same liability limits, makes it particularly attractive to shippers, which will no longer have to determine on which leg of a voyage damage occurred. The Rotterdam Rules place liability limits of 875 Special Drawing Rights (SDRs) per package and SDR 4 per kilogram for items that are not considered packages, such as automobiles and machinery.

13-3d Aircraft Containers

The types of containers used in air transport are more specifically called Unit Load Devices (ULDs) and are quite different from the types used in ocean shipping. The major differences in the way they are built and used are:

1. They are used to aggregate small individual packages rather than to form a whole shipment. Freight consolidators and airlines bundle together several different freight packages going to the same destination and unbundle them at the destination airport, sometimes to re-bundle them in another container for shipment to their final destination. In that regard, containers are used to speed up the loading and unloading of aircraft by shifting the task of loading and unloading small packages from the airplane to airport facilities. It also allows airfreight companies to use space more efficiently—for example, by building shelves in the containers, which allow more freight to be carried.

2. Although there have been some standardization attempts, most containers are designed to fit a specific aircraft. There are at least 20 different sizes, all identified by a code such as L-2 or EH, and some variants within the same size can be used as well. For example, L-2 can be used only in the belly of a Boeing 767, but EH can be used on any aircraft's main deck. Most aircraft containers, therefore, cannot be conveniently transported from one airplane to the next, and cargo must be decontainerized and recontainerized at airport facilities. This certainly removes the advantage of being able to securely pack a container and leave it undisturbed until it is unpacked by the consignee.

3. Aircraft containers are made of lightweight materials and are not designed to protect the cargo in any significant way. Most containers are made of aluminum, Plexiglas, or sometimes plywood, with "doors" that can be made of the same material, or of fabric, or even be nonexistent, with the cargo instead being held by a net. These containers offer little protection against the elements and against theft (see Figure 13-19).

4. Aircraft containers are not intermodal by intent. They are designed to be used only in aircraft and, possibly, for very short truck routes to shuttle goods to and from a freight forwarder's facilities. They are rarely used outside of the immediate vicinity of an airport.

13-4 Freight Forwarders

This complex array of alternatives is often bewildering to an occasional shipper; in those cases, it makes sense for the shipper to use the services of a **freight forwarder**, or a firm specializing in handling freight, particularly international freight.

A freight forwarder is, in layman's terms, a travel agent for freight. It knows what alternative routes are available, it knows how to determine the cost of shipping goods between two points, and it can arrange all of the paperwork necessary to ship the goods, from the exporting country's requirements to the importing country's Customs clearance.

Freight forwarders are different from Customs brokers, who specialize in clearing Customs for freight and who have to take, at least in the United States, a rigorous examination to be allowed to fulfill this role. Freight forwarders are also different

freight forwarder A company that specializes in shipping cargo on behalf of shippers (exporters or importers).

Figure 13-19
Air Cargo Containers on Dollies
Source: Photo © Hazlan Abdul Hakim. Used with permission.

from Non-Vessel-Operating Common Carriers, who buy space on liner ships or air-freighters and resell it to less-than-container-load customers, and they are regulated by the Federal Maritime Commission. Nevertheless, it is not uncommon for all three functions to be present in the same firm.

The business of freight forwarders is highly fragmented, including a large number of firms. Some are very large, with operations in just about every country. Others are quite small and, to distinguish themselves from others, end up specializing in a specific market, such as moving hazardous cargo, moving live animals, or moving what is known as project cargo.

13-5 Project Cargo

project cargo A type of cargo which requires more advance planning because of its size, weight, or volume.

The term **project cargo** is used to characterize cargo that is outside the normal realm of what shipping companies handle, specifically in terms of weight, volume, or destination. Most often, it encompasses all of the pieces of machinery or equipment required by a single project, such as the building of a dam or power plant, but can be an entire plant as well, which is being moved from a developed country, where its technology is outdated, to a developing country, where it will finish its useful life.[23] Project cargo also includes anything that requires some extra planning, such as the shipping of locomotives, railroad cars, large trucks, pleasure boats, large engines, electric generators, and so on.

In general, project cargo needs careful planning in order to reach its destination. The trucks used to transport it to the port need to trace their itineraries very carefully, not only to avoid low bridges and tunnels, but also to make sure that the proper permits can be secured. Port cranes have to be checked to make sure they can handle the load, or else floating cranes have to be rented. The ship carrying the cargo has to be selected carefully, to make sure it can accommodate the cargo. Roll-on/roll-off and lighter-aboard-ship barges are the most commonly used means of getting project cargoes to their port of destination. Finally, the final road trip has to be planned thoroughly as well. It is not unusual for such shipments to be planned more than a year in advance and to cost several million dollars because of their complexity.[24]

Such project cargo also moves quite slowly; it is difficult to make a 550,000-pound (249.5 metric tonnes) piece of equipment move quickly, especially when it involves using all lanes of a highway at once, or taking down and replacing all overhanging electric, telephone, and other utility wires.[25]

In late 2005, a 1.5-million-pound (680.4 metric tonne) hydro cracker for Canada's oil-sands project in Long Lake, Alberta (Canada), was moved by a heavy-lift ship to the Port of Duluth, Minnesota (U.S.). From the port, the unusual cargo traveled by rail on the world's largest rail car, the 36-axle German-made Schnabel car. The planning for the transportation of such a massive piece of equipment took two years. Ed Clarke, the logistician in charge of the move, said, "It's all about preplanning. At every step along the way you have to check weights, dimensions, clearances. And you have to know everything about the environment in which the equipment will be handled."[26] On a typical oversize, heavy-lift project, the logistics manager has a long list of items to check: the cargo itself, generally where it is manufactured; the docks and cargo-handling equipment (cranes) in the ports in which the cargo will be handled; the vessel on which the oversize piece will be shipped; the rail cars, the rails, and the bridges and tunnels along the trip; and even the rail beds on which the cargo will be hauled.

13-6 Alternative Means of Transportation

Despite the preponderance of the traditional means of transportation of ocean shipping, airfreight, trucking, and railroads for moving cargo internationally, a few alternative ways are used on a regular basis.

13-6a Pipelines

Probably the most easily overlooked of the alternative means of transportation are **pipelines**, which carry a substantial percentage of the world's petroleum oil and natural gas. Many of these pipelines are international. For example, Gazprom, the state-owned producer of gas in Russia, ships 525 billion cubic meters (18.5 trillion cubic feet) of gas to Europe in a single pipeline (see Figure 13-20), which meanders through Belarus, Ukraine, Poland, Slovakia, and the Czech Republic before stopping in Germany, and provides fully 20 percent of the European Union's gas needs.[27] A second pipeline is being planned. Many other pipelines crisscross the Persian Gulf area and the North American continent.

Pipelines can also be used to replace ships for some areas of the world where it is particularly hazardous to navigate. One such planned pipeline would allow oil shipped from the oil fields of southern Russia to bypass the Bosporus, a particularly congested area located in the middle of a very densely populated city, Istanbul. More than 50,000 ships travel its waters every year. The people of Istanbul and their government have been advocating such a pipeline, as they cannot control what goes through the strait—it is considered international waters—and they fear a catastrophic accident. Given the condition of some oil tankers, the treacheries of the currents in the narrow passage, and the fact that dozens of ships run aground or collide in the Bosporus every year,[28] it is not an unfounded fear. An oil and gas pipeline would remove some of this hazardous traffic.

Pipelines can be used for transporting coal as well, in the form of "slurry," a mix of water and pulverized coal that is then shipped as a liquid. Such a method can, in some cases, present some economic advantage over traditional railroad and truck transportation.

13-6b Barges

River **barges** are also commonly used to carry international cargo and are often significant sources of transportation services on certain routes and for certain

pipeline A mode of transportation consisting of a long series of pipes connected end-to-end, and used for the transport of some liquid cargo.

barge A flat-bottomed boat designed to carry cargo on rivers and canals and to be pushed or pulled.

Figure 13-20
The Russia-European Union Gas Pipeline
Source: Photo © Vladimir Kolobov. Used with permission.

merchandise. For example, 30 percent of all the containers shipped to and from Rotterdam, the ninth largest container seaport in the world—and the largest in Europe—travel by barge, with 57 percent traveling by truck and 13 percent traveling by rail.[29] The latter is a growing percentage, expected to increase with the European emphasis on low-emission means of transport. Much of the bulk cargo (ores, agricultural commodities, and petroleum-related products) travels by barges; 38 million metric tonnes traveled to and from the port by barge in 2008.[30]

More than one billion short tons (mostly commodities such as coal and grain) were carried on U.S. waterways in 2008,[31] mainly on the Mississippi and Ohio River networks. They can easily be delayed, though, by natural variations in the weather. Barges on the Mississippi River often have to wait when the river is in flood stage or when there is a drought, and the river is lower than normal. Although they are much slower, river barges offer a very economical alternative to trucks and railroads.

The barges on the North American rivers are not self-propelled. They are moved in groups of five to ten, pushed by a tugboat, and take considerable skill to maneuver (see Figure 13-21). The European and Asian barges (mostly in China) are most often self-propelled, with crews living aboard them (see Figure 13-22).

Ocean barges are also commonly used for shipping, although it is unclear how much of this mode of transportation is used for international shipping. Nevertheless, most of the traffic between the continental United States and Puerto Rico is done by barge, and so is some of the traffic with small Alaskan towns.

13-7 Ground Transportation Security

In the aftermath of the terrorist attacks of September 11, 2001, additional security efforts in ground transportation involved primarily thorough inspections by Customs and Immigration officials and other means of increased scrutiny. The strategies were similar in the European Union and in the United States.

Figure 13-21
A Barge on the Mississippi River
Source: Photo © Mike Willis. Used with permission.

Figure 13-22
A Self-Propelled Barge on the Seine River in Paris, France
Source: Photo © Pierre David.

At the U.S. border crossings, those increased inspection levels caused substantial additional delays, as there was relatively little capacity to increase the number of inspection stations. As mentioned in Chapter 3, there are only three large border crossings between the United States and Canada: (1) the Ambassador Bridge and a small tunnel between Detroit, Michigan, and Windsor, Ontario, with a combined 10 truck lanes of Customs clearance in the United States; (2) the Peace Bridge between Buffalo, New York, and Fort Erie, Ontario, with 3 Customs clearance truck lanes; and (3) the Lewiston-Queenston Bridge north of Niagara Falls, with 3 truck lanes. Altogether, these 16 truck lanes must clear about 15,000 trucks each day. That is an average of about two minutes per truck, and therefore any additional inspections beyond this very cursory review of paperwork causes delays. While there is a significantly larger number of land border crossings between the European Union and its external trading partners, as well as a smaller volume of international trade, the consequences of increased inspections were similar. Long delays and substantial frustrations were the norm at border crossings between the European Union and Albania, Belarus, Croatia, Macedonia, Russia, Serbia, Turkey, and Ukraine.

The United States and the European Union addressed these issues in similar fashion; in order to identify the shipments that could present risks, they required an advanced shipping notification of the manifest for the shipment. In the United States, since May 2008, the notification must be made at least one hour before the expected crossing of the border, and in electronic form through the Automated Commercial Environment (ACE).[32] For the European Union, since July 2009, the notification must be made two hours in advance and electronically as well.[33]

In addition, the United States implemented the Free and Secure Trade (FAST) program with Canada and Mexico, in which companies that are part of the Customs-Trade Partnership Against Terrorism (C-TPAT) can enroll. To recognize that these firms have implemented security measures in their supply chains, the U.S. Customs and Border Protection agency gives them access to a dedicated FAST lane at the border crossings, allowing them to clear Customs faster. It also allows them to send the manifest information as late as 30 minutes before crossing the border.[34] However, in order for a shipment to benefit from the FAST program, all parties involved in the transaction and the logistics of the shipment must be part of the FAST program, including the driver of the truck, who must possess a FAST card. As of April 2009, more than 90,000 commercial truck drivers had been cleared by U.S. Customs and Border Protection.[35]

Review and Discussion Questions

1. How different are the ground transport alternatives in different areas of the world? What constraints does a shipper face when shipping with ground transport?

2. What is the concept of a land bridge? What effect will such a concept have on the frequency of use of containers in shipping cargo?

3. Choose three different types of ocean containers and explain how they are used.

4. In what ways are oceangoing containers and aircraft containers different?

5. Comment on the opinion that "the number of cargo handling points is not diminished by the use of aircraft containers."

Endnotes

1. Mahieu, Yves, "Highlights of the Panorama of Transport," *Eurostat: Statistics in Focus*, European Statistical Agency, May 25, 2009, http://epp.eurostat.ec.europa.eu/cache/ITY_OFFPUB/KS-SF-09-042/EN/KS-SF-09-042-EN.PDF.

2. *Ibid.*

3. "Public Holidays with Traffic Bans," LKW Walter Transportation Company, http://www.lkw-walter.co.uk/en/driving_restrictions.aspx, accessed July 5, 2009.

4. Federal Office of Transport, "Sustainable Transport Policy: Benefiting Society, the Economy and the Environment," *Alp Transit Info*, May 2009, http://www.bav.admin.ch.

5. Dirnbauer, Franz, "The Rolling Road Has a Future Again!" *2008 UIRR Annual Report*, International Union of Combined Road-Rail Transport Companies, June 12, 2009, http://www.uirr.com/?action=page&page=47&title=N%2FP%2FA+CATEGORIES&categorie=1&year=2009&item=252.

6. Freight Transport Association, *Yearbook of Road Transport Law*. Tunbridge Wells, Kent, UK: Author.

7. Autostrada Wielkopolska, http://www.autostrada-a2.pl/en, accessed July 5, 2009.

8. Koenig, Robert, "Danes Planning to 'Flag Out' Their Trucks," *Journal of Commerce*, January 10, 2000, p. 3.

9. "Class I Railroad Statistics," Association of American Railroads, June 10, 2009, http://www.aar.org/~/media/AAR/Industry%20Info/Statistics20090610.ashx.

10. "Transport Trends—2007," *Statistics*, International Transport Forum, http://www.internationaltransportforum.org/statistics/trends/index.html#Freight_Transport, accessed July 5, 2009.

11. *Ibid.*

12. "The Year 2008 in Brief—Trends," *2008 UIRR Annual Report*, International Union of Combined Road-Rail Transport Companies, June 12, 2009, http://www.uirr.com/?action=page&page=47&title=N%2FP%2FA+CATEGORIES&categorie=1&year=2009&item=252, July 5, 2009.

13. "The Rail Freight Sector Needs EU Action Now!" *Railway Insider*, June 9, 2009, http://rinsider.clubferoviar.ro/en/afiseaza_stire.php?id=4202.

14. Lomazzi, Marc, "Le Train Passe la Grande Vitesse," *le MOCI [Moniteur du Commerce International]*, May 28, 1998, p. 31.

15. "Class I Railroad Statistics," Association of American Railroads, June 10, 2009, http://www.aar.org/~/media/AAR/Industry%20Info/Statistics20090610.ashx.

16. International Union of Railways, *The Northern East-West (N.E.W.) Freight Corridor*, Executive Project Office, Transporttutvikling AS, Narvik, 2004, http://www.transportutvikling.no/NEW_report_2004.pdf, accessed October 29, 2009.

17. *2009 IICL Annual Leased Container Fleet Survey*, Institute of International Container Lessors, June 8, 2009, http://www.iicl.org/PDF%20Docs/21st%20Container%20Fleet%20Survey.pdf.

18. Levinson, Marc, *The Box: How the Shipping Container Made the World Smaller and the World Economy Bigger*, Princeton University Press, Princeton, New Jersey, 2006.

19. Working, Russell, "Port Offers Shippers a Siberian Shortcut," *The New York Times*, December 3, 2000.

20. Witzsche, Rolf, "The Global Dimensions of the Eurasian Landbridge," http://www.rolf-witzsche.com/peace/landbridge/global-eurasian.html, accessed July 5, 2009.

21. *2008 Intermodal Market Trends and Statistics Report*, Intermodal Association of North America (IANA), http://www.intermodal.org/statistics_files/index.shtml, accessed July 5, 2009.

22. Edmonson, R.G., "Big Things from Small Rooms," *Journal of Commerce*, September 1, 2008, pp.26–27.

23. Baldwin, Tom, "Carriers Move the Immovable," *Journal of Commerce*, October 26, 1998, p. 1C.

24. *Ibid.*

25. Mathews, Anna Wilde, "Hauling Super Freight Takes Ingenuity and a Huge Rig," *Wall Street Journal*, April 13, 1998, p. B1.

26. Marciniak, Lisa, "Making the Big Jobs Look Easy" *North Star Port*, Duluth Seaway Port Authority, Winter 2005–2006 Issue.

27. Gubert, Romain, "Querelle de Gazoduc," *Le Point*, November 3, 2000, p. 25.

28. Moore, Molly, "Is the Bosporus Taking on More Than It Can Handle?" *International Herald Tribune*, November 17, 2000, p. 2.

29. *Port Statistics*, Port of Rotterdam, May 2009, http://www.portofrotterdam.com/mmfiles/Port_Statistics_2008_tcm26-60399.pdf.

30. "Hinterland Barge Statistics," *2008 Modalities*, Port of Amsterdam, http://www.portofamsterdam.nl/smartsite19897.dws, accessed July 6, 2009.

31. *The U.S. Waterway System—Transportation Facts*, December 2008, Navigation Data Center, U.S. Army Corps of Engineers, http://www.ndc.iwr.usace.army.mil/factcard/fc08/factcard.pdf.

32. United States Customs and Border Protection, *ACE Frequently Asked Questions*, June 2008, http://www.cbp.gov/linkhandler/cgov/trade/automated/modernization/ace/ace_faq.ctt/ace_faq.pdf.

33. European Commission Taxation and Customs Union, "General Overview," http://ec.europa.eu/taxation_customs/customs/security_amendment/general_overview/index_en.htm, accessed November 10, 2009.

34. United States Customs and Border Protection, "FAST: Free And Secure Trade Program," http://www.cbp.gov/xp/cgov/trade/cargo_security/ctpat/fast/, accessed November 10, 2009.

35. United States Customs and Border Protection, "FAST Driver Program," http://www.cbp.gov/xp/cgov/trade/cargo_security/ctpat/fast/fast_driver/, accessed November 10, 2009.

Packaging for Export

Chapter Fourteen

Key Terms

One of the challenging practical areas of international logistics is the packaging of goods for international shipment. This is a responsibility that always falls on the exporter, regardless of the terms of trade, or Incoterms, chosen (see Chapter 6). Unfortunately, it is a function that is oftentimes just left to the shipping department, with few guidelines other than to make sure it gets to the customers without problems, and quite often with pressures to control costs; there is rarely a strategy developed for packaging, even though it is an area that certainly has strategic implications.

This chapter makes distinctions between primary, secondary, and tertiary packaging, as seen in Figure 14-1. Primary packaging is consumer packaging, or what the consumers see when they purchase and handle the product. It is part of the marketing function of the firm and is traditionally covered in marketing management textbooks as part of the promotional efforts of the firm; primary packaging is only occasionally mentioned in this chapter. Secondary packaging is the packaging that usually groups several of the consumer goods into one unit. It is made up of one of two alternatives:

- The first is a cardboard box. Since the term used more frequently in the industry is **corrugated paperboard box**, it will be the one used in this chapter. Paperboard is categorized on several criteria, including thickness, the type of flutes used—the way the layer of paper sandwiched between the faces of the board is folded—and the number of layers: Paperboard is available in single-, double-, and triple-wall versions.

- The second is a plastic wrap that is either stretched (stretch-wrap) or heat-shrunk (shrink-wrap) over several units of the primary package. The purpose of either method is to consolidate multiple units into one and to protect them from water. The two techniques differ in the thickness of the wrap, with shrink-wrap generally much thicker than stretch-wrap, and much more resistant to multiple handlings. The term "shrink-wrap," whenever used in this chapter, will refer to either of these two techniques.

> **corrugated paperboard box**
> A type of box made of paper fibers in which two flat sheets are glued to both sides of a "wall" made of a sinusoidally shaped sheet.

Secondary packaging is what the retailer sees and handles before the goods are placed on the shelves. In discount retail stores, this secondary packaging may be seen by the consumer.

Tertiary packaging, or transportation packaging, includes all of the additional protection given to the goods to ensure their safe and efficient delivery, in sound condition, at the lowest possible cost, to their foreign purchaser.[1] Tertiary packaging for consumer goods is therefore the packaging placed around the secondary retail packaging units. For industrial goods, because there is generally no primary or secondary packaging of the products, the tertiary packaging encompasses all the packaging activities aimed at protecting them during shipment.

> **FIGURE 14-1** | Primary, Secondary, and Tertiary Packaging

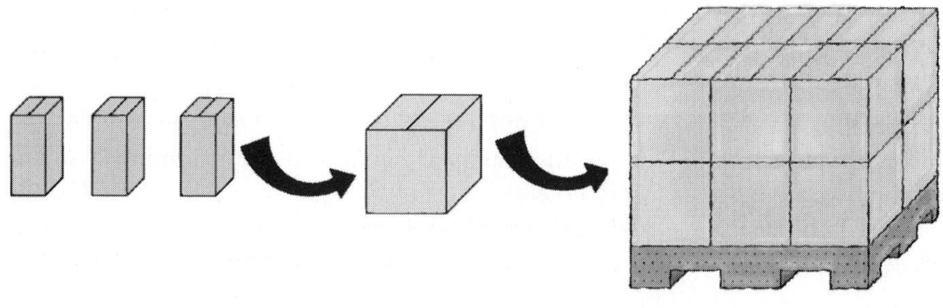

Source: Diagram courtesy of Jeff Post and Bob Iben. Used with permission.

14-1 Packaging Functions

The first function of correct packaging for export is obviously the protection of the goods from the hazards of international shipping by ocean or by air. Proper packaging has direct cost implications. On one hand, it is certain that the costs of packaging generally increase as the protection of the goods increases; however, on the other hand, the costs of losing part of the cargo to **improper packaging** are generally much higher[2] and cannot be insured against (see Chapter 10, Section 10-8 for further details), and no real trade-off exists. It is generally in the best interest of the exporter to ensure that goods are properly packaged so that they arrive undamaged to their destination. This chapter will expand on this aspect of packaging, explaining the alternatives available and their advantages and disadvantages.

The second function of correct packaging is to facilitate the handling of goods while they are in transit; well-designed packaging will allow the stevedores, the shipping line, and the trucking companies to handle the goods without difficulties, but mostly without having to improvise an inappropriate handling method. The capabilities of the equipment likely to be used in the handling of the goods must be respected (i.e., the dimensional constraints and weight constraints they place on the package, as well as the different standards and regulations used in the countries through which the goods will travel). Finally, all the handling and care instructions must be clearly marked on the package.

The third function of correct packaging, and one that is often overlooked, is that it is part of the customer service strategy of the firm. While a customer expects to receive the goods in sellable or usable condition in all cases, it also expects to be able to quickly unpack the goods and not spend considerable time and money preparing them to be used or sold. This objective is often much more difficult to achieve than just protecting the goods for transport and facilitating their handling while in transit. The packaging has to be simple enough to be opened without using specialized tools or exerting much effort, but most of all, it has to be designed so that it can be opened without damaging the goods. To a great extent, the packaging used by a firm should also reflect the image it is trying to project to customers. A well-conceived and well-constructed package is a positive reflection on the ability of a company to manufacture quality products. Similarly, more and more customers are sensitive to a packaging alternative that is easily reused or placed in the waste stream. In some cases, it is legally mandatory.

14-2 Packaging Objectives

The objective of proper packaging is to make sure that goods are protected from the three major losses that can occur in international transit:

1. Protecting the goods from mechanical damage: breakage, crushes, nicks, and dents (these perils represent roughly 43 percent of all claims made by shippers to their insurance companies)[3]
2. Protecting the goods from water damage: seawater, rain, floods, and container sweat (15 percent of claims made)
3. Protecting the goods from theft and pilferage (21 percent of claims made)

The remaining 21 percent of the claims are linked to fire, strandings, sinkings, collision, overboard losses, and jettison.

Each of these perils can be prevented to a great extent by the proper use of packaging techniques and by the correct design of the protective systems around the cargo.

However, that's not all: Another objective of packaging is to provide good customer service to the recipient of the goods. This is achieved by paying attention to

improper packaging The lack of appropriate packaging materials for an international shipment. The determination is oftentimes made by an insurance company when it refuses to pay a damage claim that it considers avoidable had proper packaging procedures been followed.

the smaller details of the packaging process and designing a "smarter" package. While it is difficult to give specific guidance, a few examples may illustrate the concept better:

- Instead of gluing—and then nailing—the plywood panels onto a crate, a customer-focused exporter would just nail them or, even better, screw them, so that they can be more easily taken apart by the receiving department of the importer. The boards can then be reused internally by the importer or by its employees rather than discarded. An exporter shipping to countries where packaging materials may end up as housing materials would be even more responsive if it considered using a slightly better grade of boards and plywood, and making sure that they have been heat-treated rather than fumigated with chemicals.

- Another way of displaying customer focus would be to include a packaging list in the recipient's language and to clearly mark all of the packages within a shipment; for example, by color-coding or letter-coding each pallet and its corresponding manifest.

- Yet another way of showing customer concern is to utilize unitized packages that match the size of the ones used by the customer, so that goods can be placed directly in its warehouse, without having to be reloaded onto the proper pallet size.

While it takes only a few extra minutes (and only a bit more money) to pack a shipment "smarter," the importer will appreciate the attention; it may actually become a strategic advantage over a competitor whose shipping department is inattentive to details. In addition, it helps prevent claims of shortages when the customer cannot locate items within a shipment.

Finally, packaging should reflect the increasing sensitivity to recycling and energy conservation present in many countries. The focus in this case should be for the exporter to use recyclable and reusable materials rather than disposable materials; for example, it should use starch "peanuts" (packaging pellets) or recycled paper cubes rather than Styrofoam,[4] or inflatable dunnage rather than scrap pallets, and it should load the goods on pallets of the size used by the customer.

14-3 Ocean Cargo

Ocean cargo can be shipped using a large number of alternative packaging alternatives. Because an increasing percentage of cargo shipped by ocean is now containerized, this particular mode will be covered first, followed by break-bulk cargo and its packaging alternatives.

14-3a Full-Container-Load (FCL) Cargo

While it is true that containers protect the cargo well against most damages, the choice of the proper container is important when shipping a **full-container-load (FCL)** shipment. An FCL shipment utilizes the entire capacity of a container, whether by weight or by volume.

Choice of Container

After having determined the correct type of container (see Chapter 13, Section 13-3a) in which the cargo will be shipped, the exporter should, as much as possible, inspect the container for a particular shipment. It is particularly important if the cargo to be placed inside will not be unitized on pallets or in crates, but will simply be placed in corrugated paperboard boxes or in their retail packaging.

The container should first be inspected from the outside for possible structural damage: A structurally unsound container could collapse under the weight of the several containers that will eventually be placed on top of it. Containers are designed to withstand the weight of up to eight other containers; a slight structural problem

full-container-load (FCL) A shipment whose volume and weight are close to the volume and weight limits of a container or for which the shipper requests that it be the only cargo in a container.

could weaken it enough to collapse under this kind of weight and a heavy sea. Hundreds of them do every year. The frame should look straight, the fittings used for lifting it and securing it on the ship or on a truck should be in place and not damaged, the doors should close properly, the repairs—if any—should appear to have been done competently, and there should be no visible structural rust. Surface rust is not pretty, but it usually does not affect the cargo carried; nevertheless, it may be a sign that the container is not very carefully maintained.

The container should also be inspected from the inside, with the doors closed, for possible light "leakage," which would indicate a water infiltration risk during shipment. Sometimes, such leakage also indicates a structural problem. The container should have a wooden floor (plywood sheathing) and ideally wooden sides as well, so as to prevent condensation damage inside the container (container "sweat") and protect the cargo from direct contact with the metal sides. The container should also have all of its inside hardware in place (tie-down rings and cleats), to allow for good securing of the cargo. The container should be inspected for foul and persistent odors. Several cargoes have been damaged by the content of a preceding shipment. Protruding nails or other fasteners should be removed to prevent an accidental puncture to the cargo. Finally, the container should be clean of grease, dirt, and other foreign material so as to keep the cargo clean.[5]

Palletization

pallet A platform of wood or plastic on which the goods are placed. The pallet allows the use of mechanical equipment to move the merchandise as a unit. Goods shipped on pallets are also called unitized packages.

It is always better for goods in a shipment to be unitized (assembled in a single larger unit) so that they can be manipulated more efficiently by using a forklift or other means of material handling. This can be done by placing the goods on **pallets**, or by building boxes in which they are placed. In either case, the unitized package includes one more layer of protection for the goods, which is better than when they are left in their original secondary package, which is often only some corrugated paperboard boxes.

The fact that the goods are placed on pallets and shrink-wrapped protects them better from water infiltration (by placing them off the floor) and from condensation in the container. It also facilitates handling and protects the goods once they have arrived at the customer's warehouse; the lower the likelihood that the goods are manipulated by hand, the greater the probability that they will be unloaded in good condition. Unitizing prevents the primary package from being crushed and therefore allows the goods to be immediately sellable; in those cases where the boxes have cosmetic damage, it is costly to repackage the goods into a new box, and therefore it is generally much cheaper to properly unitize them. Some shippers will include additional empty boxes, so that the goods can be re-packaged by the customer, if the boxes are damaged. This is a way to overcome the problem, but it is best to prevent it.

Another advantage of a palletized unit is that the secondary packaging may then be sufficient to protect the goods, as long as the pallets are protected on the corners, as seen in Figure 14-2, and the pallets are properly stacked by adding a rigid support between the lower and upper pallets. This support could be heavy corrugated multi-wall paperboard or plywood.

When unitizing the boxes onto pallets, there is another issue to take into consideration: Most pallets are built by alternating the boxes so that they constitute a "brick" pattern, as such patterns are generally believed to be stronger (see Figure 14-2). However, the stronger parts of the boxes are their corners, and therefore corners should support most of the weight of the boxes on top of them. By alternating corners, as in a brick pattern, the weaker part of the box supports the greatest weight. Such a pattern results in a greater likelihood of crushed boxes and therefore should be avoided. It is generally better to build pallets in columns, where boxes fit directly on top of one another, as such a practice results in fewer crushed or damaged boxes (see Figure 14-3).* Goods that are shipped in corrugated boxes that are not protected

---

* The authors are indebted to Professor Bud Cohan from Columbus State Community College for this point.

Figure 14-2
A Unitized, Stretch-Wrapped Pallet with Its Four Corners Protected
Source: Photo © Pierre David.

with reinforced corners or held together with stretch or shrink-wrap are much more likely to be damaged in shipment (see Figure 14-4).

Although unitized cargo is preferable, it can also present challenges. For one, the standardized size of pallets in Europe has been 80 × 120 centimeters (31.5 × 47.25 inches) since 1959. Pallet sizes in the United States are, for all intents and purposes, not standardized, even though a great percentage of them are 36 × 48 inches (91.5 × 122 centimeters). This presents difficulties, as pallets of one standard do not fit neatly into containers designed for the other. In addition, there are problems when boxes that were designed to "cover" a pallet's footprint do not conveniently fill another size; for example, a European exporter may have boxes that have a base of 40 × 40 centimeters, and while such boxes fit nicely on a European pallet, they leave a good portion of a U.S. 36-inch pallet unused. Unfortunately, a dimension that is compatible with both standards is a difficult compromise.

Non-unitized Cargo

If the goods inside the container are not unitized, for whatever reason, it is preferable that they be somewhat protected from crushing and moisture by being packaged in a higher grade of corrugated paperboard, double- or triple-walled; regular secondary packaging is generally insufficient and its use should be avoided. If the goods are to be stacked, layers of strong corrugated paperboard or sheets of plywood should be used in-between the layers to protect the lower levels from collapsing and to prevent

Figure 14-3
A Pallet with Goods Placed in Columns, for Reduced Risk of Damage
Source: Photo © Jamie Serenko. Used with permission.

crushed boxes. If the goods are to be shipped from (or to) a high-humidity area, a layer of plywood on the floor of the container or a layer of pallets should be considered. In addition, paperboard should be avoided as much as possible, as it loses up to 60 percent of its strength under those humid conditions.[6] Figure 10-5 in Chapter 10 illustrates the differences in relative humidity levels for an ocean container shipment from China to the United States.

Blocking Materials

When loading a container, it would be ideal if the goods could fill out the space as completely as possible, leaving no room for the cargo to shift. Unfortunately, that is generally unrealistic. Therefore, a number of blocking materials have been developed, collectively called **dunnage**.

dunnage Packaging material designed to prevent the cargo from moving while in transit.

The first method is to secure the goods to the container itself, if that is possible. This is normally done with hooks and straps, or wood braces, a system that is particularly good at keeping the cargo from moving inside the container (see Figure 14-5).

The second is to insert some sort of "spacer" in-between the pallets or the packages. Some companies use old pallets, some use bracing contraptions made with wooden beams (in American measurements, "4 by 4s," which measure 3.5×3.5 inches, or roughly 9×9 centimeters), and some use inflatable bags (see Figure 14-6). Before closing the door of the container, similar bracing material must be inserted between the cargo and the door to prevent shifting. Insurance claim handlers "frequently come across cargo poorly secured in a container, perhaps because void spaces are not filled, or because heavier items are not lashed down."[7] As a reminder,

Figure 14-4
A Pallet with Unprotected Corrugated Boxes Can Result in Crushed Boxes
Source: Photo © Pierre David.

insurance policies do not cover claims for improperly packaged cargo (see Chapter 10, Section 10-8).

The critical part is that the entire floor space in the container must be occupied, so that none of the cargo may move. However heavy the cargo may be, it will move and eventually be damaged if it is not braced securely. The costs of replacing damaged cargo will undoubtedly exceed whatever savings there were in not using proper dunnage.

Loading the Container
If there are different types of goods to be placed in the same container, the heavier ones should always be placed on the bottom to lower the center of gravity of the load. Similarly, great care should be taken to make sure that the center of gravity is somewhat in the center of the container. This is achieved by making sure that the goods are loaded in symmetrical fashion in the container and that the blocking material is placed between the goods, as shown in Figure 14-6. Many software packages have been designed to help exporters load mixed cargoes into containers in the most efficient manner, accounting for their volume and weight.

Figure 14-5
A Unitized Cargo Load in a Container, Correctly Braced for an Ocean Voyage
Source: Photo © Robert Crallé, Chick Packaging. Used with permission.

Figure 14-6
A Container with Inflatable Dunnage in the Center
Source: Photo © Robert Crallé, Chick Packaging. Used with permission.

14-3b Less-than-Container-Load (LCL) Cargo

Single shipments that are too small to be shipped as full containers, called **less-than-container-load (LCL)** shipments, are consolidated by a freight forwarder or a Non-Vessel-Operating Common Carrier (NVOCC) with other freight and then shipped

less-than-container-load (LCL) A shipment which volume and weight that are below the capacity of a container and for which the shipper does not request that it be the only cargo in a container.

in a full container. Because of the greater number of instances during which the freight is handled, it is mandatory that these goods be unitized on a pallet or placed in a crate or box, as well as extremely well protected from water damage. Because the nature of the freight with which the shipment is placed is never known, the greatest amount of care should be exercised in packaging such goods. In addition to the risks normally associated with a shipment by ocean, there is also the possibility of damage caused by other cargo in the container; a heavy load can inadvertently be placed on top of the pallet, or another can be poorly braced in the container and move in heavy seas. An LCL shipment can also be subjected to other cargo's leakage, odors, and other hazards. Although the consolidator is almost always quite good at packaging a container properly, with proper dunnage and protection, the owners of other cargo on board the consolidated container may not be as careful, and that represents a hazard.

14-3c Break-Bulk Cargo

Break-bulk cargo is cargo that cannot be containerized because it is too large and won't fit in a traditional container or because it exceeds the maximum weight of a container load. Great efforts have been expended to containerize as much cargo as possible, with the creation of special container sizes (see Chapter 13, Section 13-3a). However, a substantial proportion of cargo is still shipped as break-bulk.

Break-bulk cargo is placed directly in the hold of the ship and therefore has to be packaged differently than containerized cargo, which enjoys the all-around protection of the metal box. In addition, break-bulk cargo (in its tertiary packaging) is handled more frequently than containerized cargo; for example, it is loaded onto a truck or rail car on its way to the port, then unloaded in the port, loaded onto the ship, unloaded from the ship, and so on. Therefore, break-bulk cargo should be packed in such a way as to be well protected to reflect both the rigors of the journey and the extra handling.

Finally, the company responsible for shipping break-bulk cargo should ensure that the weight and dimensions of the cargo can be handled by all the facilities through which the cargo will travel; if the break-bulk cargo weighs more than the maximum capacity crane in a given port, an alternative route should be found, or arrangements should be made to rent specialized or larger equipment. If the cargo's weight exceeds the port cranes' capacity, there is a great risk that the break-bulk cargo will be taken out of its crate and dismantled so that it can be handled by the port's equipment. There is also the risk that the port personnel will try to move the cargo with the existing equipment (using it beyond its rated capacity) and damage the cargo in the process. Cigna Insurance Company publishes a guide to the equipment in place in all the ports worldwide, called *Ports of the World*,[8] so that a firm may plan the size of its shipment accordingly. Very heavy and cumbersome cargo, called "project cargo" is usually handled by specialized freight forwarders (see Chapter 13, Section 13-5) that have an excellent knowledge of all of these limitations.

Crates and Boxes

Crates and boxes—as shown in Figures 14-7 and 14-8—are very appropriate containers for either break-bulk cargo or LCL cargo to be handed to a freight consolidator. The crate or box should be built in a size that accommodates the goods without allowing them to shift. It should be very solidly built and be reinforced at those points where the crate is likely to be lifted. If the cargo needs to be kept in an upright position, the best alternative is to mount the box or crate on a pallet or to equip it with hooks or straps that allow the goods to be handled in only one direction. In order to gather evidence of mishandling, it is often a good idea to include (inside as well as outside of a box or crate) a device that records whether a shipment was handled too roughly or whether it was not kept upright during handling (See Figure 14-9).

Boxes and crates are built somewhat differently. While boxes are containers made of wood where the sides are an integral part of the structure of the container

break-bulk cargo Cargo that is unitized in a box or crate which is placed directly into the hold of a ship. It is generally too large or too heavy to be placed in a container.

crate A wooden box made especially for a product to be shipped break-bulk because it does not fit into a container, or because the exporter deems that an additional level of protection is necessary.

Figure 14-7
Loading an Oversized Box
Source: Photo © Robert Crallé, Chick Packaging. Used with permission.

Figure 14-8
An Open Crate, with Corner Reinforcements, Strapped to a Flat Rack
Source: Photo © Pierre David.

(see Figure 14-7), crates are containers built on a wooden frame and are either open or enclosed with plywood (see Figure 14-8). In general terms, well-built crates are stronger than boxes, because the wood used for the frame of the crate is of a larger size. Well-built crates are constructed with three-way corners (see Figure 14-9), which is the strongest possible corner design. Unfortunately, this technique appears to be an "art" that is disappearing, although it makes a substantial difference in the ability of the crate to resist shocks and crushing. Both crates and boxes should always be reinforced with corner strapping and with metallic bands (see Figure 14-10).

> **FIGURE 14-9**   The Three-Way Corner Design

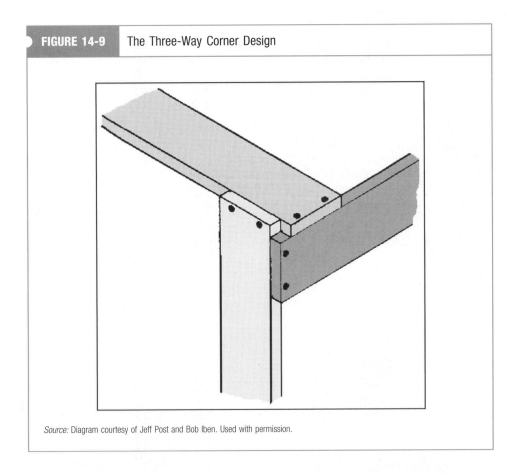

Source: Diagram courtesy of Jeff Post and Bob Iben. Used with permission.

Figure 14-10
A Well-Designed Box, Reinforced with Metal Bands
Source: Photo © Robert Crallé, Chick Packaging. Used with permission.

Open crates are obviously not appropriate for cargo that is not impervious to water. Boxes and enclosed crates protecting a shipment that is sensitive to water or moisture should be lined with a waterproof material such as polyethylene. Some packaging specialists prefer leaving the bottom of the boxes and crates free of waterproof

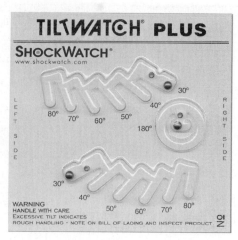

Figure 14-11
Two Means of Recording the Way a Box Was Handled in Transit
Source: Photo © Shockwatch Corporation. Used with permission.

material, while others prefer placing small holes in it to allow drainage should some water infiltration occur. To further protect crated machinery and metallic parts from water damage, it is common practice to simply spray them with oil before placing them in crates.

Since some crates and boxes are light enough to be handled by hand and are likely to be manipulated many times during an international shipment, they are sometimes mishandled despite the instructions of the shipper and the markings that they display. It is sometimes wise to determine whether rough handling occurred, and several monitoring systems have been designed to that effect. Figure 14-11 shows two such systems, one monitoring whether the goods were subjected to shocks, the other whether they were kept upright during the shipment.

Bags

Bags can also be used to transport break-bulk merchandise. The multi-wall shipping bag (which can hold around 50 pounds [25 kilograms]) is designed to be used with chemicals, plastics, and other powdered materials that are somewhat unaffected by water and unlikely to be pilfered.

The bag is made up of several layers of kraft paper and/or light polymers, and is not very good at withstanding numerous manipulations. It is recommended to add about 3 percent additional empty, slightly larger bags to contain those bags that may be damaged during an international shipment.[9] Shipping bags are quite sensitive to rough handling by dockhands (see Figure 14-12), including damage by accidental contact with mechanical equipment or other cargo with sharp angles such as boxes, crates, or pallets. The integrity of these bags is increased by palletizing and shrink-wrapping them, because mechanical equipment must then be used to handle them.

The second type of bag is a very large bag called a **flexible intermediate bulk container (FIBC)**. FIBCs are constructed of woven polymer fibers, such as polyethylene or polypropylene (see Figure 14-13). They are usually of a capacity of about 1 cubic meter and can weigh up to 1 metric tonne, but many different sizes and types exist. They are used for transporting granular cargo, such as plastics, grains, and chemicals.

Drums

Drums are used in three forms: metallic drums (steel drums), polymer drums, and fiber drums. Steel drums, shown in Figure 14-14, can be used for wet or dry cargo, and are pretty resilient containers that can withstand a good amount of abuse. They

flexible intermediate bulk container (FIBC) A type of large-capacity woven bag designed to unitize goods that would otherwise be carried as dry bulk.

Figure 14-12
Bags of Wheat Being Loaded in Port Sudan, the Sudan
Source: Photo © USAID. Used with permission.

Figure 14-13
Flexible Intermediate Bulk Containers
Source: Photo © Codefine®. Used with permission.

present great resistance to water damage and pilferage and have been used for a long time in ocean shipping. Their main disadvantage is their cost and their individual weight. Polymer drums, also shown in Figure 14-14, present the advantage of being able to carry liquid and wet cargo, but they are much less resistant to rough handling.

Figure 14-14
Three Different Types of Drums: Steel, Polymer, and Fiber
Source: Photo © Pierre David.

They should be palletized to minimize damage. Finally, fiber drums, also shown in Figure 14-14, can be used for only dry cargo, such as plastic pellets or fertilizers. They are usually lined with a polymer bag to contain the cargo.

Fiber drums are slightly more resistant to water damage than bags and are more resistant to pilferage. However, they are often damaged when port personnel handle them in the same manner as they do steel drums, such as rolling them on their sides, a practice for which they are not designed. Fiber drums are also somewhat sensitive to mechanical damage, such as that caused by careless forklift truck drivers or sharp corners.

14-3d Wood Requirements

Since March 2005, all wood products used in packaging or dunnage must conform to International Phytosanitary Measure 15, a convention that was signed by 144 countries and which is designed to further prevent the threat of wood pests, specifically the Asian long-horned beetle that attacked hardwood forests in North America and Europe, and the North American pinewood nematode, which attacked softwood forests in Europe and Asia. All wood products used in international trade must be marked with the **International Plant Protection Convention (IPPC)** symbol or face heavy fines.

The IPPC mark identifies the country in which the wood product was treated with the first two letters. Figure 14-15 shows several examples. The marking also identifies the plant at which the process was conducted with an alphanumeric code. Finally, the process used in treating the product is identified; for example, HT means that the wood was heat-treated, and MB means that the product was treated with methyl bromide. These are the only two allowable treatments to date, and although MB is a gas that the U.S. Environmental Protection Agency phased out in 2007, it continues allowing its use for IPPC purposes.[10] Three other abbreviations are used in Figure 14-15: DB stands for "debarked," and KD for "kiln-dried," which are used in many countries. The British IPPC mark also includes the abbreviation FC for the British Forestry Commission. Any wood product that has been marked with the IPPC symbol can be reused indefinitely in the international supply chain.

14-3e Markings

There are two reasons to properly mark the cargo as it is shipped: It has to be protected from poor handling, and it has to be protected from theft and pilferage.

To protect the cargo from poor handling, it is necessary to use as many of the international pictorials for cargo handling as are relevant. A number of these pictorials, as standardized by the International Organization for Standardization (ISO), are shown

International Plant Protection Convention (IPPC) An international convention, which 144 countries have ratified, that mandates that wood used for packing or dunnage be heat-treated or treated with chemicals to prevent insect infestations.

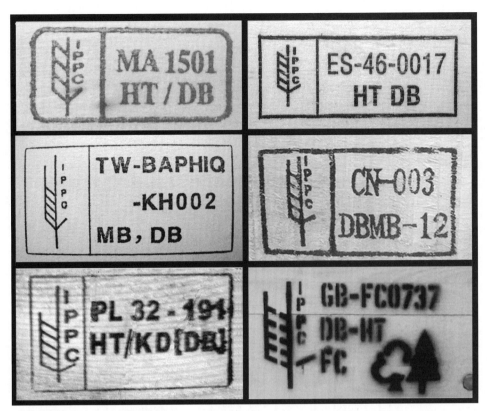

Figure 14-15
International Plant Protection Convention Marks on Several Wood Products, from Morocco, Spain, Taiwan, China, Poland, and Great Britain
Source: Photo © Pierre David.

in Figure 14-16. If at all possible, they should be accompanied by their translations in the languages of the ports through which the cargo is expected to transit. Both the net weight (the weight of the cargo alone) and the gross weight (the cargo plus the weight of the packaging) should be clearly displayed in metric units and so-called English units on the outside of the package. The outside dimensions of the goods should also be clearly displayed, both in English and in metric units. This is to prevent, as much as possible, inappropriate equipment from handling the goods at any point.

To protect break-bulk or LCL cargo from being lost or shipped to the wrong consignee, it should be clearly marked with the consignee's name—the name of the company that will pick it up at the port of the destination—as well as the shipment number. It is always a good idea to write that information on several of the sides of the load; that way, the information is never hidden from view. If at all possible, the name of the consignee should not include information that could indicate the brand or the type of the goods in the shipment, for security reasons. Such markings only increase the probability of theft or pilferage.

All the units belonging to the same shipment should be marked as such, that is, as "1 of 4," "2 of 4," and so on. Another useful practice is to mark all the units in a given shipment with a particular color—for example, on the corners of the boxes—so that they are clearly designated as parts of one shipment and so that none of them are left behind. The temptation to use a color associated with a particular company should be avoided, however, to prevent jeopardizing the firm's security efforts. For the same reason, the color should be changed regularly.

There are a number of alternatives meant to determine whether a shipment has been the victim of theft. Some shippers paint the outside of their shipments with a uniform color in order to determine whether a shipment has been tampered with. Some use shipping tape of a specific design—while avoiding using a tape marked with

Figure 14-16
International Handling Pictorials
Source: International Organization for Standards, ISO 780-1997.

their company logo—and others use a shrink-wrap of a particular color. All of these attempts have the added benefit of keeping the shipment "uniform" and therefore clearly identifiable.

Finally, it should be reiterated that markings that reveal the identity of the shipper and/or the content of the package should be avoided at all costs. "Advertising" to potential thieves the content of the cargo is foolish and can only lead to problems. Many companies use codes rather than brand markings to identify their shipments and change the code on a regular basis, without patterns, in an attempt to avoid security problems.

14-4 Air Transport

Because air transport is, by nature, less hazardous than ocean transport, packaging as a protection against damage is of lesser importance. Nevertheless, some perils still exist, such as water condensation and air pressure changes; still, the biggest problem for air cargo, by far, is theft and pilferage.

14-4a Containers

Containers used in air transport (see Figure 13-19 in Chapter 13) are much different than the ones used in ocean cargo and are not intermodal (i.e., they cannot be used conveniently in other modes of transportation, with the possible exception of one size: a 20-foot container that can be used in cargo planes and on trucks). The consequence of this situation is that cargo is usually placed (consolidated) in containers at the airport of departure, then manipulated again at the airport of arrival and placed into trucks. This additional handling should be taken into consideration when packaging goods for export by air. It is also likely that the goods will be unloaded from a container and reloaded into another at a connecting airport.

Containers used in air transport are lightweight, made of wood, Plexiglas, or aluminum, and are generally clean. As some containers are not fully enclosed, or are enclosed with netting rather than solid walls, some damage may occur in the voyage when cargo shifts. Nevertheless, most damage occurs in the handling before and after the flight; for example, while the container waits on the tarmac, the goods in the container could easily become wet from rain or snow. Such exposure should be considered when deciding on a proper package.

14-4b Packaging Materials

While most air cargo tends to be shipped by air in its secondary packaging, it is generally not an appropriate method for two reasons:

- Secondary packaging is not sufficient to protect the goods from the hazards of manipulation before and after the flight. In many cases, the airline operates on a "hub-and-spoke" model, and the goods are unloaded and manipulated at one or more hub airports. Goods in secondary packaging can be tossed by airport personnel, and boxes can fall from conveyor belts traveling at very high speeds (30 miles [45 kilometers] per hour).

- Secondary packaging often includes markings including the brand name of the goods, as well as model numbers and/or illustrations, which make them very tempting targets for thieves.

Appropriate shipping packaging would therefore be tertiary in nature and include one additional layer of corrugated paperboard, preferably double-walled, and a shrink-wrap. The United Nations established rules regarding the resistance of air packages to drops and crushes, especially for dangerous goods; these minimum requirements were last updated in 2007.[11] Nevertheless, a number of shippers still do not follow these rules.

For shipments that are fragile, the best strategy is to use a box within a box; the primary package is placed in a much larger box, which is then filled with packing material around the smaller, fragile product. While this is relatively simple, the cost of packaging in such a way can be substantial, as airlines charge a shipper on the higher of two alternatives; the actual weight of the product or its "volume-weight," which is a weight calculated on the basis of the volume of the shipment. There can therefore be a substantial cost to using a box that is slightly too large.

For cargo sensitive to humidity, a possible way of avoiding condensation damage is to add small packets of desiccant material in the box with the goods, as they are designed to absorb ambient humidity. An additional layer of shrink-wrap is always advisable, as well, to protect against other condensation, rain, or leakage caused by other cargo on the plane.

For shipments susceptible to leakage if its primary packaging breaks, such as glass or plastic bottles, the U.S. Federal Aviation Administration regulations (and United Nations rules) require that the secondary or tertiary package be capable of containing an accidental leak. Most secondary packaging is not designed for such a contingency, so adequate additional absorbent material must be packed with the goods. Importantly, the risks associated with improper packaging resulting in a leak in an aircraft are substantial: Violations of the U.S. regulations call for up to five years in prison and a U.S. $250,000 fine.[12]

14-4c Markings

Markings in international air shipments should be handled in much the same way as markings on ocean shipments. The use of the pictorials shown in Figure 14-16 is recommended.

14-5 Road and Rail Transport

In the case of international road and rail transportation, a policy of protecting the cargo in much the same way as for shipment by ocean container is most appropriate. It is always best to unitize the cargo into pallets so as to facilitate handling at the point where the goods are loaded and unloaded. The cargo pallets should be protected on all four corners, banded with nylon or steel straps, and shrink-wrapped for protection against rain and ambient humidity. As much as possible, the cargo should be blocked and braced in the truck trailer and, if applicable, in the railroad car to avoid all damage due to the cargo shifting and sudden accelerations and decelerations. Railroad companies issue very specific rules regarding the bracing of cargo in containers or truck trailers that will be carried on railroads; in particular, they mandate a very strong bracing of the cargo[13] to prevent stress against the container or trailer doors (see Figure 14-17).

Domestic shipments in the United States are almost all by truck or rail; the cargo is loaded onto a trailer that is then either driven to its destination or loaded on a railroad car (piggy-backed) to an intermediary destination and then driven to its final destination. From 1996 to 1999, the costs of goods damaged in transportation rose from U.S. $3.3 billion to U.S. $4 billion, or from 0.75 percent to 0.96 percent of gross domestic sales, according to the Grocery Manufacturers Association. Such costs increased to 1.13 percent in 2004, but decreased to 1.04 percent in 2005 and to less than 1 percent in 2007.[14] The primary cause of the decrease was attributed to "improvements in packaging."

Should the cargo be sensitive to theft, it should also be packed in unmarked boxes to prevent the possibility of pilferage.

Figure 14-17
Container Cargo Braced for Railroad Transport
Source: Photo © Robert Crallé, Chick Packaging. Used with permission.

Shipping Computers to China

The Chinese market for personal computers has always appeared very attractive to U.S. corporations because of the vast potential for sales it represents. However, there have been many difficulties for the companies involved in manufacturing personal computers in China: Compaq found that some of its distributors did not honor their debts, and AST found that many of the computer units it exported to Hong Kong were smuggled back into the United States.

IBM, meanwhile, faced charges that it was selling used machines when it was actually shipping brand new products. It turns out that the confusion arose over a packaging problem: The computers were wrapped in two layers of plastic and then shipped in paperboard boxes. However, this was not enough to protect them from the pervasive dust that floats around many Chinese cities—Beijing in particular—and the goods arrived dirty in the consumers' hands. An additional layer of shrink-wrap on the paperboard retail package solved the problem.

This was in addition to the many other problems that packaging has to solve in China. A large percentage of personal computers are delivered to their final destinations strapped on the luggage racks of bicycles (see Figure 14-18), and most deliveries to retailers and wholesalers are made in flatbed trucks, barely protected from the elements by a tarpaulin. As for units shipped to

distant cities, they go by railroads. Extremely sturdy packaging should be used in this case, as an IBM manager observed, "the [cargo handlers] virtually throw[ing] computer] cartons into trains."[15]

Figure 14-18
Computers Delivered on Bicycles in China
Source: Photo © Hui Lu. Used with permission.

14-6 Security

The issue of theft and pilferage is becoming an increasing problem for cargo shippers. It is estimated that cargo theft represents losses of at least U.S. $10 billion per year in the United States,[16] €8 billion in the European Union,[17] and more than U.S. $40 billion worldwide. The problem is that there is very little reliable data on the incidence of this type of crime, but it is a substantial concern to international shippers. Many methods have been developed to foil theft attempts against cargo; unfortunately, none has proven completely effective, but a combination of several should cover most shippers and prevent theft and pilferage.

As much as possible, the cargo should not bear the name of the shipper, especially if it is a brand that has street appeal; this issue is crucial for goods that are shipped in their secondary packaging and for which the primary packaging and the secondary packaging are one and the same, as for electronics or appliances. Such a practice jeopardizes the safety of the cargo. A possible way to prevent this problem would be to ship exclusively in full container loads (FCLs) or full truck loads (FTLs), so as to hide the cargo from anyone other than the exporter or the importer. Another is to place the goods in an additional blank paperboard box, which would be recommended for goods shipped as LCL or less-than-truck load (LTL) goods, to protect them from handling damage.

A plethora of different methods exists to place **seals** on containers, and all present advantages and disadvantages; however, all show whether the container has been opened. One critical aspect of seals is that the seal number should be written on the intermodal bill of lading so that the importer can check, upon arrival, that the seal on

seal A lock especially designed to be applied on containers and truck trailers and that the importer must break in order to get entry into the container or trailer.

Trade in Precious and Valuable Goods and Stones

Trade in precious goods and valuables is an entire branch of logistics that, although not officially calculated separately from other data, is worth millions of U.S. dollars—in the United States alone, it is estimated at U.S. $50 million. The crash of Swissair 111 on September 2, 1998, exposed some of the extent of its international scale: The airplane was carrying 110 pounds (50 kilograms) of cash, 4 pounds (1.8 kilograms) of diamonds, 4 pounds (1.8 kilograms) of watches, 11 pounds (5 kilograms) of jewelry, and an artwork by Picasso entitled "The Painter."[20] Lloyd's of London, through which this cargo was insured, has never disclosed the value of these cargoes, although there are speculations that it exceeded U.S. $300 million.

There is a substantial business in shipping precious stones internationally, such as diamonds and emeralds, because the stones are often produced, cut, set, and sold in different countries. Artwork travels from museum collections to museum exhibits (and back). Antiques and collectibles travel to and from dealers and auction houses. Cash travels to where tourists flock.

Altogether, there are few firms specializing in the shipment of precious and valuable goods, and these firms emphasize discretion—they do not advertise, do not display their names on their vehicles, and operate out of anonymous office buildings and warehouses. The addi-tional security measures they take are many: They do not ship more than a certain amount on a specific airplane or ship, they use ever-changing consignee names, and they have created a whole series of specialized packaging technologies.

Artex is such a firm. It is located in Washington, D.C., and specializes in the business of moving artwork, antiques, and jewelry collections. It employs a crew of 75 employees, most of whom are artists or art experts with museum experience. Each piece of work is moved in a crate that is specifically designed for that work of art and fitted with foam to the exact dimensions and shape of the artwork. When Artex was selected to move an African American burial site from New York City to Howard University, it took the firm's employees three months to pack the 20,000 objects this move represented.[21]

In addition, Artex's warehouse and trucks are equipped with air conditioning to keep humidity to a minimum. Each of its trucks is tracked with satellite transmitters and the Global Positioning System; this way, the firm knows at all times where the art is located. Finally, each of the trucks is driven by a team of at least two drivers equipped with cellular phones and sometimes accompanied by armed guards. Nevertheless, the best security is when no one knows that a move is occurring.

the container is the same as the seal with which the container left the exporter's premises.[18] Since October 2008, all containers shipped to the United States must be sealed with a tamper-proof seal, such as the one shown in Figure 15-4 in Chapter 15.

Altogether, though, the aspect that security experts insist is critical when shipping internationally or domestically is the personnel involved. Most thefts seem to take place with some form of insider involvement.[19] All attempts should therefore be made to limit the number of people who know the content of the shipment by making sure that the bill of lading and packaging lists are given to trusted employees only, by keeping track of non-employees on the premises, by making sure that managers are present during loading and unloading operations, and so on. Some companies keep their docks under constant video surveillance to deter crime.

14-7 Hazardous Cargo

Hazardous cargo can be shipped by ocean and by air, but, generally speaking, most dangerous goods that are flammable, explosive, or toxic are shipped by sea, and, if these shipments are containerized, they are shipped on deck rather than under deck.

The shipment of dangerous goods by sea is regulated by the International Maritime Organization (IMO), which publishes an International Maritime Danger-ous Goods (IMDG) Code every other year, in order to keep up with the rapid expansion of the types of materials created. In October 2008, the IMO's Maritime Safety Committee released its 34th amendment, valid for 2008–2010.[22] The two-volume document is quite complex; in addition to the two volumes, there is a 2008–2010 IMDG Code Supplement for additional information. Although large, the

IMDG Code was significantly reduced in size in 2000; prior to that amendment, it was a four-volume code. As its name indicates, the IMDG Code governs the packaging of all hazardous cargo, as well as their labeling, handling, and emergency responses that carriers are supposed to implement. The IMDG Code is followed by just about every country in the world, and is a *de facto* world standard.

The shipment of dangerous goods by air is regulated by a similar set of standards published by the International Air Transport Association (IATA). The IATA Dangerous Goods Regulations was developed in collaboration with the International Civil Aviation Organization (ICAO) and the standard-setting authorities of several countries and is revised every year. As of 2009, the IATA Dangerous Goods Regulations are in their 50th edition.[23] As could be expected, the shipment of hazardous cargo by air is no less complicated and cumbersome than by sea.

In addition to these international requirements, a shipper must abide by domestic regulatory agencies as well, as there often are two domestic legs to any international shipment, one in the exporter's country, the other in the importer's country. The complexity of such requirements, and their contradictory statements on occasion, makes it an obligation to contract with a specialized freight forwarder or a specialized consultant before undertaking any international shipment of hazardous goods. Shipments of products containing radioactive components are even more complicated.

14-8 Refrigerated Goods

Goods requiring refrigeration make up another category of cargo that demands particular care and specialized packaging services. It is difficult to generalize about refrigerated goods, as every commodity usually requires very specific handling; therefore, most refrigerated goods travel "alone" (i.e., different refrigerated goods are not mixed with one another, as they require different temperatures and different humidity settings). In addition, some fresh produce simply cannot be mixed together as they emit odors and other gases that would spoil the rest of the cargo. For example, a load of cucumbers should not be mixed with apples, as cucumbers are sensitive to the ethylene that the apples produce,[24] and for obvious reasons, onions and strawberries do not travel well together.

When goods needing refrigeration travel by ocean, they usually travel in a refrigerated container—also known as a "reefer." Great care should be taken in ensuring that the temperature is kept at its correct setting throughout the voyage, which is achieved with temperature-sensitive indicators. Because containers are not very effective at cooling goods—but are effective at keeping them cool—several shippers make sure that the goods are well refrigerated before they are loaded to prevent possible damage. It should also be understood that reefers cannot possibly have a completely uniform temperature: Temperatures within the box can vary by as much as five degrees Celsius (ten degrees Fahrenheit) just because air circulation cannot be made uniform. Finally, another common problem with refrigerated cargo coming in or out of the United States is the confusion between Fahrenheit and Celsius temperature settings and the errors they cause.[25]

With refrigerated cargo, the loading of the refrigerated container must allow air circulation around the cargo; this requirement means that the goods must be loaded in the center of the container, with sufficient space in between the walls of the container and the cargo for air circulation, and that the goods must be braced with a frame rather than with inflatable dunnage, for the same reason. In addition, some goods need to travel in controlled atmospheres—mixtures of oxygen and nitrogen in different percentages than ambient air—to prevent spoilage. Some experiments are being conducted to determine whether a controlled atmosphere can also be effective against some pests, and whether the right mix of humidity, temperature, and correct gas mix can divert some of the cargo that normally travels by air because of its perishable nature to ocean transport, which is much cheaper.[26]

Banana Business

In 1996, Chiquita Brands was the largest American importer (measured by the number of containers brought into the United States), with about 79,000 TEUs—20-foot equivalent units—surpassing even Wal-Mart, which imported "only" 76,000 TEUs.[28] By 2009 however, Wal-Mart's imports had grown to 720,000 TEUs, and Chiquita to 113,600 containers, all loaded with a single product, bananas.[29]

Bananas are harvested green and hard, and immediately refrigerated. They are then loaded into one of Chiquita's 15 dedicated banana ships or on a number of other ships that the firm charters. About half of these ships are completely containerized, while the others transport bananas on pallets as break-bulk cargo in refrigerated holds and in containers on deck. During their trip, the bananas are kept in a controlled atmosphere environment. At their arrival, they are then placed in a ripening environment where they acquire their yellow color before being shipped to retail stores.

Wilmington, Delaware, is by far the largest port of entry for bananas, and about 1.4 million tons of its traffic is "bananas and tropical fruits."[30] Altogether, imported fresh produce accounts for 35 percent of produce sold in the United States. See "Carnations and Cherries" in Chapter 12, Section 12-3d for more information about the U.S. reliance on Colombia in the business of cut flowers.

Fresh produce must also be kept at humidity levels of 95 to 100 percent to maintain its freshness as well as prevent weight loss due to evaporation. Most produce is made up of at least 80 percent water and is quite sensitive to water loss; for example, grapes will wrinkle and soften, and stems will turn brown with a weight loss of only 4 percent, making them more difficult to sell.[27] In addition, because produce is sold by weight, a small weight loss can translate into a substantial decrease in revenue for the importer.

For air shipments of refrigerated cargo, the challenges are different, because the cargo is not placed in refrigerated containers but in cargo holds that have different temperature settings. For example, some cargo carriers offer multiple cargo holds, kept at different temperature settings, to keep perishables in their optimum environments. However, because of the possibility that incompatible cargo might be mixed together—such as the onions and strawberries—great care should be extended to protect sensitive goods from this eventuality by keeping them in solid-wall corrugated paperboard boxes and possibly in shrink- or stretch-wrap, if applicable.

14-9 Domestic Retail Packaging Issues

In dealing with consumer products specifically, several packaging issues are also greatly influenced by primary packaging, or the design of the packaging in which the final consumer purchases the goods, as well as by secondary packaging, or the packaging designed to facilitate handling in the retail environment. Collectively, these constraints tend to be domestic in nature (i.e., they are specific to a single country or possibly a group of countries).

Adapting a firm's strategy to the different market requirements of a particular country adds substantially to the costs of manufacturing, as well as to inventory and logistical expenses. A firm has to determine whether it makes economic sense to adapt its approach to these different markets and incur those additional costs or decide to ignore them at the risk of losing potential sales. This is the same strategic dilemma faced by a firm involved in international marketing: Adapt or standardize?

Some of the factors that may affect primary and secondary packaging are explored in the following sections.

14-9a Size

Consumer packages abroad may be of a different size than consumer packages in the domestic market because of consumer preferences. They are generally smaller in those countries in which retail shopping is done frequently, and larger in those in which consumers shop at greater intervals. However, consumer packaging is complicated; consumers may demand smaller or larger packages based on preferences and customs, as well as packages of different shapes and materials. For example, sugar is sold in some countries in paper bags weighing 5 pounds (2.5 kilograms), in others in paperboard boxes weighing 1 kilogram (2.2 pounds), and yet in others in tin cans of 1 pound (0.45 kilograms). Even products that are held to be great examples of "international standardization," such as Coca-Cola® soft drinks, are sold in a myriad of sizes and therefore of primary and secondary packaging units.

Consumer packaging may also be seriously influenced by the layout of the shelves in the stores, such as their depth and the linear space allocated, constraining manufacturers to use different retail packaging.

Secondary packaging—the unit that holds several consumer packages—is influenced by the size of the retail stores and their configuration, as well as the size of the delivery trucks; the tertiary packaging unit, such as the pallet; or even the configuration of the storage area. In addition, it is influenced by the frequency and the volume of sales of the retail units.

14-9b Legal Issues

Consumer packaging may also be influenced by legal requirements. Some countries regulate sizes to be a multiple of simple metric units (1 kilogram or 1 liter), while others do not, allowing packages of any size and weight. However, the greatest requirements are in the legal constraints on handling: Many countries regulate the maximum weight an employee may carry, which influences the weight of the secondary packaging unit and, consequently, of both consumer packaging and tertiary packaging as well.

The legal constraints placed on the distribution channels can also influence consumer packaging. For example, the United States allows retail sales of some medicines "over the counter," which means that consumers buy them in drugstores, most often in a self-service environment. In France, in contrast, all drugs, including drugs not prescribed by a medical doctor, are sold exclusively through specialized stores called *pharmacies*. The primary package in a drugstore is often a blister pack or some variation of it, as the goods are sold hanging from aisle racks. Primary packages from pharmacies are usually cardboard boxes, as the pharmacist keeps them on small shelves or in large-size drawers. In addition, the drugstore may purchase goods in larger quantities than the pharmacies. In any case, the primary packaging is different and therefore the secondary and tertiary packaging will also be different.

14-9c Storage and Transportation Environment

Finally, there are a number of environmental influences on packaging, such as the dusty conditions under which transportation takes place, mentioned in "Shipping Computers to China" in Section 14-5 about IBM's packaging of personal computers in China. There are similar constraints triggered by high humidity, heat, or cold.

There are also constraints placed by the lack of refrigeration resources. The best example is probably the existence of long-conservation milk, which is sold unre-frigerated with "expiration dates" six or seven months after its production in a large number of European countries. Not only does this packaging alternative allow the use of non-refrigerated shelving in the store, but it also requires no refrigeration at all in the rest of the supply chain, from warehouses to transportation. It can also be transported safely quite far from its production location, including internationally.

All in all, several domestic issues in the importing country will also affect the packaging of goods. Companies should develop appropriate strategies to account for the possible diversity of consumer and retail packaging alternatives present in their export markets.

14-10 Packaging as a Marketing Tool

It should be relatively clear by now that good handling of the packaging requirements by the exporter will help considerably in the smooth transfer of goods from the exporter to the importer.

The most important way of looking at packaging is to prepare for the worst. The exporter should truly imagine the worst-case scenarios and the roughest possible journey in packaging the goods that it ships at export. It is only under this premise that it will adequately serve the needs of the importer to receive goods in sellable and usable condition.

The exporter should make sure that the goods are protected from physical damage by ensuring that they are packaged in sturdy cartons and loaded correctly on pallets, that the pallets are separated by appropriate dunnage such as plywood and inflatable bags, and that all goods are protected from humidity and rain by protecting them with a plastic film and by outfitting the container with desiccant strips. The container should be cleaned and inspected before it is loaded, and the seals used on the container should be of good quality. The procedures in place should be effective in keeping the paperwork in the hands of appropriate personnel only.

Although such procedures are more expensive than a more casual attitude, the benefits are substantial. Consider a hypothetical case where, from the use of an inexpensive plywood sheet spread over three pallets (a plywood sheet is 4×8 feet, or 122×244 centimeters), several boxes are slightly crushed, and the importer has to repackage the goods to make them saleable. The costs of repackaging these few boxes (labor, new boxes, calling the importer to resolve the issue) far exceed the original cost of the plywood sheet. Identical benefits can be drawn from using good pallets that do not break when the goods are unloaded, making sure that the container is watertight, and so on. In addition, because poor packaging can be used by insurance companies to deny a claim, it is to the exporter's advantage to have a track record of stellar packaging.

However, the greatest benefits from such a good packaging policy are the goodwill that it generates with the importer and the marketing benefits that can be derived from it. Because the importer is obviously not interested in having to challenge invoices or having to ask for allowances for goods that were damaged in transit, it welcomes shipments that arrive packaged carefully enough that it does not have to worry about anything. This confidence enhances the relationship between exporter and importer, and builds trust.

Finally, the exporter should make sure that the packaging is "friendly" to the employees who will unpack the goods: that the packing list is written in their language, that shipments are identified with colors that identify pallets that "belong" together, that the wood dunnage is assembled in a way that it can easily be taken apart, and so on. When shipping to countries in which the dunnage and packaging materials are likely to be recycled as housing materials, an exporter would be even more responsive if it considered using a slightly better grade of board and plywood, and making sure that they have been heat-treated rather than fumigated with methyl bromide.

 ## Review and Discussion Questions

1. What are the consequences of improper packaging for the exporter? Does your response depend on the Incoterm used? Does it depend on the insurance policy in force?

2. What are the different alternative means of packaging products that are not containerized?

3. What are some of the issues and risks that international packaging face and that are not present in a domestic shipment?

4. Use a product of your choice and ship it from one country to another in a multimodal shipment. What packaging methods would you use? Why?

Endnotes

1. Lund University, "Packaging Technology and Development," Department of Packaging Logistics, Lund, Sweden, http://www.plog.lth.se/education/master_courses/packaging_technology_and_development, accessed October 7, 2009.

2. Hensel, Bill, Jr., "A Loaded Problem," *JoC Week*, August 14–20, 2000, p. 13.

3. *Ports of the World*, 15th ed., Cigna Insurance Corporation, available from Publisher, *Ports of the World*, Cigna Companies, P.O. Box 7716, Philadelphia, Pennsylvania 19192, USA.

4. Harps, Leslie Hansen, "Popcorn! Peanuts! Bubble Wrap! Thinking Inside the Box," *Inbound Logistics*, November 2000, pp. 40–46.

5. "Container Matters" and "Any Fool Can Stuff a Container," videos published by the Thomas Miller P&I Ltd, International House, 26 Creechurch Lane, London, EC3A 5BA, United Kingdom.

6. Mottley, Robert, "Chilling out," *American Shipper*, June 2000, pp. 43–51.

7. Porter, Janet, "Insurer Warns of the Dangers of Incorrectly Packed Containers," *Journal of Commerce*, August 4, 1997, p. 16A.

8. *Ports of the World*, 15th ed., Cigna Insurance Corporation, available from Publisher, *Ports of the World*, Cigna Companies, P.O. Box 7716, Philadelphia, Pennsylvania 19192, USA.

9. *Ibid.*

10. Brindley, Chaille, "Fumigation 101," *Pallet Enterprise*, February 2004.

11. *United Nations Recommendations on the Transport of Dangerous Goods—Model Regulations*, 15th ed., 2007, United Nations Economic Commission for Europe, http://www.unece.org/trans/danger/publi/unrec/rev15/15files_e.html, accessed July 16, 2009.

12. *Electronic Code of Federal Regulations*, http://ecfr.gpoaccess.gov/cgi/t/text/text-idx?c=ecfr&rgn=div5&view=text&node=49:2.1.1.3.10&idno=49, accessed July 16, 2009.

13. BNSF Railway, Load and Ride Solution Team, *BNSF Intermodal Loading Guide*, March 2005, http://www.bnsf.com/tools/lars/intermodal_loading_guide.html.

14. Grocery Manufacturers Association, *2008 Joint Industry Unsaleables Report: The Real Causes and Actionable Solutions*, written in collaboration with the Food Marketing Institute and Deloitte, September 2008, http://www.gmabrands.com/publications/UnsaleablesFINAL091108.pdf.

15. Hamilton, David, "Untamed Frontier: PC Makers Find China Is a Chaotic Market Despite Its Potential," *Wall Street Journal*, April 8, 1996, p. A1.

16. National Commercial Vehicle and Cargo Theft Prevention Task Force, "National Commercial Vehicle and Cargo Theft Prevention Initiative," April 16, 2008, https://www.nationalcargothefttaskforce.org/ncttf/app/doc/Context_preview.action?documentId=NAT.

17. Europol, *Cargo Theft Report: Applying the Brakes to Road Cargo Crime in Europe*, 2009, http://www.europol.europa.eu/publications/Serious_Crime_Overviews/Cargo_Theft_Report.pdf.

18. "Container Matters" and "Any Fool Can Stuff a Container," videos published by the Thomas Miller P&I Ltd, International House, 26 Creechurch Lane, London, EC3A 5BA, United Kingdom.

19. Anderson, Bill, "Prevent Cargo Theft," *Logistics Today*, May 23, 2007, http://logisticstoday.com/operations_strategy/outlog_story_8744.

20. Estrin, Robin, "Swissair 111 Went Down with Millions in Valuables, Including Picasso Painting," Associated Press News Release, September 4, 1998.

21. Hull, Dana, "How a Moving Company Capitalizes on Valuable Secrets," *Washington Post*, May 5, 1997, p. F12.

22. *International Maritime Organization Dangerous Goods Code*, Amendment 34-08, 2008-2010, available from IMO Publishing, October 2008, http://www.imo.org/publications/mainframe.asp?topic_id=1642&doc_id=9928.

23. *International Air Transport Association Dangerous Goods Regulations*, 2008-2009, 50th ed., available from http://www.airseacontainers.com/prod04_Publications_01-IATA-DGR.htm.

24. Mottley, Robert, "Chilling Out," *American Shipper*, June 2000, pp. 43–51.

25. *Ibid.*

26. Seemuth, Mike, "The Ocean Alternative (Transport of Perishable Cargo by Sea)," *Journal of Commerce*, April 16, 2007.

27. Mongelluzzo, Bill, "A Cool Idea," *Journal of Commerce*, May 23, 1997, p. 1B.

28. Amerman, Don, "Keeping Chiquita Sweeter Requires Atmosphere Control as Well as Reefers," *Journal of Commerce*, June 23, 1997, p. 2C.

29. "Top 100 Importers," *Journal of Commerce*, Special Report, May 25, 2009, http://www.joc-digital.com/joc/2009top100/?pg=20.

30. "The Port of Wilmington," *World Port Source*, http://www.worldportsource.com/ports/USA_DE_The_Port_of_Wilmington_158.php, accessed July 28, 2009.

International Logistics Security

Chapter Fifteen

Key Terms

The events of September 11, 2001, tragically illustrated the vulnerability of open economies to acts of terrorism. While a large number of terrorist attacks had preceded the destruction of the New York World Trade Center towers, the scale and symbolism of their destruction made it a turning point in the way governments addressed terrorism threats. Their strategies shifted from mostly reactive attempts to a decidedly preventive and systematic approach. The response to the September 11 attacks was therefore unprecedented; within a few years, the United States, its trading partners, and a large number of international organizations implemented a series of measures designed to prevent further occurrences of acts of international terrorism. These measures have greatly influenced the way international business is now conducted.

The creation of these security measures, as well as efforts by corporations to reduce the vulnerability of their international supply chain to more traditional criminal activities, have triggered the creation of a number of corporate management functions, collectively called **security management**. This chapter outlines the way security measures imposed by governments and international organizations can be integrated with the security activities of a firm involved in international trade.

While none of these measures taken in isolation can be considered significantly effective in reducing the threat of terrorist activities, their collective implementation has resulted in a much higher level of security in international logistics.

security management
A corporate function that manages all of the security efforts of a particular company and coordinates the prevention of criminal activities against the company's employees, products, and assets.

15-1 The Impact of a Significant Disruption in International Logistics

The extent to which world trade can be seriously disrupted by a single instance of a catastrophe should not be underestimated. The closing of the U.S. ports located on the Gulf of Mexico after Hurricane Katrina delayed shipments of grain and other commodities for months.[1] The fires around Los Angeles in 2003 and the three-day power outage of August 2003 in the Midwest and Northeast of the United States cost billions of dollars in manufacturing delays and shipment disruptions.[2]

However, the greatest impact is that of a terrorist act. All North American international and domestic airline traffic was completely stopped after September 11, 2001, for 3 days; it took one complete day to reposition all of the aircraft and a couple of weeks to clear the logjam of air cargo shipments. Thirteen months later, in October 2002, the Booz-Allen-Hamilton firm conducted a "war game" simulation in which the players were told that a "dirty bomb"—a bomb containing radioactive materials that are spread by the force of the explosion—had been found in the Port of Los Angeles; they were then told that another bomb had been found in Minneapolis and that a third one had exploded in Chicago. The initial response of the 85 game participants (all from the U.S. government) was to shut down two ports for 3 days and, as the crisis worsened, to shut down all U.S. ports for 12 days.[3] The Booz-Allen-Hamilton report estimated that this single decision would have engendered a backlog of containers in U.S. ports that would have taken three months to clear, and the delays would have cost the U.S. economy $58 billion in 2002.[4] The corresponding costs in 2010 would likely be much higher, probably closer to $75 to 80 billion.

Similar disruptions could be anticipated in other parts of the world, whether they are the results of natural or man-made catastrophes. In order to prevent those occurrences, governments and international agencies have collaborated to establish security measures that address possible weaknesses in the international supply chain.

15-2 International Organizations

The first groups to implement large-scale security efforts were the international organizations that monitor agreements and treaties, such as the International Maritime Organization (IMO) and the Customs Cooperation Council.

International Ship and Port Facility Security (ISPS) Code A series of security requirements placed by the International Maritime Organization upon ports and ships.

International Convention for the Safety of Life at Sea (SOLAS) An international convention, signed by 148 countries, that outlines the safety requirements that merchant ship owners must put in place.

15-2a International Maritime Organization

One of the first international organizations to implement enhanced security measures was the IMO, when it voted to create the **International Ship and Port Facility Security (ISPS) Code** in December 2002. In order to implement this code quickly, the IMO made it a part of the **International Convention for the Safety of Life at Sea (SOLAS)**, in a section that addresses "Special Measures to Enhance Maritime Security." Since the code had already been signed by 148 countries, these changes had to be implemented by all signatory countries, and they did so relatively quickly, with most ports and ships in compliance with the ISPS Code by June 2004.

To enhance port security, the code contains two sections: One specifies the required measures that a port has to put in place (Part A), and the other is a series of recommendations for the implementation of these measures (Part B). Because ports face different threats due to their location, the types of cargo they handle, and their physical layout, the implementation of the ISPS Code has been quite different from port to port, and the costs of implementation have varied widely.[5,6] This discrepancy is also caused by the fact that the mandatory requirements are somewhat ill-defined, worded mostly in terms of questions that need to be addressed rather than specific requirements.[7] Nevertheless, the consensus of the research reports is that implementation of the ISPS Code has improved the situation everywhere and that it has many benefits in addition to the increase in the level of security. It has led to a decrease in the incidence of theft and pilferage, a substantial decline in the number of stowaways, and much smoother operations in loading and unloading ships—all of this at a cost of a few cents to a few dollars per container handled.[8]

Ports have implemented the ISPS Code in three specific ways. First, they monitor tightly who has access to the port facilities. This is achieved by mandating that workers carry identification cards, by allowing access to only authorized persons, and by requiring visitors to provide identification. The ports also monitor the activities taking place in the port, by recording them on video cameras (see Figure 15-1) and by

Figure 15-1
Monitoring of Port Facilities by Video Cameras
Source: Photo © Volodymyr Kyrylyuk. Used with permission.

keeping these records for a period of a few weeks. Finally, the ports have secure systems of communications, designed to raise the alarm whenever a threat is detected.

As it applies to ships, the ISPS Code involves the creation of a *company security officer* for each carrier and a *ship security officer* for each ship, whose responsibilities are the development of a Ship Security Assessment, as well as several ship security plans to respond to possible threats against the ship, all of which are also dependent on the type of ship and the type of cargo it carries. Ships are also required to possess certain types of equipment and to restrict onboard access. Ship owners must adhere to additional standards, such as conducting background checks before the hiring of crew members, ensuring the security of paperwork on board, training employees in security procedures, and so on.

Unfortunately, since the research on ISPS has concentrated mainly on port facilities and since the ships' implementations of the ISPS Code are private corporate decisions, little is known about the ways these measures were enacted. Nevertheless, the IMO has issued countless International Ship Security Certificates, which indicates that most ships are in compliance with the ISPS Code requirements.

15-2b World Customs Organization

Another international institution involved in security improvements in the international shipping of goods is the Customs Cooperation Council, better known as the World Customs Organization (WCO). Despite the fact that the primary role of the WCO has traditionally been the "simplification and harmonization of Customs' procedures,"[9] it has been involved in a number of initiatives designed to enhance security.

Early on, the WCO saw its role as complementing the efforts of the IMO by helping importing countries and importers identify, before the goods leave the country of export, the cargoes that should be scrutinized before they should be allowed on their international trip to the importing country. The WCO achieved that objective by encouraging the standardization of documents, by identifying the data characteristics of high-risk shipments, and by establishing guidelines that allowed Customs authorities to have access to the documents of a particular shipment before it is loaded on board the carrier's vessel or aircraft. This particular emphasis is called the Advanced Cargo Information guidelines,[10] which mirrors one of the initiatives of the U.S. Customs and Border Protection agency.

In June 2005, the WCO implemented its SAFE (Security and Facilitation in a Global Environment) initiative, a program it revised further in June 2007. The SAFE initiative further coordinates the efforts of Customs authorities worldwide in their efforts to combat terrorism. The SAFE requirements are fourfold:

- All Customs authorities have to adhere to a set of advance electronic information standards for all international shipments. What is required of shippers should be identical, regardless of country of export and country of import.

- Each country must have consistent risk management approaches to address security threats.

- Exporting countries' Customs authorities must comply with a reasonable request from the importing country's Customs authorities to inspect outgoing cargo, preferably by using non-intrusive technology (X-rays) if possible (see Figure 15-2).

- All Customs authorities must provide benefits to companies that demonstrate that they meet minimum standards of security. Such companies are called Authorized Economic Operators, and benefit from faster processing of Customs clearance and lower inspection rates.[11]

15-2c International Chamber of Commerce

The International Chamber of Commerce (ICC) also weighed in on the issues related to security initiatives in the domain of international logistics, in a policy statement

Figure 15-2
A Mobile X-Ray Scanner for Cargo Containers
Source: Photo © Gerald Nino. U.S. Customs and Border Protection. Used with permission.

dated November 2002;[12] in it, the ICC emphasized that security initiatives should be the domain of international agreements between countries, rather than initiatives imposed unilaterally by some governments. The ICC also emphasized that businesses involved in international trade have already invested considerable amounts in security initiatives and that, therefore, the rules and regulations imposed by international agreements should capitalize on these investments.

The recommendations made by the ICC reflect the organization's goals of facilitating international trade; its concerns were that country-specific requirements would place undue burdens on businesses and therefore would hamper trade. It also was concerned about the widespread dissemination of information among a number of law enforcement authorities and counseled that great care should be taken in the handling of the business information collected by security initiatives, so that no "sensitive confidential company information" would be released.[13]

15-3 National Governments

Despite the efforts undertaken by the international organizations to make international trade more secure, and the admonitions of the ICC that unilateral requirements would hinder trade, as well as the efforts of the WCO toward a common set of requirements, many governments unilaterally implemented a number of different measures in the wake of the terrorist attacks of the past two decades. While the attacks on the World Trade Center and the Pentagon in 2001 tend to be at the forefront of most Americans' consciousness, the list of tragedies is unfortunately much longer, as shown in Table 15-1. The frequency of those attacks, as well as the increasing diversity of groups intent on disrupting democratic societies, led many governments to create and enforce a number of security measures, many of which have had a substantial impact on international trade. Each government implemented those security measures because they felt that their country was specifically targeted. Unfortunately, this is not the case, as is shown in the table; terrorists have been somewhat indiscriminate in their activities, attacking multiple targets in many different countries. It has truly become a worldwide concern.

| TABLE 15-1 | Major Terrorist Acts between 1990 and 2009 | |

Terrorism Act	Date	Location
World Trade Center bombing	February 26, 1993	New York, United States
Sarin gas subway attack	March 20, 1995	Tokyo, Japan
Oklahoma City bombing	April 19, 1995	Oklahoma City, United States
Métro bombings	Summer-Fall 1995	Paris, France
Omagh bombings	August 15, 1998	Omagh, Northern Ireland
World Trade Center attacks	September 11, 2001	New York, United States
Anthrax mailings	September-October 2001	United States
Bali bombings	October 12, 2002	Bali, Indonesia
Istanbul bombings	November 15 and 20, 2003	Istanbul, Turkey
Moscow Metro bombing	February 6, 2004	Moscow, Russia
Madrid train bombings	March 11, 2004	Madrid, Spain
London subway bombings	July 7, 2005	London, United Kingdom
Mumbai train bombings	July 11, 2006	Mumbai, India
Mumbai hotel attacks	November 26, 2008	Mumbai, India

15-3a The United States

The U.S. government implemented a large number of measures to limit the country's vulnerability to terrorist attacks, focusing initially on interdiction, a strategy that the country had already been pursuing in its war against contraband street drugs and illegal immigration.

Interdiction is a strategy that attempts to eliminate all imports of a particular type of good and all entries of a specific group of persons into a country. The reasoning is relatively simple: If no terrorist can enter the country, and if no materials that can be used to cause widespread harm can be imported, then no terrorist acts are possible. The United States started to follow this approach almost immediately after the terrorist attacks of September 11, 2001, with a very strict monitoring of the flying public and of the luggage transported on airliners. The Transportation Safety Administration (TSA) was created in November 2001 by consolidating a large number of small private security firms, a move that was quite controversial at the time, as many employees of these firms did not meet federal hiring standards.[14] The interdiction policy implemented by the TSA involves a systematic inspection of all passengers and of their checked luggage, a policy which is plagued with a number of failings, as described in the following three boxes. Because of these issues, the TSA policies have increasingly been characterized as "theater," ineffective at achieving their stated goals, but presenting a reassuring presence in airports that demonstrates that "something is being done" to combat terrorism.[15,16]

interdiction A security strategy that attempts to prevent all imports of potentially dangerous goods and all entries of potentially dangerous persons.

one-hundred-percent inspection A security strategy that attempts to inspect all imported shipments for potentially dangerous goods.

The Fallacy of One-Hundred-Percent Inspections

Whenever the topic of international security is debated, there are always proponents of a **one-hundred-percent inspection** alternative, in which all imported cargo is inspected, regardless of its origin, its destination, or the means of transportation it used. This is often touted as the

safest method—since all cargo is inspected, nothing dangerous can be shipped into the country. The proponents of one-hundred-percent inspection justify their point of view with two logical reasons: The first is that everything that is dangerous will be caught by the

continued

The Fallacy of One-Hundred-Percent Inspections (Continued)

inspection process, and the other is that the fear of being caught will act as a deterrent for criminals. While a thorough inspection process may act as a deterrent, it is actually an ineffective way to increase the security of a country's borders, for several reasons.

First, it would consume an extraordinary amount of resources. Considering that each container, in order to be physically inspected, has to be opened and its cargo unloaded, inspected, and then reloaded, it is "safe" to assume that it takes a minimum of three hours to ensure that a container is carrying safe cargo. Assuming that paperwork has to be completed for each container and that the officer conducting the inspection is particularly efficient and can work alone, an average of three containers can therefore be inspected by a single inspector every day. Given a work-year of 250 days, a single inspector would be able to handle 750 containers in a year. In 2008, there were more than 10 million ocean containers that crossed the borders of the United States, and a similar number that crossed into the European Union. Just for these two economic entities, and just for ocean cargo, 20 million containers would need to be inspected, and therefore a total of 27,000 inspectors would need to be hired. Add air and road cargo, the remainder of the world's economies, and the number of inspectors would easily reach 100,000, at a cost of multiple billions of dollars.

Second, it would result in incredible delays in ports. A single port crane can handle between 15 and 40 container movements per hour. There are often three or four cranes unloading a containership. There is therefore a need for a space sufficiently large to store and inspect approximately 120 newly unloaded containers every hour. Meanwhile, the containers from the preceding two hours are still being inspected, since it takes about three hours for each, assuming that none are isolated because they are believed to be carrying dangerous goods. Ports would then need to have enough room to inspect 350 containers for each ship that calls in that port. Such room does not exist in any port. Since, in addition, there would be the need to accommodate container movements from the ship to the inspection area, and from the inspection area to the secondary means of transportation (truck or rail), this lack of infrastructure would force ships to have to wait to unload their cargoes.

Finally, a one-hundred-percent inspection program is a fallacy. Since there is no conceivable way that the required number of inspectors could be hired or that the necessary room would be made available in the ports, the inspection process would be flawed. Each container would be inspected, but so "rushed" through the process that it would not be inspected very well. There would be a perception that the system would work (after all, all containers are inspected), but inspection would never be able to uncover carefully hidden dangerous goods.

There is strong evidence that such a system does not work effectively; the TSA operates a system that is based on one-hundred-percent inspection of all passengers and all pieces of luggage. In reviews of the TSA's progress toward its interdiction mission, the U.S. Government Accountability Office (GAO) found that "TSA oversight of checked baggage screening procedures could be strengthened"[17] and "more work remains."[18] These reports are charitable; many others are much more critical and note that GAO's testers were able to bring all sorts of unauthorized items onboard aircraft, undetected.[19,20]

Customs-Trade Partnership Against Terrorism (C-TPAT) A voluntary partnership program between companies involved in international logistics and the U.S. Customs and Border Protection agency, in which companies that implement security measures obtain priority processing and reduced inspection rates.

The United States formalized further the creation of its interdiction strategy on November 25, 2002, by creating the Department of Homeland Security (DHS), consolidating 22 services that had so far operated somewhat independently. The goal was that these departments would be more effective if they were able to cooperate around a shared mission. The DHS reinforced the visibility of its mission of interdiction by renaming or regrouping many of these agencies to reflect their role in terrorism prevention: The U.S. Customs Service became Customs and Border Protection, and the investigative bureaus of the former Immigration and Naturalization Service and Customs became Immigration and Customs Enforcement. This newest department of the U.S. government counts more than 200,000 employees, third in size to the Department of Defense and the Department of Veterans Affairs, and three times larger than the Social Security Administration.

The United States complemented its interdiction approach with the creation of the **Customs-Trade Partnership Against Terrorism (C-TPAT)** in 2001; however, only a handful of companies were involved in this program in 2001 and 2002. By 2003, 137 companies joined, and in 2008, there were over 10,000 importers and logistics services providers enrolled in the program.[21]

Understanding Type I and Type II Errors

The implementation of security measures is predicated on a correct understanding of the two types of errors that can be made in statistics, called **Type I error** and **Type II error**. Although these concepts are relatively complex mathematically, they can be understood relatively easily through an illustration, using airport procedures for handling passenger luggage.

Suppose that there is a machine designed to determine whether an explosive device (a bomb) is present in a piece of luggage. Although this machine can be made particularly well, the fact that it has to process hundreds of pieces of luggage a day means that it cannot investigate thoroughly each and every piece that is loaded onto an aircraft and that it has to rely on some method that is less time-consuming and less invasive. Most of these machines take a sample of the air that surrounds a bag and analyze it to detect the presence of certain chemical molecules. If a particular type of molecule is present in a minimum concentration, the machine alerts the operator that there is the possibility of a bomb. At that time, the operator then opens the piece of luggage and conducts a more thorough, physical investigation of the piece of luggage.

However, the machine can commit two types of errors, as illustrated in Figure 15-3:

- The machine can erroneously detect a bomb where there is none; this can happen because it has to be calibrated to be extremely sensitive. After all, it has to detect minute levels of certain chemicals in a fraction of a second. Since some of these chemical molecules can be on the luggage for a number of reasons, the machine sounds the alarm even though there is actually no bomb in the luggage. Further investigation by the operator confirms that the bag is fine, and the piece of luggage is then cleared. This is called a *Type I error*. Another terminology, more commonly used in medicine, calls this type of error a "false positive": The medical device concludes that the patient has a certain disease when in reality that patient does not have it.

- The machine can erroneously clear a piece of luggage when it actually contains a bomb; this may be due to the fact that the terrorist has done a particularly good job of packaging the bomb or because the sample that the machine used did not contain, by chance alone, enough of the trace chemicals it needed to sound an alarm. In that case, the machine does not ring the alarm even though the piece of luggage is dangerous. This is called a *Type II error*. In medicine, it is called a "false negative": the medical device concludes that the patient does not have a particular disease when in reality the patient does have it.

Suppose that the "bomb-sniffing" machine in this example is designed and calibrated in such a way that it experiences a 5 percent error rate for both Type I and Type II errors. Which of the two error rates is most worrisome?

| | FIGURE 15-3 | Type I and Type II Errors |

		The piece of luggage	
		does not contain a bomb	contains a bomb
The machine	does not give an alarm		Type II error
	gives an alarm	Type I error	

The program is a shift away from interdiction and one-hundred-percent inspection; it is designed to recognize that the immense majority of the shipments that travel internationally are innocuous and, therefore, that they should not be the targets of law enforcement. The only concerns with these shipments should be the possibility that they are intercepted by criminals and the merchandise that they contain is substituted for dangerous goods. The goal of the program is therefore to encourage corporations involved in international trade to enact security measures that would prevent tampering with the shipments at any point in the supply chain; corporations are asked to evaluate their levels of security in the supply chain, determine their vulnerability, and remedy any issues.

Corporations apply for participation in the C-TPAT program, and after their applications have been accepted, they become "Tier I" members. Tier I members are also called "certified" corporations. After their supply-chain security has been

Type I error A statistical concept whereby the researcher concludes that the null hypothesis should be rejected when, in reality, the null hypothesis is true and should have been accepted.

Type II error A statistical concept whereby the researcher concludes that the null hypothesis should be accepted when, in reality, the null hypothesis is false, and should have been rejected.

The Paradox of Type I and Type II Errors As They Apply to Security Issues

When asked to evaluate a "bomb-sniffing" machine with equal Type I and Type II error rates of 5 percent, most people conclude that the Type II error rate is most worrisome; after all, a machine that misses 5 percent of all bombs is very scary indeed. However, this is an incorrect position; the Type I error rate is the problem. This is known as the paradox of Type I and Type II errors.

Suppose that there is an incidence of one bomb per one million pieces of luggage, which is also the total volume of luggage that the system processes every year; this is a rate of 0.0001 percent, which is actually much higher than the actual rate; there are, thankfully, fewer bombs and many more pieces of luggage; however, restricting the analysis to one million pieces of luggage, inspected at the rate of approximately 2,750 pieces a day, makes the paradox more understandable.

Let's assume that on a given day, a terrorist places a bomb in a piece of luggage. With a Type II error rate of 5 percent, there is a 95 percent chance that the machine will correctly detect the piece of luggage with the bomb and sound the alarm, which makes it a quasi-certainty. However, over the past year, the machine also inspected 999,999 other pieces of luggage, none of which contained a bomb; nevertheless, for approximately 50,000 of them (exactly 49,999.95 of them), the machine rang the alarm (because it committed a Type I error) and the operator had to inspect the piece of luggage manually.

Out of the 50,000 pieces of luggage that the operator has inspected up until that day, none contained a bomb. The operator has been very vigilant, looking for all possible ways a bomb could be hidden in the midst of someone's belongings, but has not found one. The single piece of luggage that does contain a well-concealed bomb will not escape scrutiny; the operator will handle it with much care. However, it is also likely that the operator will assume that it is a false alarm; after all, 100 percent of the ones inspected so far were. The dangerous piece of luggage will then be cleared, even though the bomb-sniffing machine (see Figure 15-4) identified it correctly as dangerous.

Consider that only 0.002 percent of the luggage physically inspected by the operator will contain a bomb; 99.998 percent of the inspected bags are perfectly fine. Human nature prevents most of us from paying much attention to a phenomenon that is that infrequent;[22] facing a probability of 0.002 percent is equivalent to meeting a U.S. national for the first time and assuming that this person is an undergraduate student at the University of Chicago (the ratio is roughly identical: 6,000 students in a population of 300 million); we know it's possible, but that is certainly not our first assumption.

Figure 15-4
Pieces of Luggage Entering an Explosive Detection Area
Source: Photo © Fraport AG. Used with permission.

analyzed by Customs and Border Protection and the firms' security measures have been found to be "reliable, accurate, and effective,"[23] the firms' applications are "validated," and the firms become "Tier II" members. Corporations that go beyond the minimum requirements of Customs can reach the level of "Tier III" members. As of December 2008, there were about 8,000 corporations that had Tier II status, and fewer than 300 had reached Tier III.[24]

In order to encourage corporations to participate in the C-TPAT program, Customs and Border Protection offers companies several advantages, including a lower probability of Customs inspections at the port of entry, priority scheduling of inspections when they are deemed necessary, and assistance from Customs' supply-chain security specialists to solve security challenges. Although the program was originally instituted as a voluntary program for companies involved in international trade, it has evolved into a mandatory program for all importers, carriers, and third-party logistics providers; participation is not encouraged, it is essentially expected.

The C-TPAT program operates very much within the guidelines established by the SAFE initiative enacted by the WCO. In addition, by concentrating on the analysis of shipments that can be presumed to present some level of risk (determined by their characteristics, often the fact that they are "unusual"), the C-TPAT program also meets the requirements of the ICC to be least disruptive to international commerce.

In addition to the C-TPAT program, the United States has also created a number of other initiatives, all designed to improve security:

- The Maritime Transportation Security Act (MTSA) was enacted in 2002, and is the U.S. version of the IMO's International Ship and Port Facility Security Code.

- Its follower, the Security and Accountability For Every Port (SAFE Port) Act, added additional requirements and specific enforcement responsibilities by the Coast Guard. Although it shares the same name as the WCO's initiative, it is not related.

- The Transportation Workers' Identification Credential (TWIC) program is a system of identification cards for all persons who have access to U.S. ports. It is based on biometric information. The TWIC program has been implemented from port to port, starting in 2008 (at New England ports); most ports were in compliance by April 2009.

- Other programs, such as the Container Security Initiative (CSI) and the Free and Secure Trade (FAST) program, were described in Chapters 11 and 13.

15-3b The European Union

The European Union has approached security in a significantly different way: While it recognizes that there are new security issues with the increase in terrorism and the availability of weapons of mass destruction in the hands of criminals, its primary focus has been prevention. In a paper outlining its security strategy, the European Union emphasized that the reduction of poverty, the enforcement of international agreements against arms proliferation, the restoration of democratic governments in areas of regional conflicts, and an increase in international cooperation for criminal investigations would be most effective in dealing with security threats.[25]

Therefore, it is not surprising that most of the initiatives implemented in the European Union were in response to international organizations' guidelines, first the International Ship and Port Facilities Security Code of the IMO, and then the SAFE framework of the WCO. Although there were some unilateral interpretations of these guidelines, the European Union, by and large, has responded to security threats in a relatively uniform fashion.

It is also clear that the European Union has responded to recent terrorist threats much less vigorously than the United States. This was, at least in part, because Europe had faced numerous other terrorist attacks prior to 2001—from internal as well as external elements, from criminal as well as "political" groups—and therefore had already implemented substantial countermeasures. In every decade since the 1950s, European countries have experienced significant violent attacks, from local terrorist groups such as the Organisation de l'Armée Secrète in France, the Provisional Irish Republican Army in the United Kingdom, the Baader-Meinhof Gang and the Rote Armee Fraktion in Germany, the Brigate Rosse in Italy, and the Euskadi Ta Askatasuna (Basque Separatist Party) in Spain and France, in addition to foreign groups from North Africa and the Middle East.

15-3c Other Countries

Countries outside of Europe and North America reacted with policies that mirrored those of the European Union, by implementing the ISPS Code and SAFE framework, mostly in the spirit of international cooperation rather than as a response to a perceived threat of terrorism. The prevalent viewpoint was that terrorists were targeting mostly the United States and possibly the European Union and that this was a U.S. problem, from which they could "remove" themselves.

This attitude was further reinforced by actions of the United States that often imposed additional measures on its trade partners, who were asked to implement them under the scrutiny of U.S. enforcement agencies, whether Customs and Border Protection, Immigration and Customs Enforcement, or the Coast Guard.

Many countries engaged in these changes reluctantly, as they had much more significant domestic problems and did not want to spend their resources on a "foreign" problem. The subsequent bombings in Bali, Moscow, Madrid, London, and Mumbai changed this perspective relatively quickly, and most countries today agree that terrorism is a worldwide problem, although they often see it as less significant than widespread poverty and its associated risks of significant crime and potential social unrest.

15-4 Corporate Efforts

Although governments frame the issue of supply chain security in terms of the risk of terrorism, most companies see security in a much narrower way, focusing principally on the risk of theft and other criminal activities, such as tampering, vandalism, and counterfeit products. Companies comply with requests to reduce terrorism by participating in governmental programs and other efforts to secure the international logistics' environment, but they see the benefits of such increased security mostly in terms of reduced cargo losses.

Nevertheless, the surge in government programs designed to eliminate terrorism was the impetus for many companies to engage in Total Security Management (TSM), a management philosophy based on the Total Quality Management concepts developed by W. Edwards Deming in the 1970s,[26] which encourages every employee, at every level, to recognize the importance of security within the corporation and suggest improvements in processes and procedures. By having a commitment to security that permeates all levels of responsibility within the company, security is increased greatly and becomes an essential part of the culture of the firm. Even though there are costs to making these improvements, the idea behind TSM is that these costs will be offset by the corresponding reductions in theft, damaged goods, and lost productivity, in the same way as Crosby determined that "quality is free."[27]

In order to be comprehensive in their security efforts, companies have to secure four areas in their supply chains: (1) their fixed assets (plants, warehouses, distribution centers), (2) their inbound and outbound shipments while they are in transit, (3) the information on which they rely to manage their operations, and (4) their workforce, to ensure that it is reliable and trustworthy.

In order to protect their fixed assets, companies install physical barriers designed to prevent entry by unauthorized persons. Fences are built along the perimeter of the facilities, the doors to the buildings are locked (emergency exit doors are locked from the inside so that they cannot be opened from the outside), all other points of access (e.g., roof hatches) to the buildings are secured, the number of outside lights is increased, a backup electric generator is added to prevent interruptions to lights and communication systems, and a public-address and an alarm system are installed. Companies also build gates at the entrance to the facilities, with a security guard ensuring that no unauthorized person is allowed to enter. Companies install security cameras to monitor all activities on the premises, and the videos are monitored by trained security personnel. Finally, emergency security procedures are established and training is provided for all employees, so that they know what their responsibilities are in the event of a security breach. These measures mirror the requirements of the ISPS Code for port facilities.

In order to protect their shipments while they are in transit, companies implement a different set of measures. They make sure that all cargo containers are sealed before they leave any facility, with a seal that is a good deterrent to a potential thief (see Figure 15-5), and that the seal numbers are carefully monitored. They make sure that the information on the identity of the cargo is released to as few people as possible. Companies also instruct their truck drivers to continuously monitor their surroundings and make sure that they do not stop at a rest area soon after leaving a plant, as most cargo thefts occur within a few miles of the cargo's point of origin. Many U.S. companies have put in place a "geo-fencing" system, which alerts security officials when the cargo departs from a pre-determined itinerary. Such a system is based on the Global Positioning System (GPS) and allows only slight variations in itinerary (such as a detour for construction or an accident) but sends a warning if the cargo strays more than 25 miles (40 kilometers) from the highway that the truck is supposed to take. The truck driver is then immediately contacted for further

Figure 15-5
Two Different Container Seals; Only One is Tamper Resistant (Top)
Source: Photo © Pierre David.

information, and the local police authorities are dispatched if there is a problem. Finally, an emergency plan should be developed and all employees should be trained in its application.

It is also very important for companies to guard their corporate information. While the techniques used to safeguard electronic data are quite complex, and are the subjects of a number of books,[28] a good system of procedures must ensure that information reaches only those people who need to know what is transported or what is currently in inventory. Procedures should be in place to monitor the dissemination of information (electronic and paper) within the firm.

Finally, good security measures are fundamentally predicated on good human resources practices. For instance, if employees are intent on violating the security measures put in place by a corporation, they likely will achieve their goals, as it is impossible to defend against all possibilities without affecting the normal conduct of business. It is therefore very important to verify employees' backgrounds, monitor their activities, train them to recognize security violations, and provide an anonymous system to report their concerns.

Review and Discussion Questions

1. What are the different main international logistics security programs, implemented either by international agencies or national governments?

2. What are the main differences between the alternative approaches taken by the United States and the European Union in terms of security?

3. What are the problems of a security policy that is based on one-hundred-percent inspection?

4. What are the four areas in which a corporation must enact security measures to protect itself against theft and terrorism?

5. Suppose a particular disease has an incidence of 1 percent in the population. The test used to detect this disease has a 5 percent Type I error rate; there is no Type II error rate. A physician sees test results from a patient that indicates that the patient has that disease; the probability that the patient actually has that disease is 0.01/0.0595, or about 17 percent. Explain this result.

Endnotes

1. Peige, John, "Gulf Coast Hurricanes Have Huge Impact on Shipping Flows," *MM&P Wheelhouse Weekly*, October 27, 2005, 43.

2. Ritter, Luke, J. Michael Barrett, and Rosalyn Wilson, *Securing Global Transportation Networks*. New York: McGraw-Hill, 2007.

3. Gerencser, Mark, Jim Weinberg, and Don Vincent, *Port Security War Game: Implications for U.S. Supply Chains*, Booz-Allen-Hamilton 2003, http://www.boozallen.com/media/file/128648.pdf, accessed September 21, 2009.

4. *Ibid.*

5. United Nations Conference on Trade and Development, *Maritime Security: ISPS Code Implementation, Costs and Related Financing*, Report by the UNCTAD Secretariat, March 14, 2007, http://www.unctad.org/en/docs/sdtetlb 20071_en.pdf.

6. Boske, Leigh, *Port and Supply-Chain Security Initiatives in the United States and Abroad*, Lyndon B. Johnson School of Public Affairs, University of Texas at Austin, Policy Research Project Report 150, 2006, http://www.utexas.edu/lbj/pubs/pdf/prp_150.pdf, accessed September 22, 2009.

7. Kruk, C. Burt, and Michel Luc Donner, *Review of Cost of Compliance with the New International Freight Transport Security Requirements: Consolidated Report of the Investigations Carried Out in Ports in the Africa, Europe and Central Asia, and Latin America and the Caribbean Regions*, World Bank, Transport Paper 16, February 2008, http://siteresources.worldbank.org/INTTRANSPORT/Resources/tp_16_ISPS.pdf.

8. *Ibid.*

9. World Customs Organization "About Us," http://www.wcoomd.org/home_about_us.htm, accessed September 22, 2009.

10. "The Role of Customs and the World Customs Organization in Border Management," United Nations Counter-Terrorism Committee, March 2004, http://www.osce.org/documents/sg/2004/03/2196_en.pdf.

11. World Customs Organization, *WCO SAFE Framework of Standards*, June 2007, http://www.wcoomd.org/files/1.%20Public%20files/PDFandDocuments/SAFE%20Framework_EN_2007_for_publication.pdf.

12. Policy Statement, International Chamber of Commerce's Commission on Transport and Logistics, "Supply Chain

Security," November 18, 2002, http://www.iccwbo.org/policy/transport/id518/index.html.

13. *Ibid.*

14. Roots, Roger, "Terrorized into Absurdity: the Creation of the Transportation Security Administration," *Independent Review*, March 22, 2003.

15. Stross, Randall, "Theater of the Absurd at the T.S.A.," *New York Times*, December 17, 2006.

16. Goldberg, Jeffrey, "The Things He Carried," *Atlantic Monthly*, November 2008.

17. Government Accountability Office, "TSA Oversight of Checked Baggage Screening Procedures Could Be Strengthened," July 2006, http://www.gao.gov/new.items/d06869.pdf.

18. Government Accountability Office"Screener Training and Performance Measurement Strengthened, but More Work Remains," May 2005, http://www.gao.gov/new.items/d05457.pdf.

19. Hsu, Spencer, "TSA Minimizes Failure to Detect Threats," *Washington Post*, November 16, 2007.

20. Frank, Thomas, "Most Fake Bombs Missed by Screeners," *USA Today*, October 22, 2007, http://www.usatoday.com/news/nation/2007-10-17-airport-security_N.htm.

21. Customs-Trade Partnership Against Terrorism, "2008—A Year in Review," http://www.cbp.gov/linkhandler/cgov/trade/cargo_security/ctpat/what_ctpat/2008_year_review.ctt/2008_year_review.pdf, October 10, 2009.

22. Johnson, Eric, John Hershey, Jacqueline Meszaros, and Howard Kunreuther, "Framing, Probability Distortions, and Insurance Decisions," *Journal of Risk and Uncertainty*, August 1993, pp. 35–51.

23. Boske, Leigh, *Port and Supply-Chain Security Initiatives in the United States and Abroad*, Lyndon B. Johnson School of Public Affairs, University of Texas at Austin, Policy Research Project Report 150, 2006, http://www.utexas.edu/lbj/pubs/pdf/prp_150.pdf, accessed September 22, 2009.

24. Lobdell, Karen, "C-TPAT Security Conference Overview," Client Alert, April 2009, Drinker-Biddle, http://www.drinkerbiddle.com/files/Publication/9b69895e-bed4-4110-aac3-02da16f96ed3/Presentation/PublicationAttachment/4edd430c-8d06-40fe-8bb3-00cd30f920c9/Security_Conference.pdf.

25. Solana, Javier, *A Secure Europe in a Better World: European Security Strategy*, December 12, 2003, http://www.consilium.europa.eu/uedocs/cmsUpload/78367.pdf.

26. Ritter, Luke, J. Michael Barrett, and Rosalyn Wilson, *Securing Global Transportation Networks*. New York: McGraw-Hill, 2007.

27. Crosby, Philip, *Quality Is Free*. Mentor/Penguin-Putnam, 1980.

28. Merkow, Mark, and James Breithaupt, *Information Security: Principles and Practices*. Prentice-Hall, Englewood Cliffs, NJ: Prentice-Hall, 2005.

Customs Clearance

Chapter Sixteen

Key Terms

Chapter Outline

Another aspect of international trade is the process that an importer must follow when it brings goods into a country. This process is dictated by Customs, the government office in charge of collecting taxes on imports and of enforcing a number of rules and regulations regarding what can and cannot be admitted into the country. It is generally a complex process, fraught with pitfalls and loaded with paperwork. Most countries, with very few exceptions, do not like to import goods, and they act accordingly. This chapter explains how the Customs system works in general but draws most of its examples from the process followed to import goods into the United States.

16-1 Duty

Duty is the tax that an importer must pay in order to bring goods into a country. Such duty is calculated in a number of different ways, generally based upon three criteria:

1. The type of goods imported, which is determined according to a number of rules of **classification** that essentially have been standardized worldwide
2. The value of the goods imported, which is determined not only by the invoice value, but also according to a number of rules that differ from country to country, collectively called **valuation** rules
3. The country from which the goods are imported; this determination is made according to the **rules of origin**, a process recently simplified but still quite cumbersome for manufactured products with components made in multiple countries

From these three elements, Customs calculates what **tariff** will be charged on the import, or the tax that the importer will have to pay on the imported goods. It is generally a percentage of their value, but it can also be calculated with some other method, based on the number of units shipped or their weight, for example.

16-1a Classification

The classification of goods follows a coding scheme that is essentially the same worldwide, as most countries have adopted the Harmonized Commodity Description and Coding System—also called the Harmonized System (HS) of classification—developed by the Customs Cooperation Council (also known as the World Customs Organization [WCO]). The Harmonized System is used to classify both exports and imports. The fact that a trader can use the same code when it is exporting a product from one country and importing it into another is a great simplification. At one time, almost every country had its own classification and coding system.

According to the HS, each product can have a code that uses up to ten digits. An example, taken from the tariff schedule of the United States, would be:

6402.19.05	golf shoes
30	for men
60	for women
90	for other persons

where the first six digits represent the "root" of the international coding (i.e., the code that will be identical in all the countries that have adopted the Harmonized System for the product "golf shoes"). The last four digits are country specific (i.e., every country can use them to differentiate between different subcategories of the main product, as the United States does between golf shoes for men, for women, and for "other persons," presumably children).

duty The amount of tax paid on an imported good; the duty is calculated using the tariff rate and the value of the goods.

classification The process of determining what the correct Harmonized System Number is for an import.

valuation The process of determining the value of an import, or the amount upon which the duty will be calculated.

rules of origin The rules used to determine the country of origin of a particular product.

tariff The rate at which an import is taxed; the tariff rate is dependent on the classification of the goods, as well as their country of origin. The tariff rate is also called the *duty rate*.

The Details on the Classification of Golf Shoes

The Harmonized System is divided into 21 sections, logically determined by the type of product and material, each divided into one or more chapters, with a total of 97 chapters for the entire HS nomenclature. The chapter in which the golf shoes are classified is Chapter 64, entitled "Footwear, gaiters, and the like; parts of such articles."

Each chapter is then divided into headings, which make up the first four digits of the HS number. The heading 6401 is "Waterproof footwear with outer soles and uppers of rubber or plastics, where the uppers are not assembled to the sole by means of stitching, riveting, nailing, screwing, plugging or similar process." That remark means that the soles and the uppers are "one" or "welded together," like rubber boots and downhill ski boots. The next heading is 6402, "Other footwear with outersoles and uppers of rubber or plastics." Since it is a different heading than 6401, it is easy to conclude that shoes whose uppers are stitched, riveted, nailed, or screwed to the soles would fall into this heading. They would not be considered waterproof either.

Each heading is then divided into subheadings, and this six-digit code is common to all countries that have adopted the Harmonized System. For example, heading 6401 has these two subheadings (among others):

- 6401.10 is "footwear [of the type defined in 6401] that includes a protective metal toe-cap."

- 6401.92 is "other footwear [of the type defined in 6401] covering the ankle but not the knee" (for example, downhill ski boots).

Heading 6402 has four subheadings:

- 6402.12 is "ski-boots and cross-country ski footwear and snowboard boots." They are not considered to be waterproof and their uppers are stitched or glued to the soles.

- 6402.19 is "other footwear [of the type defined in 6402] where 90 percent or more of the external surface area is rubber or plastics," where most golf shoes are classified.

- 6402.20 is "footwear with upper straps or thongs assembled to the sole by means of plugs," which are likely to be thongs/flip-flops.

- 6402.91 is "other footwear [defined in 6402] that covers the ankle."

- 6402.99 is "other footwear [defined in 6402] and that does not cover the ankles."

Golf shoes are classified as 6402.19, since they are made with rubber soles, their uppers are attached to the soles by some mechanical method, and 90 percent of the external surface area is rubber or plastics. The United States defines golf shoes yet further, with a differentiation made between men's, women's, and children's shoes.

The Harmonized System of classification is accompanied by a series of six General Rules of Interpretation, which detail how an importer should arrive at the correct HS code for an entry:[1]

1. The section, chapter, and heading serve only as guides, and the correct classification may be in a different section, chapter, and heading altogether.
2. The classification of an incomplete or unfinished product is that of the finished product. For example, shipments that contain all of the subassemblies for a final product should be classified as the final product rather than as individual parts. This is true of chemical compounds as well.
3. When in doubt between two classifications, the one with the most specific description is the correct one. However, if the product is made up of several parts, each of which would lead to a different classification, then the classification that lends the product its "essential character" is the correct one.
4. When there is no category under which a specific product can be classified, then the classification that should be used is that of a product that would be most like it.
5. Containers and packaging materials are classified with the products with which they enter. Such would be the case for camera cases, for example. However, if the container has usage beyond the product itself, then it must be entered and classified separately.

6. When comparing classifications, only descriptions at the same level should be compared; it is not appropriate to compare a heading to a subheading, for example.

Nevertheless, the correct classification is always subject to some interpretation on the part of the importer and Customs officers. Because the classification of a specific article determines at which tariff rate it will be taxed and whether it will be subjected to numerical quotas (as are some textile articles in developed countries, such as the United States; see Section 16-2a), it can be a nontrivial issue. In those cases where a U.S. importer is in doubt about a correct classification, the Customs Office will issue, prior to the entry of the goods, a **binding ruling** where it will determine the correct classification of a specific product, a decision that will be binding on both parties.[2] In early 2000, there were efforts undertaken to simplify the ten-digit classification used by the United States and to model it after some other countries' system, which uses only the six-digit subheadings of the HS.[3] However, as of 2009, the U.S. Customs tariff schedule was still using a ten-digit–based classification system.

The correct classification of an imported good is generally made by the importer and then verified by the Customs Office; however, each country has different standards, and a few put the entire classification responsibility on Customs. In any case, it is critical to have a complete description of the goods on the commercial invoice, and not just a part number or an item number. When in doubt, Customs can ask to see the merchandise before it is released, and this inspection can create substantial delays (see Figure 16-1).

binding ruling A determination, made by U.S. Customs and applicable only to the United States, that classifies a specific product and assigns it a tariff rate before the goods are imported.

> **FIGURE 16-1** | Customs Officers Conduct Random Checks to Ensure Correct Classification

Source: Photo © James Tourtellotte, Customs and Border Protection. Used with permission.

Classification Quirks

Given the multitude of products imported into the United States—and given the eclectic tastes of the U.S. population—a large number of unusual products have to be classified by importers following the Harmonized System, with some decisions that can be amusing:

A novelty item called a "necktie in a bottle" was classified by Customs as a necktie—no surprise here—and therefore was made subject to numerical quotas. However, because its bottle package was unusual, it also had to be classified separately, according to General Rule of Interpretation 5.[4]

Some Halloween costumes are classified as "articles of clothing" rather than as "toys" by Customs, and are therefore made subject to higher tariffs and some numerical quotas. This decision has obviously brought jeers from importers, who argue that children are unlikely to wear Dracula disguises to school, with the possible exception of a single holiday: Halloween.[5]

A novelty item consisting of a cloth pocket that can be wrapped on a couch's armrest to hold a TV remote control or a few magazines, and sold under the trade name "TV Duck," was classified by Customs as a bedspread—Rule of Interpretation 4—which subjected it to high tariffs and

numerical quotas. The importer disagreed, and this protracted fight went all the way to the U.S. Court of Appeals: "You had to be in the courtroom to appreciate the looks of disbelief that the judges directed toward [the Customs lawyer]."[6]

Canadian exporters have drilled holes in boards to allow their construction lumber to be classified as "finished products"—because homebuilders can fit wires and plumbing lines through them—and therefore avoid the high tariffs placed by the United States on lumber,[7] which it considers subsidized by the provincial governments of Canada. U.S. Customs and the Canadian authorities fought over this issue for four years. The U.S. even suggested to Canada that it impose an export tariff on all lumber rather than face U.S. anti-dumping duties.[8]

A company importing plastic action figures of the X-Men superheroes argued that the figures were not reproductions of human beings, which would have classified them as dolls, but rather were simply "creatures," which would classify them as toys and make them eligible for a lower tariff rate. It won its case against U.S. Customs and Border Protection.[9]

16-1b Valuation

Because most duty is collected *ad valorem* (on the value of the goods imported in a country), a correct valuation amount must be determined by the importer, following a number of valuation rules governed by the Customs Office of the country in which the goods are imported.

For all member countries of the World Trade Organization (WTO), the valuation of the goods is based on the transaction value of the sale. Therefore, the valuation of the goods must start with the value presented on the invoice sent by the exporter to the importer. For most countries, the value used is the "landed" value, or the CIF/CIP value of the goods (see Chapter 6, Sections 6-9 and 6-11 for explanations of these Incoterms), that is, the invoice value including packaging costs, transportation costs in the exporting country, international transportation costs to the country of destination, and international insurance costs. For other countries, including the United States, the value used is the FCA or FAS value (see Chapter 6, Sections 6-5 and 6-6 for explanations of these Incoterms), that is, the invoice value of the goods as well as packaging costs and transportation costs in the exporting country, but excluding the costs of international shipping and insurance.

There are obvious difficulties in reaching the correct valuation unless the commercial invoice is detailed enough to include all of these different costs in a clear, itemized fashion, regardless of the terms of trade (Incoterms) used in the transaction. For example, a CIF sale to an American importer should spell out the costs of international freight and international insurance, so that they can be deducted from the invoice value for Customs purposes.

The valuation process can be much more complicated than what has been outlined so far. Some countries used to determine value based upon the Brussels Definition of Value (BDV), or the "usual" price of a commodity, based on the price at which a product would sell in a free market between an unrelated buyer and seller. However, since 1994, BDV has slowly been replaced by the transaction value.[10] In those cases where Customs suspects that valuation based on the invoice would result in undervaluation—or, possibly, overvaluation—it can legitimately decide that valuation can be determined through other methods:

- **Comparative method**. Customs determines the value of the goods based upon the value of identical or similar goods imported in similar quantity into the same country. Note that the determination of the value of the goods is made based upon importing data and that differences in exporting countries' costs are not taken into consideration.

- **Deductive method**. Customs determines at what price identical or similar goods are sold within 90 days of importation into the importing country and determines an entry value based upon "normal" markups in the distribution channel.

- **Computed or reconstructed value method**. Customs determines the value of the goods by computing their manufacturing costs and adding "an amount for profit and general expenses equal to that usually reflected in the sales of goods of the same class or kind."[11]

- **Method of last resort**. Customs uses "well-trained" and "well-informed" Customs officials to determine the value of the goods imported. No specific guidelines are given, other than that the valuation cannot be "arbitrary." It is unlikely to be anything else, though.

The valuation of the goods imported can be increased by some items not included on the invoice—for example, a royalty to be paid by the importer to the exporter, a commission to be paid by the importer to a purchasing agent in the exporting country, or a percentage of the price at which the importer sells the goods to their final purchaser. The valuation can also be affected by the presence of what Customs calls an **assist**, or an item that the importer provided to the exporter in order to produce the goods—for example, a mold or a die that the exporter used in manufacturing the product. The value of such an assist must be added, on a *per item* basis, to the value of the goods imported.

Finally, the issue of exchange rates is relevant. Customs must arrive at the value of the goods in the importing country's currency, even though the invoice can be written in a different currency. Each national Customs Office therefore has rules to determine what exchange rate will be used to convert an invoice issued in a foreign currency. U.S. Customs uses the exchange rate of the date of export of the merchandise.

assist An item provided by the importer (customer) to the exporter (seller) so that the exporter can manufacture the goods: a mold or a die, for example.

16-1c Rules of Origin

The third element necessary to determine the duty that will be applied to a specific import is the country of origin of the goods. Goods are given a country of origin based upon the *rules of origin*, which follow one or the other of two methods, neither of which has yet been adopted universally by the WTO, despite the fact that there has been a committee working on this project since 1995.[12] So far, the committee has agreed that countries must make their rules of origin "transparent" to importers.[13]

- **Substantial transformation**. The country of origin of a product is the country in which it acquired its most substantial transformation. The determination of the "substantial transformation" is fraught with pitfalls and can lead to widely different interpretations. For example, consider a computer assembled in Mexico from parts originating in Taiwan (memory chips), the United States (CPU), China (board and hard drive), Brazil (monitor), and so on. Where did the substantial transformation take place, and what is the country of origin of the product? Although vague, this is still the method followed by the United States —with the exception of textiles—and it can lead to fairly interesting decisions (see the box "Made in Where?").

- **Change in HS classification**. The country of origin is the country in which the last change in Harmonized System classification occurred. This method is the one currently followed by the United States for textile products, and it has proven to be much easier to implement. Nevertheless, the decision can sometimes lead to a product's country of origin being a country in which a fairly inconsequential transformation took place and where little value was added. Already several exceptions have been made to this rule.

Unfortunately, there seems to be no easy way to determine what the country of origin of a complex product is. The determination of a country of origin—and the markings that are associated with it—is probably one of the most difficult issues facing firms engaged in international trade today, as different duty rates are used for different countries and as numerical quotas exist for some countries but not others. An importer can be charged very different duty rates and, in some cases, be fined substantially for having hidden the actual country of origin:

A Hong Kong clothing manufacturer was fined U.S. $388,000 for fraudulently seeking to export Chinese-made garments to the United States…. The firm pleaded guilty to ten counts of lying about the origin of 14,400 dresses. They carried Hong

Made in Where?

Under the "substantial transformation" rule of origin, U.S. Customs determined that transforming steel rods into steel wire was not substantial enough to warrant changing the country of origin but that the assembly of photo album pages into a binder was.[20] Similarly, ostrich chicks hatched in Great Britain from eggs laid in South Africa had not been subjected to "a process so substantial as to transform them into new and different articles of commerce" and therefore were coming from South Africa and subject to the then-existing embargo on imports from that country; however, ostrich feathers coming from South Africa and placed on hats made in China were considered transformed enough that their entry was permitted: They "originated" in China.[21]

Under the "change in HS number," though, there were similarly difficult situations. Underwear made for Victoria's Secret, assembled into final product in a Jordanian plant from panels cut in Israel, and shipped back across the border to Israel is officially "made in Israel," as General Rule of Interpretation 2 dictates, and benefits from the free-trade agreement between Israel and the United States.[22] Silk scarves that are finished, dyed, and hand-painted in Italy, and which used to be considered "made in Italy" under the substantial transformation rule, are now considered to be originating in China, because the HS classification for a raw silk scarf and a painted one is the

same.[23] Under pressure from the European Union, the United States relented, and those scarves are once again allowed to be "made in Italy" and fetch U.S. $200 prices,[24] a price difficult to obtain for a scarf labeled as made in China.

Sometimes, the rules are followed to the letter, but the results are disconcerting. The olive harvest in Italy is not sufficient to cover the Italian domestic needs for olive oil. Nevertheless, Italy exports a large amount of olive oil worldwide, clearly labeled as "imported from Italy." Most of the olives used in this oil come from Spain, Greece, and Tunisia. However, under both the "change in HS" rule and the "substantial transformation" rule, olive oil can be sold as "made in Italy," even though Italian companies report that as little as 20 percent of the oil comes from Italian olives.[25] In addition, under a universal rule that anything under 7 percent of a product does not affect its country of origin, the Italian olive oil can contain as much as 7 percent of oil not even processed in Italy.

All in all, even for simple products, it is often difficult to determine where a product is truly "from." Is chocolate made in Belgium from Ivory Coast cocoa beans "made in Belgium" or "made in the Ivory Coast"? Is espresso coffee made in the country in which the beans were roasted, ground, and steamed, or is it made in the country in which those beans were grown?

Kong labels but were actually made in China. The maximum penalty for such cases is U.S. $500,000 and two years in jail.[14]

U.S. Customs keeps and publishes a list of all the firms that it has found guilty of transshipping, the practice of attempting to hide the country of origin of certain products by making them transit through another country. Because of the very different conditions under which textile products from China and from Hong Kong are imported into the United States, many of these firms have been Hong Kong based.[15]

In addition, the country of origin of a good can have substantial marketing consequences, as most countries require that the goods be marked with their country of origin. For obvious reasons, importers of luxury clothing items prefer to have them marked "Made in Italy" rather than marked as made in a country not known for its designers. However, the issue is of consequence for all sorts of products, as consumers everywhere are sensitive to what international marketers call "country-of-origin effects,"[16] the perceptions that the country of origin imparts on the product.

Finally, the rules of origin can be affected by bilateral or multilateral agreements. For example, the North American Free Trade Agreement (NAFTA) between Canada, the United States, and Mexico has its own rules of origin, and such rules differ from commodity to commodity. In general, a product qualifies to enter duty free into any of the three NAFTA countries if its regional content (the percentage of its value that it acquired in any of the three countries) is at least 50 percent. For some goods, though, the maximum percentage of their value that can be outside of NAFTA is 7 percent.[17] Other free-trade agreements have their own rules of origin: The Canada-Chile Free Trade Agreement has its own rules, and so does the European Union in those agreements designed to provide EU market access to developing countries.[18] Because there are over 300 free-trade agreements worldwide, most of which have their own rules of origin, a uniform system is sorely needed.[19]

16-1d Tariffs

An importing country usually manages its imports under an "N-column tariff system," with N, the number of columns, corresponding to the number of different classes of countries that the importing country considers. The tariff rates are the same for all of the countries in a given class. Most **tariff schedules** are known as two-, three-, or four-column schedules. For example, the United States operates under a two-column tariff schedule, with the countries with which the United States has *normal trade relations* (NTR) subject to Column 1 tariffs, and others to Column 2 tariffs. In 2000, what had been the "most favored nation" (MFN) designation was officially changed to the NTR classification.

tariff schedule A document listing all the possible Harmonized System classification categories, as well as their associated tariff rates for the different types of countries.

However, the number of columns is often quite an oversimplification of the actual tariff system. Because the number and complexity of multilateral trade agreements has increased, this terminology can sometimes be confusing, as there can be many more than "N" classes. Nevertheless, the terminology has remained.

For the United States, there are only two trading partners that do not have NTR status, both of which are, at best, minor trading partners: Cuba and North Korea.[26] However, among the NTRs, there are trading partners with which the United States has free-trade relations (Canada, Mexico, Israel, Chile, Jordan, Singapore, Australia, New Zealand, as well as all Caribbean countries, all Central American countries, and all sub-Saharan African countries), and several that have a special status on specific products, such as most developing countries under the Generalized System of Preference. Add to these several bilateral agreements on specific products, and the system is much more than a two-column system. Therefore, in the United States, the first column is actually split into two subcolumns, one labeled "general" for all NTR countries, and the other "special" for all countries for which, for a given HS number, there is a special negotiated rate.

| FIGURE 16-2 | United States Tariff Schedule |

Harmonized Tariff Schedule of the United States (2009) Supplement 1 (Rev. 1)
Annotated for Statistical Reporting Purposes

XVIII

Heading / Subheading	Stat. Suf- fix	Article Description	Unit of Quantity	Rates of Duty		
				1		2
				General	Special	
9114		Other clock or watch parts:				
9114.10		Springs, including hairsprings:				
9114.10.40	00	For watches	No.	7.3%	Free (A+, AU, B, CA, D, E, IL, J, J+, JO, MA, MX, P, R) 1.8% (CL, SG)	65%
9114.10.80	00	Other	No.	4.2%	Free (A+, AU, B, CA, D, E, IL, J, J+, JO, MA, MX, P, R)	65%
9114.20.00	00	Jewels	No.	Free		10%
9114.30	00	Dials:				
9114.30.40	00	Not exceeding 50 mm in width	No.	0.4¢ each + 7.2%	Free (A+, AU, B, CA, D, E, IL, J, J+, JO, MA, MX, P, R) 0.1¢ each + 1.8%(CL, SG)	5¢ each + 45%
9114.30.80	00	Exceeding 50 mm in width	No.	4.4%	Free (A+, AU, B, CA, CL, D, E, IL, J, J+, JO, MA, MX, P, R, SG)	50%
9114.40		Plates and bridges:				
9114.40.20		Watch movement bottom or pillar plates or their				
	00	equivalent	No.	12¢ each	Free (A+, AU, B, CA, CL, D, E, IL, J, J+, JO, MA, MX, P, R) 7.5¢ each (SG)	75¢ each
9114.40.40	00	Any plate, or set of plates, suitable for assembling thereon a clock movement	No.	10¢ each	Free (A+, AU, B, CA, CL, D, E, IL, J, J+, JO, MA, MX, P, R) 2.5¢ each (SG)	38¢ each
		Other:				
9114.40.60	00	For watches	X	7.3%	Free (A+, AU, B, CA, CL, D, E, IL, J, JO, MA, MX, P, SG)	65%
9114.40.80	00	Other	X	4.2%		65%
		. . . / . . .				

Legend:

A+: Generalized System of Preference
AU: United States – Australia Free Trade Agreement
B: Automotive Product Trade Act
CA: Canada
CL: United States Chile Free Trade Agreement
D: African Growth and Opportunity Act
E: Caribbean Basin Economic Recovery Act
IL: United States – Israel Free Trade Area

J: Andean Trade Preference Act
J+: Andean Drug Eradication Act
JO: United States – Jordan Free Trade Area Implementation Act
MA: United States- Morocco Freee Trade Agreement
MX: Mexico
P: Dominican Republic – Central America US Free Trade Agreement
R: United States - Carribean Basin trade Partnership Act
SG: United States – Singapore Free Trade Agreement

Figure 16-2[27] shows this layout, with a total of 19 "special" tariffs. (Only 3 are not present in the table: the codes "C" for the Agreement on Trade in Civil Aircraft, "K" for the Agreement on Trade in Pharmaceutical Products, and "L" for the Uruguay Round Concessions on Intermediate Chemicals and Dyes.) Each product category has its own negotiated specific treatment, and the Harmonized Tariff Schedule of the United States is replete with exceptions of this nature.

Tariffs are generally calculated *ad valorem* or as a percentage tax on the value of the goods imported. Nevertheless, other methods exist, such as a fixed amount per unit imported. Some others are calculated with a mixed system, such as a fixed amount per unit in addition to a percentage of the value of the goods imported; such a tariff is called a *compound duty rate*. Figure 16-2 illustrates all these alternatives:

- A company importing springs for watches (9114.10.4000) would have to pay 7.3 percent duty on the FCA value of the goods if they came from an NTR

Web Exercise

Some countries can have very unique ways of determining tariffs. Switzerland's tariff schedule stands out in that most of its tariffs are based on the gross weight of the goods imported (per 100 kilograms) rather than their value,[28] even for products such as computers or textiles. Most countries' tariff schedules are now published electronically and can be accessed through the World Customs Organization's Web site:

- http://www.wcoomd.org/tariff/[29]

Find two (simple) products with which you are familiar, and calculate what the tariff would be for these two products if they were exported from Kenya and imported into the United States, the European Union, Switzerland, and India.

country—for example, Japan. If the springs came from India (Generalized System of Preference), Australia (U.S.-Australia Free Trade Agreement), Canada (NAFTA), Haiti (Caribbean Basin Initiative), Israel (U.S.-Israel Free Trade Agreement), Peru (U.S.-Peru Trade Promotion Agreement Implementation Act), or Mexico (NAFTA), the importer would have no duty to pay. If the springs came from North Korea, the duty rate would be 65 percent.

- A company importing small watch movement bottoms (9114.40.2000) from an NTR country, such as Germany, would have to pay U.S. $0.12 per movement, regardless of the FCA value of the movements. The same product coming from some other countries could be imported duty free, while the importer would have to pay $0.03 per movement if the shipment came from Singapore. An importer obtaining the bottoms from Cuba would be saddled with a U.S. $0.75 duty per movement.

The complexity of the tariff rate schedule in most countries is baffling, and the level of detail that is imparted to the rates of duty is simply impossible to justify. Figure 16-2 shows that the U.S. duty rate for watch springs (classified as 9114.10.4000) is reduced from 7.3 percent to zero if the country of export is in the Caribbean or in sub-Saharan Africa. However, for items classified as 9114.10.8000, "other clock parts" (not springs, jewels, or plates), those coming from the Caribbean country would have to pay the 7.3 percent duty rate, and the African country's products would be imported duty free. Similarly, it is hard to explain why dials smaller than 50 millimeters pay a compound duty rate of $0.004 per dial in addition to 7.2 percent duty, when those larger than 50 millimeters pay a duty of 4.4 percent. It is highly unlikely that it was the intent of the U.S. Congress to tax small dials at roughly twice the rate of the larger ones. Other examples abound. The level of detail and precision in the Harmonized Tariff Schedules of most countries cannot be defended.

Fortunately, this situation is likely to change, at least in the United States. Several importers of clothing products have filed lawsuits against the U.S. government, accusing it of engaging in gender discrimination. The companies are fighting the fact that bathing suits are taxed at 28 percent for men and 12 percent for women, that overalls are taxed at 9 percent for men and 14 percent for women, and that wool shirts are taxed at 18 percent for men and less than 9 percent for women.[30] The first complainant to file a lawsuit was Isotoner, an importer of gloves, which charged that the government was discriminating by charging 14 percent duty for men's gloves and 12.6 percent for "other persons." In July 2008, Isotoner's lawsuit was dismissed by the Court of International Trade. The court notified Isotoner that it needed to "allege that the government has engaged in gender-based discrimination without an exceedingly persuasive justification" in order to get relief. The court dismissed the lawsuit "without prejudice," which allows Isotoner to re-file.[31] It is likely that the other lawsuits have followed that recommendation, but none had been adjudicated as of September 2009.

16-1e Dumping

In some cases, Customs can determine that the invoice value is lower (in some rare cases, higher) than the actual value of the goods. This is generally uncovered by comparing the value of a given invoice with a database of import entries with the same Harmonized System number made in preceding year(s). For example, in the United States, the invoice value is systematically compared to existing valuations. This is one of the purposes of the column labeled "unit of quantity" in Figure 16-2 that represents the units under which the Customs computer database keeps the values of other entries under a specific HS number to determine whether a given entry is within the bounds of "normal." Should the invoice give a value outside of these bounds, a Customs import specialist will scrutinize the entry before liquidating it.

dumping The strategy followed by some exporters to sell their products at a price that is considered "too low" by the importing country's Customs office.

When the invoice's value is much below what Customs has historically accepted and when a much higher valuation is reached with one of the alternative valuation methods (see Section 16-1b), Customs can determine that the exporter is **dumping** the goods in the importing country (i.e., selling the goods at a price that is below their commercial value). The exact definition of "dumping" varies from country to country, but the most prevalent definition is that a price is set below the wholesale price of the goods in the exporting country *and* that this causes injury to competitors (or some other group, such as a labor union) located in the importing country. For some countries, such as the United States, there must be a complaint from an injured party before Customs considers that the undervaluation is a case of dumping. In addition, an organization independent of Customs—in the United States, the International Trade Commission—is asked to determine whether there is actual injury to competitors and to ascertain whether the goods are sold at below their commercial value before an exporter is found guilty of dumping.

In those cases, Customs can add an additional duty to the regular duty rate of the commodity, and this duty rate is called an "anti-dumping" duty, which can range from 1 percent to several times the value of the goods imported. Unfortunately, dumping accusations have been one of the most commonly used tools of certain countries to restrict imports, and it is still one of the most commonly used methods of protectionism. In addition, Customs can use a "countervailing" duty to tax products that the exporting government is found to have subsidized. In that case again, it will only act after an allegation of injury by an affected competitor. However, although there is strong support for such countervailing duties in some industries, the U.S. Commerce Department has declined to impose them on products coming from countries in which nonmarket economies prevail.

In the United States, there was a rash of anti-dumping duty requests in the early and mid-2000s, due to the Byrd Amendment, named for Senator Robert Byrd of West Virginia. The Byrd Amendment directed Customs to give the anti-dumping duty it collected from importers to the U.S. companies that were harmed by the dumping. In 2003, U.S. Customs and Border Protection distributed U.S. $190 million to U.S. companies, U.S. $885 million in 2004, and an estimated U.S. $3.85 billion after 2005.[32] The Timken Company, one of the largest beneficiaries of the Byrd Amendment, reported anti-dumping income of U.S. $66 million in 2003, which was an amount equal to 67 percent of its *operating* income of $98 million.[33] Although the WTO ruled against the Byrd Amendment by finding that it violated the rules of international trade,[34] the U.S. Congress did not repeal the amendment until October 2007.

16-1f Other Taxes

In addition to duties, several countries will perceive additional taxes based on the value of the goods; these additional taxes are a disguised way of creating additional revenues from imports while remaining within the boundaries of the General Agreement on Tariffs and Trade (GATT) and the rules of the WTO, which mandate systematic reductions in tariffs.

Such additional taxes can be labeled very creatively:

- **Punitive duty**. The United States, unhappy about a decision by the European Union to give preferential treatment to bananas imported from former European colonies in the Caribbean and Africa, retaliated by placing a 100 percent duty on certain items coming from any of the 15 EU countries: cashmere, blue cheese, "handbags covered in plastic sheeting," and so on.[35]

- **Border traffic tax**. Russia, in order to "make a more accurate tally of border flows of people, cargo, and means of transportation," imposes a 1 percent tax on all goods crossing its borders. Russian travelers are taxed at 0.8 percent of their monthly income.[36]

- **Safeguard tax**. Argentina, after being chastised by the WTO for having increased its duty rate on footwear, reduced them, then immediately re-imposed them through an emergency "safeguard tax" designed to protect its footwear industry against foreign competition.

- **Temporary protection tax**. The United States imposed a 33 percent additional tariff on brooms from Mexico to allow U.S. manufacturers to increase their efficiency so that they could compete against imports. It repealed this tax two years later, noting that the industry had not taken advantage of this protection period to improve its efficiency.[37]

These taxes are designed to increase revenues for the importing country, protect less efficient domestic industries, and punish importers, while respecting the letter—but certainly not the intent—of WTO agreements.

16-1g Value-Added Tax

In some countries, an additional tax is collected in addition to the duty, but is generally considered to have no bearing on importers—even if it adds up to a significant amount—because it is collected from domestic producers as well as from importers, and is eventually paid by only consumers: the **Value-Added Tax (VAT)**. The idea of VAT is somewhat simple in its concept: The tax is perceived on the value added by each firm involved in adding value to a good, from the first one in the production chain to the last one. The implementation of a VAT is somewhat complex, though.

It is probably best to explain the VAT concept and its implementation—as it is practiced in the European Union countries, at least—with a simplified example:

1. A farmer purchases seeds, fertilizer, pesticides, and fuel to produce corn. On each of her production-related purchases, she pays the VAT. She keeps track of the VAT she has paid in a special bookkeeping account, as a "debit." She then sells the corn she has produced and collects VAT from her customer, which she records in that account as a "credit." At the end of the quarter, she deducts the VAT she has paid from the VAT she has collected, and sends the difference to her government.

2. The corn is purchased by a mill that promptly transforms it into several products, including corn syrup. On all the products it sells to wholesalers and retailers, the mill collects VAT, an amount it records in a special bookkeeping account. At the end of the quarter, the mill deducts all the VAT it has paid to farmers for corn and all the VAT it has paid for its other purchases from

Value-Added Tax (VAT) A tax perceived by many countries that is very similar to a sales tax, but that is collected whenever the product's value is increased. The VAT on imports is collected at the point of entry into the country.

the VAT it has collected from its customers and sends the difference to its government.

3. The corn syrup is purchased by a consumer who uses it for cooking. The consumer pays the VAT, but has no way to collect any, so it is the consumer who bears the tax's entire burden.

For imports, the concept is the same. The VAT is collected from the importer, but the importer can deduct the value of the VAT it has paid from the VAT it eventually collects from its customers; therefore, the tax is not an actual cost to the importer. However, this is somewhat incorrect: In reality, there are substantial accounting and cash-flow costs associated with this method of garnering taxes. Nevertheless, because both domestic and imported products are taxed the same way, there are no advantages garnered by either in their final costs to the consumer. The cost is quite a substantial one for the ultimate consumer, though, as the VAT rate in the European Union is approximately 20 percent.

In the E.U., the VAT is computed on the sum of the value of the imported goods and the duty perceived at importation.

16-2 Non-Tariff Barriers

Some countries use high tariffs to attempt to limit the import of certain goods. However, steady pressure from the General Agreement on Tariffs and Trade, and now the World Trade Organization, has reduced considerably the duty paid by most goods in most countries. While there are still some exceptions, the trend is still toward ever lower duty rates, with many countries having adopted tariffs that are rarely above 10 percent for most goods.

At the same time, the WTO has also been very active in attempting to decrease the number of non-tariff trade barriers that countries can place on imports. Nevertheless, several of those alternatives are still in place, which effectively limit exporters' access to certain markets. Non-tariff trade barriers are those policies and actions that have the effect of reducing the number of items imported in a specific country. Often, not surprisingly, what is perceived as a trade barrier by an international trader is presented as an innocuous requirement by the importing country's government.

16-2a Quotas

quota A limit, set by the importing country's government, on the quantity of a specific commodity that can be imported in a given year.

The primary method used by countries to limit imports is a system of quotas, which limit the quantity of goods that can enter a particular country. A **quota** can take either of two forms:

1. *An absolute quota,* which places a yearly limit on the number of items entering a country under a specific HS number. On occasion, the quota can be implemented using the value of the goods imported by placing a ceiling on the total value of goods imported under a specific HS number. Once the quota is reached, goods in that category can no longer be imported. Some countries, whose products are subject to quotas, have established a system of visas to monitor how much of a given quota has been filled by its exporters (see Section 16-3g).

2. *A tariff-rate quota,* which places a two-tiered tariff rate on a specific category of products. Until a specific number of goods are entered, the tariff is low, but once the quota is reached, the tariff changes to a much higher percentage. Nevertheless, the goods can still be legally imported.

Quotas are usually placed on very specific items coming from a specific country of origin. For example, in 2000, no more than 147,358 dozens of articles under quota number 651-B—Harmonized System numbers 6107.22.0016 and 6108.32.0016,

The Sugar Quota

The United States has had a tariff-rate quota on sugar for many years. The total amount of raw sugar that can be imported in 2009 at the low tariff rate of U.S. $0.01406 per kilogram is 1,117,195 metric tonnes, and any amount above that is charged U.S. $0.3574 per kilogram.[42] The world market price for sugar is about U.S. $0.30 per kilogram,[43] so the tariff more than doubles the cost of sugar for U.S. importers. A number of powerful groups of sugar producers in the United States are vocal supporters of this tariff-rate quota and are substantial financial backers of both political parties, so it has never been abolished, even though the WTO has ruled against it. This group is so strong that when the United States negotiated its free-trade agreement with Australia, it covered all products, but specifically excluded sugar.

Under the 2003/2004 system, which was still in place in 2009, each producing country is allocated a given portion of the quota; for example, Haiti's share of the quota is 7,258 metric tonnes, and Brazil, the world's largest producer, is allowed 152,691 tonnes.[44] These quotas are very low, especially considering that a Handysize ship can hold 35,000 tonnes. Essentially, the largest producer of sugar in the world (36.85 million metric tonnes)[45] can ship only about four boatloads of sugar (0.4 percent of its production) to the largest market in the world, which has an annual consumption of 9,771,000 metric tonnes. Brazilian sugar imports represent therefore about 1.5 percent of the total U.S. consumption.

The quota has an impact on the sugar market in the United States. Although consumers are largely unaffected by the high price of sugar because it represents a small portion of people's expenses, the overall market size is much smaller than it would be if there were no sugar quota; many industrial users of sugar have substituted corn syrup (soft drink manufacturers) or moved abroad (candy manufacturers are producing in Mexico and Canada to ship to the U.S. market) to circumvent the artificially high cost of sugar. This restriction also distorts the export market for American products: Mexico has a retaliatory 20 percent tax on soft drinks made with corn syrup, for example.[46]

However, the impact of the sugar quota is greatest on the economies of the Caribbean and Central American countries that cannot export one of their largest agricultural crops to the United States. Table 16-1 shows the quota allocations for these countries. Note the disparities between the quotas of Haiti and the Dominican Republic, which have about the same size population; whether it is a cause or a consequence, the gross domestic product of the Dominican Republic is roughly seven times that of Haiti.[47]

TABLE 16-1	Selected Quota Quantities for Sugar (2009)[48]

Country	2009 Quota (in metric tonnes)
Barbados	7,371
Belize	11,583
Costa Rica	15,796
Dominican Republic	185,335
El Salvador	27,379
Guatemala	50,546
Guyana	12,636
Haiti	7,258
Honduras	10,530
Jamaica	11,583
Nicaragua	22,114
Panama	30,538
Trinidad and Tobago	7,371
TOTAL	400,040
Percentage of U.S. consumption	4%

A possible move to sugar-based ethanol as a substitute for gasoline in automobile engines, which is common in Brazil, may change this situation, as the United States would need to import much larger quantities of sugar; however, as of October 2009, there were no signs that ending the quota was even being considered.

corresponding to boys' and girls' blanket sleepers (a type of pajamas) made of man-made fibers—could have been imported into the United States from China.[38] This complex system of quotas for textiles and apparel was followed by the United States and other developed countries for products originating in some developing countries and was outlined in an international treaty called the Multi-Fiber Agreement (MFA). Those quotas restricted the number of textile items imported from a large number of developing countries. The WTO negotiated the Agreement on Textiles and Clothing, and all developed countries' textile quotas were supposed to have been lifted by January 1, 2005.[39]

However, within four months of that deadline,[40] both the European Union and the United States had re-imposed some quotas on textiles originating from China. These quotas were established within the WTO guidelines, which allowed for some "safeguards" should the elimination of quotas be harmful to the economies of the importing countries. Mostly, the elimination of quotas was particularly harmful to the developing countries that were competing with China. Under the MFA quota system, many countries gained access to the large markets of Europe and the United States because Chinese firms were limited in the number of products they could sell. After the quotas were lifted, the Chinese firms, being the world's chief low-cost producers of textile apparel and having seemingly unlimited capacity, would have displaced these other countries' products and created economic hardship there. Whether the imposition of quotas on Chinese goods is going to help these countries invest in increased productivity or only postpone the inevitable is unknown.

Quotas can also be aggregate, applying to all imports under an HS heading, regardless of the country of origin—for example, the United States has aggregate tariff-rate quotas on milk, cream, dried milk, cheddar cheese, ice cream, peanuts, cocoa powder, sugar, and a substantial number of other food products, that apply to all countries of origin.[41]

Quotas can also be "voluntary." Under pressure from the importing government, exporters agree to limit their exports "voluntarily" to a certain quantity. Such was the case during the early 1980s in the United States when Japanese automobile manufacturers agreed to absolute quotas for automobiles and light trucks.

Finally, quotas can come in the form of export quotas, when an exporting country limits the quantity of a certain type of good that firms can export from its territory (see Chapter 9, Section 9-3f).

16-2b Adherence to National Standards

Unfortunately, quotas are hardly the only non-tariff trade barriers placed by countries to restrict imports. In many instances, countries enact "safety measures" designed to ostensibly protect their populations from defective, dangerous, or unhealthy products from abroad. While most of these restrictions are justified and necessary, some of

The European Union's Banana Wars

In 1993, the European Union, in an effort to support the economies of some of its members' former colonies in the Caribbean and Africa, devised a complex system of quotas, preferential tariffs, and import licenses to favor bananas imported from these countries. Even though it is not an exporter of bananas, the United States got tangled in this dispute because two of the companies that were affected by these restrictions were Dole Foods and Chiquita Brands, two American firms exporting bananas grown in Central America to Europe.[55]

Even after three rulings against this practice by the WTO, the European Union still maintained this convoluted system of preferential treatment, and the United States eventually retaliated with higher tariffs on products from Europe such as pens, candles, and cheese,[56] to no avail. The "banana wars" escalated to a point where it involved the highest levels of government, and it took

years to be resolved, despite the efforts of WTO panels to ease the tension and resolve the issue.[57]

In early 2001, Chiquita Brands took the unusual step of suing the European Union for US$525 million, which the company claims were the lost profits the company had incurred because of the restrictions and which caused it to default on its bond payments.[58] The spat between the United States and the European Union is now over, and European consumers end up paying slightly less for bananas today than they did when the trade barrier was in place. However, there are still conflicts between the European Union and some of the countries in which the bananas are produced; in 2008, Ecuador won a partial victory in a lawsuit that alleged that the European Union's trade policies favored Caribbean and African producers of bananas.[59] The EU is appealing the ruling of the WTO.

them are based on dubious data and are simply a form of undisguised protectionism for less efficient domestic producers.

Countries certainly can demand that products sold within their borders meet the standards that their governments have enacted—for example, there are many requirements regarding the quality of consumer products in developed countries. The most prominent ones are the Deutsche Industrie Normen (DIN) in Germany, the Japanese Industry Standards (JIS) in Japan, the Normes Françaises (NF) in France, and the American National Standard Institute (ANSI) in the United States. A few international standards exist as well, such as those defined by the International Organization for Standardization in its ISO set of requirements. Most of these requirements are legitimate in that they reflect national preferences and sentiment toward consumer protection, health standards, and safety. For example, the European Union requires that vehicles be equipped with rear turn signals that are distinct from the brake lights, and the United States requires that automobiles be equipped with airbags. Both are obviously worthy requirements.

The point at which these requirements become non-tariff barriers is unclear. An exporter is often unwilling to incorporate into its products an additional feature that is costly or that it deems unnecessary, and claims that the requirement is a non-tariff barrier, when it may just be an unwillingness to deal with one of the differences and difficulties of selling a product in a foreign country.[49] In a parallel fashion, such a requirement may *not* be a non-tariff barrier, even if it is required only of imported products and not of domestic manufacturers, if it is to protect a country from "importing" a disease that has not yet been observed domestically. A recent example would be the so-called "mad cow disease," against which non-European countries are trying to protect themselves.

Nevertheless, countries' efforts to make imports adhere to national standards are often considered to be trade barriers. There have been lengthy spats over the safety of Mexican avocados in the United States,[50] of U.S. cherries in Mexico,[51] of New Zealand apples in Japan,[52] and of U.S. hormone-treated beef[53] and genetically-modified cereals in the European Union. The dispute with Japan over the safety of U.S. tomatoes lasted 46 years before being resolved in favor of U.S. exporters.[54]

16-2c Other Non-tariff Barriers

Countries have enacted some very creative means to slow or restrict imports without having recourse to high tariffs, quotas, or standardization requirements. Here are several examples, which certainly do not constitute an exhaustive list:

- In the very early 1980s, France decided that it needed to protect its nascent industry in videocassette recorders (VCRs). It achieved this goal by requiring that every VCR entering the country be inspected, that a sticker be placed on every machine, and that the inspection take place in Poitiers, a landlocked small town about 250 miles from the port of Le Havre, through which most VCRs were shipped. Moreover, the inspection station was a *one-man* operation.[60] Countless countries have enacted similar "slow" Customs clearance processes, in order to deter imports by increasing costs to importers for additional storage, and creating potential marketing delays.[61]

- Another tactic is to require a mind-numbing number of documents and approvals. For example, in the late 1990s, in India, "an exporter has to complete and process fifty-four documents […]: twenty-seven pre-shipment documents, fourteen for Customs clearance, and thirteen for post-shipment realization of bills. As many as 16 approvals are needed from departments of the central government."[62] The process has been largely simplified since: As of 2009, there were nine documents necessary to import in India, which is still twice the number of the average for countries that are members of the Organisation for Economic Co-operation and Development (OECD).[63]

- Another way to slow Customs entries is to request additional papers that are not readily available or that are close to impossible to gather. The United States requests the "sewing tickets" for some garments, an internal work document of the garment factory, as well as the time cards of the employees working there, in an attempt to determine the country of origin of textile products.

- South Korea has been tremendously effective at keeping foreign cars out of its domestic market. In 2008, there were 800,000 Korean-made automobiles sold on the U.S. market, but fewer than 7,000 U.S.-made automobiles sold in Korea, and only 62,000 foreign-made cars.[64] This was achieved, despite relatively low tariffs of 8 percent, with a systematic campaign designed to portray the purchase of a foreign car as unpatriotic. To bolster this perception, the South Korean government has all but threatened all purchasers of foreign cars with an income tax audit.[65]

- Russia asked the U.S. exporters of chicken parts (legs and wings) to individually inspect *every* bird—for specific diseases—before they can enter the country, effectively preventing all U.S. imports of such parts.[66]

16-2d Pre-shipment Inspections

Pre-shipment inspections (PSIs) are performed by independent companies at the point of departure of goods destined to be exported. The firm determines that the goods shipped are the ones ordered by the importer, in the correct quantity, and sufficiently well packed for an international shipment. When the independent firm has ascertained that all of these aspects conform to the invoice, it issues a Certificate of Inspection (see Chapter 9, Section 9-4c) to the importer. Inspection companies have representatives in most ports and generally can handle just about any sort of shipment; on many occasions, though, the exporter experiences delays with PSIs as the workload of inspectors can be substantial, and as the expertise needed for a specific shipment may not be available.

Pre-shipment inspections are sometimes requested by importers to ensure that exporters are shipping the correct product in the correct quantity; they are used when the importer is purchasing on a cash-in-advance basis or on a letter of credit. However, most PSIs are required by countries as part of their import process. There are several reasons for this requirement:

- The country wants an expert opinion on the classification and the value of the products that are about to enter its territory.

- The country wants to fight corruption in its own ports of entry. By having a foreign, independent firm determine the classification and value of imported goods, its own Customs authorities have lost the ability to "be flexible" and change their classifications and valuations for a bribe. Such was the motivation when Indonesia demanded that any good shipped into Indonesia had to be pre-inspected by the *Société Générale de Surveillance*.[67]

- The country wants an estimate of the currency requirements it will face in the short term, and uses the value of the shipments subject to PSI to forecast its foreign currency needs.

- The country wants to generate some revenues in addition to the tariff it charges. Most of the countries requiring PSIs have long-term contracts giving an exclusive right to a single inspection company to inspect *all* of the goods about to enter its territory. Although it is pure speculation, it is likely that inspection companies compensate the country for this exclusive right by transferring a portion of the revenues generated by inspections to the national treasury.

16-3 Customs Clearing Process

The Customs clearing process differs from country to country and tends to be arcane and cumbersome. In most countries, because of the complexity of the task, only certified Customs brokers or Customs agents are allowed to file the paperwork necessary to clear Customs. This section will give only a brief overview of the processes generally followed by Customs authorities worldwide and give examples based upon the U.S. system.

16-3a General Process

In some countries, the process starts with an application for an import license, a request for the express authorization to import a certain product. Import licenses are usually granted according to a number of criteria, most of which are based on the availability of foreign currency to pay for the import and on the availability of domestic substitutes. Generally speaking, countries with scarce foreign currency resources will attempt to limit the granting of import licenses to those companies that have generated export revenues, and to those companies purchasing goods for which no close domestic substitute is available.

For most countries, however, the process starts when an importer files an **entry** (i.e., notifies the Customs authorities that it will import—or has imported—a particular product). There is usually a paper form (see Figure 16-3) that has to be filed and which must accompany all the documentation necessary for the import: invoice, Certificate of Origin, Certificate of Inspection (when required), Certificate of Insurance, and other forms as required by the Customs rules of the importing country. In most developed countries, the importer is usually responsible for classifying the goods according to the tariff schedule of the importing country, and for determining the amount of duty. In many developing countries, this task is still left to the Customs authorities, a requirement which often delays the process of clearance. In most instances, the goods are not released to the importer (**cleared**) until after the duty is paid or after there is evidence from the importer that it will pay, a requirement often met with a Customs bond. Generally, Customs authorities will review a percentage of the entries made by importers after the goods have been cleared and will have a few months to a couple of years to challenge them. If an entry is reviewed satisfactorily, the entry is deemed **liquidated**. In some countries, such as the United States, an importer dissatisfied with the final decision of Customs authorities has a brief period of time to **protest** a liquidated entry and request a review before it is finally settled.

16-3b Customs Brokers

Because of the complexity and time-consuming nature of filling out Customs entries, many countries demand that importers delegate the task of interacting with Customs to a Customs broker, a representative of the importer that has acquired the knowledge and experience required to deal effectively and efficiently with Customs. In many countries, Customs brokers are the only entities qualified to enter goods (i.e., fill out the paperwork necessary to import goods). It is not the case in the United States, though, where importers can complete their own entries, as long as they have posted a Customs bond (see Section 16-3c). Customs brokers are usually compensated on a fee basis for each entry they handle. In the United States, Customs brokers are highly qualified individuals who have to take a grueling test on issues of classification, duty computation, and quotas before being allowed to manage importers' entries.

16-3c Customs Bonds

In most countries, the importer has to pay the duty to Customs before the shipment can be legally released. However, this can be extremely unwieldy, especially in those

entry The process by which an importer notifies Customs that it has imported a particular product.

cleared The term used to signify that goods were imported into a country and that the importer paid the duty that was due on those goods, and thus the goods were released by the Customs authorities.

liquidated entry An entry that has been successfully reviewed by Customs authorities and for which duty has been paid.

protest In a Customs transaction in the United States, the formal request by an importer to have Customs reconsider its classification, its valuation, or its determination of a country of origin.

FIGURE 16-3 The Canadian Entry Form for Food Products

Canadian Food Inspection Agency
Agence canadienne d'inspection des aliments

IMPORT DECLARATION

DÉCLARATION D'IMPORTATION

1.
- [ ] Dairy Products / Produits laitiers
- [ ] Processed Fruits and Vegetables / Fruits et légumes transfrmés
- [ ] Honey / Miel
- [ ] Maple Products / Produits de l'érable
- [ ] Pesticides / Semences
- [ ] Seeds / Semences
- [ ] Feed / Aliments du bétail
- [ ] Fertilizer * / Engrais *

* Registrable / Sujets à l'enregistrement

2. Name and Address of Manufacturer / Nom et adresse du febricant

3. Name and Address of Exporter / Nom et adresse de l'exportateur

4. Name and Canadian Address of Importer / Nom et adresse canadienne de l'importateur

Telephone Number / Numéro de téléphone ➡

5. Name and Address of Destination (consignee) / Nom et adresse du destinataire

Telephone Number / Numéro de téléphone ➡

6. Transaction No. / N° de transaction

7. Carrier / Transporteur

9. Container No. / N° de conteneur

8. Flight No. / N°de vol

10. Trailer No. / N° de remorque

PRODUCT DESCRIPTION AND PACKAGING (ATTACH LIST IF NECESSARY)
DESCRIPTION DU PRODUIT ET DE L'EMBALLAGE (ANNEXER UNE LISTEAU BESOIN)

11. Common Name / Nom usuel	12. Brand Name / Marque	13. Grade / Catégorie	14. No. of Shipping Containers / Nbre de contenants

15. No., Type and Net Contents of Individual Containers per Shipping Container / Nbre, type et contenu net des contenants individuels par contenant d'expédition	16. Total Net Quantity / Quantité totale nette	17. Label Approval No. N°. d'approbation de l'étiquette	18. Registration No. N° d'enregistrement	19. Purpose of Importation / Motif de l'importation	20. Additional documentation and other references / Documents additionnels et autres références

21. Declaration / Déclaration

I, _____ the importer of the products described on this form do hereby certify that the information provided on this form is complete, correct and accurately describes the products contained in the shipment.

By signing this declaration in the case of the food products used for human consumption, I affirm that I have read the "Regulatory Requirements for Food Products Imported into Canada" set forth in the instructions to fill out this form and that the products described on this form meet those requirements.

Je, _____ , l'importateur des Produits décrits sur ce formulaire, certifie que l'information fournie sur ce formulaire est complète et qu'elle décrit avec précision les produits contenues dans cechargement.

En signant cette déclaration, dans le cas de produits alimentaires utilisés pour consommation humaine, j'affirme que j'ai lu les "Exigences réglementaires pour les produits alimentaires importés au Canada" inscrites dans les instructions pour remplir ce formulaire et que les produits décrits sur ce formulaire satisfont ces exigences.

_____ _____
Signature   Date

GOVERNMENT USE ONLY / RÉSERVÉ A L'ADMINISTRATION

22. Stamp / Estampe

23. Instructions to Customs and Importers / Directives aux douaniers et importateurs

- [ ] Au moment de l'importation, main levée et remise sous le contrôle d'AAC (pour l'inspection à l'arrivée à destination)

Further action to be conducted on the shipment at the following place:

- [ ] _____
Autres mesures à prendre à l'égard du chargement à l'endroit suivant :

- [ ] _____
Other instruction / Instruction particulière

The information is collected by the Canadian Food Inspection Agency for the purpose of administering all Agriculture Acts. Information may be accessible or protected as required under the provisions of the **Access to information Act.**

L'information est recueillie par l'Agence canadienne d'inspectiondes aliments aux fins d'application de la législation agricole. L'information peut être accessible ou protégée en vertu des exigences de la **Loi sur l'accès à l'information.**

CFIA / ACIA 4560 (1999/06)

cases where the shipment is an express package or is time sensitive (e.g., produce). Therefore, Customs authorities allow importers (or Customs brokers entering goods on their behalf) to post a surety bond, which is a guarantee that the importer or the Customs broker will pay the duty due. A bond is generally a sum of money deposited with Customs, from which any unpaid duty can be withdrawn, or an insurance policy with a surety company that acts as a guarantor of the importer or the Customs broker, and which it would be required to pay if the duty were not paid on time. This process allows goods to be entered before the duty is paid. In some cases, actually, the goods are sold long before the entry is liquidated.

In the United States, the bond is not just a guarantee that the duty will be paid on time; it is also a contract that obligates the importer or the Customs broker to perform all Customs-related functions in a timely manner, such as filing entries that are complete and accurate, as well as presenting Customs with the goods after they have physically entered the country, generally for inspection purposes.[68]

16-3d Reasonable Care

Out of the U.S. Customs Modification Act of 1993 came the concepts of **informed compliance** and **reasonable care**, neither of which can be easily defined, but which have become pivotal to the efforts of the Customs Service in the United States.

The idea behind informed compliance is that, if an importer has been found compliant, the likelihood that one of its shipments is going to be inspected is minimal, thereby minimizing delays at entry and allowing the importer to organize its supply chain more predictably. It also lowers costs, as merchandise is cleared quickly and does not languish in some bonded warehouse while the importer and Customs argue about its correct classification, valuation, or country of origin.

In order for an importer to be found compliant, it must show that it exercised reasonable care in the filing of its Customs entries. In order to demonstrate reasonable care, the importer must follow a long list of obligations that the U.S. Customs Service provides.[69] The obligations center on making sure that the importer employs a Customs specialist, who will make sure that all—including the most recent—Customs regulations are followed and that it has put into place a process by which it correctly determines the valuation, classification, and country of origin of an import. Reasonable care is monitored through a system of compliance audits organized by U.S. Customs.[70]

16-3e Required Documentation

The documentation required by any Customs authority can be extensive. Ideally speaking, there should be only three documents required in every country to make an entry:

- A form designated for entry (specific to the record-keeping requirements of the importing country)
- A Certificate of Origin to ascertain the country of origin
- A commercial invoice with enough information to determine value and classification

However, many more can be included, from an import license to a series of certificates or other documents (most of these documents were introduced and explained in Chapter 9). One of the worst offenders was India, with about 54 documents, as shown in Section 16-2c. Many countries' requirements are published electronically; a good number of them can be accessed through www.export.gov/logistics.

The critical element of import documentation is that it is established on a *per* transaction basis. Every import, however small, needs to have its own specific entry,

informed compliance A standard of behavior, set and enforced by U.S. Customs, that is expected of importers if they want their Customs entries to be cleared quickly and Customs inspections kept to a minimum.

reasonable care A standard of behavior, set and enforced by U.S. Customs, that is expected of importers if they want their Customs entries to be cleared quickly and if they want to keep Customs inspections to a minimum.

which can lead to an inordinate amount of paperwork, under which both the importer and the Customs authorities are drowning. For example, in order to allow a shipment that landed in any of Europe's many ports to travel to another country in the EU, a form has to be filed in quintuplicate—five copies—and there were 18 million shipments of this nature in 1999, netting a "paper blizzard" of 90 million copies that the European Customs authorities must store in warehouses.[71]

There are several efforts made to simplify the process of importing merchandise and clearing Customs:

1. The most significant one is the automated (electronic) processing of entries, which was implemented by the U.S. Customs Service under the Automated Commercial System (ACS) in 1984. The ACS is in the process of being progressively replaced with the Automated Commercial Environment (ACE) system, which was completed in 2005.[72] Several countries have adopted similar programs, but to date, they are all incompatible. The WCO, with its Kyoto Protocol, and more recently the WTO are working on harmonizing Customs requirements worldwide, but so far these efforts have been only marginally successful.[73]

2. Great Britain's Customs agency has developed the International Trade Prototype with the help of U.S. Customs. The idea is that the same merchandise exported from the United States and imported into Great Britain generates two sets of paperwork, as if it were two separate, stand-alone processes. The International Trade Prototype allows the electronic documentation used for exporting the product from the United States to be used to import the product into the United Kingdom, which significantly reduces the amount of paper generated.[74] The WCO is now considering a similar setup.[75]

3. As of October 2009, the U.S. Customs and Border Protection agency was also evaluating a process that would allow an importer to file entries periodically—say, at the end of the month—rather than for every transaction. Since 2004, duties can be paid for several entries at the same time, under a program called Periodic Monthly Statement processing,[76] which is available to companies participating in ACE. Such an entry filing system would revolutionize the business of processing imports, bringing much simplification and expediency to the process.

16-3f Required Markings

Products imported into a country often require a marking—"made in [country]" or "product of [country]"—printed or affixed on the product itself or its packaging. Rules differ from country to country on the location of the marking, its size, and whether it needs to be permanently attached to the product. The determination of the country placed on the marking is also left to the country of importation. However, there are no known instances of a country on the marking being different from the country of origin for Customs duty purposes (see Section 16-1c).

In the United States, markings are required for most products, although there is a list, maintained by the U.S. Customs Office,[77] of exceptions, mostly products on which it is difficult or impossible to place a marking. All markings must be legible, conspicuous, and durable. However, the United States has an additional, unusual requirement. No product imported into the United States can have a name or package such that it may mislead the public as to its country of origin. It is therefore prohibited to include words such as "American," "United States," or "U.S.A." Inappropriate or missing markings are subject to penalties, liquidated damages, and seizures by U.S. Customs.

Finally, there is the issue of the "Made in the USA" label, which is often a marketing advantage in the U.S. market. Although the Federal Trade Commission considered lowering the minimum United States content to 75 percent of a product's value, it has maintained this content at "all or virtually all" of a product for the foreseeable future,[78] making it all but impossible to mark a product as made in the United States unless it is entirely domestically produced.

16-3g Merchandise Visas

For those products whose importation is limited by quotas, and particularly for textile products, a bilateral monitoring system has been implemented by the importing and exporting countries.

Because there is a maximum quantity of goods that can be imported into a given country in a calendar year, the government of the country of export will grant—in some cases, sell—the right to export a set quantity of a specific good to an exporting firm. Such authorization is a **merchandise visa**. The visa specifies the type of good (by Harmonized System number), the quantity, and the destination country to which the exporter is allowed to sell.

For products for which such a system is in place, the visa is one of the required documents that must be presented to the Customs authorities of the importing countries, and often to the Customs authorities of the exporting country as well. As quotas are slowly eliminated, so should be the visa requirements. Nevertheless, although merchandise visas were once predicted to become obsolete,[79] they have not disappeared, and they are often required as part of the documentation package for a given import.[80]

16-3h Duty Drawbacks

Several countries, including the United States, grant a substantial tax break to exporters who are using imported parts in the products they export. Such a tax break is called a **duty drawback**.

In the United States, the Customs Service will refund 99 percent of the duty paid by an importer in one of three cases:

- For merchandise that is rejected by the importer as non-conforming to the original purchase order
- For imported products that are re-exported unused
- For imported parts that are used—without substantial transformation—in the assembly or manufacturing of products that are eventually re-exported

Note that this duty drawback is not available for products exported to NAFTA countries.

This drawback can represent a considerable savings in many cases. However, few U.S. firms take advantage of this duty drawback opportunity, either because they do not know about it or because they fear the paperwork requirements that accompany this program.[81] Actually, the paperwork requirements used to be mind-boggling: For example, in order to take advantage of the "unused" drawback, Customs required importers to track individual items from their import to their leaving the country. However, since April 1998, the requirements have been relaxed, allowing "commercially interchangeable goods" to qualify as exports for the drawback.[82] In exchange for this flexibility, Customs has substantially stiffened penalties for illegitimate drawbacks.[83]

16-4 Foreign Trade Zones

Foreign Trade Zones (FTZs) are specific locations of a country that have acquired a special Customs status. Foreign Trade Zones—sometimes called Free Trade Zones—are areas of a country that, for Customs purposes, still are located "outside"

merchandise visa A document provided by the government of an exporting country for a product that is subject to a quota in the United States. It is a document granting the exporter the "right" to export such goods.

duty drawback A process by which the U.S. Customs and Border Protection agency refunds up to 99 percent of the duty it has collected on goods that are imported into the United States if the same goods are later exported from the United States.

of a country. Practically, that means that goods can be shipped to the FTZ without being subject to the duties, quotas, and Customs regulations of the host country. In most countries, however, including the United States, goods admitted into an FTZ must be legal in the country in which the zone is located; the exemption applies only to Customs purposes, not to other legal requirements. For example, medical devices not yet approved in the country in which the FTZ is located would not be acceptable in that FTZ, even though the devices may be perfectly legal in other countries.

Once in the FTZ, the goods can be warehoused until they are sent to their final destination, either in the host or in a foreign country. If the goods are sold in the host country, they are dutiable only at the time of that transaction. If they are sold abroad, they are dutiable only in the importing country; the country in which the FTZ is located will never collect any duty on the value of that merchandise. The country of origin used for Customs purposes remains the country from which the goods originated, and not the country in which the FTZ is located.

Foreign Trade Zones exist in one form or another in just about every country. The most common form of FTZ is a location through which cargo transits. For example, most of the ports of the world are FTZs,[84] so that cargo can be unloaded from a ship, temporarily stored in a warehouse, and then loaded onto another vessel to its final destination. Such cargo, although physically present in the country in which the port is located, never "enters" the country and is therefore never assessed duty. Because shipping companies are moving toward a system of very large containerships serving very large "hub" ports, from which smaller, so-called feeder ships are serving smaller ports, the importance of FTZs is expected to increase. Airports, which often operate on the same concept of "hub and spoke," also often possess a few warehouses in an FTZ. Because such FTZs are available to all companies involved in international trade, the United States calls them General Purpose (Foreign Trade) Zones.[85]

Foreign Trade Zones

Another type of FTZ is not located in a port or cargo area, but at the place of business of a corporation, such as a plant or a refinery. In most of these types of trade zones, some economic activity beyond simple warehousing is conducted, such as manufacturing, assembly, repackaging, and refining. The FTZ is created with the purpose of creating jobs in the host country by providing a lower cost structure to the businesses using them, because they do not have to pay duty on the goods that they are processing and eventually re-exporting. Another way a business can save money by obtaining FTZ status is when the host country has a so-called "inverted tariff structure" (i.e., the tariffs charged on parts are higher than the tariffs charged on the final product). Such FTZ locations are called "sub-zones" in the United States, affiliated for legal purposes with a General Purpose Foreign Trade Zone, because these locations are available to only one specific company and not to others.

An interesting issue arises when a substantial transformation takes place in an FTZ and the goods change from one Harmonized System (HS) classification to another. Even though the rules of origin call for the goods to be "made" in the country in which this change of HS number took place—the country in which the FTZ is located, in this case—negotiations between Customs and the company determine the country of origin that will be used for duty purposes, be it the country of origin of the parts used, or that of the main component, or yet some other alternative. In any case, it is never the country in which the change in HS took place.

Foreign Trade Zones can be quite advantageous to hold goods in inventory until they are sold, improving the cash flow of their owners, to wait for a numerical quota to open, or for an inspection by the host country's government.

However, in view of the progress made in the last few years by the WTO to lead countries toward lower tariffs and increased trade, FTZs created for other purposes than cargo transfers may have a limited future because their advantages are dwindling.

Review and Discussion Questions

1. What is the concept of a Harmonized System number? How is it used? What are the advantages of such a system?

2. Explain the concept of "valuation" from the perspective of Customs. Why is it particularly important to have a detailed commercial invoice for valuation?

3. Explain the concept of "classification" from the perspective of Customs. Why is it particularly important to have a detailed commercial invoice for classification?

4. Explain the concept of "country of origin." How is it currently determined? Why is it such a difficult concept? Why is it important?

5. What are non-tariff barriers? Why are they used? Give a few examples.

6. What types of quotas are there? How does the United States enforce the quotas it imposes? What is a "merchandise visa"?

Endnotes

1. U.S. International Trade Commission, "General Rules of Interpretation," *Harmonized Tariff Schedule of the United States (2009)*, United States International Trade Commission, Washington, District of Columbia.

2. United States Customs and Border Protection, "Requirements for Electronic Ruling Requests," June 22, 2009, http://www.cbp.gov/xp/cgov/trade/legal/rulings/eRulingRequirements.xml.

3. Lucentini, Jack, "Customs, Importers Urge ITC to Review Tariff Classifications," *Journal of Commerce*, May 1, 2000, p. 3.

4. Neville Peterson Williams (attorneys), "Cat Antlers and 'Neckties In Bottles'," *Journal of Commerce*, January 14, 1998, p. 11C.

5. Green, Paula, "A Costly Halloween Question: Are Costumes Toys or Clothing?" *Journal of Commerce*, March 26, 1998, p. 1A.

6. Rushford, Greg, "When Is a Duck Not Like a Bedspread?" *Asian Wall Street Journal*, February 24, 1997, p. 12.

7. Ungar, Ed, "Closing a Literal Loophole," *U.S. News & World Report*, April 27, 1998, p. 32.

8. Cowan, Richard, "Weyerhauser Seeks Tax to End Canada Lumber Fight," Reuters press release, November 20, 2002, http://ca.news.yahoo.com/021120/5/qdat.html, accessed December 12, 2002.

9. King, Neil Jr., "Is Wolverine Human? A Judge Answers No; Fans Howl in Protest," *Wall Street Journal*, January 20, 2003, p. A1.

10. "Customs Valuation: Agreement on Implementation of Article VII of the General Agreement on Tariffs and Trade 1994, Within the scope of the WTO," Background Note, February 2000, Agency for International Trade Information and Cooperation, http://www.acici.org/aitic/documents/Notes/note8ang.html, accessed January 11, 2001.

11. *Ibid.*

12. "The Agreement on Rules of Origin of the WTO," Background Note, June 1998, Agency for International Trade Information and Cooperation, http://www.acici.org/aitic/documents/Notes/note8ang.html, January 11, 2001.

13. "Rules of Origin: Made in Where?" in *Understanding the WTO—Non-Tariff Barriers, Red Tape, Etc.*, World Trade Organization, http://www.wto.org/English/thewto_e/whatis_e/tif_e/agrm9_e.htm#origin, accessed July 22, 2006.

14. Bangsberg, P. T., "Textile Dispute Impedes Hong Kong Export Growth," *Journal of Commerce*, February 3, 1997, p. 5A.

15. Green, Paula L., "Customs Puts 63 More Firms on Violation List," *Journal of Commerce*, November 12, 1998, p. 3A.

16. Roth, Martin S., and Jean B. Romeo, "Matching Product Category and Country Image Perceptions: A Framework for Managing Country-of-Origin Effects," *Journal of International Business Studies*, third quarter 1992, pp. 477–97.

17. "Rules of Origin," North American Free Trade Agreement, U.S. Customs and Border Protection, http://www.cbp.gov/nafta/docs/us/chap04.html, accessed July 22, 2006.

18. Brenton, Paul, and Miriam Manchin, "Making EU trade Agreements Work: The Role of Rules of Origin," CEP working document no. 183, March 2002, http://129.3.20.41/eps/it/papers/0203/0203003.pdf.

19. Gillis, Chris, "Origin Compliance Challenges Shippers," *American Shipper*, March 2004, pp. 36–37.

20. Neville Peterson Williams (attorneys), "Meeting of the Trade Minds: Discussing the Country-of-Origin Marking Travesty," *Journal of Commerce*, July 30, 1997, p. 13C.

21. Weiser, Steven S., and Arthur W. Bodek, "Which Came First, the Chicks Hatched in England or the South African Ostrich Eggs?" *Journal of Commerce*, August 19, 1998, p. 11C.

22. Jehl, Douglas, "Whose Lingerie Is It? A New Mid-East Secret," *New York Times*, December 25, 1996, p. 6.

23. Tagliabue, John, "Italian Silk Makers Upset by New U.S. Trade Law," *New York Times*, April 10, 1997.

24. Lawrence, Richard, "U.S., EU Smooth Over Differences on Country-of-Origin Regulations," *Journal of Commerce*, April 16, 1998, p. 4A.

25. Levy, Clifford, "The Olive Oil Seems Fine. Whether It's Italian Is the Issue," *New York Times*, May 7, 2004.

26. *Harmonized Tariff Schedule of the United States (2006)*, United States International Trade Commission Publication 3249, United States Government Printing Office, Washington, DC 20402. Also available at http://www.customs.gov, accessed July 21, 2006.

27. United States Tariff Schedule, 2009, Supplement 1, Revision 1, October 2, 2009, Tariff Information Center, United States International Trade Commission, http://www.usitc.gov/tata/hts/bychapter/index.htm, accessed October 17, 2009.

28. Country Commercial Guide: Switzerland, Fiscal Year 2009, U.S. & Foreign Commercial Service and U.S. Department of State, February 17, 2009, http://www.stat-usa.gov.

29. Gillis, Chris, "WCO Pushes for Customs Automation," *American Shipper*, March 2002, p. 12.

30. Barbaro, Michael, "Clothing Makers Allege Sex Discrimination in U.S. Tariffs," *New York Times*, April 29, 2007.

31. Kessinger, Jennifer, "CIT Dismisses Gender Discrimination in Tariff Classification Case," *Global Trade Expertise*, July 7, 2008, http://www.globaltradeexpertise.com/news_files/5e133639121a5208400feff89e628a20-143.php.

32. Kulish, Eric, "Dumped On," *American Shipper*, July 2004, pp. 7–16.

33. The Timken Company, *2004 Annual Report*. Canton, Ohio: Author.

34. Meller, Paul, and Elizabeth Becker, "U.S. Loses Trade Cases and Faces Penalties," *New York Times*, September 1, 2004.

35. Phillips, Michael M., "U.S. Plans Punitive Tariffs in Dispute with EU," *Wall Street Journal*, December 22, 1998, p. A2.

36. Helmer, John, "Russia Imposes Tax on Border Traffic," *Journal of Commerce*, January 27, 1997, p. 3A.

37. Lucentini, Jack, "Clinton, in Pro-Trade Move, Ends Tariffs on Brooms," *Journal of Commerce*, December 8, 1998, p. 3A.

38. *U.S. Customs Service Textile Status Report: China*, U.S. Customs Service, http://www.customs.gov/quotas/2000/cntxtpt.htm, accessed January 22, 2001.

39. Magnier, Mark, "Emerging Nations Wack U.S., Others over Protectionism," *Journal of Commerce*, May 14, 1997, p. 3A.

40. Mottley, Robert, "Quota Hangover," *American Shipper*, October 2005, pp. 14–16.

41. *Commodities Subject to Import Quotas*, U.S. Customs and Border Protection Agency, August 31, 2009, http://www.cbp.gov/xp/cgov/trade/trade_programs/textiles_and_quotas/guide_import_goods/commodities.xml.

42. United States Tariff Schedule, 2009, Supplement 1, Revision 1, October 2, 2009, Tariff Information Center, United States International Trade Commission, http://www.usitc.gov/tata/hts/bychapter/index.htm, accessed October 17, 2009.

43. "Sugar Monthly Price," http://www.indexmundi.com/commodities/?commodity=sugar, accessed October 17, 2009.

44. Customs and Border Protection, "Historical Tariff-Rate Quota/Tariff Preference Level Fill Rate," http://www.cbp.gov/xp/cgov/trade/trade_programs/textiles_and_quotas/quotatariff_fill_rates, accessed October 15, 2009.

45. "Brazil Sugar Annual Report," April 30, 2009, http://www.thebioenergysite.com/articles/343/brazil-sugar-annual-report-2009.

46. Malkin, Elisabeth, "In Mexico, Sugar vs. Corn Syrup," *New York Times*, June 9, 2004.

47. Central Intelligence Agency, *The World Fact Book*, https://www.cia.gov/library/publications/the-world-factbook, accessed October 19, 2009.

48. Customs and Border Protection, "Historical Tariff-Rate Quota/Tariff Preference Level Fill Rate," http://www.cbp.gov/xp/cgov/trade/trade_programs/textiles_and_quotas/quotatariff_fill_rates, accessed October 15, 2009.

49. Thornton, Emily, "The Japan That Says No to Cold Pills," *Business Week*, May 19, 1997, p. 34.

50. Hall, Kevin G., "Mexico Avocadoes Gain Access to U.S.," *Journal of Commerce*, November 7, 1997, p. 3A.

51. DiBenedetto, William, "Mexico Says Yes to U.S. Cherries," *Journal of Commerce*, February 12, 1997, p. 5A.

52. Shorrock, Tim, "U.S. to Investigate Japanese Barriers to Fruit Imports," *Journal of Commerce*, October 17, 1997, p. 9A.

53. Andrews, Edmund L., "WTO Overrules Europe's Ban on U.S. Hormone-Treated Beef," *New York Times*, May 9, 1997.

54. Linn, Gene, "U.S. Renews Attack on Asian Barriers to Food Exports," *Journal of Commerce*, April 23, 1998, p. 1A.

55. Weinstein, Michael M., "Banana Spat Could Have Serious Consequences for World Trade," *New York Times*, December 29, 1998.

56. Sanger, David E., "Clinton Fires First Shot in the Banana War," *New York Times*, December 22, 1998.

57. Zaroscostas, John, "EU Officials Reject Plan to Ease Banana Gridlock," *Journal of Commerce*, January 27, 1999, p. 3A.

58. DePalma, Anthony, "Chiquita Sues Europeans, Citing Banana-Quota Losses," *New York Times*, January 26, 2001.

59. "Ecuador's Banana War with Europe," *Andean Currents*, April 8, 2008, http://www.andeancurrents.com/2008/04/ecuadors-banana-war-with-europe.html.

60. "The Second Battle of Poitiers," *Time*, December 6, 1982, p. 31.

61. Greenberger, Robert S., "Some Asian Trade Barriers Likely to Fall," *Wall Street Journal*, April 10, 1998, p. A2.

62. Rao, N. Vasuki, "India to Introduce EDI to Cut Paperwork," *Journal of Commerce*, November 24, 1998, p. 3A.

63. *Business Planet: Mapping the Business Environment*, The World Bank Group, http://rru.worldbank.org/businessplanet, accessed October 19, 2009.

64. Korea Automobile Importers and Distributors Association, "61,648 Imported Cars Registered in 2008," *Kaida Plaza*, February 6, 2009 http://www.kaida.co.kr/site/kaida_eng/plaza/pressrelease_view.jsp?board_type=n4&record_seq=7773.

65. Schuman, Michael, "South Korea Acts to Discourage Imports," *Wall Street Journal*, March 7, 1997, p. A8.

66. Banerjee, Neela, and Helene Cooper, "Are Russians Playing a Game of Chicken with ... Chickens?" *Wall Street Journal*, March 18, 1996, p. B1.

67. Borsuk, Richard, "Changing of the Port Guards: Some Importers Fear a Return to Corruption," *Asian Wall Street Journal*, April 7, 1997, p. 14.

68. Fisher, Donald L., "Prompt, Accurate Marking Can Often Help to Avoid Liquidated Damage Claims," *Journal of Commerce*, July 22, 1998, p. 2C.

69. *Informed Compliance*, United States Customs Service, http://www.customs.ustreas.gov/imp-exp2/pubform/import/comply.htm, accessed October 22, 1999.

70. Mongelluzzo, Bill, "Reasonable Care Is Vital for Trade Arena under Mod Act," *Journal of Commerce*, January 29, 1999, p. 6A.

71. Freudmann, Aviva, "Customs in Europe Hopes to Cyber-Melt Paper Blizzard," *Journal of Commerce*, January 29, 1999, p. 1A.

72. Baish, Peter, "The ACE: A Good Beginning," *American Shipper*, March 2002, p. 75.

73. Freudmann, Aviva, "WTO Explores Ways to Ease Cargo Delays at Borders," *Journal of Commerce*, October 13, 1998, p. 1A.

74. Mongelluzzo, Bill, "Customs Uniformity Urged," *Journal of Commerce*, September 23, 1998, p. 1B. Freudmann, Aviva, "Britain Seeks Other 'Prototype' Partners," *Journal of Commerce*, May 1, 2000, p. 1.

75. Gillis, Chris, "WCO Pushes for Customs Automation," *American Shipper*, March 2002, p. 12.

76. U.S. Customs and Border Protection, "ACE Participants Increasingly Choose Periodic Monthly Statement Processing,"

February 5, 2009, http://www.cbp.gov/xp/cgov/trade/automated/modernization/whats_new/whats_new_ace_archives/2009/february_2009/ace_monthly.xml.

77. U.S. Customs and Border Protection, *Country of Origin Marking*, 2005 CFR Title 19, Chapter 134, http://www.access.gpo.gov/nara/cfr/waisidx_05/19cfr134_05.html, accessed October 19, 2009.

78. U.S. Federal Trade Commission, *Complying with the Made in USA Standard*, http://www.ftc.gov/bcp/edu/pubs/business/adv/bus03.shtm, accessed October 19, 2009.

79. Green, Paula, "Visa Requirements on U.S. Textiles to End Jan. 1," *Journal of Commerce*, October 9, 1998, p. 3A.

80. U.S. Customs and Border Protection, *Textile Status Report: Current Visa and Exempt Certification Requirements for Textiles*, http://www.cbp.gov/quotas/files/visa_rpt.htm, accessed October 19, 2009.

81. Imbriani, Robert, "Drawback: Learn the Rules to Earn the Refund," *Transportation and Distribution*, December 1998, p. 8.

82. Weiser, Steven S., and Ari L. Kaplan, "Unused Merchandise Drawback Offers Distinct Benefits for Importers, Exporters," *Journal of Commerce*, May 27, 1998, p. 11C.

83. Imbriani, Robert, "Drawback: Learn the Rules to Earn the Refund," *Transportation and Distribution*, December 1998, p. 8.

84. *Index to the World's Free Trade Zones*, EscapeArtist.com, http://www.escapeartist.com/ftz/ftz_index.html, accessed October 19, 2009.

85. U.S. Customs and Border Protection, *About Foreign Trade Zones and Contact Info*, http://www.cbp.gov/xp/cgov/trade/cargo_security/cargo_control/ftz/about_ftz.xml, accessed October 19, 2009.

Using International Logistics for Competitive Advantage

Chapter Seventeen

Key Terms

The preceding chapters outlined many of the challenges that an international logistics manager faces in an international environment. They covered the infrastructure of international business, the management of financial and transportation risks, and the choices related to international transportation and packaging, all of which are eminently more complex than for domestic transactions.

However, a good export manager should not see these challenges as obstacles, but as opportunities to offer a higher level of service than his or her competitors. This can be done relatively simply by following a number of elementary points. The recommendations that follow may not be sufficient to clinch the sale; however, they will certainly help in all circumstances.

Consider that an importer, in most situations, is getting several quotes from several exporters located in different countries. Although the alternative bids are likely to be evaluated on a large number of criteria (price, support, after-sale service, delivery terms, and so on), one of the most important issues will be the ease with which the purchase transaction will take place. From the importer's perspective, the easiest alternative is to purchase from a supplier who communicates clearly, who is flexible in his approach, who offers terms of sale that are convenient to the buyer, who is careful in handling paperwork and transportation, and who packages the goods carefully. When all else is the same, the well-prepared exporter will earn the sale by being better prepared on those logistical details.

The good management of international logistics is a competitive advantage.

17-1 Communication Challenges

One of the most challenging aspects of international business is effective communication. Conducting business with people in foreign countries is often hampered by language barriers. It can be quite difficult to conduct business when two people from different languages and cultures are communicating. An additional challenge for the international logistics manager is that most communications with foreign counterparts are conducted in an impersonal fashion, by e-mail, fax, and letters. This detached type of contact does not allow for the subtleties of in-person communication, such as tone of voice or gestures, which often help make communications more intelligible. There is also no opportunity to ask for immediate clarification, as there is in verbal communication, and the possibility of errors or misunderstandings is greatly increased.

The U.S. Department of State classifies languages by the degree of difficulty that they present for a native English speaker intent on learning that language. Table 17-1[1] outlines these categories and languages. The greater the differences are between two persons' languages, the greater the likelihood is that communication will be difficult. Sentences can often be interpreted differently, and both parties will then be left to wonder what the other person meant by a certain word, phrase, or sentence.

To the international logistician, the diversity of languages and associated possible misunderstandings means that extreme care should be extended to communication, to ensure that the correct meaning is conveyed every time. Conveniently for the native speaker of English, most international communication takes place in that language. English has become everybody's second language, mainly because it is the easiest language to learn,* but also because it is the language of the largest trading partners of most countries. However, the advantage of being able to communicate in one's own language means that there are significant responsibilities attached to it.

---

* Contrary to a commonly held belief, English actually is one of the easiest languages to learn because of its relatively simple grammar, its lack of gender forms, and its smaller number of tenses.

TABLE 17-1	Classification of Languages in Terms of Difficulty to Learn for a Native English Speaker

Category 1: Languages Closest to English, Easiest to Learn

Roman alphabet, similar grammar, similar syntax	Spanish, French, Dutch, Italian, Portuguese, Norwegian, Swedish, German

Category 2: Languages Difficult to Learn

Roman alphabet, different grammar, different syntax	Indonesian, Turkish, Icelandic, Czech, Hungarian, Vietnamese, Polish, Slovak, Finnish

Category 3: Languages Very Difficult to Learn

Different alphabet, different grammar, very different syntax	Hebrew, Russian, Greek, Hindi, Thai

Category 4: Languages Extremely Difficult to Learn

Complex alphabet, multiple alphabets or no alphabet, very different grammar, very different syntax	Chinese (Cantonese and Mandarin), Japanese, Korean, Arabic

17-2 International English

International English A technique of written communication in the English language that consists of removing all possible ambiguities, so that the communication can be understood by someone with a limited knowledge of English.

International logistics professionals engage mostly in written communications with their counterparts abroad (by e-mail, fax, or other written documents), and therefore it is important that they communicate clearly in writing. A specific style of writing for native English speakers has developed to increase the probability that non-native speakers of English can clearly understand what is written. This technique, dubbed **International English** by Edmond Weiss, was outlined in his outstanding book *The Elements of International English Style* in 2005.[2]

Writing in International English means following a fairly large number of rules (Weiss lists 57 of them), but the most important one is that the native English speaker should strive to make the meaning of the communication absolutely clear to the non-native speaker: "Business and technical documents intended for those who read English as their second language must be unusually simple, unambiguous, and literal. Ideally, they should be edited for ease of translation."[3] The most important rules are:

- Always assume that the person for whom English is a second language is relying on a dictionary for some words. That means that the word definition used should preferably be the first one in the dictionary and should always be un-ambiguous. For example: "The company's sales took off 25 percent last year" should be replaced with "The company's sales increased 25 percent last year," for several reasons. First, "to take" is probably one of the longest entries in the English dictionary, and the meaning of "to take off" is listed toward the end of that entry. Another reason is that one of the first meanings listed of "to take off" is "to remove (one's clothes)"; therefore there is a strong possibility that the sentence will be understood as "sales *decreased* 25 percent." A convenience sample of foreign students reinforced this point; about 30 percent of them thought it meant a decrease. By using a precise and accurate verb, "to increase," no confusion is possible. This recommendation is often contrary to the common caution to write in "simple words." In practicality, more complex words tend to be more precise and have the smallest number of alternative meanings, and therefore they are better for International English communication.

- Always proofread carefully and avoid all grammatical and spelling errors. There is a strong possibility of confusion in a sentence that reads, "The customer purchases products from company A and it's marketing services form company B." The reader is left to determine whether there are two typos ("it's" rather than "its" and "form" rather than "from") or just one ("form"). Is it that the customer purchases products from company A and marketing services from company B, or is it that it is purchasing products from company A and providing marketing services to (for) company B? Actually, a non-native speaker would probably not understand that there are possible typos in that sentence and not "get it" at all (a correct International English sentence would have used "understand" a second time, rather than "get," even if stylistically poor; the meaning is what matters). Other common misspellings result from the confusion between *there, they're,* and *their*; between *accept* and *except*; and between *effect* and *affect.* Then there is also the frequently found "should of done" instead of "should have done," which is only understandable to a native speaker who "hears" English rather than reads it. For example, it is very likely that a foreign reader will not comprehend the sentence "Our company would like to except your company's proposal," as she will not understand that the word "except" was used instead of "accept." It is just as likely that she will understand the opposite of what was meant, and that the company rejected the proposal.

- Always make sure that quantitative information will be understood without doubt. A date of 06/12/09 can be understood three different ways: A U.S. reader will understand it as June 12, 2009; a French reader will understand it as 6 December 2009; and a Chinese reader will understand it as 9 December 2006. It is best to follow the practice of spelling all dates fully: "12 June 2009" is unambiguous. The number "10^9" is "1 billion" to a North American reader, but "1,000 million" (or 1 "milliard") to a British or German reader, for whom a billion is 10^{12}; meanwhile, 10^9 is 100 crore (or 10,000 lakhs) to an Indian, Pakistani, or Nepalese. Writing the full number is always the best strategy.

- Always use simple and short sentences. As much as possible, the sentences should contain only one main idea. If there are possible "shortcuts," they should be avoided—for example, "The company requests the report be sent early in the month" should be changed to "The company requests *that* the report *should* be sent between the first and the fifth day of the month." When in doubt, punctuation should be added to enhance clarification, even if it seems too heavily punctuated to a native speaker.

- Never use idioms that are sport- or military-related, as they are rarely, if ever, understood properly. Writing that a salesperson "struck out" on a deal or that she "hit a home run" will confuse a foreigner, who, in looking it up in the dictionary will read that she "ran around the bases with one hit."[4] A correct sentence conveying the same meaning would say that she was "unsuccessful" or "successful beyond our expectations." Military terminology should also be avoided. Terms such as "plan of attack" or "price war" tend to be difficult to translate or off-putting to some cultures.[5] If there is any doubt that foreign sport terminology is incomprehensible to the uninitiated, a quick visit to a British newspaper, such as *The Guardian* (http://www.guardian.co.uk), or an Indian newspaper, such as *The Telegraph* (http://www.telegraphindia.com), and a glance at the cricket page would quickly dispel it.

The concept behind International English is that communication should be easy to understand and devoid of cultural references. One of the most effective ways to determine whether a particular message is written clearly enough to be understood by a foreign reader is to translate it using machine-translation software into another language (preferably one that is not a European language) and translate it back into English. It will rarely, if ever, be the same as the original text; however, if its original meaning is still understandable, then the text was written in an English that can be properly understood by a non-native speaker.

Web Exercise

Use the following Web sites to translate words or phrases into different languages. Translate and then back-translate some of the sentences used in this section. Compare in particular those that were used as examples of poor communication and those that were written in proper International English.

- http://babelfish.yahoo.com/
- www.google.com/language_tools

17-3 Special English

For communications conducted orally, the challenge is much greater, as there is less time to refine the sentences used and to make sure that the meaning is clear. It is important to realize that one of the greatest difficulties experienced by a non-native speaker—of any language—is to talk on the telephone. There are no visual cues that help communication and, on occasion, there are technical difficulties that hamper good communication.

In order to communicate clearly in English with foreigners, it is useful to become familiar with **Special English**, a reduced-vocabulary English developed by the Voice of America, the U.S. government-sponsored news organization that broadcasts worldwide. While the Voice of America is prohibited from broadcasting in the United States,[6] it is possible to hear its broadcast on the Internet.[7] Here are its main characteristics:

Special English A technique of oral communication in the English language that consists of a limited vocabulary and of simplified sentences, so that the communication can be understood by someone with a limited knowledge of English.

- Sentences should be short and contain only one idea. It is more effective to use two sentences ("Sentences should be short. Sentences should contain only one idea.") than to confuse the listener, who is trying to understand a particular word or sentence structure and cannot remember how the sentence started. It takes a little practice, but it is certainly easy for a native speaker to learn to speak in such a way.

- The vocabulary should be limited to correct and accurate terms. All sorts of sports-related imagery exists in American English, but it should be avoided; stating that a contract negotiation is still "in the first inning" (is in the very first stages, with only one of the two parties having made its points) or that the companies competing for a particular sale are "not on a level playing field" (one of the competitors has an unfair advantage over the other) is unlikely to ever be understood by a non-native speaker of English. The same is true of terms such as "stand up to" or "roll over," which should be replaced with their precise equivalents: "confront" or "reinvest." Even expressions that are clearly understood in one English-speaking country can be difficult for others: "carrying coals to Newcastle" makes as little sense to U.S. English speakers as "selling refrigerators to Eskimos" makes to Australians.

- The speed at which the sentences are spoken should be slower. The broadcasts of the Voice of America aim for two-thirds of the speed of normal speech. From personal experience, people from the southern part of the United States are much more easily understood than people from the north because they tend to speak at a slower pace. The U.S. southern accent is much less of an issue for foreigners, who tend to visualize the words as they are spoken.

- Finally, if a foreigner asks a native speaker to repeat a sentence, the native speaker should not repeat the sentence louder, as if the person had difficulty hearing. The issue is generally about a word that the listener did not understand or a sentence that was too complicated. It is best to just repeat the sentence using slightly different vocabulary or repeat the sentence and offer an alternative word. For example, "Our company would like to sleep on that proposal for a few days" (a sentence that violates the principles listed above, and is likely to be misunderstood) can be repeated as "Our company would like to sleep on that proposal, think about it, for a few days." In this manner, the non-native speaker better understands the sentence and gains a new bit of vocabulary.

17-4 Metric System

Communication is also better served by using what is familiar. Unfortunately, U.S. exporters and importers do not use the system of measures—the metric system—that *every other country in the world uses* (except for Liberia and Myanmar, which do not use the metric system either) but instead uses a system which even its everyday users find difficult to understand. Foreigners, thus, tend to be entirely baffled by the U.S. system of measurement.

For example, within the so-called English system of measures, there are three types of tons: (1) the short ton, which is a measure of weight and weighs 2,000 pounds; (2) the long ton, also a measure of weight at 2,240 pounds; and (3) the gross (registered) or net ton, which is a measure of volume and equal to 100 cubic feet. And there is often no indication of which ton is the correct one. Only tradition dictates which "ton" is the one that is intended.

Measurement can get much more complicated. There are five types of ounces: (1) an *avoirdupois* weight unit of 437.5 grains; (2) an apothecary or Troy weight unit of 480 grains; (3) a U.S. fluid ounce, which is a measure of volume worth six teaspoons; (4) its "equivalent" regulatory fluid ounce, which is defined as 30 milliliters or 1.5 percent more than a U.S. fluid ounce; and (5) an imperial fluid ounce, which is 4 percent smaller than the U.S. unit. There is generally no indication of which unit is the correct one in a document or regulation.[8] As if this were not enough, there are traditional units in some industries that use the same terminology very differently. For example, leather is measured in the United States in ounces, which, in this case, is a measure not of weight or volume, but of thickness: "Two-ounce leather such as calf or goat skin is about 1/32 inches thick, while eight-ounce leather is a full 1/8 inches."[9]

It is therefore to the advantage of everyone involved in a transaction to use the **metric system**, which has a very well defined set of measures, all of which are clearly and accurately established. A kilogram is a measure of mass, a liter a measure of volume, and a meter a measure of distance. There are convenient ways to cross over from one unit set to the next: One liter is exactly equal to a cube of side 0.1 meter (10^{-3} cubic meters), and a kilogram is equal to the mass of water contained in a liter. There are conventions for the names of multiples (kilo, hecto, deka) and for the names of fractions (deci, centi, and milli), all of which are decimal. More importantly, there are no ambiguous usages.

While this utilization of the metric system may represent a challenge for a U.S. exporter or importer, its customers or suppliers will understand much better what it intends to communicate, and this effort will result in a greater probability of making a sale.

Converting to the metric system, though, is more than just multiplying by the correct coefficient. Selling a product in 3.785-liter bottles (equivalent to one U.S. gallon bottle) does not satisfy the admonition to use the metric system; while it is a convenient conversion of a common English unit, it is an unusual unit of volume for a person used to the metric system, for whom products are generally sold in one- or two-liter bottles. A correct conversion would therefore use round units of measurement rather than direct "translations" of round units in the English system into awkward decimal quantities in the metric system.

metric system A decimal measuring system developed in the late eighteenth century and part of the International System of Units. Widely adopted worldwide, it is not commonly used in the United States.

Calculating Conversions

There are substantial differences between the effort extended by a shipper using the metric system and that of a shipper using the English system. Two juice manufacturers, one American, the other European, need to decide whether an identical shipment of juice boxes can fit in a 40-foot container. Will the shipment weigh less than the maximum allowable weight? Will it physically fit inside the box?

Both shipments are made of 5,000 cartons of 24 "standard" juice boxes.

The American shipper must first determine what the weight would be of this shipment of juice boxes, each containing 7 fluid ounces of apple juice. Ignoring the fact that apple juice has a slightly higher density than water, and having found that 1 fluid ounce weighs 1.04 *avoirdupois* ounce, he determines that each juice box weighs 7.28 ounces. The total weight of the shipment is therefore $5,000 \times 24 \times 7.28 = 873,600$ ounces. Because 1 pound is 16 ounces, he then divides that result by 16 to obtain the total shipment's weight of 54,600 pounds. Will that shipment fit in a container whose maximum capacity is 26.29 long tons? He needs to divide 54,600 pounds by 2,240 and ends up with 24.375 long tons. Even accounting for the additional weight of packaging and dunnage, it is well within the container's weight limit.

Each juice box measures 1⅝ inches by 2½ inches by 3½ inches. Will this shipment fit in a regular 40-foot container whose inside measurements are 39 feet 6 inches long by 7 feet 8⅛ inches wide by 7 feet 5¾ inches high? The shipper must first determine the volume of each juice box: $1.625 \times 2.5 \times 3.5 = 14$ cubic inches. Then, he determines the volume of the entire shipment: $5,000 \times 24 \times 14 = 1,680,000$ cubic inches. Finally he needs to determine the volume of the container and, for that, needs to calculate how many inches there are in each dimension: 39 feet 6 inches is $(39 \times 12) + 6$ inches or 474 inches in length, 7 feet 8⅛ inches is $(7 \times 12) + 8.125$ inches or 92.125 inches in width, and 7 feet 5¾ inches is $(7 \times 12) + 5.75$ inches or 89.75 inches in height. The entire volume of the container is therefore 3,919,136 cubic inches. The shipment of 1,680,000 cubic inches fits without problem, even accounting for the space taken by packaging and dunnage. Converting those dimensions to feet and calculating in cubic feet would not have simplified the task at all.

Using a similar shipment, the European shipper can make these calculations much faster. The capacity of each juice box is 205 milliliters and therefore it weighs 205 grams, if the slightly higher density of juice is ignored. The total shipment weighs $5,000 \times 24 \times 205$ grams = 24,600,000 grams or 24.6 tonnes. Because the capacity of the container is 26.72 tonnes, there is no issue, even after packaging and dunnage are added.

The dimensions of each juice box are $4.1 \times 6.3 \times 8.9$ centimeters. Each box therefore has a volume of 230 cubic centimeters or 230 milliliters. (This is more than the volume of the juice itself, which is 205 cubic centimeters, and that is due to the fact that the juice boxes tend to have sides that are slightly concave. This was also the case for the American juice boxes but was unnoticeable because of the units used.) The entire shipment is therefore 27,600,000 cubic centimeters or 27.6 cubic meters. The container is the same, with inside dimensions of 1,204 centimeters long by 234 centimeters wide by 228 centimeters high. Its total volume is $1,204 \times 234 \times 228 = 64,235,808$ cubic centimeters or 64.23 cubic meters, and therefore the shipment fits without difficulty, even after the packaging and dunnage are added.

Unless he knew it by heart, the American shipper needed a dictionary to find out that a fluid ounce weighs 1.04 ounces and that a long ton is 2,240 pounds. He also needed a piece of paper to keep it all straight, as well as a calculator. The European shipper only needed a calculator.

17-5 Cultural Sensitivity

Although using International English and the metric system to convey information clearly are already great ways to become a better international logistician, it is also very valuable to become savvy about others' cultures. Unfortunately, if there is one aspect of international business about which it is difficult to generalize, it is culture. There is little to culture that can be pinpointed in a few sentences, and when such an attempt is made, exceptions abound. In the long run, the best that an international logistician can do is to study intercultural communication. In the meantime, a few of these pointers can help.

One aspect of communication that is shaped by culture is the way people address each other in person, in the mail, or over the telephone. In some cultures, the forms of address are quite formal (France), and in others (Australia) quite informal. In some cultures, people are very sensitive to titles (Germany), in others much less so (Canada). U.S. culture is among those that care the least about titles and formalities, although there are a few notable exceptions to that rule. In all cases, because it is difficult to offend someone by being too formal, an astute international logistics manager will therefore always err on the side of **formality**, and communicate as politely and formally as possible until there is evidence that it is appropriate to adopt a less formal tone.

Another area in which it is easy to make quick progress is in understanding the work culture of a country. First, the international logistician should consider the separation between work and private life. In some countries, there is a considerable divide between work and family, and the two never or rarely intersect (Japan). In others, the two are closely tied to one another (Indonesia). When in doubt, it is generally better to consider that personal life and work life are separate, unless there is evidence on the part of the foreign interlocutor that it is appropriate to mention family and private life in business communications.

Another area in which there are culturally determined differences is the speed at which people operate in the workplace. In some countries, it is expected of business persons to answer an inquiry very quickly, in order to show that the inquiry is important and that it commands their full attention (Germany). A delay implies a lack of interest. In others, it is impolite to answer too quickly, as a response should be given careful thought (Saudi Arabia). There is no specific ideal way to handle these discrepancies, but the advice for international logisticians is, again, to learn the appropriate response time from what their foreign counterparts do and mirror that behavior.

Finally, culture influences the way people spend their workday; the time at which they arrive at work, leave work in the evening, and eat during the day. Culture also influences the amount of time that they spend at each meal and the days of the week that they work. Finally, it influences the different holidays that are celebrated. Countries have different holidays, and different customs during identical holidays. Sometimes it is appropriate for an exporter or importer to send a card or a greeting, in others it is not. In those cases, the *CultureGrams*[10] mentioned in Chapter 1 are most useful. In any case, for the international logistician, a delayed response to a request on a certain day may simply be due to a holiday rather than a lack of interest. Considering that India, due to its multiplicity of religions, has a total of 43 official holidays, it is more likely than not that there is some celebration during a given week.

formality A way for a person to interact with other individuals that uses conventions and regimented forms of address.

17-6 Specific Advice

In addition to the general advice presented so far, the international logistician has the opportunity to gain a competitive advantage by following a number of strategies in specific areas. Some of these strategies were presented in earlier chapters, but they bear repeating.

17-6a Terms of Payment

Although the choice of the term of sale is dependent on the level of experience of both the exporter and the importer and on the level of confidence that the exporter has in the ability of the importer to make the payment, there are some alternatives that are definitely preferable and will increase an exporter's probability to clinch the sale.

An importer, in most situations, is getting several possible quotes from several exporters located in different countries. Alternative bids are evaluated on a large number of criteria (price, specific capabilities, after-sale service, delivery terms, and so on), and on the ease with which the purchase transaction will take place. From the importer's perspective, the easiest alternative is to purchase on an open-account basis. It is likely that at least one of the potential suppliers will offer such terms, and that others will ask for a letter of credit or a documentary collection. Therefore, the supplier offering an open-account transaction has an advantage over the others. If that supplier has purchased credit insurance, that decision does not affect its probability of getting paid.

Therefore, an exporter intent on increasing its sales should choose to display that it is confident in the ability of the importer to pay for the goods by using an open account. If it is unsure about the ability of the importer to pay, it should consider purchasing a credit insurance policy.

17-6b Currency of Payment

In an international transaction, the choice of the currency exposes the exporter (or the importer) to the risk of currency exchange rate fluctuation. Rather than consider this risk to be a drawback in an international sale, a good exporter should consider it an opportunity and take advantage of the several alternatives it has to reduce its risk of currency fluctuation.

Because of the intense competition that an exporter faces in international markets, it is very likely that a significant percentage of the companies competing for the importer's business will offer quotes in the importer's currency. Because it is easier for the importer to handle a purchase in its own currency, it would place an exporter at a strategic disadvantage not to quote in that currency.

An exporter intent on increasing its sales abroad should therefore offer (all of its) quotes in the importer's currency and discuss with its banker the most appropriate hedging strategy for that particular transaction.

17-6c Incoterms

In some cases, a strategic advantage can be gained by an exporter willing to facilitate the sale of its products by assisting a novice importer in the handling of a shipment. In others, a price advantage may be obtained by an experienced importer willing to perform all or most of the tasks involved in the shipment.

Generally speaking, an exporter does not like to determine which Incoterm to use on a case-by-case basis. It adopts a "policy" to include in international quotes those services that it feels competent providing. It is difficult for an exporter to adapt its Incoterm strategy to accommodate the requirements of an importer, as it may require the exporter to be responsible for tasks that it has decided it would rather not perform. However, should the importer want to perform more tasks than what the exporter prefers, it is certainly possible for the exporter to do *less* than what it expected, and use a different Incoterm on that transaction, one for which it is responsible for less.

An exporter intent on increasing its sales should therefore offer to provide the importer with the most customer-friendly Incoterm quotes (either DDU or DDP) and, if necessary, use the services of a competent freight forwarder. Should the importer want to shoulder more responsibilities, it is always possible for the exporter to reduce its involvement and quote FCA or even EXW. The best type of quote would be one in which the exporter lists different prices for different Incoterms, leaving the importer with the decision to choose which is best for its specific case.

For example, a quote could read:

- EXW Cleveland, Ohio: $10,000
- FCA Cincinnati Airport, Covington, Kentucky: $11,000
- CIP Paris, France: $15,500

- DDU Clermont-Ferrand, France: $17,500

- DDP Clermont-Ferrand, France: $17,800

and leave the customer to decide which of the Incoterms it would like to choose. The *pro forma* invoice would then be created after that decision has been reached.

17-6d Document Preparation

Accurate and timely document preparation and delivery are an essential part of international logistics and of the smooth transfer of goods from an exporter to an importer.

Any failure to provide complete documents in a timely manner is likely to delay a shipment, generate additional costs by requiring last-minute mailings of critical documents, or create difficulties for one or more of the parties involved in the transaction. Because the responsibility of proper document preparation falls mostly on the exporter, regardless of the Incoterm used in a transaction, an exporter can turn its ability to do a good and thorough job in this aspect of international logistics into a marketing advantage.

An exporter intent on increasing its sales should therefore be thorough and meticulous in the way it prepares the documents that it provides to the importer. This should be reflected in the first contact, the *pro forma* invoice, and be communicated to the importer by emphasizing the experience of the company at providing accurate and thorough documents.

17-6e Packaging

Good handling of the packaging requirements by the exporter will also help considerably in the smooth transfer of goods from the exporter to the importer.

The most important way of looking at packaging is to prepare for the worst. The exporter should truly imagine the worst-case scenario and the roughest possible journey in packaging the goods that it ships at export. It is only under this premise that it will adequately serve the needs of the importer to receive goods in sellable and usable conditions.

Although good packaging procedures are expensive, the benefits are substantial. First, they allow the goods to arrive in perfect shape to their destination and be immediately sellable or usable by the importer. Good packaging also reduces the costs of repackaging or the costs of damaged goods. In addition, because poor packaging is always a "defense" used by insurance companies, it pays to have a track record of stellar packaging.

However, the greatest benefits from such a good packaging policy are the goodwill that it generates between the importer and the exporter, and the marketing benefits that can be derived from it. Because the importer is obviously not interested in having to challenge invoices or having to ask for allowances for goods that were damaged in transit, it welcomes shipments that arrive packaged carefully.

Careful packaging, meticulous document preparation, and considerate choices in terms of payment and Incoterm selection will enhance the relationship between exporter and importer through goodwill and trust. Learning and understanding these skills will help an international logistician gain a substantial **competitive advantage**.

competitive advantage A situation in which a company has acquired competencies and knowledge that gives it an advantage over its competitors.

Review and Discussion Questions

1. What are the advantages of learning to use International English and Special English in communicating with non-native speakers of English?

2. What are the advantages of using the metric system in international commerce?

3. What are the trade-offs between utilizing a standardized policy and remaining flexible for an exporter?

You can choose either terms of payment or Incoterms to illustrate your points.

4. In your opinion, why is it important for an exporter to sell in the importer country's currency?

5. What are the advantages of having an "environmentally friendly" packaging policy for an exporter?

Endnotes

1. Adapted from "Language Learning Difficulty for English Speakers," National Virtual Translation Center, http://www.nvtc.gov/lotw/months/november/learningExpectations.html, accessed August 15, 2006.

2. Weiss, Edmond H., *The Elements of International English Style: A Guide to Writing Correspondence, Reports, Technical Documents, Internet Pages for a Global Audience*. Armonk, NY: M.E. Sharpe, 2005.

3. *Ibid*.

4. *New College German Dictionary: German-English, English-German*. Duncan, SC: Langenscheidt, 1973.

5. Beamer, Linda, and Iris Varner, *Intercultural Communication in the Global Workplace*. New York: McGraw-Hill-Irwin, 2001.

6. Chmela, Holli, "A Language to Air News of America to the World," *New York Times*, July 31, 2006.

7. Special English News, Voice of America, http://www.voanews.com/specialenglish.

8. Food and Drug Administration, *Code of Federal Regulations*, Title 21, Volume 2, Section 101.9, "Nutrition Labeling of Food," 21 CFR 101.9, April 1, 2004, U.S. Government Printing Office, http://edocket.access.gpo.gov/cfr_2004/aprqtr/21cfr101.9.htm.

9. "Leather and Leatherworking Tips," Legio XX Online Handbook, May 6, 2003, http://www.larp.com/legioxx/leather.html.

10. *CultureGrams*, http://culturegram.stores.yahoo.net/incul.html.

Glossary

10+2 rule A set of required pieces of information that the shipper must provide to the U.S. Customs and Border Protection agency at least 24 hours prior to loading a shipment in the port of origin. Also known as the *Importer Security Filing*.

24-hour rule A rule first instituted by the U.S. Customs and Border Protection agency which requires that carriers to send Customs the manifest of all cargo destined for the United States 24 hours prior to the cargo being loaded in the port of departure. Several other countries have adopted a similar requirement.

absolute advantage An economic theory developed by Adam Smith that holds that when a nation can produce a certain type of goods more efficiently than other countries, it is in its best interest to manufacture more of those goods than it needs, and to trade with countries that produce other goods more efficiently than that nation can.

acceptance The second step in the formation of a contract. After an offer has been made by one of the parties, the contract is formed if the other party accepts the terms of the offer. Under the Convention on Contracts for the International Sale of Goods (CISG), the second party must completely agree with all the terms presented in the offer; otherwise, it is a rejection of the offer. Under the U.S. Uniform Commercial Code (UCC), however, the second party is considered to have accepted the offer if it generally agrees with its terms, even if it wants amendments to the quantity of the goods purchased, the delivery dates, and so on.

ACMI *Aircraft, Crew, Maintenance,* and *Insurance.* The term is used to refer to a type of aircraft lease where the owner is responsible for providing the aircraft, the crew, maintenance, and insurance, but not the fuel.

actuarial tables Tables used by insurance companies that illustrate the exact probability, based upon historical data, of a particular peril.

advertising A marketing term that includes all of the techniques that a firm uses to promote its products by using communication media, such as television, radio, and print. In advertising, the company retains total control over the content of the communication.

advising bank In a letter of credit transaction, the bank that determines whether the issuing bank is a legitimate bank and whether the terms of the letter of credit offered by the issuing bank on behalf of the importer are appropriate. Generally, the advising bank is the exporter's regular bank, but in some cases the exporter's bank will delegate this role to another bank which is more experienced in international trade.

agent An individual or a firm, located in an importing country, that is allowed to represent an exporter in sales negotiations. The firm being represented is called the principal.

air draft The minimum amount of space between the water and the lowest part of bridges that a ship needs in order to enter a port.

airfreighter An aircraft entirely dedicated to the transport of cargo. An airfreighter is either an aircraft that was originally designed as such or a former passenger aircraft that was retrofitted as an airfreighter.

air waybill A bill of lading used in the transportation of goods by air, domestically or internationally. An air waybill is always straight.

amendment A change to a letter of credit to which all parties to the letter of credit agree: the exporter, the importer, the issuing bank, and the advising bank. In general, amendments are made only if there are discrepancies, as every amendment costs the exporter and importer money.

applicant The firm asking the issuing bank for a letter of credit. Usually, the applicant is the importer.

arbitration A process by which the parties to a contract can settle a dispute, involving a panel of arbitrators who will follow most of the rules of a court of law, but will render a decision in a short period of time. In an international contract dispute, the arbitrators will follow the laws specified in the "Choice of Law" clause. Arbitration tends to be much cheaper than litigation.

arbitration panel A group of (generally) three arbitrators who are empowered by the parties involved in a contract dispute to reach a decision on the facts of the dispute and whose decision is binding on all parties. Generally, each of the parties chooses one arbitrator, and the third is chosen by a neutral party.

artificial currency A currency that is not in circulation. After the euro was changed into a circulating currency on January 1, 2002, the only artificial currency left was the Special Drawing Rights of the International Monetary Fund. Its value is determined by the value of a basket of four currencies: the euro (approximately 34 percent of the SDRs value), the Japanese yen (approximately 11 percent), the U.S. dollar (approximately 44 percent), and the British pound (approximately 11 percent).

assist An item provided by the importer (customer) to the exporter (seller) so that the exporter can manufacture the goods: a mold or a die, for example. The value of an assist must be included in the valuation of the imported goods for U.S. Customs purposes.

aval In a documentary collection transaction, the fact that a presenting bank is willing to sign the draft on behalf of the importer. An aval's existence is based on the creditworthiness of the importer.

average A loss incurred on an ocean voyage by a cargo owner. It can be further qualified as a *particular average* or a *general average.*

bale The end result of a packaging technique which consists of taking a commodity and unitizing it by compressing it and placing it into a bag or encircling it with string, metal, or plastic bands. Bales are used to transport cargo that is difficult to ship unless compressed: wool, cotton, tobacco, used clothing, scrap paper, and recycled plastic bottles or aluminum cans.

Baltic Exchange The world market for maritime cargo transportation, located in London, where cargo owners and ship owners negotiate the cost of moving cargo. It publishes multiple indices reflecting the market conditions for particular cargoes and types of ship.

bank guarantee A contract from a bank whereby the bank guarantees that an exporter will perform as required by its contract with the importer. If the exporter does not so perform, the bank pays a compensation to the importer. Most bank guarantees are not documentary, which means that the bank must pay without specific evidence. In other words, it pays first, and argues with the firm to which it provided a guarantee later. Bank guarantees are illegal in the United States.

banker's acceptance In a documentary collection transaction, the alternative whereby the exporter is not certain that the importer will readily accept signing a draft after being notified by the presenting bank that the documents have arrived. It therefore asks the presenting bank to "accept" the draft on behalf of the importer. Generally, this is not possible without an aval from the bank.

bareboat (or demise) charter A lease agreement (also called a *charter party*) between the owner (lessor) of a bulk cargo ship and a lessee, in which the owner provides the lessee with only the ship, without any other services or supplies. See *voyage charter* and *time charter* for alternative charter party agreements for ships.

barge A flat-bottomed boat designed to carry cargo on rivers and canals and to be pushed or pulled. Some of barges used on the rivers and canals of Europe are self-propelled.

barratry An act of disobedience or willful misconduct by the captain or the crew of a ship that causes damage to the ship or the cargo.

beneficiary The firm named in a letter of credit as the firm to which the bank is insuring payment if the importer does not pay. Usually, the beneficiary of a letter of credit is the exporter.

berth The location, in a port, where a ship is loaded and unloaded.

Bespoke Names In the Lloyd's of London vernacular, the individuals who take on the risks insured by syndicates and who have unlimited liability for those risks on their personal assets.

bill of exchange In a documentary collection transaction, another term for a draft. See *date draft* and *time draft.*

bill of lading A generic term used to describe a document issued by the carrier to the shipper. A bill of lading is (1) a contract between the carrier and the shipper whereby the carrier agrees to deliver the goods for an agreed-upon price to an agreed-upon destination; (2) a receipt for the goods, whereby the carrier certifies that it received the goods in good condition from the shipper; and (3) a certificate of title, whereby the party in possession of the original bill of lading is the owner of the goods.

binding agent An agent who can make decisions that are binding on the principal; the principal must abide by whatever statements the representative has made.

binding ruling A determination, made by U.S. Customs, and only applicable to the United States, that classifies a specific product and assigns it a tariff rate before the goods are imported. The ruling is binding on U.S. Customs, which means that it cannot "change its mind" after the product is imported.

breach In the event that one of the parties to a contract does not meet its obligation, that party can be found to have broken the terms of the contract, or to be in breach of the contract. If the party did not fulfill its obligations because of an event beyond its control, the nonperformance can be excused under the *force majeure* clause.

break-bulk cargo Cargo that is unitized in a box or crate which is placed directly into the hold of a ship. It is generally too large or too heavy to be placed in a container.

bunker The amount of fuel that a ship carries on board and that it needs to travel.

cabotage An ocean trade consisting of shipping between ports located in the same country.

call options See *currency options.*

carrier The transportation company that will provide transportation services to the shipper.

Certificate of Analysis A document provided by an independent inspection company that attests that the goods conform to the chemical description and purity levels contained in the invoice provided by the exporter. A Certificate of Analysis is always obtained by the exporter in the exporting country before the international voyage takes place.

Certificate of Certification A document provided by an independent inspection company that attests that the goods conform to the manufacturing standards of the importing country. A Certificate of Certification is always obtained by the exporter in the exporting country before the international voyage takes place.

Certificate of Conformity Another term for a Certificate of Certification. See *Certificate of Certification*.

Certificate of Free Sale A certificate that attests that the product that is exported conforms to all of the regulations in place in the exporting country and that it can be sold freely in the exporting country.

Certificate of Inspection A document provided by an independent inspection company that attests that the goods conform to the description contained in the invoice provided by the exporter. A Certificate of Inspection can also attest that the value of the goods is reflected accurately on the invoice. A Certificate of Inspection is always obtained by the exporter in the exporting country, before the international voyage takes place. Such an inspection is called a pre-shipment inspection (PSI).

Certificate of Insurance A document provided by the insurance company of the exporter that attests that the goods are insured during their international voyage. This certificate is obtained only at the request of the importer, and for transactions under certain Incoterm terms of trade, such as CIF and CIP.

Certificate of Manufacture A document provided by the exporter's chamber of commerce that attests that the goods were manufactured in the country in which the exporter is located.

Certificate of Origin A document provided by the exporter's chamber of commerce that attests that the goods originated in the country in which the exporter is located.

charter airfreight A type of freight that is shipped on a dedicated aircraft, either because it cannot be shipped on an airliner because of its weight or size, or because of its destination.

charter party A type of contract of carriage between a carrier and a shipper, in which the shipper uses all or most of the carrying capacity of the ship to transport commodities such as oil, ore, grain, or polymer pellets.

classification The process of determining what the correct Harmonized System Number is for an import. There are six rules of interpretation to help determine the correct classification.

classification society A company that is responsible for determining the seaworthiness of a particular vessel. It places a ship in a specific "class" in function of its age, maintenance records, and the availability of on-board equipment. The premium paid by the ship's owners for hull insurance is based on its class.

clean bill of lading A bill of lading that reflects the fact that the carrier received the goods in good condition. It is characterized by the presence of only a signature of the carrier's representative, and nothing else. All letters of credit require a clean bill of lading. See *soiled bill of lading*.

cleared The term used to signify that goods were imported into a country and that the importer paid the duty that was due on those goods, and thus the goods were released by the Customs authorities.

cluster An observation, first made by Michael E. Porter, that a firm can develop a substantial competitive advantage in manufacturing certain goods when a large number of its competitors and suppliers are located in close proximity, because the area then attracts the most talented employees, and the extraordinary competition between the firms generates a greater need to innovate and become efficient. Such a grouping of companies is called a cluster.

combi aircraft A type of airplane that is designed to carry both passengers and cargo on the main deck of the plane; generally, the front of the plane is equipped to accommodate passengers, and the rear is equipped to accommodate cargo. A combi aircraft cannot carry certain hazardous cargo.

Commerce Control List A list maintained by the Bureau of Industry and Security that details which commodities and products cannot be exported from the United States without the express authorization of the U.S. government. Such express authorization is called an *individual validated export license*.

commercial invoice The invoice sent by the seller to the buyer, detailing the goods purchased and the amount due. A bill. In international trade, a commercial invoice should be quite detailed and include all of the pertinent information.

commercial risk The probability of not getting paid by a certain creditor because this creditor does not have the funds to pay the debt or because the creditor refuses to pay the debt.

co-modality Another term for *intermodal* and *multimodal*.

comparative advantage An economic theory, developed by Robert Torrens and David Ricardo, that holds that nations will trade with one another as long as they can produce certain goods relatively more efficiently than one another.

competing lines In a contract between a principal and an agent or distributor, competing lines are products manufactured by a company other than the principal that compete with the products manufactured by the principal.

competitive advantage A situation in which a company has acquired competencies and knowledge that gives it an advantage over its competitors.

confidentiality In a contract between two parties, the promise by each of the parties to not divulge what it has learned about the other party's customers, manufacturing processes, and business practices.

confirmed letter of credit A payment alternative in which the exporter asks a bank to provide an additional level of payment security to a letter of credit; should the importer not pay and should the issuing bank not pay, the confirming bank will pay.

confirming bank The bank providing an additional level of payment security to the beneficiary of a letter of credit; the confirming bank certifies that it will pay the letter of credit if the importer and the issuing bank do not pay.

consignee The party named on a bill of lading as the owner of the goods, or, at least, as the party to whom the goods should be surrendered at their destination. The consignee will have the original bill of lading at the point of arrival of the goods.

consular invoice A commercial invoice that is printed on stationery provided by the consulate of the country in which the goods will be imported. The consulate sells that stationery. Some consular invoices need to be *visa*-ed by the consulate as well.

container A large metal box used in international shipments that can be loaded directly onto a truck, a railroad car, or an oceangoing vessel. The most common dimensions of containers are 8 × 8 × 20 feet and 8 × 8 × 40 feet.

Container Security Initiative A program instituted by the U.S. Customs and Border Protection agency, through which Customs agents are sent to the port of departure to inspect containers bound for the United States. Such containers are selected through screening or through suspicious activity flagged by the 24-hour rule.

contract law The set of a country's laws that govern relationships and disputes between the parties that have signed a contract. Contract law essentially dictates that the courts must settle the dispute by using the terms of the contract.

contract manufacturing A situation in which an exporter that needs to manufacture a product abroad finds a corporation in the importing country to make the product for the exporter.

contractor When used in the context of a bank guarantee, a company fulfilling a large construction contract, usually the construction of a substantial infrastructure work or a major project.

convertible currency A currency that can be converted into another currency. A convertible currency can be a hard currency (easy to convert) or a soft currency (not so easy to convert), but it can be converted.

copyright Ownership of an intangible good (intellectual property) by an individual or a firm. A copyright can be held on a work of art, a musical piece, or a written article. Copyrights, patents, and trademarks are protected by governments, preventing non-owners from using intellectual property without authorization.

Corporate Names In the Lloyd's of London vernacular, corporations that take on the risks insured by syndicates. Corporations have limited liability, unlike *Bespoke Names*, individual underwriters who have unlimited liability.

correspondent bank A foreign bank with which a domestic bank has a preferred business relationship.

corrugated paperboard box A type of box made of paper fibers in which two flat sheets are glued to both sides of a "wall" made of a sinusoidally shaped sheet. If there is only one wall, it is called a "single wall" corrugated paperboard box; if there are two walls, it is a "double wall" box; and three walls, a "triple wall" box.

counterfeit goods Goods that appear to have been produced by the legitimate manufacturer but that were actually produced by another company intent on deceiving customers and imitating the genuine goods. Counterfeit goods are generally sold for a much lower price than the authentic goods.

counteroffer An intermediary step in the formation of a contract. After an offer has been made by one of the parties, the other party may not agree with all of the terms of the offer and may want to modify them. Under the Convention on Contracts for the International Sale of Goods (CISG), this response is construed as a counteroffer. Under the U.S. Uniform Commercial Code (UCC), however, it is an acceptance of the offer.

country risk See *political risk*.

crate A wooden box made especially for a product to be shipped break-bulk because it does not fit into a container, or because the exporter deems that an additional level of protection is necessary.

credit insurance An insurance policy under which commercial risk is covered; in exchange for a premium paid by the exporter, the insurance company will bear the risk of non-payment by the importer, deducting a slight percentage of the receivable. Credit insurance does not cover political risks, unless the exporter has explicitly asked for additional political coverage, which is obtained through the Export-Import Bank.

currency The monetary unit used in a particular country for economic transactions (e.g., the dollar in the United States, the British pound in the United Kingdom, the euro in Europe, and the yen in Japan).

currency bloc A group of currencies whose values fluctuate in parallel fashion. The currencies within the group have a fixed exchange rate, but their exchange rates with currencies outside of the group float.

currency futures A method used to trade currencies; the value of a fixed quantity of foreign currency for delivery at a fixed point in the future is determined by market forces. These currencies are traded as are other commodities' futures. In the United States, they are traded on the Chicago Mercantile Exchange.

currency options A method used to speculate on the value of a currency in the future. A firm can purchase options to buy (called *call options*) or options to sell (called *put options*) a particular currency at a particular price, called the strike price, on a given date. Since the complexity of the options market is substantial, the reader is advised to learn a lot more about this alternative before venturing into the options market.

Custom-Trade Partnership Against Terrorism (C-TPAT) A voluntary partnership program between companies involved in international logistics and the U.S. Customs and Border Protection agency, in which companies that implement security measures obtain priority processing and reduced inspection rates.

damp lease A damp lease is an agreement between the owner (lessor) of an aircraft and the lessee, under which the owner provides some services in addition to the aircraft itself. For example, a damp lease could include the aircraft, maintenance, and insurance, but not the crew, which would need to be hired by the lessee.

date draft In a documentary collection transaction, a date draft is a promissory note that the importer has to pay a number of days (30, 60, 90, or 180 days) after the exporter ships the goods. The exporter controls the date at which the goods are shipped, so the draft is called a "date" draft, since the date the payment is due is known ahead of time. This is in contrast to a *time draft*, for which the importer controls the date of payment by controlling the date at which it signs the promissory note. A date draft is used in the documentary collection called *documents against acceptance (D/A)*.

deadweight tonnage (dwt) The maximum weight that a ship can carry. Since the ship also carries bunker and stores, the maximum weight that a ship can actually carry is lower than its dwt.

Destination Control Statement A formal statement which an exporter has to print on its invoice and on the Shipper's Export Declaration if the goods shipped are subject to a validated export license: "This merchandise licensed by U.S. for ultimate destination [country]; diversion contrary to U.S. law prohibited."

direct quote The value of a foreign currency expressed in units of the domestic currency; for example, the euro was worth $1.4011 as of May 25, 2009. Some currencies are traditionally expressed as direct quotes.

discrepancy A difference between the documents required by the letter of credit and the documents provided by the exporter. A discrepancy can be as simple as a misspelling and as significant as a change in the invoice amount. Since letters of credit are documentary, any discrepancy is, in theory, a violation of the terms of the letter of credit and therefore invalidates it. In practice, however, 50 percent of letters of credit have discrepancies, which are resolved through amendments.

displacement tonnage The total weight of the ship, when fully loaded, measured by the weight of the water displaced.

distribution contracts Agreements between exporters and intermediaries that can take the form of either agency or distributorship agreements.

Distribution Resources Planning (DRP) A computer-based management tool that allows a retail firm to determine what to order from its suppliers in function of what it sells to retail customers. Such information is shared with the suppliers, so that they know, in turn, what to manufacture and in what quantity.

distributor An individual or a firm, located in an importing country, that purchases goods from an exporter with the idea of reselling them for a profit.

dollarization A phenomenon whereby other countries decide to adopt the U.S. dollar as their circulating currency. Panama and Ecuador have gone through a "dollarization" of their respective economies.

draft The minimum depth of water that a ship needs in order to float.

dry-bulk cargo Dry cargo that is loaded directly into the hold of a ship, without any form of unitization. Although dry, the cargo exhibits the properties of a liquid, in that it takes the shape of the hold. Examples of dry-bulk cargo include grain, coal, plastic pellets, gravel, and iron ore.

dry lease A dry lease is an agreement between the owner (lessor) of an aircraft and a lessee, in which the owner provides only the aircraft, without any other services. See *wet lease* and *damp lease* for alternative contracts.

dumping The strategy followed by some exporters to sell the products they are exporting at a price that is considered "too low" by the importing country's Customs office. Depending on the importing country, a product's price is considered too low when it is either below its manufacturing costs or below its "normal" wholesale price.

dunnage Packaging material designed to prevent the cargo from moving while in transit.

duty The amount of tax paid on an imported good; the duty is calculated using the tariff rate and the value of the goods.

duty drawback A process by which the U.S. Customs and Border Protection agency refunds up to 99 percent of the duty it has collected on goods that are imported into the United States if the same goods are later exported from the United States.

Electronic Data Interchange (EDI) A method to send documents (invoice, certificates, packing lists, and so on) from one company to another using electronic means. EDI is different from fax transmission in that it does not transfer a copy of a sheet of paper, but sends the information it contains, which is then used by the recipient to create a document.

End-Use Certificate A document required by some governments in the case of sensitive exports, such as ammunition, to ensure that the product is used for purposes that are acceptable to the exporting country's government.

entry The process by which an importer notifies Customs that it has imported a particular product. The entry process encompasses an entry form and is accompanied by a number of other documents: invoice, Certificate of Origin, Certificate of Inspection, and so on.

euro The common currency of 16 of the 27 countries of the European Union, developed in the early 1990s and placed in circulation on January 1, 2002.

evergreen contract A contract that, by design or by default, does not have a specific term of appointment. If a contract lapses but both parties continue acting as if the contract were still in place, the contract then can be considered "evergreen."

exchange rate risk The risk represented by the fluctuation in exchange rates between the time at which two companies entered into an international contract and the time at which that contract is paid.

exclusive representative An agent or a distributor that has been granted the right to be the sole representative of the exporter in a given territory.

export quota A limit, set by the exporting country's government, on the quantity of a specific commodity that can be exported in a given year.

exposure The relative consequences of a particular risk for an exporter; the risk of a $50,000 loss would represent a greater exposure for a small exporter than for a large exporter.

express cargo Cargo shipped with a guaranteed predetermined delivery date and time.

facilities and activities In a contract between a principal and an agent or distributor, a clause that spells out what specific facilities each will maintain (retail store, warehouse, repair facilities) and what specific activities each will engage in (trade show participation, after-sale service, promotion).

factor endowment An economic theory, developed by Hecksher and Ohlin, that holds that a country will enjoy a comparative advantage over other countries if it is naturally endowed with a greater abundance of one of the factors of economic production, such as land, labor, capital, or entrepreneurship.

Fisher effect An economic theory that holds that the interest rates that businesses and individuals pay to borrow money should be uniform throughout the world and that the nominal interest rates that they actually pay in a given country are composed of this common interest rate and the inflation rate of that country.

flag of convenience Designation of the open registry of a country that has lower taxes and more lenient on-board regulations than other countries with open registries. A derogatory term.

flexible intermediate bulk container (FIBC) A type of large-capacity woven bag (of polyethylene or polypropylene fibers) designed to unitize goods that would otherwise be carried as dry bulk, such as fertilizers, plastic pellets, or grain. Depending on their size and construction, FIBCs have a carrying capacity of 1,500–6,000 pounds (680–2,000 kilograms).

floating currency A currency whose value is determined by market forces. The exchange rate of a floating currency varies frequently.

force majeure An event beyond the control of any of the parties in an agreement that prevents one of the parties from fulfilling its commitment. The affected party is then not considered to be in breach of the contract.

formality A way for a person to interact with other individuals that uses conventions and regimented forms of address.

forward exchange rate The exchange rate of a foreign currency for delivery in 30, 90, or 180 days from the date of the quote.

forward market hedge A financial technique designed to reduce exchange rate fluctuation risks in which a business agrees to purchase (or sell) a particular currency at a predetermined exchange rate at some future time (generally 30, 60, 90, 180, or 360 days later).

foul bill of lading Another term for a *soiled bill of lading*, which is a bill of lading reflecting the fact that the carrier received the goods in anything other than good condition; it is characterized by the presence of comments or notes in addition to the signature of the carrier's representative.

franchise The portion of a loss, expressed as a percentage, below which a "With Average" insurance policy will not cover a partial loss. If the amount of the partial loss exceeds the franchise, then the entire costs of the partial loss are covered.

franchisee The party granted the right to use an array of intellectual property items owned by another party in exchange for the payment of royalties.

franchising A process by which a firm possessing an array of several intellectual property items (patents, copyrights, trademarks, trade secrets) grants another company the right to use these intellectual property items in exchange for royalties. In general, the firm that is granted the rights to use the items (called the franchisee) and the firm that is granting the rights to use the items (called the franchisor) are, in the eyes of their customers, indistinguishable.

franchisor The owner of an array of several intellectual property items that grants another firm (the licensee or franchisee) the rights to use that group of intellectual property items in exchange for the payment of royalties.

freight forwarder A company that specializes in shipping cargo on behalf of shippers (exporters or importers). It is a "travel agent" for freight, finding the most appropriate itinerary and carrier, given the shipper's objectives.

freight tonne kilometer (FTK) Unit used to express the volume of cargo transported by an airline; it is the number of metric tonnes of freight, mail, passenger, and baggage carried multiplied by the distance they have been carried, in kilometers. This measure is often used interchangeably with the *revenue tonne kilometer (RTK)*.

full-container-load (FCL) A shipment whose volume and weight are close to the volume and weight limits of a container or for which the shipper requests that it be the only cargo in a container.

general average A loss incurred on an ocean voyage that involves all of the cargo owners on board, such as in the case where the captain of the ship tosses overboard some of the cargo (see *jettison*) to save the ship and the remainder of the cargo, or when the captain decides to ground the ship to prevent a total loss. The owners of the cargo saved by this action are indebted to the owners of the cargo sacrificed and to the owners of the ship.

good faith The assumption that both parties signing an agreement want to enter that agreement and have no ulterior motives. Almost all contracts have a clause specifying that the parties are entering the contract in good faith.

grain An agricultural commodity, such as corn, wheat, oats, or soybeans.

gray market A process by which entrepreneurs buy the products of a company in country A, export them to country B, and resell them to retailers and other intermediaries in country B. Since the entrepreneurs are operating outside of the normal distribution channels for these products and are not authorized distributors, the products themselves are dubbed parallel imports as well.

gross registered tonnage (GRT) The volume capacity of a ship (see *gross tonnage*), calculated in a way that meets the requirements of a specific authority, such as the Panama Canal Authority or the Suez Canal Authority.

gross tonnage The total volume of a ship's carrying capacity, measured as the space available below deck and expressed in hundreds of cubic feet. The gross tonnage is the basis upon which ships pay taxes or fees to transit through a canal.

guarantor The bank that provides a bank guarantee. If the party to which it provides a guarantee does not perform, the bank pays a compensation to the injured party. Most bank guarantees are not documentary, which means that the bank must pay without specific evidence. In other words, it pays first and argues with the firm to which it provided a guarantee later. Bank guarantees are illegal in the United States.

Hague Rules An international liability convention for ocean-going carriers that limits their liability to U.S. $500 per package. The liability convention followed by U.S. carriers until the *Rotterdam Convention* enters into force.

Hague-Visby Rules An international liability convention for ocean-going carriers that limits their liability to SDR 667 per package or SDR 2 per kilogram, whichever is higher. This liability convention is the most commonly used in the world; however, the United States did not ratify this convention.

Hamburg Rules An international liability convention for ocean-going carriers that limits their liability to SDR 835 per package or SDR 2.50 per kilogram, whichever is higher, and eliminates most of the "defenses" a carrier could use to discharge itself of liability. The Hamburg Rules have not been ratified by many countries; the United States did not ratify this convention.

hard currency A currency that can easily be converted into another currency.

hazard A situation that increases the probability of a peril and therefore of a loss. For example, a hazard would be a storm, which increases the probability of the peril of water damage; or a poorly trained crew, which increases the probability of the peril of grounding.

import license The express authorization, granted by the government of the importing country, to import a particular product in a given quantity. An import license is granted to the importer.

Importer Security Filing A set of required pieces of information that the shipper must provide to the U.S. Customs and Border Protection agency at least 24 hours prior to loading a shipment in the port of origin. Also known as the *10+2 rule*.

improper packaging The lack of appropriate packaging materials for an international shipment. The determination is oftentimes made by an insurance company when it refuses to pay a damage claim that it considers avoidable had proper packaging procedures been followed.

inconvertible currency A currency that cannot be converted into another currency.

Incoterm An International Commerce Term, or a formalized international term of trade, which specifies the responsibilities of the exporter and of the importer in an international transaction. Incoterms were first codified by the International Chamber of Commerce in 1953, and the latest revision is dated 2000.

indirect quote The value of a domestic currency expressed in units of a foreign currency; for example, the dollar was worth 94.82 yen as of May 25, 2009. Some currencies are traditionally expressed as indirect quotes.

Individual Validated Export License The express authorization, granted by the government of the exporting country, to export a particular product, or to export to a particular country or particular individual.

informed compliance A standard of behavior, set and enforced by U.S. Customs, that is expected of importers if they want their Customs entries to be cleared quickly and Customs inspections kept to a minimum.

infrastructure A collective term that refers to all of the elements in place (publicly or privately owned goods) to facilitate transportation, communication, and business exchanges.

instruction letter A document sent by an exporter to a presenting bank that spells out the exporter's instructions regarding how it expects the bank to handle the documents and how it expects the bank to handle an importer that does not accept the draft sent.

integrator An air cargo carrier that offers its customers complete door-to-door services. Such services usually include pickup, transportation, delivery, and processing, as well as numerous related tasks.

intellectual property A type of intangible good that an individual or a firm can own; it is either a copyright (the rights to a work of art, a musical piece, or a written article), a patent (the rights to a process, a material, or a design), a trademark (the rights to a commercial name or slogan), or a trade secret (a unique way to manufacture a particular product). Copyrights, patents, and trademarks are protected by governments, preventing non-owners from using intellectual property without authorization. Trade secrets are protected by being kept secret.

interdiction A security strategy that attempts to prevent all imports of potentially dangerous good and all entries of potentially dangerous persons.

Interest Rate Parity An economic theory that holds that the forward exchange rate between two currencies should reflect the differences in the interest rates in those two countries.

intermodal A shipment that takes several different means of transportation—road, rail, ocean, air—from its point of departure (seller/exporter) to its point of destination (buyer/importer). The meaning has evolved recently to limit the use of this term to freight for which a single bill of lading covering more than one of these alternatives is issued. Also called *multimodal* and *co-modality*.

intermodal bill of lading A bill of lading used in the intermodal transportation of goods, domestically or internationally. An intermodal bill of lading is generally straight.

intermodal shipment An international shipment that will use several means (modes) of transportation (rail, road, air, ocean, barge) under a single bill of lading. In most instances today, goods shipped on an intermodal bill of lading are containerized.

International Air Transport Association (IATA) A trade association comprising almost 230 airlines, representing 93 percent of all scheduled air traffic.

International Civil Aviation Organization (ICAO) An agency of the United Nations whose mission is to establish safety and security standards for international civil aviation.

International Convention for the Safety of Life at Sea (SOLAS) An international convention, signed by 148 countries, that outlines the safety requirements that merchant ship owners must put in place. It was first implemented after the sinking of the *Titanic* and has been regularly updated since.

International English A technique of written communication in the English language, developed by Edmond Weiss, that consists of removing all possible ambiguities, so that the communication can be understood by someone with a limited knowledge of English.

international factoring A means of financing international receivable accounts. The firm can ask a factoring company to advance funds on a receivable account. The factoring firm can provide the funds *with recourse*, where the owner of the account receivable is still responsible for collecting it, or *without recourse*, where the collection responsibility shifts to the factoring house.

international Fisher effect An economic theory that holds that the spot exchange rates between two countries' currencies should change in function of the differences between these two countries' nominal interest rates.

international forfaiting A means to finance an international transaction in which an exporter collects a series of drafts from the importer, all with fairly long-term due dates. The exporter sells these receivables to a forfaiting firm that buys them without recourse, which means that the forfaiting firm is responsible for collecting the funds from the importer.

International Monetary Fund (IMF) The international organization created in 1945 to oversee exchange rates and to develop an international system of payments. Today, the IMF assists countries in setting their macro-economic policies, with the view of keeping exchange rates stable and further international development.

International Plant Protection Convention (IPPC) An international convention, which 144 countries have ratified, that mandates that wood used for packing or dunnage be heat-treated or treated with chemicals to prevent insect infestations. All wood materials used in international commerce must show the IPPC mark.

International Product Life Cycle An economic theory, developed by Raymond Vernon, that holds that, over its life cycle, a product will be manufactured first in the country in which it was first developed, then in other developed countries, and eventually in developing countries.

International Ship and Port Facility Security (ISPS) Code A series of security requirements placed by the International Maritime Organization upon ports and ships.

irrevocable letter of credit A letter of credit is a document whereby a bank promises that it will pay the beneficiary (the exporter) a predetermined amount of money, should the beneficiary present a certain set of documents (bill of lading, invoice, and miscellaneous certificates) to the bank. It substitutes the creditworthiness of the importer for that of the bank. A letter of credit is irrevocable when it cannot be altered without the express consent of all parties involved (exporter, importer, issuing bank, and advising bank). Virtually all letters of credit are irrevocable, as required by the International Chamber of Commerce.

issuing bank The bank providing the letter of credit to the importer. It is that bank that, should the importer be unable to pay and should the exporter provide all the necessary documents, has the contractual obligation to pay the beneficiary (the exporter).

jettison The act of throwing overboard part of the cargo of a ship (or of the fuel of an airplane) in an attempt to lighten the ship. The purpose of such an action is to save the ship, the remainder of the cargo, and the crew.

joint venture A company jointly owned by two or more other firms.

just-in-time A management philosophy that consists of planning the manufacturing of goods in such a way that they are produced just before they are needed in the next step of the assembly process, in order to minimize the amount of inventory that a firm carries. The philosophy extends to supply parts, which need to be delivered just before they are used in the assembly process as well.

labor law A set of a country's laws that govern relationships and disputes between employers and employees; it assumes that one of the parties (employee) needs to be protected from the other (employer). Labor law can be used in settling disputes between exporters and agents, at the discretion of the courts in the country in which the agent is located, regardless of the terms of the contract between the exporter and the agent. On occasion, labor law can be used to settle disputes between exporters and distributors.

laker A cargo ship designed for the Great Lakes of the United States and Canada. Its maximum size is dictated by the size of the locks through which it will travel.

land bridge A term coined to describe the practice of shipping goods from Asia to Europe through the United States. By taking the containerized goods to a West Coast port, loading them onto trains, transporting them across the United States, and loading them again on a ship from an East Coast port, shippers avoid the costs and delays of crossing the Panama Canal.

LASH barges Floating containers measuring 18 by 9 by 3 meters that can be loaded and unloaded from a lighter-aboard-ship (LASH) mothership and can be tugged to their destination in a port or to an area without port facilities.

LASH mothership A ship equipped with cranes that is designed to carry approximately 80 lighter-aboard-ship (LASH) barges and can load and unload them at anchor (i.e., without having to be in port).

leap frogging The idea that some countries will "skip" a particular technology to adopt the most recent one available. For example, several developing countries never had a reliable telephone infrastructure; however, rather than spend funds on creating an infrastructure based on land lines, they will build a cellular-based phone system, thereby "leap frogging" the older technology.

less-than-container-load (LCL) A shipment whose volume and weight are below the capacity of a container and for which the shipper does not request that it be the only cargo in a container. LCL shipments are generally "consolidated" with other shipments to form a *full-container-load (FCL)*.

Lex Mercatoria The sum total of all the international agreements, international conventions, and other international trade customs that complement the domestic laws of any given country and to which all international trade transactions are subject. Since some countries are signatories of some treaties but not of others, the complexity associated in determining which elements of *Lex Mercatoria* apply to a given transaction can be substantial.

licensee The party that is granted the right to use an intellectual property item owned by another party (the licensor) in exchange for payment of a royalty.

licensing A process by which a firm possessing some intellectual property item (a patent, a copyright, a trademark, a trade secret) grants another company the right to use the intellectual property item in exchange for a payment, called a royalty.

licensor The owner of an intellectual property item that grants another firm (the licensee) the right to use that intellectual property in exchange for the payment of a royalty.

light tonnage The total weight of the ship, when empty, measured by using the weight of the water displaced.

lightering The process by which a large vessel's cargo is unloaded offshore into smaller vessels that then take the cargo to nearby ports. The large vessel cannot access these ports because they are not deep enough or not equipped to handle such a large ship.

liner A ship that operates on a regular schedule, traveling from a group of ports to another group of ports.

liquidated entry An entry that has been successfully reviewed by Customs authorities and for which duty has been paid; no further processing is required when an entry is liquidated.

litigation A process by which the parties to a contract can settle a dispute, involving the courts of the country chosen in the "Choice of Forum" clause of an international contract. Litigation is considered a "last resort" option, when mediation fails and when the parties in dispute cannot agree to arbitration.

manifest A document, internal to the shipping company (the carrier), that lists all cargo onboard the transportation vehicle.

Manufacturing Resources Planning (MRP II) A computer-based management tool that uses Materials Requirement Planning (MRP) at its core and allows a manufacturing firm to determine what to manufacture, and in what quantity, in function of what it sells to its customers. MRP II also includes financial and cost information and includes other functions in the firm, such as procurement and purchasing.

marketing subsidiary A firm, incorporated in the importing country and owned by the exporter, whose purpose is to sell the exporter's products.

Materials Requirement Planning (MRP) A computer-based management tool that allows a manufacturing firm to determine what to produce, and in what quantity, in function of what it sells to its customers. Such information is shared with the suppliers, so that they know, in turn, what to manufacture and in what quantity.

mediation A process by which the parties to a contract can attempt to settle a dispute, generally involving a third, independent party who can suggest a compromise solution, acceptable to all concerned. Mediation is often preferred over litigation, which is an expensive and time-consuming process in which all judicial rules must be followed and which cannot offer compromise solutions.

merchandise visa A document provided by the government of an exporting country for a product that is subject to a quota in the United States. It is a document granting the exporter the "right" to export such goods. United States Customs will not allow the import of a product subject to quotas if the shipment is not accompanied by a merchandise visa from the exporting government.

metric system A decimal measuring system developed in the late eighteenth century. Since the 1960s, it has been officially known as the International System of Units (abbreviated SI, from its French name, the *Système International d'Unités*). Widely adopted worldwide, it is not commonly used in the United States.

money market hedge A financial technique designed to reduce exchange rate fluctuation risks. When a business has to make a payment at a future date and is pursuing a money market hedge, it invests the funds in an interest-bearing account abroad. The amount invested is the amount it owes, discounted for the interest that it will earn: At maturity, the business will have sufficient funds to cover its obligations. In the case of a business anticipating a collection, the technique calls for the business to borrow from a bank abroad and reimburse the bank with the funds provided by its creditor.

multimodal A shipment that takes several different means of transportation from its point of departure (seller/exporter) to its point of destination (buyer/importer). Also called *intermodal* and *co-modality*.

Name In the Lloyd's of London vernacular, the underwriters who take on the risks insured by syndicates. Lloyd's differentiates between *Bespoke Names*, individuals who have unlimited liability for those risks, and *Corporate Names*, corporations that have limited liability.

nautical fault An error in navigation made by the crew of a ship.

negotiable bill of lading A bill of lading on which the name of the consignee has been left blank or where the words "to order" have been entered. Such a bill of lading allows the owner of the goods to sell them while in international transit. The transfer of ownership is done with the bill of lading, since it is a certificate of title to the goods. Whoever has the original bill of lading when the cargo arrives in the port is the owner of the goods.

net tonnage Obtained by subtracting the volume occupied by the engine room and the spaces necessary for the operation of the ship (crew quarters, bridge) from the gross tonnage.

Non-Vessel-Operating Common Carrier A shipment consolidator or freight forwarder that does not own any means of transportation but issues its own bills of lading and therefore acts as a carrier.

objective risk The chance of a loss that can be accurately calculated, because ample empirical data are available (e.g. the probability of a fire causing a total loss of a residence) or because a good mathematical model has been developed.

ocean bill of lading A bill of lading used in international transportation of goods on oceangoing vessels. An ocean bill of lading can be straight or negotiable and can be *clean* or *soiled*.

offer The initial step in the formation of a contract. When one of the parties to a potential sale contacts the other party, it does so with an offer to enter into a contract. Under the Convention on Contracts for the International Sale of Goods (CISG), the offer made by one of the parties is valid until its stated expiration date. Under the U.S. Uniform Commercial Code (UCC), however, an offer can be withdrawn at any time before its expiration date, without prejudice.

onboard courier (OBC) A passenger on a regularly scheduled flight who is relinquishing his or her baggage allocation, allowing companies to ship extremely urgent cargo. Such a passenger is compensated by the cargo carrier with a discount on his or her airplane ticket.

one-hundred-percent inspection A security strategy that attempts to inspect all imported shipments for potentially dangerous goods.

open registry A country that allows vessels owned by companies having no business relations in its territory to be registered in that country and carry its flag.

open-skies agreement An agreement between two or more countries whereby air carriers from one of the countries are allowed to serve any of the other countries' airports.

options market hedge A financial technique designed to reduce exchange rate fluctuation risks in which a business purchases (or sells) options in a particular currency. See *currency options*.

organized theft Theft of a cargo shipment (or part of a cargo shipment) that is due to organized criminal activity, in which one or more individuals plan and eventually commit the theft.

outright rate The exchange rate of a foreign currency for delivery in 30, 90, or 180 days from the date of the quote. The outright rate is the rate at which a commercial customer would purchase the currency. It has to be differentiated from the swap rate, which is the method used by banks and other financial institutions to express a forward exchange rate.

outsourcing A practice that consists of a business contracting other businesses to perform some of the operations that the contracting business used to handle in-house. It decided that these operations were deemed unessential to its core competency.

overloaded A mode of transportation (truck, train, barge, ship, aircraft) that carries cargo of a greater weight or greater volume than it is designed to carry.

ownership of the customers' list The list of the customers of a particular company is considered a business asset. A contract between a principal and a distributor spells out which of the two parties owns that asset.

packing list A detailed list of what is contained in a shipment.

pallet A platform made out of wood or plastic on which goods for shipment or transport are placed. The pallet allows the use of mechanical equipment to move the merchandise as a unit. Goods shipped on pallets are also called unitized packages. The pallet prevents some of the problems presented by manual handling of the goods. Pallets also offer an additional level of protection by insulating the goods from standing water.

Panamax A ship of the maximum size that can enter the locks of the Panama Canal.

particular average A partial loss incurred on an ocean voyage; the cargo may have become wet from seawater or may have been damaged from rough seas.

patent An intangible good (intellectual property) that an individual or a firm can own. A patent protects the rights to a process, material, or design. Copyrights, patents, and trademarks are protected by governments, preventing non-owners from using intellectual property without authorization.

pegged currency A currency whose value is determined by a fixed exchange rate with another, more widely traded currency. As the value of the reference currency fluctuates, so does the value of the pegged currency, but the exchange rate between the two remains constant.

peril The event that brings about a loss; for example, a fire, a collision, and a flood are all perils.

Phyto-Sanitary Certificate A document provided by an independent inspection company, or by the agriculture department of the exporting country's government, that attests that the goods conform to the agricultural standards of the importing country. A Phyto-Sanitary Certificate is always obtained by the exporter in the exporting country, before the international voyage takes place.

piggy-back A technique, developed by railroad and trucking companies, that consists of placing truck trailers on specially designed railroad cars, so that the trailers can be carried over long distances economically.

pilferage Theft of part of a cargo shipment (rarely the entire cargo shipment) due to opportunity. The thief did not plan the crime; the circumstances were such that it was possible to commit it.

pipeline A mode of transportation consisting of a long series of pipes, connected end-to-end, and used for the transport of some liquid cargo (oil, refined petroleum products, water, and natural gas).

points In a forward exchange rate, the difference between the outright rate and the swap rate. Points are not fixed units; their value depends on the way a currency is expressed, but is the smallest decimal value in which that currency is traded. For example, the indirect quote for the Japanese yen/U.S. $ exchange rate was 94.82 yen as of May 25, 2009. A "point" for this currency rate is therefore worth 0.01 yen. The direct quote for the European euro/U.S. $ exchange rate was $1.4011 on the same date; a "point" for this currency is therefore worth U.S. $0.0001.

political risk The probability of not getting paid by a certain creditor because the creditor's country does not have the funds to pay the debt (insufficient foreign exchange reserves) or because the creditor is not legally allowed to pay the debt (political embargo). Political risk can also mean the probability of nationalization of a firm's subsidiary by the host country. Political risk is also known as *country risk*.

post-Panamax A ship whose size is too large to enter the locks of the Panama Canal.

presenting bank In a documentary collection transaction, the bank that interacts with the importer on behalf of the exporter. The presenting bank is the one receiving the documents from the exporter or from the remitting bank and that holds them until the importer either signs a draft or pays the exporter.

pre-shipment inspection (PSI) An inspection conducted by an independent inspection company before goods are shipped internationally. The inspection is conducted at the request of the importer or of the importing country's government to ensure that the invoice reflects accurately the type of goods shipped by the exporter and their value. A pre-shipment inspection generates a Certificate of Inspection.

principal The party represented by an agent in an international agency agreement; the exporter.

pro forma **invoice** A quote provided by the exporter to the importer for the purpose of the importer obtaining a letter of credit. The *pro forma* invoice should contain exactly the same information as the future commercial invoice, for the same total cost, so as to prevent discrepancies at the time of the letter of credit settlement.

project cargo A type of cargo which requires more advance planning because of its size, weight, or volume. Project cargo generally moves through unconventional means.

Protection and Indemnity club (P&I) A group of ship owners who agree to mutually share the costs of a member's liabilities to other parties; for example, the club members would be individually responsible for the costs of a single member's liability in the event of an oil spill. If the costs of the oil spill exceed the ability of a specific P&I club to cover them, other P&I clubs are contractually obligated to cover them.

protest (1) In a documentary collection transaction, if the drawee (importer) does not pay a draft that it has signed, the presenting bank will file a protest, a legal document that notifies other parties that the drawee is not honoring its debts. In many countries, the filing of a protest effectively cuts the drawee's ability to have access to any credit. (2) In a Customs transaction in the United States, the formal request by an importer to have Customs reconsider its classification, its valuation, or its determination of a country of origin. A protest is generally filed when an importer feels that the amount of duty paid is excessive, or when a good is not allowed in the United States because a quota has been met.

Purchasing Power Parity An economic theory that holds that exchange rates should reflect the price differences of each and every product between countries. The idea is that a set amount of money (regardless of the currency in which it is expressed) would purchase the same goods in any country of the world.

pure risk The chance or the probability of a loss only. Pure risks can be insured against (i.e., transferred to an insurance company).

put options See *currency options*.

quick-change aircraft An aircraft that can very quickly be converted between passenger and freight operations through the use of palletized sections of seats.

quota A limit, set by the importing country's government (sometimes in agreement with the governments of the concerned exporting countries), on the quantity of a specific commodity that can be imported in a given year. There are two different types of quotas: (1) an absolute quota, which limits the quantity of goods imported, and beyond which no good can be imported, and (2) a tariff-rate quota, which places a low duty rate on goods imported until the quota is reached, and a very high duty rate on quantities of the goods imported beyond the quota. See also *export quota*.

reasonable care A standard of behavior, set and enforced by U.S. Customs, that is expected of importers if they want their Customs entries to be cleared quickly and Customs inspections kept to a minimum.

registration A process whereby an agent or a distributor has to notify the government of the importing country that it has entered into an agency agreement or a distributorship agreement with a foreign manufacturer.

rejection An intermediary step in the formation of a contract. After an offer has been made by one of the parties, the other party may not agree with all of the terms of the offer and may want to modify them. Under the Convention on Contracts for the International Sale of Goods (CISG), this response is construed as a rejection of the original offer, to which a counteroffer can be made.

remitting bank In a documentary collection transaction, the bank that interacts with the exporter and with the presenting bank in the importing country. The remitting bank is the one that receives the documents from the exporter and then sends them to the presenting bank. It has no obligation to render judgment or advice on the quality of the packet of documents; it just transmits them to the presenting bank.

revenue tonne kilometer (RTK) Unit used to express the volume of cargo transported by an airline; it is the number of metric tonnes of freight, mail, passengers, and baggage carried multiplied by the distance they have been carried, in kilometers. This measure is often used interchangeably with the *freight tonne kilometer (FTK)*.

reverse logistics The management of the logistical activities involved in the return of a product (or parts of it, including the packaging) to a manufacturer.

risk The chance or the probability of a loss.

risk retention A risk management strategy in which a company elects to retain a certain type of risk and decides not to insure that risk.

risk transfer A risk management strategy in which a company elects not to retain a risk and asks an insurance company to take that risk in exchange for a premium.

road-train An Australian trucking technique, consisting of having one tractor pulling multiple trailers. Road-trains are the conceptual equivalent of trains, but operating on a road. Road-trains have between three and seven trailers.

roller deck The configuration of the deck of an aircraft when it is designed to accept cargo shipments; the deck is equipped with rollers and bearings that allow cargo to be moved in any direction without much friction.

Rotterdam Rules A liability convention for intermodal shipments, implemented by the United Nations, but which only fifteen countries (including the United States) had ratified as of September 2009.

royalty The amount of money paid by a licensee to a licensor for the right to use the licensor's intellectual property. Royalty fees are generally determined in function of the number of times that the licensee or franchisee used the intellectual property.

rules of origin The rules used to determine the country of origin of a particular product. Two commonly-used interpretations for country of origin are (1) the country where the Harmonized System Number classification of a product changed for the last time, and (2) the country in which the greatest value was added to the product.

seal Lock especially designed to be applied on containers and truck trailers and that the importer must break in order to get entry into the container or trailer. Locks have an identification number that is recorded on the bill of lading, and that number must be checked by the importer as well, to ensure that the seal was not "replaced" during the voyage. Seals can be a simple loop of braided steel or a reinforced steel pin. Some seals are electronic and record attempted entries.

secondary registry A response by developed countries to the threat of open registries and flags of convenience: These developed countries created a secondary registry with lower on-board standards and taxes to entice ship owners to carry their flags and not defect to flag-of-convenience countries.

security management A corporate function that manages all of the security efforts of a particular company and coordinates the prevention of criminal activities against the company's employees, products, and assets.

ship's rail An imaginary rail that circles the entire hull of a ship. Should a cargo item fall from a crane onto the ship while it is being loaded, the determination of whose responsibility it is hinges on which side of the ship's rail it falls on. Under CIF, for example, if the cargo falls on the outside of the ship's rail, it is the exporter's responsibility; if it falls on the inside, it is the importer's.

shipper The party to an international transaction that is responsible for arranging the transportation of the goods. Depending on the Incoterm used and on the leg of the journey in consideration, the shipper is either the exporter or the importer.

Shipper's Export Declaration (SED) A document collected by U.S. Customs designed to keep track of the type of goods exported from the United States, as well as their destination and their value.

Shipper's Letter of Instruction A document in which the shipper spells out how it wants the carrier to handle the goods while they are in transit.

sight draft In a documentary collection or a letter of credit transaction, a sight draft is a promise by the importer that it will pay immediately, "at sight." A sight draft is used in the documentary collection called *documents against payment (D/P)*.

soft currency A currency that cannot be easily converted into another currency; either it is inconvertible, it is only convertible into other soft currencies, or it has an exchange rate that differs substantially between sales of the currency and purchases of the currency.

soiled bill of lading A bill of lading that reflects the fact that the carrier received the goods in anything other than good condition; it is characterized by the presence of comments or notes in addition to the signature of the carrier's representative. See *clean bill of lading*.

Special Drawing Right (SDR) An artificial currency (it does not circulate, see *artificial currency*) of the International Monetary Fund. Its value is determined by the value of a basket of four currencies: the euro (approximately 34 percent of the SDR's value), the Japanese yen (approximately 11 percent), the U.S. dollar (approximately 44 percent), and the British pound (approximately 11 percent).

Special English A technique of oral communication in the English language, developed by the Voice of America, that consists of a limited vocabulary and of simplified sentences, so that the communication can be understood by someone with a limited knowledge of English.

speculative risk The chance or probability of a loss or a gain (e.g., an investment in the stock market).

spot exchange rate The exchange rate of a foreign currency for immediate delivery (within 48 hours).

stand-by letter of credit A type of letter of credit that covers more than one shipment; for example, a large transaction would normally necessitate a letter of credit for each shipment, since a separate bill of lading is generated for each shipment. A stand-by letter of credit allows for multiple bills of lading, issued on different dates. A stand-by letter of credit can also be used to secure the performance of the seller. Upon evidence that the seller is not performing according to the terms of the contract it has with the importer, the issuing bank has to pay the importer; this latter type of stand-by letter of credit is often used in large construction projects involving U.S. firms, since U.S. banks cannot legally provide bank guarantees.

stevedore A company or a person whose responsibility is to load and unload ships in a port.

stores All the supplies that a ship carries and that it needs to function.

straight bill of lading A bill of lading on which the name of the consignee has been entered. Such a bill of lading is non-negotiable, which means that the ownership of the goods cannot change in transit.

strike price See *currency options.*

subjective risk The perceived risk of a loss by an individual or company. Whether this perception is correct can be settled only by calculating the objective risk.

subsidiary A corporation entirely owned by another corporation.

surveyor An individual or company whose responsibility it is to determine the extent and the circumstances of a marine cargo loss. A surveyor is an independent party who is not working for the shipper, the carrier, or the insurance company.

sustainability A deliberate attempt at using resources, including aircraft, in such a way as to preserve and protect the environment and meet the needs of future generations.

swap rate The exchange rate of a foreign currency for delivery in 30, 90, or 180 days from the date of the quote. The swap rate is the difference between the current spot rate and the rate at which a commercial customer would purchase the currency. It is expressed in points that must be subtracted or added to the spot rate. The swap rate is the method used by banks and other financial institutions to express a forward exchange rate. The sum of the swap rate and the spot rate yields the outright rate, which is the rate paid by a commercial customer for the currency.

syndicate Under the Lloyd's concept of an insurance market, a group of Names who agree to insure a certain type of loss. The risks are shared by all the members of the syndicate.

system's theft Theft that is perpetrated by someone who also gains access to a computer in the information system of the supply chain and deletes the files related to that shipment. The theft is then likely to go undetected for a period of time.

tariff The rate at which an import is taxed; the tariff rate is dependent on the classification of the goods, as well as their country of origin. The tariff rate is also called the duty rate.

tariff schedule A document listing all the possible Harmonized System classification categories, as well as their associated tariff rates for the different types of countries. Most tariff schedules have two or more "columns," which refers to the number of categories of countries of origin the tariff schedule uses.

term of sale An element in a contract of sale that specifies the method of payment to which an exporter and an importer have agreed. Specifically, the term of sale will specify cash in advance, letter of credit, documentary collection, open account, or TradeCard transaction.

term of trade An element in a contract of sale that specifies the responsibilities of the exporter and of the importer. Specifically, the term of trade will specify which activities must be performed by the exporter and which by the importer, which activities are paid by the exporter and which by the importer, and where in the international transportation process the transfer of responsibility for the merchandise takes place.

termination for "convenience" The unilateral decision, by one of the parties to a contract, to end a contract before its term of appointment expires, for reasons unrelated to the performance of the contract by the other party(ies). The term is also used when one party decides not to renew the contract even if the preset criteria for renewal have been met by the other party(ies).

termination for "just cause" The unilateral decision, by one of the parties to a contract, to end a contract before its term of appointment expires, because the other party has not met some of the terms of the contract that it had agreed to perform. The term is also used when one party decides to not renew the contract because the preset criteria for renewal have not been met.

time charter A lease agreement (also called a charter party) between the owner (lessor) of a bulk cargo ship and a lessee in which the owner provides the lessee with the ship, the crew, and all other services or supplies, for an agreed-upon period of time. See *voyage charter* and *bareboat charter* for alternative charter party contracts for ships.

time-definite shipment Cargo or package shipments that must be delivered by a guaranteed, pre-determined time and day.

time draft In a documentary collection transaction, a time draft is a promissory note that the importer has to pay a number of days (30, 60, 90, or 180 days) after it accepts the draft by signing it. A time draft is different from a date draft because the importer controls the date at which it will sign the note, whereas in a *date draft*, the exporter controls the date of payment by controlling the date at which the goods are shipped. A time draft is used in the documentary collection called *documents against acceptance (D/A).*

to order bill of lading A bill of lading on which the name of the consignee has been left blank, or where the words "to order" have been entered. Such a bill of lading allows the owner of the goods to sell them while in international transit. The transfer of ownership is done with the bill of lading, because it is a certificate of title to the goods. Whoever has the original bill of lading when the cargo arrives in the port is the owner of the goods.

tractor The part of an articulated semi truck that is in the front and whose engine pulls the trailer.

trade acceptance In a documentary collection transaction, the alternative whereby the exporter expects the importer to readily accept signing a draft after being notified by the presenting bank that the documents have arrived. The importer (trader) "accepts" the draft.

trademark An intangible good (intellectual property) that an individual or a firm can own. A trademark represents the rights to a commercial name or slogan. Copyrights, patents, and trademarks are protected by governments, preventing non-owners from using intellectual property without authorization.

trailer The part of an articulated semi truck that is in the rear and is pulled by the tractor.

tramp A ship that does not operate on a regular schedule and is available to be chartered for any voyage, from any port to any port.

transaction exposure The risk represented by the financial impact of fluctuations in exchange rates in an international transaction. A small exposure means that the firm is likely to be largely unaffected by a change in exchange rates, because the amount of the transaction is small relative to the company's size.

trot-on/trot-off A ship designed to carry livestock. It possesses a ramp that the animals can use to walk on-board and exit the vessel.

tweendeck In a combination ship, a deck located below the main deck that is used to carry smaller-size break-bulk cargo, such as vehicles.

Type I error A statistical concept whereby the researcher concludes that the null hypothesis should be rejected when, in reality, the null hypothesis is true and should have been accepted (e.g., in security management, concluding that a shipment is dangerous when in reality it is harmless).

Type II error A statistical concept whereby the researcher concludes that the null hypothesis should be accepted when, in reality, the null hypothesis is false and should have been rejected (e.g., in security management, concluding that a shipment is harmless when in reality it is dangerous).

underwriter The company, syndicate, or Name that assumes the risk of a loss for another party, in exchange for a premium.

uniform bill of lading A bill of lading used in the transportation of goods on trucks and trains, either domestically or internationally. A uniform bill of lading is generally straight.

valuation The process of determining the value of an import, or the amount upon which the duty will be calculated. The value of an import generally includes not only the value of the goods but also the value of some of the transportation services used to get the goods into the importing country.

Value-Added Tax (VAT) A tax perceived by many countries that is very similar to a sales tax, but that is collected whenever the product's value is increased. Only the final consumer eventually pays the tax, but every company involved in the production or supply chain is required to collect the VAT that its customers pay and pay the VAT to its suppliers. The difference between what a firm collects and what it pays must be sent to the government. The VAT on imports is collected at the point of entry into the country. The basis for the tax is the sum of the value of the goods and of the duty paid.

variant A modification to one of the Incoterms codified by the International Chamber of Commerce. Variants are generally used to further clarify the responsibilities of the exporter and importer in a given transaction. For example, the variant "EXW loaded" clarifies that the exporter agrees to load the goods onto the vehicle provided by the importer when the official Incoterm is silent on that specific point.

visa A process by which the consulate of the country in which the goods will be imported reviews and approves the consular invoice for a fee. A visa shows on the consular invoice as a rubber stamp or a seal.

volume-weight (dimensional weight) A weight, calculated based upon the dimensions of a shipment, used by airlines to determine the tariff to be charged to a shipper when a shipment is not very dense. The volume-weight equivalency is that 6,000 cubic centimeters is 1 kilogram (or that 1 cubic meter is 166.67 kilograms). In all instances, an airline charges the higher of the actual weight and the volume-weight. Volume-weight is also called dimensional weight.

voyage charter A lease agreement (also called a *charter party*) between the owner (lessor) of a bulk cargo ship and a lessee, in which the owner provides the lessee with the ship, the crew, and all other services or supplies for a single voyage. See *time charter* and *bareboat charter* for alternative charter party contracts for ships.

wet-bulk (liquid) cargo Liquid cargo that is loaded directly into the hold of a ship, without any form of unitization. Examples of liquid bulk cargo include crude oil, vegetable oil, alcohol, and molasses, as well as liquid chemicals, such as chlorine or caustic soda.

wet lease An agreement under which the owner (lessor) of an aircraft provides the airplane, insurance, maintenance services, fuel, and a flight crew to the lessee, who has to cover all of the other variable costs, such as airport fees.

World Trade Organization (WTO) The international organization that replaced the General Agreement on Tariffs and Trade in 1995. It is responsible for enforcing international trade agreements and for ensuring countries deal fairly with one another.

Index

An *italic f* next to a page number (e.g., 177*f*) identifies information that appears in a figure. An *italic n* next to a page number (e.g., 177*n*) indicates information that appears in a footnote or endnote. An *italic t* next to a page number (e.g., 188*t*) identifies information that appears in a table.